System,
Change,
and Conflict

System, Change, and Conflict

A Reader on Contemporary Sociological Theory and the Debate Over Functionalism

EDITED BY

N. J. Demerath III

AND

Richard A. Peterson

The Free Press, New York

Collier-Macmillan Limited, London

HM
24
D43

TO JUDY AND CLAIRE

Contents

System,
Change,
and Conflict

General
Introduction

*T*HE grand tradition of sociological theory is among the most prestigeful
and the most yawned-at aspects of the discipline. Its scholarly trappings and
philosophical cast add elegance to a field accused of crassness. But elegance
must never be confused with relevance, and many see this theory as graceful
shadow-boxing with little bearing on the action within the bloody ring itself.
Courses in "sociological theory" are required of undergraduate and graduate
students alike. Yet many such courses raise more dust than debate, for theory
is often a nod to the past, and students are more frequently asked to revere a
period piece than to argue a point of current import.

None of this need be the case. For one thing, it is restricted to an exalted
conception of theory and overlooks the sort of theorizing that is crucial to the
most close-cropped empirical study. And even more, abstract theory has
excitement for exploitation. It is *not* true that "theorists" must be Western
Europeans and forty years in the grave. Nor have contemporary theorists
ignored the "big issues" of the world; international conflict, societal change,
the kaleidoscope of inequality, and problems of individual self-fulfillment
have all been confronted at this level, though without panaceas or even
unanimity. Here too is a plane on which sociology's own path has been
charted, recharted, and charted again. Abstraction does not preclude passion,

and debates have been shrill and implacable. Indeed, this volume focuses upon one of these in presenting the arguments both for and against "functionalism." Our objective is not to contrive harmony out of dissonance but to let the dissonance swing to its own beat.

Functionalism itself has served different purposes for different scholars. Its most general characteristic is an assumption that society can be analyzed as a systemic whole with constituent parts in search of a mutually adjusted equilibrium. Some "functionalists" treat the assumption as an indisputable description of the "real world"; others see it as a usefully artificial model or a hypothesis open to test. Some stress analysis of the whole society; others use the whole as a background for examining certain "parts" in detail, whether religion, the family, the economic firm, or the like. All of these interpretations and more are manifest in the selections to follow. And then there are the equally heterogeneous critics. Some charge that functionalism offers an ill-conceived utopia; others argue that it portrays a social hell uncritically. Some fault functionalism for betraying scientific procedures; others argue that it merely overstates common scientific practice and evokes artificial criticism that jeopardizes the baby as well as the bathwater.

This book is not a brief for any of these positions. For our purposes, functionalism is most important as a goad to the most far-reaching, continuous examination of sociology that the field has yet witnessed. The following recurrent questions are typical: Can societies be viewed as "systems," and, if so, systems of what sort and with what degree of integration and equilibrium? To what extent is a basic assumption of conflict a more appropriate departure for the analysis of societies? What are the fundamental aspects of social change and the most fruitful ways of analyzing them? Can one speak meaningfully of a finite number of prerequisites for society, and, in their absence, of societal death? Are some institutions more necessary for the maintenance of society than others, and, if so, what are they? What has and ought to have highest priorities for explanation in sociological theory: taxonomy or proposition building? What are the logical and substantive differences between various levels of analysis, ranging from the societal to the individual? Finally, is there an inevitable articulation of politics and theory; if so, what are the consequences of our present ideologies? Each of these issues ramifies beyond functionalism and concerns the sociological enterprise as a whole; each would remain an issue even if functionalism itself were expunged.

In our view functionalism is not a fad soon to be recessed. Its model of social systems is too valuable as both a foil and a stimulant. What seems more likely is that contemporary functionalism will evolve into the sociological theory of the future just as functionalism itself evolved out of nineteenth-century organicism, the grand but value-laden notion that society is an organism with liver, heart, and vitalistic goals. Of course, the evolution of ideas is rarely smooth or even gentlemanly, and the respecification of functionalism is likely to have all the fire, invective, and insight that has characterized its development thus far. It is to this sort of debate that the present volume is devoted.

But there is a certain *hubris* in editing a book on the functionalist controversy, much less one that seeks to probe sociological theory in general. Most readers will have preformed opinions, and no two readers are likely to have the same reaction. Some will be disturbed by our exclusions, others by our inclusions. Many may quarrel with the organization, a number with our commentary. For this reason it is important to set forth a manifesto of policy so that the reader can at least distinguish between what was attempted and what was not.

First, of course, the book attempts to raise issues instead of settling them. Rather than end the debate, we seek to focus it. For this reason, the book is not organized to chart the chronological development of ideas. The format features the direct confrontation of divergent perspectives. Each chapter stresses a different aspect of the wider disagreement. Within each, we have paired writings whose differences are sometimes subtle, sometimes blatant. Most of these writings have been scattered in the literature and have heretofore sent both scholars and students scurrying through the stacks. For some this is especially unfortunate, since some pieces were meant specifically as rebuttals to others: Nagel's "Commentary on Merton," Mills' "Critique of Parsons," and Dore's "Reply to Davis," are several examples. Argument and appreciation are compatible, and we hope to stress the former in order to cultivate the latter.

A *second* policy concerns the forefathers of the functionalist debate. Early protagonists such as Spencer, Lilienfield, Pareto, Durkheim, Radcliffe-Brown and Malinowski have their opposite numbers in Weber, Marx and a host of others.[1] It would be appropriate to include all of these men, but, in fact, we have included none. This is hardly typical of volumes on theory, and the exclusion is far from a denigration. Because these men are reprinted over and over in other collections, because they are frequently cited and explicated in the articles we have included, and because we want to empha-

---

[1] The historical development of functionalism is recorded well at various points in the literature. See, for example, Walter Buckley, "Structural-Functional Analysis in Modern Sociology," in Howard Becker and Alvin Boskoff, eds., *Modern Sociological Theory in Continuity and Change* (New York: Holt, Rinehart and Winston, 1957), pp. 236–59; Don Martindale, *The Nature and Types of Sociological Theory* (Boston: Houghton Mifflin, 1960), pp. 441–522; Lewis A. Coser and Bernard Rosenberg, eds., *Sociological Theory: A Book of Readings,* second edition (New York: The Macmillan Co., 1964), pp 615–665 for some classic early statements of the school; and Talcott Parsons, *The Structure of Social Action* (Glencoe: The Free Press, 1949) for a monumental analysis of the rise of contemporary sociological theory generally.

size that this is an ongoing pursuit that did not end with World War 1—for all these reasons we have given the space to more recent and less attended volleys in the exchange. All but three of the selections have appeared since 1950 as befits a volume on "contemporary theory."

A *third* goal concerns the relation between sociology and the social sciences more generally. Sociology is not alone in reaping the benefits and bearing the cross of functionalism. Although sociology has often been accused of parochialism, it should help to realize that other "churches" harbor similar doctrines and similar heresies.[2] To this end we have included selections from diverse disciplines, including political science, anthropology, economics, and the philosophy of science. These selections not only provide bibliographic paths into the controversy within their own disciplines, but they contribute trenchantly to the wider debate as a whole.

A *fourth* matter concerns the troublesome distinction between "theory" and "empirical analysis." Certainly much of the best and worst in the functionalist tradition is found in analyses of concrete phenomena. And if there is truth in the axiom that all sociological analysis is functional, then all studies are candidates for inclusion. Precisely because of this abundance of material, we have decided to include only work that is self-consciously addressed to wider issues in the debate. This leads to such unfortunate exclusions as the Davis–Moore theory of stratification and the controversy surrounding it. Not only is this material substantive in focus, but it has grown to such proportions as to defy brief representation in a collection such as this one. On the other hand, Geertz's article on the Javanese funeral is included despite its substantive flavor because it offers a major critique of the functional analysis of social change generally. The policy of cutting empirical detail as far as possible also has merits in confining the discussion to a common level of abstraction. The debate as constituted appeals more to logic and perspective than to detailed knowledge of a particular society or a particular institution. Insofar as data are relevant, they are generally data to which we all are privy.

A *fifth* judgment concerns the editing of specific articles. Here questions of space, relevance, and redundancy have been our guide. Approximately half of the articles have been reprinted in their entirety. In some instances extended examples have been cut, in others we have excised "reviews of the literature" which are now readily available to the reader of this collection. In no case was the editing task easily accomplished; the attempt has been to

---

[2] For more extended analysis of functionalism in areas other than sociology, see Don Martindale, ed., *Functionalism in the Social Sciences: The Strengths and Limits of Functionalism in Anthropology, Economics, Political Science, and Sociology* (Monograph 5 in a series sponsored by The American Academy of Political and Social Science, Philadelphia, 1965).

preserve the integrity of each article while including as many articles as possible. Of course, a collection is inevitably incomplete and represents only one step in mastering a set of ideas.

Finally, a *sixth* judgment concerns the book's organization. Order is scarce in a debate as far-reaching as this one. Issues frequently blur, and articles often overlap. Nevertheless, each chapter is intended to be self-contained, presenting a particular topic from a number of divergent viewpoints. In effect each chapter represents as far as possible the larger debate in microcosm. The intent is to sharpen the debate in terms of a limited number of specific issues. Thus, while the collection was assembled for the cover-to-cover reader, each chapter stands alone as a relatively coherent whole.

The book begins with an exchange covering the gamut of issues in the debate at large. *Chapter I* includes Robert K. Merton's classic delineation and defense of contemporary functionalism and Ernest Nagel's critical reply as a philosopher of science. Merton's essay marks the contemporary resurgence of the functional debate in American sociology. Nagel's response is a model of logical critiques generally and attempts to establish the boundaries of functional analysis on logical grounds. To those who are unfamiliar with the controversy, this chapter offers a probing introduction.

Chapter II establishes the pattern for its successors in addressing a specific topic. The concept of "system" is pivotal for the remainder of the volume; Pitirim Sorokin, Ludwig von Bertalanffy, Talcott Parsons and Neil J. Smelser, Alvin W. Gouldner, and C. Wright Mills contribute a variety of perspectives suggested by the polarized terms, "System and Saturnalia."

Chapter III considers "Change and Process," two disputed alternatives in the analysis of social dynamics. Here Parsons, S. N. Eisenstadt, Clifford Geertz, and Wayne Hield suggest divergent approaches. Concepts such as equilibrium, differentiation, institutionalization, and disjunction are strategic.

Chapter IV turns to the closely related area of "Conflict and Consensus." Irving Louis Horowitz, David Lockwood, Pierre Van den Berghe, and Lewis Coser offer contrasting views. None subscribes to a consensual view of society in which conflict is an afterthought or an epiphenomenon. Yet they differ in their judgments concerning the gap between "conflict theory" and functionalism generally.

Chapter V considers a classic tenet of functionalism: the possibility of stipulating "Functional Needs and System Requisites." The chapter begins with the well-known statement of David Aberle, Albert Cohen, Arthur K. David, Marion J. Levy, and Francis Sutton. Critical considerations ensue from Barrington Moore, Jr., Gideon Sjoberg, George Homans, and Harry Bredemeier. Several of these authors doubt the validity of universal needs;

others find contradictions in these needs; still others quarrel concerning the level of analysis implied by such an approach.

Chapter VI explores the concept of function in a different light under the title "Teleology and Explanation." The focus here is on the logic of functional analysis. The articles by Kingsley Davis and Ronald Dore dispute its uniqueness as an analytic approach. Dorothy Emmet, Abraham Kaplan, and Ernest Haas raise further questions concerning the legitimacy of the approach and the relationship between key terms such as "function," "purpose," and "explanation."

Chapter VII confronts a theme that is sotto voce throughout: the implication of "Values and Ideology" in functional analysis. Harold Fallding, Fritz Machlup, Ralf Dahrendorf, and Andrew Hacker raise a number of questions on this score. The first applauds the articulation of values in functional analysis. The second condemns normative intrusions on general grounds. The third is more specific in attacking fuctionalism for a putative bias that is analytically misleading and politically offensive. Finally, the last author suggests that there are indeed specific biases, but raises questions about their presumed conservative direction.

Demerath's "Epilogue" is a commentary on the debate as a whole. It seeks a de-escalation of the tone and a fresh look at some of the specific issues involved in structural-functionalism. It suggests that functionalism is not a single stance but rather many postures, each of which has advantages and disadvantages. This neutral *denouement* is uncharacteristic in a volume that chronicles impassioned advocacy and heated exchange. Yet, we have been content to provide the arena without serving either as lions or Christians.

Finally, we should put our own editorial contribution in perspective. Insofar as this is "our" book, we are reminded of a Harvard professor, renowned for his many edited volumes, who was introduced before his professional colleagues this way: "Most of you are familiar with the professor's works; in fact, most of you have written them."

Chapter I

Overview

Introduction

*T*HE debate over functionalism has spawned such a variety of issues that it is difficult to begin with any one of them. Alternatively, we shall begin with them all. No single piece spans these issues more completely than Robert K. Merton's seminal article, "Manifest and Latent Functions." Ernest Nagel's "Formalization of Functionalism" evaluates Merton's work from the vantage point of the philosophy of science. Taken together, the two provide a trenchant introduction to the confrontations which follow. They also exemplify the cogency of cross-disciplinary exchange.

Merton's essay first appeared in the *American Sociological Review* in 1945 but was considerably revised and extended to form the first chapter of his book of essays, *Social Theory and Social Structure.* To borrow one of its own terms, this essay serves "multiple functions." It notes the prevalent confusion in functionalist terminology; it comments on the history of functionalism and surveys its application in fields other than sociology. It reviews judiciously both the three "prevailing postulates" of functionalism and shows the extent to which they are necessary. It includes a lengthy explication of "manifest and latent functions," drawing upon several classic illustrations, not the least of which is Merton's own analysis of the political machine. It argues that, contradictory to the assertions of many of functionalism's critics, there is no special ideological bias inherent in functionalism. Finally, the work attends to dilemmas of methodology and offers a "paradigm for functional analysis" that is a Larousse among cookbooks.

It is precisely this paradigm that attracts Nagel's formal scrutiny. Philosophers of science often intimidate the sociological theorist. In our overreaction, we tend to see the philosopher as a logical hound who delights in treeing sociological possums. This threat is minimized if we can persuade ourselves that the hound lacks not only sympathy with sociology but also detailed knowledge of its obstacles and nuances. Nagel is the first of several philosophers in this volume who put the lie to these images[1]; he is both sympathetic and knowledgeable. Still, he differs with Merton on a number of issues. For example, he demurs at a simple distinction between manifest and latent functions, arguing that all functions are technically latent except under limited conditions that Merton fails to specify. Nagel also takes a suggestive step in the functional analysis of change by pointing out that change itself may be a property of some systems, one that is preserved as part of general self-maintenance. As a last instance, Nagel is among the rare critics who finds ideological commitment on the part of the theorist "quite innocuous" so long as the commitment is specified. In all of this, Nagel uses a formal rhetoric that concerns environments (E), systems (S), properties of systems (G), and "state co-ordinates," which are independent variables influencing these properties. The vocabulary has the advantage of departing from our conventional concepts and their limiting connotations; but, since the reading is difficult, it is worth noting that a partial explication is available in Francesca Cancian's "Functional Analysis of Change," *American Sociological Review*, 25 (December, 1960).

To some it may appear that the comprehensiveness of both Merton and Nagel affords them not only the first word but also the last. It is true that they raise the major issues in the debate, and yet subsequent chapters offer more than recapitulation. There is ample disagreement in store even on the issues raised. Not only do later authors have divergent answers, but they also ask different questions. If Merton focuses on what functionalism *ought to be* and Nagel elucidates what it *logically can be*, others are concerned with *what it is* and the consequences of *what it has been*. If Merton and Nagel are primarily concerned with saving functionalism for the scientific world, others are more interested in saving the world from functionalism.

---

[1] This volume does suffer from one conspicuous omission among philosophers of science who have confronted functionalism: Carl G. Hempel. Hempel's essay, "The Logic of Functionalism," challenges Nagel's work in incisiveness and breadth of coverage. Unhappily, the piece was not available for reprinting, though it can be obtained in its original publication as part of Llewellyn Gross, ed., *Symposium on Sociological Theory* (Evanston: Row, Peterson and Co., 1959), pp. 271–307, and also as part of Hempel's own recent collection of his work, *Aspects of Scientific Explanation and Other Essays in the Philosophy of Science* (New York: The Free Press, 1965).

Robert K. Merton

Manifest and Latent Functions

Toward the Codification of Functional Analysis in Sociology

*F*UNCTIONAL analysis is at once the most promising and possibly the least codified of contemporary orientations to problems of sociological interpretation. Having developed on many intellectual fronts at the same time, it has grown in shreds and patches rather than in depth. The accomplishments of functional analysis are sufficient to suggest that its large promise will progressively be fulfilled, just as its current deficiencies testify to the need for periodically overhauling the past the better to build for the future. At the very least, occasional re-assessments bring into open discussion many of the difficulties which otherwise remain tacit and unspoken.

Like all interpretative schemes, functional analysis depends upon a triple alliance between theory, method and data. Of the three allies, method is by all odds the weakest. Many of the major practitioners of functional analysis have been devoted to theoretic formulations and to the clearing up of concepts; some have steeped themselves in data directly relevant to a functional frame of reference; but few have broken the prevailing silence regarding how one goes about the business of functional analysis. Yet the plenty and variety of functional analyses force the conclusion that *some* methods have been employed and awaken the hope that much may be learned from their inspection.

Although methods can be profitably examined without reference to theory or substantive data—methodology or the logic of procedure of course has precisely that as its assignment—empirically oriented disciplines are more fully served by inquiry into procedures if this takes due account of their theoretic problems and substantive findings. For the use of "method" involves not only logic but, unfortunately perhaps for those who must struggle with the difficulties of research, also the practical problems of aligning data with the requirements of theory. At least, that is our premise. Accordingly, we shall interweave our account with a systematic review of some of the chief conceptions of functional theory.

The Vocabularies of Functional Analysis

From its very beginnings, the functional approach in sociology has been caught up in terminological confusion. *Too often, a single term has been used to symbolize different concepts, just as the same concept has been symbolized by different terms.* Clarity of analysis and adequacy of communication are both victims of this frivolous use of words. At times, the analysis suffers from the unwitting shift in the conceptual content of a given term, and communication with others breaks down when the essentially same content is obscured by a battery of diverse terms. We have only to follow, for a short distance, the vagaries of the concept of "function" to discover how conceptual clarity is effectively marred and communication defeated by competing vocabularies of functional analysis.

SINGLE TERM, DIVERSE CONCEPTS

The word "function" has been preempted by several disciplines and by popular speech with the not unexpected result that its connotation often becomes obscure in sociology proper. By confining ourselves to only five connotations commonly assigned to this one word, we neglect numerous others. There is first, popular usage, according to which function refers to some public gathering or festive occasion, usually conducted with ceremonial overtones. It is in this connection, one must assume, that a newspaper headline asserts: "Mayor Tobin Not Backing Social Function," for the news account goes on to explain that "Mayor Tobin announced today that he is not interested in any social function, nor has he authorized anyone to sell tickets or sell advertising for any affair." Common as this usage is, it enters into the academic literature too seldom to contribute any great share to the prevailing chaos of terminology. Clearly, *this* connotation of the word is wholly alien to functional analysis in sociology.

A second usage makes the term function virtually equivalent to the term occupation. Max Weber, for example, defines occupation as "the mode of specialization, specification and combination of the functions of an individual so far as it constitutes for him the basis of a continual opportunity for income or for profit." [1] This is a frequent, indeed almost a typical, usage of the term by some economists who refer to the "functional analysis of a group" when they report the distribution of occupations in that group. Since this is the case, it may be expedient to follow the suggestion of Sargant Florence,[2] that the more nearly descriptive phrase "occupational analysis" be adopted for such inquiries.

A third usage, representing a special instance of the preceding one, is found both in popular speech and in political science. Function is often used to refer to the activities assigned to the incumbent of a social status, and more particularly, to the occupant of an office or political position. This gives rise to the term functionary, or official. Although function in this sense overlaps the broader meaning assigned the term in sociology and anthropology, it had best be excluded since it diverts attention from the fact that functions are performed not only by the occupants of designated positions, but by a wide range of standardized activities, social processes, culture patterns and belief-systems found in a society.

Since it was first introduced by Leibniz, the word function has its most precise significance in mathematics, where it refers to a variable considered in relation to one or more other variables in terms of which it may be expressed or on the value of which its own value depends. This conception, in a more extended (and often more imprecise) sense, is expressed by such phrases as "functional interdependence" and "functional relations," so often adopted by social scientists.[3] When Mannheim observes that "every social fact is a function of the time and place in which it occurs," or when a demographer states that "birth-rates are a function of economic status,"

[1] Max Weber, *Theory of Social and Economic Organization* (edited by Talcott Parsons), (London: William Hodge and Co., 1947), 230.

[2] P. Sargant Florence, *Statistical Method in Economics,* (New York: Harcourt, Brace and Co., 1929), 357–58n.

[3] Thus, Alexander Lesser: "In its logical essentials, what is a functional relation? Is it any different in kind from functional relations in other fields of science? I think not. A genuinely functional relation is one which is established between two or more terms or variables such that it can be asserted that under certain defined conditions (which form one term of the relation) certain determined expressions of those conditions (which is the other term of the relation) are observed. The functional relation or relations asserted of any delimited aspect of culture must be such as to explain the nature and character of the delimited aspect under defined condition." "Functionalism in social anthropology," *American Anthropologist,* N.S. 37 (1935), 386–93, at 392.

they are manifestly making use of the mathematical connotation, though the first is not reported in the form of equations and the second is. The context generally makes it clear that the term function is being used in this mathematical sense, but social scientists not infrequently shuttle back and forth between this and another related, though distinct, connotation, which also involves the notion of "interdependence," "reciprocal relation" or "mutually dependent variations."

It is this fifth connotation which is central to functional analysis as this has been practiced in sociology and social anthropology. Stemming in part from the native mathematical sense of the term, this usage is more often explicitly adopted from the biological sciences, where the term function is understood to refer to the "vital or organic processes considered in the respects in which they contribute to the maintenance of the organism." [4] With modifications appropriate to the study of human society, this corresponds rather closely to the key concept of function as adopted by the anthropological functionalists, pure or tempered.[5]

Radcliffe-Brown is the most often explicit in tracing his working conception of social function to the analogical model found in the biological sciences. After the fashion of Durkheim, he asserts that "the function of a recurrent physiological process is thus a correspondence between it and the needs (*i.e.*, the necessary conditions of existence) of the organism." And in the social sphere where individual human beings, "the essential units," are connected by networks of social relations into an integrated whole, "the function of any recurrent activity, such as the punishment of a crime, or a funeral ceremony, is the part it plays in the social life as a whole and therefore the contribution it makes to the maintenance of the structural continuity." [6]

Though Malinowski differs in several respects from the formulations of

---

[4] See for example, Ludwig von Bertalanffy, *Modern Theories of Development*, (New York: Oxford University Press, 1933), 9 ff., 184 ff.; W. M. Bayliss, *Principles of General Physiology* (London, 1915), 706, where he reports his researches on the functions of the hormone discovered by Starling and himself; W. B. Cannon, *Bodily Changes in Pain, Hunger, Fear and Rage* (New York: Appleton & Co., 1929), 222, describing the "emergency functions of the sympathetico-adrenal system."

[5] Lowie makes a distinction between the "pure functionalism" of a Malinowski and the "tempered functionalism" of a Thurnwald. Sound as the distinction is, it will soon become apparent that it is not pertinent for our purposes. R. H. Lowie, *The History of Ethnological Theory* (New York: Farrar & Rinehart, 1937), Chapter 13.

[6] A. R. Radcliffe-Brown, "On the concept of function in social science," *American Anthropologist*, 1935, 37, 395–6. See also his later presidential address before the Royal Anthropological Institute, where he states: "... I would define the social function of a socially standardized mode of activity, or mode of thought, as its relation to the social structure to the existence and continuity of which it makes some contribution. Analogously, in a living organism, the physiological function of the beating of the heart, or the secretion of gastric juices, is its relation to the organic structure . . . . "On social structure," *The Journal of the Royal Anthropological Institute of Great Britain and Ireland*, 1940, 70, Pt. I, 9–10.

Radcliffe-Brown, he joins him in making the core of functional analysis the study of "the part which [social or cultural items] play in the society." "This type of theory," Malinowski explains in one of his early declarations of purpose, "aims at the explanation of anthropological facts at all levels of development by *their function, by the part which they play within the integral system of culture, by the manner in which they are related to each other within the system. . . .*" [7]

As we shall presently see in some detail, such recurrent phrases as "the part played in the social or cultural system" tend to blur the important distinction between the concept of function as "interdependence" and as "process." Nor need we pause here to observe that the postulate which holds that every item of culture has *some* enduring relations with other items, that it has *some* distinctive place in the total culture scarcely equips the field-observer or the analyst with a specific guide to procedure. All this had better wait. At the moment, we need only recognize that more recent formulations have clarified and extended this concept of function through progressive specifications. Thus, Kluckhohn: ". . . a given bit of culture is 'functional' insofar as it defines a mode of response which is adaptive from the standpoint of the society and adjustive from the standpoint of the individual." [8]

From these connotations of the term "function," and we have touched upon only a few drawn from a more varied array, it is plain that many concepts are caught up in the same word. This invites confusion. And when many different words are held to express the same concept, there develops confusion worse confounded.

SINGLE CONCEPT, DIVERSE TERMS

The large assembly of terms used indifferently and almost synonymously with "function" presently includes use, utility, purpose, motive, intention, aim, consequences. Were these and similar terms put to use to refer to the same strictly defined concept, there would of course be little point in noticing their numerous variety. But the fact is that the undisciplined use of these terms, with their ostensibly similar conceptual reference, leads to successively greater departures from tight-knit and rigorous functional analysis. The connotations of each term which differ from rather than agree with the connotation that they have in common are made the (unwitting) basis for inferences which become increasingly dubious as they become progressively remote from the central concept of function. One or two illustrations will

---

[7] B. Malinowski, "Anthropology," *Encyclopaedia Britannica,* First Supplementary Volume, (London and New York, 1926), 132–133 [italics supplied].

[8] Clyde Kluckhohn, *Navaho Witchcraft,* Papers of the Peabody Museum of American Archaeology and Ethnology, Harvard University, (Cambridge: Peabody Museum, 1944), XXII, No. 2, 47a.

bear out the point that a shifting vocabulary makes for the multiplication of misunderstandings.

   In the following passage drawn from one of the most sensible of treatises on the sociology of crime, one can detect the shifts in meaning of nominally synonymous terms and the questionable inferences which depend upon these shifts. (The key terms are italicized to help in picking one's way through the argument.)

> *Purpose* of Punishment. Attempts are being made to determine the *purpose or function* of punishment in different groups at different times. Many investigators have insisted that some one *motive* was *the motive* in punishment. On the other hand, the *function* of punishment in restoring the solidarity of the group which has been weakened by the crime is emphasized. Thomas and Znaniecki have indicated that among the Polish peasants the punishment of crime is *designed primarily* to restore the situation which existed before the crime and renew the solidarity of the group, and that revenge is *a secondary consideration.* From this point of view punishment *is concerned primarily* with the group and only *secondarily* with the offender. On the other hand, expiation, deterrence, retribution, reformation, income for the state, and other things have been posited as *the function* of punishment. In the past as at present it is not clear that any one of these is *the motive* ; punishments seem to grow from *many motives* and to perform *many functions.* This is true both of the individual victims of crimes and of the state. Certainly the laws of the present day are not consistent in *aims or motives* ; probably the same condition existed in earlier societies.[9]

   We should attend first to the list of terms ostensibly referring to the same concept: purpose, function, motive, design, secondary consideration, primary concern, aim. Through inspection, it becomes clear that *these terms group into quite distinct conceptual frames of reference.* At times, some of these terms—motive, design, aim and purpose—clearly refer to the *explicit ends-in-view of the representatives of the state.* Others—motive, secondary consideration—refer to the *ends-in-view of the victim of the crime.* And both of these sets of terms are alike in referring to the *subjective anticipations of the results of punishment.* But the concept of function involves the standpoint of *the observer,* not necessarily that of the participant. Social function refers to *observable objective consequences,* and not to *subjective dispositions* (aims, motives, purposes). And the failure to distinguish between the objective sociological consequences and the subjective dispositions inevitably leads to confusion of functional analysis, as can be seen from the following excerpt (in which the key terms are again italicized):

> The extreme of unreality is attained in the discussion of the so-called "functions" of the family. The family, we hear, performs important *functions*

J. B. Lippincott, 1939), 349–350.
   [9] Edwin H. Sutherland, *Principles of Criminology,* third edition, (Philadelphia:

in society ; it provides for the perpetuation of the species and the training of the young ; it performs economies and religious functions, and so on. Almost we are encouraged to believe that *people marry and have children because* they are eager to perform these needed societal functions. In fact, people marry *because* they are in love, or for other less romantic but no less personal reasons. The *function* of the family, *from the viewpoint of individuals,* is to satisfy their wishes. The *function* of the family or any other social institution is *merely what people use it for.* Social *"functions"* are mostly *rationalizations of established practices* ; *we* act first, explain afterwards ; *we* act for *personal reasons,* and justify *our* behavior by social and ethical *principles.* Insofar as these *functions* of institutions have any real basis, it must be stated in terms of the social processes in which people engage *in the attempt* to satisfy their wishes. Functions arise from the inter-action of concrete human beings and concrete *purposes.*[10]

This passage is an interesting medley of small islets of clarity in the midst of vast confusion. Whenever it mistakenly identifies (subjective) motives with (objective) functions, it abandons a lucid functional approach. For it need not be assumed, as we shall presently see, that the *motives* for entering into marriage ("love," "personal reasons") are identical with the *functions* served by families (socialization of the child). Again, it need not be assumed that the *reasons* advanced by people for their behavior ("*we* act for personal reasons") are one and the same as the observed consequences of these patterns of behavior. The subjective disposition may coincide with the objective consequence, but again, it may not. The two vary independently. When, however, it is said that people are motivated to engage in behavior which may give rise to (not necessarily intended) functions, there is offered escape from the troubled sea of confusion.[11]

This brief review of competing terminologies and their unfortunate consequences may be something of a guide to later efforts at codification of the concepts of functional analysis. There will plainly be occasion to limit the use of the sociological concept of function, and there will be need to distinguish clearly between subjective categories of disposition and objective categories of observed consequences. Else the substance of the functional orientation may become lost in a cloud of hazy definitions.

---

10 Willard Waller, *The Family,* (New York: Cordon Company, 1938), 26.

11 These two instances of confusion between motive and function are drawn from an easily available storehouse of additional materials of the same kind. Even Radcliffe-Brown, who ordinarily avoids this practice, occasionally fails to make the distinction. For example: "... the exchange of presents did not serve the same *purpose* as trade and barter in more developed communities. The *purpose* that it did serve is a moral one. The *object* of the exchange was to produce a friendly feeling between the two persons concerned, and unless it did this it failed of its *purpose.*" Is the "object" of the transaction seen from the standpoint of the observer, the participant, or both? See A. R. Radcliffe-Brown, *The Andaman Islanders,* (Glencoe, Illinois: The Free Press, 1948), 84 [italics supplied].

Prevailing Postulates in Functional Analysis

Chiefly but not solely in anthropology, functional analysts have commonly adopted three interconnected postulates which, it will now be suggested, have proved to be debatable and unnecessary to the functional orientation.

Substantially, these postulates hold first, that standardized social activities or cultural items are functional for the *entire* social or cultural system; second, that *all* such social and cultural items fulfill sociological functions; and third, that these items are consequently *indispensable*. Although these three articles of faith are ordinarily seen only in one another's company, they had best be examined separately, since each gives rise to its own distinctive difficulties.

POSTULATE OF THE FUNCTIONAL UNITY OF SOCIETY

It is Radcliffe-Brown who characteristically puts this postulate in explicit terms:

The function of a particular social usage is the contribution it makes to the *total social life* as the functioning of the *total social system*. Such a view implies that a social system (*the total social structure* of a society together with the totality of social usages, in which that structure appears and on which it depends for its continued existence) has a certain kind of unity, which we may speak of as a functional unity. We may define it as a condition in which all parts of the social system work together with a sufficient degree of harmony or internal consistency, *i.e.*, without producing persistent conflicts which can neither be resolved nor regulated.[12]

It is important to note, however, that he goes on to describe this notion of functional unity as a hypothesis which requires further test.

It would at first appear that Malinowski was questioning the empirical acceptability of this postulate when he notes that "the sociological school" (into which he thrusts Radcliffe-Brown) "exaggerated the social solidarity of primitive man" and "neglected the individual." [13] But it is soon apparent that Malinowski does not so much abandon this dubious assumption as he succeeds in adding another to it. He continues to speak of standardized practices and beliefs as functional "for culture as a whole," and goes on to assume that they are *also* functional for every member of the society. Thus, referring to primitive beliefs in the supernatural, he writes:

Here the functional view is put to its acid test. . . . It is bound to show in what way belief and ritual work for social integration, technical and economic

---

12 Radcliffe-Brown, "On the concept of function," *op. cit.*, 397 [italics supplied].
13 See Malinowski, "Anthropology," *op. cit.*, 132 and "The group and the individual in functional analysis," *American Journal of Sociology*, 1939, 44, 938–64, at 939.

efficiency, for *culture as a whole*—indirectly therefore for the biological and mental welfare *of each individual member*.[14]

If the one unqualified assumption is questionable, this twin assumption is doubly so. Whether cultural items do uniformly fulfill functions for the society viewed as a system and for all members of the society is presumably an empirical question of fact, rather than an axiom.

Kluckhohn evidently perceives the problem inasmuch as he extends the alternatives to include the possibility that cultural forms "are adjustive or adaptive . . . for the members of the society *or* for the society considered as a perduring unit." [15] This is a necessary first step in allowing for variation in the *unit* which is subserved by the imputed function. Compelled by the force of empirical observation, we shall have occasion to widen the range of variation in this unit even further.

It seems reasonably clear that the notion of functional unity is *not* a postulate beyond the reach of empirical test; quite the contrary. The degree of integration is an empirical variable,[16] changing for the same society from time to time and differing among various societies. That all human societies must have *some* degree of integration is a matter of definition—and begs the question. But not all societies have that *high* degree of integration in which *every* culturally standardized activity or belief is functional for the society as a whole and uniformly functional for the people living in it. Radcliffe-Brown need in fact have looked no further than to his favored realm of analogy in order to suspect the adequacy of his assumption of functional unity. For we find significant variations in the degree of integration even among individual biological organisms, although the commonsense assumption would tell us that here, surely, all the parts of the organism work toward a "unified" end. Consider only this:

One can readily see that there are *highly integrated organisms* under close control of the nervous system or of hormones, the loss of any major part of which will strongly affect the whole system, and frequently will cause death, but, on the other hand, there are the lower *organisms much more loosely correlated*, where the loss of even a major part of the body causes only temporary inconvenience pending the regeneration of replacement tissues. Many of these more

---

14 Malinowski, "Anthropology," *op. cit.,* 135, Malinowski maintained this view, without essential change, in his later writings. Among these, consult, for example, "The group and the individual in functional analysis," *op. cit.,* at 962–3: ". . . we see that every institution contributes, on the one hand, toward the integral working of *the community as a whole,* but it also satisfies the derived and basic needs of the individual . . . everyone of the benefits just listed is enjoyed *by every individual member.*" [italics supplied].

15 Kluckhohn, *Navaho Witchcraft,* 46b [italics supplied].

16 It is the merit of Sorokin's early review of theories of social integration that he did not lose sight of this important fact. *Cf.* P. A. Sorokin, "Forms and problems of culture-integration," *Rural Sociology,* 1936, 1, 121–41; 344–74.

loosely organized animals are *so poorly integrated that different parts may be in active opposition to each other*. Thus, when an ordinary starfish is placed on its back, part of the arms may attempt to turn the animal in one direction, while others work to turn it in the opposite way. . . . On account of its *loose integration*, the sea anemone may move off and leave a portion of its foot clinging tightly to a rock, so that the animal suffers serious rupture.[17]

If this is true of single organisms, it would seem *a fortiori* the case with complex social systems.

One need not go far afield to show that the assumption of the complete functional unity of human society is repeatedly contrary to fact. Social usages or sentiments may be functional for some groups and dysfunctional for others in the same society. Anthropologists often cite "increased solidarity of the community" and "increased family pride" as instances of functionally adaptive sentiments. Yet, as Bateson[18] among others has indicated, an increase of pride among individual families may often serve to disrupt the solidarity of a small local community. Not only is the postulate of functional unity often contrary to fact, but it has little heuristic value, since it diverts the analyst's attention from possible disparate consequences of a given social or cultural item (usage, belief, behavior pattern, institution) for diverse social groups and for the individual members of these groups.

If the body of observation and fact which negates the assumption of functional unity is as large and easily accessible as we have suggested, it is interesting to ask how it happens that Radcliffe-Brown and others who follow his lead have continued to abide by this assumption. A possible clue is provided by the fact that this conception, in its recent formulations, was developed by social *anthropologists*, that is, by men primarily concerned with the study of non-literate societies. In view of what Radin has described as "the highly integrated nature of the majority of aboriginal civilizations," this assumption may be tolerably suitable for some, if not all, non-literate societies. But one pays an excessive intellectual penalty for moving this possibly useful assumption from the realm of small non-literate societies to the realm of large, complex and highly differentiated literate societies. In no field, perhaps, do the dangers of such a transfer of assumption become more visible than in the functional analysis of religion. This deserves brief review, if only because it exhibits in bold relief the fallacies one falls heir to by sympathetically adopting this assumption without a thorough screening.

The Functional Interpretation of Religion.—In examining the price paid for the transfer of this tacit assumption of functional unity from the field of relatively small and relatively tightknit non-literate groups to the field of

---

[17] G. H. Parker, *The Elementary Nervous System,* quoted by W. C. Allee, *Animal Aggregation,* (University of Chicago Press, 1931), 81–82.

[18] Gregory Bateson, *Naven,* (Cambridge [England] University Press, 1936), 31–32.

more highly differentiated and perhaps more loosely integrated societies, it is useful to consider the work of sociologists, particularly of sociologists who are ordinarily sensitized to the assumptions on which they work. This has passing interest for its bearing on the more general question of seeking, without appropriate modification, to apply to the study of literate societies conceptions developed and matured in the study of non-literate societies. (Much the same question holds for the transfer of research procedures and techniques, but this is not at issue here.)

The large, spaceless and timeless generalizations about "the integrative functions of religion" are largely, though not of course wholly, derived from observations in non-literate societies. Not infrequently, the social scientist implicitly adopts the findings regarding such societies and goes on to expatiate upon the integrative functions of religion *generally*. From this, it is a short step to statements such as the following:

> *The reason why religion is necessary* is apparently to be found in the fact that human society *achieves its unity* primarily through the possession by its members of certain ultimate values and ends in common. Although these values and ends are subjective, they influence behavior, and their integration enables this society to operate as a system.[19]
> In an extremely advanced society built on scientific technology, the priesthood tends to lose status, because sacred tradition and supernaturalism drop into the background . . . [but] *No society* has become so completely secularized as to liquidate *entirely* the belief in transcendental ends and supernatural entities. Even in a secularized society *some system* must exist for the integration of ultimate values, for their ritualistic expression, and for the emotional adjustments required by disappointment, death, and disaster.[20]

Deriving from the Durkheim orientation which was based largely upon the study of non-literate societies, these authors tend to single out *only* the apparently integrative consequences of religion and to neglect its possibly disintegrative consequences *in certain types of social structure*. Yet consider the following very well-known facts and queries. (1) When different religions co-exist in the same society, there often occurs deep conflict between the several religious groups (consider only the enormous literature on inter-religious conflict in European societies). In what sense, then, does religion make for integration of "the" society in the numerous multi-religion societies? (2) It is clearly the case that "human society achieves its unity [insofar as it exhibits such unity] primarily through the possession by its members of certain ultimate values and ends in common." But what is the evidence indicating that "non-religious" people, say, in our own society less often

---

[19] Kingsley Davis and Wilbert E. Moore, "Some principles of stratification," *American Sociological Review,* April 1945, 10, 242–49, at 244. [italics supplied].
[20] *Ibid.,* 246. [italics supplied].

subscribe to certain common "values and ends" than those devoted to religious doctrines? (3) In what sense does religion make for integration of the larger society, if the content of its doctrine and values is at odds with the content of other, non-religious values held by many people in the same society? (Consider, for example, the conflict between the opposition of the Catholic Church to child-labor legislation and the secular values of preventing "exploitation of youthful dependents." Or the contrasting evaluations of birth control by diverse religious groups in our society.)

This list of commonplace facts regarding the role of religion in contemporary literate societies could be greatly extended, and they are of course very well known to those functional anthropologists and sociologists who describe religion as integrative, without limiting the range of social structures in which this is indeed the case. It is at least conceivable that a theoretic orientation derived from research on non-literate societies has served to obscure otherwise conspicuous data on the functional role of religion in multi-religion societies. Perhaps it is the transfer of the assumption of functional unity which results in blotting out the entire history of religious wars, of the Inquisition (which drove a wedge into society after society), of internecine conflicts among religious groups. For the fact remains that all this abundantly known material is ignored in favor of illustrations drawn from the study of religion in non-literate society. And it is a further striking fact that the same paper, cited above, that goes on to speak of "religion, which provides integration in terms of sentiments, beliefs and rituals," does not make a single reference to the possibly divisive role of religion.

Such functional analyses may, of course, mean that religion provides integration of those who believe in the *same* religious values, but it is unlikely that this is meant, since it would merely assert that integration is provided by any consensus on any set of values.

Moreover, this again illustrates the danger of taking the assumption of functional unity, which *may* be a reasonable approximation for some non-literate societies, as part of an implicit model for *generalized* functional analysis. Typically, in non-literate societies, there is but one prevailing religious system so that, apart from individual deviants, the membership of the total society and the membership of the religious community are virtually co-extensive. Obviously, in this type of social structure, a common set of religious values may have as *one* of its consequences the reinforcement of common sentiments and of social integration. But this does not easily lend itself to defensible generalization about other types of society.

We shall have occasion to return to other theoretic implications of current functional analyses of religion but, for the moment, this may illustrate the dangers which one inherits in adopting the unqualified postulate of functional unity. This unity of the total society cannot be usefully posited in advance of observation. It is a question of fact, and not a matter of opinion. The theoretic framework of functional analysis must expressly require that there be *specification* of the *units* for which a given social or cultural item is functional. It must expressly allow for a given item having diverse consequences, functional and dysfunctional, for individuals, for subgroups, and for the more inclusive social structure and culture.

POSTULATE OF UNIVERSAL FUNCTIONALISM

Most succinctly, this postulate holds that all standardized social or cultural forms have positive functions. As with other aspects of the functional conception, Malinowski advances this in its most extreme form:

The functional view of culture *insists* therefore upon the principle that in *every type of civilization, every custom, material object, idea and belief fulfills some vital function. . . .*[21]

Although, as we have seen, Kluckhohn allows for variation in the unit subserved by a cultural form, he joins with Malinowski in postulating functional value for all surviving forms of culture. ("My basic postulate . . . is that *no* culture forms survive unless they constitute responses which are adjustive or adaptive, in some sense . . ." [22] This universal functionalism may or may not be a heuristic postulate; that remains to be seen. But one should be prepared to find that it too diverts critical attention from a range of non-functional consequences of existing cultural forms.

In fact, when Kluckhohn seeks to illustrate his point by ascribing "functions" to seemingly functionless items, he falls back upon a type of function which would be found, *by definition* rather than by inquiry, served by all persisting items of culture. Thus, he suggests that

The at present mechanically useless buttons on the sleeve of a European man's suit subserve the "function" of preserving the familiar, of maintaining a tradition. People are, in general, more comfortable if they feel a continuity of behavior, if they feel themselves as following out the orthodox and socially approved forms of behavior.[23]

This would appear to represent the marginal case in which the imputation of function adds little or nothing to the direct description of the culture pattern or behavior form. It may well be assumed that all *established* elements of culture (which are loosely describable as "tradition") have the minimum, though not exclusive, function of "preserving the familiar, of

---

[21] Malinowski, "Anthropology," *op. cit.*, 132. [The italics, though supplied, are perhaps superfluous in view of the forceful language of the original.]
[22] Kluckhohn, *Navaho Witchcraft*, 46 [italics supplied].
[23] *Ibid.*, 47.

maintaining a tradition." This is equivalent to saying that the "function" of conformity to *any* established practice is to enable the conformist to avoid the sanctions otherwise incurred by deviating from the established practice. This is no doubt true but hardly illuminating. It serves, however, to remind us that we shall want to explore the *types of functions* which the sociologist imputes. At the moment, it suggests the provisional assumption that, although any item of culture or social structure *may* have functions, it is premature to hold unequivocally that every such item *must* be functional.

The postulate of universal functionalism is of course the historical product of the fierce, barren and protracted controversy over "survivals" which raged among the anthropologists during the early part of the century. The notion of a social survival, that is, in the words of Rivers, of "a custom . . . [which] cannot be explained by its present utility but only becomes intelligible through its past history," [24] dates back at least to Thucydides. But when the evolutionary theories of culture became prominent, the concept of survival seemed all the more strategically important for reconstructing "stages of development" of cultures, particularly for non-literate societies which possessed no written record. For the functionalists who wished to turn away from what they regarded as the usually fragmentary and often conjectural "history" of non-literate societies, the attack on the notion of survival took on all the symbolism of an attack on the entire and intellectually repugnant system of evolutionary thought. In consequence, perhaps, they over-reacted against this concept central to evolutionary theory and advanced an equally exaggerated "postulate" to the effect that "every custom [everywhere] . . . fulfills some vital function."

It would seem a pity to allow the polemics of the anthropological forefathers to create splendid exaggerations in the present. Once discovered, ticketed and studied, social survivals cannot be exorcized by a postulate. And if no specimens of these survivals can be produced, then the quarrel dwindles of its own accord. It can be said, furthermore, that even when such survivals are identified in contemporary literate societies, they seem to add little to our understanding of human behavior or the dynamics of social change. Not requiring their dubious role as poor substitutes for recorded history, the sociologist of literate societies may neglect survivals with no apparent loss. But he need not be driven, by an archaic and irrelevant controversy, to adopt the unqualified postulate that all culture items fulfill vital functions. For this, too, is a problem for investigation, not a conclusion in

---

24 W. H. R. Rivers, "Survival in sociology," *The Sociological Review,* 1913, 6, 293–305. See also E. B. Tylor, *Primitive Culture,* (New York, 1874), esp. I, 70–159; and for a more recent review of the matter, Lowie, *The History of Ethnological Theory,* 44 ff., 81 f. For a sensible and restrained account of the problem, see Emile Durkheim, *Rules of Sociological Method,* Chapter 5, esp. at 91.

advance of investigation. Far more useful as a directive for research would seem the provisional assumption that persisting cultural forms have a *net balance of functional consequences* either for the society considered as a unit or for subgroups sufficiently powerful to retain these forms intact, by means of direct coercion or indirect persuasion. This formulation at once avoids the tendency of functional analysis to concentrate on positive functions and directs the attention of the research worker to other types of consequences as well.

Postulate of Indispensability

The last of this trio of postulates common among functional social scientists is, in some respects, the most ambiguous. The ambiguity becomes evident in the aforementioned manifesto by Malinowski to the effect that

in every type of civilization, every custom, material object, idea and belief fulfills some *vital* function, has some task to accomplish, represents an *indispensable part* within a work whole.[25]

From this passage, it is not at all clear whether he asserts the indispensability of the *function*, or of the *item* (custom, object, idea, belief) fulfilling the function, or *both*.

This ambiguity is quite common in the literature. Thus, the previously cited Davis and Moore account of the role of religion seems at first to maintain that it is the *institution* which is indispensable: "The reason why religion is necessary . . ."; ". . . religion . . . plays a unique and indispensable part in society." [26] But it soon appears that it is not so much the institution of religion which is regarded as indispensable but rather the functions which religion is taken typically to perform. For Davis and Moore regard religion as indispensable only insofar as it functions to make the members of a society adopt "certain ultimate values and ends in common." These values and ends, it is said,

must . . . appear to the members of the society to have some reality, and it is the role of religious belief and ritual to supply and reinforce this appearance of reality. Through ritual and belief the common ends and values are connected with an imaginary world symbolized by concrete sacred objects, which world in turn is related in a meaningful way to the facts and trials of the individual's life.

---

[25] Malinowski, "Anthropology," *op. cit.,* 132 [italics supplied].
[26] Kingsley Davis and Wilbert E. Moore, *op. cit.,* 244, 246. See the more recent review of this matter by Davis in his Introduction to W. J. Goode, *Religion Among the Primitives* (Glencoe, Illinois: The Free Press, 1951) and the instructive functional interpretations of religion in that volume.

Through the worship of the sacred objects and the beings they symbolize, and the acceptance of *supernatural prescriptions* that are at the same time codes of behavior, a powerful control over human conduct is exercised, guiding it along lines sustaining the institutional structure and conforming to the ultimate ends and values.[27]

The alleged indispensability of religion, then, is based on the assumption of fact that it is through "worship" and "supernatural prescriptions" *alone* that the necessary minimum of "control over human conduct" and "integration in terms of sentiments and beliefs" can be achieved.

In short, the postulate of indispensability as it is ordinarily stated contains two related, but distinguishable, assertions. First, it is assumed that there are certain *functions* which are indispensable in the sense that, unless they are performed, the society (or group or individual) will not persist. This, then, sets forth a concept of *functional prerequisites,* or *preconditions functionally necessary* for a society, and we shall have occasion to examine this concept in some detail. Second, and this is quite another matter, it is assumed that *certain cultural or social forms* are indispensable for fulfilling each of these functions. This involves a concept of specialized and irreplaceable structures, and gives rise to all manner of theoretic difficulties. For not only can this be shown to be manifestly contrary to fact, but it entails several subsidiary assumptions which have plagued functional analysis from the very outset. It diverts attention from the fact that alternative social structures (and cultural forms) have served, under conditions to be examined, the functions necessary for the persistence of groups. Proceeding further, we must set forth a major theorem of functional analysis; *just as the same item may have multiple functions, so may the same function be diversely fulfilled by alternative items.* Functional needs are here taken to be permissive, rather than determinant, of specific social structures. Or, in other words, there is a range of variation in the structures which fulfill the function in question. (The limits upon this range of variation involve the concept of structural constraint, of which more presently).

In contrast to this implied concept of indispensable cultural forms (institutions, standardized practices, belief-systems, etc.), there is, then, the concept of *functional alternatives,* or *functional equivalents,* or *functional substitutes.* This concept is widely recognized and used, but it should be noted that it cannot rest comfortably in the same theoretical system which entails the postulate of indispensability of particular cultural forms. Thus, after reviewing Malinowski's theory of "the functional necessity for such mechanisms as magic," Parsons is careful to make the following statement:

---

[27] Ibid., 244–245 [italics supplied].

. . . wherever such uncertainty elements enter into the pursuit of emotionally important goals, if not magic, at least *functionally equivalent* phenomena could be expected to appear.[28]

This is a far cry from Malinowski's own insistence that

Thus magic fulfills *an indispensable function* within culture. It satisfies a definite need *which cannot be satisfied by any other factors of primitive civilization.*[29]

This twin concept of the indispensable function and the irreplaceable belief-and-action pattern flatly excludes the concept of functional alternatives.

In point of fact, the concept of functional alternatives or equivalents has repeatedly emerged in every discipline which has adopted a functional framework of analysis. It is, for example, widely utilized in the psychological sciences, as a paper by English admirably indicates.[30] And in neurology, Lashley has pointed out on the basis of experimental and clinical evidence, the inadequacy of the "assumption that individual neurons are specialized for particular functions," maintaining instead that a particular function may be fulfilled by a range of alternative structures.[31]

Sociology and social anthropology have all the more occasion for avoiding the postulate of indispensability of given structures, and for systematically operating with the concept of functional alternatives and functional substitutes. For just as laymen have long erred in assuming that the "strange" customs and beliefs of other societies were "mere superstitions," so functional social scientists run the risk of erring in the other extreme, first, by being quick to find functional or adaptive value in these practices and beliefs, and second, by failing to see which alternative modes of action are ruled out by cleaving to these ostensibly functional practices. Thus, there is not seldom a readiness among some functionalists to conclude that magic or certain religious rites and beliefs are functional, because of their effect upon the state of mind or self-confidence of the believer. Yet it may well be in some instances, that these magical practices obscure and take the place of accessible secular and more adaptive practices. As F. L. Wells has observed,

To nail a horseshoe over the door in a smallpox epidemic may bolster the morale of the household but it will not keep out the smallpox; such beliefs

---

[28] Talcott Parsons, *Essays in Sociological Theory, Pure and Applied,* (Glencoe, Illinois: The Free Press, 1949), 58.

[29] Malinowski, "Anthropology," *op. cit.,* 136 [italics supplied].

[30] Horace B. English, "Symbolic versus functional equivalents in the neuroses of deprivation," *Journal of Abnormal and Social Psychology,* 1937, 32, 392–94.

[31] K. S. Lashley, "Basic neural mechanisms in behavior," *Psychological Review,* 1930, 37, 1–24.

and practices will not stand the secular tests to which they are susceptible, and the sense of security they give is preserved only while the real tests are evaded.[32]

Those functionalists who are constrained by their theory to attend to the effects of such symbolic practices *only* upon the individual's state of mind and who therefore conclude that the magical practice is functional, neglect the fact that these very practices may on occasion take the place of more effective alternatives.[33] And those theorists who refer to the indispensability of standardized practices or prevailing institutions because of their observed function in reinforcing common sentiments must look first to functional substitutes before arriving at a conclusion, more often premature than confirmed.

Upon review of this trinity of functional postulates, several basic considerations emerge which must be caught up in our effort to codify this mode of analysis. In scrutinizing, first, *the postulate of functional unity,* we found that one cannot assume full integration of all societies, but that this is an empirical question of fact in which we should be prepared to find a range of degrees of integration. And in examining the special case of functional interpretations of religion, we were alerted to the possibility that, though human nature may be of a piece, it does not follow that the structure of non-literate societies is uniformly like that of highly differentiated, "literate" societies. A difference in degree between the two—say, the existence of

---

[32] F. L. Wells, "Social maladjustments: adaptive regression," in Carl A. Murchison, ed., *Handbook of Social Psychology,* Clark University Press, 1935), 880. Wells's observation is far from being antiquarian. As late as the 1930's smallpox was not "being kept out" in such states at Idaho, Wyoming, and Montana which, lacking compulsory vaccination laws, could boast some 4,300 cases of smallpox in a five-year period at the same time that the more populous states of Massachusetts, Pennsylvania and Rhode Island, states with compulsory vaccination laws, had no cases of smallpox at all. On the shortcomings of "common sense" in such matters, see Hugh Cabot, *The Patient's Dilemma* (New York: Reynal & Hitchcock, 1940), 166–167.

[33] It should perhaps be noted that this statement is made with full cognizance of Malinowski's observation that the Trobrianders did not *substitute* their magical beliefs and practices for the application of rational technology. The problem remains of assessing the degree to which technological development is slackened by the semi-dependence on magic for dealing with the "range of uncertainty." This area of uncertainty is presumably not fixed, but is itself related to the available technology. Rituals designed to regulate the weather, for example, might readily absorb the energies of men who might otherwise be reducing that "area of uncertainty" by attending to the advancement of meteorological knowledge. Each case must be judged on its merits. We refer here only to the increasing tendency among social anthropologists and sociologists to confine themselves to the observed "morale" effects of rationally and empirically ungrounded practices, and to forego analysis of the alternatives which would be available in a given situation, did not the orientation toward "the transcendental" and "the symbolic" focus attention on other matters. Finally, it is to be hoped that all this will not be mistaken for a re-statement of the sometimes naive rationalism of the Age of Enlightenment.

several disparate religions in the one and not in the other—may make hazardous the passage between them. From critical scrutiny of this postulate, it developed that a theory of functional analysis must call for *specification* of the social units subserved by given social functions, and that items of culture must be recognized to have multiple consequences, some of them functional and others, perhaps, dysfunctional.

Review of the second *postulate of universal functionalism*, which holds that all persisting forms of culture are inevitably functional, resulted in other considerations which must be met by a codified approach to functional interpretation. It appeared not only that we must be prepared to find dysfunctional as well as functional consequences of these forms but that the theorist will ultimately be confronted with the difficult problem of developing an organon for assessing the net balance of consequences if his research is to have bearing on social technology. Clearly, expert advice based only on the appraisal of a limited, and perhaps arbitrarily selected, range of consequences to be expected as a result of contemplated action, will be subject to frequent error and will be properly judged as having small merit.

The postulate of indispensability, we found, entailed two distinct propositions: the one alleging the indispensability of certain functions, and this gives rise to the concept of *functional necessity* or *functional prerequisites*; the other alleging the indispensability of existing social institutions, culture forms, or the like, and this when suitably questioned, gives rise to the concept of *functional alternatives, equivalents or substitutes*.

Moreover, the currency of these three postulates, singly and in concert, is the source of the common charge that functional analysis inevitably involves certain ideological commitments. Since this is a question which will repeatedly come to mind as one examines the further conceptions of functional analysis, it had best be considered now, if our attention is not to be repeatedly drawn away from the analytical problems in hand by the spectre of a social science tainted with ideology.

Functional Analysis as Ideology

FUNCTIONAL ANALYSIS AS CONSERVATIVE

In many quarters and with rising insistence, it has been charged that, whatever the intellectual worth of functional analysis, it is inevitably committed to a "conservative" (even a "reactionary") perspective. For some of these critics, functional analysis is little more than a latter-day version of the eighteenth century doctrine of a basic and invariable identity of public and private interests. It is viewed as a secularized version of the doctrine set forth by Adam Smith, for example, when in his *Theory of Moral Senti-ments*, he wrote of the "harmonious order of nature, under divine guidance, which promotes the welfare of man through the operation of his individual propensities."[34] Thus, say these critics, functional theory is merely the orientation of the conservative social scientist who would defend the present order of things, just as it is, and who would attack the advisability of change, however moderate. On this view, the functional analyst systematically ignores Tocqueville's warning not to confound the familiar with the necessary: ". . . what we call necessary institutions are often no more than institu-tions to which we have grown accustomed. . . ." It remains yet to be shown that functional analysis inevitably falls prey to this engaging fallacy but, having reviewed the postulate of indispensability, we can well appreciate that *this* postulate, if adopted, might easily give rise to this ideological charge. Myrdal is one of the most recent and not the least typical among the critics who argue the inevitability of a conservative bias in functional analysis:

> . . . if a thing has a "function" it is good or at least essential.* The term "function" can have a meaning *only* in terms of an assumed *purpose*** ; if that purpose is left undefined or implied to be the "interest of society" which is not further defined,*** a considerable leeway for arbitrariness in practical implica-tion is allowed but the main direction is given: *a description of social institutions in terms of their functions must lead to a conservative teleology.*[35]

Myrdal's remarks are instructive less for their conclusion than for their premises. For, as we have noted, he draws upon two of the postulates so often adopted by functional analysts to reach the unqualified charge that he who describes institutions in terms of functions is unavoidably committed to "a conservative teleology." But nowhere does Myrdal challenge the inevitability of the postulates themselves. It will be interesting to ask how ineluctable the commitment when one has escaped from the premises.

In point of fact, if functional analysis in sociology were committed to teleology, let alone a conservative teleology, it would soon be subjected, and properly so, to even more harsh indictments than these. As has so often happened with teleology in the history of human thought, it would be subjected to a *reductio ad absurdum*. The functional analyst might then

---

34 Jacob Viner, "Adam Smith and Laissez Faire," *Journal of Political Economy*, 1937, 35, 206.

* Here, be it noted, Myrdal gratuitously *accepts* the doctrine of indispensability as intrinsic to any functional analysis.

* * This, as we have seen, is not only gratuitous, but false.

* * * Here, Myrdal properly notes the dubious and vague postulate of functional unity.

35 Gunnar Myrdal, *An American Dilemma* (New York: Harper and Brothers, 1944) II, 1056 [italics and parenthetical remarks supplied].

meet the fate of Socrates (though not for the same reason) who suggested that God put our mouth just under our nose so that we might enjoy the smell of our food.[36] Or, like the Christian theologians devoted to the argument from design, he might be cozened by a Ben Franklin who demonstrated that God clearly "wants us to tipple, because He has made the joints of the arm just the right length to carry a glass to the mouth, without falling short of or overshooting the mark: 'Let us adore, then, glass in hand, this benevolent wisdom; let us adore and drink.' "[37] Or, he might find himself given to more serious utterances, like Michelet who remarked "how beautifully everything is arranged by nature. As soon as the child comes into the world, it finds a mother who is ready to care for it."[38] Like any other system of thought which borders on teleology, though it seeks to avoid crossing the frontier into that alien and unproductive territory, functional analysis in sociology is threatened with a reduction to absurdity, once it adopts the postulate of all existing social structures as indispensable for the fulfillment of salient functional needs.

FUNCTIONAL ANALYSIS AS RADICAL

Interestingly enough, others have reached a conclusion precisely opposed to this charge that functional analysis is intrinsically committed to the view that whatever is, is right or that this is, indeed, the best of all possible worlds. These observers, LaPiere for example, suggest that functional analysis is an approach inherently critical in outlook and pragmatic in judgment:

> There is . . . a deeper significance than might at first appear in the shift from structural description to functional analysis in the social sciences. This shift represents a break with the social absolutism and moralism of Christian theology. If the important aspect of any social structure is its functions, it follows that no structure can be judged in terms of structure alone. In practice this means, for example, that the patriarchal family system is collectively valuable *only if and to the extent that* it functions to the satisfaction of collective ends. As a social structure, *it has no inherent value*, since its functional value will vary from time to time and from place to place.
>
> The functional approach to collective behavior will, undoubtedly, *affront all those who believe that specific sociopsychological structures have inherent values*. Thus, to those who believe that a church service is good because it is a church service, the statement that some church services are formal motions which are devoid of religious significance, that others are functionally com-

---

[36] Farrington has some further interesting observations on pseudo-teleology in his *Science in Antiquity* (London: T. Butterworth, 1936), 160.

[37] This, in a letter by Franklin to the Abbé Morellet, quoted from the latter's *mémoires* by Dixon Wecter, *The Hero in America*, (New York: Scribner, 1941), 53–54.

[38] It is Sigmund Freud who picked up this remark in Michelet's *The Woman*.

parable to theatrical performances, and that still others are a form of revelry and are therefore comparable to a drunken spree will be an affront to common sense, an attack upon the integrity of decent people, or, at the least, the ravings of a poor fool.[39]

The fact that functional analysis can be seen by some as inherently conservative and by others as inherently radical suggests that it may be *inherently* neither one nor the other. It suggests that functional analysis may involve no *intrinsic* ideological commitment although, like other forms of sociological analysis, it can be infused with any one of a wide range of ideological values. Now, this is not the first time that a theoretic orientation in social science or social philosophy has been assigned diametrically opposed ideological implications. It may be helpful, therefore, to examine one of the most notable prior instances in which a sociological and methodological conception has been the object of the most varied ideological imputations, and to compare this instance, so far as possible, with the case of functional analysis. The comparable case is that of dialectical materialism; the spokesmen for dialectical materialism are the nineteenth century economic historian, social philosopher and professional revolutionary, Karl Marx, and his close aide and collaborator, Friedrich Engels.

The Ideological Orientations of Dialectical Materialism

1. "The mystification which dialectic suffers at Hegel's hands by no means prevents him from being the first to present *its general form* of working in a comprehensive and conscious manner. With him it is standing on its head. It must be turned right side up again if you would discover the *rational kernel* within the *mystical shell*.

2. *"In its mystified form* dialectic became the fashion in Germany, *because it seemed to transfigure and to glorify the existing state of things.*

3. *"In its rational form* it is a scandal and an abomination to bourgeois-

Comparative Ideological Orientations of Functional Analysis

1. *Some* functional analysts have gratuitously *assumed* that *all* existing social structures fulfill indispensable social functions. This is sheer faith, mysticism, if you will, rather than the final product of sustained and systematic inquiry. The postulate must be earned, not inherited, if it is to gain the acceptance of men of social science.

2. The three postulates of functional unity, universality and indispensability comprise a system of premises which must inevitably lead to a glorification of the existing state of things.

3. In its more empirically oriented and analytically precise forms, func-

---

[39] Richard LaPiere, *Collective Behavior,* (New York: McGraw-Hill, 1938), 55–56 [italics supplied].

The Ideological Orientations of Dialectical Materialism

dom and its doctrinaire professors, because *it includes in its comprehensive and affirmative recognition of the existing state of things,* at the same time also, *the recognition of the negation of* that state [of affairs], of its inevitable breaking up ;

Comparative Ideological Orientations of Functional Analysis

tional analysis is often regarded with suspicion by those who consider an existing social structure as eternally fixed and beyond change. This more exacting form of functional analysis includes, not only a study of the *functions* of existing social structures, but also a study of their *dysfunctions* for diversely situated individuals, subgroups or social strata, and the more inclusive society. It provisionally assumes, as we shall see, that when *the net balance of the aggregate of consequences* of an existing social structure is clearly dysfunctional, there develops a strong and insistent pressure for change. It is possible, though this remains to be established, that beyond a given point, this pressure will inevitably result in more or less predetermined directions of social change.

4. "because it regards *every historically developed form* as in fluid movement, and therefore takes into account *its transient nature* not less than *its momentary existence* ; because it lets nothing impose upon it, and is *in its essence* critical and revolutionary."[40]

4. Though functional analysis has often focused on the *statics* of social structure rather than the *dynamics* of social change, this is not intrinsic to that system of analysis. By focusing on dysfunctions as well as on functions, this mode of analysis can assess not only the bases of social stability but the potential sources of social change. The phrase "historically developed forms" may be a useful reminder that social structures are typically undergoing discernible change. It remains to discover the pressures making for various types of change. To the extent that functional analysis focuses wholly on functional consequences, it leans toward an ultraconservative ideology ; to the extent that it focuses wholly on dysfunctional consequences, it leans

---

[40] The passage to this point is quoted, without deletion or addition but only with the introduction of italics for appropriate emphasis, from that fount of dialectical materialism, Karl Marx, *Capital,* (Chicago : C. H. Kerr, 1906), I, 25–26.

The Ideological Orientations of
Dialectical Materialism

Comparative Ideological Orientations
of Functional Analysis

toward an ultra-radical utopia. "In its essence," it is neither one nor the other.

5. ". . . all successive historical situations are *only transitory stages* in the endless course of development of human society from the lower to the higher. *Each stage is necessary, therefore justified for the time and conditions to which it owes its origin.*

5. Recognizing, as they must, that social structures are forever changing, functional analysts must nevertheless explore the interdependent and often mutually supporting elements of social structure. In general, it seems that most societies are integrated to the extent that many, if not all, of their several elements are reciprocally adjusted. Social structures do not have a random assortment of attributes, but these are variously interconnected and often mutually sustaining. To recognize this, is not to adopt an uncritical affirmation of every *status quo* ; to fail to recognize this, is to succumb to the temptations of radical utopianism.

6. "But in the newer and higher conditions which *gradually develop in its own bosom, each loses its validity and justification.* It must give way to a higher form which will also in its turn decay and perish . . .

6. The strains and stresses in a social structure which accumulate as dysfunctional consequences of existing elements are not cabin'd, cribb'd and confined by appropriate social planning and will in due course lead to institutional breakdown and basic social change. When this change has passed beyond a given and not easily identifiable point, it is customary to say that a new social system has emerged.

7. "It [dialectical materialism] reveals the transitory character of everything and in everything ; nothing can endure before it except the uninterrupted process of becoming and of passing away . . . *It* [dialectic] *has, of course, also a conservative side: it recognizes that definite stages of knowledge and society are justified for their time and circumstances ; but only so far. The conservatism of this mode of outlook is relative ; its revolutionary*

7. But again, it must be reiterated: neither change alone nor fixity alone can be the proper object of study by the functional analyst. As we survey the course of history, it seems reasonably clear that all major social structures have in due course been cumulatively modified or abruptly terminated. In either event, they have not been eternally fixed and unyielding to change. But, at a given moment of observation, any such social structure

The Ideological Orientations of Dialectical Materialism	Comparative Ideological Orientations of Functional Analysis
character is absolute—the only absolute it admits."41	may be tolerably well accommodated both to the subjective values of many or most of the population, and to the objective conditions with which it is confronted. To recognize this is to be true to the facts, not faithful to a pre-established ideology. And by the same token, when the structure is observed to be out of joint with the wants of the people or with the equally solid conditions of action, this too must be recognized. Who dares do all that, may become a functional analyst, who dares do less is none.42

This systematic comparison may be enough to suggest that functional analysis does not, any more than the dialectic, *necessarily* entail a specific ideological commitment. This is not to say that such commitments are not often implicit in the works of functional analysts. But this seems extraneous rather than intrinsic to functional . theory. Here, as in other departments of intellectual activity, abuse does not gainsay the possibility of use. *Critically* revised, functional analysis is neutral to the major ideological systems. To this extent, and only in this limited sense,43 it is like those theories or instruments of the physical sciences which lend themselves indifferently to use by opposed groups for purposes which are often no part of the scientists' intent.

IDEOLOGY AND THE FUNCTIONAL ANALYSIS OF RELIGION

Again, it is instructive to turn, however briefly, to discussions of the functions of religion to show how the *logic* of functional analysis is adopted by people otherwise opposed in their ideological stance.

The social role of religion has of course been repeatedly observed and interpreted over the long span of many centuries. The hard core of continuity

---

41 Similarly, the subsequent passage is quoted, with deletion only of irrelevant material and again with italics supplied, from Friedrich Engels, in *Karl Marx, Selected Works,* (Moscow: Cooperative Publishing Society, 1935), I, 422.

42 It is recognized that this paraphrase does violence to the original intent of the bard, but it is hoped that the occasion justifies the offense.

43 This should not be taken to deny the important fact that the values, implicit and openly acknowledged, of the social scientist may help fix his choice of problems for investigation, his formulation of these problems and, consequently, the utility of his findings for certain purposes, and not for others. The statement intends only what it affirms: functional analysis had no *intrinsic* commitment to any ideological camp, as the foregoing discussion at least illustrates.

in these observations consists in an emphasis on religion as an institutional means of social control, whether this be in Plato's concept of "noble lies," or in Aristotle's opinion that it operates "with a view to the persuasion of the multitude" or in the comparable judgment by Polybius that "the masses . . . can be controlled only by mysterious terrors and tragic fears." If Montesquieu remarks of the Roman lawmakers that they sought "to inspire a people that feared nothing with fear of the gods, and to use that fear to lead it whithersoever they pleased," then Jawaharlal Nehru observes, on the basis of his own experience, that "the only books that British officials heartily recommended [to political prisoners in India] were religious books or novels. It is wonderful how dear to the heart of the British Government is the subject of religion and how impartially it encourages all brands of it."[44] It would appear that there is an ancient and abiding tradition holding, in one form or another, that religion has served to control the masses. It appears, also, that the language in which this proposition is couched usually gives a clue to the ideological commitment of the author.

How is it, then, with some of the current functional analyses of religion? In his critical consolidation of several major theories in the sociology of religion, Parsons summarizes some of the basic conclusions which have emerged regarding the "functional significance of religion":

. . . if moral norms and the sentiments supporting them are of such primary importance, what are the mechanisms by which they are maintained *other than external processes of enforcement?* It was Durkheim's view that religious ritual was of primary significance as a mechanism for *expressing and reinforcing* the *sentiments* most essential to the *institutional integration* of the society. It can readily be seen that this is clearly linked to Malinowski's views of the significance of funeral ceremonies as *a mechanism for reasserting the solidarity of the group* on the occasion of severe emotional strain. Thus Durkheim worked out certain aspects of the specific relations between *religion and social structure* more sharply than did Malinowski, and in addition put the problem in a different functional perspective in that he applied it to the society as a whole in abstraction from particular situations of tension and strain for the individual.[45]

And again, summarizing an essential finding of the major comparative study in the sociology of religion, Parsons observes that "perhaps the most striking feature of Weber's analysis is the demonstration of the extent to which precisely the variations in socially sanctioned values and goals in secular life correspond to the variations in the dominant religious philosophy of the great civilizations." [46]

---

[44] Jawaharlal Nehru, *Toward Freedom,* (New York: John Day, 1941), 7.
[45] Talcott Parsons, *Essays in Sociological Theory,* 61 [italics supplied].
[46] *Ibid.,* 63.

Similarly, in exploring the role of religion among racial and ethnic sub-groups in the United States, Donald Young in effect remarks the close correspondence between their "socially sanctioned values and goals in secular life" and their "dominant religious philosophy":

One function which a minority religion may serve is that of *reconciliation with inferior status and its discriminatory consequences.* Evidence of religious service of this function may be found among all American minority peoples. On the other hand, religious institutions may also develop in such a way as to be *an incitement and support of revolt against inferior status.* Thus, the Christian-ized Indian, with due allowance for exceptions, has tended to be *more submissive* than the pagan. Special cults such as those associated with the use of peyote, the Indian Shaker Church, and the Ghost Dance, all three containing both Christian and native elements, were foredoomed attempts to develop *modes of religious expression adapted to individual and group circumstances.* The latter, with its emphasis on an assured millennium of freedom from the white man, encouraged forceful revolt. The Christianity of the Negro, in spite of appreciable encour-agement of verbal criticism of the existing order, *has emphasized acceptance of present troubles in the knowledge of better times to come in the life hereafter.* The numerous varieties of Christianity and the Judaism brought by immigrants from Europe and Mexico, in spite of common nationalistic elements, also *stressed later rewards rather than immediate direct action.*[47]

These diverse and scattered observations, with their notably varied ideological provenience, exhibit some basic similarities. First, they are all given over to the consequences of specific religious systems for prevailing sentiments, definitions of situations and action. These consequences are rather consistently observed to be those of reinforcement of prevailing moral norms, docile acceptance of these norms, postponement of ambitions and gratifications (if the religious doctrine so demands), and the like. However, as Young observes, religions have also served, under determinate conditions, to provoke rebellion, or as Weber has shown, religions have served to motivate or to canalize the behavior of great numbers of men and women toward the modification of social structures. It would seem premature, there-fore, to conclude that all religion everywhere has only the one consequence of making for mass apathy.

Second, the Marxist view implicitly and the functionalist view explicitly affirm the central point that systems of religion *do affect behavior,* that they are *not merely* epiphenomena but partially independent determinants of behavior. For presumably, it makes a difference if "the masses" do or do not

---

[47] Donald Young, *American Minority Peoples,* (New York: Harper, 1937), 204 [italics supplied]. For a functional analysis of the Negro church in the United States, see George Eaton Simpson and J. Milton Yinger, *Racial and Cultural Minorities* (New York: Harper & Brothers, 1953), 522–530.

accept a particular religion just as it makes a difference if an individual does or does not take opium.

Third, the more ancient as well as the Marxist theories deal with the *differential* consequences of religious beliefs and rituals for various sub-groups and strata in the society—*e.g.*, "the masses"—as, for that matter, does the non-Marxist Donald Young. The functionalist is not confined, as we have seen, to exploring the consequences of religion for "society as a whole."

Fourth, the suspicion begins to emerge that the functionalists, with their emphasis on religion as a *social mechanism* for "reinforcing the sentiments most essential to the institutional integration of the society," may not differ materially in their *analytical framework* from the Marxists who, if their metaphor of "opium of the masses" is converted into a neutral statement of social fact, also assert that religion operates as a social mechanism for reinforcing certain secular as well as sacred sentiments among its believers.

The point of difference appears only when *evaluations* of this commonly accepted fact come into question. Insofar as the functionalists refer only to "institutional integration" without exploring the diverse consequences of integration about very different types of values and interests, they confine themselves to purely *formal* interpretation. For integration is a plainly formal concept. A society may be integrated around norms of strict caste, regimentation, and docility of subordinated social strata, just as it may be integrated around norms of open mobility, wide areas of self-expression and independence of judgment among temporarily lower strata. And insofar as the Marxists assert, without qualification, that all religion everywhere, whatever its doctrinal content and its organizational form, involves "an opiate" for the masses, they too shift to purely formal interpretations, without allowing, as the excerpt from Young shows to be the case, for particular religions in particular social structures serving to activate rather than to lethargize mass action. It is in the *evaluation* of these functions of religion, rather than in the logic of analysis, then, that the functionalists and the Marxists part company. And it is the *evaluations* which permit the pouring of ideological content into the bottles of *functionalism*.[48] The bottles themselves are neutral to their contents, and may serve equally well as containers for ideological poison or for ideological nectar.

---

[48] This type of talking-past-each-other is perhaps more common than one is wont to suspect. Often, the basic agreement in the *analysis* of a situation is plentifully obscured by the basic disagreement in the *evaluation* of that situation. As a result, it is erroneously assumed that the opponents differ in their cognitive procedures and findings, whereas they differ only in their sets of values. Consider, for example, the recent striking case of the public debates and conflicts between Winston Churchill and Harold Laski, where it was generally assumed, among others by Churchill himself, that the two disagreed on the substantive premise that social change is more readily accepted

in time of war than in time of peace. Yet compare the following excerpts from the writings of the two men:

"The former peace-time structure of society had for more than four years been superseded and life had been raised to a strange intensity by the war spell. Under that mysterious influence, men and women had been appreciably exalted above death and pain and toil. *Unities and comradeships had become possible* between men and classes and nations and grown stronger *while the hostile pressure and the common cause endured*. But now the spell was broken: too late for some purposes, too soon for others, and too suddenly for all! *Every victorious country subsided to its old levels and its previous arrangements;* but these latter were found to have fallen into much disrepair, their fabric was weakened and disjointed, they seemed narrow and out of date."

"*With the passing of the spell there passed also,* just as the new difficulties were at their height, *much of the exceptional powers of guidance and control....* To the faithful, toil-burdened masses the victory was so complete that no further effort seemed required.... *A vast fatigue dominated collective action.* Though every subversive element endeavored to assert itself, *revolutionary rage like every other form of psychic energy burnt low.*"

"The intensity of the exertions evoked by the national danger far exceeded the ordinary capacities of human beings. All were geared up to an abnormal pitch. *Once the supreme incentive had disappeared, everyone became conscious of the severity of the strain. A vast and general relaxation and descent to the standards of ordinary life was imminent.* No community could have gone on using up treasure and life energy at such a pace. *Most of all was the strain apparent in the higher ranks of the brain workers.* They had carried on uplifted by the psychological stimulus which was now to be removed. 'I can work until I drop' was sufficient while the cannon thundered and armies marched. *But now it was peace: and on every side exhaustion,* nervous and physical, unfelt or unheeded before, became evident."

"The atmosphere of war permits, and even compels, innovations and experiments that are not possible when peace returns. The invasion of our wonted routine of life accustoms us to what William James called the vital habit of breaking habits.... *We find ourselves stimulated to exertions, even sacrifices,* we did not know we had it in us to make. *Common danger builds a basis for a new fellowship* the future of which is dependent wholly upon whether its foundations are temporary or permanent. If they are temporary, then the end of the war sees the resumption of all our previous differences exacerbated tenfold by the grave problems it will have left." "I am, therefore, arguing that the changes which we require we can make by consent in a period in which, as now, conditions make men remember their identities and not their differences."

"We can begin those changes now because the atmosphere is prepared for their reception. It is highly doubtful *whether we can make them by consent when that atmosphere is absent.* It is the more doubtful because the effort the war requires will induce in many, above all in those who have agreed to the suspension of privilege, *a fatigue, a hunger for the ancient ways, which it will be difficult to resist.*"

"In all revolutions there comes a period of inertia when *the fatigue of the effort compels a pause in the process of innovation.* That period is bound to come with the cessation of hostilities. *After a life on the heights the human constitution seems to demand tranquility and relaxation.* To insist, in the period of pause, that we gird up our loins for a new and difficult journey, above all for a journey into the unknown, is to ask the impossible.... When hostilities against Nazism cease, *men will want, more than anything, a routine of thought and habit which does not compel the painful adaptation of their minds to disturbing excitement.*"

The Gibbonesque passages in the first column are, of course, by Churchill, the

The Logic of Procedure

PREVALENCE OF THE FUNCTIONAL ORIENTATION

The functional orientation is of course neither new nor confined to the social sciences. It came, in fact, relatively late on the sociological scene, if one may judge by its earlier and extended use in a great variety of other disciplines.[49] The central orientation of functionalism—expressed in the practice of interpreting data by establishing their consequences for larger structures in which they are implicated—has been found in virtually all the sciences of man—biology and physiology, psychology, economics and law, anthropology and sociology.[50] The prevalence of the functional outlook is

---

Winston Churchill between the Great Wars, writing in retrospect about the aftermath of the first of these: *The World Crisis:* Volume 4, *The Aftermath,* (London: Thornton Butterworth, 1928), 30, 31, 33. The observations in the second column are those of Harold Laski, writing during the Second Great War to say that it is the policy of Mr. Churchill to make "the conscious postponement of any issue deemed 'controversial' until the victory is won [and] this means . . . that the relations of production are to remain unchanged until peace comes, and that, accordingly, none of the instruments for social change on a large scale, will be at the national disposal for agreed purposes." *Revolution of Our Time,* (New York: Viking Press, 1943), 185, 187, 193, 227–8, 309. Unless Churchill had forgotten his analysis of the aftermath of the first war, it is plain that he and Laski were *agreed on the diagnosis* that significant and deliberately enacted social change was unlikely in the immediate post-war era. The difference clearly lay in the appraisal of the desirability of instituting designated changes at all. (The italics in both columns were by neither author.)

It may be noted, in passing, that the very expectation on which both Churchill and Laski were *agreed—i.e.* that the post-war period in England would be one of mass lethargy and indifference to planned institutional change—was not altogether borne out by the actual course of events. England after the second great war did not exactly repudiate the notion of planned change.

[49] The currency of a functionalist outlook has been repeatedly noted. For example: "The fact that in all fields of thinking the same tendency is noticeable, proves that there is now a general trend toward interpreting the world in terms of interconnection of operation rather than in terms of separate substantial units. Albert Einstein in physics, Claude Bernard in physiology, Alexis Carrel in biology, Frank Lloyd Wright in architecture, A. N. Whitehead in philosophy, W. Koehler in psychology, Theodor Litt in sociology, Hermann Heller in political science, B. Cardozo in law: these are men representing different cultures, different countries, different aspects of human life and the human spirit, and yet all approaching their problems with a sense of 'reality' which is looking not to material substance but to functional interaction for a comprehension of phenomena." G. Niemeyer, *Law Without Force,* (Princeton University Press, 1941), 300. This motley company suggests anew that agreement on the functional outlook need not imply identity of political or social philosophy.

[50] The literature commenting on the trend toward functionalism is almost as large and considerably more sprawling than the diverse scientific literatures exemplifying the

in itself no warrant for its scientific value, but it does suggest that cumulative experience has forced this orientation upon the disciplined observers of man as biological organism, psychological actor, member of society and bearer of culture.

More immediately relevant is the possibility that prior experience in other disciplines may provide useful methodological models for functional analysis in sociology. To learn from the canons of analytical procedure in these often more exacting disciplines is not, however, to adopt their specific conceptions and techniques, lock, stock and barrel. To profit from the logic

---

trend. Limitations of space and concern for immediate relevance limit the number of such references which must here take the place of an extended review and discussion of these collateral developments in scientific thought.

For *biology,* a general, now classical, source is J. H. Woodger, *Biological Principles: A Critical Study,* (New York: Harcourt Brace and Co., 1929), esp. 327 ff. For correlative materials, at least the following are indicated: Bertalanffy, *Modern Theories of Development, op. cit.,* particularly 1–46, 64 ff., 179 ff.; E. S. Russell, *The Interpretation of Development and Heredity: A Study in Biological Method,* (Oxford: Clarendon Press, 1930), esp. 166–280. Foreshadowing discussions will be found in the less instructive writings of W. E. Ritter, E. B. Wilson, E. Ungerer, J. Schaxel, J. von Uexküll, etc. The papers of J. Needham—e.g., "Thoughts on the problem of biological organization," *Scientia,* August 1932, 84–92—can be consulted with profit.

For *physiology,* consider the writings of C. S. Sherrington, W. B. Cannon, G. E. Coghill, Joseph Barcroft, and especially the following: C. S. Sherrington, *The Integrative Action of the Nervous System,* (New Haven: Yale University Press, 1923); W. B. Cannon, *Bodily Changes in Pain, Hunger, Fear and Rage,* chapter 12, and *The Wisdom of the Body,* (New York: W. W. Norton, 1932), all but the unhappy epilogue on "social homeostasis"; G. E. Coghill, *Anatomy and the Problem of Behavior,* (Cambridge University Press, 1929); Joseph Barcroft, *Features in the Architecture of Physiological Function,* (Cambridge University Press, 1934).

For *psychology,* virtually any of the basic contributions to dynamic psychology are in point. It would not only be low wit but entirely true to say that Freudian conceptions are instinct with functionalism, since the major concepts are invariably referred to a functional (or dysfunctional) framework. For a different order of conception, see Harvey Carr, "Functionalism," in Carl Murchison, ed. *Psychologies of 1930,* (Clark University Press, 1930); and as one among many articles dealing with substantially this set of conceptions, see J. M. Fletcher, "Homeostasis as an explanatory principle in psychology," *Psychological Review,* 1942, 49, 80–87. For a statement of application of the functional approach to personality, see chapter I in Clyde Kluckhohn and Henry A. Murray, ed. *Personality in Nature, Society and Culture,* (New York: A. A. Knopf, 1948), 3–32. The important respects in which the Lewin group is oriented toward functionalism have been widely recognized.

For *law,* see the critical paper by Felix S. Cohen, "Transcendental nonsense and the functional approach," *Columbia Law Review,* 1935, XXXV, 809–849, and the numerous annotated references therein.

For *sociology and anthropology,* see the brief sampling of references throughout this chapter. The volume edited by Robert Redfield provides a useful bridge across the chasm too often separating the biological from the social sciences. Levels of Integration in Biological and Social Systems, *Biological Symposia,* 1943, VIII. For an important effort to set out the conceptual framework of functional analysis, see Talcott Parsons, *The Social System,* (Glencoe, Illinois: Free Press, 1951).

of procedure successfully employed in the biological sciences, for example, is not to backslide into accepting the largely irrelevant analogies and homologies which have so long fascinated the devotees of organismic sociology. To examine the *methodological* framework of biological researches is not to adopt their *substantive* concepts.

The *logical structure* of experiment, for example, does not differ in physics, or chemistry or psychology, although the substantive hypotheses, the technical tools, the basic concepts and the practical difficulties may differ enormously. Nor do the near-substitutes for experiment—controlled observation, comparative study and the method of "discerning"—differ in their *logical structure* in anthropology, sociology or biology.

In turning briefly to Cannon's logic of procedure in physiology, then, we are looking for a methodological model which might possibly be derived for sociology, without adopting Cannon's unfortunate homologies between the structure of biological organisms and of society.[51] His procedures shape up somewhat as follows. Adopting the orientation of Claude Bernard, Cannon first indicates that the organism *requires* a relatively constant and stable state. One task of the physiologist, then, is to provide "a concrete and detailed account of the modes of assuring steady states." In reviewing the numerous "concrete and detailed" accounts provided by Cannon, we find that the *general mode of formulation* is invariable, irrespective of the specific problem in hand. A typical formulation is as follows: *"In order that* the blood shall . . . serve as a circulating medium, fulfilling the various *functions* of a common carrier of nutriment and waste . . ., *there must be* provision for holding it back whenever there is danger of escape." Or, to take another statement: *"If* the life of the cell is to continue . . ., the blood . . . *must* flow with sufficient speed to deliver to the living cells the (necessary) supply of oxygen."

Having established the *requirements* of the organic system, Cannon then proceeds to describe *in detail* the various *mechanisms* which operate to meet these requirements (*e.g.,* the complicated changes which lead to clotting, the local contraction of injured blood vessels that lessen the severity of bleeding; accelerated clot formation through the secretion of adrenin and the action of adrenin upon the liver, etc.). Or again, he describes the various biochem-

---

[51] As previously implied, Cannon's epilogue to his *Wisdom of the Body* remains unexcelled as an example of the fruitless extremes to which even a distinguished mind is driven once he sets about to draw *substantive* analogies and homologies between biological organisms and social systems. Consider, for example, his comparison between the fluid matrix of the body and the canals, rivers and railroads on which "the products of farm and factory, of mine and forest, are borne to and fro." This kind of analogy, earlier developed in copious volumes by René Worms, Schaeffle, Vincent, Small, and Spencer among others, does *not* represent the distinctive value of Cannon's writings for the sociologist.

ical arrangements which ensure a proper supply of oxygen to the normal organism and the compensating changes which occur when some of these arrangements do not operate adequately.

If the logic of this approach is stated in its more general terms, the following interrelated sequence of steps becomes evident. First of all, certain functional requirements of the organisms are established, requirements which must be satisfied if the organism is to survive, or to operate with some degree of effectiveness. Second, there is a concrete and detailed description of the arrangements (structures and processes) through which these requirements are typically met in "normal" cases. Third, if some of the typical mechanisms for meeting these requirements are destroyed, or are found to be functioning inadequately, the observer is sensitized to the need for detecting compensating mechanisms (if any) which fulfill the necessary function. Fourth, and implicit in all that precedes, there is a detailed account of the structure *for which* the functional requirements hold, as well as a detailed account of the arrangements *through which* the function is fulfilled.

So well established is the logic of functional analysis in the biological sciences that these requirements for an adequate analysis come to be met almost as a matter of course. Not so with sociology. Here, we find extraordinarily varied conceptions of the appropriate design of studies in functional analysis. For some, it consists largely (or even exclusively) in establishing empirical interrelations between "parts" of a social system; for others, it consists in showing the "value for society" of a socially standardized practice or a social organization; for still others, it consists in elaborate accounts of the purposes of formal social organizations.

As one examines the varied array of functional analyses in sociology, it becomes evident that sociologists in contrast, say, to physiologists, do not typically carry through operationally intelligible procedures, do not systematically assemble needed types of data, do not employ a common body of concepts and do not utilize the same criteria of validity. In other words, we find in physiology, a body of standard concepts, procedures and design of analysis and in sociology, a variegated selection of concepts, procedures and designs, depending, it would seem, on the interests and tastes of the individual sociologist. To be sure, this difference between the two disciplines has *something*—perhaps, a good deal—to do with differences in the character of the data examined by the physiologist and the sociologist. The relatively large opportunities for experimental work in physiology are, to be trite about it, scarcely matched in sociology. But this scarcely accounts for the systematic ordering of procedure and concepts in the one instance and the disparate, often uncoordinated and not infrequently defective character of procedure and concepts in functional sociology.

A Paradigm for Functional Analysis in Sociology

As an initial and admittedly tentative step in the direction of codifying functional analysis in sociology, we set forth a paradigm of the concepts and problems central to this approach. It will soon become evident that the chief components of this paradigm have progressively emerged in the foregoing pages as we have critically examined the vocabularies, postulates, concepts and ideological imputations now current in the field. The paradigm brings these together in compact form, thus permitting simultaneous inspection of the major requirements of functional analysis and serving as an aid to self-correction of provisional interpretations, a result difficult to achieve when concepts are scattered and hidden in page after page of discursive exposition.[52] The paradigm presents the hard core of concept, procedure and inference in functional analysis.

Above all, it should be noted that the paradigm does not represent a set of categories introduced *de novo,* but rather a *codification* of those concepts and problems which have been forced upon our attention by critical scrutiny of current research and theory in functional analysis. (Reference to the preceding sections of this chapter will show that the groundwork has been prepared for every one of the categories embodied in the paradigm.)

1. *The item(s) to which functions are imputed*—The entire range of sociological data can be, and much of it has been, subjected to functional analysis. The basic requirement is that the object of analysis represent a *standardized* (*i.e.* patterned and repetitive) item, such as social roles, institutional patterns, social processes, cultural pattern, culturally patterned emotions, social norms, group organization, social structure, devices for social control, *etc.*

BASIC QUERY: What must enter into the protocol of observation of the given item if it is to be amenable to systematic functional analysis?

2. *Concepts of subjective dispositions (motives, purposes)*—At some point, functional analysis invariably assumes or explicitly operates with some conception of the motivation of individuals involved in a social system. As the foregoing discussion has shown, these concepts of subjective disposition are often and erroneously merged with the related, but different, concepts of objective consequences of attitude, belief and behavior.

BASIC QUERY: In which types of analysis is it sufficient to take observed motivations as *data,* as given, and in which are they properly considered as *problematical,* as derivable from other data?

3. *Concepts of objective consequences (functions, dysfunctions)*—We have observed two prevailing types of confusion enveloping the several current conceptions of "function":

(1) The tendency to confine sociological observations to the *positive* contri-

---

[52] For a brief statement of the purpose of analytical paradigms such as this, see the note on paradigms elsewhere in this volume.

butions of a sociological item to the social or cultural system in which it is implicated ; and

(2) The tendency to confuse the subjective category of *motive* with the objective category of *function*.

Appropriate conceptual distinctions are required to eliminate these confusions.

The first problem calls for a concept of *multiple consequences* and *a net balance of an aggregate of consequences*.

Functions are those observed consequences which make for the adaptation or adjustment of a given system ; and *dysfunctions,* those observed consequences which lessen the adaptation or adjustment of the system. There is also the empirical possibility of *nonfunctional* consequences, which are simply irrelevant to the system under consideration.

In any given instance, an item may have both functional and dysfunctional consequences, giving rise to the difficult and important problem of evolving canons for assessing the net balance of the aggregate of consequences. (This is, of course, most important in the use of functional analysis for guiding the formation and enactment of policy.)

The second problem (arising from the easy confusion of motives and functions) requires us to introduce a conceptual distinction between the cases in which the subjective aim-in-view coincides with the objective consequence, and the cases in which they diverge.

Manifest functions are those objective consequences contributing to the adjustment or adaptation of the system which are intended and recognized by participants in the system ;

Latent functions, correlatively, being those which are neither intended nor recognized.*

BASIC QUERY: What are the effects of the transformation of a previously latent function into a manifest function (involving the problem of the role of knowledge in human behavior and the problems of "manipulation" of human behavior)?

4. *Concepts of the unit subserved by the function*—We have observed the difficulties entailed in *confining* analysis to functions fulfilled for "the society," since items may be functional for some individuals and subgroups and dysfunctional for others. It is necessary, therefore, to consider a *range* of units for which the item has designated consequences: individuals in diverse statuses, subgroups, the larger social system and culture systems. (Terminologically, this

---

* The relations between the "unanticipated consequences" of action and "latent functions" can be clearly defined, since they are implicit in the foregoing section of the paradigm. The unintended consequences of action are of three types:

   (1) those which are functional for a designated system, and these comprise the latent functions;

   (2) those which are dysfunctional for a designated system, and these comprise the latent dysfunctions; and

   (3) those which are irrelevant to the system which they affect neither functionally nor dysfunctionally, *i.e.,* the pragmatically unimportant class of nonfunctional consequences.

For a preliminary statement, see R. K. Merton, "The unanticipated consequences of purposive social action," *American Sociological Review* 1936, 1, 894–904; for a tabulation of these types of consequences see Goode, *Religion Among the Primitives,* 32–33.

implies the concepts of psychological function, group function, societal function, cultural function, *etc*.)

5. *Concepts of functional requirements (needs, prerequisites)*—Embedded in every functional analysis is some conception, tacit or expressed, of the functional requirements of the system under observation. As noted elsewhere,[53] this remains one of the cloudiest and empirically most debatable concepts in functional theory. As utilized by sociologists, the concept of functional requirement tends to be tautological or *ex post facto* ; it tends to be confined to the conditions of "survival" of a given system ; it tends, as in the work of Malinowski, to include biological as well as social "needs."

This involves the difficult problem of establishing *types* of functional requirements (universal vs. specific) ; procedures for validating the assumption of these requirements ; *etc*.

BASIC QUERY : What is required to establish the validity of such a variable as "functional requirement" in situations where rigorous experimentation is impracticable?

6. *Concepts of the mechanisms through which functions are fulfilled*— Functional analysis in sociology, as in other disciplines like physiology and psychology, calls for a "concrete and detailed" account of the mechanisms which operate to perform a designated function. This refers, not to psychological, but to social, mechanisms (*e.g.*, role-segmentation, insulation of institutional demands, hierarchic ordering of values, social division of labor, ritual and ceremonial enactments, *etc*.).

BASIC QUERY : What is the presently available inventory of social mechanisms corresponding, say, to the large inventory of psychological mechanisms? What methodological problems are entailed in discerning the operation of these social mechanisms?

7. *Concepts of functional alternatives (functional equivalents or substitutes)*—As we have seen, once we abandon the gratuitous assumption of the functional indispensability of particular social structures, we immediately require some concept of functional alternatives, equivalents, or substitutes. This focuses attention on the *range of possible variation* in the items which can, in the case under examination, subserve a functional requirement. It unfreezes the identity of the existent and the inevitable.

BASIC QUERY : Since scientific proof of the equivalence of an alleged functional alternative ideally requires rigorous experimentation, and since this is not often practicable in large-scale sociological situations, which practicable procedures of inquiry most nearly approximate the logic of experiment?

8. *Concepts of structural context (or structural constraint)*—The range of variation in the items which *can* fulfill designated functions in a social structure is not unlimited (and this has been repeatedly noted in our foregoing discussion). The interdependence of the elements of a social structure limits the effective possibilities of change or functional alternatives. The concept of structural constraint corresponds, in the area of social structure, to Goldenweiser's "principle of limited possibilities" in a broader sphere. Failure to recognize the relevance of interdependence and attendant structural restraints leads to utopian thought in which it is tacitly assumed that certain elements of a social system can be

---

[53] R. K. Merton, "Discussion of Parsons' 'Position of sociological theory,' " *American Sociological Review,* 1949, 13, 164–168.

eliminated without affecting the rest of that system. This consideration is recognized by both Marxist social scientists (*e.g.* Karl Marx) and by non-Marxists (*e.g.* Malinowski).[54]

BASIC QUERY: How narrowly does a given structural context limit the range of variation in the items which can effectively satisfy functional requirements? Do we find, under conditions yet to be determined, an area of indifference, in which any one of a wide range of alternatives may fulfill the function?

9. *Concepts of dynamics and change*—We have noted that functional analysts *tend* to focus on the statics of social structure and to neglect the study of structural change.

This emphasis upon statics is not, however, *inherent* in the theory of functional analysis. It is, rather, an adventitious emphasis stemming from the concern of early anthropological functionalists to counteract preceding tendencies to write conjectural histories of non-literate societies. This practice, useful at the time it was first introduced into anthropology, has disadvantageously persisted in the work of some functional sociologists.

The concept of dysfunction, which implies the concept of strain, stress and tension on the structural level, provides an analytical approach to the study of dynamics and change. How are observed dysfunctions contained within a particular structure, so that they do not produce instability? Does the accumulation of stresses and strains produce pressure for change in such directions as are likely to lead to their reduction?

BASIC QUERY: Does the prevailing concern among functional analysts with the concept of *social equilibrium* divert attention from the phenomena of *social disequilibrium*? Which available procedures will permit the sociologist most adequately to gauge the accumulation of stresses and strains in a social system?

---

54 Previously cited excerpts from Marx document this statement, but these are, of course, only a few out of many places in which Marx in effect stresses the importance of taking account of the structural context. In *A Contribution to the Critique of Political Economy* (appearing in 1859 and republished in Karl Marx, *Selected Works, op. cit.*, I, 354–371), he observes for example: "No social order ever disappears before all the productive forces for which there is room in it have been developed; and new higher relations of production never appear before the material conditions of their existence have matured in the womb of the old society itself. Therefore, mankind always sets itself only such tasks as it can solve; since, looking at the matter more closely, we will always find that the task itself arises only when the material conditions necessary for its solution already exist or are at least in the process of formation." (p. 357) Perhaps the most famous of his many references to the constraining influence of a given social structure is found in the second paragraph of *The Eighteenth Brumaire of Louis Napoleon:* "Man makes his own history, but he does not make it out of whole cloth: he does not make it out of conditions chosen by himself, but out of such conditions as he finds close at hand." (From the paraphrase of the original as published in Marx, *Selected Works*, II, 315.) To my knowledge, A. D. Lindsay is the most perceptive among the commentators who have noted the theoretic implications of statements such as these. See his little book, *Karl Marx's Capital: An Introductory Essay*, (Oxford University Press, 1931), esp. at 27–52.

And for other language with quite different ideological import and essentially similar theoretic implications, see B. Malinowski, "Given a definite cultural need, the means of its satisfaction are small in number, and therefore the cultural arrangement which comes into being in response to the need is determined within narrow limits." "Culture," *Encyclopedia of the Social Sciences, op. cit.*, 626.

To what extent does knowledge of the structural context permit the sociologist to anticipate the most probable directions of social change?

10. *Problems of validation of functional analysis*—Throughout the paradigm, attention has been called repeatedly to the *specific* points at which assumptions, imputations and observations must be validated.[55] This requires, above all, a rigorous statement of the sociological procedures of analysis which most nearly approximate the *logic* of experimentation. It requires a systematic review of the possibilities and limitations of *comparative* (cross-cultural and cross-group) *analysis*.

BASIC QUERY: To what extent is functional analysis limited by the difficulty of locating adequate *samples of social systems* which can be subjected to comparative (quasi-experimental) study?[56]

11. *Problems of the ideological implications of functional analysis*—It has been emphasized in a preceding section that functional analysis has no intrinsic commitment to an ideological position. This does not gainsay the fact that *particular* functional analyses and *particular* hypotheses advanced by functionalists may have an identifiable ideological role. This, then, becomes a specific problem for the sociology of knowledge: to what extent does the social position of the functional sociologist (*e.g.,* vis-à-vis a particular "client" who has authorized a given research) evoke one rather than another formulation of a problem, affect his assumptions and concepts, and limit the range of inferences drawn from his data?

BASIC QUERY: How does one detect the ideological tinge of a functional analysis and to what degree does a particular ideology stem from the basic assumptions adopted by the sociologist? Is the incidence of these assumptions related to the status and research role of the sociologist?

Before proceeding to a more intensive study of some parts of this paradigm, let us be clear about the uses to which it is supposed the paradigm can be put. After all, taxonomies of concepts may be multiplied endlessly without materially advancing the tasks of sociological analysis. What, then, are the purposes of the paradigm and how might it be used?

---

[55] By this point, it is evident that we are considering functional analysis as a method for the *interpretation* of sociological data. This is not to gainsay the important role of the functional orientation in sensitizing sociologists to the *collection* of types of data which might otherwise be neglected. It is perhaps unnecessary to reiterate the axiom that one's concepts *do* determine the inclusion or exclusion of data, that, despite the etymology of the term, *data* are not "given" but are "contrived" with the inevitable help of concepts. In the process of evolving a functional interpretation, the sociological analyst invariably finds it necessary to obtain data other than those initially contemplated. Interpretation and the collection of data are thus inextricably bound up in the array of concepts and propositions relating these concepts. For an extension of these remarks, see Chapter II.

[56] George P. Murdock's *Social Structure,* (New York: Macmillan, 1949), is enough to show that procedures such as those involved in the cross-cultural survey hold large promise for dealing with certain methodological problems of functional analysis. See also the procedures of functional analysis in George C. Homans and David M. Schneider, *Marriage, Authority, and Final Causes* (Glencoe: The Free Press, 1955).

Purposes of the Paradigm

The first and foremost purpose is to supply a provisional codified guide for adequate and fruitful functional analyses. This objective evidently implies that the paradigm contains the minimum set of concepts with which the sociologist must operate in order to carry through an adequate functional analysis and, as a corollary, that it can be used here and now as a guide for the critical study of existing analyses. It is thus intended as an all-too-compact and elliptical guide to the formulation of researches in functional analysis and as an aid in locating the distinctive contributions and deficiencies of earlier researches. Limitations of space will permit us to apply only limited sections of the paradigm to a critical appraisal of a selected list of cases in point.

Secondly, the paradigm is intended to lead directly to the postulates and (often tacit) assumptions underlying functional analysis. As we have found in earlier parts of this chapter, some of these assumptions are of central importance, others insignificant and dispensable, and still others, dubious and even misleading.

In the third place, the paradigm seeks to sensitize the sociologist not only to the narrowly scientific implications of various types of functional analysis, but also to their political and sometimes ideological implications. The points at which a functional analysis presupposes an implicit political outlook and the points at which it has bearing on "social engineering" are concerns which find an integral place in the paradigm.

It is obviously beyond the limits of this chapter to explore in detail the large and inclusive problems involved in the paradigm. This must await fuller exposition in a volume devoted to this purpose. We shall, therefore, confine the remainder of the present discussion to brief applications of only the first parts of the paradigm to a severely limited number of cases of functional analysis in sociology. And, from time to time, these few cases will be used as a springboard for discussion of special problems which are only imperfectly illustrated by the cases in hand.

Items Subjected to Functional Analysis

At first glance, it would appear that the sheer *description* of the item to be analyzed functionally entails few, if any, problems. Presumably, one should describe the item "as fully and as accurately" as possible. Yet, at second thought, it is evident that this maxim provides next to no guidance for the observer. Consider the plight of a functionally oriented neophyte armed only with this dictum as an aid to answering the question: *what* am I to observe, *what* am I to incorporate into my field notes, and *what* may I safely omit?

Without assuming that a detailed and circumstantial answer can now be supplied to the field worker, we can nevertheless note that the question itself is legitimate and that *implicit* answers have been partly developed. To tease out these implicit answers and to codify them, it is necessary to approach cases of functional analysis with the query: *what kinds of data have been consistently included, no matter what the item undergoing analysis, and why have these rather than other data been included?*

It soon becomes apparent that the functionalist orientation largely determines what is included in the description of the item to be interpreted. Thus, the description of a magical performance or a ceremonial is not confined to an account of the spell or formula, the rite and the performers. It includes a systematic account of the people participating and the onlookers, of the types and rates of interaction among performers and audience, of changes in these patterns of interaction in the course of the ceremonial. Thus, the description of Hopi rain ceremonials, for example, entails more than the actions seemingly oriented toward the intervention of the gods in meteorological phenomena. It involves a report of the persons *who* are variously involved in the pattern of behavior. And the description of the participants (and on-lookers) is in *structured terms,* that is, in terms of locating these people in their inter-connected social statuses.

Brief excerpts will illustrate how functional analyses begin with a systematic inclusion (and, preferably, charting) of the statuses and social interrelations of those engaging in the behavior under scrutiny.

Chiricahua puberty ceremonial for girls: the extended domestic family (parents and relatives financially able to help) bear the expense of this four-day ceremony. The parents select the time and place for the ceremonial. "All the members of the *girl's encampment* attend and nearly all the *members of the local group.* A goodly sprinkling of visitors from *other local groups* and some *travelers from outside bands* are to be seen, and their numbers increase as the day wears on." The *leader of the local group* to which the girl's family belongs speaks, welcoming all visitors. In short, this account explicitly calls attention to the following statuses and groups variously involved in the ceremonial: the girl; her parents and immediate family; the local group, especially through its leader; the band represented by members of outside local groups, and the "tribe by members of other bands."[57]

As we shall see in due course, although it bears stating at this point, *the sheer description* of the ceremony in terms of the statuses and group affiliations of those variously involved *provides a major clue to the functions* performed by this ceremonial. In a word, we suggest that the structural

---

[57] Morris E. Opler, "An outline of Chiricahua Apache social organization," in Fred Eggan ed. *Social Anthropology of North American Tribes,* (Chicago: University of Chicago Press, 1937), 173–239, esp. at 226–230 [italics supplied].

description of participants in the activity under analysis provides hypotheses for subsequent functional interpretations.

Another illustration will again indicate the nature of such descriptions in terms of role, status, group affiliation and the interrelations among these.

Patterned responses to mirriri (hearing obscenity directed at one's sister) among the Australian Murngin. The standardized pattern must be all too briefly described: when a husband swears at his wife in the presence of her brother, the brother engages in the seemingly anomalous behavior of throwing spears at the wife (not the husband) and her sisters. The description of this pattern goes on to include status descriptions of the participants. The *sisters* are members of the brother's *clan* ; the husband comes from another clan.

Note again that participants are *located* within social structures and this location is basic to the subsequent functional analysis of this behavior.[58]

Since these are cases drawn from non-literate society, it might be assumed that these requirements for description are peculiar to non-literate materials. Turning to other instances of functional analyses of patterns found in modern Western society, however, we can identify this same requirement as well as additional guides to "needed descriptive data."

The "romantic love complex" in American society: although all societies recognize "occasional violent emotional attachments," contemporary American society is among the few societies which capitalize upon romantic attachments and in popular belief, at least, make these the basis for choice of a marriage partner. This characteristic pattern of choice minimizes or eliminates the selection of one's mate by parents or the wider kinship group.[59]

Note that the emphasis upon one pattern of choice of mates thereby excludes alternative patterns of choice known to occur elsewhere.

This case suggests a *second* desideratum for a type of data to be included in the account of the item subjected to functional analysis. In describing the characteristic (modal) pattern for handling a standardized problem (choice of marriage-partner), the observer, wherever possible, indicates the principal alternatives which are thereby excluded. This, as we shall see,

---

58 W. L. Warner, *A Black Civilization—A Social Study of an Australian Tribe,* (New York: Harper & Bros., 1937), 112–113.

59 For various approaches to a functional analysis of the "romantic love complex," see Ralph Linton, *Study of Man,* (New York: D. Appleton-Century Co., 1936), 174–5; T. Parsons, "Age and sex in the social structure of the United States," *American Sociological Review,* Oct. 1942, 7, 604–616, esp. at 614–15; T. Parsons, "The kinship system of the contemporary United States," *American Anthropologist,* 1943, 45, 22–38, esp. at 31–32, 36–37, both reprinted in his *Essays in Sociological Theory, op. cit.;* T. Parsons, "The social structure of the family," in Ruth N. Ashen, ed., *The Family: Its Function and Destiny,* (New York: Harper, 1949), 173–201; R. K. Merton, "Intermarriage and the social structure," *Psychiatry,* 1941, 4, 361–74, esp. at 367–8; and Isidor Thorner, "Sociological aspects of affectional frustration," *Psychiatry,* 1943, 6, 157–173, esp. at 169–172.

provides direct clues to the structural context of the pattern and, by suggesting pertinent comparative materials, points toward the validation of the functional analysis.

A *third* integral element of the description of the problematical item preparatory to the actual functional analysis—a further requirement for preparing the specimen for analysis, so to speak—is to include the *"meanings"* (or cognitive and affective significance) of the activity or pattern for members of the group. In fact, as will become evident, a fully circumstantial account of the meanings attached to the item goes far toward suggesting appropriate lines of functional analysis. A case drawn from Veblen's many functional analyses serves to illustrate the general thesis:

> *The cultural pattern of conspicuous consumption:* the conspicuous consumption of relatively expensive commodities "means" (symbolizes) the possession of sufficient wealth to "afford" such expenditures. Wealth, in turn, is honorific. Persons engaging in conspicuous consumption not only derive gratification from the direct consumption but also from the heightened status reflected in the attitudes and opinions of others who observe their consumption. This pattern is most notable among the leisure class, *i.e.*, those who can and largely do refrain from productive labor [this is the status or role component of the description]. However, it diffuses to other strata who seek to emulate the pattern and who likewise experience pride in "wasteful" expenditures. Finally, consumption in conspicuous terms tends to crowd out other criteria for consumption (*e.g.* "efficient" expenditure of funds). [This is an explicit reference to alternative modes of consumption obscured from view by the cultural emphasis on the pattern under scrutiny.][60]

As is well known, Veblen goes on to impute a variety of functions to the pattern of conspicuous consumption—functions of aggrandizement of status, of validation of status, of "good repute," of display of pecuniary strength. These consequences, as experienced by participants in the patterned activity, are gratifying and go far toward explaining the continuance of the pattern. *The clues to the imputed functions are provided almost wholly by the description of the pattern itself* which includes explicit references to (1) the status of those differentially exhibiting the pattern, (2) known alternatives to the pattern of consuming in terms of display and "wastefulness" rather than in terms of private and "intrinsic" enjoyment of the item of consumption; and (3) the diverse meanings culturally ascribed to the behavior of conspicuous consumption by participants in and observers of the pattern.

These three components of the description of the specimen to be analyzed are by no means exhaustive. A full descriptive protocol, adequate for subsequent functional analysis, will inevitably spill over into a range of immediate

---

[60] Thorstein Veblen, *The Theory of the Leisure Class,* (New York: Vanguard Press, 1928), esp. chapters 2–4.

psychological and social consequences of the behavior. But these may be more profitably examined in connection with the concepts of function. It is here only necessary to repeat that the description of the item does not proceed according to whim or intuition, but must include at least these three characteristics of the item, if the descriptive protocol is to be of optimum value for functional analysis. Although much remains to be learned concerning desiderata for the descriptive phase of the total analysis, this brief presentation of models for descriptive content may serve to indicate that procedures for functional analysis *can* be codified—ultimately to the point where the sociological field worker will have a chart guiding observation.

Another case illustrates a further desideratum for the description of the item to be analyzed.

> *Taboo on out-marriage:* the greater the degree of group solidarity, the more marked the sentiment adverse to marriage with people outside the group. "It makes no difference what is the cause of the desire for group solidarity. . . ." Outmarriage *means* either losing one's group-member to another group or incorporation into one's own group of persons who have not been thoroughly socialized in the values, sentiments and practices of the in-group.[61]

This suggests a *fourth* type of datum to be included in the description of the social or cultural specimen, prior to functional analysis. Inevitably, participants in the practice under scrutiny have *some* array of motives for conformity or for deviation. *The descriptive account should, so far as possible, include an account of these motivations, but these motives must not be confused, as we have seen, with (a) the objective pattern of behavior or (b) with the social functions of that pattern.* Inclusion of motives in the descriptive account helps explain the *psychological* functions subserved by the pattern and often proves suggestive with respect to the social functions.

Thus far, we have been considering items which are clearly patterned practices or beliefs, patterns recognized as such by participants in the society. Thus, members of the given society can, in varying degrees, describe the contours of the Chiricahua puberty ceremony, the Murngin mirriri pattern, the choice of mates on the basis of romantic attachments, the concern with consuming conspicuously and the taboos on out-marriage. These are all parts of the overt culture and, as such, are more or less fully known to those who share in this culture. The social scientist, however, does not confine himself to these overt patterns. From time to time, he uncovers a covert cultural pattern, a set of practices or beliefs which is as consistently pat-

---

[61] Romanzo Adams, *Interracial Marriage in Hawaii*, esp. at 197–204; Merton, "Intermarriage . . .," *op. cit.*, esp. at 368–9; K. Davis "Intermarriage in caste societies," *American Anthropologist*, 1941, 43, 376–395.

terned as overt patterns, but which is not regarded as a normatively regulated pattern by the participants. Examples of this are plentiful. Thus, statistics show that in a quasi-caste situation such as that governing Negro-white relations in this country, the prevailing pattern of interracial marriage (when it occurs) is between white females and Negro males (rather than between Negro females and white males). Although this pattern, which we may call caste hypogamy, is not institutionalized, it is persistent and remarkably stable.[62]

Or consider another instance of a fixed but apparently unrecognized pattern. Malinowski reports that Trobrianders cooperatively engaged in the technological task of building a canoe are engaged not only in that explicit technical task but also in establishing and reinforcing inter-personal relations among themselves in the process. Much of the recent data on those primary groups called "informal organizations" deals with these patterns of relations which are observed by the social scientist but are unrecognized, at least in their full implications, by the participants.[63]

All this points to a *fifth* desideratum for the descriptive protocol: regularities of behavior *associated* with the nominally central activity (although not part of the explicit culture pattern) should be included in the protocols of the field worker, since these *unwitting regularities* often provide basic clues to distinctive functions of the total pattern. As we shall see, the inclusion of these "unwitting" regularities in the descriptive protocol directs the investigator almost at once to analysis of the pattern in terms of what we have called latent functions.

In summary, then, the descriptive protocol should, so far as possible, include:

1) location of participants in the pattern within the social structure—differential participation;

2) consideration of alternative modes of behavior excluded by emphasis on the observed pattern (*i.e.* attention not only to what occurs but also to what is neglected by virtue of the existing pattern);

3) the emotive and cognitive meanings attached by participants to the pattern;

4) a distinction between the motivations for participating in the pattern and the objective behavior involved in the pattern;

---

[62] *Cf.* Merton, "Intermarriage . . .," *op. cit.;* Otto Klineberg ed., *Characteristics of the American Negro,* (New York: Harper, 1943).

[63] The rediscovery of the primary group by those engaged in sociological studies of industry has been one of the chief fillips to the functional approach in recent sociological research. Reference is had here to the work of Elton Mayo, Roethlisberger and Dickson, William Whyte, and Burleigh Gardner, among many others. There remain, of course, the interesting differences in *interpretation* to which these data lend themselves.

5) regularities of behavior not recognized by participants but which are nonetheless associated with the central pattern of behavior.

That these desiderata for the observer's protocol are far from complete is altogether likely. But they do provide a tentative step in the direction of *specifying* points of observation which facilitate subsequent functional analysis. They are intended to be somewhat more specific than the suggestions ordinarily found in general statements of procedure, such as those advising the observer to be sensitive to the "context of situation."

Manifest and Latent Functions

As has been implied in earlier sections, the distinction between manifest and latent functions was devised to preclude the inadvertent confusion, often found in the sociological literature, between conscious *motivations* for social behavior and its *objective consequences.* Our scrutiny of current vocabularies of functional analysis has shown how easily, and how unfortunately, the sociologist may identify *motives* with *functions.* It was further indicated that the motive and the function vary independently and that the failure to register this fact in an established terminology has contributed to the unwitting tendency among sociologists to confuse the subjective categories of motivation with the objective categories of function. This, then, is the central purpose of our succumbing to.the not-always-commendable practice of introducing new terms into the rapidly growing technical vocabulary of sociology, a practice regarded by many laymen as an affront to their intelligence and an offense against common intelligibility.

As will be readily recognized, I have adapted the terms "manifest" and "latent" from their use in another context by Freud (although Francis Bacon had long ago spoken of "latent process" and "latent configuration" in connection with processes which are below the threshold of superficial observation).

The distinction itself has been repeatedly drawn by observers of human behavior at irregular intervals over a span of many centuries.[64] Indeed, it would be disconcerting to find that a distinction which we have come to regard as central to functional analysis had not been made by any of that numerous company who have in effect adopted a functional orientation. We need mention only a few of those who have, in recent decades, found it necessary to distinguish in their specific interpretations of behavior between the end-in-view and the functional consequences of action.

---

[64] References to some of the more significant among these earlier appearances of the distinction will be found in Merton, "Unanticipated consequences . . .," *op. cit.*

George H. Mead[65]: ". . . that attitude of hostility toward the law-breaker has the unique advantage [read: latent function] of uniting all members of the community in the emotional solidarity of aggression. While the most admirable of humanitarian efforts are sure to run counter to the individual interests of very many in the community, or fail to touch the interest and imagination of the multitude and to leave the community divided or indifferent, the cry of thief or murderer is attuned to profound complexes, lying below the surface of competing individual efforts, and citizens who have [been] separated by divergent interests stand together against the common enemy."

Emile Durkheim's[66] similar analysis of the social functions of punishment is also focused on its latent functions (consequences for the community) rather than confined to manifest functions (consequences for the criminal).

W. G. Sumner[67]: ". . . from the first acts by which men try to satisfy needs, each act stands by itself, and looks no further than the immediate satisfaction. From recurrent needs arise habits for the individual and customs for the group, but these results are consequences which were never conscious, and never foreseen or intended. They are not noticed until they have long existed, and it is still longer before they are appreciated." Although this fails to locate the latent functions of standardized social actions for a designated social structure, it plainly makes the basic distinction between ends-in-view and objective consequences.

R. M. MacIver[68]: In addition to the direct effects of institutions, "there are further effects by way of control which lie outside the direct purposes of men . . . this type of reactive form of control . . . may, though unintended, be of profound service to society."

W. I. Thomas and F. Znaniecki[69]: "Although all the new [Polish peasant cooperative] institutions are thus formed with the definite purpose of satisfying

---

[65] George H. Mead, "The psychology of punitive justice," *American Journal of Sociology*, 1918, 23, 577–602, esp. 591.

[66] As suggested earlier in this chapter, Durkheim adopted a functional orientation throughout his work, and he operates, albeit often without explicit notice, with concepts equivalent to that of latent function in all of his researches. The reference in the text at this point is to his "Deux lois de l'évolution penale," *L'année sociologique*, 1899–1900, 4, 55–95, as well as to his *Division of Labor in Society* (Glencoe, Illinois: The Free Press, 1947).

[67] This one of his many such observations is of course from W. G. Sumner's *Folkways*, (Boston: Ginn & Co., 1906), 3. His collaborator, Albert G. Keller retained the distinction in his own writings; see, for example, his *Social Evolution*, (New York: Macmillan, 1927), at 93–95.

[68] This is advisedly drawn from one of MacIver's earlier works, *Community*, (London: Macmillan, 1915). The distinction takes on greater importance in his later writings, becoming a major element in his *Social Causation*, (Boston: Ginn & Co., 1942), esp. at 314–321, and informs the greater part of his *The More Perfect Union*, (New York: Macmillan, 1948).

[69] The single excerpt quoted in the text is one of scores which have led to *The Polish Peasant in Europe and America* being deservedly described as a "sociological classic." See pages 1426–7 and 1523 ff. As will be noted later in this chapter, the insights and conceptual distinctions contained in this one passage, and there are many others like it in point of richness of content, were forgotten or never noticed by those industrial sociologists who recently came to develop the notion of "informal organization" in industry.

certain specific needs, their social function is by no means limited to their explicit and conscious purpose . . . every one of these institutions—commune or agricultural circle, loan and savings bank, or theater—is not merely a mechanism for the management of certain values but also an association of people, each member of which is supposed to participate in the common activities as a living, concrete individual. Whatever is the predominant, official common interest upon which the institution is founded, the association as a concrete group of human personalities unofficially involves many other interests; the social contacts between its members are not limited to their common pursuit, though the latter, of course, constitutes both the main reason for which the association is formed and the most permanent bond which holds it together. Owing to this combination of an abstract political, economic, or rather rational mechanism for the satisfaction of specific needs with the concrete unity of a social group, the new institution is also the best intermediary link between the peasant primary-group and the secondary national system."

These and numerous other sociological observers have, then, from time to time distinguished between categories of subjective disposition ("needs, interests, purposes") and categories of generally unrecognized but objective functional consequences ("unique advantages," "never conscious" consequences, "unintended . . . service to society," "function not limited to conscious and explicit purpose").

Since the occasion for making the distinction arises with great frequency, and since the purpose of a conceptual scheme is to direct observations toward salient elements of a situation and to prevent the inadvertent oversight of these elements, it would seem justifiable to designate this distinction by an appropriate set of terms. This is the rationale for the distinction between manifest functions and latent functions; the first referring to those objective consequences for a specified unit (person, subgroup, social or cultural system) which contribute to its adjustment or adaptation and were so intended; the second referring to unintended and unrecognized consequences of the same order.

There are some indications that the christening of this distinction may serve a heuristic purpose by becoming incorporated into an explicit conceptual apparatus, thus aiding both systematic observation and later analysis. In recent years, for example, the distinction between manifest and latent functions has been utilized in analyses of racial intermarriage,[70] social stratification,[71] affective frustration,[72] Veblen's sociological theories,[73] pre-

---

[70] Merton, "Intermarriage and the social structure," *op. cit.*

[71] Kingsley Davis, "A conceptual analysis of stratification," *American Sociological Review,* 1942, 7, 309–321.

[72] Thorner, *op. cit.,* esp. at 165.

[73] A. K. Davis, *Thorstein's Veblen's Social Theory,* Harvard Ph.D. dissertation, 1941, and "Veblen on the decline of the Protestant Ethic," *Social Forces,* 1944, 22, 282–86; Louis Schneider, *The Freudian Psychology and Veblen's Social Theory,* (New York: King's Crown Press, 1948), esp. Chapter 2.

vailing American orientations toward Russia,[74] propaganda as a means of
social control,[75] Malinowski's anthropological theory,[76] Navajo witchcraft,[77] problems in the sociology of knowledge,[78] fashion,[79] the dynamics
of personality,[80] national security measures,[81] the internal social dynamics of
bureaucracy,[82] and a great variety of other sociological problems.

The very diversity of these subject-matters suggests that the theoretic
distinction between manifest and latent functions is not bound up with a
limited and particular range of human behavior. But there still remains
the large task of ferreting out the specific uses to which this distinction
can be put, and it is to this large task that we devote the remaining pages
of this chapter.

Heuristic Purposes of the Distinction

Clarifies the analysis of seemingly irrational social patterns.—In the
first place, the distinction aids the sociological interpretation of many social
practices which persist even though their manifest purpose is clearly not
achieved. The time-worn procedure in such instances has been for diverse,
particularly lay, observers to refer to these practices as "superstitions,"
"irrationalities," "mere inertia of tradition," *etc.* In other words, when group
behavior does not—and, indeed, often cannot—attain its ostensible purpose
there is an inclination to attribute its occurrence to lack of intelligence, sheer
ignorance, survivals, or so-called inertia. Thus, the Hopi ceremonials
designed to produce abundant rainfall may be labelled a superstitious
practice of primitive folk and that is assumed to conclude the matter. It
should be noted that this in no sense accounts for the group behavior. It is

[74] A. K. Davis, "Some sources of American hostility to Russia," *American Journal of Sociology,* 1947, 53, 174–183.

[75] Talcott Parsons, "Propaganda and social control," in his *Essays in Sociological Theory.*

[76] Clyde Kluckhohn, "Bronislaw Malinowski, 1884–1942," *Journal of American Folklore,* 1943, 56, 208–219.

[77] Clyde Kluckhohn, *Navaho Witchcraft, op. cit.,* esp. at 46–47 and ff.

[78] Merton, Chapter XII of this volume.

[79] Bernard Barber and L. S. Lobel, " 'Fashion' in women's clothes and the American social system," *Social Forces,* 1952, 31, 124–131.

[80] O. H. Mowrer and C. Kluckhohn, "Dynamic theory of personality," in J. M. Hunt, ed., *Personality and the Behavior Disorders,* (New York: Ronald Press, 1944), 1, 69–135, esp. at 72.

[81] Marie Jahoda and S. W. Cook, "Security measures and freedom of thought: an exploratory study of the impact of loyalty and security programs," *Yale Law Journal,* 1952, 61, 296–333.

[82] Philip Selznick, *TVA and the Grass Roots* (University of California Press, 1949); A. W. Gouldner, *Patterns of Industrial Bureaucracy* (Glencoe, Illinois: The Free Press, 1954); P. M. Blau, *The Dynamics of Bureaucracy* (Chicago: University of Chicago Press, 1955); A. K. Davis, "Bureaucratic patterns in Navy officer corps," *Social Forces* 1948, 27, 142–153.

simply a case of name-calling; it substitutes the epithet "superstition" for an analysis of the actual role of this behavior in the life of the group. Given the concept of latent function, however, we are reminded that this behavior *may* perform a function for the group, although this function may be quite remote from the avowed purpose of the behavior.

The concept of latent function extends the observer's attention beyond the question of whether or not the behavior attains its avowed purpose. Temporarily ignoring these explicit purposes, it directs attention *toward* another range of consequences: those bearing, for example, upon the individual personalities of Hopi involved in the ceremony and upon the persistence and continuity of the larger group. Were one to confine himself to the problem of whether a manifest (purposed) function occurs, it becomes a problem, not for the sociologist, but for the meteorologist. And to be sure, our meteorologists agree that the rain ceremonial does not produce rain; but this is hardly to the point. It is merely to say that the ceremony does not have this technological use; that this purpose of the ceremony and its actual consequences do not coincide. But with the concept of latent function, we continue our inquiry, examining the consequences of the ceremony not for the rain gods or for meteorological phenomena, but for the groups which conduct the ceremony. And here it may be found, as many observers indicate, that the ceremonial does indeed have functions—but functions which are non-purposed or latent.

Ceremonials may fulfill the latent function of reinforcing the group identity by providing a periodic occasion on which the scattered members of a group assemble to engage in a common activity. As Durkheim among others long since indicated, such ceremonials are a means by which collective expression is afforded the sentiments which, in a further analysis, are found to be a basic source of group unity. Through the systematic application of the concept of latent function, therefore, *apparently* irrational behavior may *at times* be found to be positively functional for the group. Operating with the concept of latent function, we are not too quick to conclude that if an activity of a group does not achieve its nominal purpose, then its persistence can be described only as an instance of "inertia," "survival," or "manipulation by powerful sub-groups in the society."

In point of fact, some conception like that of latent function has very often, almost invariably, been employed by social scientists observing *a standardized practice designed to achieve an objective which one knows from accredited physical science cannot be thus achieved*. This would plainly be the case, for example, with Pueblo rituals dealing with rain or fertility. *But with behavior which is not directed toward a clearly unattainable objective, sociological observers are less likely to examine the collateral or latent functions of the behavior.*

Directs attention to theoretically fruitful fields of inquiry.—The distinction between manifest and latent functions serves further to direct the attention of the sociologist to precisely those realms of behavior, attitude and belief where he can most fruitfully apply his special skills. For what is his task if he confines himself to the study of manifest functions? He is then concerned very largely with determining whether a practice instituted for a particular purpose does, in fact, achieve this purpose. He will then inquire, for example, whether a new system of wage-payment achieves its avowed purpose of reducing labor turnover or of increasing output. He will ask whether a propaganda campaign has indeed gained its objective of increasing "willingness to fight" or "willingness to buy war bonds," or "tolerance toward other ethnic groups." Now, these are important, and complex, types of inquiry. But, so long as sociologists *confine* themselves to the study of manifest functions, their inquiry is set for them by practical men of affairs (whether a captain of industry, a trade union leader, or, conceivably, a Navaho chieftain, is for the moment immaterial), rather than by the theoretic problems which are at the core of the discipline. By dealing primarily with the realm of manifest functions, with the key problem of whether deliberately instituted practices or organizations succeed in achieving their objectives, the sociologist becomes converted into an industrious and skilled recorder of the altogether familiar pattern of behavior. *The terms of appraisal are fixed and limited by the question put to him by the non-theoretic men of affairs,* e.g., has the new wage-payment program achieved such-and-such purposes?

But armed with the concept of latent function, the sociologist extends his inquiry in those very directions which promise most for the theoretic development of the discipline. He examines the familiar (or planned) social practice to ascertain the latent, and hence generally unrecognized, functions (as well, of course, as the manifest functions). He considers, for example, the consequences of the new wage plan for, say, the trade union in which the workers are organized or the consequences of a propaganda program, not only for increasing its avowed purpose of stirring up patriotic fervor, but also for making large numbers of people reluctant to speak their minds when they differ with official policies, *etc.* In short, it is suggested that the *distinctive* intellectual contributions of the sociologist are found primarily in the study of unintended consequences (among which are latent functions) of social practices, as well as in the study of anticipated consequences (among which are manifest functions).[83]

---

[83] For a brief illustration of this general proposition, see Robert K. Merton, Marjorie Fiske and Alberta Curtis, *Mass Persuasion,* (New York: Harper, 1946), 185–189; Jahoda and Cook, *op. cit.*

There is some evidence that it is precisely at the point where the research attention of sociologists has shifted from the plane of manifest to the plane of latent functions that they have made their *distinctive* and major contributions. This can be extensively documented but a few passing illustrations must suffice.

The Hawthorne Western Electric Studies.[84]—As is well known, the early stages of this inquiry were concerned with the problem of the relations of "illumination to efficiency" of industrial workers. For some two and a half years, attention was focused on problems such as this: do variations in the intensity of lighting affect production? The initial results showed that within wide limits there was no uniform relation between illumination and output. Production output increased *both* in the experimental group where illumination was increased (or *decreased*) *and* in the control group where no changes in illumination were introduced. In short, the investigators confined themselves wholly to a search for the manifest functions. Lacking a concept of latent social function, no attention whatever was initially paid to the social consequences *of the experiment* for relations among members of the test and control groups or for relations between workers and the test room authorities. In other words, the investigators lacked a sociological frame of reference and operated merely as "engineers" (just as a group of meteorologists might have explored the "effects" upon rainfall of the Hopi ceremonial).

Only after continued investigation, did it occur to the research group to explore the consequences of the new "experimental situation" for the self-images and self-conceptions of the workers taking part in the experiment, for the interpersonal relations among members of the group, for the coherence and unity of the group. As Elton Mayo reports it, "the illumination fiasco had made them alert to the need that very careful records should be kept of everything that happened in the room in addition to the obvious engineering and industrial devices. Their observations therefore included not only records of industrial and engineering changes but also records of physiological or medical changes, and, *in a sense,* of social and anthropological. This last took the form of a 'log' that gave as full an account as possible of the actual events of every day. . . ."[85] In short, it was only after a long series of experiments which wholly neglected the latent social func-

---

[84] This is cited as a case study of how *an elaborate research was wholly changed in theoretic orientation and in the character of its research findings by the introduction of a concept approximating the concept of latent function.* Selection of the case for this purpose does not, of course, imply full acceptance of the *interpretations* which the authors give their findings. Among the several volumes reporting the Western Electric research, see particularly F. J. Roethlisberger and W. J. Dickson, *Management and the Worker,* (Cambridge, Mass.: Harvard University Press, 1939).

[85] Elton Mayo, *The Social Problems of an Industrial Civilization,* (Harvard University Press, 1945), 70.

tions of the experiment (as a contrived social situation) that this distinctly sociological framework was introduced. "With this realization," the authors write, "the inquiry changed its character. No longer were the investigators interested in testing for the effects of single variables. In the place of a controlled experiment, they substituted the notion of a social situation which needed to be described and understood as a system of interdependent elements." Thereafter, as is now widely known, inquiry was directed very largely toward ferreting out the latent functions of standardized practices among the workers, of informal organization developing among workers, of workers' games instituted by "wise administrators," of large programs of worker counselling and interviewing, *etc.* The new conceptual scheme entirely altered the range and types of data gathered in the ensuing research.

One has only to return to the previously quoted excerpt from Thomas and Znaniecki in their classical work of some thirty years ago, to recognize the correctness of Shils' remark:

. . . indeed the history of the study of primary groups in American sociology is a supreme instance of the *discontinuities of the development of this discipline:* a problem is stressed by one who is an acknowledged founder of the discipline, the problem is left unstudied, then, some years later, it is taken up with enthusiasm as if no one had ever thought of it before.[86]

For Thomas and Znaniecki had repeatedly emphasized the sociological view that, whatever its major purpose, "the association as a concrete group of human personalities unofficially involves many other interests; the social contacts between its members are not limited to their common pursuit. . . ." In effect, then, it had taken years of experimentation to turn the attention of the Western Electric research team to the latent social functions of primary groups emerging in industrial organizations. It should be made clear that this case is not cited here as an instance of defective experimental design; that is not our immediate concern. It is considered only as an illustration of the pertinence for *sociological* inquiry of the concept of latent function, and the associated concepts of functional analysis. It illustrates how the inclusion of this concept (whether the term is used or not is inconsequential) can sensitize sociological investigators to a range of significant social variables which are otherwise easily overlooked. The explicit ticketing of the concept may perhaps lessen the frequency of such occasions of discontinuity in future sociological research.

The discovery of latent functions represents significant increments in sociological knowledge.—There is another respect in which inquiry into

---

[86] Edward Shils, *The Present State of American Sociology,* (Glencoe, Illinois: The Free Press, 1948), 42 [italics supplied].

latent functions represents a distinctive contribution of the social scientist. It is precisely the latent functions of a practice or belief which are *not* common knowledge, for these are unintended and generally unrecognized social and psychological consquences. As a result, findings concerning latent functions represent a greater increment in knowledge than findings concerning manifest functions. They represent, also, greater departures from "common-sense" knowledge about social life. Inasmuch as the latent functions depart, more or less, from the avowed manifest functions, the research which uncovers latent functions very often produces "paradoxical" results. The seeming paradox arises from the sharp modification of a familiar popular preconception which regards a standardized practice or belief *only* in terms of its manifest functions by indicating some of its subsidiary or collateral latent functions. The introduction of the concept of latent function in social research leads to conclusions which show that "social life is not as simple as it first seems." For as long as people confine themselves to *certain* consequences (*e.g.* manifest consequences), it is comparatively simple for them to pass moral judgments upon the practice or belief in question. Moral evaluations, generally based on these manifest consequences, tend to be polarized in terms of black or white. But the perception of further (latent) consequences often complicates the picture. Problems of moral evaluation (which are not our immediate concern) and problems of social engineering (which are our concern[87]) both take on the additional complexities usually involved in responsible social decisions.

An example of inquiry which implicitly uses the notion of latent function will illustrate the sense in which "paradox"—discrepancy between the apparent, merely manifest, function and the actual, which also includes latent functions—tends to occur as a result of including this concept. Thus, to revert to Veblen's well-known analysis of conspicuous consumption, it is no accident that he has been recognized as a social analyst gifted with an eye for the paradoxical, the ironic, the satiric. For these are frequent, if not inevitable, outcomes of applying the concept of latent function (or its equivalent).

The Pattern of Conspicuous Consumption.—The manifest purpose of buying consumption goods is, of course, the satisfaction of the needs for which these goods are explicitly designed. Thus, automobiles are obviously intended to provide a certain kind of transportation; candles, to provide light; choice articles of food to provide sustenance; rare art products to provide aesthetic pleasure. Since these products *do* have these uses, it was largely

---

[87] This is not to deny that social engineering has direct moral implications or that technique and morality are inescapably intertwined, but I do not intend to deal with this range of problems in the present chapter. For some discussion of these problems see chapters VI, XV and XVII; also Merton, Fiske and Curtis, *Mass Persuasion,* chapter 7.

assumed that these encompass the range of socially significant functions. Veblen indeed suggests that this was ordinarily the prevailing view (in the pre-Veblenian era, of course): "The end of acquisition and accumulation is conventionally held to be the consumption of the goods accumulated. . . . This is at least felt to be the economically legitimate end of acquisition, *which alone it is incumbent on the theory to take account of.*" [88]

However, says Veblen in effect, as sociologists we must go on to consider the latent functions of acquisition, accumulation and consumption, and these latent functions are remote indeed from the manifest functions. "But, it is only when taken in a sense far removed from its naive meaning [*i.e.* manifest function] that the consumption of goods can be said to afford the incentive from which accumulation invariably proceeds." And among these latent functions, which help explain the persistence and the social location of the pattern of conspicuous consumption, is its symbolization of "pecuniary strength and so of gaining or retaining a good name." The exercise of "punctilious discrimination" in the excellence of "food, drink, shelter, service, ornaments, apparel, amusements" results not merely in direct gratifications derived from the consumption of "superior" to "inferior" articles, but also, and Veblen argues, more importantly, it results in a *heightening or reaffirmation of social status*.

The Veblenian paradox is that people buy expensive goods not so much because they are superior but because they are expensive. For it is the latent equation ("costliness = mark of higher social status") which he singles out in his functional analysis, rather than the manifest equation ("costliness = excellence of the goods"). Not that he denies manifest functions *any* place in buttressing the pattern of conspicuous consumption. These, too, are operative. "What has just been said must not be taken to mean that there are no other incentives to acquisition and accumulation than this desire to excel in pecuniary standing and so gain the esteem and envy of one's fellowmen. The desire for added comfort and security from want is present as a motive at every stage. . . ." Or again: "It would be hazardous to assert that a useful purpose is ever absent from the utility of any article or of any service, however obviously its prime purpose and chief element is conspicuous waste" and derived social esteem.[89] It is only that *these direct, manifest functions*

---

88 Veblen, *Theory of Leisure Class, op. cit.,* p. 25.

89 *Ibid.,* 32, 101. It will be noted throughout that Veblen is given to loose terminology. In the marked passages (and repeatedly elsewhere) he uses "incentive," "desire," "purpose," and "function" interchangeably. Since the context usually makes clear the denotation of these terms, no great harm is done. But it is clear that the expressed purposes of conformity to a culture pattern are by no means identical with the latent functions of the conformity. Veblen occasionally recognizes this. For example, "In strict accuracy nothing should be included under the head of conspicuous waste but such expenditure as is incurred on the ground of an invidious pecuniary compar-

do not fully account for the prevailing patterns of consumption. Otherwise put, if the latent functions of status-enhancement or status-reaffirmation were removed from the patterns of conspicuous consumption, these patterns would undergo severe changes of a sort which the "conventional" economist could not foresee.

In these respects, Veblen's analysis of latent functions departs from the common-sense notion that the end-product of consumption is "of course, the direct satisfaction which it provides": "People eat caviar because they're hungry; buy Cadillacs because they want the best car they can get; have dinner by candlelight because they like the peaceful atmosphere." The common-sense interpretation in terms of selected manifest motives gives way, in Veblen's analysis, to the collateral latent functions which are also, and perhaps more significantly, fulfilled by these practices. To be sure, the Veblenian analysis has, in the last decades, entered so fully into popular thought, that these latent functions are now widely recognized. [This raises the interesting problem of the changes occurring in a prevailing pattern of behaviour when its *latent* functions become generally recognized (and are thus no long latent). There will be no occasion for discussing this important problem in the present publication.]

The discovery of latent functions does not merely render conceptions of the functions served by certain social patterns more precise (as is the case also with studies of manifest functions), but introduces a *qualitatively different increment in the previous state of knowledge.*

Precludes the substitution of naive moral judgments for sociological analysis.—Since moral evaluations in a society tend to be largely in terms of the manifest consequences of a practice or code, we should be prepared to find that analysis in terms of latent functions at times runs counter to prevailing moral evaluations. For it does not follow that the latent functions will operate in the same fashion as the manifest consequences which are ordinarily the basis of these judgments. Thus, in large sectors of the American population, the political machine or the "political racket" are judged as unequivocally "bad" and "undesirable." The grounds for such moral judgment vary somewhat, but they consist substantially in pointing out that political machines violate moral codes: political patronage violates the code of selecting personnel on the basis of impersonal qualifications rather than on grounds of party loyalty or contributions to the party war-chest; bossism violates the code that votes should be based on individual appraisal of the qualifications of candidates and of political issues, and not on abiding loyalty

---

ison. But in order to bring any given item or element in under this head *it is not necessary that it should be recognized as waste in this sense by the person incurring the expenditure.*" (*Ibid*, 99; italics supplied). *Cf.* A. K. Davis, "Veblen on the decline of the Protestant Ethic," *op. cit.*

to a feudal leader; bribery, and "honest graft" obviously offend the pro-
prieties of property; "protection" for crime clearly violates the law and the
mores; and so on.

In view of the manifold respects in which political machines, in varying
degrees, run counter to the mores and at times to the law, it becomes pertinent to inquire how they manage to continue in operation. The familiar
"explanations" for the continuance of the political machine are not here in
point. To be sure, it may well be that if "respectable citizenry" would live up
to their political obligations, if the electorate were to be alert and enlightened; if the number of elective officers were substantially reduced from the
dozens, even hundreds, which the average voter is now expected to appraise
in the course of town, county, state and national elections; if the electorate
were activated by the "wealthy and educated classes without whose participation," as the not-always democratically oriented Bryce put it, "the best-
framed government must speedily degenerate";—if these and a plethora of
similar changes in political structure were introduced, perhaps the "evils" of
the political machine would indeed be exorcized.[90] But it should be noted
that these changes are often not introduced, that political machines have had
the phoenix-like quality of arising strong and unspoiled from their ashes,
that, in short, this structure has exhibited a notable vitality in many areas of
American political life.

Proceeding from the functional view, therefore, that we should *ordinarily*
(not invariably) expect persistent social patterns and social structures to
perform positive functions *which are at the time not adequately fulfilled by
other existing patterns and structures*, the thought occurs that perhaps this
publicly maligned organization is, *under present conditions*, satisfying basic
latent functions.[91] A brief examination of current analyses of this type of

---

[90] These "explanations" are "causal" in design. They profess to indicate the social
conditions under which political machines come into being. Insofar as they are
empirically confirmed, these explanations of course add to our knowledge concerning
the problem: how is it that political machines operate in certain areas and not in
others? How do they manage to continue? *But these causal accounts are not sufficient.*
The functional consequences of the machine, as we shall see, go far toward supple-
menting the causal interpretation.

[91] I trust it is superfluous to add that this hypothesis is not "in support of the
political machine." The question whether the dysfunctions of the machine outweigh
its functions, the question whether alternative structures are not available which may
fulfill its functions without necessarily entailing its social dysfunctions, still remain
to be considered at an appropriate point. We are here concerned with documenting
the statement that moral judgments based *entirely* on an appraisal of manifest functions of a social structure are "unrealistic" in the strict sense, *i.e.,* they do not take
into account other actual consequences of that structure, consequences which may
provide basic social support for the structure. As will be indicated later, "social
reforms" or "social engineering" which ignore latent functions do so on pain of
suffering acute disappointments and boomerang effects.

structure may also serve to illustrate additional problems of functional analysis.

Some Functions of the Political Machine.—Without presuming to enter into the variations of detail marking different political machines—a Tweed, Vare, Crump, Flinn, Hague are by no means identical types of bosses—we can briefly examine the functions more or less common to the political machine, as a generic type of social organization. We neither attempt to itemize all the diverse functions of the political machine nor imply that all these functions are similarly fulfilled by each and every machine.

The key structural function of the Boss is to organize, centralize and maintain in good working condition "the scattered fragments of power" which are at present dispersed through our political organization. By this centralized organization of political power, the boss and his apparatus can satisfy the needs of diverse subgroups in the larger community which are not adequately satisfied by legally devised and culturally approved social structures.

To understand the role of bossism and the machine, therefore, we must look at two types of sociological variables: (1) the *structural context* which makes it difficult, if not impossible, for morally approved structures to fulfill essential social functions, thus leaving the door open for political machines (or their structural equivalents) to fulfill these functions and (2) the subgroups whose distinctive needs are left unsatisfied, except for the latent functions which the machine in fact fulfills.[92]

Structural Context.—The constitutional framework of American political organization specifically precludes the legal possibility of highly centralized power and, it has been noted, thus "discourages the growth of effective and responsible leadership. The framers of the Constitution, as Woodrow Wilson observed, set up the check and balance system 'to keep government at a sort of mechanical equipoise by means of a standing amicable contest among its several organic parts.' They distrusted power as dangerous to liberty: and therefore they spread it thin and erected barriers against its concentration." This dispersion of power is found not only at the national level but in local areas as well. "As a consequence," Sait goes on to observe, "when *the people or particular groups* among them demanded positive action, no one had adequate authority to act. The machine provided an antidote." [93]

The constitutional dispersion of power not only makes for difficulty of effective decision and action but when action does occur it is defined and

---

[92] Again, as with preceding cases, we shall not consider the possible dysfunctions of the political machine.

[93] Edward M. Sait, "Machine, Political," *Encyclopedia of the Social Sciences*, IX, 658 b [italics supplied]; *cf.* A. F. Bentley, *The Process of Government* (Chicago, 1908), Chap. 2.

hemmed in by legalistic considerations. In consequence, there developed "a much *more human system* of partisan government, whose chief object soon became the circumvention of government by law. . . . The lawlessness of the extra-official democracy was merely the counterpoise of the legalism of the official democracy. The lawyer having been permitted to subordinate democracy to the Law, the Boss had to be called in to extricate the victim, which he did after a fashion and for a consideration." [94]

Officially, political power is dispersed. Various well-known expedients were devised for this manifest objective. Not only was there the familiar separation of powers among the several branches of the government but, in some measure, tenure in each office was limited, rotation in office approved. And the scope of power inherent in each office was severely circumscribed. Yet, observes Sait in rigorously functional terms, "Leadership is necessary; and *since* it does not develop readily within the constitutional framework, the Boss provides it in a crude and irresponsible form from the outside." [95]

Put in more generalized terms, *the functional deficiences of the official structure generate an alternative (unofficial) structure to fulfill existing needs somewhat more effectively.* Whatever its specific historical origins, the political machine persists as an apparatus for satisfying otherwise unfulfilled needs of diverse groups in the population. By turning to a few of these subgroups and their characteristic needs, we shall be led at once to a range of latent functions of the political machine.

Functions of the Political Machine for Diverse Subgroups.—It is well known that one source of strength of the political machine derives from its roots in the local community and the neighborhood. The political machine does not regard the electorate as an amorphous, undifferentiated mass of voters. With a keen sociological intuition, the machine recognizes that the voter is a person living in a specific neighborhood, with specific personal problems and personal wants. Public issues are abstract and remote; private problems are extremely concrete and immediate. It is not through the generalized appeal to large public concerns that the machine operates, but through the direct, quasi-feudal relationships between local representatives of the machine and voters in their neighborhood. Elections are won in the precinct.

The machine welds its link with ordinary men and women by elaborate networks of personal relations. Politics is transformed into personal ties. The precinct captain "must be a friend to every man, assuming if he does not feel sympathy with the unfortunate, and utilizing in his good works the resources

---

[94] Herbert Croly, *Progressive Democracy*, (New York, 1914), p. 254, cited by Sait, *op. cit.*, 658 b.

[95] Sait, *op. cit.*, 659 a. [italics supplied].

which the boss puts at his disposal." [96] The precinct captain is forever a friend in need. In our prevailingly impersonal society, the machine, through its local agents, fulfills the important social *function of humanizing and personalizing all manner of assistance* to those in need. Foodbaskets and jobs, legal and extra-legal advice, setting to rights minor scrapes with the law, helping the bright poor boy to a political scholarship in a local college, looking after the bereaved—the whole range of crises when a feller needs a friend, and, above all, a friend who knows the score and who can do something about it,—all these find the ever-helpful precinct captain available in the pinch.

To assess this function of the political machine adequately, it is important to note not only that aid *is* provided but *the manner in which it is provided.* After all, other agencies do exist for dispensing such assistance. Welfare agencies, settlement houses, legal aid clinics, medical aid in free hospitals, public relief departments, immigration authorities—these and a multitude of other organizations are available to provide the most varied types of assistance. But in contrast to the professional techniques of the welfare worker which may typically represent in the mind of the recipient the cold, bureaucratic dispensation of limited aid following upon detailed investigation of *legal* claims to aid of the "client" are the unprofessional techniques of the precinct captain who asks no questions, exacts no compliance with legal rules of eligibility and does not "snoop" into private affairs.[97]

For many, the loss of "self-respect" is too high a price for legalized assistance. In contrast to the gulf between the settlement house workers who so often come from a different social class, educational background and ethnic group, the precinct worker is "just one of us," who understands what it's all about. The condescending lady bountiful can hardly compete with the understanding friend in need. In *this struggle between alternative structures for fulfilling the nominally same function* of providing aid and support to those who need it, it is clearly the machine politician who is better integrated with the groups which he serves than the impersonal, professionalized, socially distant and legally constrained welfare worker. And since the politician can at times influence and manipulate the official organizations for the dis-

---

96 *Ibid.,* 659 a.

97 Much the same contrast with official welfare policy is found in Harry Hopkins' open-handed and non-political distribution of unemployment relief in New York State under the governorship of Franklin Delano Roosevelt. As Sherwood reports: "Hopkins was harshly criticized for these irregular activities by the established welfare agencies, which claimed it was 'unprofessional conduct' to hand out work tickets without thorough investigation of each applicant, his own or his family's financial resources and probably his religious affiliations. 'Harry told the agency to go to hell,' said [Hopkins' associate, Dr. Jacob A.] Goldberg." Robert E. Sherwood, *Roosevelt and Hopkins, An Intimate History,* (New York: Harper, 1948), 30.

pensation of assistance, whereas the welfare worker has practically no influence on the political machine, this only adds to his greater effectiveness. More colloquially and also, perhaps, more incisively, it was the Boston ward-leader, Martin Lomasny, who described this essential function to the curious Lincoln Steffens: "I think," said Lomasny, "that there's got to be in every ward somebody that any bloke can come to—no matter what he's done—and get help. *Help, you understand; none of your law and justice, but help.*" [98]

The "deprived classes," then, constitute one subgroup for whom the political machine satisfies wants not adequately satisfied in the same fashion by the legitimate social structure.

For a second subgroup, that of business (primarily "big" business but also "small"), the political boss serves the function of providing those political privileges which entail immediate economic gains. Business corporations, among which the public utilities (railroads, local transportation and electric light companies, communications corporations) are simply the most conspicuous in this regard, seek special political dispensations which will enable them to stabilize their situation and to near their objective of maximizing profits. Interestingly enough, corporations often want to avoid a chaos of uncontrolled competition. They want the greater security of an economic czar who controls, regulates and organizes competition, providing that this czar is not a public official with his decisions subject to public scrutiny and public control. (The latter would be "government control," and hence taboo.) The political boss fulfills these requirements admirably.

Examined for a moment apart from any moral considerations, the political apparatus operated by the Boss is effectively designed to perform these functions with a minimum of inefficiency. Holding the strings of diverse governmental divisions, bureaus and agencies in his competent hands, the Boss rationalizes the relations between public and private business. He serves as the business community's ambassador in the otherwise alien (and sometimes unfriendly) realm of government. And, in strict businesslike terms, he is well-paid for his economic services to his respectable business clients. In an article entitled, "An Apology to Graft," Lincoln Steffens suggested that "Our economic system, which held up riches, power and acclaim as prizes to men bold enough and able enough to buy corruptly timber, mines, oil fields and franchises and 'get away with it,' was at fault." [99] And, in a conference with a hundred or so of Los Angeles business leaders, he described a fact well known to all of them: the Boss and his machine were an *integral part* of

---

[98] *The Autobiography of Lincoln Steffens,* (Chautauqua, New York; Chautauqua Press, 1931), 618. Deriving largely from Steffens, as he says, F. Stuart Chapin sets forth these functions of the political machine with great clarity. See his *Contemporary American Institutions,* (New York: Harper, 1934), 40–54.

[99] *Autobiography of Lincoln Steffens,* 570.

the organization of the economy. "You cannot build or operate a railroad, or a street railway, gas, water, or power company, develop and operate a mine, or get forests and cut timber on a large scale, or run any privileged business, without corrupting or joining in the corruption of the government. You tell me privately that you must, and here I am telling you semi-publicly that you must. And that is so all over the country. And that means that we have an organization of society in which, *for some reason*, you and your kind, the ablest, most intelligent, most imaginative, daring, and resourceful leaders of society, are and must be against society and its laws and its all-around growth." [100]

Since the demand for the services of special privileges are built into the structure of the society, the Boss fulfills diverse functions for this second subgroup of business-seeking-privilege. These "needs" of business, as presently constituted, are not adequately provided for by conventional and culturally approved social structures; consequently, the extra-legal but more-or-less efficient organization of the political machine comes to provide these services. To adopt an *exclusively* moral attitude toward the "corrupt political machine" is to lose sight of the very structural conditions which generate the "evil" that is so bitterly attacked. To adopt a functional outlook is to provide not an apologia for the political machine but a more solid basis for modifying or eliminating the machine, *providing* specific structural arrangements are introduced either for eliminating these effective demands of the business community or, if that is the objective, of satisfying these demands through alternative means.

A third set of distinctive functions fulfilled by the political machine for a special subgroup is that of providing alternative channels of social mobility for those otherwise excluded from the more conventional avenues for personal "advancement." Both the sources of this special "need" (for social mobility) and the respect in which the political machine comes to help satisfy this need can be understood by examining the structure of the larger culture and society. As is well known, the American culture lays enormous emphasis on money and power as a "success" goal legitimate for all members of the society. By no means alone in our inventory of cultural goals, it still remains among the most heavily endowed with positive affect and value. However, certain subgroups and certain ecological areas are notable for the relative absence of opportunity for achieving these (monetary and power) types of success. They constitute, in short, sub-populations where "the cultural em-

---

100 *Ibid.,* 572–3 [italics supplied]. This helps explain, as Steffens noted after Police Commissioner Theodore Roosevelt, "the prominence and respectability of the men and women who intercede for crooks" when these have been apprehended in a periodic effort to "clean up the political machine." *Cf.* Steffens, 371, and *passim.*

phasis upon pecuniary success has been absorbed, but where there is *little access to conventional and legitimate* means for attaining such success. The conventional occupational opportunities of persons in (such areas) are almost completely limited to manual labor. Given our cultural stigmatization of manual labor,[101] and its correlate, the prestige of white-collar work, it is clear that the result is a tendency to achieve these culturally approved objectives *through whatever means are possible.* These people are on the one hand, "asked to orient their conduct toward the prospect of accumulating wealth [and power] and, on the other, they are largely denied effective opportunities to do so institutionally."

It is within this context of social structure that the political machine fulfills the basic function of providing avenues of social mobilty for the otherwise disadvantaged. Within this context, even the corrupt political machine and the racket "represent the triumph of amoral intelligence over morally prescribed 'failure' when the channels of vertical mobility are closed or narrowed *in a society which places a high premium on economic affluence,* [*power*] *and social ascent for all its members.*" [102] As one sociologist has noted on the basis of several years of close observation in a slum area:

The sociologist who dismisses racket and political organizations as deviations from desirable standards thereby neglects some of the major elements of slum life. . . . *He does not discover the functions they perform for the members* [of the groupings in the slum]. The Irish and later immigrant peoples have had the greatest difficulty in finding places for themselves in our urban social and economic structure. Does anyone believe that the immigrants and their children could have achieved their present degree of social mobility without gaining control of the political organization of some of our largest cities? The same is true of the racket organization. *Politics and the rackets have furnished an important means of social mobility for individuals, who, because of ethnic background and*

---

101 See the National Opinion Research Center survey of evaluation of occupations which firmly documents the general impression that the manual occupations rate very low indeed in the social scale of values, *even among those who are themselves engaged in manual labor.* Consider this latter point in its full implications. In effect, the cultural and social structure exacts the values of pecuniary and power success even among those who find themselves confined to the stigmatized manual occupations. Against this background, consider the powerful motivation for achieving this type of "success" by any means whatsoever. A garbage-collector who joins with other Americans in the view that the garbage-collector is "the lowest of the low" occupations can scarcely have a self-image which is pleasing to him; he is in a "pariah" occupation in the very society where he is assured that "all who have genuine merit can get ahead." Add to this, his occasional recognition that "he didn't have the same chance as others, no matter what they say," and one perceives the enormous psychological pressure upon him for "evening up the score" by finding some means, whether strictly legal or not, for moving ahead. All this provides the structural and derivatively psychological background for the "socially induced need" in *some* groups to find some accessible avenue for social mobility.

102 Merton, "Social structure and anomie," chapter IV of this volume.

low class position, are blocked from advancement in the "respectable" channels.[103]

This, then, represents a third type of function performed for a distinctive subgroup. This function, it may be noted in passing, is fulfilled by the *sheer* existence and operation of the political machine, for it is in the machine itself that these individuals and subgroups find their culturally induced needs more or less satisfied. It refers to the services which the political apparatus provides for its own personnel. But seen in the wider social context we have set forth, it no longer appears as *merely* a means of self-aggrandizement for profit-hungry and power-hungry *individuals,* but as an organized provision for *subgroups* otherwise excluded from or handicapped in the race for "getting ahead."

Just as the political machine performs services for "legitimate" business, so it operates to perform not dissimilar services for "illegitimate" business: vice, crime and rackets. Once again, the basic sociological role of the machine in this respect can be more fully appreciated only if one temporarily abandons attitudes of moral indignation, to examine in all moral innocence the actual workings of the organization. In this light, it at once appears that the subgroup of the professional criminal, racketeer or gambler has basic similarities of organization, demands and operation to the subgroup of the industrialist, man of business or speculator. If there is a Lumber King or an Oil King, there is also a Vice King or a Racket King. If expansive legitimate business organizes administrative and financial syndicates to "rationalize" and to "integrate" diverse areas of production and business enterprise, so expansive rackets and crime organize syndicates to bring order to the otherwise chaotic areas of production of illicit goods and services. If legitimate business regards the proliferation of small business enterprises as wasteful

---

[103] William F. Whyte, "Social organization in the slums," *American Sociological Review,* Feb. 1943, 8, 34–39 (italics supplied). Thus, the political machine and the racket represent a special case of the type of organizational adjustment to the conditions described in chapter IV. It represents, note, an *organizational* adjustment: definite structures arise and operate to reduce somewhat the acute tensions and problems of individuals caught up in the described conflict between the "cultural accent on success-for-all" and the "socially structured fact of unequal opportunities for success." As chapter IV indicates, other types of *individual* "adjustment" are possible: lone-wolf crime, psychopathological states, rebellion, retreat by abandoning the culturally approved goals, etc. Likewise, other types of *organizational adjustment* sometimes occur; the racket or the political machine are not *alone* available as organized means for meeting this socially induced problem. Participation in revolutionary organizations, for example, can be seen within this context, as an alternative mode of organizational adjustment. All this bears theoretic notice here, since we might otherwise overlook the basic functional concepts of functional substitutes and functional evquivalents, which are to be discussed at length in a subsequent publication.

and inefficient, substituting, for example, the giant chain stores for hundreds of corner groceries, so illegitimate business adopts the same businesslike attitude and syndicates crime and vice.

Finally, and in many respects, most important, is the basic similarity, if not near-identity, of the economic role of "legitimate" business and of "illegitimate" business. *Both are in some degree concerned with the provision of goods and services for which there is an economic demand.* Morals aside, they are both business, industrial and professional enterprises, dispensing goods and services which some people want, for which there is a market in which goods and services are transformed into commodities. And, in a prevalently market society, we should expect appropriate enterprises to arise whenever there is a market demand for certain goods or services.

As is well known, vice, crime and the rackets *are* "big business." Consider only that there have been estimated to be about 500,000 professional prostitutes in the United States of 1950, and compare this with the approximately 200,000 physicians and 350,000 professional registered nurses. It is difficult to estimate which have the larger clientele: the professional men and women of medicine or the professional men and women of vice. It is, of course, difficult to estimate the economic assets, income, profits, and dividends of illicit gambling in this country and to compare it with the economic assets, income, profits and dividends of, say, the shoe industry, but it is altogether possible that the two industries are about on a par. No precise figures exist on the annual expenditures on illicit narcotics, and it is probable that these are less than the expenditures on candy, but it is also probable that they are larger than the expenditure on books.

It takes but a moment's thought to recognize that, *in strictly economic terms*, there is no relevant difference between the provision of licit and of illicit goods and services. The liquor traffic illustrates this perfectly. It would be peculiar to argue that prior to 1920 (when the 18th amendment became effective), the provision of liquor constituted an economic service, that from 1920 to 1933, its production and sale no longer constituted an economic service dispensed in a market, and that from 1934 to the present, it once again took on a serviceable aspect. Or, it would be *economically* (not morally) absurd to suggest that the sale of bootlegged liquor in the dry state of Kansas is less a response to a market demand than the sale of publicly manufactured liquor in the neighboring wet state of Missouri. Examples of this sort can of course be multiplied many times over. Can it be held that in European countries, with registered and legalized prostitution, the prostitute contributes an economic service, whereas in this country, lacking legal sanction, the prostitute provides no such service? Or that the professional abortionist is in the economic market where he has approved legal status and that he is out of the economic market where he is legally taboo? Or that gambling satisfies a specific demand for entertainment in Nevada, where it constitutes the largest business enterprise of the larger cities in the state, but that it differs essentially in this respect from motion pictures in the neighboring state of California?[104]

The failure to recognize that these businesses are only *morally* and not *economically* distinguishable from "legitimate" businesses has led to badly scrambled analysis. Once the economic identity of the two is recognized, we may anticipate that if the political machine performs functions for "legitimate big business" it will be all the more likely to perform not dissimilar functions for "illegitimate big business." And, of course, such is often the case.

The distinctive function of the political machine for their criminal, vice and racket clientele is to enable them to operate in satisfying the economic demands of a large market without due interference from the government. Just as big business may contribute funds to the political party war-chest to ensure a minimum of governmental interference, so with big rackets and big crime. In both instances, the political machine can, in varying degrees, provide "protection." In both instances, many features of the structural context are identical: (1) market demands for goods and services; (2) the operators' concern with maximizing gains from their enterprises; (3) the need for partial control of government which might otherwise interfere with these activities of businessmen; (4) the need for an efficient, powerful and centralized agency to provide an effective liaison of "business" with government.

Without assuming that the foregoing pages exhaust either the range of functions or the range of subgroups served by the political machine, we can at least see that *it presently fulfills some functions for these diverse subgroups which are not adequately fulfilled by culturally approved or more conventional structures.*

Several additional implications of the functional analysis of the political machine can be mentioned here only in passing, although they obviously require to be developed at length. First, the foregoing analysis has direct implications for *social engineering*. It helps explain why the periodic efforts at "political reform," "turning the rascals out" and "cleaning political house" are typically (though not necessarily) short-lived and ineffectual. It

---

[104] Perhaps the most perceptive statement of this view has been made by Hawkins and Waller. "The prostitute, the pimp, the peddler of dope, the operator of the gambling hall, the vendor of obscene pictures, the bootlegger, the abortionist, all are productive, all produce services or goods which people desire and for which they are willing to pay. It happens that society has put these goods and services under the ban, but people go on producing them and people go on consuming them, and an act of the legislature does not make them any less a part of the economic system." "Critical notes on the cost of crime," *Journal of Criminal Law and Criminology*, 1936, 26, 679–94, at 684.

exemplifies a basic theorem: *any attempt to eliminate an existing social structure without providing adequate alternative structures for fulfilling the functions previously fulfilled by the abolished organization is doomed to failure.* (Needless to say, this theorem has much wider bearing than the one instance of the political machine.) When "political reform" confines itself to the manifest task of "turning the rascals out," it is engaging in little more than sociological magic. The reform may for a time bring new figures into the political limelight; it may serve the casual social function of re-assuring the electorate that the moral virtues remain intact and will ultimately triumph; it may actually effect a turnover in the personnel of the political machine; it may even, for a time, so curb the activities of the machine as to leave unsatisfied the many needs it has previously fulfilled. But, inevitably, unless the reform also involves a "re-forming" of the social and political structure such that the existing needs are satisfied by alternative structures or unless it involves a change which eliminates these needs altogther, the political machine will return to its integral place in the social scheme of things. *To seek social change, without due recognition of the manifest and latent functions performed by the social organization undergoing change, is to indulge in social ritual rather than social engineering.* The concepts of manifest and latent functions (or their equivalents) are indispensable elements in the theoretic repertoire of the social engineer. In this crucial sense, these concepts are not "merely" theoretical (in the abusive sense of the term), but are eminently practical. In the deliberate enactment of social change, they can be ignored only at the price of considerably heightening the risk of failure.

A second implication of this analysis of the political machine also has a bearing upon areas wider than the one we have considered. The paradox has often been noted that the supporters of the political machine include both the "respectable" business class elements who are, of course, opposed to the criminal or racketeer and the distinctly "unrespectable" elements of the underworld. And, at first appearance, this is cited as an instance of very strange bedfellows. The learned judge is not infrequently called upon to sentence the very racketeer beside whom he sat the night before at an informal dinner of the political bigwigs. The district attorney jostles the exonerated convict on his way to the back room where the Boss has called a meeting. The big business man may complain almost as bitterly as the big racketeer about the "extortionate" contributions to the party fund demanded by the Boss. Social opposites meet—in the smoke-filled room of the successful politician.

In the light of a functional analysis all this of course no longer seems paradoxical. Since the machine serves both the businessman and the criminal man, the two seemingly antipodal groups intersect. This points to a more general theorem: *the social functions of an organization help determine the structure (including the recruitment of personnel involved in the structure), just as the structure helps determine the effectiveness with which the functions are fulfilled.* In terms of social status, the business group and the criminal group are indeed poles apart. But status does not fully determine behavior and the inter-relations between groups. Functions modify these relations. Given their distinctive needs, the several subgroups in the large society are "integrated," whatever their personal desires or intentions, by the centralizing structure which serves these several needs. In a phrase with many implications which require further study, *structure affects function and function affects structure.*

Concluding Remarks

This review of some salient considerations in structural and functional analysis has done little more than indicate some of the principal problems and potentialities of this mode of sociological interpretation. Each of the items codified in the paradigm require sustained theoretic clarification and cumulative empirical research. But it is clear that in functional theory, stripped of those traditional postulates which have fenced it in and often made it little more than a latter-day rationalization of existing practices, sociology has one beginning of a systematic and empirically relevant mode of analysis. It is hoped that the direction here indicated will suggest the feasibility and the desirability of further codification of functional analysis. In due course each section of the paradigm will be elaborated into a documented, analyzed and codified chapter in the history of functional analysis.

Ernest Nagel

A Formalization of Functionalism

WITH SPECIAL REFERENCE TO
ITS APPLICATION IN THE SOCIAL SCIENCES

*I*T is the aim of the present essay to examine Merton's paradigm in the light of a schema of distinctions derived from an analysis of functional explanations in biological science. This examination is undertaken with one primary objective in mind: to exhibit the several items in Merton's codification as intimately related features in a coherent pattern of analysis, and thereby to make more evident than he has done the indispensable requirements which an adequate functional account in sociology must seek to satisfy. . . .

It is notorious that in many disciplines (e.g., modern physics) functional statements rarely occur. No modern student of electricity, for example, would feel comfortable with a proposed reformulation of Ohm's Law (At constant temperature, the current in a wire is proportional to the electromotive force) into a functional statement such as "At constant temperature, the current in a wire varies in order to remain proportional to the electromotive force." Several reasons can be advanced to account for this sense of discomfort, but perhaps the most important one is the following. There is a prima facie difference between most systems investigated in the physical sciences and those studied in biology. In the former, the properties and activities of the systems are dependent upon a set of factors in such a way that when these factors undergo any considerable variation the properties and activities of the system cease to exist. In the latter, however, the systems appear to be self-maintaining with respect to the continued manifestation of certain of their traits, despite fairly extensive variations in the factors upon which those traits causally depend. For example, the temperature of a stone will fluctuate with the temperature of its environment. But because the human body possesses mechanisms of regulation, it can maintain a fairly constant internal temperature despite quite considerable variations in the temperature of its environment. Accordingly, functional statements are regarded as appropriate in connection with systems possessing self-maintaining mechanisms for certain of their traits, but seem pointless and even misleading when used with reference to systems lacking such self-regulatory devices.[1]

We now turn to a closer inspection of the general character of such "directively organized" (sometimes also called "goal-directed") systems. . . . Let S be such a system and E its "external" environment. Just how the line between S and E is to be drawn need not concern us; it is a problem which must be settled on the basis of the special facts in individual cases, though it is conceivable that in some cases the line is drawn quite arbitrarily. We are supposing that S is a "functional" (or "self-maintaining," or "directively organized," or "goal-directed") system with respect to a certain trait (property, state, process) G. That is, S either possesses G at some time or during some period, or S is undergoing a series of alterations terminating in G, such that S is preserved in the state G or in its development to acquire G, despite some fairly extensive class of changes whether in E or in certain parts of S itself. We are therefore assuming that unless S contains some mechanism which produces effects compensating for these changes, it will cease to exhibit G or the tendency to acquire G; and it will be our primary task to make this assumption more articulate.

It is of utmost importance to specify in each concrete case both the system S and the trait G. For in the first place, a system may be self-maintaining with respect to one trait but not with respect to some other. Thus, the human organism exhibits homeostasis with respect to its internal temperature, but apparently not with respect to the diameter of the iris of the eye. In the second place, S may be a part of some more inclusive system S^1,

---

[1] For a more extended discussion of the question raised in this paragraph and of related matters, cf. Ernest Nagel, "Teleological Explanation and Teleological Systems" in *Vision and Action* (Sidney Ratner, editor), New Brunswick, 1953.

and though S is directly organized relative to G, S^1 may not be. In the third place, there may be several G's with respect to all of which S is a functional system. Nevertheless, as will become clearer in the sequel, the circumstances under which S is self-maintaining with respect to some of these G's may not coincide with the circumstances under which it is self-maintaining with respect to the others. Moreover, some of the G's with respect to which S is self-maintaining may constitute some kind of "hierarchy"—the hierarchy might be based on relations of causal dependence, temporal precedence, relations of inclusiveness or specificity, importance in some scale of values, and so on—and the conditions under which S is self-maintaining with respect to one member of the hierarchy may or may not be compatible with the self-maintenance of S with respect to another member of the hierarchy. Each of these possibilities will be found to have considerable relevance for the subsequent discussion.

To continue the analysis we require the notions of "state co-ordinate" (or "state variable") and "state description" which play such important roles in theoretical physics; and we must stop to explain them.

Imagine a physical system Σ to be completely isolated from external influences and to exhibit at some initial time t_0 specific forms of the set of properties Γ (which may or may not be exhaustive of all the properties of Σ), which will be denoted by "Γ_0." If left undisturbed until time t_1, the system will exhibit the same or different specific forms of these properties Γ, which will be denoted by "Γ_1." Suppose now that Σ is brought back into its initial state Γ_0, and that after an interval of time $(t_1 - t_0)$ it once again exhibits Γ_1. If Σ behaves in an analogous way, no matter what state is taken as the initial state and no matter how large the temporal interval, it will be called a "deterministic system with respect to Γ" (or more briefly, when there is no danger of confusion, a "deterministic system"). The set of properties Γ may be quite extensive, perhaps far too numerous for convenient observation. However, assume that there are n (a relatively small finite number) properties in Γ, whose specific forms can be taken as values of the variables "x_1," "x_2" . . ., "x_n," such that the specific forms of *all* the properties in Γ at any time are uniquely determined by these n properties at that time, and such that n is the smallest number of properties for which this holds. Accordingly, if at some initial time t_0 these variables have the values $x_1 t_0, \ldots, x_1 t_0$ (so that Σ is in the state Γ_0), while at some subsequent time t_1 the variables have the values $x_1 t^1, \ldots, x_n t^1$ (so that Σ is the state Γ_1), then since Σ is a deterministic system the second set of values of the variables (and hence the second state of Σ) are uniquely determined by the first set. Such variables will be called "state co-ordinates," and the set of variables will be referred to as a "state description." It is explicitly postulated that the values of the state co-ordinates at a given time are independent of one another, even though their values at one time depend on their values at another time. . . .

With this schematic formulation of the distinctive traits of functional systems before us, we now examine Merton's codification of the "concepts and problems which have been forced upon our attention by critical scrutiny of current research and theory in functional analysis." We shall first reproduce in turn each item in his paradigm; identify as far as it is possible to do so the distinctions each contains with elements in the formal analysis of the preceding section; indicate whenever necessary possible ambiguities in his discussion; and show at what points in his paradigm the special subject matter of sociology raises problems and requires distinctions for which there appear to be no counterparts in our generalized formulation of functional systems.

1. *The item (s) to which functions are imputed*

The entire range of sociological data can be, and much of it has been, subjected to functional analysis. The basic requirement is that the object of analysis represent a *standardized* (i.e., patterned and repetitive) item, such as social roles, institutional patterns, social processes, cultural pattern, culturally patterned emotions, social norms, group organization, social structure, devices for social control, etc.

Basic query: what must enter into the protocol of observation of the given item if it is to be amenable to systematic functional analysis?

(a) The "data" and "items" here mentioned appear to have a status in inquiry analogous to the parts and processes of organisms whose functions are being investigated in biology. If the inquiry is successfully completed, and its findings are formulated, some of these items could presumably be represented by *state co-ordinates* for some trait of the system.

(b) However, Merton's attention appears to be directed primarily to the preliminary stage of a functional analysis, rather than to the completed outcome of such an inquiry—to the stage at which crude and tentative discriminations are being explored, and gross relations of dependence between the discriminated items are being established. There is usually quite a distance between this exploratory state and the formulation of a satisfactory list of state co-ordinates for some trait of system. Indeed, a proposed list of state co-ordinates does not become definitive until an adequate theory (or system of general laws) has been established to account for a given set of traits of the subject matter. It is well known that in the development of a science it is often necessary to add to or subtract from an initial list of state co-ordinates. For ideally the state co-ordinates must describe completely the state of a system that is causally relevant to the occurrence of a given property. There are no rules for discovering the appropriate set of co-ordinates; and there is no assurance whatever that they are contained in a catalogue of miscellaneous items discriminated in a subject matter, no matter how exhaustive such a catalogue may seem to be and no matter how carefully the items are observed and collected. It is in fact by no means the case that the most obvious or even the immediately observable parts or features of a system are the features which correspond to an adequate list of state co-ordinates; and the history of science supplies ample evidence to show that the pertinent co-ordinates of a system are often related to matters of direct observation only indirectly.

(c) It has already been explained, and merits some emphasis, that the state co-ordinates for a given trait of a system must be mutually independent variables—in the sense that their respective values at a given time are not derivable from one another. It is not entirely clear from Merton's statement whether the items he mentions are intended as a possible list of co-ordinates for some *one* state of a system, or whether they are a juxtaposition of several partial lists for *different* states. If the former is intended, the question whether the items cited satisfy the requirement just noted for state co-ordinates is a factual issue, upon which the present study has nothing to say. There is, however, some prima facie ground for doubt whether, for example, "social structure" and "institutional patterns"—if taken as state co-ordinates for some one state—do meet this requirement.

(d) A partial though formal answer can be given to Merton's Basic Query, on the assumption that it is addressed to the requirements for proto-cols of observation relating to the values of state co-ordinates. The notion of state co-ordinate would have no significant application to empirical inquiry unless at least the following conditions are fulfilled. (i) A rule must be speci-fied for each state co-ordinate (or for certain combinations of them) which connects it (or the combinations) with matters of gross observation, however involved and indirect the connection may be. (ii) Different hypothetical values of a given state co-ordinate (or of a given combination of state co-ordinates) must be discriminable in observation—at any rate, with some degree of approximation. For example, if the co-ordinate is a distance, one must be able to distinguish observationally between a distance of, say, two and two hundred meters, though perhaps not between a tenth and an eleventh of a millimeter. (iii) The traits represented by different state co-ordinates (or different combinations of co-ordinates) must be distinguishable by some form of observation—for example, what is denoted by "position" must be distinguishable from what is denoted by "momentum."

2. Concepts of subjective dispositions (motives, purposes)

At some point, functional analysis invariably assumes or explicitly operates with some conception of the motivation of individuals involved in a social system. As the foregoing discussion has shown, these concepts of subjective disposition are often and erroneously merged with the related, but different, concepts of objective consequences of attitude, belief and behavior.

Basic query: in which types of analysis is it sufficient to take observed motivations as *data*, as givens, and in which are they properly considered as *problematical*, as derivable from other data?

(a) It seems reasonable to suppose that reference is here being made to motives and purposes as causally relevant for the occurrence of some phenomena. Accordingly, the reference is to a *special* state co-ordinate for some state of a system. However, as a state co-ordinate "subjective disposition" is on par with any other co-ordinates (such as those mentioned in the first number of the paradigm); and it is not evident why it should be listed under a special category in what is ostensibly a *general* paradigm of functional analysis.

Whether, in point of fact, "subjective disposition" is a suitable state co-ordinate in the study of social systems, is of course not a formal question, and it can be decided only on the basis of the special facts and established laws of the social sciences.

(b) Moreover, not only can the Basic Query receive no answer in general or formal terms; it must also be cleared of some ambiguities to be quite definite. (i) If "subjective disposition" is one state co-ordinate among others in a system, and since the values of state co-ordinates at a given time are (by definition) independent of one another, the specific value of this co-ordinate at a given time will not be "derivable" from the corresponding values of the other co-ordinates at that time. In this sense of the Query, observed motivations must be taken "as data, as givens."

(ii) On the other hand, still on the assumption that "subjective disposition" is a state co-ordinate, the specific character of subjective dispositions at one time must be derivable from the values of the state co-ordinates at some previous time—provided, of course, that suitable laws for the system have already been established. In this sense of the Query, observed motivations can always be "properly considered as problematical."

(iii) However, it may be that "subjective disposition" is not a suitable variable to count as a state co-ordinate in a given system, perhaps because it does not enter in that capacity into known laws or theories. Two cases can then be distinguished. (α) Although "subjective disposition" is not a state co-ordinate, it may be related by some known laws to variables that are state co-ordinates. In this case, observed motivations will be "derivable from other data." (β) It may be that it is related by no known laws to other variables. In this case, motives and purposes will have to be taken as "data, as givens."

(iv) Finally, there is the possibility that two alternate but equivalent analyses (or theories) are available for a given system, in one of which "subjective disposition" is a state variable but in the other not. Accordingly, when

considered within the framework of one mode of analyses, subjective dispositions will be "givens" or "derivable," depending on whether one is raising
the question mentioned under (i) or under (ii); but when considered within
the framework of the second mode of analysis, they could always be properly
regarded as derivable from other data—that is, from the values of the state
co-ordinates of the second theory.

3. *Concepts of objective consequences (functions, dysfunctions)*

We have observed two prevailing types of confusion enveloping the several
current conceptions of 'function':

(1) the tendency to confine sociological observations to the *positive* contributions of a sociological item to the social or cultural system in which it is implicated ; and

(2) the tendency to confuse the subjective category of *motive* with the objective category of *function*.

Appropriate conceptual distinctions are required to eliminate these
confusions.

The first problem calls for a concept of *multiple consequences* and *a net
balance of an aggregate of consequences*.

Functions are those observed consequences which make for the adaptation or
adjustment of a given system ; and *dysfunctions*, those observed consequences
which lessen the adaptation or adjustment of the system. There is also the
empirical possibility of *nonfunctional* consequences, which are simply irrelevant
to the system under consideration.

In any given instances, an item may have both functional and dysfunctional
consequences, giving rise to the difficult and important problem of evolving
canons for assessing the net balance of the aggregate of consequences. (This is,
of course, most important in the use of functional analysis for guiding the formation and enactment of policy.)

The second problem (of confusion between motives and functions) requires
us to introduce a conceptual distinction between the cases in which the subjective
aim-in-view coincides with the objective consequences, and the cases in which
they diverge.

Manifest functions are those objective consequences contributing to the
adjustment or adaptation of the system which are intended and recognized by
participants in the system ;

Latent functions, correlatively, being those which are neither intended nor
recognized.

Basic query: what are the effects of seeking to transform a previously latent
function into a manifest function (involving the problem of the role of
knowledge in human behavior and the problems of 'manipulation' of human
behavior)?

(a) Despite the general clarity of Merton's observations in connection
with the first problem, several distinguishable things seem to be covered
by them.

(i) By the "function" of an item (or set of items) in *S* one may understand simply some trait G which that item succeeds in maintaining in S. The item can then be represented as a state co-ordinate for G, and its function is the preservation of G in S. In this sense of the word, a function of an item is a role it plays in S, so that "function" is being employed in the first of the three meanings of the word that have been distinguished above.

(ii) However, the word could be understood to have a more inclusive meaning, and to refer to some or all of the effects (immediate as well as indirect) that are produced by a change in a state variable, provided only that the change falls into some class K_G of variations which preserve S in a G state for some indicated G. Thus, suppose S to have two G's, G_1 and G_2, where A_1 and B_1 are state co-ordinates for the first, and A_2 and B_2 are state co-ordinates for the second. A change in A_1 may bring forth compensating changes in B_1 so as to maintain G_1; but it may also bring about a variation in A_2 that in turn is followed by a G_2-preserving variation in B_2. All these changes in these several co-ordinates, and not only the maintenance of G_1 and G_2, will then be "objective consequences" of the initial change in A_1, "which make for the adaptation or adjustment of a given system," and may be intended by the phrase "function of A_1." In this sense of the word, "function" is being employed in approximately the third meaning previously distinguished.

(b) In terms of the distinctions of our generalized account of functional systems, a dysfunction can be identified as one of the following kinds of change.

(i) If A is a state co-ordinate for G in S, and A varies so that despite additional changes in other co-ordinates for G, the variations fall outside the class K_{AG} of G-preserving changes, and thereby take S out of its G state.

(ii) If A varies so as to remain within the class K_{AG} of G-preserving variations, but for some reason another co-ordinate B changes so that its new value falls outside the class K_{BG} (and so takes S out of the G state).

(iii) If, as before, S has two G's, G_1 and G_2, where A_1 and B_1 are co-ordinates for the first while A_2 and B_2 are co-ordinates for the second, and if A_1 varies with compensating variations in B_1 so as to preserve G_1, but induces a variation in A_2 which is not compensated by a G_2-preserving variation in B_2 (so that S moves out of the G_2 state). In this third case, the change in A_1 can perhaps be regarded as only a partially dysfunctional one.

(c) Nonfunctional changes can be specified as follows: A system S will in general possess an indefinite number of properties that are not exhausted by the set of state co-ordinates for a given G (or class of G's). Suppose S to possess the class of G's: G_1, G_2, . . ., G_n and that X is a property of S which does not belong to any set of state co-ordinates for these G's nor is it a constituent element in any of the G's. If a change in X induces no functional or dysfunctional variations in any of these co-ordinates, the change may be said to be nonfunctional with respect to these G's. An important point to be observed is that just as the claim that a given change is functional or dysfunctional must be understood as being relative to a specified G (or sets of G's), so the claim that a change is nonfunctional must similarly be construed as being relative to a specified set of G's. A change which is non-functional with respect to G_1 may be functional, or dysfunctional, or non-functional relative to G_2.

(d) A similar relational formulation is required for explicating the sense in which "an item may have both functional and dysfunctional conse-quences." Thus, as just noted, a variation in a co-ordinate may be functional with respect to G_1, but dysfunctional with respect to G_2. Moreover, a system S may undergo development over a period of time (whether as a consequence of a "natural" growth or of an altered environment); and it is quite possible that though a variation in an item at one time is functional relative to G_1, a similar variation in that item at another time is dysfunctional with respect to G_1. Should such a case arise, it might become a matter of debate whether one is investigating the "same" system S at different times, or two different systems S_1 and S_2 which happen to stand to one another in some relation of causal continuity.

It is also pertinent to mention in this connection the possibility that some hierarchy has been established for various G's which a system may exhibit. Suppose, for example, that a set of four G's is arranged in the order: G_1, G_2, (G_3, G_4), where the first takes precedence over the second, the second over the other two, but G_3 and G_4 have the same rank. If a change in S is G_1-preserving but not G_2-preserving, it may perhaps count as "on the whole" functional rather than dysfunctional. If the change is dysfunctional with respect to G_1, it may count as dysfunctional "on the whole," even if it is functional relative to G_2. However, if the change is nonfunctional with respect to G_1 and G_2, but is functional relative to G_3 and dysfunctional rela-tive to G_4, it would doubtless be regarded as quite arbitrary to characterize the change as being "on the whole" one kind rather than another.

(e) Merton's second problem concerns a confusion which involves matters specific to the social sciences, and is not covered by the distinctions developed in the generalized account of functional systems. Thus, it has already been noted that "subjective aim-in-view" (or "subjective disposi-tion" more generally) is at best a special state co-ordinate which, in a formal analysis of such systems, counts simply as one co-ordinate among others. Accordingly, unless "subjective aim-in-view" is explicitly introduced as a special state co-ordinate, Merton's distinction between manifest and latent functions is vacuous, and all functions fall under the head of "latent functions."

However, if "subjective aim-in-view" is recognized as a special variable, it becomes possible to formulate the question raised in the Basic Query within the framework of such a slightly enlarged formal analysis. For let A_x be this state co-ordinate, B some other co-ordinate for a given G of $S;$ and use the notation A_B to represent the intended and recognized consequences of a certain variation in B, also X_B to represent the actual consequences of this change in B. To say that the intended and recognized consequences of a given change in B is the same as the actual consequences of the change, could then be represented as: $A_B = X_B$; and to say that the intended and recognized consequences of the change is different from the actual ones, could be represented as: $A_B \neq X_B$. The question in the Basic Query may then be put as follows. If at time t_0, $A_B \neq X_B$, but at the subsequent time t_1 $A_B = X_B$, what consequences does the change in the two values of A_x have for the system S or some designated part of it?

4. *Concepts of the unit subserved by the function*

We have observed the difficulties entailed in *confining* analysis to functions fulfilled for 'the society,' since items may be functional for some individuals and subgroups and dysfunctional for others. It is necessary, therefore, to consider a *range* of units affected by the given item: individuals in diverse statuses, subgroups, the larger social system and culture systems. (Terminologically, this implies the concepts of psychological function, group function, societal function, cultural function, etc.)

(a) The two important points that are apparently being made in this number of the paradigm can be identified in the abstract statement of functional systems as follows. In a functional analysis, it is essential to specify (i) the system S which is being investigated, as well as (ii) the G of S which is maintained by indicated items in S.

(b) Enough has been said about the second of these points; but the first, despite its obviousness, perhaps deserves a brief elaboration.

(i) A given item will in general be an element in several systems. Suppose that an item belongs to the three systems S_1, S_2, S_3, where the first is a part of the second, the second a part of the third, and G_1, G_2 and G_3 are G's in them respectively. Assume that the item is causally relevant to G_1 and G_2, but not to G_3, and that it is represented by the co-ordinate A. Then a change in A will be nonfunctional with respect to G_3; but it may be functional in relation to both G_1 and G_2, dysfunctional in relation to both, or functional relative to one and dysfunctional relative to the other.

(ii) A given item may be an element in a system S_1, which is part of the environment of another system S_2. If this item is causally relevant to G_1 of S_1, and if S_2 exhibits G_2, a variation in this item may be either functional or dysfunctional with respect to G_1, and at the same time functional, dysfunctional or nonfunctional with respect to G_2.

(iii) A system S_1 that exhibits G_1 may contain two subordinate systems S_2 and S_3 as parts, where these parts exhibit G_2 and G_3 respectively. If an item which is an element of S_2 (and hence of S_1) but not of S_3 is causally relevant to both G_1 and G_2, a variation in it may be functional with respect to all three G's, or dysfunctional with respect to all of them, or nonfunctional with respect to G_3 and functional with respect to one of the other G's but dysfunctional in relation to the third one.

5. *Concepts of functional requirements (needs, prerequisites)*

Embedded in every functional analysis is some conception, tacit or expressed, of functional requirements of the system under observation. As noted elsewhere, this remains one of the cloudiest and empirically most debatable concepts in functional theory. As utilized by sociologists, the concept of functional requirement tends to be tautological or *ex post facto ;* it tends to be confined to conditions of 'survival' of a given system ; it tends, as in the work of Malinowski, to include biological as well as social 'needs.'

This involves the difficult problem of establishing types of functional requirements (universal vs. highly specific) ; procedures for validating the assumption of these requirements ; etc.

Basic query: what is required to establish the validity of such an intervening variable as 'functional requirement' in situations where rigorous experimentation is impracticable?

(a) The main point that appears to be noted here is the variety of G's which a given system S may exhibit, and the importance for a clear-headed functional analysis of specifying which one of the several G's is under discussion.

It is of course not an easy matter to establish the complete set of state co-ordinates for a given G. But it is also evident that a proposed list will tend to be used tautologically, as Merton observes, unless the G for which they are alleged co-ordinates is carefully indicated. For a variation in *any* item in S will have *some* consequences in S; and any item could easily be made to count as a state co-ordinate if the *sole* ground for such a designation were the fact that its variation produces some changes in S.

(b) However, the notion of "functional requirements" suggests something further—a classification of the various G's of a system on the basis of some principle, and perhaps the establishment of a hierarchy among them.

(i) It may be supposed that for a given system S there are certain comprehensive G's corresponding to the "vital functions" of biological organisms (i.e., respiration, reproduction, etc.) which are "indispensable" to the "survival" of S. A list of such G's is in effect a *definition* (or part of a definition) of what is to be understood by a given S, so that if G_1 is on this list, to say that G_1 is essential to the survival of S is to utter a tautology. Now although in principle it is quite easy to construct such a defining list of G's, and although in some areas of study (*e.g.*, biology) there is general agreement on the membership of such a list, in other domains, as Merton observes, agreement is difficult to obtain and the specification of such "vital functions" may remain debatable for an indefinite period.

(ii) In any event, the construction of a typology for the G's of a system, or the establishment of a hierarchy among them, requires special material assumptions depending on the S that is being considered. A generalized account of functional analysis cannot be expected to resolve these problems. However, it is possible within the framework of such an account to make explicit the pattern of relations that are involved in the distinction between "universal" and "highly specific" functional requirements, perhaps in the following manner.

Suppose that G_1, G_2, . . ., G_n are a set of n mutually exhaustive and exclusive G's for a given S, in the sense that at a given time or period one of them is realized in S but that the occurrence of one of them in S at a given time excludes the occurrence in S at that time of any of the others. Suppose further that the occurrence in S of some one G_i ($i=1, 2, . . ., n$) at any time implies the occurrence in S at that time of G^*, but not conversely. Under the conditions supposed, we may say that G^* is a "universal" functional requirement for S during a specified period, while any of the G_i's are "more specific" functional requirements.

(c) The question raised in the Basic Query does not appear to be specific to functional analysis, and can be pertinently raised in any causal inquiry where "rigorous experimentation" is precluded. For to ask whether a given item A contributes to the maintenance of a specified G in S, or whether G is indispensable to S, is either to ask whether the occurrence of G is dependent on A and its interrelations with other items, or whether some other (defining) traits of S are dependent on the preservation of G. And these are questions which, though they may be difficult to answer, arise in all domains of inquiry, and not only in the study of directively organized systems.

6. *Concepts of the mechanisms through which functions are fulfilled*

Functional analysis in sociology, as in other disciplines like physiology and psychology, calls for a 'concrete and detailed' account of the mechanisms which operate to perform a given function. This refers, not to psychological, but to social, mechanisms (e.g. role-segmentation, insulation of institutional demands, hierarchical ordering of values, social division of labor, ritual and ceremonial enactments, etc.)

Basic query: what is the presently available inventory of social mechanisms corresponding, say, to the large inventory of psychological mechanisms? What are the methodological problems entailed in discerning the operation of these social mechanisms?

(a) This number of the paradigm is prima facie simply a call for an explicit listing of the state co-ordinates for the various G's of social systems, and thus seems in part to be but a restatement of a point already noted in the preceding number.

(b) It should be added, however, that any inquiry into functional systems would doubtless not come to an end with the mere discovery of a complete set of state co-ordinates for a given G, but would also seek to establish the detailed modes of dependence between the states of the system at different times as well as the specific conditions under which the G occurs. If we employ the notation of the mathematical formulation of directively organized systems given earlier, the point of the present number of the paradigm can then be restated as the following threefold requirement for functional analysis: the specification of the state co-ordinates $x_1, \ldots, x_n$ for a given G; the formulation of the relations of dependence $f_1, \ldots, f_n$, which holds between the co-ordinates at different times; and the discovery of the conditions $g_1, \ldots, g_r$ under which the G occurs.

(c) Merton's apparent insistence upon social rather than psychological mechanisms is obviously predicated upon the assumption that a distinction can be drawn between them which is sufficiently clear for the purposes at hand. Moreover, although this is far less certain, he seems to adopt the further material assumption that in sociology an adequate list of state co-ordinates for a given G will contain only co-ordinates referring to distinctively social items. But these assumptions, whether or not Merton is actually committed to them, involve factual issues that fall outside the scope of this study.

7. *Concepts of functional alternatives (functional equivalents or substitutes)*

As we have seen, once we abandon the gratuitous assumption of the functional indispensability of given social structures, there is immediately required some concept of functional alternatives, equivalents, or substitutes. This focuses attention on the *range of possible variation* in the items which can, in the given instance, subserve a functional requirement. It unfreezes the identity of the existent and the inevitable.

Basic query: since scientific proof of the equivalence of an alleged functional alternative ideally requires rigorous experimentation, and since this is not often practicable in large-scale sociological situations, which practicable procedures of inquiry most nearly approximate the logic of experiment?

(a) The point here noted is easily recognized as central in the analysis of directively organized systems, and as an expression of the basic idea upon which the generalized account of the preceding section is built. Stated in the notation of that formulation, the point is that if the class K_G of possible G states for a specified G of a system contains more than one member (and this condition may be supposed to be contained in the assumption that the system is directively organized with respect to G), G can occur as a consequence of different configurations of elements in S (or its environment) and in relative independence of the variations in any one of the causally relevant elements.

However, though this point is by now quite familiar, a few further ampliative comments may be useful.

(i) A system may "grow" or "develop" in time, so that although a given G may be maintained throughout the development, the state co-ordinates for G and the mode of the mutual dependence of their values at different times may change. This possibility and its obvious consequences can be made formally explicit as follows: Suppose that $X_1, \ldots, X_n$ is a hypothetically complete list of state co-ordinates in S for a given G. It may happen that during a certain period T_1, or under certain conditions c_1, G is preserved in S, though the item X_n is inoperative (whether because it does not occur in S in that period or because other circumstances cause it to be simply a "sleeping partner"). But it may turn out that during a subsequent period T_2, or under other conditions c_2, while G is still preserved in S, X_n is no longer inoperative although X_1 now becomes inactive (whether because of its disappearance from S or because of some induced quiescence). The quiescence of X_n in S during T_1 and its activity during T_2 can be taken in the present context as a formal representation of growth or other modes of development in S; and the inverse supposition for X_1 can be used to represent senescence or other modes of decay in S. But however this may be, the possibility that at different times and under different circumstances different items in S are causally operative for maintaining a given G in S, makes further evident that a given G may be preserved through the operation of different instrumentalities.

(ii) A different though analogous possibility is contained in the supposition that a certain G^* in S is "universal" (in the sense explained above) in relation to the "more specific" traits $G_1, \ldots, G_n$. Since in this case the occurrence of G^* is contingent upon the realization of some one of the G_i's, but is independent of the realization of any particular G_i, the point stressed in this number of the paradigm immediately follows.

(b) In the generalized account of functional systems presented earlier, explicit recognition was given to the fact that a system S has an environment E. Since E is generally the locus of some of the items represented by the state co-ordinates for a given G, and therefore contributes something to the range of G-preserving variations in the items causally relevant to G, the recognition of *E* appears to be of considerable importance for the point stressed in this number of the paradigm.

However, for reasons that are not obvious, Merton makes no explicit mention of the environment in which an object of functional analysis in sociology is embedded, though presumably every such object does have an environment. This reminder of one missing item in Merton's codification applies not only to the present number of his paradigm, but to others as well.

8. *Concepts of structural context (or structural constraint)*

The range of variation in the items which *can* fulfill designated functions within a given instance is not unlimited (and this has been repeatedly noted in our foregoing discussion). The interdependence of the elements of a social structure limit the effective possibilities of change or functional alternatives. The concept of structural constraint corresponds, in the area of social structure, to Goldenweiser's 'principle of limited possibilities' in a broader sphere. Failure to recognize the relevance of interdependence and attendant structural restraints leads to utopian thought in which it is tacitly assumed that certain elements of a social system can be eliminated without affecting the rest of the system. This consideration is recognized by both Marxist social scientists (e.g., Karl Marx) and by non-Marxists (e.g., Malinowski).

Basic query: how narrowly does a given structural context limit the range of variation in the items which can effectively satisfy functional requirements? Do we find, under conditions yet to be determined, an area of indifference, in which any one of a wide range of alternatives may fulfill the function?

(a) Our generalized account of functional systems has distinguished two kinds of constraints upon the state co-ordinates of such systems, though only one of them appears to be explicitly recognized in this number of the paradigm.

(i) The structure of a given system *S* imposes certain "boundary conditions" or general constraints upon the items represented by a set of state co-ordinates, in virtue of which the values of the co-ordinates *A*, *B*, etc. must all fall into certain ranges of values K_A, K_B, etc., respectively. Alternatively, the possible states of *S* must fall into a certain class K_S. This type of constraint is not mentioned in the present number of the paradigm.

(ii) Since there are certain conditions which the values of the state co-ordinates *A*, *B*, etc., must satisfy if they are to be the values that determine a *G* state *of S*, these values must fall into certain restricted classes K_{AG}, K_{BG}, etc. Alternatively, the possible *G* states of *S* must all be members of a restricted class K_G. This is apparently the type of constraint to which Merton is calling attention; and the analogue he suggests for Goldenweiser's principle of limited possibilities is an immediate corollary to it.

(iii) If G^* is universal in *S* with respect to the more specific G_1, . . ., G_n, the latter constitute a set of "indifferent" alternatives, any one of which entails the realization of G^*. Accordingly, though both types of constraints must be recognized for the co-ordinates for each of the G_i's the existence of these alternatives in a sense can mitigate the practical force of the restraints by permitting a choice between them and yet preserving G^*.

(b) However, it is conceivable that Merton has in mind more involved forms of constraint that are analyzable as compounded out of restraints of the second type. Two of the large number of such more complex forms will be mentioned.

(i) Suppose S to be capable of maintaining two distinct G's, G_1 and G_2, and that A is a state co-ordinate for both of them. Suppose, moreover, that though a variation in A is functional with respect to G_1 as long as the change falls into the class K_{AG1}, it is dysfunctional with respect to G_2 unless the change falls into the narrower class $K_{AG1\ G2}$. Accordingly, for the maintenance of both G's, more severe restrictions are placed upon the possible variation of an item than for the maintenance of one of them.

Moreover, as a consequence of ignorance as to what is the complete set of state co-ordinates for G_1, a variation in a known co-ordinate may produce compensating variations in an unknown one so as to preserve G_1 though at the same time giving rise to certain "side effects" that are dysfunctional with respect to G_2. Here too, more restrictive limits must be supposed to hold for the variation of the first variable if both G's are to be preserved.

(ii) On the other hand, though a proposed list of co-ordinates for a given G may be complete, it may contain redundant items (in the sense that their values at a given time are not mutually independent, so that in effect the proposed co-ordinates fail to satisfy a requirement for state co-ordinates). Or again, though a proposed list of co-ordinates is complete without redundancy, it may contain items that are causally irrelevant to a given G. In either case, mistaken ideas can easily arise as to the limits of possible G-preserving changes in S, in some cases the supposed limits being perhaps wider than the actual ones, in other cases narrower.

9. *Concepts of dynamics and change*

We have noted that functional analysts *tend* to focus on the statics of social structure and to neglect the study of structural change. The concept of dysfunction, which implies the concept of strain, stress and tension on the structural level, provides an analytical approach to the study of dynamics and change. How are observed dysfunctions contained within a given structure, so that they do not produce instability? Does the accumulation of stresses and strains produce pressure for change in such directions as are likely to lead to their reduction?

Basic query: does the prevailing concern among functional analysts with the concept of *social equilibrium* divert attention from the phenomena of *social disequilibrium?* Which available procedures will permit the sociologist most adequately to gauge the accumulation of stresses and strains in a given social system? To what extent does the structural context permit the sociologist to anticipate the most probable directions of social change?

Several distinguishable though related problems are conceivably covered by this number of the paradigm.

(a) Changes in the co-ordinates for a given G of S which fall outside the limits of the class K_G of G-preserving changes, are dysfunctional with respect to that G. One problem is therefore the investigation of those circumstances, whether their locus is in S or in E, which bring about such changes.

(b) Changes that are dysfunctional relative to a given G may nevertheless be instrumental for the maintenance or the emergence of some other G (which may be a foreseen or an unforeseen consequence of those changes). Attentive scrutiny of S with a view to discovering such suspected G's is thus suggested by the occurrence of variations that are dysfunctional with respect to a given G.

(c) The mode of dependence of a set of co-ordinates upon one another (i.e., the f_i's in the mathematical formulation of functional systems) may change with time, whether as a consequence of alterations in other items of S or in E; and such a change may give rise to alterations in the conditions under which a given G can occur (i.e., in the g_i's of the mathematical formulation). Accordingly, the class K_G of G-preserving variations for a given G may not remain constant. Should K_G shrink to nothing, the given G will no longer be realizable in S; should it become enlarged, G will be capable of being maintained under a more flexible set of circumstances than previously. The discussion therefore suggests the study of possible variations in the conditions under which a given G can occur.

(d) If G_1 and G_2 are related to G^* as more specific functions to a universal one, a change in a co-ordinate which is dysfunctional with respect to G_1 may nevertheless eventuate in the occurrence of G_2. Accordingly, S will remain stable with respect to G^*, despite an initial dysfunctional change relative to G_1. The problem is thus suggested whether prima facie dysfunctional changes in a system may nevertheless not be entirely compatible with the preservation of some assumed "vital function" of the system.

(e) A system S may exhibit at different times a series G_1, G_2, . . . of mutually incompatible G's, which succeed each other because of certain "built in" features of S or because of certain progressive changes in E or both. The double problem then would be to (i) ascertain the order of the succession of the G_i's, with the aim of formulating their law of development, and (ii) discover the state co-ordinates which control the development.

10. *Problems of validation of functional analysis*

Throughout the paradigm, attention has been called repeatedly to the *specific* points at which assumptions, imputations and observations must be validated. This requires, above all, a rigorous statement of the sociological procedures of analysis which most nearly approximate the *logic* of experimentation. It requires a systematic review of the possibilities and limitations of *comparative* (cross-cultural and cross-group) *analysis*.

Basic query: to what extent is functional analysis limited by the difficulty of locating adequate *samples of social systems* which can be subjected to comparative (quasi-experimental) study?

The questions here raised are factual ones, requiring for their answer familiarity with currently available techniques of sociological study. Nothing said in this paper can throw any light upon them.

11. *Problems of the ideological implications of functional analysis*

It has been emphasized in a preceding section, that functional analysis has no intrinsic commitment to a given ideological position. This does not gainsay the fact that *particular* hypotheses advanced by functionalists may have an identifiable ideological role. This, then, becomes a specific problem for the sociology of knowledge: to what extent does the social position of the functional sociologist (e.g., *vis-à-vis* a particular "client" who has authorized a given research) evoke one rather than another formulation of a problem, affect his assumptions and concepts, and limit the range of inferences drawn from his data?

Basic query: how does one detect the ideological tinge of a given functional analysis and to what degree does a particular ideology stem from the basic assumptions adopted by the sociologist? Is the incidence of these assumptions related to the status and research of the sociologist?

(a) These questions again deal with substantive matters, and they are obviously relevant to all sociological inquiry, and not to functional analysis in sociology exclusively.

(b) It is perhaps worth noting at this place that the commitment of a functional analyst in sociology to some "ideological position" is quite innocuous, if the analyst makes clear what *G* of a system he is investigating, and if he indicates explicitly to the maintenance of what *G* a given item in a system allegedly contributes. Functional analyses in all domains, and not only in sociology, run a similar risk of dogmatic provincialism which characterizes some analyses in sociology, when the relational character of functional statements is ignored, and when it is forgotten that a system may exhibit a variety of *G*'s or that a given item may be a member of a variety of systems.

Chapter II

System

and

Saturnalia

Introduction

*T*HE first chapter postponed the choice of a leading issue by beginning with them all. Now a choice is necessary, but perhaps we have overestimated its difficulty. Earlier in the General Introduction we referred to the concept of "system" as the central element in functionalism. Certainly it is a fulcrum in the debate. Is society a system? If so, a system of what sort? If not, to what extent is it profitable to treat it as if it were? Virtually every other facet of the controversy has its roots in this one. An author's position here portends his position on change, conflict, functional needs, teleology, and even the role of ideology in sociology. But precisely because of its centrality, the question of system poses an editorial quandary. The problem is not to decide which readings belong here, but rather which readings do not. We have selected five that address the issue most directly while representing a variety of perspectives on it.

Pitirim Sorokin's discussion of "Causal-Functional and Logico-Meaningful Integration" initiates the exchange. This essay forms the first chapter of a four-volume treatise on *Social and Cultural Dynamics*. While the selection summarizes neither the book nor the man, it offers a broad taxonomy that is compelling in its own right. Here Sorokin distinguishes four types of social and cultural integration: "spatial adjacency," "adjacency due to an external factor," "causal or functional integration," and "logico-meaningful unity." The former two are not "systems" at all, and Sorokin resists the tendency to view all societies and all aspects of society from a system perspective. And yet properties of systems are entailed in both functional and logico-meaningful integration, the differences between which comprise the core of the essay. In part, these differences reflect a distinction between culture and social structure, at least in the sense that "logico-meaningful integration" is discussed almost exclusively within the context of "high culture" and the arts. The differences also follow the classic distinction between objective study and subjective understanding or *"verstehende."* Thus, causal-functional integration can be ascertained objectively; logico-meaningful integration is only subjectively discernible as a gestalt in the eye of the beholder. In a similar fashion, the distinction anticipates Merton's delineation of latent and manifest functions. Causal integration is latent, remaining to be uncovered by scientific scrutiny; logico-meaningful integration is nothing if not manifest to the artist and the relevant audience. (If this last parallel is instructive, it should come as no surprise since Merton is among Sorokin's most celebrated pupils.) And yet none of these parallels is exact. Certainly the work must be read on its own terms. Its merit as an introduction is that it moves beyond the all-or-nothing question of whether society is a system to the more sophisticated issues of system in what sense and of what sort.

Ludwig von Bertalanffy both broadens and intensifies the matter as a philosopher of science. To von Bertalanffy, the system concept is equally relevant to every science. Indeed, he sees it as a scientific common denominator and proceeds to sharpen and expand it in terms of a "General System Theory." Just as Sorokin ranges between cultures, von Bertalanffy ranges across disciplines. Physics, biology, mathematics, ecology, psychology, economics, and sociology are all within his ambience. His vocabulary cross-cuts these with its multiple applications. Concepts such as "open vs. closed systems," "equifinality," "isomorphism," "servo mechanism," and "homeostasis," are useful, if intimidating. Other concepts such as "equilibrium," "feedback," and "reductionism" are less arcane and will reoccur frequently in the discussions to follow. In all of this, von Bertalanffy enriches the discussion by widening its boundaries, specifying its ground-rules, and providing relevant criteria for evaluation.

Talcott Parsons and Neil J. Smelser pursue a theory that is only slightly less general than von Bertalanffy's. The selection in this chapter refers only to "social systems" but the essential framework is intended to apply to cultural systems, biological systems, and personality systems as well. Actually Parsons is paradoxical within the functionalist controversy. Although he is central to the debate, he seldom enters it explicitly and is misunderstood by critics and defenders alike. Part of the misunderstanding involves a level of abstraction to which few are accustomed. Another source is ambiguity on the question of whether Parsons is discussing society itself or a strategically distorted model of it. Finally, there are problems concerning "which Parsons" is at issue—early Parsons or late Parsons, substantive Parsons or analytic Parsons, Parsons the sociologist or Parsons as "homo politicus." Passionate arguments go past one another as the Parsonian referents vary. Thus while most of the critics represented concentrate upon the "early analytic" Parsons of *The Social System* (Gouldner, Mills, Lockwood, Dahrendorf), the selections from Parsons in this volume represent the "late analytic" phase of *Economy and Society* and *Theories of Society*. This is not to say that earlier criticism is irrelevant; surely Parson's first steps produced his ultimate directions. At the same time, there have been important changes of path and pace along the way. Not the least of these has been the influence of Smelser, co-author of the selection in this chapter. Smelser's subsequent independent work on social change and collective behavior suggests his influence on Parsons in the general area of social dynamics. In any event, in the selection reprinted here, the two provide a concise summary of the fabled A-G-I-L schema and consider the "boundary interchanges" between these alphabetical sub-systems. We have included illustrative discussion of only two of the six interchanges, though all six are marked in detail in the accompanying diagram. While the selection includes much that is new in Parsons, it does not provide the full intellectual history of either the scheme or its authors. Much of this may be had from Edward Devereaux's excellent and eminently readable explication in Max Black, ed., *The Social Theories of Talcott Parsons* (Prentice-Hall, 1961). Short of that, even those who are familiar with Parsons may want to read his essay in Chapter III before going on to the ensuing criticisms here.

Alvin W. Gouldner's "Reciprocity and Autonomy in Functional Theory" departs from many earlier analyses of "systems" by treating the concept as a variable rather than a type, however "ideal." Gouldner points out that there are different degrees of "systemness" according to the amount of reciprocity, interdependence, and autonomy that exists between the parts and the whole. He not only explores instances and mechanisms of articulation and avoidance, but he uses the perspective as a criterion for assessing the divergent theoretical styles of Parsons and Merton among others. Gouldner is among the few who explore differences *within* the functionalist camp instead of aggregating all functionalists under a single judgment, whether damned or saved. Certainly his essay contributes a new flexibility to classical functionalism. But Gouldner does more than relieve the system concept of its more onerous baggage. He goes on to discuss the promising benefits which may accrue to functionalism from new developments in mathematics and methodology. Here he is at pains to bridge the void between functionalism's abstractions and the world's realities.

C. Wright Mills despaired of the possibility of any such bridge. His remarks on "Grand Theory" drawn from his book, *The Sociological Imagination,* make this quite clear. The essay has two main thrusts. First, Mills argues that Parsons and the system theorists are so abstract that they have burnt bridges behind them thereby losing touch with the reality around them. Not only have they failed to attend the momentous problems of the day, but they have misinterpreted the commonplace. Here in fact is the second prong of Mills' offensive. Insofar as the "grand theorists" do comment upon social reality their commentary is wrong more often than not. Thus, their emphasis on "normative order" as opposed to "power" is more fantasy than fact. Indeed, their emphasis on order itself is a projection of wishes rather than an induction from experience. Mills' overriding point is that the demands of a "grand theory" are at odds with the demands of an informed and relevant sociology. The theory places artificial constraints for elegance at the expense of accuracy, for unity at the expense of verity.

Certainly these sentiments will reoccur in the volume. In most cases, they are placed at the rear of their respective chapters, just as Mills is here. This is not to afford them a "last word" or to dismiss them as an "afterthought." Rather it is because they are criticisms that can only be evaluated after an exposure to what is being criticized.

Pitirim Sorokin

Causal-Functional
and Logico-Meaningful Integration

*A*LL the numerous interrelations of the various elements of culture can be reduced to four basic types: (1) *Spatial or Mechanical Adjacency,* ranging from a loose and accidental concurrence of two or more cultural objects to a mechanical union of the elements into one structural unity (say, glued or cemented or sewn or tied together); (2) *Association Due to an External Factor;* (3) *Causal or Functional Integration;* (4) *Internal or Logico-meaningful Unity.*

A.   SPATIAL OR MECHANICAL ADJACENCY (CONGERIES).

This means any conglomeration of cultural elements (objects, traits, values, ideas) in a given area of social and physical space, with spatial or mechanical concurrence as the only bond of union. A dump in which are fragments of a great variety of objects—pieces of paper, broken bottles, empty cans, fragments of clothing, discarded spoons, wire, garbage, furniture, ashes, coal, tools—offers an example of such a combination. All these objects just drifted or were thrown together, and this is the only bond that unites them. An untidy attic, with its miscellaneous array of many articles, is yet another example. The same thing can be said of the cases of the spatial conglomeration of various architectural styles and of the logically unrelated discussions of various social problems within the limits of one book. Two pieces of paper (say, a page from Plato's *Republic* and the advertisement of an automobile company) glued together into one meaningless mechanical unity; a piece of wood nailed to a remnant of a shoe without any meaning or function as an instrument for anything; an Ionic or Corinthian column attached to a flat-roofed garage without architectural, aesthetic, or structural significance—these and hundreds of similar combinations are examples of the spatial and purely mechanical congeries of various cultural objects and values. As a matter of fact, what anthropologists call a culture area is often nothing more than a spatial adjacency of the traits and complexes of the area in question. . . .

B.   INDIRECT ASSOCIATION THROUGH A COMMON EXTERNAL FACTOR.

A somewhat greater unification occurs in such cases where two or more culture elements, spatially adjacent but with no functional or logical connection, are also related to one another through the association of each with a common factor external to both or all of them. In the northern part of Vologda province in North Russia, for example, the following culture elements exist together: *vodka* as a beverage, skis used by the peasants in the winter time, houses built out of heavy timber, large stoves for heating, felt winter boots, the gathering together during the winter evenings of the boys and girls in each of their houses in turn, the performance of plays, singing, and love making. None of these elements requires the others either logically or functionally. *Vodka* as such does not require skis or felt boots; felt boots do not require a large stove or specific forms of winter-evening entertainment. But all of these traits are perceptibly connected with the climatic conditions of the area with its cold and its long winters. Each trait, through its connection with the climatic factor, is likewise affiliated indirectly with the other traits. As a result we have a unification of heterogeneous culture elements, not only spatially, but also through their connection with one common external factor: That is the unification talked of by many sociological and anthropological integrators. . . .

C.   CAUSAL OR FUNCTIONAL INTEGRATION.

By this is meant a combination of cultural elements in which they compose one causal (functional) unity. Usually, where the elements are "material," functional unity is superimposed upon spatial adjacency and external association, but not every spatially adjacent or externally related combination will be a functionally integrated unity. The parts of an automobile spread over the floor of a factory or packed into one box before being assembled into one functional whole, the finished automobile, are a mere spatial array. When they are assembled into one whole, their combination becomes functional and operates so that every important part depends upon the others. The same can be said of the house in contradistinction to the sum of the materials of which it is built: stone, cement, bricks, timber, paint, nails, and so on. Dumped together in one yard these elements form a mere heap of contiguous parts. When the house is built, it is a structural and functional unity.

Similarly, causal or functional unity is likewise of a far higher degree of integration than that of a number of elements spatially adjacent but also related through a common external factor. In a functional array as a rule the parts are related to one another directly, or, if indirectly, by several internal "centers" which are closer to them in essential nature than would be the case in a purely external integration. Not every cell of an organism or bolt in a car is adjacent or directly related to all the other cells or parts. But all the cells are directly connected through the nervous system, the blood circulation, and the organs, just as the bolts or other parts are united through the whole frame of the car, the electric system, and so on. And these unifying factors are all internal to the system itself.

But the simple cases we have been considering are far from exhausting the problems of the functional integration of cultural elements. The field is infinitely larger and more important. In order to make this clear, a few diagnostic criteria of the functional relationship between the parts of a cultural configuration should be pointed out. Simply stated, they consist chiefly of the *tangible, noticeable, testifiable, direct interdependence (mutual or one-sided) of the variables or parts upon one another and upon the whole system.* If variation A is always followed by B (under the same conditions and in a large enough number of cases so that mere chance is eliminated), we say that they are functionally related. *This means that any cultural synthesis is to be regarded as functional, when, on the one hand, the elimination of one of its important elements perceptibly influences the rest of the synthesis in its functions (and usually in its structure); and when, on the other hand, the separate element, being transposed to a quite different combination, either cannot exist in it or has to undergo a profound modification to become a part of it.* Such is the symptomatic barometer of internal integration, a barometer which simply applies the principle of causality or functionalism to each case in question.

One can now see the profound difference between mere spatial adjacency, between external unification, and the deeper synthesis of functional unity. A bolt or spring taken from an unassembled pile of automobile parts does not modify the pile essentially; removed from an assembled car, it may completely impede the performance of the car. Moreover, the bolt or spring itself does not change in significance when removed from a miscellaneous heap, but if it be detached from a machine in which it performs an essential function, it loses that function entirely.

Let us now pass on to more complex examples. Can we take, say, the stock-market system of Wall Street from the modern capitalistic type of economic organization and transpose it, say, to the society of the Trobriands? The answer is that as soon as this is done, the capitalist system of economy here fails to function normally for lack of the stock market, while among the Trobriands, Wall Street does not have any chance to exist or survive generally in the form which it has in the United States. This means that the stock market is essentially a functional part of the American economic system. Suppose we should take the parliamentary regime in its English form, together with the principles of contractual relations and of the equality of all citizens before the law, and the other democratic tenets of Victorian England, and transplant them in the Hindu caste society. The results would be similar; the democratic politico-juridical complex can hardly be grafted on the caste-society tree and yet retain the same form which it had; it would either die or be changed enormously. On the other hand, the rest of the Victorian democratic sociopolitical system could hardly function as it did without the aid of the transplanted parts of the complex. As a matter of fact, even in Continental European societies, where the configuration of cultural elements differs from that of England, though by less than does the Hindu, the parliamentary system has never functioned in the way in which it does in England. One has only to glance at the history of parliamentarism in Germany, Austria, Russia, or Italy to perceive the difference. . . .

In brief, in any culture area there are always present in the totality of the traits, patterns, objects, and values of which it consists, complexes which represent a functional integration. . . .

There is no need to stress the fact that *the degree of functional unity or functional interdependence is everywhere not the same:* it fluctuates from unity to unity; in some cases it is exceedingly close, in others looser, until finally it imperceptibly passes into either a mere external unity or even a mere spatial adjacency.

In sociology and the social sciences there is a multitude of theories that attempt to describe and interpret culture generally along the lines of functional unity. All the theories that take some specific variable internal to a culture (whether it be modes of production, technique and invention, religion, morals, art and science, philosophy and forms of government) and try to "explain" all or the majority of the other characteristics of the culture in question as a "function" or "superstructure" or "effect" of this variable: all such theories, as I have already suggested, assume the existence of a causal-functional integration between the parts. In other words, their promulgators appear to be partisans of the view of the functional unity of all culture elements. . . .

In view of the virtual unanimity of opinion it is unnecessary to insist upon the existence of the causal-functional sort of integration as a form *sui generis*. But the application of the theory is to be somewhat moderated. We have seen and shall see that not all the components of any culture are linked together causally, but only a part of them. In any culture there are also spatial and external unities where no causal association in the narrow sense can be found. And in many cultural complexes there are "logico-meaningful" unities, different from the causal-functional. Therefore it is fallacious to assume, as many causalists do, that every conglomeration of cultural objects is a functional unity and that there must be a functional connection between all of the components. . . .

D. LOGICO-MEANINGFUL INTEGRATION OF CULTURE

Having beclouded the true nature of functional integration by being unable to distinguish its elements from those of spatial adjacency and external association in highly heterogeneous conglomerations of cultural elements, many integrators have also failed to see that above functional integration proper there is an additional form of association quite different from it, and more different still from the spatial and external types of unification. For lack of a better term, I style this the Logico-meaningful Integration of Culture. This is integration in its supreme form. In what does it consist? What are its qualities? Suppose we have before us the scattered pages of a great poem, or of Kant's *Critique of Pure Reason*, or fragments of the statue of Venus of Milo, or the scattered pages of the score of Beethoven's *Third Symphony*. If we know the proper patterns of meaning and value, we can put these pages or parts together into a significant unity in which each page or fragment takes its proper place, acquires a meaning, and in which all together give the supremely integrated effect that was intended. I say "supremely integrated" because in such instances each part, when set in its designated position, is no longer noticeable as a part, but all the parts together form, as it were, a seamless garment. Their unification is far closer than that of mere functional association. The connection is similar in nature to that between the premises, "All human beings are mortal," and "Socrates is a human being," and the conclusion, "Ergo, Socrates is mortal." Is this connection functional? Hardly, unless we broaden the meaning of functional to such an extent that it loses distinct meaning altogether. . . .

What must be used are the *logical* laws of identity, contradiction, consistency; and it is these laws of logic which must be employed to discover whether any synthesis is or is not *logico-meaningful*. Side by side with such logical laws, in the narrow sense, the broader principles of "keeping," of internal consistency, must also be used to determine the existence of this higher unity, or the lack of it. These are the principles expressed in the terms "consistent style," "consistent and harmonious whole," in contradistinction to "inconsistent mingling of styles," "hodgepodge," "clashing" patterns or forms, and they apply especially to the examination of artistic creation. Many such superlative unities cannot be described in analytical verbal terms; they are just felt as such, but this in no way makes their unity questionable. One cannot prove by mere words—no matter what they are—the inner consistency and supreme integration of the Cathedral of Chartres, or the Gregorian chant, or the musical compositions of Bach or Mozart or Beethoven, or the tragedies of Shakespeare, or the sculpture of Phidias, or the pictures of Dürer or Raphael or Rembrandt, or many other logico-meaningful unities. But not being completely describable in terms of language, their supreme unity is felt by competent persons as certainly as if they could be analyzed with mathematical or logical exactness. All such unities are covered here by the term logico-meaningful, though many are not logical unities in the formal sense of the word logic.

A few concrete illustrations will make still clearer the nature of this sort of integration. Suppose we find side by side in some cultural conglomeration a highly developed ascetic-monastic life and a materialistic-Sensate philosophy. At once we feel that the two are inconsistent; they do not belong together; they do not make any sense; their combination is not integrated in a logico-meaningful unity. This conclusion will remain valid no matter how frequently such a coexistence of these two variables is found. Asceticism and a purely idealistic philosophy of life, on the contrary, do belong to each other logically. If we find together in a given cultural area the strictest caste system and the equalitarian ideology shared by all castes, it once again becomes evident that we are faced with inconsistency. These opposing elements, though they may form a spatial or some other form of congeries, cannot be integrated in a logico-meaningful unity. . . .

Logico-Meaningful Integration and the Method of Its Study

A.   The causal-functional and the logico-meaningful methods of integration both act as the *means of ordering into comprehensible systems the infinitely numerous and complex phenomena of the sociocultural world.* What we style the sociocultural world consists of endless millions of individual objects, events, processes, fragments, having an infinite number of forms, properties, and relationships. With a proper modification we can say of it what is said of the whole universe: "The universe is infinite: unbounded in space and time and infinitely complex. In its infinite complexity it cannot be known and understood through direct sensory perception." . . .

The same is true of the sociocultural universe. To our perception it also is given as a complicated and inexhaustible chaos of infinitely numerous, diverse, and seemingly unrelated fragments. . . . None of us perceives directly the culture of any area as something whole which is bound compactly and comprehensively in a book, or packed in a box, or depicted upon a single canvas. . . .

One way of ordering the chaos of the whole universe as well as of the cultural world is furnished by the causal-functional or probablistic formulas of integration. They give us the *patterns of uniformity* that are to be found in the relationships of a vast number of individual components of this infinite chaos. By means of these formulas we can reduce the chaos to a series of comprehensive systems, in which we are more easily oriented and which permit us to distinguish more important from less important aspects. Causal-functional formulas like the Newtonian Law of Gravitation sum up briefly a prodigious number of separate relationships. They are like a beam of light that cuts across chaotic darkness through all its unlimited depths. This, with proper reservations, can be said of any causal formula. It achieves its purpose by establishing a *uniformity* of relationship between the variables under scrutiny. Through it a vast concurrence of fragmentary events, forms, objects, and relationships becomes a comprehensive whole. When the formula shows that the variables A and B—depression and birth rate, modes of production and ideological forms, isolation and suicide, urbanization and crime—are more or less uniformly associated with each other in the sense that B normally follows A or changes with A, this *uniformity* binds the variables together, introduces a readily understood causal order into disorder.

Different in nature, but similar in function, is the role of the *logico-meaningful method of ordering chaos*. Here, however, the ordering element is not uniformity of relationship between the fragmentary variables, but *identity of meaning* or *logical coalescence*. Hidden behind the empirically different, seemingly unrelated fragments of the cultural complex lies an identity of meaning, which brings them together into consistent *styles*, typical *forms*, and significant *patterns*. If, therefore, *uniformity of relationship is the common denominator of causally united phenomena, in the logico-meaningful union it is identity of central meaning or idea.*

The procedure involved in arranging the scattered pages of a treatise or putting into a comprehensible unity the individually meaningless fragments of a jigsaw puzzle is, as we have seen, a concrete example of such a logically meaningful ordering. Of course, if the sociocultural conglomeration—the scattered pages or the fragments of the puzzle—do not belong together, the procedure is impossible. But this means only that where there is no factual logical unity in the cultural conglomeration one cannot find it; and if one tries to impose it upon the mass, one commits an error similar to that of finding or imposing a causal relationship where it does not exist.

We thus see that the ordering natures of the causal and of the logico-meaningful principle are different, but that their cognitive functions are similar: both serve the same purpose, each in its own way; both sum up in their formulas large accumulations of events, objects, relationships; both connect into a unity chaotic masses of fragments. Both are necessary for a study of the sociocultural phenomena, each in its own field. . . .

B.   The causal method, especially in the natural sciences, obtains its formulas mainly through breaking up the complex phenomena into their simpler units; and the more general the formula, the further the reduction of complex to simple, until ultimate simplicity—the atom, electron, proton—is reached. Studying the relationships between these simplest and therefore universal units and discovering the nature of their uniformity, the causal method offers *eo ipso* formulas of uniformity which are also universal in their application. . . .

In the logico-meaningful method of formulating the unifying principles, such a procedure is impossible. Despite the endless efforts of a legion of social scientists, simple social atoms or units have not been found, and cannot be found, so far as the logically integrated part of culture is concerned. One cannot indicate what is the cultural atom in literature, painting, music, science, philosophy, architecture, or in any other similar compartment of culture. Instead, however, the logico-meaningful method has its own common denominator of all relevant phenomena: *it is the identity (or similarity) of central meaning, idea, or mental bias that permeates all the logically related fragments.* Because of this all the fragments in question are identical or similar in their significance, all of them have the same common denominator, which binds them together, conditions their relationship, makes them a unity. . . .

C.   The functional or causal or probablistic connection of separate units is almost always inferential and external; it rarely gives us an internal comprehension of the connection. Through experimental or observational or statistical manipulations we find that two variables, A and B, seem always to go together: they either coexist, or follow each other, or vary together. But why they do so—why, for instance, the force of gravitation is in direct ratio to the mass and in inverse ratio to the square of the distance; why the volume of gas varies in inverse ratio to the pressure; why oxygen and hydrogen in certain conditions turn into H_2O—we do not know. All we know is that within the limits of our perception they have usually done so, and that they will probably continue to do so in the future. Beyond this externally observed connection, we do not have any intimate understanding of such associations. . . .

Different is the feeling we have in regard to logically integrated unities. The properly trained mind apprehends, feels, perceives, senses, and understands the supreme unity of Euclid's or Lobachevski's geometry of perfect mathematical deduction; of Platonic metaphysics; of Phidias's Athena; of a suite or concerto by Bach; of a Shakespeare drama; of the architecture of the Parthenon or the Cathedral of Chartres. Such a mind comprehends their sublime unity internally, intimately; often feels it immediately and directly, senses it without any experimental or statistical manipulations and without indirect reasoning. It is given to such a mind axiomatically, so to speak, as the supreme certainty to which no inference can add anything. . . .

D. The primary difference between the causal and logico-meaningful connection leads to a further derivative difference between them. The essentially external nature of the causal association in many cases precludes our grasping the relationship between discrete variables in time or space. If variables A and B are not met with regularly, nor coexist, nor follow each other in immediate sequence, nor vary uniformly, such variables cannot be declared to be connected causally. Even if theoretically such a causal chain exists between them (as is possible from the standpoint of "singularistic causality"), it cannot be discovered and understood and, therefore, for the observer is practically nonexistent. Considerably different is the situation in regard to logico-meaningful connection. Theoretically (and not infrequently in fact) this sort of association is comprehensible even when the interrelated fragments are met with at quite different periods, and in quite different places, and only once or a few times. Conversely, the mere fact of our regular observation of the variables A and B in causal association does not necessarily force us to recognize that they are logically and meaningfully integrated.

If one meets only once and only in one culture (say, the Egyptian) a belief in the hereafter, funeral rites, and the practice of mummifying the body, this one case is sufficient to establish the logical connection between these three elements. Or if one finds only once the association of a dominant philosophical materialism, the naturalistic style of painting, and the economic and mechanistic interpretation of history, this case is sufficient to make clear that they belong logically together, though on the basis of one case we cannot say anything of their causal connection. Contrariwise, a scientist could prove, on the basis of a large number of "cases," that the variables A and B—say, the number of yellow leather shoes in use and the divorce rate—always vary together. And yet such an exceptionless causal association in no way forces us to conclude that the elements are united also logically and meaningfully. A competent person could listen as many times as you like to a musical

composition where jazz and crooning are interspersed with bars from Tschai-
kovsky, Stravinsky, or Wagner. Any number of repetitions of these bars
would not oblige him in any way to declare that such musical compositions
are logical and consistent unities. Suppose we find a large number of houses
in the classical style upon which is superimposed a Gothic tower. This does
not prevent our declaring such houses architectural "hash." For the same
reason we would declare illogical the conclusion, "Socrates is immortal,"
from the premises which should establish his mortality; or the answer, "Six,"
to the question, "How much do two and two make?" There certainly must
be *causes* for such illogicality; but no matter how frequent such answers are
or how many people make them, they still remain illogical. This shows once
again that the causal and logical forms of connection are governed by entirely
different principles.

Now it frequently happens in fact . . . that the presence of the logical
connection between variables is accompanied by their causal cohesion. It
thus comes about that the discovery of a logico-meaningful relationship is
often one of the best heuristic symptoms of a probable causal link as well.
But not every causal association is followed necessarily by a logical connection. All the causal-functional connections in the field of the natural
sciences, for example, and many in the field of human culture are free from
additional logical bonds. And this throws light on the mixture of different
architectural forms, opposing musical styles, disparate premises and conclusions which were cited above as examples of alogical, nonlogical, and
illogical combinations which might yet be causally explicable.

E. Causal-functional or probablistic connections vary so in *degree of
intensity* that we not only have cases in which we can be fairly certain of the
causal nature of the association, but also others in which we are not certain
whether the association is really causal or merely incidental (*post hoc propter
hoc* and the like). Similarly, the closeness of logico-meaningful integration
also varies from the sublime unity to one barely perceptible and merging into
the lower grades of association. The greatest values in all the important compartments of culture represent, as a rule, the logico-meaningful synthesis in
its most intense form. A mere heaping-up of various bits of information, on
the contrary, hardly ever has acquired the distinction of being considered
a great scientific or philosophical contribution; nor has a mere hodge-podge
of various styles made great music, painting, or poetry.

F. Causal integration, being external and inferential, exists supposedly
in the inorganic, organic, and superorganic worlds. The logico-meaningful
unities can be looked for only in the field of the phenomena that involve
human thought and imagination; that is, in the field of human culture, and
there only in that part which is a result of the activity of the human mind,
whether this activity is scientific, religious, artistic, philosophical, moral, or

technical. *Meaningful and logical integration by definition can only exist where there is mind and meaning. . . .*

G.   As a corollary to this statement it is to be pointed out that, since the highest values and complexes of values in any great culture belong to the class of the logico-meaningful unities, *this level gives it its sociocultural* and *logico-meaningful individuality; its specific style; its physiognomy and personality.* When we talk of the Greek culture of the fifth century B.C. as something peculiar and distinct, what we in fact mean first and most of all is the totality of the specific logico-meaningful systems created by their great men of genius—such men as Phidias, Praxiteles, Aeschylus, Pindar, Sophocles, Polygnotus, Socrates, and later, Plato. And this is true of any other culture or cultural period so far as its highest form of individuality is concerned.

H.   Causal relationships and the formulas which describe their uniformities vary widely in the *extent of their applicability.* Some have a very limited range of pertinence; others are relevant to an infinitely great number of cases. Newton's Law of Gravitation is more general, covers a much larger class of phenomena, than Kepler's laws. . . .

In a similar fashion the logico-meaningful principles of integration in the cultural world vary in range of applicability, beginning with the narrow principle which describes the coalescence of a few components of infrequent occurrence and in a limited cultural scheme—as, for example, the concurrence of images of anchor, dove, and olive branch in the frescoes of the Catacombs with the peculiar contents of the early Christian funeral prayer— and ending with the principle that explains and fits together millions of cultural fragments of wide distribution in space and time. The hedonistic or utilitarian principle may give sense and unity to many scattered phenomena in a large cultural conglomeration, which includes such elements as large-scale kidnaping, "get-rich-quick" schemes, emphasis on the *useful* in arts and science, "wine, women, and song" morality, and the philosophy of pragmatism with its utilitarian tenet to the effect that if the belief in God is useful, God exists; if not, God does not exist. But there may be a still broader principle in which that of utilitarianism itself becomes only one of the small subordinate fragments. In this sense we may speak of a long gradation of logico-meaningful formulas from the very limited to the most general. . . .

I.   From everything that has thus far been said, it follows that the investigation of each type of culture integration requires its own special procedure and brings about its characteristic results. *A study of any purely spatial and mechanical congeries cannot give anything but a mere descriptive catalogue of the parts.* Since these are not united causally, no formula of causal uniformity, no causal or functional generalization, can be made for them. . . .

In a study of cultural syntheses the parts of which are united causally or functionally, the causal-functional method with its more or less general causal formulas provides the proper procedure. . . .

Finally, in the study of logico-meaningful relationships, the proper method is neither a mere concrete description nor a causal formula, but the appropriate unification of the fragments into a whole according to their logical significance or their logical cobelonging. . . .

The essence of the logico-meaningful method of cognition is, as has already been mentioned, in the finding of the central principle (the "reason") *which permeates all the components, gives sense and significance to each of them, and in this way makes cosmos of a chaos of unintegrated fragments.* If in a given concurrence of cultural elements such unity exists, and if it is correctly discovered and the unifying principle accurately formulated, the formula is as important in its field from the cognitive standpoint as any causal formula in a case of causal coalescence. . . .

J.   If the fruitfulness of this method depends upon the discovery of the unifying principle that permeates a large or small portion of the components of a given cultural synthesis, the questions now arise: *How can such a principle be discovered? What are the guarantees that it is an adequate principle and not the mere phantasy of a "speculative" mind superimposed upon a reality in which it does not actually occur? If different investigators offer quite different principles, how can it be ascertained which of them is valid, which not, or which is more valid than the others?*

The first question is almost superfluous. As is true also of scientific or causal investigation, the principle may be suggested by observation, statistical study, meditation, logical analysis, even by dreaming and by what is called mere "chance," or "intuition." All of these ways, alone or in various combinations, have been operative in the first stages of most scientific discovery.

More important is the question: *How can it be ascertained that a given principle of logical integration is valid?* The criteria of validity are virtually the same as for any scientific law. First of all, the principle must by nature be logical; and second, it must stand successfully the test of the "relevant facts," that is, it must fit and represent them. . . .

Here the comparative value of the principles is decided by the same criteria as those used in the natural sciences. *Of several rival theories, that theory is best which describes the field of the phenomena in question most accurately and embraces in its description the largest number of phenomena.* For these reasons the Copernican system is better than the Ptolemaic, Newton's laws than Kepler's. Similarly, in the realm of sociocultural phenomena, where several different principles of integration may be formulated, some may be more correct and more broadly applicable than others. Some, for example, may fit only a limited set of phenomena, while others will apply to several sets. But one will stand forth as giving the most satisfactory meaning to the larger part of the elements. And this is the theory we must choose. . . .

These remarks clarify sufficiently the nature of the logico-meaningful form of integration, the situations in which it is relevant, and the methods of its application.

It is hardly necessary to add that the method is not new: it has been used, and used effectively, by the great social thinkers of the remote, as well as the more recent, past. . . .

Some Results of the Preceding Analysis

If it is valid that there are at least four different types of cultural integration—spatial, external, functional, and logical—each with the properties described, then one may draw a definite series of conclusions.

A. All the cultural conglomerations can be ranged theoretically upon a scale beginning with those which are a mere spatial congeries, that is, are unintegrated in the proper sense of the word, and ending with those which are completely integrated logically. . . .

B. If spatial adjacency and, in part, external unification are present in nearly every cultural complex, the same cannot be said of the functional and logical forms of synthesis. It is probable that at least some of the elements are bound either functionally or logically; but what they are, and how great a part of the whole they compose depends upon the culture and the period, and must be found by special study. No generalization equally applicable to all cultures is possible here. . . .

C. If propositions A and B are valid, then the following theories widely accepted are fallacious:

(1) That every culture is an integrated unity (unless, of course, by integration is meant a mere spatial congeries, a meaning which in its turn not only destroys the significance of the term, but also leads to other errors and illogicalities).

(2) That any change in any component of a given cultural configuration functionally or logically affects all the other components and therefore the whole of the given culture. . . .

D. The nature of the change of a spatial congeries differs from that of functionally or logically unified systems. In the congeries the change would mean mainly a mechanical addition or subtraction of elements, or their rearrangement chiefly through external forces. In the unified cultural

systems the change would mean a transformation of the system as a whole
or in its greater part. . . .

Change in spatial congeries is almost always accidental. It does not have
any inner logic and is the result of the interplay of various external
factors. . . .

Somewhat similar is the situation in a cultural congeries. A force external
to the heap may dump into it some additional elements or carry away some
of the objects which were there; it may change their mechanical order. The
congeries remains passive through all these changes, does not have initiative,
preferences, attraction and repulsion. . . .

The difference between the merely spatial accumulation and the
genuinely integrated system is so profound that the nature and methods of
their change are also profoundly different. . . .

E.   So far as the logically and functionally integrated systems are concerned, because they are real systems, they possess several fundamental
traits and give rise to a number of important considerations which are usually
neglected.

(1) Any functional or logical system as a unity has a certain degree of
autonomy and inherent self-regulation in its functioning and change
("equilibrium" of the imitators of mechanics). Any system, whether it be a
mechanism like an automobile, an organism like even the paramecium, or a
cultural system, has a certain degree of independence of, or immunity to,
external conditions. In some cases this freedom may be large, in others
narrow, but it is possessed to some extent by every system which pretends
to integration. . . .

(2) The autonomy of any system means further the existence of some
margin of choice or selection on its part with regard to the infinitely great
number of varying external agents and objects which may influence it. It
will ingest some of these and not others. It has an affinity for some and a
repulsion for others.

(3) Autonomy means further still that the functions, change, and
destiny of the system are determined not only and not so much by the
external circumstances (except in the case of catastrophic accidents), but by
the nature of the system itself and by the relationship between its parts. . . .

A cultural system has its own logic of function, change, and destiny,
which is a result not only (and regularly not so much) of the external conditions, but of its own nature. This does not deny the influence of the external
circumstances; neither does it deny the possibility of occurrence of the most
decisive, catastrophic accidents caused by an external force; but it stresses
what seems to have been forgotten for the last few decades, namely, that
one of the most important "determinators" of the functioning and course of
any system lies within the system itself, is inherent in it. In this sense any

inwardly integrated system is an autonomous self-regulating, self-directing, or, if one prefers, "equilibrated" unity. Its life course is set down in its essentials when the system is born. This is one of the specific aspects of the larger principle which may be called "immanent self-regulation and self-direction."

(4) If this is true, then it is incorrect to "explain" any true system as the mere plaything of external conditions and reduce the explanation of the change in the system to this or that external factor. . . .

(5) Reliance upon one element of an integrated combination as a main factor in explaining changes within the combination, as many investigators in the field have done, is a serious error in procedure. The partisans of the economic interpretation of history make the economic factor the source of change in all the compartments of culture; partisans of religion, of race, of heredity, and of other factors, make each of these respectively the chief source. But, in the meantime, if a given culture is a unity in which economic, religious, populational, and other compartments are but single elements, its change can be explained through such a main factor procedure with as little accuracy as, for instance, the change of the human organism as it passes from childhood to puberty could be explained through increase in stature or some other such "factor." . . .

At a certain point of its history (slightly accelerated or retarded by the external circumstances) the cultural system must undergo its inwardly ordained change. When this begins, all the main compartments of the culture change. It is therefore equally futile to argue that the transformation of one factor causes another, or all the others, to change, or vice versa.

From these conclusions it is apparent that the investigators of cultural phenomena who have sought to explain the transformations of an integrated system by means of a factor which is merely a symptom or result have failed to recognize the true nature of change in such a system. In addition if their main factor is dependent on something external and accidental, they are also guilty of failing to discriminate between a genuine integration of cultural elements and a mere spatial congeries.

Ludwig von Bertalanffy

General System Theory

The Quest for a General System Theory

MODERN science is characterized by its ever-increasing specialization, necessitated by the enormous amount of data, the complexity of techniques and of theoretical structures within every field. This, however, has led to a breakdown of science, as an integrated realm: The physicist, the biologist, the psychologist and the social scientist are, so to speak, encapsulated in a private universe, and it is difficult to get word from one cocoon to the other.

There is, however, another remarkable aspect. If we survey the evolution of modern science, as compared to science a few decades ago, we are impressed by the fact that similar general viewpoints and conceptions have appeared in very diverse fields. Problems of organization, of wholeness, of dynamic interaction, are urgent in modern physics, chemistry, physical chemistry, and technology. In biology, problems of an organismic sort are everywhere encountered: it is necessary to study not only isolated parts and processes, but the essential problems are the organizing relations that result from dynamic interaction and make the behavior of parts different when studied in isolation or within the whole. The same trend is manifest in

Reprinted from Ludwig von Bertalanffy, "General System Theory," *Main Currents of Modern Thought*, 71, 75 (1955), by permission.

gestalt theory and other movements as opposed to classical psychology, as well as in modern conceptions of the social sciences. These parallel developments in the various fields are even more dramatic if we consider the fact that they are mutually independent and largely unaware of each other.

Up to recent times, the corpus of laws of nature was almost identical with theoretical physics. Few attempts to state exact laws in non-physical fields have gained universal recognition. However, the impact and the development of the biological, behavioral, and social sciences seem to make necessary an expansion of our conceptual schemes in order to allow for systems of laws in fields where application of physics is not sufficient or possible.

Such trend towards generalized theories is taking place in many fields and in a variety of ways. For example, an elaborate theory of the dynamics of biological populations, the struggle for existence and biological equilibria has developed starting with the pioneering work by Lotka and Volterra.[1] The theory operates with biological notions such as individuals, species, coefficients of competition, and the like. A similar procedure is applied in quantitative economics and econometrics.[2] The models of families of equations here applied happen to be similar to those of Lotka or, for that matter, of chemical kinetics, but the model of interacting entities and forces is at a different level. To take another example: living organisms are essentially open systems, that is, systems exchanging matter with their environment. Conventional physics and physical chemistry deal with closed systems, and only in recent years has theory been expanded to include irreversible processes, open systems, and states of non-equilibrium. If, however, we want to apply the model of open systems to, say, the phenomena of animal growth, we autimolicaly come to a generalization of theory referring not to physical but to biological units.[3] In other words, we are dealing with generalized systems. The same is true of the fields of cybernetics and theory of information which have gained so much interest in the past few years.

Thus, there exist models, principles, and laws that apply to generalized systems or their subclasses, irrespective of their particular kind, the nature of their component elements, and the relations of "forces" between them. It seems legitimate to ask for a theory, not of systems of a more or less special kind, but of universal principles applying to systems in general.

In this way we come to postulate a new discipline, called General System

---

[1] Cf. the recent survey: U. D'Ancona, *The Struggle for Existence*. Leiden 1954.

[2] e.g., K. Boulding, *A Reconstruction of Economics*, New York 1950; G. Tintner, *Econometrics*. New York 1952.

[3] For a brief survey of this theory, cf. L. von Bertalanffy, Problems of Organic Growth. *Nature 163*, 156 1949; Metabolic Types and Growth Types. *Amer. Naturalist* 85, 111, 1951.

Theory. Its subject matter is the formulation and derivation of those principles which are valid for "systems" in general.

(1) A first consequence of the existence of general system properties is the appearance of structural similarities or isomorphies in different fields. There are correspondences in the principles which govern the behavior of entities that are intrinsically, widely different. This correspondence is due to the fact that they all can be considered, in certain respects, as "systems," that is, complexes of elements standing in interaction. The fact that the fields mentioned, and many others as well, are concerned with "systems," leads to a correspondence in general principles and even in special laws when the conditions correspond in the phemonena under consideration.

In fact, similar concepts, models and laws have often appeared in widely different fields, independently and based upon totally different facts. There are many instances where identical principles were discovered several times because the workers in one field were unaware that the theoretical structure required was already well developed in some other field.[4] General System Theory will go a long way towards avoiding such unnecessary duplication of labor.

System isomorphies also appear in problems which are recalcitrant to quantitative analysis but nevertheless of great intrinsic interest. There are, for example, isomorphies between biological systems and "epiorganisms" (Gerard) like animal communities and human societies.[5] Which principles are common to the several levels of organization and so may legitimately be transferred from one level to another, and which are specific so that transfer leads to dangerous fallacies? Can civilizations and cultures be considered as systems?

It seems, therefore, that a general theory of systems would be a useful tool providing, on the one hand, models that can be used in, and transferred to, different fields, and safeguarding, on the other hand, from vague analogies which often have marred the progress in these fields.[6]

(2) There is, however, another and possibly more important aspect of General System Theory. To use an expression of W. Weaver,[7] classical science was highly successful in developing the theory of unorganized or disorganized complexity which stems from statistics, the laws of chance, and, in the last resort, the second law of thermodynamics. Today our main problem is that of organized complexity. Concepts like those of organization,

[4] Cf. N. Wiener, *Cybernetics*. New York 1948.

[5] Cf. R. W. Gerard, this *Yearbook;* A. E. Emerson, Supraorganismic Aspects of the Society. *Colloques Internat., Centre Nat. de la Recherche scientifique, 34,* 333, 1952.

[6] For a discussion of "analogy," "logical homology," and "explanation proper," see L. von Bertalanffy, Problems of General System Theory. *Human Biology 23,* 302, 1951.

[7] W. Weaver, Science and Complexity. *Amer. Scientist 36,* 4, 1948.

wholeness, directiveness, teleology, control, self-regulation, differentiation and the like are alien to conventional physics. However, they pop up everywhere in the biological, behavioral, and social sciences, and are, in fact, indispensable for dealing with living organisms or social groups. Thus, a basic problem posed to modern science is a general theory of organization. General System Theory is in principle capable of giving exact definitions for such concepts and, in suitable cases, of putting them to quantitative analysis.

(3) If we have briefly indicated what General System Theory means, it will avoid misunderstanding also to state what it is not. It is not pure mathematics or identical with the triviality that mathematics of some sort can be applied to any sort of problem; instead it poses specific problems which are far from being trivial. Further, General System Theory is not a search for vague and superficial analogies between physical, biological, and social systems. Analogies as such are of little value, since beside similarities between phenomena, dissimilarities always can be found as well. The isomorphy we have mentioned is a consequence of the fact that, in certain aspects, corresponding abstractions and conceptual models can be applied to different phenomena. It is only in view of these aspects that system laws will apply. This does not mean that physical systems, organisms and societies are all the same. In principle, it is the same situation as when the law of gravitation applies to Newton's apple, the planetary system, and the phenomenon of tide. This means that in view of some rather limited aspects a certain theoretical system, that of mechanics, holds true; it does not mean that there is a particular resemblance between apples, planets, and oceans in a great number of other aspects.

Aims of General System Theory

Summarizing, the aims of General System Theory can be indicated as follows:

(a) There is a general tendency towards integration in the various sciences, natural and social.

(b) Such integration seems to be centered in a general theory of systems.

(c) Such theory may be an important means for aiming at exact theory in the non-physical fields of science.

(d) Developing unifying principles running "vertically" through the universes of the individual sciences, this theory brings us nearer to the goal of the unity of science.

(e) This can lead to a much-needed integration in scientific education.

A remark as to the delimitation of the theory here discussed seems to be appropriate. The term and program of a General System Theory was introduced by the present author a number of years ago.[8] It has turned out, however, that quite a large number of workers in various fields have been led to similar conclusions and ways of approach. It is suggested, therefore, to maintain this name which is now coming into general use, be it only as a convenient label.

It looks, at first, as if the definition of systems as "sets of elements standing in interaction" is so general and vague that not much can be learned from it. This, however, is not true. Systems can, for example, be defined by certain families of differential equations and if, in the usual way of mathematical reasoning, more specified conditions are introduced, many important properties can be found of systems in general and more special cases.

This mathematical approach followed in General System Theory is not the only possible or most general one. There are a number of related modern approaches, such as information theory, cybernetics, game, decision, and net theories, stochastic models, operations research, to mention only the most important ones. However, the fact that differential equations cover extensive fields in the physical, biological, economical, and probably also the behavioral sciences, makes them a suitable access to the study of generalized systems.

I am now going to illustrate General System Theory by way of some examples.

---

[8] It seems that A. Lotka (*Elements of Physical Biology*. Baltimore 1925) was the first to advance the idea of general system laws, introducing the simultaneous differential equations for the definition of general systems which were used by the later authors (Bertalanffy, Ashby, see below). The idea of a General System Theory was developed by Bertalanffy in the late thirties and presented in various lectures, but this material remained unpublished until 1945 (Zu einer allgemeinen Systemlehre. *Blaetter f. Deutsche Philosophie 18,* 3/4), which publication got lost in the turmoil of this time. General System Theory was then presented at various places (Vom Sinn und der Einheit der Wissenschafte. *Der Student, Wien, 2, No. 7/8,* 10, 1947. Das Weltbild der Biologie. In: *Weltbild und Menschenbild,* III. Internat. Hochschulwochen des Oesterr. College 1947, Salzburg, p. 251; Zu einer allgenmeinen Systemlehre. *Biologia Generalis 19,* 114, 1949; An Outline of General System Theory. *Brit J. Philos. Sci. 1,* 139, 1950; (with C. G. Hempel, R. E. Bass and H. Jonas) General System Theory: A New Approach to Unity of Science. 1–6. *Human Biology 23,* 302, 1951). Without using the term, General System Theory, but in a similar intention, the same mathematical frame has been used by W. R. Ashby (Effect of controls on stability. *Nature 155,* 242, 1945; The Physical Origin of Adaptability by Trial and Error. *J. Gen. Psychol. 32,* 13, 1945; Principles of the Self-Organizing Dynamic System. *J. Gen. Psychol. 37,* 125, 1947; Dynamic of the cerebral cortex. XIII. *J. Comp. Physiol. Psychol. 40,* 1, 1947; Summarized in his book, *Design for a Brain.* London 1952). Some of the characteristics and their mathematical expressions of general systems as developed by Bertalanffy, *loc. cit.,* are discussed in *art.* Hall and Fagen, this *Yearbook.*

Closed and Open Systems:
Limitations of Conventional Physics

My first example is that of closed and open systems. Conventional physics deals only with closed systems, that is, systems which are considered to be isolated from their environment. Thus, physical chemistry tells us about the reactions, their rates, and the chemical equilibria eventually established in a closed vessel where a number of reactants is brought together. Thermodynamics expressly declares that its laws only apply to closed systems. In particular, the second principle of thermodynamics states that, in a closed system, a certain quantity, called entropy, must increase to a maximum, and eventually the process comes to a stop at a state of equilibrium. The second principle can be formulated in different ways, one being that entropy is a measure of probability, and so a closed system tends to a state of most probable distribution. The most probable distribution, however, of a mixture, say, of red and blue glass beads, or of molecules having different velocities, is a state of complete disorder; having separated all red beads on one hand, and all blue ones on the other, or having, in a closed space, all fast molecules, that is, a high temperature on the right side, and all slow ones, a low temperature, at the left, is a highly improbable state of affairs. So the tendency towards maximum entropy or the most probable distribution is the tendency to maximum disorder.

However, we find systems which by their very nature and definition are not closed systems. Every living organism is essentially an open system. It maintains itself in a continuous inflow and outflow, building up and breaking down of components, never being, so long as it is alive, in a state of chemical and thermodynamic equilbrium but maintained in a so-called steady state which is distant from the latter. This is the very essence of that fundamental phenomenon of life which is called metabolism, the chemical processes within living cells. What now? Obviously, the conventional formulations of physics are, in principle, inapplicable to the living organism *qua* open system and steady state, and we may well suspect that many characteristics of living systems which are paradoxical in view of the laws of physics, are precisely a consequence of this fact.

It is only in recent years that an expansion of physics, in order to include open systems, has taken place.[9] This theory has shed light on many obscure

---

[9] Although the idea of the organism as a "dynamic equilibrium" goes back, at least, to Johannes Müller and Dubois-Raymond, the concept of "open system," so far as can be ascertained, was first used in thermodynamics by R. Defay (Introduction à la thermodynamique des systèms ouverts. *Acad. Roy. de Belgique. Bull. Classe des Sciences, 53 Serie 15*, 678, 1929). In 1932, L. von Bertalanffy introduced the same concept in biology, emphasizing that an expansion of the theory of physical chemistry

phenomena in physics and biology, and has also led to important general conclusions of which I will mention only two.

The first is the principle of equifinality.[10] In any closed system, the final state is unequivocally determined by the initial conditions: for example, the motion in a planetary system where the positions of the planets at a time t are unequivocally determined by their positions at a time t_0. Or in a chemical equilibrium, the final concentrations of the reactants naturally depend on the initial concentrations. If either the initial conditions or the process is altered, the final state will also be changed. This is not so in open systems. Here, the same final state may be reached from different initial conditions and in different ways. This is what is called equifinality, and it has a significant meaning for the phenomena of biological regulation. Those who are familiar with the history of biology will remember that it was just equifinality that led the German biologist Driesch to embrace vitalism, that is, the doctrine that vital phenomena are inexplicable in terms of natural science. Driesch's argument was based on experiments on embryos in early development. The same final result, a normal individual of the sea urchin, can develop from a complete ovum, from each half of a divided ovum, or from the fusion product of two whole ova. The same applies to embryos of many other species, including man, where identical twins are the product of the splitting of one ovum. Equifinality, according to Driesch, contradicts the laws of physics, and can be accomplished only by a soul-like vitalistic

---

is needed in order to deal adequately with the steady state of the organism (*Theoretische Biologie*. Erster Band. Berlin 1932; Untersuchungen ueber die Gesetzlichkeit des Wachstums. *Roux' Archiv 131*, 613, 1934). Kinetic principles of open systems were first developed, concurrently, by A. C. Burton (The Properties of the Steady State Compared to those of Equilibrium as Shown in Characteristic Biological Behavior. *J. Cell. Comp. Physiol. 14*, 327, 1939) and L. von Bertalanffy (Der Organismus als physikalisches System betrachtet. *Naturwissenschaften 28*, 521, 1940). The kinetics of open systems can be found, in the present *Yearbook,* in *art.* Bradley and Calvin. The thermodynamics of open systems in part of the recent development of "Irreversible Thermodynamics," mainly due, in Germany, to J. Meixner (*Thermodynamik der irreversiblen Prozesse. Arbeiten* 1941–1949. Aachen 1954), and to the work of the Belgian school. Comprehensive presentations: I. Prigogine, *Etude thermodynamique des phénomènes irréversibles*. Paris 1947; Introduction to Thermodynamics of Irreversible Processes. Amer. Lecture Series 185. Springfield (Ill.) 1955; S. R. de Groot, *Thermodynamics of Irreversible Processes.* New York 1951; K. G. Denbigh, *The Thermodynamics of the Steady State*. London and New York 1951. The most important recent development, generalizing and surpassing the last-mentioned work, is the introduction of a "Time Axiom" into irreversible thermodynamics by H. G. Reik (Zur Theorie irreversibler Vorgaenge. I-IV. *Annalen der Physik 11*, 270, 407, 420, *13*, 73). A presentation of the theory of open systems from the biologist's standpoint is L. von Bertalanffy, *Biophysik des Fliessgleichgewichts*. (Transl. by W. Westphal). Braunschweig 1953. A good introduction is H. G. Bray and K. White, Organisms as Physico-Chemical Machines. *New Biology 16*, 70, 1954.

[10] Introduced by Bertalanffy, Der Organismus als physikalisches System betrachtet, *loc. cit.*

factor which governs the processes in foresight of the goal, the normal organism to be established. It can be shown, however, that open systems, insofar as they attain a steady state, must show equifinality, so the supposed violation of physical laws disappears.[11]

Another apparent contrast between inanimate and animate nature is what sometimes was called the violent contradiction between Lord Kelvin's degradation and Darwin's evolution, between the law of dissipation in physics and the law of evolution in biology. According to the second principle of thermodynamics, the general trend of events in physical nature is toward states of maximum disorder and levelling down of differences, with the so-called heat death of the universe as the final outlook, when all energy is degraded into evenly distributed heat of low temperature, and the world process comes to a stop. In contrast, the living world shows, in embryonic development and in evolution, a transition towards higher order, heterogeneity, and organization.[12] But on the basis of the theory of open systems, the apparent contradiction between entropy and evolution disappears. In all irreversible processes, entropy must increase. Therefore, the change of entropy in closed systems is always positive, order is continually destroyed. In open systems, however, we have not only production of entropy due to irreversible processes, but also import of the entropy which may well be negative. This is the case in the living organism which imports complex molecules high in free energy. Thus, living systems, maintaining themselves in a steady state, can avoid the increase of entropy, and may even develop towards states of increased order and organization.

From these examples, you may guess the bearing of the theory of open systems. Among other things, it shows that many supposed violations of physical laws in living nature do not exist, rather that they disappear with the generalization of physical theory. In a generalized version the concept

---

[11] It should perhaps be mentioned that equifinality is not a mathematical characteristic but a physical characteristic of (certain) open systems. It does not depend on the structure of the system equations but on the meaning of the parameters so that formally identical equations may apply to non-equifinal closed systems as well as to equifinal open systems. However, the equifinal case where the final state depends only on the reaction and transport parameters and not on the initial conditions, is found only in open systems. On the conditions of equifinality, cf. Bertalanffy, *Biophysik des Fliessgleichgewichts, op. cit.*

[12] The contrast between inanimate and living nature has been formulated by L. Brillouin (Life, Thermodynamics, and Cybernetics. *Amer. Scientist 37*, 554, 1949) as follows: "How is it possible to understand life, when the whole world is ruled by such a law as the second principle of thermodynamics which points towards death and annihilation?" This apparent paradox has often been used as the basis for vitalistic or theological arguments (e.g., H. Adams, *The Degradation of the Democratic Dogma*. New York 1920, Woltereck, R., *Ontologie des Lebendigen*. Stuttgart 1939; E. Schroedinger, *What is Life?* Cambridge (Engl.) 1945; Lecomte du Noüy, *Human Destiny*. New York 1947; R. E. D. Clark, *Darwin: Before and After*. London 1948).

of open systems can be applied to non-physical levels. Examples are its use in ecology and the evolution towards a climax formation (Whittacker),[13] in psychology where "neurological systems" were considered as "open dynamic systems" (Krech),[14] in philosophy where the trend toward "transactional" as opposed to "self-actional" and "inter-actional" viewpoints closely corresponds to the open-system model (Bentley).[15]

Information and Entropy

Another development which is closely connected with system theory is that of the modern theory of communication. It has often been said that energy is the currency of physics, just as economic values can be expressed in dollars or pounds. There are, however, certain fields of physics and technology where this currency is not readily acceptable. This is the case in the field of communication which, due to the development of telephones, radio, radar, calculating machines, servomechanisms and other devices, has led to the rise of a new mathematical field.[16]

The general notion in Communication Theory is that of information. Information is measured in terms of decisions. Take the game of Twenty Questions, where we are supposed to find out an object by having questions answered about it by yes or no. The amount of information conveyed in one answer is a decision between two alternatives, such as animal or non-animal. With two questions, it is possible to decide for one out of four possibilities, for example, mammal—non-mammal, or flowering plant—non-flowering plant. With three questions it is a decision out of eight, and so forth. Thus, the logarithm at the basis 2 of the possible answers can be used as a measure of information, the unit being the so-called binary unity or bit. The information contained in two answered questions is $\log_2 4 = 2$ bits, of three answers, $\log_2 8 = 3$ bits, and so forth. This measure of information happens to be similar to that of entropy or rather negative entropy, since entropy also is defined as a logarithm of probability. But entropy, as we have already heard, is a measure of disorder; hence negative entropy or information is a measure of order or of organization since the latter, compared to distribution at random, is an improbable state. In this way information theory comes close to the theory of open systems, which may increase in

[13] R. H. Whitacker, A Consideration of Climax Theory: The Climax as a Population and Pattern. *Ecol. Monographs 23*, 41, 1953.

[14] D. Krech, this *Yearbook*; cf. also L. von Bertalanffy, Theoretical Models in Biology and Psychology. *J. Personality 20*, 24, 1951.

[15] A. F. Bentley, Kennetic Inquiry. *Science 112*, 775, 1950.

[16] See: C. E. Shannon and W. Weaver, *The Mathematical Theory of Communication*. Urbana (Ill.) 1949; Wiener, *Cybernetics, op. cit.*

order and organization, or show negative entropy. But negative entropy can be considered a measure of decisions, taken out of equally probable ones, a measure of improbability or information.

Another central concept of Communication Theory is that of feedback. A simple scheme for feedback is the following. In the classical case of stimulus-response, a stimulus affects a receptor; the message of the receptor is transmitted to some controlling apparatus, and from this to an effector which gives the response. In feedback, the result of the effector's activity is monitored back to the receptor so that the system is self-regulating.

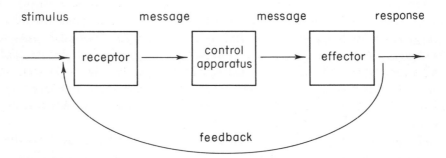

Feedback arrangements are used in modern technology to a wide extent for the stabilization of a certain action, as in thermostats or in radio receivers; or for the direction of actions towards a goal where the aberration from that goal is fed back, as information, till the goal or target is reached. This is the case in self-propelled missiles which seek their target, anti-aircraft fire control systems, ship-steering systems, and other so-called servo-mechanisms.

There is a large number of biological phenomena which correspond to the feedback scheme. First, there are the phenomena of so-called homeo-stasis,[17] or maintenance of balance in the living organism, the prototype of which is thermo-regulation in warm-blooded animals. Cooling of the blood stimulates certain centers in the brain which "turn on" heat producing mechanisms of the body, and the body temperature is monitored back to the center so that temperature is maintained at a constant level. Similar homeostatic mechanisms exist in the body for maintaining the constancy of a great number of physico-chemical variables. Furthermore, feedback systems comparable to the servomechanisms of technology exist in the animal and human body for the regulation of actions. If we want to pick up a pencil, report is made to the central nervous system of the amount of

---

[17] W. B. Cannon, Organization for Physiological Homeostasis. *Physiol. Rev. 9*, 397, 1929.

which we have failed the pencil in the first instance; this information then is fed back to the central nervous system so that the motion is controlled till it reaches its aim.

So a great variety of systems in technology and in living nature follow the feedback scheme, and it is well known that a new discipline, called Cybernetics, was introduced by Norbert Wiener to deal with these phenomena. The theory tries to show that mechanisms of a feedback nature are at the basis of teleological or purposeful behavior in man-made machines as well as in living organisms, and in social systems.

It should be borne in mind, however, that the feedback scheme is of a rather special nature. It presupposes structural arrangements of the type mentioned. There are, however, many regulations in the living organism which are of essentially different nature, namely, those where the order is effectuated by a dynamic interplay of processes. Remember the classical example of embryonic regulation where the whole is re-established from the parts in an equifinal process. It can be shown that the *primary* regulations in organic systems, that is, those which are most fundamental and primitive in embryonic development as well as in evolution, are of such nature of dynamic interaction. They are based upon the fact that the living organism is an open system, maintaining itself in, or approaching a steady state. Superimposed are those regulations which we may call *secondary,* and which are controlled by fixed arrangements, especially of the feedback type. This state of affairs is a consequence of a general principle of organization which may be called progressive mechanization. At first, systems—biological, neurological, psychological or social—are governed by dynamic interaction of their components; later on, fixed arrangements and conditions of constraint are established which render the system and its parts more efficient, but also gradually diminish and eventually abolish its equipotentiality.[18] Thus, dynamics is the broader aspect, since we can always arrive from general system laws to machinelike function by introducing suitable conditions of constraint, but the opposite way is not practicable.

Causality and Teleology

Another point I would like to make is the change the scientific world-picture has undergone in the past few decades.[19] In the world view called

---

[18] For a more detailed discussion of dynamic and feedback regulation, see L. von Bertalanffy, Towards a Physical Theory of Organic Teleology. *Human Biology 23*, 346, 1941; progressive mechanization: An Outline of General System Theory, *loc. cit.*; *Problems of Life.* New York 1952; and Hall and Fagen, this *Yearbook*.

[19] Cf. L. K. Frank, G. E. Hutchinson, W. K. Livingstone, W. S. McCulloch and N. Wiener, *Teleological Mechanisms*. Ann. N.Y. Acad. Scie. *50*, 1948.

mechanistic, born of classical physics of the 19th century, the aimless play of the atoms, governed by the inexorable laws of mechanical causality, produced all phenomena in the world, inanimate, living, and mental. No room was left for any directiveness, order, or telos. The world of the organisms appeared a mere product of chance, accumulated by the senseless play of mutation at random and selection; the mental world as a curious and rather inconsequential epiphenomenon of material events.

The only goal of science appeared to be the analytical, that is, the splitting-up of reality into ever smaller units and the isolation of individual causal trains. Thus, physical reality was split up into mass points or atoms, the living organism into cells, behavior into reflexes, perception into punctual sensations, and so forth. Correspondingly, causality was essentially one-way: one sun attracts just one planet, one gene in the fertilized ovum produces such and such inherited character, one sort of bacterium produces this or that disease, mental elements are lined up, like the beads in a string of pearls, by the law of association. Remember Kant's famous table of the categories which attempts to systematize the fundamental notions of classical science: it is symptomatic that the notion of interaction and of organization were only space-fillers or did not appear at all.

Now we may state as characteristic of modern science that this scheme of isolable units acting in one-way causality has proved to be insufficient. Hence the appearance, in all fields of science, of notions like wholeness, holistic, organismic, *gestalt* and so forth which all signify that in the last resort, we must think in terms of systems of elements in mutual interaction.

Similarly, notions of teleology and directiveness appeared to be outside the scope of science and the playground of mysterious, super-natural or anthropomorphic agencies; or else, a pseudo-problem, intrinsically alien to science, and merely a misplaced projection of the observer's mind into a nature governed by purposeless laws. Nevertheless, these aspects exist, and you cannot conceive of a living organism, not to speak of behavior and human society, without taking into account what variously and rather loosely is called adaptiveness, purposiveness, goal-seeking and the like.

It is characteristic of the present view that these aspects are taken seriously as a legitimate problem for science; moreover, we can well indicate models showing such behavior.

Two such models we have already mentioned. One is equifinality, the tendency towards a characteristic final state from different initial states in different ways, based upon dynamic interaction in an open system attaining a steady state; the second, feedback, the homeostatic maintenance of a characteristic state or the seeking of a goal, based upon circular causal chains and mechanisms monitoring back information on deviations from the state to be attained or the goal to be reached. A third model for adaptive behavior, a *Design for a Brain,* was developed by Ashby, who incidentally starts with the same mathematical definitions and equations for a general system as were used by the present author. Both writers have developed their systems independently and, following different lines of interest, have arrived at different theorems and conclusions. Ashby's model for adaptiveness is, roughly, that of step functions defining a system, that is, functions which, after a certain critical value is overstepped, jump into a new family of differential equations. This means that, having passed a critical state, the system starts off in a new way of behavior. Thus, by means of step functions, the system shows adaptive behavior by what the biologist would call trial and error: it tries different ways and means, and eventually settles down in a field where it does not come any more in conflict with critical values of the environment. Such a system adapting itself by trial and error was actually constructed by Ashby as an electromagnetic machine, called the homeostat.

I am not going to discuss the merits and shortcomings of these models of teleological or directed behavior. What should be stressed, however, is the fact that teleological behavior directed towards a characteristic final state or goal is not something off limits of natural science and an anthropo-morphic misconception of processes which, in themselves, are undirected and accidental. Rather it is a form of behavior which can well be defined in scientific terms and for which the necessary conditions and possible mechanisms can be indicated.

What Is Organization?

Similar considerations apply to the concept of organization. Organization also was alien to the mechanistic world. The problem did not appear in classical physics, mechanics, electrodynamics and so forth. Even more, the second principle indicated destruction of order as the general direction of events. It is true that this is different in modern physics. An atom, a crystal, or a molecule are organizations, as Whitehead never failed to emphasize. In biology, organisms, by definition, are organized things. But although we have an enormous amount of data on biological organization, from biochemistry to cytology, to histology and anatomy, we do not have a real theory of biological organizations, that is, a conceptual system which permits explanation of the empirical facts.

Characteristic of organization, that of a living organism or a society, are notions like those of wholeness, growth, differentiation, hierarchical order, dominance, control, competition, and so forth. Such notions do not appear in conventional physics. System theory is well capable of dealing with these matters. It is possible to define such notions within the mathematical model of a system;[20] moreover, in some respects, detailed theories can be developed which deduce, from general assumptions, the possible special cases. A good example is the theory of biological equilibria, cyclic fluctuations, and so forth, as initiated by Lotka, Volterra, Gauss, and others. It will certainly be found that Volterra's biological theory and the theory of quantitative economics are isomorphic in many respects.

There are, however, many aspects of organizations which do not easily lend themselves to quantitative interpretation. This difficulty is not unknown in natural science. Thus, the theory of biological equilibria or that of natural selection are highly developed fields of mathematical biology, and nobody doubts that these theories are legitimate, essentially correct, and an important part of the theory of evolution and of ecology. It is hard, however, to apply them in the field because the parameters chosen, such as selective value, rate of destruction and generation and the like cannot easily be determined. So we have to content ourselves with a qualitative argument which, however, may lead to interesting consequences.

As an example of the application of General System Theory to human society, I would like to quote a recent book by Boulding, entitled *The Organizational Revolution*.[21] Boulding starts with a general model of organization and states what he calls Iron Laws holding good for any organization. Such Iron Laws are, for example, the malthusian law that the increase of a population is greater than that of its resources. Then there is a law of the optimum size of organizations: the larger an organization grows, the longer is the way of communication and this, depending on the particular nature of the organization, acts as a limiting factor and does not allow an organization to grow beyond a certain critical size. According to the law of instability, many organizations are not in a stable equilibrium but show cyclic fluctuations which result from the interaction of subsystems. This, incidentally, could probably be treated in terms of the Volterra theory, Volterra's so-called first law being that of periodic cycles. The important law of oligopoly states that, if there are competing organizations, the instability of their relations and hence the danger of friction and conflicts increase with the decrease of the number of those organizations. Thus, so long as they are relatively small and numerous, they muddle through in some way to coexistence. But if only a few or a competing pair is left, as is the case with the colossal political blocks at the present day, conflicts become devastating to the point of complete mutual destruction. The number of

[20] See Bertalanffy, An Outline of General System Theory, *loc. cit.*
[21] K. E. Boulding, *The Organizational Revolution*. New York 1953.

such general theorems for organization can easily be enlarged. They are well capable of being developed in an exact way, as it actually was done for certain aspects.[22]

General System Theory and the Unity of Science

Let me close these remarks with a few words about the general implications of interdisciplinary theory.

The integrative function of General System Theory can perhaps be summarized as follows. So far, the unification of science has been seen in the reduction of all sciences to physics, in the final resolution of all phenomena into physical events. From our point of view, unity of science gains a more realistic aspect. A unitary conception of the world may be based, not upon the possibly futile and certainly far-fetched hope finally to reduce all levels of reality to the level of physics, but rather on the isomorphy of laws in different fields. Speaking in what has been called the "formal" mode, that is, looking at the conceptual constructs of science, this means structural uniformities of the schemes we are applying. Speaking in "material" language, it means that the world, that is, the total of observable phenomena, shows structural uniformities, manifesting themselves by isomorphic traces of order in its different levels of realism.

We come, then, to a conception which in contrast to reductionism, we may call perspectivism.[23] We cannot reduce the biological, behavioral, and social levels to the lowest level, that of the constructs and laws of physics. We can, however, find constructs and possibly laws within the individual levels. The world is, as Aldous Huxley once put it, like a Neapolitan ice cake where the levels, the physical, the biological, the social and the moral universe, represent the chocolate, strawberry, and vanilla layers. We cannot reduce strawberry to chocolate—the most we can say is that possibly in the last resort, all is vanilla, all mind or spirit. The unifying principle is that we find organization on all levels. The mechanistic world view, taking the play of physical particles for ultimate reality, found its expression in a civilization glorifying physical technology which eventually has led to the catastrophies of our time. Possibly the model of the world as a great organization can help to re-enforce the sense of reverence for the living which we have almost lost in the last sanguinary decades of human history.

---

[22] Cf. also: Ch. A. McClelland, Applications of General System Theory in International Relations. *Currents in Modern Thought 12*, 27, 1955.

[23]. Cf. L. von Bertalanffy, An Essay on the Relativity of Categories. *Philos. of Sci.* 22, 243, 1955.

Talcott Parsons and Neil J. Smelser

The Primary Sub-Systems of Society

*O*UR most general proposition is that total societies *tend* to differentiate into sub-systems (social structures) which are specialized in each of the four primary functions. Where concrete structures cannot be identified, as is often the case, it is still often possible to isolate types of processes which are thus specialized.

The economy is the primary sub-system specialized in relation to the *adaptive* function of a society. If this proposition is correct, three other cognate sub-systems in a differentiated society should correspond to the other three functional problems. The sub-system goal of each of the three should be defined as a primary *contribution* to the appropriate functional need of the total society. For instance, the goal of the economy is the production of income which is at the disposal of the society.[1] In these terms, the other three societal sub-systems cognate with the economy are: (1) a goal-attainment sub-system, (2) an integrative sub-system, and (3) a pattern-maintenance and tension-management sub-system—all three of which possess the characteristics of social systems. Let us discuss each in turn.

The goal-attainment sub-system focuses on the political (in a broader sense) functions in a society. Since these functions are not coterminous with the governmental structure, it seems appropriate to term this sub-sector the "polity," parallel with the economy. The goal of the economy, as we have

---

[1] Secondarily, such a sub-system is then defined by *its* own adaptive exigencies, integrative exigencies, and type of institutionalized value pattern (as a specialization of the value pattern of the total society).

Reprinted with permission of Routledge and Keegan Paul Ltd. and of The Free Press from *Economy and Society* by Talcott Parsons and Neil J. Smelser. First published in the United States of America in 1959 by The Free Press.

noted, is to *produce* generalized facilities, as means to an indefinite number of possible uses. The important feature of this production is not only the quantity of such facilities (in a "physical" sense), but their *generalizability*, i.e., their adaptability to these various uses. The goal of the polity, however, is the *mobilization* of the necessary prerequisites for the *attainment* of given system goals of the society. Wealth is *one* of the indispensable prerequisites, but as we shall see, there are other equally important ones.

To put it in a slightly different way, the goal of the polity is to maximize the capacity of the society to attain its system goals, i.e., collective goals. We define this capacity as *power* as distinguished from wealth. We will discuss wealth as an ingredient of power presently; suffice it to say that the use of wealth for collective goals means a sacrifice of the *general* disposability of wealth, and hence its availability for other sub-systems than the polity.

The polity is related to government in approximately the same way that the economy is to "business." The analytical system does not coincide with concrete organization but political goals and values tend to have primacy over others in an organ of government, much the same as economic goals and values tend to have primacy in a business organization. . . .

The integrative sub-system of the society relates the cultural value-patterns to the motivational structures of individual actors in order that the larger social system can function without undue internal conflict and other failures of coordination. These processes maintain the institutionalization of value patterns which define the main structural outline of the society in the first instance. Sociologists refer to specialized integrative mechanisms primarily as mechanisms of social control.[2]

The integrative system of the society is the "producer" of another generalized capacity to control behaviour analogous to wealth and power. Some sociologists, notably Durkheim, refer to this capacity as "solidarity." [3] Wealth, therefore, is a generalized capacity to command goods and services, either as facilities or as reward objects for any goal or interest at any level in society. Power is the generalized capacity to mobilize the resources of the society, including wealth and other ingredients such as loyalties, "political responsbility," etc., to attain particular and more or less immediate collective goals of the system. Correspondingly, solidarity is the generalized capacity of agencies in the society to "bring into line" the behaviour of system units in accordance with the integrative needs of the system, to check or reverse disruptive tendencies to deviant behaviour, and to promote the conditions of harmonious cooperation.

Wealth or income is an output of the economy *to* other sub-systems of the

---

[2] Cf. Parsons *The Social System*, Chapt. VII.
[3] Another term is "cohesion."

society. Thus only in a secondary sense should we describe an economy as "wealthy"; the appropriate adjective is "productive." The *society* is wealthy or not wealthy. Similarly, a polity is not powerful, but a society is. The polity is more or less effective in the "production of power." Finally, the society has a high level of solidarity, but the integrative sub-system itself does not. The integrative system "contributes" solidarity to the social system. In the case of all three, "factors" analogous to the factors of production combine to produce the appropriate output or contribution; similarly, the output itself is distributed by shares among the different sub-systems of the society.

The pattern-maintenance and tension-management sub-system stands relative to the society as the land complex stands relative to the economy. At the societal level, this sub-system focuses on the institutionalized culture, which in turn centres on patterns of value orientations.[4] Such patterns are relevant to all social action. For any system, however, they are most nearly constant and relatively independent of the urgency of immediate goal needs and the exigencies of adaptive and integrative problems imposed on the system.

This relative constancy and insulation from exigencies does not mean that pattern maintenance occurs "automatically," i.e., without mechanisms. On the contrary, such patterns are institutionalized only through organization of potentially very unstable elements (in the process of socialization), and to be successful this organization requires complex "maintenance operations."

Pattern maintenance and tension management differ from the integrative problem in the sense that they focus on the *unit* of the system, not the system itself.[5] Integration is the problem of *inter*unit relationships, pattern maintenance of *intra*unit states and processes. Of course such a distinction depends on the degree of differentiation between system units. In the present context the distinction raises questions of the importance of the differentiation of the economy from other sub-systems in any given case. The differentiation is very clear in the modern industrial case. Hence it is essential to discriminate between the processes by which the basic economic commitments are *maintained* and the processes by which the boundary relations between the economy and other social sub-systems are *adjusted*. To take a specific case, a sharp fall in production occasioned by a deficit in consumer spending (a Keynesian depression) differs vastly from a fall occasioned by a breakdown in the fundamental motivation to work productively. In the latter case

---

[4] For the general theoretical background, cf. *Toward a General Theory of Action*, *The Social System*, and *Working Papers in the Theory of Action*.

[5] This is what is implied by referring to *latent* pattern maintenance and tension management. Essential *conditions* of the larger system functioning, rather than the functioning itself, are involved.

"pump-priming" measures are irrelevant; it is a problem of maintaining patterns of value.

The functioning of a unit in an interaction system ultimately depends on the motivation of the individual actors participating in the unit. The "tension-management" aspect of the pattern-maintenance sub-system concerns this motivation. The primary adaptive exigencies *of this sub-system* lie in those personality elements which maintain adequate motivation to conform with cultural values. The tension which is managed is individual motivation,[6] in actual or potential conflict with the fulfilment of behaviour expectations in institutionally defined roles. Unless controlled or managed, such tension disorganizes the relevant unit and thereby interferes with its functioning in the system.

The pattern-maintenance sub-system also has a type of "product" or contribution of generalized significance throughout the total social system. This is a type of "respect" accorded as a reward for conformity with a set of values. In cases when degrees of this respect are compared to others, we might call it *prestige*. Prestige, therefore, is the "product" of successful pattern maintenance or tension management in the interest of pattern conformity; it is a *capacity* to act in such a way as to implement the relevant system of institutionalized values.

The exact mechanisms of tension management and pattern maintenance vary from system to system. The primary function of the latency sub-system is always relative to a given superordinate system reference. It defines the conditions of stability of the units of this superordinate system, whatever the units happen to be. But the units themselves, at the next level down in an analytic breakdown, have the properties of systems. The definition of the conditions of stability therefore depend empirically on the system level in question.

The Boundaries Between the Sub-systems of Society

The four primary functional sub-systems of a society—the economy, the polity, the integrative sub-system, and the pattern-mainenance and tension-management sub-system. In what relation do they stand to each other? As we have suggested, each constitutes part of the *situation* for each of the others. From the point of view of any one sub-system, the primary cognate *social* situation or environment consists of the other three. For the economy,

---

[6] It does not matter, for purposes of the present analysis, what proportion of this motivation is constitutionally given and what proportion is affected by learning.

for instance, the polity, the integrative system and the pattern-maintenance system constitute the primary social situation.

But is not the relationship between system and social situation more specific? We introduced an element of specificity in the above analysis of the economic classification of the factors of production and the shares of income, in which we tried to demonstrate that these constitute the inputs and outputs, respectively, between the economy and the rest of society. This brief statement can be developed further.

Certainly the boundaries of the economy are not completely undifferentiated with respect to the relative concentration of *types* of input and output. Labor services, for instance, do not come from the same sources as capital resources; similarly, wages are not paid to the same elements as "interest" and other capital returns. To be sure, in the history of economics, there have been difficulties in identifying the sources of the factors and the recipients of the shares as sociologically distinct "classes." That there is *some* correspondence between these economic differentiations and those of social structure, however, seems beyond doubt, though the concrete social structures vary from one society to another.

If this is true for the economy's boundaries, then it should be true for the boundaries of the other sub-systems of the society. Furthermore, there should be a cognate classification of types of input and output in each of the *other* sub-systems. This follows from the general postulate that the scheme of functional differentiation is grounded in the *general* theory of social systems and therefore applies to the economy and to its cognate sub-systems in society.

If this reasoning is accepted, what is the nature of the "matching" between inputs and outputs among the various sub-systems of the society? Let us first take the goal-attainment sub-system of the economy, i.e., the production of goods and services for the "satisfaction" of consumers' wants, as one of the economy's specialized outputs. Is it a *specialized input* into another specific sub-system of the society? Or is it simply "spread" over the whole range of boundaries of the other sub-systems? The latter assumption is altogether incompatible with a vast amount of evidence for the relatively determinate structuring of social systems. But how can we demonstrate a specific "matching"?

We have one obvious empirical clue at the outset. The output of consumers' goods and services from the economy is (in concrete social structure terms) primarily to the family or household; conversely the input of labor services into the economy is an input from the household.

But what is the household or family? In sociological terms, the family (in our society, specifically the nuclear family) is not simply a "random sample" of the non-economic parts of the social structure. It is specifically located in the pattern-maintenance sub-system of the society.[7] It follows that the output of the economy over its goal-attainment boundary (A_G) goes *primarily* to some branch of the pattern-maintenance sub-system, at least in the modern industrial type of society.

If this boundary identification is correct empirically, what is its theoretical rationale? Certain classical economists sensed the appropriate line of reasoning, albeit in a vague and largely untenable way. This is that the household's primary output, from the societal perspective, is the organization of human motivation. In sociological terms this involves the socialization of children and the tension management of adults, both understood with reference to the central value patterns of the society.[8] The primary function (though by no means the only one) of consumers' wealth at the societal level is as an ingredient for this process. This is not merely because man, as organism, must meet biological needs: sociologically more important, it is because man, as human personality, must be provided with the symbolic media for learning and implementing values in human relations. The "style of life" of a household cannot be an abstract entity. It must have concrete content—actual premises in which everyday life is lived, the equipment of the home, clothing and many other things. Biological needs are, of course, met in this context; but they and their modes of realization occur within a cultural pattern.

Here we might note again the applicability of a distinction we believe to be fundamental to our analysis: the distinction between analytical sub-system and concrete structure of the economy. The relationship between the economy and the latent pattern-maintenance and tension-management sub-system is essentially analytical, i.e., it illustrates the crucial point of interaction between two differentiated functional sub-systems. But the economy does not "end" at the market for consumer goods. Indeed a good deal of the working capital of the economy is, even in our society, located concretely in households in the form of consumer durables in the process of depreciation. The functional differentiation of society and the concrete structure of collectivities, therefore, are overlapping classifications. As we have pointed out, our analysis deals primarily with the analytical sub-systems.

What are the reciprocal inputs from the household, i.e., labor services? Clearly they are in some sense "products" of the functioning household. It is possible, we think, to interpret them as the primary goal output of the pattern-maintenance sub-system to the economy (L_G).

The naïve economic version of this hypothesis is that the only serious

---

[7] Cf. *Working Papers,* Chapt. V., Sec. viii, and Parsons, T., Bales, R. F., *et al. Family, Socialization and Interaction Process,* 1955, Chapt. I.

[8] *Family, Socialization and Interaction Process,* Chapt. I, pp. 16 ff.

function of the human services is in their contribution to the production of wealth and that socialization itself is simply a form of economic production. The alternative to this untenable interpretation is that while an aspect of the life of the household is self-sufficient and in certain respects the household is directly integrated with "community structures," its social function *vis-à-vis* the division of labor is institutionalized as occupational roles in so far as it is institutionalized in specialized role-performance form at all.

In a highly differentiated society, the occupational role system is by no means coterminous with the economy; it extends beyond role involvements only in organizations with economic primacy (business firms). Nevertheless, occupational roles connect closely with the economy even when the organization in question is not a business firm. The basis of this connection is that occupational roles, which are always subject to the contract of employment, are subject at least to limited control by economic sanctions. Thus production of wealth has the goal primacy of occupational performance over only part of the range of occupational structure, but over the whole range labor market mechanisms control occupational performance and the allocation of personnel between occupational roles.[9] This is the sense in which labor service is always *channeled through* the economy in the transition from household to non-household role functions in the society. Also, the terms relating to income which a household receives are always important in the contract of employment.

To sum up, the boundary relationships between the economy and the pattern-maintenance sub-system are symmetrically reciprocal; each exchanges "primary goal outputs" with the other. The household—in its occupational role aspect—institutionalizes the function of "producer" of labor service to the society via the economy. The goal of the economy is to produce income primarily for the satisfaction of consumer wants.[10] . . .

Figure 1 shows the entire social system and the primary boundary interchanges. The three boundary interchanges we have developed [in sections not reproduced here] are: (1) the goal-attainment boundary of the economy *vis-à-vis* the goal-attainment boundary of the pattern-maintenance system (A_G—L_G); (2) the adaptive boundary of the economy *vis-à-vis* the adaptive boundary of the polity (A_A—G_A); and (3) the integrative boundary of the

---

[9] There are different *types* of markets, however. Cf. Chapt. III, pp. 146 ff.

[10] It will be noted that we have been careful *not* to assert or imply that consumers are "located" only in the household or that they are in any general sense a category of individuals. The state is clearly one of the major consumers in modern societies—e.g., of military equipment. We do not think that the benefits (or costs) of this military consumption can in any sensible way be allocated among the individual members of the society. It is the government as *collectivity* which is the consumer. But in this capacity or "role" the government is acting as part of the pattern-maintenance sub-system, not of the polity, as it does in other respects.

economy *vis-à-vis* the integrative boundary of the integrative sub-system $(A_I—I_I)$. At each of these three a factor of production for the economy is exchanged primarily for an output from the economy to the appropriate sub-system.

Besides these three, we would expect cognate boundary-structures for the three remaining interchanges. That is, (1) the polity and integrative system have contiguous goal-attainment sub-systems $(G_G—I_G)$; (2) the integrative and pattern-maintenance systems have contiguous adaptive sub-systems $(I_A—L_A)$; and (3) the polity and pattern-maintenance systems have contiguous integrative sub-systems $(G_I—L_I)$. After considerable study we are convinced that these three boundary relationships make good sociological sense and illuminate many problems not relevant to the present volume. We indicate them by dotted lines only, to complete the schematic outline of the major input-output categories among the major sub-systems of society.[11]

To complete the theoretical sketch of the boundary relations we must return to the economy's latent pattern-maintenance and tension-management sub-system $(A_L$, which deals with "land" factors). The latency sub-system of any larger system is always a special case relative to the other three systems in the sense that it is "insulated" from sensitivity to the current performance-sanction interplay of the larger system with its cognate systems. To be sure, the latency sub-system of the society has boundary relations with the economy and the other two non-latent systems, as shown in Figure 1. But *its own* latency sub-system is not contiguous to any sub-system of any other primary system. What is the status of this "special" latency boundary?

The "special" boundary of the latency sub-system at any given system level is a *cultural* rather than an interaction boundary.[12] The latency sub-system, as we have noted, maintains value patterns. But cultural patterns are not isolated atoms, each institutionalized in connection with its own particular system or sub-system. The cultural value system of a society is more or less integrated. In particular the value patterns applicable to any given sub-system are *differentiated value sub-systems* of the general value system of the total society. The relations between these cultural sub-systems are, of course,

---

[11] This is the first publication which incorporates the analysis of the boundary relations between the primary functional sub-systems of a society. It is thus not possible to refer the reader to other sources; subsequent publications by one or both of the authors should contribute to filling this gap in the not-too-distant future.

[12] In no sense is the latency boundary an "external" boundary, however. This view is tempting, since land involves physical resources. But according to the general theory of action, relations to the physical environment are not the function of *any* primary sub-system of an interaction system, but are resultant functions of all of them. So far as external relations in general are specialized, of course, they belong in the adaptive and goal-attainment systems (cf. Chapt. I. pp. 17–18.)

FIGURE 1

BOUNDARY INTERCHANGES BETWEEN THE
PRIMARY SUB-SYSTEMS OF A SOCIETY*

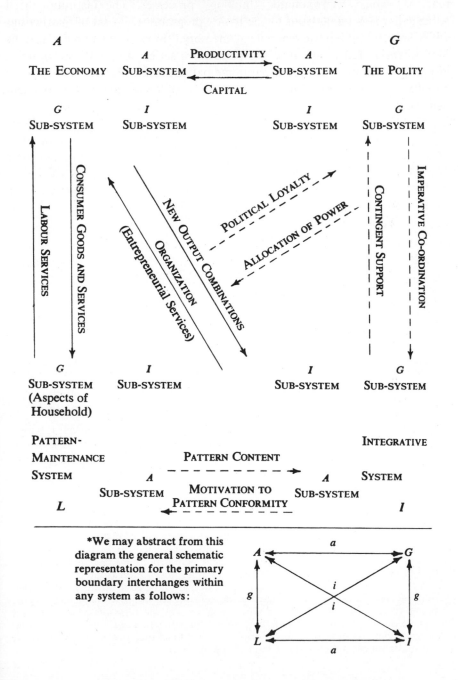

*We may abstract from this diagram the general schematic representation for the primary boundary interchanges within any system as follows:

not interactive; they include relations of consistency, level of generality, differentiation of relevant context of application, etc.

The role of the cultural value patterns is analogous to those modern machines which approximate "thinking" processes. The institutionalized value patterns are analogous to the basic "programme" or set of instructions which are "stored" in the machine's "memory." In response to more specific "information" fed in, the machine performs a series of operations to arrive at particular results. But the programme pattern cannot be derived from the specific operational procedures or vice versa; they are analytically independent factors.

Alvin W. Gouldner

Reciprocity and Autonomy
in Functional Theory

*T*HE intellectual fundament of functional theory in sociology is the concept of a "system." Functionalism is nothing if it is not the analysis of social patterns as parts of larger systems of behavior and belief. Ultimately, therefore, an understanding of functionalism in sociology requires an understanding of the resources of the concept of "system." Here, as in other embryo disciplines, the fundamental concepts are rich in ambiguity.

The recurrent use of organismic models by leading contributors to functionalism, such as Durkheim and Radcliffe-Brown, has its major intellectual justification in the fact that organisms are *examples* of systems. To the extent that the organismic model has proved fruitful in sociological analysis it has been so because the organism was a paradigmatic case of a system. It has been easier to unravel the implications of system-thinking by the direct inspection of a concrete case of a system, such as an organism or, for that matter, a machine, than it has been to analyze formally the implications of the concept of a system treated in full abstraction.

Yet the occasional vulgarities of those using organismic models clearly indicated the hazards of this procedure.[1] Indeed, we might say that the organismic model has been misleading in sociological analysis precisely insofar as it led to a focus on characteristics which were peculiar to the organism but not inherent in a generalized notion of a "system." Thus the need to distinguish between the concrete case, namely the organism, and the thing it was a case of, namely a "system," became increasingly evident to functional theorists.

Yet in one sense the organismic theorists were correct. That is, if social behavior is to be understood by application of system models, a generalized concept of a system alone is insufficient. For there is always a question of the *kind* of system model that shall be employed in the understanding of social behavior. There are at least two ways of approaching this problem. One is the strategy of the organismic theorists, namely to take a concrete case of a system and use it as a guide. But even this is ambiguous because biological organisms vary enormously and there remains the difficult problem of stipulating *which* organism is to be used as a model. A second route, to be followed here, is to make explicit the most generalized dimensions in terms of which systems, formally construed, may vary and then to stipulate the conjunction of formal system dimensions which are to be applied to social behavior.

From a sociologist's standpoint, the two most important aspects of a "system" are the "interdependence" of a number of "parts" and the tendency of these to maintain an "equilibrium" in their relationships. Consequently, much of system analysis and functional theory resolves itself into questions about "interdependence" and "equilibrium." As shall be indicated later, equilibrium necessarily implies interdependence, but interdependence does not necessarily imply equilibrium. Agreeing with Parsons that "the most general and fundamental property of a system is the interdependence of parts or variables," this paper shall therefore focus on the concept of interdependence, leaving the equilibrium problem for later analysis.[2]

There is another problem to be considered here. It is implicit in the

---

[1] Many of the early users of the organismic analogy were well aware of its difficulties and by no means deluded themselves into believing that society *was* an organism. Indeed, some of the classic organismic theorists were far more methodologically astute than some who reject the organismic analogy with the banal and irrelevant criticism that it does not seem intuitively fitting. For a methodologically wise use of the organismic analogy see A. R. Radcliffe-Brown, *Structure and Function in Primitive Society* (Glencoe, Ill.: Free Press, 1952), ch. IX.

[2] For a tentative and partial statement of my views on the problematics of the equilibrium model see A. W. Gouldner, "Some Observations on Systematic Theory, 1945–1955," in H. L. Zetterberg, ed., *Sociology in the United States of America* (Paris: UNESCO, 1956), pp. 34–42.

concept of system, and becomes manifest as soon as an effort is made to apply it to any given subject matter. This is the problem of identifying the interdependent parts. That is, what elements shall be held to constitute the system and on what grounds shall a decision be made to include certain elements in the system?

System Models in Merton and Parsons

It has been suggested above that system analysis is central to sociological functionalism. This will be documented by examination of the two leading American contributors to functional theory in sociology, Robert K. Merton and Talcott Parsons. As shall be seen, system concepts play a pivotal role in both their formulations of functional theory. It will also be noted, however, that the nature of their commitment to a system model differs, Parsons' being what may be called a total commitment, while Merton's can be regarded as a strategy of minimal commitment.

With characteristic cogency, Robert Merton has stated his conception of the "central orientation of functionalism." This he finds is "expressed in the practice of interpreting data by establishing their consequences for larger structures in which they are implicated. . . ." [3] It is instructive to contrast this with the more extended formulation by Talcott Parsons: "The most essential condition of successful dynamic analysis is continual and systematic reference of every problem to the state of the system as a whole. . . . Functional significance in this context is inherently teleological. A process or set of conditions either 'contributes' to the maintenance (or development) of the system or it is 'dysfunctional' in that it detracts from the integration and effectiveness of the system. It is thus the functional reference of all particular conditions and processes to the state of the total system as a going concern which provides the logical equivalent of simultaneous equations in a fully developed system of analytical theory." [4]

Without doubt, there is substantial convergence in these two statements concerning the fundamentals of functional analysis. Both Merton and Parsons agree that in accounting for any social or cultural pattern an effort must be made to relate this to the context in which it occurs, so that it may not be understood in isolation but must be analyzed in its relation to other

---

[3] R. K. Merton, *Social Theory and Social Structure* (Glencoe, Ill.: Free Press, rev. ed., 1957), pp. 46–47.

[4] T. Parsons, *Essays in Sociological Theory Pure and Applied* (Glencoe, Ill.: Free Press, 1949), p. 21.

patterns. In short, both postulate a system model that is dealing with social and cultural phenomena.

There is, however, a notable difference in emphasis in Merton's and Parsons' formulations. This is expressed in Parsons' stress on the notion of a "system" while Merton persistently avoids explicit use of this concept. In fact, there is but one reference to it in the index to Merton's volume on *Social Theory and Social Structure*. More importantly, Merton's avoidance of the system concept is above all suggested by the architecture of his basic paradigm of functional analysis.[5] This does not begin with an analysis of "social systems," but, rather, with a directive to identify the "units" which are problematic in any given case. For Merton, the first step in functional analysis involves stipulation of "some standardized (i.e., patterned and repetitive) item, such as social roles, institutional patterns, social processes, cultural patterns, ..." [6] In brief, for Merton functional analysis is focused on some delimited unit of human behavior or belief, with a view to accounting either for its persistence or change by establishing its consequences for environing social or cultural structures.

System analysis could have entered into Merton's directives for functional analysis in at least two major ways: either by treating the structural context to which the unit is linked as a system, and/or by analyzing the unit itself as a subsystem composed of interdependent parts. Neither of these courses is explicitly stressed in Merton's formulations.

When Merton does take up the structural context in his paradigm, his comments are primarily devoted to a consideration of the ways in which this context generates constraints, limiting the range of variation in the problematic pattern with which the functional analyst is directed to begin. He does indicate that social structures are composed of interdependent elements, and to this extent acknowledges their systemic character, but this never becomes an object of formal analysis.

Furthermore, the problematic unit pattern with which Merton's paradigm of functional analysis begins is not itself explicitly identified as subject to system analysis. In the operational protocols which follow the paradigm, Merton states that the unit pattern on which the analysis focuses must be seen as implicated in the behavior of people who are differently located in the larger social structure. He indicates also that it is necessary to locate "these people in their inter-connected social statuses." The emphasis here, however, seems to involve a structural location of the component elements rather than a focus on the systemic character of the structure itself.

For example, Merton does not require that the problematic unit be

---

[5] Merton, *ibid.*, p. 50 *et seq.*
[6] Merton, *ibid.*, p. 50.

related to any postulated "need" of the contextual structure *as a system.* Indeed, while Merton concedes that "in every functional analysis [there] is some conception of the functional requirements of the system under observation," he goes on to insist that the notion of functional requirements or needs of the social system "remains one of the cloudiest and empirically most debatable concepts in functional theory." [7]

For Parsons the central theoretical and empirical problems are those which involve a social system as such, and which explain how it is maintained as a going system. Empirically delimitable units become important for him primarily as they enter into the maintenance of the social system, in the satisfaction of its needs, or in their resolution of its problems. In contrast to Merton, Parsons does not focus on the explanation of empirically delimited units of social behavior or belief, but instead centers attention directly on analysis of the contextual structure as a system.

The Selection of System Parts

Parsons' assumption is that it is impossible to understand adequately any single pattern except by referring it to some larger systemic whole. He therefore assumes that the *whole* system must be conceptually constituted prior to the investigation and analysis of specific patterns. In consequence, Parsons is led forthwith to the analysis of the *total* anatomy of social systems in an effort to identify their constituent elements and relationships. This presumably makes it possible to refer any given problematic pattern in a systematic manner to all the component structures constituting the system. The theoretical strategy here requires that all the constituents of the whole system be *immediately* constituted in an *ex cathedra* manner.

But whether or not a given structure in the social anatomy is in fact there, or whether it is useful to postulate it, is an important part resolvable only by empirical research. The specification of the component elements of social systems is, in principle, no more attainable by theoretical postulation alone than are the attributes of "living" systems, which the biologist regards as the systems with which his discipline deals. What seems to have been neglected is that the elements of social systems cannot be merely constituted *a priori,* but must also be inductively sought and empirically validated.

It is in large measure because of their differing orientations to the role of empirical operations not in science in general, but in theory construction in particular, that Parsons and Merton differ in this regard. That is, part of the problem here is how one identifies and provides a warrant for the elements

---

[7] Merton, *ibid.,* p. 52.

held to be constitutive of a social system. In large measure, Merton differs from Parsons because he feels that *empirical* operations are necessarily involved in the very admission of elements as part of a social system. He does not regard this problem as solely resolvable by theoretical postulation. Although he has not committed himself on this specific point in any extended manner, Merton's emphasis on theories of the "middle range," which he counterposes to Parsons' stress on systematic, all-encompassing theories,[8] indicates that he takes a much more empirical and heuristic approach to the process of constituting a social system.

Pursuing Merton's strategy of middle-range theories, no commitment would be made to any variable which could not pay its way empirically. The expectation is that cumulative research would, through successive approximations, sift out a battery of explanatory variables and establish their interrelations.[9] This is by no means a new species of empiricism, nor a new espousal of the prerogatives of research against those of theory. It is simply an insistence that theoretical considerations alone cannot provide scientifically legitimate grounds for the admission of elements to a social system.

Objection may be lodged against this approach on the grounds that, not having staked out in advance *all* the constituent elements of the social system, the problematic pattern cannot then be related to the system as a whole. The procedure can therefore yield only incomplete explanations of any particular pattern. This is quite true, but it is an objection just as applicable to Parsons' strategy. For although Parsons takes cognizance of the "total" social system, this is by no means a closed and complete system, but an open and partial one. Many of the things accounting for variance in particular patterns of social behavior will, also, fall outside of its jurisdiction and it, too, can account for no more than part of the variance.

The basic gain of the Mertonian strategy is that it prevents either premature commitment to, or premature exclusion of, any given structure as an element in the social system. The latter, the exclusion of structures from the social system, is as vital a decision as that of inclusion, and would seem no more susceptible to a purely theoretical resolution.

As Parsons formulates his conception of the social system, elements in the biological constitution and physiological functioning of man, as well as

---

[8] Merton, *ibid.*, p. 4 *et seq.*

[9] Cf. Merton's critical appreciation of the method of "successive approximations" in P. F. Lazarsfeld and R. K. Merton, "Friendship as Social Process," in M. Berger, T. Abel, and C. H. Page, eds., *Freedom and Control in Modern Society* (New York: D. Van Nostrand Company, Inc., 1954), pp. 60–62. Contrast this with Parsons' statement that, "In a system of interdependent variables . . . the value of any one variable is not *completely* determined unless those of *all* the others are known." T. Parsons, *The Structure of Social Action* (New York: McGraw-Hill Book Company, Inc., 1937), p. 25. (Our emphases—A.W.G.)

features of the physical and ecological environment, are excluded. So, too, seems to be the historically developing cultural complexes of material arti-facts. To a Malinowski it might well seem that this is a form of academic monasticism in which men are cleansed of their baser passions for sex, food, and material possessions by theoretical purification.

Among other tendencies, Parsons' theory of the social system leads research attention away from *systematic* efforts to develop and validate generalized propositions concerning the manner in which ecological and other properties of the physical environment of groups structure patterns of social organization. In exiling these from the social system, Parsons at best derives a purely formal advantage, namely that of establishing a distinct class of systems which may form the object of an independent social science. But in doing this he fails to make a systematic place for numerous cogent researches which, if lacking in formal elegance in this sense, do illuminate the important ways in which social behavior is structured by ecological forces. To constitute the social system thusly may well accomplish the objective of establishing a charter for an independent social science. But it may be a Pyhrric victory bought at the cost of a scientific ritualism, where logical elegance is substituted for empirical potency.

The systematic omission of such ecological forces from models which seek to account for variance in social and cultural behavior would, moreover, seem to have varying degrees of appropriateness, depending on the society under study. Evans-Pritchard's[10] and Steward's[11] studies of primitive groups clearly demonstrate the potency of ecological forces in shaping social organ-ization in folk societies. In societies with advanced technologies and urban centers, however, these forces are patently less powerful in structuring social behavior. Thus Parsons' model of a social system may have an *unequal* capacity to account for variance in social behavior in different social systems. It may, because of its exclusion of ecological elements, be a more powerful tool in dealing with industrially advanced urban societies than with "under-developed" primitive groups which have much less control over nature.

While it is for this reason tempting to think of Parsons' model as essen-tially one of an industrially developed social system, we cannot do so because no systematic provision is made for some of the very elements which charac-terize these. In particular, Parsons' model of the social system excludes all "material" elements, including tools and machines. This would seem dubious on several interlocking grounds: First, precisely because these are man's own unique and distinctive creations, the very products of his social interaction.

---

10 E. E. Evans-Pritchard, *The Nuer* (Oxford: Clarendon Press, 1940).
11 J. H. Steward, *Theory of Culture Change* (Urbana: University of Illinois Press, 1955), especially chs. 6–10.

Secondly, because they enter intimately as mediating instruments of communication and hence of symbolic social interaction. Thirdly, because they are also instruments of transportation, often making possible the very interchanges among social parts which enable them to establish interdependences. Fourth and last, because modern electronic and cybernetic devices have developed to the point where the distinction between human thinking and machine operation is no longer so radical as was assumed in the organismic tradition from which functionalism grew.[12]

The line between the interaction of man with man, on the one side, and the interaction of men with machines, on the other, has begun to grow wavery. Parsons holds that "a social system consists of a plurality of individual actors, interacting with each other in a situation . . . and whose relations . . . [are] defined and mediated in terms of a system of culturally structured and shared symbols."[13] If this is so, then it may well be that modern machinery qualifies, not simply as the environment in which social interaction occurs, but as a *party* to the interaction itself, as a member of the social system, as well as a cultural artifact which, like shared symbols, mediates communication.

Here again it is necessary to insist that the matter cannot be decided by *a priori* postulation alone. Whether we want to constitute a model of the social system as a man-made system or, instead, as a men-machine system, depends in important part on the empirical consequences stemming from the inclusion or exclusion of machines. Internal consistency and parsimony, such as they are in modern social theory, are necessary but not sufficient criteria of the postulate sets of an empirical sociology. One might well remember Ruskin's sarcasms about a fictitious science of gymnastics which postulated that men had no skeletons.

In one respect, Parsons' work manifests a fairly widespread tendency among sociologists, namely an inclination to rest content with a demonstration that some sociological variable "makes a difference." If a variable can be shown to control even the smallest proportion of variance in a problematic pattern it is all too readily regarded as a memorable contribution to sociology and all too ceremoniously ushered into its theoretical hall of fame. It is surely no treason to theory to suggest that, in the last analysis, not only empirical researches in general, but mathematical ones in particular, will have a voice

---

[12] Among a spate of recent literature on this see W. R. Ashby, *Design for a Brain* (New York: John Wiley and Sons, Inc., 1952); N. Wiener, *Cybernetics* (New York: John Wiley and Sons, Inc., 1948); L. A. Jefress, ed., *Cerebral Mechanisms in Behavior* (New York: John Wiley and Sons, Inc., 1951); H. Von Foerster, ed., *Cybernetics, Transactions of the 6th, 7th, and 8th Conferences* (New York: Josiah Macy, Jr., Foundation, 1950, 1951, 1952); perhaps the most cogent popular account is that of W. Sluckin, *Minds and Machines* (London: Penguin Books, Inc., 1954).

[13] T. Parsons, *The Social System* (Glencoe, Ill.: Free Press, 1951), pp. 5–6.

in legitimating conceptual innovation. For unless sustained interest is manifested in the *degree* of variance which a variable controls, and, unless, further, we can identify sociological variables that certifiably control *substantial* proportions of variance in specified patterns of human behavior, sociology will remain scientifically immature and practically ineffectual.

The Principle of Functional Reciprocity

It would seem clear from the foregoing that the ways in which Merton and Parsons seek to apply the notion of a "system" to sociological analysis differs and, particularly so, with reference to the manner in which constituents shall be identified and admitted to or excluded from the system. Yet it needs to be stressed that this involves no necessary difference in principle with respect to the strategic place of the concept of a system, especially as an *explanatory* tool.

This can be documented by reference to Merton's analysis of the latent functions of political machines in the United States.[14] He opens this by inquiring how it is that political machines manage to continue operating, despite the fact that they frequently run counter to both the mores and the law. In the more generalized terms of his paradigm of functional analysis, Merton begins by identifying a social pattern, the political machine, and seeks to explain its persistence by establishing its consequences for the larger social structures in which it is implicated. The *general* form of his explanation of the persistence of the political machine is to demonstrate that it performs "positive functions which are at the same time not adequately fulfilled by other existing patterns and structures." [15]

Among these are (1) the organization and centralization of power so that it can be mobilized to "satisfy the needs of diverse subgroups in the larger community. . . ," (2) including personalized forms of assistance—jobs, legal aid, foodbaskets, for deprived, lower-class groups, (3) political privileges and aid to business groups, (4) channels of social mobility for disadvantaged groups in the society, and (5) "protection" for illicit rackets.

Now insofar as the objective of the above analysis was to provide an *explanation of the persistence* of the political machine, then the mere establishment of the consequences of the machine for the larger structures in which it is involved provides only a partial and one-sided answer. The explanation is incomplete insofar as the analyst has not explicitly traced the manner in which the groups or structures, whose needs have been satisfied, in

---

14 Merton, *ibid.*, p. 71 *et seq.*
15 Merton, *ibid.*, p. 73.

turn "reciprocate" and repay the political machine for the gains it provides them. In this particular case, the patterns of reciprocity are so largely evident and well documented that it would be belaboring the obvious to dwell upon them, and were perhaps for this reason omitted. The reciprocities involved are all too clearly implied in the notion of the "corruption" of the machine.

Ordinarily, however, the formal adequacy of a functional *explanation* of the persistence of a social pattern would seem to require that the analyst demonstrate not merely the consequences of *A* for *B*, but, also, the reciprocal consequences of *B* for *A*. The only logically stable terminal point for a functional analysis is not the demonstration of a social pattern's function for others, but the demonstration of the latter's reciprocal functionality for the problematic social pattern.

In short, functional analysis premises the operation of a "principle of functional reciprocity," a principle variously employed by Marx,[16] by Mauss,[17] by Malinowski,[18] by Lévi-Strauss,[19] and by Homans[20] in different

---

[16] The principle of reciprocity enters Marx's theoretical analysis not in peripheral but in central ways; it is most importantly implicated in his concept of "exploitation"; this is rendered technically specific in the manner of nineteenth century political economy in his analysis of "surplus value." If one puts aside Marx's moral condemnations of exploitation and considers only its sociological substance, it is clear that it refers to a breakdown in reciprocal functionality. It is a basic implication of Marx's analysis that exploitation in class societies induces social instabilities. Characteristically, however, Marx is interested in the sources of instabilty and change and thus focuses on the contrary of functional reciprocity. Marx is also concerned to analyze the compensatory mechanisms in modern society which conceal the breakdown in functional reciprocity and, in this connection, his concept of "fetishism" is clearly relevant. See especially K. Marx, *Capital*, vol. I, tr. by Eden and Cedar Paul (New York: E. P. Dutton and Co., Inc., 1930), pp. 43–59.

[17] See M. Mauss, *The Gift* (Glencoe, Ill.: Free Press, 1954). Mauss stresses that there is a universally recognized obligation to reciprocate gifts which have been accepted. In his last chapter, Mauss also seems to be verging on a concept of "exploitation" when he comments that people have "a strong desire to pursue the thing they have produced once they realize that they have given their labour without sharing in the profit." P. 64.

[18] This comes out most clearly in Malinowski's discussion of Trobriand society concerning which he remarks that its whole structure is arranged into "well-balanced chains of reciprocal services." Discussing the exchanges between the coastal fisherman and the inland gardeners, of fish and vegetables, respectively, he notes that such *reciprocity is a mechanism which underlies and induces conformity with the obligations they have to each other*. B. Malinowski, *Crime and Custom* (London: Paul, Trench, Trubner, 1926), pp. 46, 23 *et seq*. There is no doubt that Radcliffe-Brown also assumed a principle of reciprocity which he called "the principle of equivalent return." This he held was expressed in the *lex talionis*, in the principle of indemnification for injury, and in the principle that those who give benefits should receive equivalent benefits. From his Chicago University seminar, "The Nature of a Theoretical Natural Science of Society," 1937.

[19] C. Lévi-Strauss, *Les Structures élémentaires de la parenté* (Paris: Presses Universitaires, 1949). In this volume, which owes so much to Mauss and Durkheim, Lévi-Strauss presents his now near-classic theory of the "exchange" of women.

[20] G. C. Homans and D. M. Schneider, *Marriage, Authority, and Final Causes*

empirical contexts. This underlying functionalist assumption might just as well be made explicit and could be stated in the following generalized form: (1) Any one structure is more likely to persist if it is engaged in reciprocally functional interchanges with some others; (1.1) the less reciprocal the functional interchange between structures, the less likely is either structure, or the patterned relation between them, to persist—(1.2) *unless compensatory mechanisms are present.*

Essentially, the principle of reciprocity implies a system of interdependent parts engaged in mutual interchanges. It is in this sense that the notion of a system is necessarily involved in Merton's analysis of the political machine as, we think, it must be in any functional analysis.

It needs to be stressed, however, that "mutual interchange" does not necessarily imply that the relations among parts of a social system are invariably those of symmetrical functional reciprocity. It does, however, imply either that such functional reciprocity exists, or that there has developed some compensatory mechanism for coping with the lack of or breakdown in it. It is, we suspect, precisely because Merton saw that the relations between parts were not invariably those of symmetrical functional reciprocity that he did not commit himself to a generalized principle of reciprocity. Nonetheless, it is implied by his analysis. It is only by chancing an explicit formulation of the assumption and laying it open to critical examination, that it can be tempered and refined, or invalidated and rejected.

There is something of a tactical dilemma here which needs to be resolved. It seems evident, on the one hand, that to cease analysis before attempting to *establish empirically* the reciprocal functionality of B for A, and to explain the persistence of A by demonstrating its functions for B, is to substitute postulation for research. On the other hand, there are substantial empirical grounds for rejecting an unqualified principle of reciprocity. For this would involve the dubious assumption that structures which derive gains from others are invariably "grateful" and that power-constrained services, with little or no reciprocity, are not merely unstable but totally impossible.

An unqualified principle of reciprocity diverts attention from the specific social or cultural mechanisms which may compensate for the lack of functional reciprocity. Among such compensatory mechanisms may be culturally shared prescriptions of unconstrained "generosity" such as the Christian notion of "turning the other cheek," the feudal concept of *noblesse*

(Glencoe, Ill.: Free Press, 1955). This represents a criticism of particulars of Lévi-Strauss's theory. Homans' forthcoming work on a systematic theory of "exchange" is also fundamentally based on the principle of reciprocity.

oblige, or the Roman notion of "clemency."[21] There may also be cultural prohibitions banning the examination of certain interchanges from the standpoint of their reciprocity, such as the sociologically wise cliché, "It's not the gift but the sentiment that counts." Again, power arrangements may serve to compel continuances of services for which there is little functional reciprocity. Although these may be expected, from the present standpoint, to be less stable than those where functional reciprocity motivates continued performances, they are certainly not for that reason sociologically unimportant.

Another arrangement which may serve to prevent or control failures in functional reciprocity is the mutual sharing of structures *A* and *B*, of some third structure *C*. To use Lévi-Strauss' terminology[22] in a broader sense, we would say that a situation of "generalized interchange"—where *A* supplies *B*'s needs, *B* supplies *C*'s, and *C* supplies *A*'s needs—may be more stable than that of a "restricted interchange" between *A* and *B* alone. This case is relevant to Parsons' discussion of the basic equilibrium model of the social system. The minimal social system, comprised of two role players, Ego and Alter, is postulated by Parsons to be in equilibrium when each conforms to the other's expectation and is rewarded by him for such compliant behavior. It is clear, first, that this model implicitly utilizes the principle of reciprocity and may be regarded as a special case of it. More to the point here, however, note that Ego may in fact continue to comply with Alter's expectations, not because Alter reciprocates or rewards such compliances, but because Ego's compliances are expected and rewarded by a third role player. In short, the system may be maintained, and guarded against defaults in functional reciprocity, through the intervention of "third" structures which perform what may be termed a "policing" function.

It is impossible to do justice here to the question of whether this implies that the minimal model of a social system should be constituted of three rather than two role players. As a conservative inference from the foregoing, however, it would seem that an important focus of functional analysis couched in role terms should be centered on the stabilizing activities of such "third parties" as the witness, *amicus curiae,* police, friend of the family, arbitrators, or ritual adjudicators such as "old men of the earth."[23] In complex social systems it may be expected that such third party roles will be structurally specialized and differentiated from others; in simpler

---

[21] For a discussion of such a mechanism in a modern industrial setting, see the analysis of the "indulgency pattern" in A. W. Gouldner, *Wildcat Strike* (Yellow Springs, Ohio: Antioch Press, 1954), pp. 18–26.

[22] Lévi-Strauss, *ibid.,* p. 548.

[23] See the discussion in Max Gluckman, *Custom and Conflict in Africa* (Glencoe, Ill.: Free Press, 1955).

social systems it may be that such policing functions will be conjoined with others.

It is clear from all this, then, that in explaining any social pattern it cannot be merely assumed that functional reciprocity will operate in any given case, but it is necessary to establish empirically its occurrence. Failing in this, it is necessary to search out compensatory arrangements which provide a functional substitute for reciprocity.

There are important connections between the principle of functional reciprocity and the older anthropological concept of a vestigial "survival." A social pattern was commonly regarded as a "survival" if it could not be established that it made any contributions to the adaptation of a going system in which it was *presently* implicated. The polemical opposition of the earlier functionalists to this concept logically rested on the tacit assumption of an *unqualified* principle of reciprocity. That is, they premised that a structure which persisted was obviously securing satisfaction of its needs from others, and, if it continues to receive these, this can only be because this structure somehow reciprocally contributed to the others' adaptation. The anthropological functionalist was therefore enjoined to exercise his ingenuity to search out what were, in effect, hidden reciprocities.

The early functionalists' polemical opposition to the notion of a survival, however, tended to obscure the significance of varying *degrees* of functional reciprocity, and to neglect the mechanisms which might control the instabilities resulting from a breakdown in functional reciprocity. The early functionalist neglected the fact that a "survival" was simply a limiting case of a larger class of phenomena, much deserving of study, namely, relations between structures in which there is little functional reciprocity. Essentially, the early functionalists' opposition to the concept of a "survival" now has unwarranted survival in the neglect of the problem of asymmetrical patterns of functional reciprocity.

Interdependence as Problematic

It is one of the central implications of these comments that the notion of interdependence, so crucial to the concept of a system, needs to be taken as problematic rather than as given, if a system model adequate to the analysis of social behavior is to be developed. One of the reasons why this has not been systematically done in Parsons' analysis is related to the distinction which he makes between a "theoretical" and an "empirical" system. The former refers to a logically interrelated conceptual scheme or a set of propositions. An empirical system, on the other hand, "has to do with the criteria for coherence and harmony to be applied to some specific body of subject matter."[24]

There are, it would seem, two meanings which might be attributed to Parsons' use of the term "empirical system." One is that it unwittingly retains vestiges of eighteenth century usage, referring to a "natural" system which is somehow there "in itself" in a realistic sense, that is, apart from any particular conceptualization. Despite the fact that this would be radically at variance with Parsons' methodological position, which is predominantly constructionist, there are uneasy moments when a reader may feel that such an inference is not altogether outlandish. Insofar, however, as an "empirical system" is held to consist of "criteria" to be applied to some subject matter, it is clear that the empirical system cannot be the referent of the theory, but must instead be a set of assumptions in terms of which these referents are to be studied.

A second and by far the most acceptable interpretation, therefore, is that what Parsons means by an "empirical system" is, perversely enough, what philosophers of science commonly term a "formal system." Purely formal systems, as in mathematics and logic, are those devoid of any kind of empirical content, and this is much the way in which Parsons uses the notion of an empirical system. When a formal system is applied to a specific subject matter it is said to be "interpreted"; some formal systems have many interpretations, others have none. The nub of the issue here is the nature of the interpretation to be given to the formal and empty notion of a "system" when it is applied to human relations. In order for a formal system to be successfully applied, it would seem necessary that the interpretation to which it is subjected be explicitly examined.

The significant point, however, is that the notion of a theoretical system denotes what Parsons regards as analytically problematical, while the formal concept of an "empirical system," is largely unexplored or taken simply as setting the terms within which the theoretical system must develop. As a result of this, the notion of "empirical system" does not become systematically problematic for Parsons, and he fails to explore the alternative interpretations which are possible even within such a commitment.

We, on the contrary, would stress that even on a formal level of system analysis, there are different elements involved in the conception of an "empirical system" and, combined or interpreted differently, they may constitute different types of empirical systems.[25] It is therefore necessary to

---

[24] T. Parsons and E. A. Shils, eds., *Toward a General Theory of Action* (Cambridge: Harvard University Press, 1951), p. 49.

[25] For systematic efforts pointing in this direction see J. Feibleman and J. W. Friend,

choose among competing formal models and to identify those that constitute a better "fit" for the known, relevant data.

As mentioned above, the two key elements involved in the concept of system are first, "interdependence," and secondly, "self-maintenance" or equilibrium. It makes a good deal of difference whether interdependence and equilibrium are treated as undifferentiated attributes, or whether they are viewed as dimensions capable of significant variation in degree.

Unless the latter procedure is followed and unless, further, it is clearly seen that interdependence and equilibrium are not synonymous terms but are independently variable, then there is a compelling tendency to by-pass the possibility that there are significantly different types of empirical systems even on the most formal level of analysis. Mere use of the concept of an empirical system is much as if a mathematical physicist were to commit himself only to the use of "geometry" in general, without stipulating the specific system of geometry he proposes to employ in solving his particular problems.

Viewed in Parsons' way,[26] the concept of an empirical system is essentially an "ideal type" and is subject to the liabilities inherent in all such concepts. That is, it obscures the underlying continua involved in its constituents, and focuses attention on particular, and especially extreme, values of the dimensions. To speak of systems as characterized by an interdependence of parts and their equilibrium tends to obscure the fact that these are things which can vary in degree. Moreover, it tends to create a presumption that they universally covary in the same direction.

One may find, however, a conjunction of low interdependence with high equilibrium, where the low interdependence permits a localized absorption of externally induced trauma, thus guarding the remainder of the system elements from ramifying damage. It is this kind of a conjunction which would seem to be implied in the notion of "insulation," which Parsons, along with other functionalists, regards as a "defense mechanism" of social systems. In brief, the lowering of the degree of interdependence may contribute to an increase in the degree of equilibrium, or in restoring it to a higher level.

Conversely, an instance of a conjunction of high interdependence and low equilibrium would seem to be implied in the notion of a "vicious cycle."

"The Structure and Function of Organization," *Philosophical Review*, 54 (Jan., 1945), pp. 19–44, and A. Angyal, "The Structure of Wholes," *Philosophy of Science*, 6 (Jan., 1939), pp. 25–37.

[26] Cf. Parsons and Shils, *ibid.*, p. 107. "The most general and fundamental property of a system is the interdependence of parts or variables. . . . This order must have a tendency to self-maintenance, which is very generally expressed in the concept of equilibrium. . . ."

Here, the very interdependence of elements enables negative feedback cycles to develop with cumulative impairment of the system's equilibrium. From these considerations it seems clear that equilibrium and interdependence may vary independently and, consequently, conjunctions of different values of these two variables may be postulated concerning the character of social systems.

Functional Autonomy and Degrees of Interdependence

A crucial assumption of the analysis here is that there are *varying degrees* of interdependence which may be postulated to exist among the parts of a system. At one extreme, each element may be involved in a mutual interchange with all others; at the opposite extreme, each element may be involved in mutual interchanges with only one other.[27] The former may be regarded as defining maximal interdependence and "systemness," the latter as defining minimal interdependence or "systemness."

Still another way of viewing interdependence is from the standpoint of the parts' dependence upon the system. The parts may have varying amounts of their needs satisfied by, and thus varying degrees of dependence upon, other system elements. A number of parts which are engaged in mutual interchanges may, at one extreme, all be totally dependent on each other for the satisfaction of their needs. In this case the *system* they comprise can be said to be "highly" interdependent, while these *parts* can be said to possess "low" functional autonomy. Conversely, a system may be composed of parts all of which derive but little satisfaction of their needs from each other; here the system would be minimally interdependent and the parts would be high on functional autonomy. Operationally speaking, we might say that the functional autonomy of a system part is the probability that it can survive separation from the system.

A conceptualization of "systemness" in terms of functional autonomy has been suggested here because the notion of mutual interdependence commonly used in definitions of systems tends toward a focus primarily on the "whole" or on the relations between parts, and on their functionally reciprocated need for each other. "Functional autonomy," however, focuses on the *parts*, albeit in their relation to each other; it directs attention to the possibility that any part may have little, as well as great, need for another, and that the mutual need of parts need not be symmetrical. In short, it

---

[27] For an excellent discussion of this by a sociologist see G. Shapiro, *The Formulation and Verification of a Theory of Primary Social Integration*, unpublished doctoral dissertation, Cornell University, 1954, especially ch. 2.

focuses attention on interchanges where functional reciprocity may not be symmetrical, and thus directs analysis to tension-producing relationships.

In these terms, the question becomes, "What can be predicated about the functional autonomy of the parts of social systems, and in what ways does the problem of the functional autonomy of the parts enter into the analysis of social systems?" In the following comments, which explore several of these implications, it will be emphasized that the problem of functional autonomy is of considerable significance for the analysis of tension within social systems, and thus for the analysis of social change.

Functional Autonomy and System Tension

To the degree that parts possess some measure of functional autonomy, they must be expected to seek to maintain this. In short, the equilibrium assumptions, applied to a social system as a whole, would seem equally applicable in principle to its parts. Thus, the parts of a social system should be expected to "maintain their boundaries." It must then be assumed that parts with some degree of functional autonomy will resist full or complete integration into the larger system. Conversely, the system itself, straining toward integration, can be expected to seek submission of the parts to the requirements of the position they occupy. Consequently, there may be some tension between the part's tendency to maintain an existent degree of functional autonomy and the system's pressure to control the part.

It would seem that this or some similar model underlies various theories, such as the Freudian, which postulate an endemic conflict between the individual and the society or group. Essentially, these have been answered by formulations counterstressing the malleability of the individual organism, the potency of the socialization process, and the inability of the organism to become a full "human being" apart from society.

Actually, however, the very malleability of the organism which makes it susceptible to socialization by one social system also allows it to be resocialized by another; its malleability is thus actually a condition of its functional autonomy. Furthermore, the relevant question here is the ability of the already socialized individual to remain such after separation from any given social system, not merely to become such without involvement in some society.

More pointedly, it would seem that, once socialized, many individuals do have a capacity to generate an "escape velocity"; and that human beings are not invariably characterized by a total dependence upon any one social system.[28] *Socialized* individuals have some measure of mobility, vertical and horizontal, among the social systems within their society, moving with varying degrees of ease or stress from one to another. They may and do also migrate to, or sojourn in, societies different from those in which they were originally socialized. They have, in our terms, considerable, if varying, degrees of functional autonomy in relation to any given social system. Consequently, if we think of the "socialized individual" as in some sense a "part," and not merely as the raw material, of social systems, it would seem necessary to eschew models which overstress the interdependence of the parts and to select those which systematically include concern with their functional autonomy. To fit the data of social behavior, the system model required must be such as to facilitate not only the analysis of the interdependence of the system as a whole, but also the analysis of the functional autonomy of its parts, and the concrete strains which efforts to maintain this autonomy may induce.

Two lines of sociological analysis which have recently been developed are highly relevant to these assumptions about functional autonomy. One stems from the study of occupations made by E. C. Hughes and his students, in which the repeated observation of diverse occupations—both noble and profane—indicates that their occupants typically strive to maintain a degree of functional autonomy. As Hughes puts it, they seek to maintain a degree of social distance or freedom, not merely from all in the same social system in which they operate but, most particularly, "from those people most crucially concerned with [their] work."[29]

A second and more generalized direction from which the problem of functional autonomy has been approached in sociological terms is that developed by Erving Goffman. Utilizing materials from his study of a mental hospital, Goffman distinguishes between two types of deference behavior, that is, the expression of appreciation of one person to and for another. One type, "avoidance rituals," refers to those forms of deference stipulating what one may *not* do to another, and which leads actors to maintain social distance from each other. The second, "presentational rituals," specify what *is* to be done and involve expressions of positive appreciation and regard. Goffman sums up his analysis as follows:

---

[28] In this connection, the significance of Asch's experiments on the effects of group influence on perception would not only be that some 33 per cent of his subjects distorted their perception to conform with the pressures of others in their group, but also that 67 per cent of them did *not* do so. See S. E. Asch, *Social Psychology* (New York: Prentice-Hall, Inc., 1952), ch. 16.

[29] E. C. Hughes, "Work and the Self," in J. H. Rohrer and M. Sherif, eds., *Social Psychology at the Crossroads* (New York: Harper and Brothers, 1951), p. 322.

I have mentioned four very common forms of presentational deference: salutations, invitations, compliments, and minor services. Through all of these the recipient is told that he is not an island unto himself and that others are, or seek to be, involved with him and with his personal concerns . . . avoidance rituals, taking the form of proscriptions, interdictions, and taboos . . . imply acts the actor must refrain from lest he violate the right of the recipient to keep him at a distance. . . .

In suggesting that there are things which must be said and done to a recipient, and things that must not be said and done, it should be plain that there is an inherent opposition and conflict between these two forms of deference. . . . There is an inescapable opposition between showing a desire to include an individual and showing respect for his privacy. As an implication of this dilemma, we must see that social intercourse involves a constant dialectic between presentational rituals and avoidance rituals. A peculiar tension must be maintained for these opposing requirements of conduct must somehow be held apart from one another and yet realized together in the same interaction ; the gestures which carry an actor to a recipient must also signify that things will not be carried too far.[30]

It would seem that a system model which focused solely on the "wholeness" of the system and neglected the functional autonomy of the parts would be unable to fit the kind of data obtained in either Hughes's or Goffman's researches. Nor, above all, would it systematically cue the analyst to the tensions which result in social systems by virtue of the parts' strain toward functional autonomy, or to the analysis of the ways in which they maintain their functional autonomy. From the standpoint of the kind of system model which Parsons favors, the emphasis on interdependence would conduce to a one-sided focus—in Goffman's terms—on the "presentational rituals." That is, it conduces to a preoccupation with the mechanisms of social integration, and to a neglect of the avoidance rituals which constitute proper ways in which socialized individuals are enabled to resist total inclusion in a social system and total loss of their functional autonomy.

In Parsons' system model, concern is largely focused on the needs of the system as a whole, and the stability of this system is viewed as dependent upon their satisfaction. The implication here, however, is that there is a sense in which the very striving of the system to satisfy its needs may generate tension for it, insofar as this impairs the functional autonomy of the parts. This means that a need of systems, which possess parts having degrees of functional autonomy, is to inhibit its own tendencies to subordinate and fully specialize these parts. In short, it must inhibit its own tendencies toward "wholeness" or complete integration if it is to be stable. The system model thus indicated for the analysis of social behavior is not one in

---

[30] E. Goffman, "The Nature of Deference and Demeanor," *American Anthropologist*, 58 (June, 1956), pp. 486–88

which the system is viewed as a "plunger" playing an all-or-none game, but as a mini-max player seeking to strike a federalizing balance between totalitarian and anarchist limits.[31]

It is commonly assumed that the "organization" of the system, that is, the particular arrangement of its parts, provides primarily for the avenues of integration among them. In our terms, however, "organization" not only serves to link, control, and interrelate parts but also functions to separate them and to maintain and protect their functional autonomy. Organization is seen then as shaped by a conflict, particularly by the tensions between centripetal and centrifugal pressures, as limiting control over parts as well as imposing it, as establishing a balance between their dependence and independence, and as separating as well as connecting the parts.[32]

Social organizations, insofar as they involve role systems, manifest the dualism indicated above. It is of the essence of social roles that they never demand total involvements by the actors, but only segmental and partial involvements. To say that a person is an actor in a social system and that he plays a role there implies, on the one side, that he is subject to some system controls and to the requirements of the role, and that he has obligations to the collectivity of which his role is a part. On the other side, however, it also implies that his obligations to that system are somehow limited. Even when the actor is involved in a primary social system, where the role obligations are diffuse and numerous, he is never exposed to unlimited obligations.

One of the most common ways in which consideration of the functional autonomy of parts has implicitly entered into current sociological analysis has been as an element in the generation of system tension. The drive of the subpart to maintain or to extend its functional autonomy has been frequently understood as a source of tensions for the system. In "organizational analysis," in the technical sociological sense, the tensions between the "field offices" and the "main office," between the various departments within an organization, as well as in the commonly noted oscillation between centralization and decentralization, all imply cognizance of the significance of functional autonomy. Similarly, concern with the development of "organized deviance" and its potentially disruptive impact on the system again token a tacit appreciation of the tension-provoking potential of functionally autonomous parts.

Because parts have or strive to maintain different degrees of functional autonomy, it cannot be assumed that all have an equal role in the generation

---

[31] The philosophic posture here parallels that developed in E. Cassirir, *An Essay on Man* (New Haven: Yale University Press, 1944).

[32] For discussion of some of the problems here from a philosopher's viewpoint see R. B. Winn, "The Nature of Relations," *Philosophical Review*, 50 (Jan., 1941), pp. 20–35.

of tensions for the system. It would seem reasonable to suppose that those parts in a social system with most functional autonomy can more readily become loci of organized deviance and of effective resistance to system controls.

If it is reasonable to assume that some system parts have a greater role as loci of system tension, it would also seem consistent to maintain that not all have an equally deep involvement in the resolution of the tensions of the system, or in the mobilization of defenses against these. That is, those parts with least functional autonomy, those which cannot survive separation from a social system, are more likely to be implicated in its conservation than those which can.

Contrariwise, those with most autonomy are most able to press for or to accept changes, when these are consistent with their own autonomy. For example, it is evident that the eighteenth century French nobility had a greater involvment in the maintenance of the *ancien régime* than did the French *bourgeoisie,* which could and did survive separation from the older social system and acted as a stimulant to its basic reorganization. It would seem, then, to put the matter differently, that not all parts of a system have an equal "vested interest" in its maintenance. The concept of the differential functional autonomy of parts directs attention to the need to distinguish between parts having a greater or lesser vested interest in system maintenance.

The Strategies of Parts and Systems

Among other things, the functional autonomy of a part implies that it is not totally contingent upon the parasystem for the satisfaction of its own needs. There are at least three importantly different strategies with which this situation can be played, from the standpoint of the part. One is the strategy of withdrawal. The part can, so to speak, go into business for itself and resist such a high degree of specialization that it loses power to service its own minimal metabolic needs. A second strategy is to spread its risks, so that its needs may be normally satisfied by a number of systems in which it is involved.

Both of these strategies for the maintenance of the functional autonomy of a part presents difficulties and sources of tension for the parasystem. The functional autonomy of a part, whichever strategy it employs, allows it a degree of refractoriness to the imposition of controls from the system. This may be exemplified by the case of bureaucratic resistance to higher-echelon policy decisions.

A special source of tension derives from the part's involvement in multiple systems. To the degree that two systems share a part then the laws of both will affect the behavior of the part. This means not only that such a functionally autonomous part will be refractory to system steering, but that it will tend to oscillate and initiate changes for either system.

For example, it is not simply that the socialized human being may be refractory to the controls of a social system because he is involved in a biological system and is consequently required to eat, sleep, or breathe. But being involved in a biological system, the human being is also subject to various mundane liabilities such as illness, injury, and death. These are far from entirely governed by the laws of any social system and thus their occurrence is random relative to the functioning of social systems. Although social systems may develop mechanisms for cushioning their effects, for example, through "understudies" or prescribed rules of succession,[33] these effects must always, in some measure, be actively disruptive to the social systems, even if only to the personalized relations within them.

While we have here stressed the sharing of a part between a social and a biological system, the point is much the same in the case of parts shared between two or more social systems. The shared parts are more likely to engage in oscillations disruptive to one or both systems. In sociological analysis, this has been recognized in the concern with multiple role involvements in general, and "cross-pressure" situations in particular.

There is a third strategy which a functionally autonomous part may adopt, in addition to withdrawal and spreading the risk. That is, it may undertake a reorganization of the entire system in which it finds itself, so that it may secure fuller satisfaction of its distinctive needs and so that these are now higher on the schedule of priorities to which the new system orients itself. In short, functionally autonomous parts may have a "vested interest" in changing the system. Here, again, is an important source of tension for the system.

There is, from this standpoint, an inherent ambiguity in a conflict between a part and its encompassing system. Such a tension may signify one of two different things: either (1) that the part generating the tension has not yet been controlled by or excluded from the larger system, but that it ultimately will, or (2) that the friction-generating part is the harbinger of a new reorganization of the whole system.

There seems to be at least three empirically important strategies which a system can adopt to cope with the potentialities of tensions thus induced. One is to insulate itself and withdraw its parts from the environing system, excluding or "alienating" parts possessing significant functional autonomy,

---

[33] On the problem of succession in social systems see A. W. Gouldner, *Patterns of Industrial Bureaucracy* (Glencoe, Ill.: Free Press, 1954), pp. 59–104.

admitting only those it can highly control, and refusing to share parts with other systems. Demands for deep occupational involvement, separation between family and work life, and highly selective programs of recruitment would be examples of such a strategy as practiced by many modern businesses. A second strategy is that of expansion, in which the system attempts to engulf others which share its parts and thereby tighten control over them. This is also exemplified by the tendency of certain modern industries to develop an interest in the employee's personal life, to concern itself with the character of his wife, and to influence and regulate his residential living.[34] A third strategy is that of "selective risk." That is, the system will maximize its security by delegating its basic metabolic needs to structures within it which have minimal functional autonomy. This statement, however partial, of the specific and diverse strategies by means of which systems may respond to tensions is, it would seem, a formulation appreciatively more determinate than the mere assertion that systems attempt to "maintain their boundaries."

On the level of social systems, these considerations imply that distinctions will be made between core functions and peripheral ones,[35] and between "reliable" and "unreliable" or disloyal personnel,[36] the former functions being allocated to the former personnel. One would also look for tendencies of limited purpose organizations to transform themselves into "total institutions," or for total institutions to be transformed into limited purpose organizations by functional differentiation, specialization, and insulation of parts. Finally, the above considerations of system strategy would imply that it is necessary for the sociologist to identify and examine the particular policy which a social system has adopted in its relations to environing systems. It is to be expected that all social systems, not merely governments, but families, schools, or factories, will also develop some kind of a "foreign policy," tacit or explicit, which regulates its relations with surrounding social systems.[37]

It may be noted in passing that the threats to which the system is seen here to be variously responding derive from the defenses of its functionally autonomous parts. In this connection what is a threat from the system's standpoint is a defensive maneuver from the part's standpoint. Conversely, the system's defenses against these are, in turn, threats to the part's

---

[34] A stimulating if impressionistic account of this pattern is to be found in W. H. Whyte, *Is Anybody Listening?* (New York: Simon and Schuster, Inc., 1952).

[35] For a case of this see the discussion in A. W. Gouldner, *Wildcat Strike, ibid.*, p. 24.

[36] This is more extensively developed in A. W. Gouldner, "The Problem of Loyalty in Groups Under Tension," *Social Problems*, 2 (Oct., 1954), pp. 82–87.

[37] Cf. K. Mannheim, *Man and Society in an Age of Reconstruction* (New York: Harcourt, Brace and Company, Inc., 1941), p. 245.

defenses.[38] Consequently, it is to be expected that efforts to reduce the threatening behavior of either the part or the system will be resisted. In short, not only efforts to change the system, but also those directed at *maintaining* it are likely to entail conflict and resistance.

Functional Autonomy and Structural Dedifferentiation

Insofar as a system is composed of some parts which have a degree of functional autonomy, it possesses potentialities for certain types of changes, or responses to tensions, which would not exist if it had no functionally autonomous parts. A system with no functionally autonomous parts would have only one of two dodges when confronted with powerful disruptions. It could either dissolve and be completely destroyed or it would have to undergo radical structural reorganization.

However, given a system some of whose parts have a measure of functional autonomy, there is a third response available to an extremely disruptive stimulus, namely dedifferentiation. That is, the system can surrender higher levels of integration and permit its functionally autonomous parts to regroup on a lower level of complexity. Sociologically speaking, this means that when a complex social system's defensive mechanisms do not permit it to cope adaptively with threats, it may destructure itself into component primary groupings, surrendering its sovereignty to the parts.

Julian Steward's theory of "levels of sociocultural integration" is, in effect, a statement of this possibility. As he remarks, "In culture, simple forms such as those represented by the family or band, do not wholly disappear when a more complex stage of development is reached, nor do they merely survive fossil-like. . . . They gradually become specialized, dependent parts of new total configurations. . . ." [39] Steward holds that it is useful to look upon the larger, more complex, social systems, such as the nation state, as a distinctive level of organization but one which is, nonetheless, composed of parts—families and communities—which continue to retain a significant measure of functional autonomy. In the event that the larger more complex system is dissolved, they may survive separation from it.

Steward has analyzed several anthropologically interesting cases in which this happened, one of the best documented of which is that of Cuna-Cueva Indians of the Isthmus of Panama. The evidence indicates that at the time of the Hispanic conquest, this tribe had a fairly complex state structure, with a

---

[38] For fuller discussion see A. W. Gouldner, *ibid.*, ch. 10, and especially p. 171.
[39] J. H. Steward, "Levels of Sociocultural Integration," *Southwestern Journal of Anthropology*, 7 (Winter, 1951), p. 379.

ruling class of nobles and priests. The conquest, however, destroyed these national and state institutions of the Cuna. Neither Spanish governance nor Catholic religion effectively substituted for these, as the Cuna moved back into regions to which the Spanish were unwilling to follow. There Cuna life reorganized itself on a simpler communal basis, with the village becoming the largest unit of political life. It is clear, however, that such dedifferentiations of social structure are not peculiar to primitive peoples and have not infrequently occurred in historical European societies, most notably following the fall of the Roman Empire.

The phenomenon of dedifferentiation indicates that the functional autonomy of system parts may not only be *conducive* to system tensions, but can also provide a basis for responding to them. Indeed, the functional autonomy of the parts of a *social* system, allowing as it does for structural dedifferentiation, may be functional to the maintenance of the integrity of the *cultural* system. For the cultural system, the historically accumulated heritage of beliefs and skills may be maintained at least in some part in the smaller units into which the larger one has been dedifferentiated. To make this possible, however, the part must always be invested with more of the culture than it requires for the performance of its distinctive system function. In short, the part must not be overly specialized. It can be thus seen from another perspective why the parts of social systems *must be allowed* measures of functional autonomy by the system. The functional autonomy of parts then is not an unmitigated source of difficulty for the system, but may provide a basis for a defensive strategy of last resort, structural dedifferentiation.

Sociologists have, of course, long been aware of processes of structural dedifferentiation. In thinking of this, however, they have tended to focus primarily on the level of the atomization of the anomic individual, and to regard this as a purely pathological phenomenon. The existence of masses of men who are anomically cut adrift from larger social systems does, of course, imply that these systems are experiencing serious difficulty in maintaining themselves.

But such anomic dedifferentiation can also be seen as a desperate expedient through which the system is striving to maintain itself. As Merton states, "some [unknown] degree of deviation from current norms is probably functional for the basic goals of all groups. A certain degree of 'innovation,' for example, may result in the formation of new institutionalized patterns of behavior which are more adaptive than the old in making for realization of the primary goals." [40]

Tensionful as it may be, the anomic dedifferentiation of a social system need not be a requiem of its total dissolution, but a necessary prelude to its

---

[40] Merton, *ibid.*, p. 182.

reorganization. For anomic disorder may make possible a ferment of innovation which can rescue the system from destruction.[41] When a system has exhausted its routine solutions for an important problem and when these have failed, then, at that point, anomic randomness is more functional than the treadmill and orderly plying of the old structures. The anomic individual may not merely be an uncontrolled "social cancer," but a seed pod of culture which, if only through sheer chance, may fall upon fertile ground. In short, *limited* increases in randomness, by way of structural dedifferentiation, may be the ultimate defense of systems in the face of extremity.

It has been suggested that the discrimination of functionally autonomous parts within a social system is significant because these aid in identifying possible loci of strain within the system, as well as marking out the boundaries along which dedifferentiation may occur. In the role terms so central to social system analysis, then, it would seem that the identification of the most and least functionally autonomous roles within the system may be a valuable point of departure for the analysis of strains within the system. We may speak of roles which have relatively great functional autonomy as "cosmopolitans" while those having little can be termed "locals." I have, in another connection, attempted to develop the thesis that certain important strains in social systems can be analyzed as an outcome of tensions between cosmopolitans and locals.[42] Not merely roles, however, but other kinds of parts within social systems can be examined from the standpoint of their functional autonomy, and systematic consideration of these can aid in the analysis of system tension and change.

System Theories Versus Factor Theories

In the analysis of system changes, a distinction is commonly made between endogenous and exogenous sources of change, that is, between forces internal and external to the system. Our emphasis here on *degrees* of functional autonomy and *degrees* of system interdependence may be linked up with this distinction between exogenous and endogenous forces, and seen in its further ramifications for the analysis of change.

In noting that the functional autonomy of parts and system interdepend-

---

[41] Of similar import are Morris Ginsberg's comments in his essay on "Moral Progress": "There is no reason, it seems to me, for believing that the men of this age are suffering from a weakening of moral fibre." Again, some of modern man's bewilderment "is a sign not of moral decay but rather of moral ferment." M. Ginsberg, *Reason and Unreason in Society* (Cambridge: Harvard University Press, 1948), pp. 317–18.

[42] A. W. Gouldner, "Cosmopolitans and Locals: Toward an Analysis of Latent Social Roles," *Administrative Science Quarterly*, 2 (Dec., 1957), pp. 281–306 and (March, 1958), pp. 444–80.

ence are matters of degree we, in effect, state that exogenous and endogenous factors are not qualitatively but quantitatively different. That is, they are simply at opposite ends of the same continuum of interdependence and functional autonomy. Hence, specific system parts may be both *partly* exogenous and *partly* endogenous. Thus, if exogenous forces are peculiarly important to the understanding of system change, as they are commonly held to be in Parsons' and other system models, *any* element *in* the system may be important in understanding system change to the extent that it possesses a degree of exogenousness, though all need not be equally so.

In some measure this may be regarded as a partial resolution of the classical tension between two lines of sociological theory. One of these, the position stemming from Comte and passing through Durkheim to Parsons, stresses that system change has to be thought of as deriving from exogenous forces, the system *model* itself not being conceived of as possessing internal sources of disequilibrium. The other, deriving from the Marxian tradition, stresses that the system can change due to its "internal contradictions," that is, endogenous forces. Here the point stressed is that social systems may be looked upon as composed of parts having varying degrees of functional autonomy and interdependence; thus the difference between the external and internal, the "inside" and "outside" of the system, is not an absolute distinction, and the thickness or permeability of the system boundaries varies at different zones.

It is in this sense that some system parts can be thought of as having relatively greater *independence* than others, vis-à-vis the system under study, and may thus be of strategic importance in accounting for system changes. In *Structure of Social Action*, Parsons has stressed that independent parts are also interdependent, but he has tended to treat both independence and interdependence as "constants" rather than as variables.[43] We, on the contrary, have emphasized that they are variables. To say that two parts are interdependent is not to imply that they are *equally* so and thus, even within a system of interdependent parts, various parts can have *varying* degrees of independence or freedom.

Having gone this far, it is now evident that a stress on the "web of interdependence" within a system by no means relieves the analyst of the problem of factor weighting or loading. The analyst must still cope with the task of determining the differential contribution made by different system parts to the state of the system as a whole. In short, different system parts make different degrees of contribution to either the stability or the change of the system, and these need to be analytically and empirically distinguished.

As a matter of fact, this tends to be done, even by Parsons, with respect

---

[43] T. Parsons, *The Structure of Social Action, ibid.*

to the analysis of system stability when he utilizes the notion of "defense mechanisms." In effect, this constitutes an effort at the qualitative analysis of components of the system which play a particularly important role in enabling it to maintain its integrity. Logically, a parallel analysis of those system elements which make more important contributions to system *change* would seem to be equally desirable. It may be that the notion of the differential functional autonomy of system parts may provide an analytic tool for the qualitative discrimination of factors contributing importantly to system change.

It is one implication of these comments that the divergence between analytic models conceiving of social behavior in terms of social systems of interdependent parts—long a cardinal doctrine of functionalists—and models stressing the importance of certain "factors" is not so radical as is often assumed. Although there are general grounds for believing that there are "no one or two inherently primary sources of impetus to change in social systems," there are equally plausible grounds for asserting that not all elements in a social system contribute equally to its change. There is nothing inherently incompatible between an effort to develop a *generalized* theory of social change along these lines and one which stresses, as does Parsons, "the plurality of possible origins of change." [44]

Historically speaking, it seems that as a result of the empirical difficulties which older and methodologically unsophisticated factor theories encountered, functionalists polemically counterposed a stress on the system as such. In taking systemness as problematic, and focusing solely on the question of an unclarified "interdependence" of elements, they were led to neglect the problem of the *differential* significance which various parts of the system had in determining changes in the system.

Although the methodological position of earlier functionalists commonly affirmed an amorphous interdependence of parts within a social system, it does not follow that the specific empirical analyses in which they engaged actually utilized this principle. In particular, the classic contributors, from Comte to Parsons, have often gone out of their way to stress the significance of "shared value elements" in maintaining the equilibrium of social systems.[45]

Contrariwise, some of the early "factor" theories can be regarded not as having denied, but as having taken system interdependence as given, and as having focused their analysis on the problem of identifying and weighting the

---

44 T. Parsons, *The Social System, ibid.*, p. 494.

45 See the cognate analysis of Parsons' theory in the excellent piece by David Lockwood, "Some Remarks on 'The Social System,' " *British Journal of Sociology*, 7 (June, 1956), pp. 134–45, where the nub of the criticism is the neglect of structured but nonnormative elements in Parsons' work.

various parts within it.[46]. If this view of the matter is correct, it may be that the distinction between social theories has not so much been between system and factor theories, but rather between overt and covert factor theories, or between implicit and explicit system theories.

Factor theories are intrinsically difficult to demonstrate rigorously without the use of mathematical tools. For they imply a quantitative difference between two or more elements in determining a given outcome. Insofar as system models simply make a vague affirmation of the "interdependence" of parts they are more readily given empirical application in a purely qualitative manner.

It may be, therefore, that earlier functionalists neglected the problem of weighting system parts, because they then lacked the mathematical tools requisite for a rigorous resolution of the problem. Today, however, mathematical and statistical developments may be on the verge of making this possible and have, therefore, demanded that this dormant issue be reopened.[47]

---

[46] One of the most interesting cases of this is, of course, that of Marxism, which is commonly interpreted as a factor theory. It is clear, however, if not from Marx himself then at least from Engels, that they were deeply concerned about system analysis. Among Engels' frequent references to the matter are the following: "Marx and I are ourselves partly to blame for the fact that younger writers sometimes lay more stress on the economic side than is due it. We had to emphasize this main principle in opposition to our adversaries, who denied it, and we had not always the time, the place, or the opportunity to allow the other elements involved in the interaction to come into their rights." Again, "According to the materialist conception of history the determining element in history is *ultimately* the production and reproduction in real life. More than this neither Marx nor I have ever asserted." Finally, "In nature nothing happens alone. Everything has an effect on something else and vice versa...." K. Marx and F. Engels (tr. by D. Torr), *Selected Correspondence, 1846–1895* (New York: International Publishers, 1942), pp. 477, 475, 114. N. Bukharin was one of the first of later Marxists to develop formally the use of system analysis on a sociological level. For example, a society "may be regarded as a whole consisting of parts (elements) related to each other; in other words, the whole may be regarded as a system." N. Bukharin, *Historical Materialism: a System of Sociology* (New York: International Publishers, 1925), p. 87.

[47] For example, Paul Lazarsfeld is developing a statistical model which "provides a procedure for discovering which of the interacting elements preponderate...." Lazarsfeld and Merton, *ibid.*, p. 59.

C. Wright Mills

Grand Theory

*T*HE basic cause of grand theory is the initial choice of a level of thinking so general that its practitioners cannot logically get down to observation. They never, as grand theorists, get down from the higher generalities to problems in their historical and structural contexts. This absence of a firm sense of genuine problems, in turn, makes for the unreality so noticeable in their pages. One resulting characteristic is a seemingly arbitrary and certainly endless elaboration of distinctions, which neither enlarge our understanding nor make our experience more sensible. This in turn is revealed as a partially organized abdication of the effort to describe and explain human conduct and society plainly.

When we consider what a word stands for, we are dealing with its *semantic* aspects; when we consider it in relation to other words, we are dealing with its *syntactic* features.[1] I introduce these shorthand terms because

---

[1] We can also consider it in relation to its users—the pragmatic aspect, about which we have no need to worry here. These are three 'dimensions of meaning' which Charles M. Morris has so neatly systematized in his useful 'Foundations of the Theory of Signs,' *International Encyclopedia of United Science*, Vol. I, No. 2. University of Chicago Press, 1938.

they provide an economical and precise way to make this point: Grand theory is drunk on syntax, blind to semantics. Its practitioners do not truly understand that when we define a word we are merely inviting others to use it as we would like it to be used; that the purpose of definition is to focus argument upon fact, and that the proper result of good definition is to transform argument over terms into disagreements about fact, and thus open arguments to further inquiry.

The grand theorists are so preoccupied by syntactic meanings and so unimaginative about semantic references, they are so rigidly confined to such high levels of abstraction that the 'typologies' they make up—and the work they do to make them up—seem more often an arid game of Concepts than an effort to define systematically—which is to say, in a clear and orderly way—the problems at hand, and to guide our efforts to solve them.

One great lesson that we can learn from its systematic absence in the work of the grand theorists is that every self-conscious thinker must at all times be aware of—and hence be able to control—the levels of abstraction on which he is working. The capacity to shuttle between levels of abstraction, with ease and with clarity, is a signal mark of the imaginative and systematic thinker.

Around such terms as 'capitalism' or 'middle class' or 'bureaucracy' or 'power elite' or 'totalitarian democracy,' there are often somewhat tangled and obscured connotations, and in using these terms, such connotations must be carefully watched and controlled. Around such terms, there are often 'compounded' sets of facts and relations as well as merely guessed-at factors and observations. These too must be carefully sorted out and made clear in our definition and in our use.

To clarify the syntactic and the semantic dimensions of such conceptions, we must be aware of the hierarchy of specificity under each of them, and we must be able to consider all levels of this hierarchy. We must ask: Do we mean by 'capitalism,' as we are going to use it, merely the fact that all means of production are privately owned? Or do we also want to include under the term the further idea of a free market as the determining mechanism of price, wages, profit? And to what extent are we entitled to assume that, by definition, the term implies assertions about the political order as well as economic institutions?

Such habits of mind I suppose to be the keys to systematic thinking and their absence the keys to the fetishism of the Concept. Perhaps one result of such an absence will become clearer as we consider, more specifically now, a major confusion of Parsons' book [*The Social System*].

Claiming to set forth 'a general sociological theory,' the grand theorist in fact sets forth a realm of concepts from which are excluded many structural features of human society, features long and accurately recognized as fundamental to its understanding. Seemingly, this is deliberate in the interest of making the concern of sociologists a specialized endeavor distinct from that of economists and political scientists. Sociology, according to Parsons, has to do with 'that aspect of the theory of social systems which is concerned with the phenomena of the institutionalization of patterns of value-orientation in the social system, with the conditions of that institutionalization; and of changes in the patterns, with conditions of conformity with and deviance from a set of such patterns, and with motivational processes in so far as they are involved in all of these.'[2] Translated and unloaded of assumption, as any definition should be, this reads: Sociologists of my sort would like to study what people want and cherish. We would also like to find out why there is a variety of such values and why they change. When we do find a more or less unitary set of values, we would like to find out why some people do and others do not conform to them. (end of translation)

As David Lockwood has noted,[3] such a statement delivers the sociologist from any concern with 'power,' with economic and political institutions. I would go further than that. This statement, and, in fact, the whole of Parsons' book, deals much more with what have been traditionally called 'legitimations' than with institutions of any sort. The result, I think, is to transform, by definition, all institutional structures into a sort of moral sphere—or more accurately, into what has been called 'the symbol sphere.' [4] In order to make the point clear, I should like first to explain something about this sphere; second to discuss its alleged autonomy; and third, to indicate how Parsons' conceptions make it quite difficult even to raise several of the most important problems of any analysis of social structure.

Those in authority attempt to justify their rule over institutions by linking it, as if it were a necessary consequence, with widely believed-in moral symbols, sacred emblems, legal formulae. These central conceptions may refer to a god or gods, the 'vote of the majority,' 'the will of the people,' 'the aristocracy of talent or wealth,' to the 'divine right of kings,' or to the allegedly extraordinary endowment of the ruler himself. Social scientists, following Weber, call such conceptions 'legitimations,' or sometimes 'symbols of justification.'

Various thinkers have used different terms to refer to them: Mosca's 'political formula' or 'great superstitions,' Locke's 'principle of sovereignty,' Sorel's 'ruling myth,' Thurman Arnold's 'folklore,' Weber's 'legitimations,'

---

[2] Parsons, op. cit. p. 552.

[3] Cf. his excellent 'Some Remarks on "The Social System," ' *The British Journal of Sociology*, Vol. VII, 2 June 1956.

[4] H. H. Gerth and C. Wright Mills, *Character and Social Structure*, New York, Harcourt, Brace, 1953, pp. 274–7, upon which I am drawing freely in this section and in section 5, below.

Durkheim's 'collective representations,' Marx's 'dominant ideas,' Rousseau's 'general will,' Lasswell's 'symbols of authority,' Mannheim's 'ideology,' Herbert Spencer's 'public sentiments'—all these and others like them testify to the central place of master symbols in social analysis.

Similarly in psychological analysis, such master symbols, relevant when they are taken over privately, become the reasons and often the motives that lead persons into roles and sanction their enactment of them. If, for example, economic institutions are publicly justified in terms of them, then references to self-interest may be acceptable justification for individual conduct. But, if it is felt publicly necessary to justify such institutions in terms of 'public service and trust,' the old self-interest motives and reasons may lead to guilt or at least to uneasiness among capitalists. Legitimations that are publicly effective often become, in due course, effective as personal motives.

Now, what Parsons and other grand theorists call 'value-orientations' and 'normative structure' has mainly to do with master symbols of legitimation. This is, indeed, a useful and important subject. The relations of such symbols to the structure of institutions are among the most important problems of social science. Such symbols, however, do not form some autonomous realm within a society; their social relevance lies in their use to justify or to oppose the arrangement of power and the positions within this arrangement of the powerful. Their psychological relevance lies in the fact that they become the basis for adherence to the structure of power or for opposing it.

We may not merely assume that some such set of values, or legitimations, *must* prevail lest a social structure come apart, nor may we assume that a social structure must be made coherent or unified by any such 'normative structure.' Certainly we may not merely assume that any such 'normative structure' as may prevail is, in any meaning of the word, autonomous. In fact, for modern Western societies—and in particular the United States— there is much evidence that the opposite of each of these assumptions is the more accurate. Often—although not in the United States since World War II—there are quite well organized symbols of opposition which are used to justify insurgent movements and to debunk ruling authorities. The continuity of the American political system is quite unique, having been threatened by internal violence only once in its history; this fact may be among those that have misled Parsons in his image of The Normative Structure of Value-Orientation.

'Governments' do not necessarily, as Emerson would have it, 'have their origin in the moral identity of men.' To believe that government does is to confuse its legitimations with its causes. Just as often, or even more often, such moral identities as men of some society may have rest on the fact that institutional rulers successfully monopolize, and even impose, their master symbols.

Some hundred years ago, this matter was fruitfully discussed in terms of the assumptions of those who believe that symbol spheres are self-determining, and that such 'values' may indeed dominate history: The symbols that justify some authority are separated from the actual persons or strata that exercise the authority. The 'ideas,' not the strata or the persons using the ideas, are then thought to rule. In order to lend continuity to the sequence of these symbols, they are presented as in some way connected with one another. The symbols are thus seen as 'self-determining.' To make more plausible this curious notion, the symbols are often 'personalized' or given 'self-consciousness.' They may then be conceived of as The Concepts of History or as a sequence of 'philosophers' whose thinking determines institutional dynamics. Or, we may add, the Concept of 'normative order' may be fetishized. I have, of course, just paraphrased Marx and Engels speaking of Hegel.[5]

Unless they justify institutions and motivate persons to enact institutional roles, 'the values' of a society, however important in various private milieux, are historically and sociologically irrelevant. There is of course an interplay between justifying symbols, institutional authorities, and obedient persons. At times we should not hesitate to assign causal weight to master symbols— but we may not misuse the idea as *the* theory of social order or of the unity of society. There are better ways to construct a 'unity,' as we shall presently see, ways that are more useful in the formulation of significant problems of social structure and closer to observable materials.

So far as 'common values' interest us, it is best to build up our conception of them by examining the legitimations of each institutional order in any given social structure, rather than to *begin* by attempting first to grasp them, and in their light 'explain' the society's composition and unity.[6] We may, I suppose, speak of 'common values' when a great proportion of the members of an institutional order have taken over that order's legitimations, when such legitimations are the terms in which obedience is successfully claimed, or at least complacency secured. Such symbols are then used to 'define the situations' encountered in various roles and as yardsticks for the evaluations of leaders and followers. Social structures that display such universal and central symbols are naturally extreme and 'pure' types.

At the other end of the scale, there are societies in which a dominant set

---

[5] Cf. Karl Marx and Frederick Engels, *The German Ideology*, New York, International Publishers, 1939, pp. 42 ff.

[6] For a detailed and empirical account of the 'values' which American businessmen, for example, seek to promulgate, see Sutton, Harris, Kaysen and Tobin, *The American Business Creed*, Cambridge, Mass., Harvard University Press, 1956.

of institutions controls the total society and superimposes its values by violence and the threat of violence. This need not involve any breakdown of the social structure, for men may be effectively conditioned by formal discipline; and at times, unless they accept institutional demands for discipline, they may have no chance to earn a living.

A skilled compositor employed by a reactionary newspaper, for example, may for the sake of making a living and holding his job conform to the demands of employer discipline. In his heart, and outside the shop, he may be a radical agitator. Many German socialists allowed themselves to become perfectly disciplined soldiers under the Kaiser's flag—despite the fact that their subjective values were those of revolutionary Marxism. It is a long way from symbols to conduct and back again, and not all integration is based on symbols.[7]

To emphasize such conflict of value is not to deny 'the force of rational consistencies.' The discrepancy between word and deed is often characteristic, but so is the striving for consistency. Which is predominant in any given society cannot be decided *a priori* on the basis of 'human nature' or on the 'principals of sociology' or by the fiat of grand theory. We might well imagine a 'pure type' of society, a perfectly disciplined social structure, in which the dominated men, for a variety of reasons, cannot quit their prescribed roles, but nevertheless share none of the dominator's values, and thus in no way believe in the legitimacy of the order. It would be like a ship manned by galley slaves, in which the disciplined movement of the oars reduces the rowers to cogs in a machine, and the violence of the whipmaster is only rarely needed. The galley slaves need not even be aware of the ship's direction, although any turn of the bow evokes the wrath of the master, the only man aboard who is able to see ahead. But perhaps I begin to describe rather than to imagine.

Between these two types—a 'common value system' and a superimposed discipline—there are numerous forms of 'social integration.' Most occidental societies have incorporated many divergent 'value-orientations'; their unities involve various mixtures of legitimation and coercion. And that, of course, may be true of any institutional order, not only of the political and economic. A father may impose demands upon his family by threatening to withhold inheritance, or by the use of such violence as the political order may allow him. Even in such sacred little groups as families, the unity of 'common values' is by no means necessary: distrust and hatred may be the very stuff needed to hold a loving family together. A society as well may of course flourish quite adequately without such a 'normative structure' as grand theorists believe to be universal.

I do not here wish to expound any solution to the problem of order, but

---

[7] Gerth and Mills, op. cit. p. 300.

merely to raise questions. For if we cannot do that, we must, as demanded by the fiat of quite arbitrary definition, *assume* the 'normative structure' which Parsons imagines to be the heart of 'the social system.'

'Power,' as the term is now generally used in social science, has to do with whatever decisions men make about the arrangements under which they live, and about the events which make up the history of their period. Events that are beyond human decision do happen; social arrangements do change without benefit of explicit decision. But in so far as such decisions are made (and in so far as they could be but are not) the problem of who is involved in making them (or not making them) is the basic problem of power.

We cannot assume today that men must in the last resort be governed by their own consent. Among the means of power that now prevail is the power to manage and to manipulate the consent of men. That we do not know the limits of such power—and that we hope it does have limits—does not remove the fact that much power today is successfully employed without the sanction of the reason or the conscience of the obedient.

Surely in our time we need not argue that, in the last resort, coercion is the 'final' form of power. But then we are by no means constantly at the last resort. Authority (power justified by the beliefs of the voluntarily obedient) and manipulation (power wielded unbeknown to the powerless) must also be considered, along with coercion. In fact, the three types must constantly be sorted out when we think about the nature of power.

In the modern world, I think we must bear in mind, power is often not so authoritative as it appeared to be in the medieval period; justifications of rulers no longer seem so necessary to their exercise of power. At least for many of the great decisions of our time—especially those of an international sort—mass 'persuasion' has not been 'necessary'; the fact is simply accomplished. Furthermore, such ideologies as are available to the powerful are often neither taken up nor used by them. Ideologies usually arise as a response to an effective debunking of power; in the United States such opposition has not been recently effective enough to create a felt need for new ideologies of rule.

Today, of course, many people who are disengaged from prevailing allegiances have not acquired new ones, and so are inattentive to political concerns of any kind. They are neither radical nor reactionary. They are inactionary. If we accept the Greeks' definition of the idiot as an altogether private man, then we must conclude that many citizens of many societies are indeed idiots. This—and I use the word with care—this spiritual condition seems to me the key to much modern malaise among political intellectuals, as well as the key to much political bewilderment in modern society. Intellectual 'conviction' and moral 'belief' are not necessary, in either the rulers or the ruled, for a structure of power to persist and even to flourish. So far as

the role of ideologies is concerned, the frequent absence of engaging legitimation and the prevalence of mass apathy are surely two of the central political
facts about the Western societies today.

In the course of any substantive research, many problems do confront
those who hold the view of power that I have been suggesting. But we are not
at all helped by the deviant assumptions of Parsons, who merely assumes that
there is, presumably in every society, such a 'value hierarchy' as he imagines.
Moreover, its implications systematically impede the clear formulation of
significant problems:

To accept his scheme we are required to read out of the picture the facts
of power and indeed of all institutional structures, in particular the economic,
the political, the military. In this curious 'general theory,' such structures of
domination have no place.

In the terms provided, we cannot properly pose the empirical question of
the extent to which, and in what manner, institutions are, in any given case,
legitimated. The idea of the normative order that is set forth, and the way it
is handled by grand theorists, leads us to assume that virtually all power is
legitimated. In fact: that in the social system, 'the maintenance of the complementarity of role-expectations, once established, is not problematical. . . .
No special mechanisms are required for the explanation of the maintenance
of complementary interaction-orientation.' [8]

In these terms, the idea of conflict cannot effectively be formulated.
Structural antagonisms, large-scale revolts, revolutions—they cannot be
imagined. In fact, it is assumed that 'the system,' once established, is not only
stable but intrinsically harmonious; disturbances must, in his language, be
'introduced into the system.' [9] The idea of the normative order set forth leads
us to assume a sort of harmony of interests as the natural feature of any
society; as it appears here, this idea is as much a metaphysical anchor point
as was the quite similar idea among the eighteenth-century philosophers of
natural order.[10]

The magical elimination of conflict, and the wondrous achievement of
harmony, remove from this 'systematic' and 'general' theory the possibilities
of dealing with social change, with history. Not only does the 'collective
behavior' of terrorized masses and excited mobs, crowds and movements
—with which our era is so filled—find no place in the normatively created
social structures of grand theorists. But any systematic ideas of how history
itself occurs, of its mechanics and processes, are unavailable to grand theory,

---

[8] Parsons, op. cit. p. 205.

[9] Ibid. p. 262.

[10] Cf. Carl Becker, *The Heavenly City;* and Lewis A. Coser, *Conflict*, Glencoe, Illinois, The Free Press, 1956.

and accordingly, Parsons believes, unavailable to social science: 'When such a theory is available the millennium for social science will have arrived. This will not come in our time and most probably never.' [11] Surely this is an extraordinarily vague assertion.

Virtually any problem of substance that is taken up in the terms of grand theory is incapable of being clearly stated. Worse: its statement is often loaded with evaluations as well as obscured by sponge-words. It is, for example, difficult to imagine a more futile endeavor than analyzing American society in terms of 'the value pattern' of 'universalistic-achievement' with no mention of the changing nature, meaning and forms of success characteristic of modern capitalism, or of the changing structure of capitalism itself; or, analyzing United States stratification in terms of 'the dominant value system' without taking into account the known statistics of life-chances based on levels of property and income.[12]

I do not think it too much to say that in so far as problems are dealt with realistically by grand theorists, they are dealt with in terms that find no place in grand theory, and are often contradictory to it. 'Indeed,' Alvin Gouldner has remarked, 'the extent to which Parsons' efforts at theoretical and empirical analysis of change suddenly lead him to enlist a body of Marxist concepts and assumptions is nothing less than bewildering. . . . It almost seems as if two sets of books were being kept, one for the analysis of equilibrium and another for the investigation of change.' [13] Gouldner goes on to remark how in the case of defeated Germany, Parsons recommends attacking the Junkers at their base, as 'a case of exclusive class privilege' and analyzes the civil service in terms of 'the class basis of recruitment.' In short, the whole economic and occupational structure—conceived in quite Marxian terms, not in terms of the normative structure projected by grand theory—suddenly rises into view. It makes one entertain the hope that grand theorists have not lost all touch with historical reality.

I now return to the problem of order, which in a rather Hobbesian version, seems to be the major problem in Parsons' book. It is possible to be brief about it because in the development of social science it has been redefined, and in its most useful statement might now be called the problem of social integration; it does of course require a working conception of social structure and of historical change. Unlike grand theorists, most social scientists, I think, would give answers running something like this:

First of all, there is no *one* answer to the question, What holds a social

---

[11] Parsons, taken from Alvin W. Gouldner, 'Some observations on Systematic Theory, 1945–55,' *Sociology in the United States of America*, Paris, UNESCO, 1956, p. 40.

[12] Cf. Lockwood, op. cit. p. 138.

[13] Gouldner, op. cit. p. 41.

structure together? There is no one answer because social structures differ profoundly in their degrees and kinds of unity. In fact, types of social structure are usefully conceived in terms of different modes of integration. When we descend from the level of grand theory to historical realities, we immediately realize the irrelevance of its monolithic Concepts. With these we cannot think about the human variety, about Nazi Germany in 1936, Sparta in seventh century B.C., the United States in 1836, Japan in 1866, Great Britain in 1950, Rome at the time of Diocletian. Merely to name this variety is surely to suggest that whatever these societies may have in common must be discovered by empirical examination. To predicate anything beyond the most empty formalities about the historical range of social structure is to mistake one's own capacity to talk for all that is meant by the work of social investigation.

One may usefully conceive types of social structure in terms of such institutional orders as the political and kinship, the military and economic, and the religious. Having defined each of these in such a way as to be able to discern their outlines in a given historical society, one asks how each is related to the others, how, in short, they are composed into a social structure. The answers are conveniently put as a set of 'working models' which are used to make us more aware, as we examine specific societies at specific times, of the links by which they are 'tied together.'

One such 'model' may be imagined in terms of the working out in each institutional order of a similar structural principle; think for example of Tocqueville's America. In that classical liberal society each order of institutions is conceived as autonomous, and its freedom demanded from any co-ordination by other orders. In the economy, there is *laissez faire;* in the religious sphere, a variety of sects and churches openly compete on the market for salvation; kinship institutions are set up on a marriage market in which individuals choose one another. Not a family-made man, but a self-made man, comes to ascendancy in the sphere of status. In the political order, there is party competition for the votes of the individual; even in the military zone there is much freedom in the recruitment of state militia, and in a wide sense—a very important sense—one man means one rifle. The principle of integration—which is also the basic legitimation of this society—is the ascendancy within each order of institutions of the free initiative of independent men in competition with one another. It is in this fact of correspondence that we may understand the way in which a classic liberal society is unified.

But such 'correspondence' is only one type, only one answer to the 'problem of order.' There are other types of unity. Nazi Germany, for example, was integrated by 'co-ordination.' The general model can be stated as follows: Within the economic order, institutions are highly centralized; a few big units more or less control all operations. Within the political order there is more fragmentation: Many parties compete to influence the state, but no one of them is powerful enough to control the results of economic concentration, one of these results—along with other factors—being the slump. The Nazi movement successfully exploits the mass despair, especially that of its lower middle classes, in the economic slump and brings into close correspondence the political, military, and economic orders. One party monopolizes and remakes the political order, abolishing or amalgamating all other parties that might compete for power. To do this requires that the Nazi party find points of coinciding interest with monopolies in the economic order and also with certain elites of the military order. In these main orders there is, first, a corresponding concentration of power; then each of them coincides and co-operates in the taking of power. President Hindenburg's army is not interested in defending the Weimar Republic, or in crushing the marching columns of a popular war party. Big business circles are willing to help finance the Nazi party, which, among other things, promises to smash the labor movement. And the three types of elite join in an often uneasy coalition to maintain power in their respective orders and to co-ordinate the rest of society. Rival political parties are either suppressed and outlawed, or they disband voluntarily. Kinship and religious institutions, as well as all organizations within and between all orders, are infiltrated and co-ordinated, or at least neutralized.

The totalitarian party-state is the means by which high agents of each of the three dominant orders co-ordinate their own and other institutional orders. It becomes the over-all 'frame organization' which imposes goals upon all institutional orders instead of merely guaranteeing 'government by law.' The party extends itself, prowling everywhere in 'auxiliaries' and 'affiliations.' It either breaks up or it infiltrates, and in either case it comes to control all types of organizations, including the family.

The symbol spheres of all institutions are controlled by the party. With the partial exception of the religious order, no rival claims to legitimate autonomy are permitted. There is a party monopoly of formal communications, including educational institutions. All symbols are recast to form the basic legitimation of the co-ordinated society. The principle of absolute and magical leadership (charismatic rule) in a strict hierarchy is widely promulgated, in a social structure that is to a considerable extent held together by a network of rackets.[14]

But surely that is enough to make evident what I should think an obvious

---

[14] Franz Neumann, *Behemoth*, New York, Oxford, 1942, which is a truly splendid model of what a structural analysis of an historical society ought to be. For the above account, see Gerth and Mills, op. cit. pp. 363 ff.

point: that there is no 'grand theory,' no one universal scheme in terms of which we can understand the unity of social structure, no one answer to the tired old problem of social order, taken *überhaupt*. Useful work on such problems will proceed in terms of a variety of such working models as I have outlined here, and these models will be used in close and empirical connection with a range of historical as well as contemporary social structures.

It is important to understand that such 'modes of integration' may also be conceived as working models of historical change. If, for example, we observe American society at the time of Tocqueville and again in the middle of the twentieth century, we see at once that the way the nineteenth century structure 'hangs together' is quite different from its current modes of integration. We ask: How have each of its institutional orders changed? How have its relations with each of the others changed? What have been the tempos, the varying rates at which these structural changes have occurred? And, in each case, what have been the necessary and sufficient causes of these changes? Usually, of course, the search for adequate cause requires at least some work in a comparative as well as an historical manner. In an over-all way, we can summarize such an analysis of social change, and thus formulate more economically a range of larger problems, by indicating that the changes have resulted in a shift from one 'mode of integration' to another. For example, the last century of American history shows a transition from a social structure largely integrated by correspondence to one much more subject to co-ordination.

The general problem of a theory of history can not be separated from the general problem of a theory of social structure. I think it is obvious that in their actual studies, working social scientists do not experience any great theoretical difficulties in understanding the two in a unified way. Perhaps that is why one *Behemoth* is worth, to social science, twenty *Social Systems*. . . .

The withdrawal into systematic work on conceptions should be only a formal moment within the work of social science. It is useful to recall that in Germany the yield of such formal work was soon turned to encyclopedic and historical use. That use, presided over by the ethos of Max Weber, was the climax of the classic German tradition. In considerable part, it was made possible by a body of sociological work in which general conceptions about society were closely joined with historical exposition. Classical Marxism has been central to the development of modern sociology; Max Weber, like so many other sociologists, developed much of his work in a dialogue with Karl Marx. But the amnesia of the American scholar has always to be recognized. In grand theory we now confront another formalist withdrawal, and again, what is properly only a pause seems to have become permanent. As they say in Spain, 'many can shuffle cards who can't play.'[15]

---

[15] It must be evident that the particular view of society which it is possible to dig out of Parsons' texts is of rather direct ideological use; traditionally, such views have of course been associated with conservative styles of thinking. Grand theorists have not often descended into the political arena; certainly they have not often taken their problems to lie within the political contexts of modern society. But that of course does not exempt their work from ideological meaning. I shall not analyze Parsons in this connection, for the political meaning of *The Social System* lies so close to its surface, when it is adequately translated, that I feel no need to make it any plainer. Grand theory does not now play any direct bureaucratic role, and as I have noted, its lack of intelligibility limits any public favor it might come to have. This might of course become an asset: its obscurity does give it a great ideological potential.

The ideological meaning of grand theory tends strongly to legitimate stable forms of domination. Yet only if there should arise a much greater need for elaborate legitimations among conservative groups would grand theory have a chance to become politically relevant. I began this chapter with a question: Is grand theory, as represented in *The Social System*, merely verbiage or is it also profound? My answer to this question is: It is only about 50 per cent verbiage; 40 per cent is well-known textbook sociology. The other 10 per cent, as Parsons might say, I am willing to leave open for your own empirical investigations. My own investigations suggest that the remaining 10 per cent is of possible—although rather vague—ideological use.

Chapter III

Change
and
Process

Introduction

*E*VERY discipline develops a set of critical shibboleths that are awesome in their invocation and are calculated to bring one's opponent to his knees blushing. In sociology these include "reductionism," "determinism," "empiricism," "the ecological fallacy," and "static bias." The last has haunted functionalism since its inception. But to what extent *does* contemporary functionalism harbor a static bias? More accurately, what sorts of change can it handle and what sorts does it fumble? These are the guiding questions of the present chapter. Of course, the answers vary.

It is perhaps appropriate that Talcott Parsons should be the sole author represented twice in this volume for he has served the debate both as fulcrum and fodder for more than twenty-five years. Note, however, that Parsons is not functionalism incarnate. Not only does he differ from others of the label, but he has modified his own views over the years. Once again it is worth mentioning that many of his critics focus on an earlier stage than the one represented in the present selection. This should not eclipse their insights or compromise their vigor. Rather it should alert the reader to a sub-theme in the chapter: To what extent has Parsons accomodated earlier criticism? His essay here is from his lengthy introduction to *Theories of Society*. Compared to his earlier treatments of change in *The Social*

System, this is more extensive and detailed in discussing various types of dynamics. Whereas the earlier Parsons tended to deemphasize "endogenous" change generated from within the system, the current Parsons features an extended discussion of internally-induced differentiation. Structural differentiation has come to have a central place in Parson's paradigm, yet he indicates that it neither exhausts nor minimizes change. He also discusses "exogamous" change in connection with developing areas as well as equilibrating mechanisms that involve flux but no structural change at all. To provide a framework for this elaborate taxonomy, Parsons begins with three sets of distinctions that are crucial to his work as a whole. These include the distinctions between structure and function, between equilibrium and change, and between system and the subsystems of which it is composed.

S. M. Eisenstadt's article, "Social Change, Differentiation, and Evolution," identifies the Parsonian focus on structural differentiation as a sophisticated new form of evolutionism. Eisenstadt faults both the differentiationists and the older evolutionists for a faith that what is new is both better and more stable. Some changes are neither; even if they are one, they need not be the other. The key variable for Eisenstadt is "institutionalization," and not all change is institutionalized. Unless it becomes institutionalized, it is not likely to increase the system's adaptive potential in accord with evolutionary postulates. Even if it is institutionalized, Eisenstadt argues, it may become maladaptive and give rise to further change. In short, differentiation is no more a theoretical panacea than its more naive predecessor, evolutionism. While theories of differentiation mark an advance in the study of change, we must be careful to guard against overestimation and uncritical acceptance. As evolutionism itself attests, today's scientific vogue may become tomorrow's scientific whipping-boy.

An anthropologist, Clifford Geertz, seems to take an opposite tack. His charge against functionalist theories of change is not that they have overestimated differentiation, but precisely that they have underestimated differentiation of one particular sort. Geertz argues that functionalism treats culture and social structure as all-too perfectly interconnected. Some sociologists see culture as a derivative of social structure; others commit the opposite fallacy. Geertz suggests not only that the two domains are frequently independent but also frequently disjunctive. It is precisely this disjunctiveness that is both cause and symptom of major social change. The argument is in the tradition of Sorokin's distinction between causal and logico-meaningful integration. It is buttressed by an extensive anthropological case-study of a Javanese funeral ceremony. The ceremony failed, to the dismay of its participants and to the surprise of functional theorists who, following Malinowski, hold that ceremonies are successful almost by definition. In explicating the failure, Geertz is led to his theoretical critique.

Note, however, that the case material is lengthy, and at one point we have substituted our own synopsis of the crucial events. This is not to deny the importance of ethnography, but rather to focus on the theory that emerges from it.

Wayne Hield challenges functionalist conceptions of change on grounds that are partly analytic but also partly normative. His concern is that the functionalists articulate an interest in change but manifest a stake in order. While they are aware of deviance and disruption, Hield asserts, their perspectives are subverted by two considerations. First, they tend to regard disorder as an unnatural intrusion upon the pursuit of order itself. Second, they tend to applaud order once it is achieved. Hield argues that the former is analytically distorting and that the latter is normatively offensive. The quest for order becomes an apology for regimentation. Instead of seeking its supports, we should cultivate its obstacles. Switching clients from Hobbes to Rousseau, we should change our research from the search for stability to the search for liberation, from the conditions of changelessness to the pursuit of autonomy through change. Of course, much of this is redolent of C. Wright Mills. Yet it is no mere recapitulation, and Hield is especially distinctive in his emphasis on the individual as an agent in his own behalf. Neo-Marxists and Functionalists alike share a view of the individual as the product of institutional monoliths in an overpowering matrix. Hield retains a faith in the rational man to resist the conspiracy and assert his own destiny.

Finally, we have mentioned repeatedly the problems of partitioning issues into separate chapters as each topic encroaches upon every other. Change is a particularly important instance of this. It is a dominant motif throughout the volume and is particularly important to Chapters IV and VII in their concern with conflict and ideology. For that matter, of course, both conflict and ideology are heavily implicated here.

Talcott Parsons

A Paradigm for the Analysis
of Social Systems and Change

*L*ET us now turn to a more detailed discussion of our conception of a
social system. First, the concept of interpenetration implies that, however
important *logical* closure may be as a theoretical ideal, *empirically* social
systems are conceived as *open* systems, engaged in complicated processes of
interchange with environing systems. The environing systems include, in this
case, cultural and personality systems, the behavioral and other subsystems
of the organism, and, through the organism, the physical environment. The
same logic applies internally to social systems, conceived as differentiated
and segmented into a plurality of subsystems, each of which must be treated
analytically as an open system interchanging with environing subsystems of
the larger system.

The concept of an open system interchanging with environing systems
also implies *boundaries* and their maintenance. When a set of interdependent
phenomena shows sufficiently definite patterning and stability over time, then
we can say that it has a "structure" and that it is fruitful to treat it as a

"system." A boundary means simply that a theoretically and empirically significant difference between structures and processes internal to the system and those external to it exists and tends to be maintained. In so far as boundaries in this sense do not exist, it is not possible to identify a set of interdependent phenomena as a system; it is merged in some other, more extensive system. It is thus important to distinguish a set of phenomena not meant to constitute a system in the theoretically relevant sense—e.g., a certain type of statistical sample of a population—from a true system.

Structural and Functional Modes of Analysis.—Besides identifying a system in terms of its patterns and boundaries, a social system can and should be analyzed in terms of three logically independent—i.e., cross-cutting —but also interdependent, bases or axes of variability, or as they may be called, bases of selective abstraction.

The first of these is best defined in relation to the distinction between "structural" and "functional" references for analysis. However relative these two concepts may be, the distinction between them is highly important. The concept of structure focuses on those elements of the patterning of the system which may be regarded as independent of the lower-amplitude and shorter time-range fluctuations in the relation of the system to its external situation. It thus designates the features of the system which can, in certain strategic respects, be treated as constants over certain ranges of variation in the behavior of other significant elements of the theoretical problem.

Thus, in a broad sense, the American Constitution has remained a stable reference point over a period of more than a century and a half. During this time, of course, the structure of American society has changed very greatly in certain respects; there have been changes in legal terms, through legislation, through legal interpretations, and through more informal pro- cesses. But the federal state, the division between legislative and executive branches of government, the independent judiciary, the separation of church and state, the basic rights of personal liberty, of assembly, and of property, and a variety of other features have for most purposes remained constant.

The functional reference, on the other hand, diverges from the structural in the "dynamic" direction. Its primary theoretical significance is integrative; functional considerations relate to the problem of *mediation* between two fundamental sets of exigencies: those imposed by the relative constancy or "givenness" of a structure, and those imposed by the givenness of the environing situation external to the system. Since only in a theoretically limiting case can these two be assumed to stand in a constant relation to each other, there will necessarily exist a system of dynamic processes and mechanisms.

Concepts like "structure" and "function" can be considered as either concrete or analytical. Our present concern is with their analytical meaning;

we wish to state in a preliminary way a fundamental proposition about the structure of social systems that will be enlarged upon later—namely, that their structure as treated within the frame of reference of action *consists* in institutionalized patterns of normative culture. It consists in components of the organisms or personalities of the participating individuals only so far as these "interpenetrate" with the social and cultural systems, i.e., are "internalized" in the personality and organism of the individual. I shall presently discuss the problem of classifying the elements of normative culture that enter into the structure of social systems.

The functional categories of social systems concern, then, those features in terms of which systematically ordered modes of adjustment operate in the changing relations between a given set of patterns of institutionally established structure in the system and a given set of properties of the relevant environing systems. Historically, the most common model on which this relationship has been based is that of the behaving organism, as used in psychological thinking. From this point of view, the functional problem is that of analyzing the mechanisms which make orderly response to environmental conditions possible. When using this model in analyzing social systems, however, we treat not only the environment but the structure of the system as problematical and subject to change, in a sense which goes farther than the traditional behavior psychologist has been accustomed to go.[1]

In interpreting this position, one should remember that the immediately environing systems of a social system are not those of the physical environment. They are, rather, the other primary subsystems of the general system of action—i.e., the personalities of its individual members, the behaviorally organized aspects of the organisms underlying those personalities, and the relevant cultural systems in so far as they are not fully institutionalized in the social system but involve components other than "normative patterns of culture" that are institutionalized.[2]

"Dynamic" Modes of Analysis.—The importance of the second basis or axis of empirical variability, and hence of theoretical problem formulation, follows directly. A fundamental distinction must be made between two orders of "dynamic" problems relative to a given system. The first of these concerns the processes which go on under the assumption that the structural patterns of institutionalized culture are given, i.e., are assumed to remain constant. This is the area of problems of *equilibrium* as that concept has

---

[1] In addition, of course, our analysis is couched explicitly in terms of action and not of the type of physiology which has so preoccupied many behavior psychologists.

[2] It is too technical an issue to discuss here, but we would take the position that a social system in the *analytical* sense has *no* immediate and direct input-output interchange with the physical environment; all such interchange, which is of crucial importance empirically, is mediated through the "behavioral organism."

been used by Pareto, Henderson, and others, and of homeostasis as used by Cannon. The significance of such problems is directly connected with both the concept of system and the ways in which we have defined the relation between structure and function.

The concept of equilibrium is a fundamental reference point for analyzing the processes by which a system either comes to terms with the exigencies imposed by a *changing* environment, without essential change in its own structure, or fails to come to terms and undergoes other processes, such as structural change, dissolution as a boundary-maintaining system (analogous to biological death for the organism), or the consolidation of some impairment leading to the establishment of secondary structures of a "pathological" character. Theoretically, the concept of equilibrium has a normative reference in only one sense. Since the structure of social systems consists in institutionalized normative culture, the "maintenance" of these normative patterns is a basic reference point for analyzing the equilibrium of the system. However, whether this maintenance actually occurs or not, and in what measure, is entirely an empirical question. Furthermore, "disequilibrium" may lead to structural change which, from a higher-order normative point of view, is desirable.

The second set of dynamic problems concerns processes involving change in the structure of the system itself. This involves, above all, problems of interchange with the cultural system, however much these may in turn depend upon the internal state of the social system and its relations to other environing systems. Leaving distinctions within the category of internal adjustive processes aside for the moment, one can say that, with respect to its external interchanges, problems of equilibrium for the social system involve primarily its relations to its individual members as personalities and organisms, and, through these, to the physical environment. Problems of structural change, on the other hand, primarily involve its relations to the cultural systems affecting its patterns of institutionalized normative culture.

However fundamental the distinction between dynamic problems which do and do not involve structural change may be, the great importance of an intermediate or mixed case should be emphasized. This is the problem of change involving the structure of subsystems of the social system, but not the over-all structural pattern. The most important case in this category is that of processes of structural differentiation. Structural differentiation involves genuine *reorganization* of the system and, therefore, fundamental structural change of various subsystems and their relations to each other. Its analysis therefore presents problems of structural change for the relevant subsystems, but not in the same sense for the system as a whole. The problems involved concern the organization of the structural components of social systems, particularly the hierarchical order in which they are placed. Further discussion will have to await clarification of these problems.

The Hierarchy of Relations of Control.—The third of the three essential axes of theoretical analysis may be defined as concerning a hierarchy of relations of control. The development of theory in the past generation in both the biological and the behavioral sciences has revealed the primary source of the difficulty underlying the prominent reductionism of so much earlier thought. This was the reductionist tendency to ignore the importance of the ways in which the organization of living systems involved structures and mechanisms that operated as agencies of control—in the cybernetic sense of control—of their metabolic and behavioral processes. The concept of the "behavioral organism" put forward above is that of a cybernetic system located mainly in the central nervous system, which operates through several intermediary mechanisms to control the metabolic processes of the organism and the behavioral use of its physical facilities, such as the motions of limbs.

The basic subsystems of the general system of action constitute a hierarchical series of such agencies of control of the behavior of individuals or organisms. The behavioral organism is the point of articulation of the system of action with the anatomical-physiological features of the physical organism and is its point of contact with the physical environment. The personality system is, in turn, a system of control over the behavioral organism; the social system, over the personalities of its participating members; and the cultural system, a system of control relative to social systems.

It may help if we illustrate the nature of this type of hierarchical relationship by discussing the sense in which the social system "controls" the personality. There are two main empirical points at which this control operates, though the principles involved are the same in both cases. First, the situation in which any given individual acts is, far more than any other set of factors, composed of *other* individuals, not discretely but in ordered sets of relationship to the individual in point. Hence, as the source of his principal facilities of action and of his principal rewards and deprivations, the concrete social system exercises a powerful control over the action of any concrete, adult individual. However, the *patterning* of the motivational system in terms of which he faces this situation also depends upon the social system, because his own personality *structure* has been shaped through the internalization of systems of social objects and of the patterns of institutionalized culture. This point, it should be made clear, is independent of the sense in which individuals are concretely autonomous or creative rather than "passive" or "conforming," for individuality and creativity are, to a considerable extent, phenomena of the institutionalization of expectations. The social system which controls the personality is here conceived analytically, not concretely. . . .

Control Relations within the Social System.—The same basic principle of cybernetic hierarchy that applies to the relations between general subsystems of action applies again *within* each of them, notably to social systems, which is of primary concern here. The principle of the order of cybernetic priority, combined with primacy of relevance to the different boundary-interchange exigencies of the system, will be used as the fundamental basis for classifying the components of social systems. The relevance of this hierarchy applies, of course, to all the components distinguished according to the first of our three ranges of variation, to structures, functions, mechanisms, and categories of input and output.

The most strategic starting point for explaining this basic set of classifications is the category of functions, the link between the structural and the dynamic aspects of the system. I have suggested that it is possible to reduce the essential functional imperatives of any system of action, and hence of any social system, to four, which I have called pattern-maintenance, integration, goal-attainment, and adaptation. These are listed in order of significance from the point of view of cybernetic control of action processes in the system type under consideration. . . .

The problem of systematizing the morphology of living—i.e., biological, psychological, social, and cultural—systems is intrinsically easier to solve than that of their dynamics. . . . Dynamic analysis must, in our theoretical scheme, be referred to morphological premises, or else be subject to complete loss of orientation. The statement that everything empirical is subject to change may be metaphysically correct; but this is often translated into the scientifically untenable doctrine condemning as invalid a heuristic assumption that any reference point is structurally given, on the grounds that such an assumption would commit the investigator to deny the fluidity of ultimate reality. Science is not a photographic reproduction of reality, but is a highly selective mode of organizing man's orientation to reality—however philosophers define the latter. The scientifically specific component of this organization depends on ability to establish reference-points structurally stable enough to justify the *simplification* of dynamic problems prerequisite to logically manageable analysis. Empirically, these reference-points are relative and may be expected to change as the science develops. The categorical assertion that any assumptions about structure are scientifically inadmissible, because in the last analysis everything is in flux, denies the legitimacy of science. In any science, and in sociology in particular, the concept of change is meaningful only in terms of a definable *something,* i.e., something which can be described in structural terms.

The Problem of Structural Change

According to the program laid out above, the last major problem area is the analysis of processes of structural change in social systems. The process of structural change may be considered the obverse of equilibrating process; the distinction is made in terms of boundary-maintenance. Boundary implies both that there is a difference of state between phenomena internal and external to the system; and that the type of process tending to maintain that difference of state is different from the type tending to break it down. In applying this concept to social systems, one must remember that their essential boundaries are those vis-à-vis personalities, organisms, and cultural systems, and not those directly vis-à-vis the physical environment.

A boundary is thus conceived as a kind of watershed. The control resources of the system are adequate for its maintenance up to a well-defined set of points in one direction: beyond that set of points, there is a tendency for a *cumulative* process of change to begin, producing states progressively farther from the institutionalized patterns. The metaphor of the watershed, however, fails to demonstrate the complexity of the series of control levels and, hence, of the boundaries of subsystems within larger systems. The mechanisms discussed earlier are involved in the dynamic aspects of such a hierarchical series of subboundaries; if a subboundary is broken, resources within the larger system counteract the implicit tendency to structural change. This is most dramatically shown in the capacity of social control mechanisms, in a narrow sense, to reverse cumulative processes of deviance. The conception of the nature of the difference between processes of equilibration and processes of structural change seems inherent in the conception of a social system as a cybernetic system of control over behavior.

As observed, structural change in subsystems is an inevitable part of equilibrating process in larger systems. The individual's life-span is so short that concrete role-units in any social system of societal scope must, through socialization, continually undergo structural change. Closely bound to this is a low-order collectivity like the nuclear family. Though the institutional norms defining "the family" in a society or a social sector may remain stable over long periods, *the family* is never a collectivity; and real families are continually being established by marriages, passing through the "family cycle," and, eventually, disappearing, with the parents' death and the children's dispersion. Similar considerations apply to other types of societal subsystems.

Within this frame of reference, the problem of structural change can be considered under three headings, as follows: (1) the sources of tendencies toward change; (2) the impact of these tendencies on the affected structural components, and the possible consequences; and (3) possible generalizations about trends and patterns of change.

THE SOURCES OF STRUCTURAL CHANGE

The potential sources of structural change are exogenous and endogenous—usually in combination. The foregoing discussion has stressed the instability of the relations between any system of action and its situation, because this is important for defining the concepts of goal and the political function. We were emphasizing *relation,* and a relation's internal sources of instability may derive from external tendencies to change.

Exogenous Sources of Change.—The exogenous sources of social structural change consist in endogenous tendencies to change in the organisms, personalities, and cultural systems articulated with the social systems in question. Among such sources are those operating through genetic changes in the constituent human organisms and changes in the distribution of genetic components within populations, which have an impact on behavior as it affects social role-performance, including the social system's capacities for socialization. Changes in the physical environment are mediated most directly either through the organism—e.g., through perception—or through appropriate aspects of the cultural system—e.g., technological knowledge.

One particularly important source of exogenous change is a change originating in other social systems. For the politically organized society, the most important are other politically organized societies. To consider change in this context, it is essential to treat the society of reference as a unit in a more inclusive social system. Even when the system's level of integration is relatively low and chronic conflicts between its subunits continually threaten to break into war, *some* element of more or less institutionalized order always governs their interrelations—otherwise, a concept like "diplomacy" would be meaningless. Of course, exogenous cultural borrowing and diffusion are mediated through interrelations among societies.

Endogenous Sources: "Strains."—The most general, commonly used term for an endogenous tendency to change is "strain." *Strain* here refers to a condition in the *relation* between two or more structured units (i.e., subsystems of the system) that constitutes a tendency or pressure toward changing that relation to one incompatible with the equilibrium of the relevant part of the system. If the strain becomes great enough, the mechanisms of control will not be able to maintain that conformity to relevant normative expectations necessary to avoid the breakdown of the structure. A strain is a tendency to disequilibrium in the input-output balance between two or more units of the system.

Strains can be relieved in various ways. For the system's stability, the ideal way is resolution—i.e., restoring full conformity with normative expectations, as in complete recovery from motivated illness. A second relieving mechanism is arrestation or isolation—full conformity is not restored, but some accommodation is made by which less than normal performance by the deficient units is accepted, and other units carry the resulting burden. However, it may be extremely difficult to detect a unit's failure to attain full potentiality, as in the case of handicap contrasted with illness. Completely eliminating the unit from social function is the limiting case here.

Strain may also be relieved by change in the structure itself. Since we have emphasized strain in the *relations* of units (instability internal to the unit itself would be analyzed at the next lower level of system reference), structural change must be defined as alteration in the normative culture defining the expectations governing that relation—thus, at the systematic level, comprising all units standing in strained relations. The total empirical process may also involve change in the structure of typical units; but the essential reference is to *relational pattern*. For example, chronic instability in a typical kind of market might lead to a change in the norms governing that market; but if bargaining units change their tactics in the direction of conforming with the old norms, this would not constitute *structural* change of *this* system. In line with the general concepts of inertia and of the hierarchy of controls, we may say that endogenous change occurs only when the lower-order mechanisms of control fail to contain the factors of strain.

Factors in Change.—In introducing our discussion of the factors in structural change, we must establish the essential point that the conception of a system of interdependent variables, on the one hand, and of units or parts, on the other, by its nature implies that there is no necessary order of teleological significance in the sources of change. This applies particularly to such old controversies as economic or interest explanations *versus* explanations in terms of ideas or values. This problem is logically parallel to the problem of the relations between heredity and environment. Of a set of "factors," *any or all may be sources of change,* whose nature will depend on the ways an initial impetus is propagated through the system by the types of dynamic process analyzed under subhead III, above. [The analysis referred to, "The Dynamics of Social Equilibrium," is omitted here—*Editor.*]

To avoid implying a formless eclecticism we must add two other points. First, careful theoretical identifications must be made of the nature of the factors to which an impetus to structural change is imputed. Many factors prominent in the history of social thought are, according to the theory of social systems, exogenous—including factors of geographical environment and biological heredity, and outstanding personalities, as "great men," who are never conceived of simply as products of their societies. This category of exogenous factors also includes cultural explanations, as those in terms of religious ideas. Furthermore, these different exogenous sources are not alike in the nature of their impact on the social system.

Among these exogenous sources of change is the size of the population of any social system. Perhaps the most important relevant discussion of this was Durkheim's, in the *Division of Labor,* where he speaks of the relations between "material" and "dynamic" density. Populations are partially result- ants of the processes of social systems, but their size is in turn a determinant.[3]

The second, related point concerns the implications of the hierarchy of control in social systems. It may be difficult to define magnitude of impact; however, given approximate equality of magnitude, the probability of pro- ducing structural change is greater in proportion to the position in the order of control at which the impact of its principal disturbing influence occurs. This principle is based on the assumption that stable systems have mechan- isms which can absorb considerable internal strains, and thus endogenous or exogenous variabilities impinging at lower levels in the hierarchy of control may be neutralized before extending structural changes to higher levels. It follows that the crucial focus of the problem of change lies in the stability of the value system.

The analytical problems in this area are by no means simple. Difficulties arise because of the complex ways in which societies are composed of inter- penetrating subsystems, and because of the ways in which the exogenous factors impinge somehow on every role, collectivity norm, and subvalue. Thus the collectivity component of social structure has been placed, in general analytical terms, only third in the general control hierarchy. Yet every society must be organized as a whole on the collectivity level, integrat- ing goal-attainment, integrative, and pattern-maintenance functions. Hence an important change in the leadership composition of the over-all societal collectivity *may* have a far greater impact on the norms and values of the society generally than would a value change in lower-order subsystems. Hence a naïve use of the formula, the higher in the control hierarchy the greater the impact, is not recommended.

The Impact of the Forces of Change

Our approach to the problem of impact has already been foreshadowed. Disturbance may result from deficient or excessive input at a given point in the system. The generalization about the disturbing effects of excess is a direct corollary of the concept of equilibrium; it seems contrary often to common sense, but it has been clearly validated for many cases in social

---

[3] We have recently been reminded by Schnore of the importance of this aspect of Durkheim's analysis. See Leo Schnore, "Social Morphology and Human Ecology," *American Journal of Sociology*, May, 1958, pp. 620–34.

interaction. One of the best known cases is the Keynesian point about the relation between oversaving and unemployment; another is Durkheim's generalization about the positive relation between increasing economic prosperity and rates of suicide; a third would be the pathogenic effect of maternal overprotection on a developing child. The point is crucial for present purposes, because, in any important boundary relation of a society, the stability of both systems is a function of a *balancing* of rates of input and output which go *both* ways. This consideration also clearly applies to both exogenous and endogenous sources of change.

Impact will vary as a function of at least five ranges of variation in the nature of the impinging process, as described below: (1) the magnitude of the disturbance—not an absolute quantity, but magnitude of *change* from previous customary input-output rates, which have become accommodated to the system's conditions of equilibrium. (2) The proportion of units in the system at the relevant levels that are affected. (3) The strategic character of the unit's functional contribution to the system—e.g., the sudden death of 50 per cent of the unskilled workers would not have the same impact as the death of 50 per cent of the highest 10 per cent of political leaders. (4) The incidence of the disturbance on analytically distinguishable components of the system's structure. Given the strategic significance of a structural unit, roles are most readily replaceable or reparable, subcollectivities less so, norms even less so, and value-commitments least. The reverse order holds for exposure to the impact of change; the conditions of individuals' role-performances are most exposed and therefore most likely to "give," whereas value-commitments are least exposed because they are neither function- nor situation-specific. Finally, (5) there is the degree of resistance by the relevant parts of the system to the impact of forces of change—i.e., the level of effectiveness of the mechanisms of control. A relatively large disturbance may not lead to major change in a very stable system; a much smaller disturbance may lead to drastic change in an unstable system. Stability is variable both quantitatively and qualitatively.

Empirically, forces making for change seldom operate neatly according to discrete analytical categories; their impact is diffused. Thus the Cold War's impact on American society operates primarily on two levels. One is by its effect on national security—primarily a political problem. Since the United States can no longer rely on a stable European power system for its security, as it did through the nineteenth century, the Cold War is the immediate cause for maintaining a large military establishment and attempting to foster the rapid development of military technology—with all the repercussions that this essentially new peacetime situation has throughout the society. The Cold War also has an important impact at the level of commitments to values and the most generalized level of norms. Without this "challenge of communism"—not just the challenge of a strong military power, but a challenge to the *legitimacy* of the "American way"—the current situation would be far less disturbing.

These two components are empirically associated. But they are analytically distinguishable, and their proportionate importance may vary, in the same case over time as well as in different cases. A comparably serious military threat to national security, unaccompanied by the ideological factor, would be much less disturbing at present to the United States, because internal changes in American society have produced factors of instability at integrative levels that were not previously so acute. Our problem in really accepting our universalistic values, for example, is clearly shown in the present segregation-desegregation issue. A major development of societal political responsibility, as a function of both internal development and changed international position, is necessary. Without special sensitivities to the symbolic reverberations of "communism"—independent of "realistic" dangers—a phenomenon like McCarthyism would be incomprehensible.

Analytical discrimination of factors within the framework of empirical variation makes more precision about matters of impact possible. Thus technological processes concerning the physical environment have quite a different significance from problems of the motivational commitments of individuals and collective subunits to functional performance in the system. For example, in America there has allegedly been a major shift recently in this respect—in Riesman's terms, from "inner-directed" to "other-directed"; in Kluckhohn's, a "decline of the Protestant Ethic."[4] Both interpretations suggest a retreat from occupational contributions into the sphere of private preoccupations. Though discussions of such problems are often couched in the terminology of values, this problem belongs more at the level of motivation to functional contribution. Whether or not a change in the societal value-system underlies this at a higher level of control is an analytically distinguishable part of the empirical problems.[5]

By present definition, a change in the structure of a social system is a change in its normative culture. At the most general level, it is a change in the paramount value system. From this level through the series of differentiation, segmentation, and specification, it involves changes in the normative culture of subsystems, of progressively lower order, that are increasingly specific with reference to function in the larger system and to situation.

----

[4] See David Riesman, *The Lonely Crowd;* Clyde Kluckholm, "Have There Been Discernible Shifts in American Values during the Past Generation?" in Elting Morrison (ed.), *The American Style* (New York: Harper, 1958) pp. 145–217.

[5] I have attempted to deal more fully with this problem in "The Link between Character and Society" (with Winston White), in Lipset and Lowenthal (eds.), *Culture and Social Character: The Work of David Riesman Reviewed* (Glencoe: The Free Press, 1961).

Through specification we arrive eventually at the *role* level and, with this, at the psychological motivation of the individual. It is my thesis that *any* major disturbance will occasion widespread disturbances in individuals' motivations at the role level, and under the requisite conditions will lead to structural changes at least there. But it does not follow either from the presence of widespread symptoms of disturbance, or from important structural changes in such motivational patterning, that the structure of the system at all levels—especially in the paramount value system—has changed.

In considering the general problem of impact, we must remember that every structurally distinguished subsystem of a society is both complex and never fully integrated. Moreover, the structural components are interlarded in all the different subsystems; yet even minimal integration requires some measure of consistency between values and norms both at the higher and lower levels of specification and across the lines of functional differentiation. Such considerations help account for the facts that many processes of change occur simultaneously at several levels, and that influences are propagated through the levels of control in the system from one to another.

An important example is presented by underdeveloped societies at the present time. If we take economic development, in the sense of industrialization, as the focal content of the process, the two primary foci of the impact of inputs are political and cultural, in the value-sense; they are not, in the usual analytical sense, economic. Both focus primarily on the relations of underdeveloped societies to economically advanced societies.

The great stirring which has been going on focuses first on national independence and power, as evidenced by the acute sensitivity to the negative symbol of "imperialism." This political preoccupation's effect then seems to be propagated in two directions: to economic development as *instrumental* to political power (and as a symbol of collective achievement); and to the *functional* value-systems associated with political power and economic productivity. The highest-level values will still be carefully *contrasted* with those of the societies serving as models of political and economic development. Another important symbolic expression of this is the common imputation of materialism to Western societies, whereas it is alleged that India, for example, can somehow have all the advantages of high industrialization without being infected with the materialistic values of the Western world. Further—contrary to the explicit content of Marxian ideology—it is often alleged that communism, because collectivistic, is less materialistic than so-called "capitalism," though communist societies have been marked by a far more exclusive dedication to economic development than *any* capitalistic society. The essential point here is the tendency to maintain the highest-level values while permitting major changes in the next level of value-specification, i.e., that of the primary functional subsystem.[6]

It is difficult to see how, in the longer run, this can fail to engender major strains; however, there is a twofold proximate ideological defense, namely, the instrumental character of political and economic development, and the bridging of the implicit conflict by symbols like "socialism." The important point analytically is that, without at least two different orders of input beyond normal levels, impetus for major change is unlikely to occur. One order is the *real* political inferiority, symbolized as "colonial dependency," of the disturbed society. The other is the existence, in the social environment, of a *model* of instrumentally appropriate reorganization, whose partial functional values can be adopted, initially allegedly without disturbing the highest-level values of the system.[7]

TYPES OF PROCESS OF STRUCTURAL CHANGE

Finally, we must attempt to determine whether any important generalizations can be made about the types of process of change found at the structural level. The phenomena of the institutionalization of normative culture imply internalization in the personality structures of constituent personalities, which in turn implies that institutionalization is embedded in the non-rational layers of motivational organization. It is not accessible to change simply through the presentation, to an actor, of rational advantages in the external definition of the situation.

In social structure, the relation of normative culture to personality is expressed by the fundamental distinction between two types of integrative mechanisms in the social system—those allocative mechanisms, operating through media like money and power, that affect the balance of advantages and disadvantages in the situation of an acting unit; and those which, like integrative communication, operate through affecting the motivational state of the unit, concerning the definition of what he wants and not how he can get it.

Only when strain impinges on and involves this level of the system of behavioral control can structural change in the present sense become

---

[6] Further analysis of these problems is contained in the paper "Some Reflections on the Sociological Framework of Economic Development," *Structure and Process in Modern Societies* (Glencoe, Ill.: Free Press, 1959), Chapter III.

[7] Naturally in the total picture, specifically economic factors of production are also necessary inputs, from other societies or from other "systems" operating in the territory of the society, like motivation, capital, etc. But because of the relation to the hierarchical structure of social systems, the inputs of political urgency and functional value-commitment are far more critical in what Rostow calls the "take-off" phenomenon than is the availability of adequate factors of production in the strictly economic sense.

possible. Once it has occurred, the question is whether the impetus to change goes "over the watershed" or, under the countervailing impact of the mechanisms of social control, falls back again.

In either case, strain at this level is manifested by a series of symptoms of disturbance showing the psychological marks of irrationality. These will be organized along the major axes of hope and fear, of "wishful thinking" and "anxiety" showing unrealistic trends in *both* respects. Psychologically, this goes back to the ambivalent structure of motivation to deviance already mentioned.

The directions of this positive-negative polarization are defined in terms of the structural possibilities of deviance.[8] The most important variables are the polarizations between activity and passivity, between compulsive alienation and compulsive conformity, that yields the types of rebelliousness, withdrawal, "ritualism," and compulsive performance. In other words, there will be fantasies of utopian ideal future states, of idealized past states, of security in a status quo from which sources of disturbance could conveniently be banished, and of eliminating sources of disturbance directly within the framework of the old structure. There will be corresponding foci of anxiety.

These motivational components are common to all symptoms of disturbance in the institutionalization of social structures. The symbols to which they become attached will depend on the appropriate system references and situations. At the societal level, it is not difficult to detect the utopian element in "communism," in the sense of an alleged actual type of society; or, on the other side, a complete "free enterprise" system. The socially regressive idealization of an unrealistically conceived past appears in such symbols as the simple, unspoiled "Americanism" of the McCarthyites, or in the *Volksgemeinschaft* of German Romantics (particularly in its most extreme version, Naziism). Such symbols as "imperialism," "capitalism," and "communism" are foci of irrational anxiety and aggression.

Another symbolic content is found where the focus of disturbance is a different order of social system. "Authoritarianism" and "conformity" are good examples of anxiety-laden symbols widely current in our society. Some of the irrational symbols in this context have functions in social systems analogous to those of the personality's mechanisms of defense. The equivalents of displacement and projection are found in the imputation of the sources of disturbance to exogenous systems—particularly similar systems—when much of the motivation really arises from internal strain. Indeed, dis-

---

8 See Merton, "Social Structure and Anomie," *Social Theory and Social Structure*, revised and extended edition, Free Press, 1957; and Parsons, *The Social System*, Free Press, 1951, Chap. VII.

placement and/or projection on *personalities* of the products of strain in social systems cause much of the attributing of ill-will to, e.g., "ruling circles."

Symptoms of disturbance, with the kind of structure just sketched, are common to processes which do and do not result in structural change. Whether or not the change occurs depends on the *balance* between the strength of the disturbing forces and the kinds of reception they meet—i.e., the balance between acts motivated by response to disturbance and the sanctions that they stimulate in both endogenous and exogenous agencies. This statement is not a tautology if these conceptions are given content through definition of the nature of the performances and sanctions, and of the strategic significance of content for the equilibrium of the system.

Structural change is possible only when a certain level of strain on institutionalized structure is reached. Such strain may be propagated from technological, economic, and political levels; but the fact that a system is faced with severe problems on those levels is never *by itself* a sufficient explanation of structural change. It is necessary to trace the repercussions of these strains on the higher levels of the control system.

Even when the institutional level is reached, severity of strain is never alone an adequate explanation of change. Structural change is only one possible outcome of strain. Other results are the resolution of the strain, through mechanisms of control, that leaves the old structure intact; and the isolation of disturbing forces, at the cost of some impairment of the system's functioning—and, of course, radical dissolution of the system.

Besides the generalized strength-weakness balance of the disturbances and controls respectively, the most important factors favoring structural change are the following: (1) Adequate mechanisms for overcoming the inevitable resistances of institutionalized structural patterns (vested interests) to abandonment. Overwhelming force or political coercion may impose very severe strains, but, in the absence of such mechanisms, they lead only to active or passive resistance, even though the resistance is realistically hopeless.[9] Endogenously, the balance between positive and negative components in the symptoms of disturbance is the primary factor. For example, if the negative side outweighs the positive, anxiety and aggression will block new institutionalization. (2) Among the positive reactions, there must be combinations with adequate constructive possibilities. The component of alienation must be strong enough to motivate detachment from the older patterns,

---

[9] In certain respects, the Hungarian crisis of 1956 seems to fit this pattern, so far as institutionalization of the new patterns of Stalinist communism is concerned. The social system equivalents of the therapeutic mechanisms centering on permissiveness and support seem particularly crucial in this connection.

but not so closely connected with other negative components that it motivates only destructive behavior. On the other hand, too great passivity would motivate only withdrawal. (3) A model, from exogenous sources or endogenously produced, of the pattern to be newly institutionalized is necessary. In socializing the child, the parents, older peers, teachers, and others serve as "role-models" whose personalities and actions embody the patterns of value and norms which the child is expected to internalize; without such adequate models, the internalization would be impossible. (4) The pattern of sanctions evoked by behavior in the transitional phases must selectively reward action conforming with the new model (and must not reward action in terms of the old pattern), and must be sufficiently consistent over a period to bring about the coinciding of the values of units and their self-interest that is the hallmark of institutionalization.

The socialization of the child actually constitutes a process of structural change in one set of structural components of social systems, namely, the role-patterns of the individual—indeed, much of the foregoing paradigm has been derived from this source.[10] These considerations may then be extended to the next level: the corollary of the proposition that the child internalizes new roles in the process of socialization is that the social systems in which this process occurs, e.g., the mother-child system and the nuclear family, must undergo processes of structural change. Thus, the nuclear family with one infant is, structurally speaking, not the same system as that with two adolescent children and one latency-period child, though in another perspective it may still be the same family.

For a more general sociological analysis, however, it may be better to illustrate by two types of process of structural change close to the societal level, in one of which the "model" is predominantly endogenous to the system, in the other, exogenous. The first is the case usually referred to as "structural differentiation" affecting the level of primary functional subsystems; the second, the case involving change in the value-system at the societal level.

The Differentiation of Occupational from Kinship Roles.—In the above discussion, reference has often been made to the relative "functional diffuseness" of many social structures. The process of functional differentiation is one of the fundamental types of social change, and has evolutionary aspects and implications. In its bearing on the type of system, it involves more than increasing complexity—e.g., the fact that flexible disposability of resources

---

10 This assumption is based largely on Freud's work. See Parsons and Olds, Chapter IV of Parsons and Bales, *Family, Socialization and Interaction Process*, Free Press, 1955, and Parsons, "Social Structure and the Development of Personality: Freud's Contribution to the Integration of Psychology and Sociology," *Psychiatry*, November, 1958.

depends on such differentiation. This dependence requires higher-order mechanisms of integration, substituting the more specialized processes of control associated with markets, power systems, etc., for control through embeddedness in diffuse structures.

Perhaps the best example is the differentiation of occupational roles, in the ideal sense already discussed, from embeddedness in kinship structures which have enjoyed ascribed claims to the functional equivalents of such services. On the role-structure level, the change means that what has been one role of an individual in a single kinship collectivity (which may, however, be internally differentiated) becomes differentiated into two roles in two distinct collectivities, the kinship group and the employing organization.[11]

The first prerequisite of change is disengagement from the preceding pattern.[12] In other words, some order of relative deprivation becomes attached to following the old way. The impingement of the deprivation is on the individual and on the kinship collectivity. The impingement may take such forms as deterioration of previously assumed market conditions, or of the availability of new opportunities which cannot be utilized within the old structural framework. Such severe and prolonged relative deprivation would eventually give rise to symptoms of disturbance of the sort discussed.

In order to prevent the overwhelming consolidation of the negative components of the reactions to disturbance, there must be an adequate range of institutionalized permissiveness and support, in addition to the imposition of deprivations for following the old pattern. There should not be too great immediate pressure for abandoning the old ways precipitately and totally. In the Industrial Revolution in England, this institutionalized permissiveness, as Smelser shows, comprised considerable remaining realistic opportunity in the old domestic pattern of industrial organization, compromise organizational patterns whereby whole families were hired by the cotton mills as units, and considerable "romantic" ideological support for the value of the old ways.

A positive model for the new patterning of work contribution must be demonstrated, first on the immediately relevant organizational level—e.g., factories are organized and jobs made available which offer advantages, i.e., various components of reward, including but not confined to money wages, to the worker and his household. But one crucial problem concerns

---

[11] The operation of this process at the "working class" level has, to my knowledge been most thoroughly analyzed in Neil J. Smelser, *Social Change or the Industrial Revolution*, U. of Chicago Press, 1959.

[12] The general paradigm of the process of differentiation somewhat elliptically followed here was set forth in Parsons and Smelser, *Economy and Society*, Free Press, 1956, Chap. V, and much more extensively developed and applied in Smelser, *op. cit.*

the ways in which this new model can be made legitimate in terms of the relevant values.

As Smelser shows, it was very important in the British case that the structural changes in the role-organization of the labor force of the late eighteenth century were preceded, and for some time accompanied, by a marked revival, in precisely the geographical section and population groups involved, of the Puritan religion. According to the famous Weber hypothesis, Puritanism has legitimized both profit-making and more broadly effective contribution to instrumental function in society. More immediately, the main justification of the factory system was its greater productive effectiveness. In the typical working-class household, there was promise of both realistic opportunity to organize work in a new way, and legitimation of that way in terms of a firmly institutionalized religious tradition. A steady pattern of sanctions operated to reinforce the change, whose most tangible aspect was the steady increase of real wages, largely derived from the productivity of the new industry.[13]

The outcome of the process was the incorporation of a very large new group of the working-class labor force into the factory system, in fully differentiated occupational roles, with the concomitant loss of most of the function of family economic production. Working in factory premises, for an individual wage and under factory rather than kinship discipline, was a main structural feature of the outcome. Smelser makes it clear that this was not a simple matter of attracting workers by better wages than could be offered elsewhere—it was only possible through a major restructuring of the institutional structure of the working-class kinship system.

For the larger system, the part played by the *endogenous* sources of the model components of the process was particularly important. It is not necessary to question the common belief that the immediate impetus came from mechanical inventions. Implementing this impetus at levels bearing on the structure of occupational roles, however, was mainly the work of entrepreneurs—some of whom, like Arkwright, were also the inventors. But the legitimation of the new opportunities could be derived by *specification*, in the

---

13 A tragic case of the misfiring of such a process of change, illustrating the importance of the balance of these factors, was the case of the hand-loom weavers. The original impetus for greatly increased productivity came in spinning. The resulting greatly increased supply of yarn put pressure on the weaving branch. But in the absence of usable inventions—which came later—and of other aspects of reorganization in this field, the main result was an enormous quantitative expansion of the weaving trade on the *old* basis of social structure. When the power loom took over, the unrestructured weaving trade was left high and dry. It is not surprising that this group was the main center of disturbance in North England in that period. Smelser, *op. cit.*, treats this case in some detail.

light of the new opportunities, of an already firmly institutionalized value-system. The essential point is that enhanced economic productivity was defined as good, in a way justifying the major disturbances of institutional structures at lower levels necessary for taking advantage of the greater opportunities. The legitimation of profit-making is only part of a larger complex, whose focus is on the valuation of productivity.

The distinction between the process of structural differentiation and that involving the value-system of a society is relative. In complex societies, processes of differentiation are continually going on at relatively low levels of specification and high levels of structural segmentation. The differentiation of occupational roles from embeddedness in kinship should, however, be placed among the very important processes having repercussions in the society extending far beyond their immediate locations. It is clearly a function of great extension in the division of labor and, consequently, in the extent of markets. It makes salient a whole series of new problems with respect to the institution of contract and the conditions of employment—including the beginnings of large-scale union organization and collective bargaining, and various other questions about the status of the working classes. When a process occurs of the magnitude of the rise of the cotton textile industry until about 1840—*magnitude* not only absolutely but in terms of its place in the total economy of Great Britain—it constitutes a major change in the structure of the society. It is not surprising that the disturbances associated with it included much agitation in national politics and noticeable "effervescence" in religion. At the same time, the change did not involve introducing a new value system at the national level—i.e., the fundamentals of Puritan orientation and its place in British national values had been settled in the sixteenth and seventeenth centuries.

Change in the Societal Value System.—At the highest normative level, two main types of structural change may be distinguished. The first, already described, is the one where the principal model component comes from outside the society. This has been true of the contemporary underdeveloped areas, as outlined. To some degree, it was true of all the post-British cases of industrialization, including the American.

The American case went farthest in accepting the British model of free enterprise, though with some important qualifications. This can be attributed first to the fact that the value system deriving mainly from the ethic of ascetic Protestantism had been strongly institutionalized in this country by the early nineteenth century; furthermore, the basic structural position of religion had been settled by the adoption of the Constitutional separation of church and state that paved the way for denominational pluralism. The British model, therefore, posed no serious problem of value-orientation; the American case was considerably closer to a pure culture of the ascetic branch of Protestantism most involved in industrialization than was the British. The problem in our case was primarily the process of structural differentiation. Many religious movements, especially revivalist ones, played an important part on the fringes of the spread of industrialization. These have been essentially similar to Methodism in the north of England in the later eighteenth century.

This is probably one of the major causes of the relatively small role of political agency in the American case, though political agency played a greater part in such fields as the subsidizing of railway building in America than in Britain. Essentially, there was no very serious problem of gaining general acceptance of the functional values necessary for industrialization, as there was in underdeveloped areas or even in most Continental European countries. It is probably not entirely fortuitous that both Japan and the Soviet Union, although very different, became industrialized under very heavy governmental pressure; in both cases, the ideological justification of the requisite value-commitments played a particularly important part. In Japan, the nationalistic connotations of aspects of the Shinto religious tradition were particularly important.[14] In the Soviet case, the revolutionary force of the Communist movement was grafted onto a Russian social structure that had always emphasized the priority of the state over private interests— far more strongly than in most Western countries. The Party functioned as the primary agency of ideological indoctrination which, under the utopian conception of communism, has inculcated the values necessary for high commitment to economic productivity—values which seem to have been relatively weak in pre-Revolutionary Russia.

The combination of practical urgency and the absence of the functional-level value commitment constitutes a major reason that, for the underdeveloped countries, governmental agency and the importance of the ideological symbol of "socialism" play such an important role in industrialization. Even the rigid authoritarianism of Communist organizational practices occasions far less resistance in these circumstances, since there is both the factor of urgency, to an extent which we do not feel, and, perhaps even more important, the necessity of counterbalancing, in the inevitable ambivalent structure, the profound resistance to value change.[15]

---

[14] On the political primacy of Japanese society and its role in industrialization, as well as its relation to the religious background, see R. N. Bellah, *Tokugawa Religion* (Glencoe, Ill.: Free Press, 1957).

[15] The most conspicuous example of a failure to overcome this resistance, very probably because of the failure to provide the necessary permissiveness and support to ease

The second main type of societal value-change is that occurring when the cultural model cannot be supplied from a socially exogenous source, but must, so far as the social system reference is concerned, be evolved from within the society. This is the situation to which Max Weber's famous category of charismatic innovation applies. The focus of the change must be in the cultural system's religious aspects. It must concern alterations in the definition of the meaning of the life of the individual in society and of the character of the society itself.

In the process of development, a cultural change which could change values at a societal level would arise, through some complex process involving the interaction and interdependence of social and cultural systems. Considerations such as those reviewed by Weber in his writings on classes, status groups and religion (see end of Section B in Part Four) would be highly relevant insofar as they concern society. The whole system of action, and the action-exogenous environment impinging upon it, is also relevant to this problem. The special role of the charismatic personality may involve problems specific to personality theory and not reducible either to sociological or cultural terms.

The obverse is the process of institutionalizing new religious values. The first question arising concerns the specification of the values from the cultural to the social system level, that is, defining of the implications of the cultural premises for the *kind of society* considered desirable. The second basic problem concerns the processes by which, once such a set of societal values is available, the strategically most important elements in the population may be motivationally committed to them. In other words, these elements must be socialized in the new definition of the situation if they are to exert the leverage necessary for extending the institutionalization of the values to all the important levels of specification and areas of differentiated function in the society.

A few points may be mentioned that are pertinent. The bearers of the new values must somehow become established in such a way that they cannot be reabsorbed in the older system. Religious or semi-religious movements, churches, etc., must be structurally independent of the paramount politically organized collectivity. Once consolidated, however, the institutionalization of new values in the secular society is possible only when these bearers can acquire a fundamental influence over the leadership elements of the paramount political system, through conversion of these elements

---

the process of relinquishment of old values, is probably the case of the Russian peasantry. Agriculture is clearly the main sore spot of Soviet productivity, and this seems to go back to the violently coercive procedures adopted in the collectivization program. See Bauer, Inkeles, and Kluckhohn, *How the Soviet System Works* (Cambridge: Harvard Press, 1957).

through infiltration, or through revolution. In early medieval Europe, the Church was the main locus of the values which later underlay the activism of modern Western society. The religious orders were the main locus of the values' growth and consolidation. If the Church and its orders had merely been a part of the political organization, this would not have occurred. In the great period from Gregory VII to Innocent III, the Church was able to impose much more of its values on a reluctant political laity than it otherwise could have. This did not happen without a good deal of direct interpenetration of political and religious leadership; but the basic principle of differentiation of church and state, though under considerable strain, was not abandoned.

A variety of other considerations about this process could be discussed, but perhaps these are enough to show the general nature of the process of change involved in the institutionalization of new values at the societal level.

CONCLUSION

Although it may seem long, relative to the task the above outline is obviously just a sketch, and a very tentative one. It is a statement of what seems to *one* particular author at *one* particular time to be the most useful way of organizing his view of the complex problems and materials which must somehow enter into the analysis of social systems. We have emphasized, throughout the introductory materials of this Anthology, that in our opinion sociology, as a theoretical as well as an empirical science, is in an early stage of development. We hold, therefore, that *any* statement made in our generation, even in outline, is in the nature of the case destined to be superseded, and relatively quickly. Any other view would contradict the established fact that science is an *inherently* evolving thing; if it should stop developing and become fixated on any particular set of "doctrines," it would *ipso facto* cease to be science.

This is the statement of our fundamental conviction. It does not imply, as is sometimes suggested, that, in the theory of sociology as in other sciences, there is an indefinite plurality of equally legitimate positions on all questions, an eclecticism which is the counterpart, for the sociology of science, of radical cultural relativism in a broader context. Such an implication would directly contradict our equally fundamental conviction that there has been a definite emerging structure of problems in our field, and a cumulative development of analytical thinking relative to them.

We have conscientiously tried to avoid the Scylla of dogmatism in presenting a theoretical view which is inevitably selective and incomplete, but is the best *we* can do at this time. We think it equally necessary to avoid the Charybdis of that formless eclecticism, common at least by implication in contemporary discussions, according to which in our field "anything goes," or "you pays your money and you takes your choice"; according to which there are alleged to be *no* serious professional criteria of theoretical excellence on any generalized level.[16]

---

[16] It is perhaps pertinent to note (January, 1961) that this Introduction was written in the late summer and early fall of 1958. Sufficient developments have taken place in the interim so that had it been written two years later, it would have been somewhat different and we hope better. It was not, however, possible to undertake extensive revisions at that time. For the interested reader there are two places where some of the pertinent further theoretical developments are available, namely "Pattern Variables Revisited: A Response to Professor Dubin," *American Sociological Review*, August, 1960; and "The Point of View of the Author," the final chapter in Max Black (ed.), *The Social Theories of Talcott Parsons* (New York: Prentice-Hall, 1961).

S. N. Eisenstadt

Social Change, Differentiation and Evolution

*E*VOLUTIONARY theory dominated sociological thought in the 19th and early 20th centuries, but since about 1920 interest in it has, on the whole, given way to preoccupation with systematic analysis of social systems, analysis of broad social and demographic trends, and investigation of the social determinants of behavior. The recent tentative revival of interest in an evolutionary perspective is closely related to growing interest in historical and comparative studies. It does not, of course, denote a mere "return" to the assumptions of the older schools, but it does imply revision and reappraisal of evolutionary theory in the light of recent advances in sociological theory and research.

The older evolutionary models broke down mainly on two stumbling blocks. The first was the assumption that the development of human societies is unilinear, and the major "stages" of development universal.[1] The second

---

Reprinted from S. N. Eisenstadt, "Social Change, Differentiation and Evolution," *American Sociological Review*, 29 (June, 1964), pp. 375–386, by permission of the author and The American Sociological Association.

[1] One of the best expositions of the strength and limitations of the classical evolutionary approach was written by a prominent contemporary sociologist identified with that approach. See Morris Ginsberg, "On the Concept of Evolution in Sociology" in

stumbling block was the failure to specify fully the systematic characteristics of evolving societies or institutions, as well as the mechanisms and processes of change through which the transition from one "stage" to another was effected. Most of the classical evolutionary schools tended, rather, to point out general causes of change (economic, technological, spiritual, etc.) or some general trends (e.g., the trend to complexity) inherent in the development of societies. Very often they confused such general tendencies with the causes of change or assumed that the general tendencies explain concrete instances of change.[2]

Hence, reappraisal of an evolutionary perspective is contingent on systematic explanation of the processes of change within a society, the processes of transition from one type of society to another, and especially the extent to which such transition may crystallize into different types or "stages" that evince some basic characteristics common to different societies. Despite contrary claims, the conceptual tools recently developed for the analysis of systematic properties of societies and social institutions may be used to analyze the concrete processes of change within them.

First, tendencies to change are inherent in all human societies, because they face basic problems to which no overall continuous solutions exist. These problems include uncertainties of socialization, perennial scarcity of resources relative to individual aspirations and different, contrasting, types of social orientation or principles of social organization (e.g., *Gemeinschaft* vs. *Gesellschaft*) within the society.[3] Second, specific processes of change in any concrete society are closely related to the specific characteristics of its institutional structure and can be explained largely in terms of the crystallization of this structure and the problem of maintaining it. Moreover, the directions of change in any given society are greatly influenced and limited by its basic systematic characteristics and by the specific problems resulting from its institutionalization.[4]

---

idem, Essays on Sociology and Social Philosophy, Vol. I, (London: William Heinemann, 1957), and *idem, Diversity of Morals*, (London: William Heinemann, 1956), chs. 11 and 12. For a more recent summary, see T. B. Bottomore, *Sociology, A Guide to Problems and Literature*, (London: Unwin University Books, 1962), chs. 7 and 16.

[2] See Kenneth E. Bock, "Evolution, Function and Change," *American Sociological Review*, 28 (April, 1963), pp. 229–237. The use of general causes or trends for explanation of evolution can be found also in Marshall D. Sahlins and Elman R. Service (eds.), *Evolution and Culture*, Ann Arbor, Mich.: University of Michigan Press, 1960, who follow Leslie A. White, *The Evolution of Culture*, New York: McGraw-Hill, 1959. However, their distinction between general and specific evolution indicates that they are aware at least of some of the difficulties in such an assumption.

[3] See Wilbert E. Moore, "A Reconsideration of Theories of Social Change," *American Sociological Review*, 25 (December, 1960), pp. 817 ff.

[4] See Shmuel N. Eisenstadt, "Institutionalization and Change," *American Sociological Review*, 29 (April, 1964), pp. 49–59.

From the point of view of reappraising evolutionary theory, however, the more crucial problem concerns the extent to which change from one type of society to another is not accidental or random but evinces overall evolutionary or "developmental" trends in the society's adaptability to an extending environment. In other words, the main problem here is the extent to which such changes may be envisaged as crystallizing into developmental "stages"—the key concept in classical evolutionary thought.

In the older evolutionary school such stages have been construed mostly in terms of "specialization" and "complexity." In recent works these concepts have been to a large extent replaced by that of "differentiation."[5] This replacement is not merely semantic: it reflects an important theoretical advance in the study of society—an advance that greatly facilitates critical re-evaluation of the evolutionary perspective in the social sciences.

Differentiation is, like complexity or specialization, first of all a classificatory concept. It describes the ways through which the main social functions or the major institutional spheres of society become disassociated from one another, attached to specialized collectivity and roles, and organized in relatively specific and autonomous symbolic and organizational frameworks within the confines of the same institutionalized system.

In broad evolutionary terms, such continuous differentiation has been usually conceived as a continuous development from the "ideal" type of the primitive society or band in which all the major roles are allocated on an ascriptive basis, and in which the division of labor is based primarily on family and kinship units.[6] Development proceeds through various stages of specialization and differentiation.

Specialization is manifest first when each of the major institutional spheres develops, through the activities of people placed in strategic roles within it, its own organizational units and complexes, and its specific criteria of action. The latter tend to be more congruent with the basic orientations of a given sphere, facilitating the development of its potentialities—technological innovation, cultural and religious creativity, expansion of political power or participation, or development of complex personality structure.[7]

---

5 See, for instance, Robert M. MacIver and Charles Page, *Society*, New York: Rinehart, 1947; Talcott Parsons, *The Social System*, Glencoe, Ill.: The Free Press, 1951, chs. 4, 5; and Marion J. Levy, Jr., *The Structure of Society*, Princeton: Princeton University Press, 1952, especially ch. 7.

6 For a recent discussion of primitive societies from an evolutionary point of view, see Elman R. Service, *Primitive Social Organization, An Evolutionary Perspective*, New York: Random House, 1962.

7 For an earlier approach, see Pitirim A. Sorokin, *Society, Culture and Personality*, New York: Harper, 1947, and for one of the fullest recent analytic approaches, see Talcott Parsons and Edward A. Shils (eds.), *Toward a General Theory of Action*, Cambridge, Mass.: Harvard University Press, 1951, p. 2.

Secondly, different levels or stages of differentiation denote the degree to which major social and cultural activities, as well as certain basic resources —manpower, economic resources, commitments—have been disembedded or freed from kinship, territorial and other ascriptive units. On the one hand, these "free-floating" resources pose new problems of integration, while on the other they may become the basis for a more differentiated social order which is, potentially at least, better adapted to deal with a more variegated environment.

Differentiation and Problems of Integration

The more differentiated and specialized institutional spheres become more interdependent and potentially complementary in their functioning within the same overall institutionalized system. But this very complementarity creates more difficult and complex problems of integration. The growing autonomy of each sphere of social activity, and the concomitant growth of interdependence and mutual interpretation among them, pose for each sphere more difficult problems in crystallizing its own tendencies and potentialities and in regulating its normative and organizational relations with other spheres.[8] And at each more "advanced" level or stage of differentiation, the increased autonomy of each sphere creates more complex problems of integrating these specialized activities into one systematic framework.[9]

Continuous regulation of these more specialized units and of the flow of "free-floating" resources among them necessitates the institutionalization of certain symbolic, normative and organizational patterns[10]—written language, generalized legal systems, and various types of complex social organization— which evince, at each more complex level of differentiation, a greater scope of generalization.

Perhaps the best indication of the importance of these macrosocietal integrative problems is the emergence of a "center," on which the problems of different groups within the society increasingly impinge.[11] The emergence

---

[8] For an analysis of these problems in one major cultural and social sphere, see Robert N. Bellah's companion article in this issue on evolution in religion.

[9] For an analysis of one such case see Shmuel N. Eisenstadt, *The Political Systems of Empires*, New York: The Free Press, 1963.

[10] Talcott Parsons describes these as "evolutionary universals" in his companion article in this issue.

[11] On the concept of "center of society" and on the problems of macrosociological analysis, see Edward A. Shils, "Epilogue," in Talcott Parsons, Edward A. Shils, Kaspar D. Naegele, and Jesse R. Pitts (eds.), *Theories of Society*, New York: The Free Press, 1961, Vol. 2, especially pp. 1441–1445. For special developments in modern societies

of a political or religious "center" of a society, distinct from its ascriptive components, is one of the most important break-throughs of development from the relatively closed kinship-based primitive community. In some of the archaic societies of the ancient Near East, Pre-Han China, and various pre-liminary stages of City States, the center in these first stages of differentiation was not only structurally differentiated from the major ascriptive groups but also distinct from them, being largely identical with relatively closed but already differentiated higher-status groups.

With growing differentiation in later city states and in feudal and central-ized Imperial systems, impingement of the broader groups and strata on the center increased somewhat. This is most clearly visible at the onset of modernization, when broader groups and strata tend to be drawn into the center, demanding greater participation.

Recognition of the integrative problems that are attendant on new levels of differentiation constitutes the main theoretical implication of the concept of differentiation. How does this analytical implication affect the possibility of reappraising the evolutionary perspective in sociological theory?

Such a reappraisal is contingent on the explication of three major problems. First, the occurrence of changes that facilitate growing differentia-tion must be explained. Second, we must understand the conditions that ensure institutionalization of more differentiated, generalized, and adaptable systems, and third, the possibility that parallel systems will develop within different societies should be evaluated. We are as yet far from any definitive answers to these questions, but at least we can point out some of the most important problems.

The passage of a given society from one stage of differentiation to another is contingent on the development within it of certain processes of change which create a degree of differentiation that cannot be contained within the pre-existing system. Growing differentiation and the consequent structural break-throughs may take place through a secular trend of differen-tiation, or through the impact of one or a series of abrupt changes, or both. These tendencies may be activated by the occupants of strategic roles within the major institutional spheres as they attempt to broaden the scope and develop the potentialities of their respective spheres. The extent to which these changes are institutionalized, and the concrete form they take in any given society, necessarily depend on the basic institutional contours and

---

see Daniel Lerner, *The Passing of Traditional Society*, Glencoe, Ill.: The Free Press, 1958; Talcott Parsons, *Structure and Process in Modern Societies*, Glencoe, Ill.: The Free Press, 1960, ch. 4; Edward A. Shils, *Political Development in New States*, The Hague: Mouton, 1963; and Shmuel N. Eisenstadt, *Modernization, Growth and Diver-sity*, The Carnegie Faculty Seminar on Political and Administrative Development, Indiana University, Bloomington, Ind., 1963.

premises of the pre-existing system, on its initial level of differentiation, and on the major conflicts and propensities for change within it.[12]

But we need not assume that all changes in all societies necessarily increase differentiation. On the contrary, the available evidence shows that many social changes do not give rise to overall changes in the scope of differentiation, but instead result mainly in changes in the relative strength and composition of different collectivities or in the integrative criteria of a particular institutional sphere. Largely because the problem has not yet been fully studied we do not know exactly what conditions facilitate or precipitate these different types of change in different societies.[13]

Similarly we need not assume that the successful, orderly institutionalization of a new, more differentiated social system is a necessary outcome of every instance of social change or of increased social differentiation within a society. Moreover, the concrete contours of such institutionalization may greatly vary among different societies at similar or parallel stages of differentiation.

The degree of differentiation refers mainly to the "division of labor" in any social system. It denotes the extent to which a society has been transformed from something approximating Durkheim's "mechanical" model to a potentially more "organic" one; it also denotes the extent to which new regulative or integrative problems cannot be dealt with by pre-existing institutions. Growing differentiation entails extension of the scope and depth of internal problems and of external environmental exigencies to which any social system is sensitive and with which it may or may not be able to deal.

The growing autonomy of the different institutional spheres, and the extension of their organizational scope, not only increases the range and depth of "social" and human problems, but it opens up new possibilities for development and creativity—for technological development, expansion of political power or rights, or cultural, religious, philosophical, and personal creativity. Growing differentiation also enhances systemic sensitivity to a much wider physical-technical environment and to more comprehensive intersocietal relations. But the growth of systemic sensitivity to a broader and more variegated environment, to new problems and exigencies, does not necessarily imply the development of the ability to deal with these problems, nor does it indicate the ways in which these problems may be solved. At any given level of differentiation, an institutional sphere may or may not achieve an adequate degree of integration, and the potentialities unfolded through

---

12 See Eisenstadt, "Institutionalization and Change," *op. cit.*

13 But see Fred Eggan, "Cultural Drift and Social Change," *Current Anthropology*, 4 (October, 1963), pp. 347–360. For a preliminary attempt to analyze this problem in one

the process of differentiation may be wasted"—i.e., fail to become crystallized into an institutional structure.

Responses to Growing Differentiation

The possibility that similar processes of change and institutionalization of different levels of differentiation may occur in different societies can be explained only so far as the available evidence bears out the assumption that the tendencies of major social spheres to autonomy and some of the basic potentialities for development in these spheres are characteristic of all societies.

Unlike the classical evolutionary writers, however, most "recent" theorists, from Weber on, do not assume that the types of social system characteristic of a given level of differentiation take on the same concrete institutional contours in all societies.[14] But the implications of this position have not yet been fully explicated.

At any level of development, response to the problems created by the process of differentiation may take one of several different forms. The most extreme outcome is failure to develop any adequate institutional solution to the new problems arising from growing differentiation. Aside from biological extinction, the consequences may be total or partial disintegration of the system, a semi-parasitic existence at the margin of another society, or total submersion within another society.

Thus, for instance, the Greek City States at the end of the Periclean period—in contrast to the late Roman Republic—did not produce a political leadership capable of building new types of political regime; as distinct sociopolitical units they became extinct. Similarly, many societies undergoing modernization lack the ability to crystallize new, viable regimes in the economic, political or cultural fields. In Bulgaria, for instance, Gerschenkron has analyzed an interesting case of what he calls "missed opportunity." The Congo constitutes perhaps the most extreme instance of this problem among contemporary new states.[15]

---

14 See Max Weber, *The Theory of Social and Economic Organization*, London: William Hodge, 1941, especially ch. 3. More recent works dealing with these problems include Robert Redfield, *The Primitive World and Its Transformations*, Ithaca, N.Y.: Cornell University Press, 1953; MacIver and Page, *op. cit.*, especially chs. 2 and 3; Talcott Parsons, *Structure and Process in Modern Societies, op. cit.*, ch. 3; and Verne F. Ray (ed.), *Intermediate Societies, Social Mobility and Communication*, Proceedings of the 1959 Annual Spring Meeting of the American Ethnological Society, Seattle: University of Washington Press, 1959.

15 See Alexander A. Gerschenkron, *Economic Backwardness in Historical Perspective*, Cambridge, Mass.: Harvard University Press, 1962, ch. 8, and also Shmuel N. Eisenstadt, "Breakdowns of Modernization," *Economic Development and Cultural Change*, forthcoming.

A less extreme type of response tends to lead to "regression," i.e., to the institutionalization of less differentiated systems. Examples include the establishment of small patrimonial or semi-feudal chiefdoms on the ruins of the Ahmenid Empire, the development of dispersed tribal-feudal systems at the downfall of the Roman Empire, and similar developments on the ruins of Greek City States.[16] Many such regressive developments are only partial in the sense that within some parts of the new institutional structure some nuclei of more differentiated and creative orientations may survive or even develop. Sometimes, but certainly not always, these nuclei "store" entreprenurial ability for possible—but not inevitable—future developments.

Another possibility, which perhaps overlaps with the last one but is not always identical to it, is the development of a social system in which the processes of differentiation and change go on relatively continuously in one part or sphere of a society without yet becoming fully integrated into a stable wider framework. In such situations a continuous process of unbalanced change may develop, resulting either in a breakdown of the existing institutional framework, or in stabilization at a relatively low level of integration.

Perhaps the best examples of such developments can be found in various dual conquest societies (e.g., conquest of the sedentary population by nomads in the Mongol Empire) and especially in the pre-independence stages of modern colonial societies. In the colonial societies, changes in the "central" areas have not been congruent with changes at the local level. Most changes introduced either directly or indirectly by the colonial powers have been focused on the central political or economic institutions of the society. Central political structures and orientations have been greatly altered by the introduction of unitary systems of administration, the unification or regularization of taxation, the establishment of modern court procedures, and at later stages, the introduction of limited types of representation. Similarly, many changes have been effected in the economy, notably the change to a market economy.

At the same time, however, the colonial powers (or indigenous traditional rulers) saw it as part of their task to effect these changes only within the limits set by the existing institutions and their own interests. The rulers tried to contain the changes taking place in the local rural and urban communities within the pre-existing traditional systems, and at the local level most of their administrative efforts were aimed at strengthening existing organizations and relations, maintaining peace and order, and reorganizing the system of taxation. Thus, while the administration attempted to introduce innovations —particularly new taxes and improved methods of revenue administration—

---

16 For analysis of some of the relevant societies, see Eisenstadt, *The Political Systems of Empires, op. cit.,* including full bibliographical references.

it did so within a relatively unchanged social setting, with the implicit goal of limiting changes to technical matters.

These processes of uneven change in colonial societies, unlike parallel but less intensive and continuous processes in the older conquest societies, could not be frozen at a given stage. Attempts at indirect rule, on the one hand, and the widespread efforts of indigenous rulers to limit changes to purely technical matters, on the other, reflect attempts to stop development at a particular stage, but such devices did not usually succeed for long. The economic needs of the colonial powers or the indigenous ruling groups, their growing dependency on continuously changing international markets and international political organization, precluded any freezing of development, and tended to draw wider strata of the colonial societies into the orbit of modern institutional settings. This in turn facilitated the development of social movements that tended to focus on solidary symbols to the exclusion of other problems.[17]

A fourth, and perhaps the most variegated, type of response to growing differentiation consists of some structural solution which is on the whole congruent with the relevant problems. But within this broad type a wide variety of concrete institutional arrangements is possible. Such different solutions usually have different structural results and repercussions. Each denotes a different structure crystallized according to different criteria, and different modes of interpenetration of the major social spheres.

Thus, drawing again on examples from the great centralized Empires, we see that although the initial stages of socio-economic differentiation were relatively similar in Byzantium, in the later (Abbasid) Caliphate, and in post-Han China, each of these societies developed different overall institutional structures. The Byzantine Empire became a highly militarized and politically oriented system, while in the Caliphate a theocratic structure, based on continuous attempts to institutionalize a new type of universalistic politico-religious community, developed. China developed a centralized system based, at the center, on the power of the Emperor and the bureaucracy, and at the local level, on the relative predominance of the gentry. The selective channels of the examination and the literati were the major mechanisms integrating the local and central levels.[18]

Among modern and modernizing societies an even wider variety of concrete institutional types can be found at all stages of modernization. Modern societies differ, as is well known, not only in the degree of economic or poli-

---

[17] On the Nomad Empires, see Owen Lattimore, *Studies in Frontier History*, London: Oxford University Press, 1962, especially chs. 3 and 4. On the processes of unbalanced change in colonial societies see Shmuel N. Eisenstadt, *Essays on Sociological Aspects of Political and Economic Development*, The Hague: Mouton, 1961.

[18] See Eisenstadt, *The Political Systems of Empires, op. cit.*

tical differentiation, but also in the basic integrative criteria and symbols in the political, economic or cultural spheres. At each level of differentiation a great variety of institutional patterns occurs.[19]

One very interesting and intriguing possibility is the development of a relatively stable system in which the major institutional spheres vary in degree of differentiation. One of the most important examples of such variation occurs in feudal systems, which are characterized by a relatively high degree of differentiation in some of the central cultural roles as against a much smaller degree of differentiation in the economic and political roles.[20] Similar instances of "uneven" differentiation which have not yet crystallized into stable overall institutional systems exist in some of the more differentiated tribal and patrimonial societies.

One interesting aspect of uneven differentiation is that the more differentiated units of such related societies (e.g., the church in feudal or patrimonial systems) develop a sort of international system of their own apart from that of their "parent" societies.

Similarly, various aspects of modernization may develop in different degrees in the major spheres of modernizing societies. As one example, in many new states today—especially in Africa but also in Asia—we witness a continuous extension of political modernization, which is not usually accompanied by anything approaching a similar degree of development in the economic sphere, even where economic development is an important slogan. In many of these societies these varying degrees of modernization seem to coalesce into ongoing social and political systems, though at a minimal level of efficiency and integration.[21] This structural type may sometimes be similar to, or a derivative of, the product of continuous "unbalanced" change described above. But much more research is needed to elucidate the exact relations between the two.

The variety of integrative criteria and institutional contours at any level of differentiation is, of course, not limitless. The very notion of interdependence among major institutional spheres negates the assumption that

---

[19] On the varieties of modern societies see Parsons, *Structure and Process in Modern Societies, op. cit.,* ch. 3, and "A Revised Analytical Approach to the Theory of Social Stratification," in *Essays in Sociological Theory* (rev. ed.), Glencoe, Ill.: The Free Press, 1954, pp. 386–441; Clifford Geertz (ed.), *Old Societies and New States,* New York: The Free Press, 1963; and Eisenstadt, *Modernization, Growth and Diversity, op. cit.*

[20] See Otto Hintze, "Wesen un Verbreitung des Feudalismus," *Sitzungsbertichte der Preussischen Akademie der Wissenschaften, Phil. Hist. Klasse,* 1929, 5, 321–347, and Rushton Coulborn (ed.), *Feudalism in History,* Princeton: Princeton University Press, 1956, p. 1. C. L. Cahen, "Réflexions sur L'usage du mot de 'Féodalite,' " *Journal of the Economic and Social History of the Orient,* 3 (April, 1960), pp. 1–20.

[21] See Eisenstadt, *Modernization, Growth and Diversity, op. cit.*

any number of levels of differentiation in different institutional spheres can coalesce into a relatively stable institutionalized system. The level of differentiation in any one sphere necessarily constitutes, within broad limits, a precondition for the effective institutionalization of certain levels of differentiation in other social spheres. But within these broad limits of mutual preconditioning a great deal of structural variety is possible.

Constricted Development

Not only may different institutional contours and integrative mechanisms develop at each level of differentiation, but each such structure, once institutionalized, creates its own boundary-maintaining mechanisms, its own directions of change, and its potential for further development or for breakdown and regression. Each such institutional system tends to develop specific tendencies toward "de-differentiation," or the constriction of the new potentialities for further development. The growing differentiation and increasing interdependence among the various more autonomous and diversified institutional spheres increases the probability that one sphere will attempt to dominate the other coercively, by restricting and regimenting their tendencies toward autonomy.

This probability is especially strong with respect to the political and religious (or value) spheres, because these spheres are especially prone to "totalistic" orientations that tend to negate the autonomy of other spheres. Religious and political elites may attempt to dominate other spheres, imposing rigid frameworks based on their own criteria. The aim of such policies is usually an effective de-differentiation of the social system, and they may result in rigidity and stagnation, or precipitate continual breakdown of the system. These tendencies to de-differentiation are usually very closely related to the specific processes of change that may develop within any institutionalized system.

Thus, in the Byzantine Empire, the centralistic tendencies of the monarchs and the Church alternated with the more centrifugal tendencies of the aristocracy and some peasant groups, while the relatively high levels of political commitment demanded by the polity conflicted with the strong tendencies toward passivity and "other-worldliness" among elements within the Church. In the long run, the predominance of the latter alternatives contributed to the downfall of the Byzantine Empire and the "ossification" of the Eastern Church.

This outcome was also facilitated by the weakness of later Emperors who oscillated between repressive policies and giving in to the aristocratic forces, in both cases without developing a consistent new institutional framework.

The situation was different in the early Caliphate. On the one hand there was a strong universalistic emphasis on the state as the framework of the religious community but in a way subordinate to it. On the other hand, no comprehensive, independent, and cohesive organization of the religious groups and functionaries developed. Political participation was confined mostly to court cliques, and neither participation in the bureaucracy nor the religious check on political authority was effective because no machinery other than revolt existed to enforce it. Indeed, various religious sects and movements continually arose, very often contributing to the downfall of the state.

This aspect of the early Caliphates gave rise to a continual oscillation between "totalistic" political-religious movements, aiming at the total transformation of the political regime through various illegitimate means—assassinations, rebellions—and an otherworldly passivity that only helped to maintain the despotic character of the existing political regimes.

In the later Caliphate, various sects tried to overthrow the more differentiated polity and establish simple, de-differentiated political communities; these attempts alternated with military-bureaucratic usurpations. These movements, which often overlapped, blocked further political development.[22]

Similarly, breakdowns of relatively differentiated frameworks and attempts to "de-differentiate" have also occurred in various modern modernizing societies. In the more recent period such processes have developed in several "new states" like Burma, Indonesia or Pakistan. These developments are not entirely dissimilar from other less recent examples. The initial modernization of China, so often used as a negative example in comparison with the more successful initial modernization of Japan, comes to mind here. Similarly, the long histories of several Latin American countries represent a similar process. Although in many of them only the very minimal structural or socio-demographic features of modernization developed over a very long time, in other cases, as in Chile and especially in pre-Peron Argentina, evident progress toward modernization was halted or reversed.

Lastly, the rise of militarism in Japan and especially the European Fascism and Nazism of the twenties and thirties should be mentioned here as perhaps the most important case of a breakdown of modernization at a much more advanced level of development.

In each of these cases we witness the breakdown of a relatively differentiated and modern framework, the establishment of a less differentiated framework or the development of blockages and eruptions leading to institutionalized stagnation, rigidity, and instability.[23]

---

[22] See Eisenstadt, *The Political Systems of Empires, op. cit.,* and "Institutionalization and Change," *op. cit.*

[23] See Eisenstadt, "Breakdowns of Modernization," *op. cit.*

Thus, specific processes of institutional change open up some potentialities but may block others, and in some cases the institutionalization of a given solution may "freeze" further development or give rise to stagnation or continual breakdown. In these cases the new systems are unable to adapt effectively to the wider and more variegated environments to which they became exposed as a result of the differentiation they have undergone.[24]

Causes of Different Evolutionary Paths

The great variety of institutional and integrative contours of different societies arriving at similar levels or stages of differentiation may be due to several different, yet interconnected, reasons. First, different societies arrive at the same level of differentiation through different historical paths and through a variety of concrete structural forms. Thus, for instance, the political systems of centralized Empires could develop from city states, or from patrimonial or feudal regimes. These different antecedents greatly affected the social composition and the concrete organization of the new centralized structure as well as the basic orientations and problems of its rulers.

Similarly, the process of modernization may begin in tribal groups, in caste societies, in different types of peasant society, and in societies with different degrees and types of prior urbanization. These groups differ greatly with regards to resources and abilities for setting up and implementing relatively differentiated goals, and for regulating the increasingly complex relations among different parts of the society.

One aspect of the variety among these antecedents of differentiation is of special interest. Within many relatively undifferentiated societies exist enclaves of much more differentiated and specialized activities, especially in the economic and cultural spheres. Thus, cities function in many societies not only as administrative or cultural centers but very often as distinct entities, to some extent separated from the rest of society evincing a much higher degree of differentiation and specialization in the cultural or economic field. Similarly, monasteries and monastic orders, sects and academies, and very often special ethnic and religious minorities and special religious-tribal federations, may to some extent be detached from the wider society and evince, at least in certain spheres, a higher degree of differentiation. In more modern times

---

[24] One of the most interesting recent comparative analyses of the development of different institutional structures and different potentialities for further change, at a similar level of differentiation is Marshal D. Sahlins, "Poor Man, Rich Man, Big Man, Chief: Political Types in Melanesia and Polynesia," *Comparative Studies in Society and History*, 5 (April, 1963), pp. 285–304.

various political, religious and intellectual sects and elites may constitute important enclaves of more differentiated activities.[25]

Very often enclaves of this sort constitute parts of an international system of their own which transcends, at any given time, the confines of the total society to which they belong as well as its own international system.

Such enclaves may be very important sources of innovation within a society. Their presence or absence in any "antecedent" stage may greatly influence the scope and nature of the different integrative solutions that may be institutionalized at a later stage of differentiation.

Third, the variability of institutional contours at the same level of differentiation also stems from differences among predominant elites. Elites may develop either in different institutional spheres or in the same sphere but with different ideologies and orientations of action. Some of them may be more influential than others in establishing the detailed contours of the new institutional system.

Thus, to return to our earlier example, the major differences in the institutional contours among the Chinese, Byzantine and Abbasside Empires has been to no small degree influenced by the different types of predominant elites—the bureacratic-literati in China, the separate military and religious elites in Byzantium and the militant sectarian elite in the Caliphate.

Similarly, Shils' analysis of the different institutional patterns of modern and modernizing societies—political democracy, tutelary democracy, modernizing oligarchy, totalitarian oligarchy and traditional oligarchy— shows how the crystallization of each such type is influenced not only by the broad structural conditions of these societies but also, to a very large degree, by the composition and orientation of the leading elites in each type of society.[26] Kerr and associates have shown in a recent analysis that different modernizing elites tend to develop different strategies with regard to some major problems of social and economic policy, such as the pace of industrialization, sources of funds, priorities in development, pressures on enterprises and managers, the educational system, policies of agriculture, methods of allocation of labor and many others.[27]

---

[25] For an analysis of some modern intellectual sectarian groups see, in addition to Weber's classical analysis of the Protestant Ethic, Franco Venturi, *Roots of Revolution*, New York: Alfred A. Knopf, 1960; Vladimir C. Nahirny, "The Russian Intelligentsia From Men of Ideas to Men of Convictions," *Comparative Studies in Society and History*, 4 (July, 1962), pp. 403–436; Harry J. Benda, "Non-Western Intelligentsia as Political Elites," in John H. Kautsky (ed.), *Political Change in Underdeveloped Countries, Nationalism and Communism*, New York: Wiley, 1962, pp. 235–252.

[26] Shils, *Political Development in the New States, op. cit.*

[27] Clark Kerr, *et al., Industrialism and Industrial Man*, Cambridge, Mass.: Harvard University Press, 1960.

Innovating Elites

These considerations—especially recognition of the complex relations between the processes of social change and structural differentiation, on the one hand, and viable institutionalization of different types of structure, on the other—are crucial to the critical re-evaluation of the evolutionary perspective in the social sciences.

How can we explain the variability of institutionalized solutions to the problems arising from the development of a given level of structural differentiation? We must first recognize that the emergence of a solution, i.e., the institutionalization of a social order congruent with the new range of problems, is not necessarily given in the process of differentiation. We must discard the assumption—underlying, even if only implicitly, many studies of comparative institutions in general and of modernization in particular—that the conditions giving rise to structural differentiation, and to "structural sensitivity" to a greater range of problems, also create the capacity to solve these problems or determine the nature of such solutions.

The crucial problem is the presence or absence, in one or several institutional spheres, of an active group of special "entrepreneurs," or an elite able to offer solutions to the new range of problems. Among modern sociologists Weber came closest to recognizing this problem when he stressed that the creation of new institutional structures depends heavily on the "push" given by various "charismatic" groups or personalities and that the routinization of charisma is critical for the crystallization and continuation of new institutional structures. The development of such "charismatic" personalities or groups constitutes perhaps the closest social analogy to "mutation."

A number of questions pertaining to such elites and their relation to the broader social strata and structure in which they operate should be considered here, as possible guides to further research.

First, under what conditions do leaders or entrepreneurs with the requisite vision and organizational ability appear at all? Second, what is the nature of this "vision," or the proposed institutional solution to the problems attendant on growing differentiation? This problem has two aspects. One has to do with the particular institutional sphere within which an elite develops and is most active, or the values and orientations it especially emphasizes and attempts to institutionalize or "impose" as the dominant values of the new social structure. The other aspect is the nature of the concrete solution that the emerging elite proposes within this particular institutional framework. At any level of differentiation a given social sphere contains not one but several, often competing, possible orientations and potentialities for development. Again, Weber saw this most clearly when he showed that religious institutions may take several forms, often contradictory, at any level of differentiation of the religious sphere from other institutions. Thus, at the stage when autonomous religious orientations and organizations break away from the relatively closed "primitive" community, prophets or mystagogues may arise, and at higher levels of differentiation, sectarian developments may compete with tendencies to establish Churches, or strong "other-worldly" orientations, with "this-worldly" ones.[28]

Finally, we should consider readiness of competing elites and various wider segments of the society to accept the new elite's solutions, i.e., to provide at least the minimal resources necessary for the institutionalization of the proposed solutions. Within broad limits, the degree of correspondence between the elite's "vision" and the needs of other groups varies; it is not fully determined by the existing or developing level of differentiation.

As yet, we know little about the specific conditions, as distinct from the more general trend to structural differentiation, that facilitate the rise of new elites, and which influence the nature of their basic orientations, on the one hand, and their relations with broader strata, on the other. Available indications, however, are that factors beyond the general trend to differentiation are important. For example, various special enclaves, such as sects, monasteries, sectarian intellectual groups or scientific communities, play an important role in the formation of such elites. And a number of recent studies have indicated the importance of certain familial, ideological and educational orientations and institutions.[29]

Within this context the whole problem of the extent to which institutional patterns are crystallized not through "independent invention" within a society but through diffusion from other societies, should be reexamined. Cases of diffusion might be partially due to the successful "importation," by entrepreneurial groups on the margins of a given society, of acceptable solutions to latent problems or "needs" within that society.

Thus, at any given level of differentiation the crystallization of different

---

[28] See Max Weber, *The Sociology of Religion*, translated by Ephraim Fischoff, Boston: Beacon Press, 1963, especially chs. 4, 10, 11. For an interesting modern case study bearing on this problem see Ernest Gellner, "Sanctity, Puritanism, Secularism and Nationalism in North Africa," *Archives de Sociologie des Religions*, 15 (Janvier-Juin, 1963), pp. 71–87.

[29] See David C. McClelland, *The Achieving Society*, Princeton, N.J.: Van Nostrand, 1960, and "National Character and Economic Growth in Turkey and Iran," in Lucien W. Pye (ed.), *Communication and Political Development*, Princeton, N.J.: Princeton University Press, 1963, pp. 152–182; and Everett Hagen, *On the Theory of Social Change*, Homewood, Ill.: The Dorsey Press, 1962; Clifford Geertz, "Modernization in Moslem Society: The Indonesian Case," in *Cultural Motivation to Progress and the Three Great World Religions in South and South East Asia*, An International Seminar sponsored by the University of the Philippines, Manila, and The Congress for Cultural Freedom, Manila, 1963 (mimeo.), and *idem. Peddlers and Princes*, Chicago; University of Chicago Press, 1963.

institutional orders is shaped by the interaction between the broader structural features of the major institutional spheres, on the one hand and, on the other hand, the development of elites or entrepreneurs in some of the institutional spheres of that society, in some of its enclaves, or even in other societies with which it is in some way connected.

The variability in the concrete components of such interaction helps to explain the great—but not limitless—variety of structural and integrative forms that may be institutionalized at any given level of differentiation. It indicates also that while different societies may arrive at broadly similar stages of evolution in terms of the differentiation of the major institutional and symbolic spheres, yet the concrete institutional contours developed at each such step, as well as the possible outcomes of such institutionalization in terms of further development, breakdown, regression or stagnation, may greatly differ among them.

Clifford Geertz

Ritual and Social Change

A JAVANESE EXAMPLE

*A*S in so many areas of anthropological concern, functionalism, either of the sociological sort associated with the name of Radcliffe-Brown or of the social-psychological sort associated with Malinowski, has tended to dominate recent theoretical discussions of the role of religion in society. Stemming originally from Durkheim's *The Elementary Forms of the Religious Life*[1] and Robertson-Smith's *Lectures on the Religion of the Semites*[2], the sociological approach (or, as the British anthropologists prefer to call it, the social anthropological approach) emphasizes the manner in which belief and particularly ritual reinforce the traditional social ties between individuals; it stresses the way in which the social structure of a group is strengthened and perpetuated through the ritualistic or mythic symbolization of the underlying social values upon which it rests. The social-psychological approach, of which Frazer and Tylor were perhaps the

---

[1] Emile Durkheim, *The Elementary Forms of the Religious Life*, Glencoe, Illinois, 1947.

[2] W. Robertson-Smith, *Lectures on the Religion of the Semites*, Edinburgh, 1894. From Clifford Geertz, "Ritual and Social Change: A Javanese Example," *American Anthropologist*, 59 (February, 1957), pp. 32–54. Reprinted by permission of the author and the journal.

pioneers but which found its clearest statement in Malinowski's classic *Magic, Science and Religion*[3], emphasizes what religion does for the individual—how it satisfies both his cognitive and affective demands for a stable, comprehensible, and coercible world, and how it enables him to maintain an inner security in the face of natural contingency. Together, the two approaches have given us an increasingly detailed understanding of the social and psychological "functions" of religion in a wide range of societies.

Where the functional approach has been least impressive, however, is in dealing with social change. As has been noted by several writers (Leach[4]; Merton[5]), the emphasis on systems in balance, on social homeostasis, and on timeless structural pictures, leads to a bias in favor of "well-integrated" societies in a stable equilibrium and to a tendency to emphasize the functional aspects of a people's social usages and customs rather than their disfunctional implications. In analyses of religion this static, ahistorical approach has led to a somewhat over-conservative view of the role of ritual and belief in social life. Despite cautionary comments by Kluckhohn[6] and others on the "gain and cost" of various religious practices such as witchcraft, the tendency has been consistently to stress the harmonizing, integrating, and psychologically supportive aspects of religious patterns rather than the disruptive, disintegrative, and psychologically disturbing aspects; to demonstrate the manner in which religion preserves social and psychological structure rather than the manner in which it destroys or transforms it. Where change had been treated, as in Redfield's work on Yucatan, it has largely been in terms of progressive disintegration: "The changes in culture that in Yucatan appear to 'go along with' lessening isolation and homogeneity are seen to be chiefly three: disorganization of the culture, secularization and individualization."[7] Yet even a passing knowledge of our own religious history makes us hesitate to affirm such a simply "positive" role for religion generally.

It is the thesis of this paper that one of the major reasons for the inability of functional theory to cope with change lies in its failure to treat sociological and cultural processes on equal terms; almost inevitably one of the two is either ignored or is sacrificed to become but a simple reflex, a "mirror image," of the other. Either culture is regarded as wholly derivative

---

[3] Bronislaw Malinowski, *Magic, Science and Religion and Other Essays*, Glencoe, Illinois, and Boston, Massachusetts, 1948.

[4] E. R. Leach, *Political Systems of Highland Burma*, Cambridge, Massachusetts, 1954.

[5] Robert Merton, *Social Theory and Social Structure*, Glencoe, Illinois, 1949.

[6] Clyde Kluckhohn, *Navaho Witchcraft*, Peabody Museum Papers, No. XXII, Cambridge, Massachusetts, 1944.

[7] Robert Redfield, *The Folk Culture of Yucatan*, Chicago, Illinois, 1941, p. 339.

from the forms of social organization—the approach characteristic of the British structuralists as well as many American sociologists; or the forms of social organization are regarded as behavioral embodiments of cultural patterns—the approach of Malinowski and many American anthropologists. In either case, the lesser term tends to drop out as a dynamic factor and we are left either with an omnibus concept of culture ("that complex whole . . .") or else with a completely comprehensive concept of social structure ("social structure is not an aspect of culture, but the entire culture of a given people handled in a special frame of theory.")[8] In such a situation, the dynamic elements in social change which arise from the failure of cultural patterns to be perfectly congruent with the forms of social organization are largely incapable of formulation. "We functionalists," E. R. Leach has recently remarked, "are not really 'anti-historical' by principle; it is simply that we do not know how to fit historical materials into our framework of concepts."[9]

A revision of the concepts of functional theory so as to make them capable of dealing more effectively with "historical materials" might well begin with an attempt to distinguish analytically between the cultural and social aspects of human life, and to treat them as independently variable yet mutually interdependent factors. Though separable only conceptually, culture and social structure will then be seen to be capable of a wide range of modes of integration with one another, of which the simple isomorphic mode is but a limiting case—a case common only in societies which have been stable over such an extended time as to make possible a close adjustment between social and cultural aspects. In most societies, where change is a characteristic rather than an abnormal occurrence, we shall expect to find more or less radical discontinuities between the two. I would argue that it is in these very discontinuities that we shall find some of the primary driving forces in change.

One of the more useful ways—but far from the only one—of distinguishing between culture and social system is to see the former as an ordered system of meaning and of symbols, in terms of which social interaction takes place; and to see the latter as the pattern of social interaction itself.[10] On the one level there is the framework of beliefs, expressive symbols, and values in terms of which individuals define their world, express their feelings, and make their judgments; on the other level there is the ongoing process of interactive behavior, whose persistent form we call social structure. Culture

---

8 Meyer Fortes, *The Structure of Unilineal Descent Groups, American Anthropologist*, 55: 17–41.

9 Leach, *op. cit.*, p. 282.

10 Talcott Parsons and Edward A. Shils, *Toward a General Theory of Action*, Cambridge, Massachusetts, 1951.

is the fabric of meaning in terms of which human beings interpret their experience and guide their action; social structure is the form that action takes, the actually existing network of social relations. Culture and social structure are then but different abstractions from the same phenomena. The one considers social action in respect to its meaning for those who carry it out, the other considers it in terms of its contribution to the functioning of some social system.

The nature of the distinction between culture and social system is brought out more clearly when one considers the contrasting sorts of integration characteristic of each of them. This contrast is between what Sorokin[11] has called "logico-meaningful integration" and what he has called "causal-functional integration." By logico-meaningful integration, characteristic of culture, is meant the sort of integration one finds in a Bach fugue, in Catholic dogma, or in the general theory of relativity; it is a unity of style, of logical implication, of meaning and value. By causal-functional integration, characteristic of the social system, is meant the kind of integration one finds in an organism, where all the parts are united in a single causal web; each part is an element in a reverberating causal ring which "keeps the system going." And because these two types of integration are not identical, because the particular form one of them takes does not directly imply the form the other will take, there is an inherent incongruity and tension between the two and between both of them and a third element, the pattern of motivational integration within the individual which we usually call personality structure:

"Thus conceived, a social system is only one of three aspects of the structuring of a completely concrete system of social action. The other two are the personality systems of the individual actors and the cultural system which is built into their action. Each of the three must be considered to be an independent focus of the organization of the elements of the action system in the sense that no one of them is theoretically reducible to terms of one or a combination of the other two. Each is indispensable to the other two in the sense that without personalities and culture there would be no social system and so on around the roster of logical possibilities. But this interdependence and interpenetration is a very different matter from reducibility, which would mean that the important properties and processes of one class of system could be theoretically *derived* from our theoretical knowledge of one or both of the other two. The action frame of reference is common to all three and this fact makes certain "transformations" between them possible. But on the level of theory here attempted they do not constitute a single system, however this might turn out to be on some other theoretical level."[12]

---

11 Pitrim Sorokin, *Social and Cultural Dynamics*, 3 vols, New York, 1937.
12 Talcott Parsons, *The Social System*, Glencoe, Illinois, 1951.

I will attempt to demonstrate the utility of this more dynamic functionalist approach by applying it to a particular case of a ritual which failed to function properly. I shall try to show how an approach which does not distinguish the "logico-meaningful" cultural aspects of the ritual pattern from the "causal-functional" social structural aspects is unable to account adequately for this ritual failure, and how an approach which does so distinguish them is able to analyze more explicitly the cause of the trouble. It will further be argued that such an approach is able to avoid the simplistic view of the functional role of religion in society which sees that role merely as structure-conserving, and to substitute for it a more complex conception of the relations between religious belief and practice and secular social life. Historical materials can be fitted into such a conception, and the functional analysis of religion can therefore be widened to deal more adequately with processes of change.

The Setting

The case to be described is that of a funeral held in Modjokuto, a small town in eastern Central Java.[13] A young boy, about ten years of age, who was living with his uncle and aunt, died very suddenly but his death, instead of being followed by the usual hurried, subdued, yet methodically efficient Javanese funeral ceremony and burial routine, brought on an extended period of pronounced social strain and severe psychological tension. The complex of beliefs and rituals which had for generations brought countless Javanese safely through the difficult post-mortem period suddenly failed to work with its accustomed effectiveness. To understand why it failed demands knowledge and understanding of a whole range of social and cultural changes which have taken place in Java since the first decades of this century. This disrupted funeral was in fact but a microcosmic example of the broader conflicts, structural dissolutions, and attempted reintegrations which, in one form or another, are characteristic of contemporary Indonesian society.

The religious tradition of Java, particularly of the peasantry, is a compo-

---

[13] The names of the town and of all individuals mentioned in this paper are pseudonyms. The field work extended from May 1953 until September 1954, with a two-month gap in July and August of 1953, and was undertaken as part of a co-operative project of six anthropologists and a sociologist under the sponsorship of the Center for International Studies of the Massachusetts Institute of Technology. A full description of the town and of the villages around it, prepared by the entire team, is in the process of publication. I wish to thank Victor Ayoub, Robert Bellah, Hildred Geertz, Arnold Green, Robert Jay, and Elizabeth Tooker for reading and criticizing various drafts of this paper.

site of Indian, Islamic, and indigenous Southeast Asian elements.[14] The rise
of large, militaristic kingdoms in the inland rice basins in the early centuries
of the Christian era was associated with the diffusion of Hinduist and
Buddhist culture patterns to the island; the expansion of international mari-
time trade in the port cities of the northern coast in the fifteenth and sixteenth centuries was associated with the diffusion of Islamic patterns. Working their way into the peasant mass, these two world religions became fused
with the underlying animistic traditions characteristic of the whole Malaysian
culture area. The result was a balanced syncretism of myth and ritual in
which Hindu gods and goddesses, Moslem prophets and saints, and local
place spirits and demons all found a proper place.

The central ritual form in this syncretism is a communal feast, called
the *slametan*. Slametans, which are given with only slight variations in
form and content on almost all occasions of religious significance—at
passage points in the life cycle, on calendrical holidays, at certain stages of
the crop cycle, on changing one's residence, etc.—are intended to be both
offerings to the spirits and commensal mechanisms of social integration for
the living. The meal, which consists of specially prepared dishes, each symbolic of a particular religious concept, is cooked by the female members of
one nuclear family household and set out on mats in the middle of the living-
room. The male head of the household invites the male heads of the eight
or ten contiguous households to attend; no close neighbor is ignored in
favor of one further away. After a speech by the host explaining the spiritual
purpose of the feast and a short Arabic chant, each man takes a few hurried,
almost furtive, gulps of food, wraps the remainder of the meal in a banana-
leaf basket, and returns home to share it with his family. It is said that the
spirits draw their sustenance from the odor of the food, the incense which is
burned, and the Moslem prayer; the human participants draw theirs from
the material substance of the food and from their social interaction. The
result of this quiet, undramatic little ritual is twofold: the spirits are
appeased and neighborhood solidarity is strengthened.[15]

The ordinary canons of functional theory are quite adequate for the
analysis of such a pattern. It can rather easily be shown that the slametan
is well designed both to "tune up the ultimate value attitudes" necessary to
the effective integration of a territorially-based social structure, and to fulfill
the psychological needs for intellectual coherence and emotional stability
characteristic of a peasant population. The Javanese village (once or twice a
year, village-wide slametans are held) is essentially a set of geographically

---

[14] K. Landon, *Southeast Asia, Crossroad of Religions*, Chicago, Illinois, 1949.

[15] A fuller description of the slametan pattern, and of Javanese religion generally,
will be found in my contribution to the forthcoming project report on the Modjokuto
community study: Geertz, in press.

contiguous, but rather self-consciously autonomous, nuclear family households whose economic and political interdependence is of roughly the same
circumscribed and explicitly defined sort as that demonstrated in the
slametan. The demands of the labor-intensive rice and dry-crop agricultural
process require the perpetuation of specific modes of technical co-operation
and enforce a sense of community on the otherwise rather self-contained
families—a sense of community which the slametan clearly reinforces. And
when we consider the manner in which various conceptual and behavioral
elements from Hindu-Buddhism, Islam, and "animism" are reinterpreted
and balanced to form a distinctive and nearly homogeneous religious style,
the close functional adjustment between the communal feast pattern and
the conditions of Javanese rural life is even more readily apparent.

But the fact is that in all but the most isolated parts of Java, both the
simple territorial basis of village social integration and the syncretic basis
of its cultural homogeniety have been progressively undermined over the
past fifty years. Population growth, urbanization, monetization, occupational
differentiation, and the like, have combined to weaken the traditional ties of
peasant social structure; and the winds of doctrine which have accompanied
the appearance of these structural changes have disturbed the simple uniformity of religious belief and practice characteristic of an earlier period.
The rise of nationalism, Marxism, and Islamic reform as ideologies, which
resulted in part from the increasing complexity of Javanese society, has
affected not only the large cities where these creeds first appeared and have
always had their greatest strength, but has had a heavy impact on the smaller
towns and villages as well. In fact, much of recent Javanese social change is
perhaps most aptly characterized as a shift from a situation in which the
primary integrative ties between individuals (or between families) are
phrased in terms of geographical proximity to one in which they are phrased
in terms of ideological like-mindedness.

In the villages and small towns these major ideological changes appeared
largely in the guise of a widening split between those who emphasized the
Islamic aspects of the indigenous religious syncretism and those who
emphasized the Hinduist and animistic elements. It is true that some difference between these variant subtraditions has been present since the arrival
of Islam; some individuals have always been particularly skilled in Arabic
chanting or particularly learned in Moslem law, while others have been
adept at more Hinduistic mystical practices or specialists in local curing
techniques. But these contrasts were softened by the easy tolerance of the
Javanese for a wide range of religious concepts, so long as basic ritual
patterns—i.e., slametans—were faithfully supported; whatever social

divisiveness they stimulated was largely obscured by the over-riding commonalities of rural and small-town life.

However, the appearance after 1910 of Islamic modernism (as well as vigorous conservative reactions against it) and religious nationalism among the economically and politically sophisticated trading classes of the larger cities strengthened the feeling for Islam as an exclusivist, antisyncretic creed among the more orthodox element of the mass of the population. Similarly, secular nationalism and Marxism, appearing among the civil servants and the expanding proletariat of these cities, strengthened the pre-Islamic (i.e., Hinduist-animist) elements of the syncretic pattern, which these groups tended to prize as a counterweight to puristic Islam and which some of them adopted as a general religious framework in which to set their more specifically political ideas. On the one hand, there arose a more self-conscious Moslem, basing his religious beliefs and practices more explicitly on the international and universalistic doctrines of Mohammed; on the other hand there arose a more self-conscious "nativist," attempting to evolve a generalized religious system out of the material—muting the more Islamic elements—of his inherited religious tradition. And the contrast between the first kind of man, called a *santri*, and the second, called an *abangan*, grew steadily more acute, until today it forms the major cultural distinction in the whole of the Modjokuto area.[16]

It is especially in the town that this contrast has come to play a crucial role. The absence of pressures toward interfamilial co-operation exerted by the technical requirements of wet-rice growing, as well as lessened effectiveness of the traditional forms of village government in the face of the complexities of urban living, severely weaken the social supports of the syncretic village pattern. When each man makes his living—as chauffeur, trader, clerk, or laborer—more or less independently of how his neighbors make theirs, his sense of the importance of the neighborhood community naturally diminishes. A more differentiated class system, more bureaucratic and impersonal forms of government, greater heterogeneity of social background, all tend to lead to the same result: the de-emphasis of strictly geographical ties in favor of diffusely ideological ones. For the townsman, the distinction between santri and abangan becomes even sharper, for it emerges as his primary point of social reference; it becomes a symbol of his social identity,

---

[16] For a description of the role of the santri-abangan distinction in the rural areas of Modjokuto, see Robert Jay, *Local Government in Rural Central Java, The Far Eastern Quarterly*, XV: 215–227. A third religious variant which I have discriminated elsewhere, the *prijaji*, is mainly confined to upper-class civil servants, teachers, and clerks, and so will not be dealt with here. For reference, see Clifford Geertz, "Religious Belief and Economic Behavior in a Central Javanese Town: Some Preliminary Considerations," *Economic Development and Cultural Change*, IV: 134–158, and *Religion in Modjokuto*, Cambridge, Massachusetts, 1957.

rather than a mere contrast in belief. The sort of friends he will have, the sort of organizations he will join, the sort of political leadership he will follow, the sort of person he or his son will marry, will all be strongly influenced by the side of this ideological bifurcation which he adopts as his own.

There is thus emerging in the town—though not only in the town—a new pattern of social living organized in terms of an altered framework of cultural classification. Among the elite this new pattern has already become rather highly developed, but among the mass of the townspeople it is still in the process of formation. Particularly in the *kampongs,* the off-the-street neighborhoods in which the common Javanese townsmen live crowded together in a helter-skelter profusion of little bamboo houses, one finds a transitional society in which the traditional forms of rural living are being steadily dissolved and new forms steadily reconstructed. In these enclaves of peasants-come-to-town (or of sons and grandsons of peasants-come-to-town), Redfield's folk culture is being constantly converted into his urban culture, though this latter is not accurately characterized by such negative and residual terms as "secular," "individualized," and "culturally disorganized." What is occurring in the kampongs is not so much a destruction of traditional ways of life, as a construction of a new one; the sharp social conflict characteristic of these lower-class neighborhoods is not simply indicative of a loss of cultural consensus, but rather indicative of a search, not yet entirely successful, for new, more generalized, and flexible patterns of belief and value.

In Modjokuto, as in most of Indonesia, this search is taking place largely within the social context of the mass political parties, as well as in the women's clubs, youth organizations, labor unions, and other sodalities formally or informally linked with them. There are several of these parties (though the recent general election severely reduced their number), each led by educated urban elites—civil servants, teachers, traders, students, and the like—and each competing with the others for the political allegiance of both the half rural, half urban kampong dwellers and of the mass of the peasantry. And almost without exception, they appeal to one or another side of the santri-abangan split. Of this complex of political parties and sodalities, only two are of immediate concern to us here: Masjumi, a huge, Islam-based political party; and Permai, a vigorously anti-Moslem politico-religious cult.

Masjumi is the more or less direct descendant of the pre-war Islamic reform movement. Led, at least in Modjokuto, by modernist santri intellectuals, it stands for a socially conscious, antischolastic, and somewhat puritanical version of back-to-the-Koran Islam. In company with the other Moslem parties, it also supports the institution of an "Islamic State" in Indonesia in place of the present secular republic. However, the meaning of this ideal is not entirely clear. Masjumi's enemies accuse it of pressing for an intolerant, medievalist theocracy in which abangans and non-Moslems will be persecuted and forced to follow exactly the prescripts of the Moslem law, while Masjumi's leaders claim that Islam is intrinsically tolerant and that they only desire a government explicitly based on the Moslem creed, one whose laws will be in consonance with the teachings of the Koran and Hadith. In any case, Masjumi, the country's largest Moslem party, is one of the major spokesmen on both the national and the local levels for the values and aspirations of the santri community.

Permai is not so impressive on a national scale. Though it is a nation-wide party, it is a fairly small one, having strength only in a few fairly circum-scribed regions. In the Modjokuto area however, it happened to be of some importance, and what it lacked in national scope it made up in local inten-sity. Essentially, Permai is a fusion of Marxist politics with abangan religious patterns. It combines a fairly explicit anti-Westernism, anti-capitalism, and anti-imperialism with an attempt to formalize and generalize some of the more characteristic diffuse themes of the peasant religious syncretism. Permai meetings follow both the slametan pattern, complete with incense and symbolic food (but without Islamic chants), and modern parliamentary procedure; Permai pamphlets contain calendrical and numerological divin-atory systems and mystical teachings as well as analyses of class conflict; and Permai speeches are concerned with elaborating both religious and political concepts. In Modjokuto, Permai is also a curing cult, with its own special medical practices and spells, a secret password, and cabalistic inter-pretations of passages in the leaders' social and political writings.

But Permai's most notable characteristic is its strong anti-Moslem stand. Charging that Islam is a foreign import, unsuited to the needs and values of the Javanese, the cult urges a return to "pure" and "original" Javanese beliefs, by which they seem to mean to the indigenous syncretism with the more Islamic elements removed. In line with this, the cult-party has initiated a drive, on both national and local levels, for secular (i.e., non-Islamic) marriage and funeral rites. As the situation stands now, all but Christians and Balinese Hindus must have their marriages legitimatized by means of the Moslem ritual.[17] Funeral rites are an individual concern but, because of the long history of syncretism, they are so deeply involved with Islamic customs that a genuinely non-Islamic funeral tends to be a practical impossibility.

---

[17] Actually, there are two parts to Javanese marriage rites. One, which is part of the general syncretism, is held at the bride's home and involves a slametan and an elaborate ceremonial "meeting" between bride and groom. The other, which is the official ceremony in the eyes of the Government, follows the Moslem law and takes place at the office of the subdistrict religious officer, or Naib. For reference, see Geertz, *Religion in Modjokuto,* Cambridge, Massachusetts, 1957.

Permai's action on the local level in pursuit of non-Islamic marriage and funeral ceremonies took two forms. One was heavy pressure on local government officials to permit such practices, and the other was heavy pressure on its own members to follow, voluntarily, rituals purified of Islamic elements. In the case of marriage, success was more or less precluded because the local officials' hands were tied by Central Government ordinances, and even highly ideologized members of the cult would not dare an openly "illegitimate" marriage. Without a change in the law, Permai had little chance to alter marriage forms, though a few abortive attempts were made to conduct civil ceremonies under the aegis of abangan-minded village chiefs.

The case of funerals was somewhat different, for a matter of custom rather than law was involved. During the year I was in the field, the tension between Permai and Masjumi increased very sharply. This was due in part to the imminence of Indonesia's first general elections, and in part to the effects of the cold war. It was also influenced by various special occurrences—such as a report that the national head of Permai had publically called Mohammed a false prophet; a speech in the nearby regional capital by a Masjumi leader in which he accused Permai of intending to raise a generation of bastards in Indonesia; and a bitter village-chief election largely fought out on santri vs. abangan grounds. As a result, the local subdistrict officer, a worried bureaucrat trapped in the middle, called a meeting of all the village religious officials, or Modins. Among many other duties, a Modin is traditionally responsible for conducting funerals. He directs the whole ritual, instructs the mourners in the technical details of burial, leads the Koran chanting, and reads a set speech to the deceased at the graveside. The subdistrict officer instructed the Modins—the majority of whom were village Masjumi leaders—that in the case of the death of a member of Permai, they were merely to note the name and age of the deceased and return home; they were not to participate in the ritual. He warned that if they did not do as he advised, they would be responsible if trouble started and he would not come to their support.

This was the situation on July 17, 1954, when Paidjan, nephew of Karman, an active and ardent member of Permai, died suddenly in the Modjokuto kampong in which I was living.

The mood of a Javanese funeral is not one of hysterical bereavement, unrestrained sobbing, or even of formalized cries of grief for the deceased's departure. Rather, it is a calm, undemonstrative, almost languid letting go, a brief ritualized relinquishment of a relationship no longer possible. Tears are not approved of and certainly not encouraged; the effort is to get the job done, not to linger over the pleasures of grief. The detailed busy-work of the funeral, the politely formal social intercourse with the neighbours pressing in from all sides, the series of commemorative slametans stretched out at intervals for almost three years—the whole momentum of the Javanese ritual system is supposed to carry one through grief without severe emotional disturbance. For the mourner, the funeral and postfuneral ritual is said to produce a feeling of *iklas,* a kind of willed affectlessness, a detached and static state of "not caring"; for the neighborhood group it is said to produce *rukun,* "communal harmony."

[Editors' Summary: Very much in contrast to the conventional funeral, this one produced emotional upheaval, open conflict, and a residue of hostility. The intrusion of political divisiveness centered around the *Modin's* unwillingness to supervise the ceremony in the *Permai* home of the deceased boy's uncle. The deceased's relatives were visibly confused and upset by the interruption in the ceremonial flow, as were the attendant neighbors—both *santris* and *abangans,* who clustered in two distinct groups. Smoldering confusion turned to overt emotionalism with the arrival of the deceased's parents from out-of-town. To the dismay of all, his mother not only sobbed hysterically but insisted on seeing the corpse and fell to kissing it about the genitals. Finally, however, a local *santri* tailor, Abu, renewed his attempt to smooth the difficulties and complete the burial. By-passing the deceased's uncle and turning directly to the more Islamic father, he was able to secure a request for the return of the *Modin.* Finally, the body was interred, although this did little to pacify dissatisfactions and disgraces arising out of the ceremony itself. Indeed these flared up anew three days later at a *slametan* ceremony to commemorate the death. Much of the evening was consumed by a *Permai* political oration, drawing upon texts from Marx, Sukarno, and nativism. The boy's father finally spoke of his embarrassment and dishonor. This unusual public expression produced still more discomfort and the meeting disbanded silently shortly thereafter. When Geertz left four months later tensions had not eased and everyone wondered what would happen the next time a death occurred in a *Permai family.*]

Analysis

"Of all the sources of religion," wrote Malinowski, "the supreme and final crisis of life—death—is of the greatest importance."[18] Death, he argued, provokes in the survivors a dual response of love and loathing, a deep-going emotional ambivalence of fascination and fear which threatens both the psychological and social foundations of human existence. The survivors are drawn toward the deceased by their affection for him, repelled from him

---

[18] Malinowski, *op. cit.,* p. 29.

by the dreadful transformation wrought by death. Funeral rites, and the mourning practices which follow them, focus around this paradoxical desire both to maintain the tie in the face of death and to break the bond immediately and utterly, and thus insure the domination of the will to live over the tendency to despair. Mortuary rituals maintain the continuity of human life by preventing the survivors from yielding either to the impulse to flee panic-stricken from the scene or to the contrary impulse to follow the deceased into the grave:

"And here into this play of emotional forces, into this supreme dilemma of life and final death, religion steps in, selecting the positive creed, the comforting view, the culturally valuable belief in immortality, in the spirit independent of the body, and in the continuance of life after death. In the various ceremonies at death, in commemoration and communion with the departed, and worship of ancestral ghosts, religion gives body and form to the saving beliefs . . . Exactly the same function it fulfills also with regard to the whole group. The ceremonial of death which ties the survivors to the body and rivets them to the place of death, the beliefs in the existence of the spirit, in its beneficent influences or malevolent intentions, in the duties of a series of commemorative or sacrificial ceremonies—in all this religion counteracts the centrifugal forces of fear, dismay, demoralization, and provides the most powerful means of reintegration of the group's shaken solidarity and of the re-establishment of its morale. In short, religion here assures the victory of tradition over the mere negative response of thwarted instinct."[19]

To this sort of theory, a case such as that described above clearly poses some difficult problems. Not only was the victory of tradition and culture over "thwarted instinct" a narrow one at best, but it seemed as if the ritual were tearing the society apart rather than integrating it, were disorganizing personalities rather than healing them. To this the functionalist has a ready answer, which takes one of two forms depending upon whether he follows the Durkheim or the Malinowski tradition: social disintegration or cultural demoralization. Rapid social change has disrupted Javanese society and this is reflected in a disintegrated culture; as the unified state of traditional village society was mirrored in the unified slametan, so the broken society of the kampong is mirrored in the broken slametan of the funeral ritual we have just witnessed. Or, in the alternate phraseology, cultural decay has led to social fragmentation; loss of a vigorous folk tradition has weakened the moral ties between individuals.

It seems to me that there are two things wrong with this argument, no matter in which of the two vocabularies it is stated: it identifies social (or cultural) conflict with social (or cultural) disintegration; it denies independent roles to both culture and social structure, regarding one of the two as a mere epiphenomenon of the other.

---

[19] *Ibid.,* pp. 33–35.

In the first place, kampong life is not simply anomic. Though it is marked by vigorous social conflicts, as is our own society, it nevertheless proceeds fairly effectively in most areas. If governmental, economic, familial, stratificatory, and social control institutions functioned as poorly as did Paidjan's funeral, a kampong would indeed be an uncomfortable place in which to live. But though some of the typical symptoms of urban upheaval—such as increased gambling, petty thievery, and prostitution—are to some degree present, kampong social life is clearly not on the verge of collapse; everyday social interaction does not limp along with the suppressed bitterness and deep uncertainty we have seen focused around burial. For most of its members most of the time, a semiurban neighborhood in Modjokuto offers a viable way of life, despite its material disadvantages and its transitional character; and for all the sentimentality which has been lavished on descriptions of rural life in Java, this is probably as much as one could say for the village. As a matter of fact, it is around religious beliefs and practices—slametans, holidays, curing, sorcery, cult groups, etc.—that the most seriously disruptive events seem to cluster. Religion here is somehow the center and source of stress, not merely the reflection of stress elsewhere in the society.[20]

Yet it is not a source of stress because commitment to the inherited patterns of belief and ritual has been weakened. The conflict around Paidjan's death took place simply because all the kampong residents did share a common, highly integrated, cultural tradition concerning funerals. There was no argument over whether the slametan pattern was the correct ritual, whether the neighbors were obligated to attend, or whether the supernatural concepts upon which the ritual is based were valid ones. For both santris and abangans in the kampongs, the slametan maintains its force as a genuine sacred symbol; it still provides a meaningful framework for facing death—for most people the only meaningful framework. We cannot attribute the failure of the ritual to secularization, to a growth in skepticism, or to a disinterest in the traditional "saving beliefs," any more than we can attribute it to anomie.

We must rather, I think, ascribe it to a discontinuity between the form of integration existing in the social structural ("causal-functional") dimension and the form of integration existing in the cultural ("logico-meaningful") dimension—a discontinuity which leads not to social and cultural disintegration, but to social and cultural conflict. In more concrete, if somewhat aphoristic terms, the difficulty lies in the fact that socially kampong people are urbanites, while culturally they are still folk.

---

[20] For a description of a somewhat disrupted celebration of the end of the Fast holiday, Hari Raya (id al-fitr) in Modjokuto, which shows many formal similarities to Paidjan's funeral, see Geertz, *Religion in Modjokuto.*

I have already pointed out that the Javanese kampong represents a transitional sort of society, that its members stand "in between" the more or less fully urbanized elite and the more or less traditionally organized peasantry. The social structural forms in which they participate are for the most part urban ones. The emergence of a highly differentiated occupational structure in place of the almost entirely agricultural one of the countryside; the virtual disappearance of the semihereditary, traditional village government as a personalistic buffer between the individual and the rationalized central government bureaucracy, and its replacement by the more flexible forms of modern parliamentary democracy; the evolution of a multiclass society in which the kampong, unlike the village, is not even a potentially self-sufficient entity, but is only one dependent subpart—all this means that the kampong man lives in a very urban world. Socially, his is a *Gesellschaft* existence.

But on the cultural level—the level of meaning—there is much less of a contrast between the kampong dweller and the villager; much more between him and a member of the urban elite. The patterns of belief, expression, and value to which the kampong man is committed—his world-view, ethos, ethic, or whatever—differ only slightly from those followed by the villager. Amid a radically more complex social environment, he clings noticeably to the symbols which guided him or his parents through life in rural society. And it is this fact which gave rise to the psychological and social tension surrounding Paidjan's funeral.

The disorganization of the ritual resulted from a basic ambiguity in the meaning of the rite for those who participated in it. Most simply stated, this ambiguity lay in the fact that the symbols which compose the slametan had both religious and political significance, were charged with both sacred and profane import. The people who came into Karman's yard, including Karman himself, were not sure whether they were engaged in a sacralized consideration of first and last things or in a secular struggle for power. This is why the old man (he was a graveyard keeper, as a matter of fact) complained to me that dying was nowadays a political problem; why the village policeman accused the Modin not of religious but of political bias for refusing to bury Paidjan; why the unsophisticated Karman was astonished when his ideological commitments suddenly loomed as obstacles to his religious practices; why Abu was torn between his willingness to submerge political differences in the interest of a harmonious funeral and his unwillingness to trifle with his religious beliefs in the interest of his own salvation; why the commemorative rite oscillated between political diatribe and a poignant search for an adequate explanation of what had happened—why, in sum, the slametan religious pattern stumbled when it attempted to "step in" with the "positive creed" and "the culturally valuable belief."

As emphasized earlier, the present severity of the contrast between santri and abangan is in great part due to the rise of nationalist social movements in twentieth-century Indonesia. In the larger cities where these movements were born, they were originally of various sorts: tradesmen's societies to fight Chinese competition; unions of workers to resist plantation exploitation; religious groups trying to redefine ultimate concepts; philosophical discussion clubs attempting to clarify Indonesian metaphysical and moral notions; school associations striving to revivify Indonesian education; co-operative societies trying to work out new forms of economic organization; cultural groups moving toward a renaissance of Indonesian artistic life; and, of course, political parties working to build up effective opposition to Dutch rule. As time wore on, however, the struggle for independence absorbed more and more the energies of all these essentially elite groups. Whatever the distinctive aim of each of them—economic reconstruction, religious reform, artistic renaissance—it became submerged in a diffuse political ideology; all the groups were increasingly concerned with one end as the prerequisite of all further social and cultural progress—freedom. By the time the revolution began in 1945, reformulation of ideas outside the political sphere had noticeably slackened and most aspects of life had become intensely ideologized, a tendency which has continued into the post-war period.

In the villages and small town kampongs, the early, specific phase of nationalism had only a minor effect. But as the movement unified and moved toward eventual triumph, the masses too began to be affected and, as I have pointed out, mainly through the medium of religious symbols. The highly urbanized elite forged their bonds to the peasantry not in terms of complex political and economic theory, which would have had little meaning in a rural context, but in terms of concepts and values already present there. As the major line of demarcation among the elite was between those who took Islamic doctrine as the overall basis of their mass appeal and those who took a generalized philosophical refinement of the indigenous syncretic tradition as such a basis, so in the countryside santri and abangan soon became not simply religious but political categories, denoting the followers of these two diffuse approaches to the organization of the emerging independent society. When the achievement of political freedom strengthened the importance of factional politics in parliamentary government, the santri-abangan distinction became, on the local level at least, one of the primary ideological axes around which the process of party maneuvering took place.

The effect of this development has been to cause political debate and religious propitiation to be carried out in the same vocabulary. A koranic chant becomes an affirmation of political allegiance as well as a paean to

God; a burning of incense expresses one's secular ideology as well as one's sacred beliefs. Slametans now tend to be marked by anxious discussions of the various elements in the ritual, of what their "real" significance is; by arguments as to whether a particular practice is essential or optional; by abangan uneasiness when santris lift their eyes to pray and santri uneasiness when abangans recite a protective spell. At death, as we have seen, the traditional symbols tend both to solidify individuals in the face of social loss and to remind them of their differences; to emphasize the broadly human themes of mortality and undeserved suffering and the narrowly social ones of factional opposition and party struggle; to strengthen the values the participants hold in common and to "tune up" their animosities and suspicions. The rituals themselves become matters of political conflict; forms for the sacralization of marriage and death are transformed into important party issues. In such an equivocal cultural setting, the average kampong Javanese finds it increasingly difficult to determine the proper attitude toward a particular event, to choose the meaning of a given symbol appropriate to a given social context.

The corollary of this interference of political meanings with religious meanings also occurs: the interference of religious meanings with political ones. Because the same symbols are used in both political and religious contexts, people often regard party struggle as involving not merely the usual ebb and flow of parliamentary maneuver, the necessary factional give-and-take of democratic government, but involving as well decisions on basic values and ultimates. Kampong people in particular tend to see the open struggle for power explicitly institutionalized in the new republican forms of government as a struggle for the right to establish different brands of essentially religious principles as official: "if the abangans get in, the koranic teachers will be forbidden to hold classes"; "if the santris get in, we shall all have to pray five times a day." The normal conflict involved in electoral striving for office is heightened by the idea that literally everything is at stake: the "if we win, it is our country" idea that the group which gains power has a right, as one man said, "to put his own foundation under the state." Politics thus takes on a kind of sacralized bitterness; and one village election in a suburban Modjokuto village actually had to be held twice because of the intense pressures generated in this way.

The kampong man is, so to speak, caught between his ultimate and his proximate concepts. Because he is forced to formulate his essentially metaphysical ideas, his response to such basic "problems" as fate, suffering, and evil, in the same terms as he states his claims to secular power, his political rights and aspirations, he experiences difficulty in enacting either a socially and psychologically efficient funeral or a smoothly running election.

But a ritual is not just a pattern of meaning; it is also a form of social interaction. Thus, in addition to creating cultural ambiguity, the attempt to bring a religious pattern from a relatively less differentiated rural background into an urban context also gives rise to social conflict, simply because the kind of social integration demonstrated by the pattern is not congruent with the major patterns of integration in the society generally. The way kampong people go about maintaining solidarity in everyday life is quite different from the way the slametan insists that they should go about maintaining it.

As emphasized earlier, the slametan is essentially a territorially based ritual; it assumes the primary tie between families to be that of residential propinquity. One set of neighbors is considered a significant social unit (politically, religiously, economically) as against another set of neighbors; one village as against another village; one village-cluster as against another village-cluster. In the town, this pattern has in large part changed. Significant social groups are defined by a plurality of factors—class, political commitment, occupation, ethnicity, regional origins, religious preference, age, and sex, as well as residence. The new urban form of organization consists of a careful balance of conflicting forces arising out of diverse contexts: class differences are softened by ideological similarities; ethic conflicts by common economic interests; political opposition, as we have seen, by residential intimacy. But in the midst of all this pluralistic checking and balancing, the slametan remains unchanged, blind to the major lines of social and cultural demarcation in urban life. For it, the primary classifying characteristic of an individual is where he lives.

Thus when an occasion arises demanding sacralization—a life-cycle transition, a holiday, a serious illness—the religious form which must be employed acts not with but against the grain of social equilibrium. The slametan ignores those recently devised mechanisms of social insulation which in daily life keep group conflict within fixed bounds, as it also ignores the newly evolved patterns of social integration among opposed groups which balance contradictory tensions in a reasonably effective fashion. People are pressed into an intimacy they would as soon avoid; where the incongruity between the social assumptions of the ritual ("we are all culturally homogeneous peasants together") and what is in fact the case ("we are several different kinds of people who must perforce live together despite our serious value disagreements") leads to a deep uneasiness of which Paidjan's funeral was but an extreme example. In the kampong, the holding of a slametan increasingly serves to remind people that the neighborhood bonds they are strengthening through a dramatic enactment are no longer the bonds which most emphatically hold them together. These latter are ideological, class, occupation, and political bonds, divergent ties which are no longer adequately summed up in territorial relationships.

In sum, the disruption of Paidjan's funeral may be traced to a single source: an incongruity between the cultural framework of meaning and the patterning of social interaction, an incongruity due to the persistence in an urban environment of a religious symbol system adjusted to peasant social structure. Static functionalism, of either the sociological or social psychological sort, is unable to isolate this kind of incongruity because it fails to discriminate between logico-meaningful integration and causal-functional integration; because it fails to realize that cultural structure and social structure are not mere reflexes of one another but independent, yet interdependent, variables. The driving forces in social change can be clearly formulated only by a more dynamic form of functionalist theory, one which takes into account the fact that man's need to live in a world to which he can attribute some significance, whose essential import he feels he can grasp, often diverges from his concurrent need to maintain a functioning social organism. A diffuse concept of culture as "learned behavior," a static view of social structure as an equilibrated pattern of interaction, and a stated or unstated assumption that the two must somehow (save in "disorganized" situations) be simple mirror images of one another, is rather too primitive a conceptual apparatus with which to attack such problems as those raised by Paidjan's unfortunate but instructive funeral.

Wayne Hield

The Study of Change in Social Science

O*NE* of the more significant changes in the social sciences to-day is the way the subject of "social change" is being redefined for investigation. In the eighteenth and nineteenth centuries social scientists were interested in the problem of how to mould a society characterized by rational order and progress for all. The assumption of human nature underlying the theories of such figures as Marx and Lester Ward, for example, lay in the belief that man was fundamentally a rational being capable of coming to grips with the laws of social reality as they perceived them and resolutely working for the change of broad social and political structures. Their theoretical systems were designed to demonstrate the possibility of man's controlling his physical and social environment for human betterment. As such their theoretical positions presented alternative programmes and methods for the patterning of societal action.[1]

To-day, social scientists are predominantly occupied with the reverse

From Wayne Hield, "The Study of Change in Social Science," *The British Journal of Sociology,*[5] (March, 1964), pp. 1–11. Reprinted by permission of the author and the journal.

[1] Cf. Reinhard Bendix, "The Image of Man in the Social Sciences," *Commentary,* February, 1951, for a discussion of earlier theorists in this connection.

emphasis of how to help man successfully adjust to the existing social and political order. The theoretical basis of research begins with the Hobbesian problem of how to maintain social control. The subject of change as treated by Talcott Parsons and Robert K. Merton, undoubtedly the leading social theorists in the field of sociology to-day, is defined as a by-product in the malfunctioning of social control or order. Though both theorists have made notable contributions to our understanding of the mechanisms involved in social control, their approach is similar to the earlier anthropologists, Malinowski and Radcliffe-Brown, both of whom were primarily concerned with maintaining a stable, integrated and harmonious social equilibrium. By taking as their research problem the task of explaining how it is that various social institutions of preliterate societies function interdependently in an integrated whole, these earlier anthropologists either neglected the question of change in direction or control of institutional structures or studied social change as evidence of breakdown in social control and consequently studied means by which control was restored. Thus in the study of certain laws and customs of these preliterate societies, attention was centred in the conditions leading to the perpetuation of codes of behaviour and to the impact of crime or delinquency, for example, in either strengthening or serving to reinforce societal sanctions. Interest in the stability and order of such communities tended to preclude study of social and political change, and particularly, changes of the distribution of power. . . .

Although Parsons and Merton in their stress on the problem of "social control" claim to be equally interested in social deviance in so far as this increases our understanding of the mechanisms of permanence and change, the perhaps unforeseen consequence of this theoretic position is leading to a deluge of inquiries of various forms of social adjustment, or how it is that man adapts himself to certain institutional structures exercising social control. This may be due in part to the way they define their system of "structural-functional" analysis. Much of the systematic elaboration of this system involves the formulation of "normative patterns" of behaviour or ideal-types representing alternative ways that people might think or behave when confronted with certain structural or institutional settings. . . . It becomes the task of the social scientist to investigate means of maintaining social control or reducing tensions or conflicts to restore a condition of harmony and equilibrium. By defining in this way what is problematic in research, deviant attitudes and behaviours become speculatively interesting if somewhat pathological consequences of certain "dysfunctional" elements in social order. Where deviance presents itself, the theoretic concern is with the processes involved in restoring or re-equilibrating a condition of equilibrium or social control.

Essentially this position in sociology is following the tradition of the psychologists, social psychologists, and anthropologists in their emphasis on social adjustment. Mental hygienists are busy in smoothing over the sharp, asocial edges of the personality to allow its successful marketability in the white-collar world.[2] The flood of interest in "psychologizing" now explains away the curious idea systems of the deviant, the abnormal, the malcontent, as "personality" problems. Such deviants are not to be taken at their face value when continued demands are made for wage raises, for example, rather are their statements taken as symptoms of underlying exaggerated personality needs requiring the therapy of understanding the "psychological" reasons for their fixated ideas in order to be "saved" and turned back into society without them.

Industrial sociologists, in the tradition of Elton Mayo, are dishing out the morning coffee and the morale-building essay contest on "My Job and Why I Like to Work Here" to better adjust the morale of the worker to his business of tending the machine. The work of Kurt Lewin in dynamics of small group behaviour has been followed by J. L. Moreno's sociometric methods utilized for tracking down the "social isolate" or other deviants to adjust them to the larger whole, be it the schoolroom, factory, church, or the armed forces. . . .

Again in the area of social class studies, Lloyd Warner and his followers in their surveys of social circles in various small towns, have offered their findings as a means for aiding those who are not contented with their lot to fit into the desired stratum. Their "subjective" approach to social class leads to generalizations that one's class position is somehow equated with whatever level the person feels he is in; if you think of yourself as middle-class, you are middle-class. Typically the focus of this type of research are the attitudes of the "average" small town man. What people think or feel about each other is now regarded as more important than the "objective" approach by Marx in the study of economic position or relation to the means of production as index of class. Thus Parsons gives this definition of stratification: "The ranking system in terms of esteem is what we may call the system of stratification of the society." [3] While paying lip-service to "objective" elements in determining class position, Parsons together with the Lloyd Warner school devote little attention to the consideration of economic or technological variables in the study of social class nor to the distribution of economic and political power in determining the bases of stratification.

For the most part, the reaction to Marx manifest in the reliance on the

---

[2] See Kingsley Davis, "Mental Hygiene and the Class Structure," *A Study of Interpersonal Relations,* edited by Patrick Mullahy (New York: Hermitage Press, 1949).
[3] Parsons, *The Social System,* p. 132. See also his *Essays in Sociological Theory,* chap. VII.

works of Max Weber has resulted in an orientation stressing the role of ideologies or value-orientations as motivating factors of behaviour in such a manner that economic and technological variables are by-passed. The study of how people feel about other people in their work or in their community position is creating an imbalance and one-sided social psychological view in the field of sociology. . . .

Throughout these works, the "man-on-the-street," or the worker in the factory, or the soldier in the armed forces, become the central object of investigation. The mass man becomes the irrational object to be manipulated by the social scientist or by outside interests through the aid of social science techniques in adjusting his personality needs to the desired condition of conformity or harmony. It does not take much vision to realize that the human relations experts of the next fifty years are, however unintended, going to constitute the main drift in this area with their new found occupation of building the morale of the disenchanted, fitting the unfit, and adjusting the maladjusted.

Social Adjustment in Social Science Theory

The key theoretical concepts in social psychology and sociology preordain the nature of these studies of social adjustment. In both fields there is a convergence of theory with suggestions for research proceeding from nearly identical theoretical constructs: the tension-need theory of behaviour. In this view, as developed through the works of the gestaltists, Lewin, Tolman, H. A. Murray, and more recently, Krech and Crutchfield, the personality is ideally conceptualized in his most restful moments as being in a state of "psychic homeostasis," or a relative absence of needs. The basic postulate of this approach is that a need does not become dominant in a personality if there is no obstruction to its satisfaction. When the person does not receive enough affection, for example, a tension develops in the personality and we speak of a *need* for affection. Resulting behaviour constitutes an attempt to release tension; all obstructions to need satisfactions, or reduction in tension, are considered to be hedonically negative, while the "greatest pleasure seems to be associated with a relatively rapid lowering of need tension." Normal functioning is linked with the state of "psychic homeostasis."

In research, the logical question to be asked follows: "What social conditions give rise to a state of exaggerated need-tension and how can such tension be reduced to a state of homeostasis?" From this one can see that it is readily adapted to any condition or scene of conflict representing tension, and to the means by which such conflict may be attenuated. The problem of change is that of reducing intensified need-dispositions or altering the expectations of the subjects with the interest in restoring a condition of equilibration or social order. Illustrative case studies of this method are provided by Krech and Crutchfield and by Kurt Lewin in considering conflict between management and labour to be the reflection of certain underlying social tensions and needs not met in the work situation. Remedies for these conditions hark back to those of Elton Mayo, T. N. Whitehead, and Burleigh Gardner by suggesting the use of more psychological rewards, praise and recognition, as a means for reducing conflicts between labour and management.[4]

The tension-need theory has now been incorporated in the major theoretical works of Talcott Parsons. In his recent work, *The Social System*, the basic problem outlined is that of explaining the adjustment of individuals or social groups to one another. As Parsons indicates, the social system is characterized by a plurality of individual actors who interact with each other in terms of a tendency to the "optimization of gratification." The focus of his work is that of the "gratification-deprivation" balance of the ego personality (me) in relation to alter (you). Motivation is defined as orientation to improvement of the "gratification-deprivation" balance of the actor.[5] Thus, his thesis develops from the same hedonistic calculus found in the tension-need theory of behaviour. Deviant behaviour, for Parsons, is defined as the abnormal in psychological terms:

> We may say that the need for *security* in the motivational sense is the need to preserve stable cathexes of social objects, including collectivities. Tendencies to dominance or submission, aggressiveness or compulsive independence, then, may be interpreted as manifestations of insecurity. The need for a feeling of *adequacy* on the other hand, we may say, is the need to feel able to live up to the normative standards of the expectation system, to conform in that sense. The compulsive enforcer, the perfectionist, the incorrigible and the evader, then, could be interpreted as motivated by a sense of inadequacy.[6]

With this operational definition of deviance as "insecurity" and "inadequacy," Parsons stresses ways in which deviance can be mitigated. In this he offers explanations for the origins of deviant behaviour; the genesis of

---

[4] Krech and Crutchfield, *Theory and Problems of Social Psychology* (New York: McGraw Hill, 1948), chap. XIV; Kurt Lewin, *Resolving Social Conflicts* (New York: Harpers, 1948), chap. 8.

[5] The opposite thesis is, of course, equally plausible that real gratification is found particularly in the state of tension or in various states of deprivation. While this hypothesis has not been the subject of research, it would seem that extensive documentation of the idea could be found in such societies as our own that thrive on a constant high level of tension in "inter-personal" relationships to say nothing of the consistent tensions evident in international diplomacy. For a suggestive consideration of this problem, see Fyodor Dostoevsky, "Notes from Underground," *The Short Novels of Dostoevsky* (edited by Thomas Mann), (New York: Dial Press, 1951), pp. 129–156.

[6] Parsons, *The Social System*, p. 261.

value orientations making for conflict between ego and alter; discussion of conflicts in roles; and possible structural determinants of deviance. In each case he proceeds to means for re-equilibrating the system of order. It is no accident, then, that Parsons' discussion of the "Mechanisms of Social Control" follows that of his treatment of deviant behaviour.

In light of the foregoing, it is hardly a surprise that Parsons draws upon an extensive analogy of social control to the role of psychotherapy as a means illustrating suggested treatment of deviance. He states that psychotherapy may serve "as a prototype of the mechanisms of social control."[7] . . .

All this fits into the larger societal trends Parsons anticipates in our society. As a student of Max Weber, Parsons sees a growing rationalization of our societal life, a strain towards objectivity, systematization, and organizational efficiency in the calculation of appropriate means to achieve desired goals. While both Weber and Parsons agree in recognizing this vast directional factor in the nature of modern life, their evaluations of this trend are quite different. Weber was appalled by the implications for human freedom in this development of rationalization in bureaucratic structures. Bureaucratization, as Weber studied it, proceeds hand-in-hand with a growing concentration of economic and political power at the apex of large organizational structures together with the economic and social levelling of the masses. The important policy-making functions of the modern bureaucratic organization are appropriated by the top officials of the hierarchy while below an army of technicians and clerks perform routine tasks of administration carrying out decisions made at higher levels. The immediate implication perceived by Weber is the threat of such concentration of authority to the democratic process as those who are governed find themselves levelled to a state of apathetic mediocrity. It was to this problem of how to maintain freedom or independent exercise of discretion in modern life that Weber devoted much of his writing and his activity in political life:

This passion for bureaucracy, as we have heard it expressed here, is enough to drive one to despair. It is as if in politics the spectre of timidity—which has in any case always been rather a good standby for the German—were to stand alone at the helm ; as if we were deliberately to become men who need "order" and nothing but order, who become nervous and cowardly if for one moment this order wavers, and helpless if they are torn away from their total incorporation in it. That the world should know no men but these: it is in such an evolution that we are already caught up, and the great question is therefore not how can we promote and hasten it, but what can we oppose to this machinery in order to keep a portion of mankind free from this parcelling-out of the soul, from this supreme mastery of the bureaucratic way of life.[8]

---

[7] Parsons, *The Social System,* p. 301.

[8] From a lecture by Max Weber on Bureaucratization in J. P. Mayer, *Max Weber and German Politics* (Faber & Faber, Ltd., 1943), p. 97.

In contrast to Weber who constantly asked this question above of how to regulate and control bureaucratic machinery in maintaining the dignity of man, Parsons neglects this as a basic problem to be dealt with by social scientists. Instead he seems to agree with the big change and direction of these changes in modern life. The nature of modern scientific investigation in its objective quest for laws of human behaviour is considered a prime leader in this respect. There are certain non-empirical elements such as philosophy, ideologies, and religious beliefs which will in turn act back on the progress of rationalization in science as obstacles in its development. . . . "Making this allowance for this factor, however, we may speak of the process of rationalization with considerable confidence as a general directional factor in the change of social systems." [9]

At one point, Parsons recognizes certain conflicts between his "virtual certainty" that there is an "inherent factor of the general directionality of change in the process of rationalization" and certain expressive symbols of our age. The forced "affective neutrality" of our technological and bureaucratic system finds release in spectator amusements: comics, T.V., radio, movies. Technological change, says Parsons, force new reward systems and new distributions of roles, however, "It is probable that the strains imposed by these processes much more than any inherent 'conflict of interests' is the primary factor in the genesis of so-called 'class-conflicts' in modern Western society." [10]

In a few brief paragraphs the "dysfunctional" elements in the rationalization of our society are accounted for and brushed aside. For the most part, Americans are getting along well enough; if there are occasional conflicts and disturbances, these are epiphenomena. Thus we may infer from Parsons' position that frustration in our society is explained as a momentary zigzag in the course of progressing rationalization. It only remains to adjust our societal groups to the "normative pattern."

Since "adjustment" is the major problem in question, suggestions for research centre on ideologies, beliefs, and expectations in their proper structural-functional settings in the analysis of conformity or deviance of social groups from societal norms, for, operating with the assumptions of the psychotherapeutic process, these are what must be changed by the therapists in maintaining social control. The researcher of late in his study of small group behaviour and of the mass man wants to know who and what the subject is thinking about when he expresses a certain attitude or behaviour; this is what is referred to as "reference group" theory in the social sciences.[11]

---

[9] Parsons, *The Social System*, p. 499.

[10] Parsons, *ibid.*, p. 513.

[11] See T. H. Newcomb, *Social Psychology* (Tavistock Publications, 1952), p. 225 ff., for elaboration of this theoretical construct.

What determines the extent of internalizing certain attitudes of parents, peers, or authority figures and how is this reflected in behaviour? Through an understanding of the ego-cathected identifications of the individual, the applied scientist can work towards changing the subject's identifications with people who have been significant to him and thereby change the way in which he defines the situation. . . .

In this orientation, theorists have turned to the concepts of "status" and "role" developed by the anthropologist, Ralph Linton, as valuable tools for examining how people adjust to their formally prescribed positions in various institutional or social settings. "Status," as defined by Linton, refers to a place in a social structure recognized by society such as age, sex, occupation, position in family unit, and so forth. "Role" designates the behaviour expected by society or certain groups or individuals in carrying out one's status position. The concept of "role" is the dynamic aspect of "status" suggesting analysis of how the individual interprets his status position.[12]

These concepts originally employed in the study of small, relatively static preliterate communities imply a state of stability and definity which is hardly present in "status" and "role" positions in our highly complex and changing society. One can, of course, formally delimit certain "status" positions for the purpose of defining what is to be studied in an organizational structure. However, this imputed concreteness to position in an organization is misleading and tends to neglect the fact that definitions of behaviour expected in certain "status" and "role" positions are continually changing not only in the minds of those who perform them but in the expectations of those who recruit and control the behaviours of subordinates. As these concepts have been defined, the aspect of "role" which is the dynamic interpretation by the subject of his "status" position leads the scientist to the investigation of background factors, ideologies, or other elements brought to his present "status" position resulting in more or less successful adjustment to the defined constant variable, his "status" position. In this, the interacting effect of change in the expectations of the leaders and the led as they influence one another is avoided by devoting attention essentially to the adjustment of the subordinate to the super-ordinate. Should the actors manifest so-called "deviant" or "dysfunctional" behaviour in a more dynamic interpretation of their position, the very labels employed in the approach of Parsons appear to assume that the given set of institutional norms or the given power structure is the normal and correct state of affairs. Man is a helpless creature to be adapted and adjusted to the *status quo* or what is called "social control." Evidence of conflict or tension or anything which might be considered "compulsive" and

---

12 Ralph Linton, *The Cultural Background of Personality* (Routledge & Kegan Paul, 1946), pp. 77–82.

motivated by a sense of inadequacy prompts the social scientist to fit him into the ubiquitous "social equilibrium." Such deviants, by definition, are "dysfunctional" to the larger order of harmony.

The study of change has thus been obscured by the formulation of theoretical constructs stressing order and stability. While it is interesting and useful to learn how a complex society manages to get along without complete chaos, our society among others, is, in the meantime, moving in the direction of more centralized controls over the areas of human freedom. In the opinion of the writer, the problem of modern society is not altogether that of Plato, Machiavelli, Hobbes, Locke, Rousseau and others who sought the foundations of a stable order to restrain what appeared to be impending societal chaos. Social control *to-day* is on the increase as large-scale bureaucracy proceeds to engulf modern man in the struggle to hold such structures accountable to society. It is this very rigidity and inflexibility of the bureaucracy and the consequent apathy of the employee that is now beginning to stimulate interest in "The Lonely Crowd" and in "Man for Himself." [13]

Research is needed in the problem of how to make man a rational being, an agent of change with the power to effect deliberate modification of his own environment rather than to view him as an irrational, passive adjuster to the contemporary scene. Problems for research would investigate, for example, the conditions for developing a personality with the "nerve of failure" to withstand pressures for ethical and behavioural conformity without being morally destroyed. What kind of family, peer group, or occupational background is conducive to the active and autonomous individual who has the moral strength or actual power to act back upon pressures for conformity.[14] Under what conditions do individuals or groups become active and effective in altering the given definition of the situation. What contributes to the recognition and acceptance of alternative views within and between large-scale organizations.[15] How are significant changes in policy made and carried out in large-scale bureaucracy. Such questions necessarily involve a consideration of the bases of power to accomplish change while assuming a certain amount of tension or conflict to be "normal" and perhaps inevitable in the study of change.

---

[13] David Riesman, *The Lonely Crowd* (New Haven: Yale University Press, 1950); Erich Fromm, *Man for Himself* (New York: Rinehart and Company, Inc., 1947).

[14] For specific propositions in research along these lines, see Marie Jahoda, "Toward a Social Psychology of Mental Health," *Problems of Infancy and Childhood,* Fourth Conference Supplement II (Josiah Macy, Jr. Foundation, New York: 1950).

[15] Seymour M. Lipset deals with this problem in a forthcoming work on the International Typographical Union. [Lysset, Trew and Coleman, *Union Democracy,* Glencoe: Free Press, 1956.—Editor's Note].

Chapter IV

Conflict

and

Consensus

Introduction

*O*NE of sociology's clearest mandates is to substitute facts for fancies, yet sociology is often accused of providing more fancies than facts. This is nowhere more evident than in the abstract debate which contrasts *consensus* and *conflict* as dominant images for characterizing society. Here sociologists and their social-philosophical predecessors have had as much to do with establishing myths as destroying them. The debate has frequently been more ideological than analytic, more polemical than scholarly. One consequence is the tendency to polarize positions artificially. We often speak of "consensus theory" in the singular without specifying particular "consensus theorists." As commonly, we discuss "conflict theory" without inspecting its internal variations. This chapter focuses on these variations. Each of the authors is nominally a conflict theorist, and yet there are clear differences among them. While each is critical of functionalism, the criticisms stem from different perspectives and point to divergent corrections.

Irving Louis Horowitz begins by providing both an historical background and a contemporary judgment. The history concerns antecedents on both sides of the issue, Socrates, Marsilius, Hobbes, Marx and Simmel, on the one hand; Aristotle, de Tocqueville, Dewey, and Parsons, on the other. The judgment deplores the implicit tendency of the latter thinkers to equate organization with consensus and, in turn, consensus with equilibrium. Horowitz finds conflict shunted to the side as incompatible with structure. He argues that the incompatibility is spurious since conflict operates within the social structure and not outside of it. At the same time, Horowitz is also concerned that consensus loses the conceptual potency that it might have because it is defined too broadly. In particular he distinguishes between consensus and cooperation, arguing that the latter is empirically more common, politically more feasible, and analytically less value-laden. Rather than plump for a perspective of either consensus or conflict, Horowitz urges the analysis of cooperation as a mediating concept that can bridge the gap between them.

David Lockwood criticizes only one particular "consensus theorist" and this on somewhat different grounds than Horowitz. Lockwood's extended review of Parsons' *The Social System* is a classic of the genre. He suggests that Parsons' approach is only an incomplete, if vital, segment of a larger social theory. Although Parsons' work on the normative aspect of society is seminal, Lockwood argues that this focus neglects whole chunks of social reality. The empirical realm of social structure requires a different pattern of analysis, one that accounts for the discrepancies between the normative wish and the structural fact. It is here that *power* and *conflict* rear their tousled heads; it is here that the Parsonian scheme must give ground to a less idealistic model. Note, however, that several caveats are in order. First, as we have mentioned earlier, Parsons is no official spokesman of functionalism, and may be less representative than his renown would indicate. Second, Parsons has altered many of his views since the publication of *The Social System*, and his more recent selections in the volume are worth reconsideration in the light of Lockwood's trenchancies. (See particularly his defense of the *priority* of the study of social statics as the only firm basis for the analysis of social change, a defense which appears in the selection reprinted in Chapter III.) But Lockwood does not seek to replace Parsons' view. He argues simply that Parsons' model has a more limited utility than is claimed for it. Lockwood prefers the Marxian alternative not because its predictions are more accurate but rather because its theoretical scope is wider and more provocative.

Pierre L. van den Berghe examines this reasoning and takes specific issue with the juxtaposition of Parsons and Marx. As common as the polarity has become, van den Berghe points to a possible rapprochement between functionalism and the Hegelian–Marxian dialectic. Thus, both views treat society holistically; both stress the continuum of consensus and cleavage with recent insights suggesting that consensus may be dysfunctional just as conflict may be functional; both have an evolutionary perspective on social change; and both stress equilibrium since the dialectical term "synthesis" has much in common with the functionalist emphasis on "integration." In all of this, van den Berghe is an exception to the tendency noted earlier to treat conflict and consensus theory as polar opposites with contradictory analytic styles as well as divergent ideological leanings. At a time when sociologists frequently feel compelled to declare themselves one way or the other, van den Berghe seeks to indicate that the divergencies are more polemically apparent than sociologically real.

As if to confirm this judgment, the last selection represents the wheel come full circle. Here Lewis Coser indicates that conflict may indeed have consensual and eminently "functional" consequences. Coser's essay forms the last chapter of his well-known book, *The Functions of Social Conflict*. A concise summary of the book's insights, the elegance of the ideas should more than compensate for the terse expression. These ideas are in large part the legacy of George Simmel, although Coser has organized and extended them. They suggest that internal conflict has a range of salutary consequences including stabilizing group relations by bringing simmering grievances to a more manageable boil, and revitalizing norms that have lost their saliency. The consequences of external conflict are equally plumbed. Thus, groups engaged in conflict are able to claim greater membership commitment and are apt to join in association with other groups, previously regarded with hostility.

In all of this, the question "*which* conflict theory?" is underscored. Clearly there are sharp differences among the authors represented in this chapter. One line of cleavage is between those who assert that "consensus" and "conflict" theory are two sides of one scheme soon to be merged and those who insist that conflict theory is distinct and incompatible with consensus theory. Between these two views is yet a third, that conflict and consensus are incompatible *but mutually fruitful* views of society, both of which must be taken into account for the fullest development of social theory. This latter view is suggested by Reinhard Bendix and Bennett Berger in their joint, "Images of Society and Problems of Concept Formation in Sociology," in Llewellyn Gross's *Symposium on Sociological Theory* (Row, Peterson, 1959). An awareness of these differences should help to deescalate the debate into a more profitable discussion. Again, however, this chapter does not exhaust conflict theory in this volume, let alone conflict theory generally. One conspicuous omission that is only alluded to is the area of "game theory" and the growing literature on the sociology of international conflict. For a lead on the latter, see the article by Ernst Haas in Chapter VI.

Irving Louis Horowitz

Consensus, Conflict, and Co-operation

*F*EW WORDS in the vocabulary of contemporary sociology appear as soothing or as reassuring as consensus. The chain of agreeable associations of the term symbolize the final mating of the science of sociology and a theory of social equilibrium. What stands in need of investigation is the price paid for this essentially recent turn in sociological theory. Specifically it must be asked whether the movement away from traditional theories of conflict and conflict resolution represents a genuinely new stage in the secularization of social science or is in fact a narrowing down of the field brought about by social pressures.

Whatever its meaning, the notion of consensus is an impressively stated although inadequately explored reference point in present day sociology. The resilient strength of consensus theories stems in part from some vague sense that they are connected to functionalism. For those skeptical of this fusion of consensus and function, analysis of the issues is blunted by the plethora of definitions the unwary examiner is greeted with. The fact is that there is an

From Irving Louis Horowitz, "Consensus, Conflict and Cooperation: A Sociological Inventory," *Social Forces,* 41 (Dec., 1962), pp. 177–188. Reprinted by permission of the author and the journal.

absence of consensus in sociological theory as to just what does and does not constitute consensus or a consensual matrix.

There are at least seven shadings of meaning which currently attaches to the term consensus beyond the common-sense usage of the word as a proper synonym for agreement between people. First and perhaps most commonly, sociologists define consensus as "adjustment of social dissension." This usage is borrowed from the present psychoanalytic definition of normality as social adjustment and neurosis as the absence of adjustment.[1] The second view has its point of departure in role theory. Consensus is seen as an accord between role behavior and role expectation.[2] The third position, while having a point of contact with an adjustment approach to consensus, lifts it out of the individual realm into a cultural framework. "Where an opinion is very widely held and cuts across all groups in society" there you must have consensus.[3] The fourth theory sees our term as affiliated to hedonistic impulse, as "possible only when two or more parties want to maintain a relationship which each regards as in its own interest." [4] A cognate definition is offered by the same writer in terms of game theory. "Two parties or groups are playing to gain a maximum, but they are prepared to settle for less within the recognized limits." [5] The sixth account identifies consensus with the curbing of hedonistic impulse and instinct, and with the Durkheim notion of solidarity and social cohesion generally.[6] Our last author sees consensus in its barest atomic terms as a sharing of perspectives, as "nothing more or less than the existence on the part of two or more persons, of similar orientations toward something." [7]

Examining these definitions dispassionately, and leaving aside the truth content of each, it is difficult to understand why the concept of consensus has aroused such intense sociological interest. No logical unravelling of the above definitions will explain why consensus, barely a meaningful word in the sociological lexicon of previous decades, is now viewed as a fully matured theory. An accounting of the term is therefore required on extra philological

---

[1] J. O. Hertzler, *American Social Institutions : A Sociological Analysis* (Boston: Allyn and Bacon, 1961), p. 63.

[2] Neal Gross, "The Sociology of Education," *Sociology Today : Problems and Prospects,* ed. by R. K. Merton, L. Broom, L. S. Cottrell, Jr. (New York: Basic Books, 1959), p. 140.

[3] Leonard Broom and Philip Selznick, *Sociology : A Text with Adapted Readings* (Evanstown, Ill.: Row, Peterson & Co., 1958, second edition), p. 278.

[4] Arnold W. Green, *Sociology : An Analysis of Life in Modern Society* (New York: McGraw-Hill Book Co., 1960, third edition), p. 65.

[5] Arnold W. Green, *ibid.,* p. 67.

[6] Ely Chinoy, *Society, An Introduction to Sociology* (New York: Random House, 1961), pp. 344–46.

[7] Theodore Newcomb, "The Study of Consensus," *Sociology Today, op. cit.,* p. 279.

grounds. The expanding uses and abuses of consensus theory overshadows the existing definitional ambiguities.

Consensus theory is now employed to settle a wide range of sociological problems. What is most frequently encountered is the identification of consensus with functional efficiency, and no less with the social requisites of political democracy.[8] In its simplest form, the bivariate equation is that increase in the amount of social consensus yields an increase in functional efficacy and democratic polity; while inversely, decrease in the amount of social consensus creates social disorganization and dysfunction. On a broader front, advocates of consensus theory see this as a new turn in sociology—away from the knotty issue of how conflicts arise and are settled to the spatially and temporally more durable issue of how men cooperate with one another. By defining the core of social action in terms of two functional references: (a) the maintenance of a pattern of orientation, and (b) the definition of the meaning of one or more situational objects, consensus comes to be equated with social equilibrium.[9]

Before proceeding to the substance of my remarks, an historical observation is in order. It is clear that the early development of sociology from Marx to Simmel takes as its point of departure the idea that society is best understood as a selective and collective response to the needs of social interaction in a nonequilibriated world. This involved a rejection, conscious or otherwise, of the idea that society is best understood as a contractual or informal agreement made between equals to secure common goals. As such, the Roman Empire for Simmel is not a union of the general will with particularized wills, but rather an illustration of the efficiency, the functionality of political superordination, of what he terms Caesaristic types of rule. Thus what consensus exists is for Simmel the "tendency of domination by means of leveling." This apparent consensual apparatus is but *disguised* superordination. In discussing Philip the Good of Burgundy, he notes that "legal differences were created exclusively by the arbitrary pleasure of the ruler. They thus marked all the more distinctly the common, unalterable subordination of his subjects." [10]

Similarly for Marx, the economic system called capitalism does not come into existence in consequence of the clamor of public opinion, or to express

---

[8] Seymour M. Lipset, "Political Sociology," *Sociology Today, op. cit.,* p. 114.

[9] Talcott Parsons, *The Social System* (Glencoe: The Free Press, 1951), p. 507. This same view is even more forcefully developed in "The Point of View of the Author," *The Social Theories of Talcott Parsons,* ed. by Max Black (Englewood Cliffs, New Jersey: Prentice-Hall, 1961), p. 327.

[10] Georg Simmel, "Subordination under an Individual," *The Sociology of Georg Simmel,* edited and translated by K. H. Wolff (Glencoe: The Free Press, 1950), pp. 201–207.

the general will (although those who do come to power exercise such rational-izations) but simply to satisfy the historical process which brings a social class to power. The welding of such power to a new social class is the purpose of the State, which in turn enters the historical picture as the central agency of coercion while posing as the agency of social consensus.

> The *practical* struggle of these particular interests, which constantly *really* run counter to the communal and illusory communal interests, makes *practical* intervention and control necessary through the illusory "general interest" in the form of the state. The social power, i.e., the multiplied productive force, which arises through the cooperation of different individuals as it is determined within the division of labor, appears to these individuals, since their cooperation is not voluntary but natural, not as their own united power, but as an alien force exist-ing outside them, of the origin and end of which they are ignorant, which they thus cannot control.[11]

Consensus is thus the idealization of coercion.

The roots of conflict theory reach back in time to Hobbes and the forma-tion of the modern nation-State, Marsilius of Padua in the medieval world, and Thrasymachus, Socrates and Plato in ancient Greek society. In essence, the position holds that social organization does not flow from the consensus of *vox populi*, but from the contradictory yet interrelated needs and designs of men. It is interesting to note that the debate between Thrasymachus and Socrates in *The Republic* concerning the nature of justice (the dialogue on power versus virtue) at no point assumes society to be the consequence of popular will or common agreement. Nonetheless, it cannot be said that the history of social and political theory has been a one-sided acceptance of con-flict theory and its underlying power thesis as the only explanation of social structure and social action. Such an assertion would have to discount the bulk of writings from Aristotle's "golden mean" to Dewey's "common faith." Thus the history of conflict and consensus has been a dialogue between exclusive frames of reference seeking to explain the same phenom-enon—human cooperation.

From the point of view of sociological history, however, it is pertinent to bear in mind its close affiliation with conflict theorists: Marx on *Klassen-kampf*, Gumplowicz on *Rassenkampf*, Mosca's ruling and ruled classes, and Simmel on *Superordnung* and *Unterordnung*. Only now, with sociology in the full passion of its empiricist revolt against European systems of sociology and social philosophy, has a strenuous effort been made to overcome theories of conflict—what has come to be termed "crisis ideologies." Part of this

---

[11] Karl Marx and Friedrich Engels, *The German Ideology,* in *Basic Writings on Politics and Philosophy : Marx and Engels,* ed. by L. S. Feuer (Garden City : Double-day and Co., 1959), pp. 255–256, also p. 253.

cleansing process has been the promotion of consensus theory. With this promotion has come the inevitable search for new sociological hero images. The brilliant social historian deTocqueville in particular has been elevated in current estimates.[12]

The rallying point in de Tocqueville is the comment that "a society can exist only when a great number of men consider a great number of things from the same point of view; when they hold the same opinions upon many subjects, when the same occurrences suggest the same thoughts and impressions to their minds." [13] Here then seems to be the historical progenitor of the new theory of consensus, and the repudiation of those political sociologies which seek to define social structure in terms of holders and seekers of power, of the ability to command and to coerce. We must now focus attention on current efforts to convert deTocqueville's insight into a theory.

Perhaps the most widespread axiom of consensus theory holds that it is a necessary condition for social structure.[14] The social structure has come to be defined as excluding those patterns of human action which are spontaneous and unstructured. Social structure is said to consist in a "set of statuses" defined by relatively stable relationships between people. What follows is a mechanical notion of the relation of consensus and conflict as structured and unstructured modes of behavior respectively. Consensus involves objectification of position, group cohesion, collective representations, common traditions, and rules for inducting and indoctrinating new members; while conflict is seen as external to social structure, as spontaneity, impulsive action, lack of organization, intuitive response to immediate situations. In short, consensus differs from conflict as organization differs from deviance.[15] Thus to discuss social structure is by definition not to examine conflict situations, and of course, the pernicious *vice versa*, to examine conflict situations is to discuss something extraneous to social structure.

To place conflict outside the framework of social structure, or to go beyond that and see conflict as necessarily destructive of the social organism, is to place a definite premium on social equilibrium. It strongly implies that a

---

12 Seymour M. Lipset, *Political Man : The Social Bases of Politics* (Garden City: Doubleday and Co., 1960), pp. 26–28, 65–66. Lipset's continual juxtaposition of deTocqueville and Marx is a strong indication that the differences between consensus and conflict theories involve something more than scientific requirements. Indeed, he has made them ideological poles: consensus representing democracy and conflict representing authoritarianism.

13 Alexis deTocqueville, *Democracy in America,* trans. by H. Reeve (New York: Century and Co., 1899), v. I, p. 398.

14 cf. Robert E. Park, "Reflections on Communication and Culture," *The American Journal of Sociology,* XLIV (1939), 191–205.

15 Kurt Lang and Gladys E. Lang, *Collective Dynamics* (New York: Thomas Y. Crowell Co., 1961), pp. 13–14.

society can be changed only by apocalyptic or spontaneous methods. The identification of consensus with social structure reinforces the stereotyped view that change does not emanate from the Establishment and, keeping within the boundaries it informally sets, is deviant in relation to social order as such. Consensus theory thus tends to become a metaphysical representation of the dominant ideological matrix. It rests on a principle of "general interests" which every member of society is supposed to imbibe if he wishes to avoid the onus of being a deviant or an unconnected isolate. The sociology of small groups has been especially active in pushing this view; the implication being that a condition of social conflict necessarily is a world of deviants and isolates quite incapable of attending to problems of functional survival.[16] The possibility that differing goal orientations are consonant with a single functional agency is too rarely entertained.[17] . . .

Briefly then, only when social function is narrowly defined as social equilibrium can a sociological theory of conflict be viewed as an overt or hidden menace to the social system.

A series of considerations which are increasingly being adduced to demonstrate the singular advantages of consensus theory over conflict theory relates to the difficulties of a social examination of unstable relations. Three factors in particular are pointed out: (a) the transitory nature of conflict situations, that is the actual behavior of a mass in an extreme situation, such as civil war or revolution, is so short lived and capricious that predicting conclusions or consequences of conflict situations is impossible; (b) the necessity for dealing with conflict situations in their natural social environment has as its corollary the absence of controlled experiments such as one finds in strictly delineated types of research; (c) the consequent necessity of presenting evaluations in terms of second and third hand materials such as newspaper reports, autobiographical sketches, and historical studies of unique events—all of which clearly involve the sociological researcher in commitments beyond the empirical confines of the sampling situation.[18]

The scrutiny of this series of objections reveals a transparency and shallowness that poses a serious threat to sociological research as such. The criteria of scientific analysis have never been reducible to the simplicity of an investigatory context. What the above objections fail to take account of is the

---

[16] Theodore Newcomb, "The Study of Consensus," *Sociology Today, op. cit.,* p. 284.

[17] Gideon Sjoberg, "Contradictory Functional Requirements and Social Systems," *Journal of Conflict Resolution,* IV (1960), 198–208; also see, Eugene Litwak, "Models of Bureaucracy which permit Conflict," *The American Journal of Sociology,* LXVII (1961), 177–184.

[18] A fuller catalogue of objections to the study of conflict situations is contained in Kurt Lang and Gladys Lang, *op. cit.,* pp 545–53.

need for a criterion of significance, of the importance of any specific undertaking to the general growth of sociological knowledge. While it is correct that conflict situations, even of major proportions, are generally of "short" duration (at least in relation to the consequences), this is not a serious objection either to the empirical study of conflict situations, or more to the point, of a causal analysis of the genesis and sources of such situations. Sheer brevity of the conflict situation in relation to the consensual consolidation which may follow only indicates that certain sampling devices are ineffectual to resolve certain kinds of social events. To reason that any step beyond the borders of current methodological safeguards is to step beyond sociology as such is sheer casuistry; justifying the deep fears of many scholars in cognate social sciences that sociologists are too interested in domination and too little interested in cooperation.

The objection to the study of conflict situations because such situations have no well defined contours or boundaries is equally transparent. For this is very nearly always the case of the anthropologist in relation to a given culture. Would it seriously be contended that the "natural" setting of anthropological research makes it a lesser social science? The surest guarantee against provincialism and ethnocentricism would be a greater effort by sociologists to develop techniques of study suitable to this "natural" social setting. The failure to do so has too frequently placed the sociologist in the position of offering questionnaires devised for particular situations as uniformly (if not universally) valid in other cultural and social settings. The natural setting within which conflict arises, far from being an obstacle, should provide a powerful incentive to move beyond the highly structured but hardly universal, world of the small group. That this opportunity has not been seized is more a reflection of the limits of the "opinion leaders" among sociologists than a true delimiting of the legitimate boundaries of sociology.

The pernicious notion that the sociologist somehow has a unique tool of investigation that entitles him to ignore or downgrade the value of journalistic reports or historical surveys is insupportable on scientific grounds. Criteria for sound analysis are fairly constant throughout the spectrum of the social and historical sciences. The same questions can be asked about newspaper clippings as about questionnaires. Lasswell has done just that in his *Language of Politics.*

Can we assume that a scholar read his sources with the same degree of care throughout this research? Did he allow his eye to travel over the thousands upon thousands of pages of parliamentary debates, newspapers, magazines and other sources listed in his bibliography or notes? Or did he use a sampling system, scanning some pages superficially, though concentrating upon certain periods? Was the sampling system for the *Frankfurter Zeitung,* if one was employed, comparable with the one for the *Manchester Guardian?* Were the leaflets chosen simply because they were conveniently available to the scholar, or were they genuinely representative of the most widely circulated propaganda leaflets?[19]

These are, to be sure, correctly framed sociological questions. But they carry no implication that results are inferior if they are gathered from one source and not another. There is a difference between *resolving* a case for a position on the basis of news reports and *employing* such reports in attempting to arrive at some position.

To equate the worth of a theory (such as consensus theory *or* conflict theory) with ease of study, is a sophistical device which leads to a situation in which only those things are studied for which data already exists—which may help to account for that fantastic sameness and duplication of research efforts in present day small-group sociology. The greatest sociological requirement is precisely to fashion methods adequate to the tasks of studying problems of social order in a world of conflicting interests, standards, and values. Social order must itself be defined, and no less define, the larger universe of social change. The sociologist can hardly run the risk of being surprised by events of common currency in consequence of a theory of society bewitched by order and befuddled by change.

The faith in consensus theory as operationally more worthwhile than conflict theory often takes the form of a deep respect for the amazing complexity of social organization in industrial economies: the automation of production, the automation of human responsibilities, the precision of "chain of command" and "line" matrices, and the auto-regulative capacities of man in mass society to continually adjust to (and make adjustments in) bureaucratic procedures. The Parsonian school of sociology in particular seems impressed with the regularities which obtain between organization and society as such. Here the dilemma lies in equating organization to consensus. The stress and strain of organizational life gives rise to a definition of social action as that auto-regulative mechanism which adjusts for such "alienative" factors.

Such a view suffers from the master problem in traditional laissez-faire economics; namely, the assumption that automatic marketing "laws" somehow operate over and above the actual desires and ends of men. To meet the laissez-faire implications in the theory of social consensus, certain functionalists have developed a theory of the "safety-value," such that organizations "provide substitute objects upon which to displace hostile sentiments as well as means of abreaction of aggressive tendencies."[20] But this sub-theory only

---

[19] Harold D. Lasswell, "Why be Quantitative," in *Reader in Public Opinion and Communication*, enlarged edition, edited by Bernard Berelson and Morris Janowitz (Glencoe: The Free Press, 1953), p. 267.

[20] Lewis A. Coser, *op. cit.*, pp. 155–156.

reinforces the "metaphysical pathos" surrounding the theory of social organization since, far from being challenged, the assumption of institutional omnipotence and omniscience is reinforced. One is forced to conclude that the "clever" organization can even program small scale conflicts situations in order to guarantee the consensual apparatus as a whole.

The wide uses of consensus theory, particularly as a replacement for conflict theory, shows a close historical and analytical connection to the displacement of the language of social class with an alternate language of social status. It is a shift in viewing industrial society as susceptible to many and varied forms, to a vision of the industrial complex as growing omnipotent with time. Essentially, the Weberian theory of bureaucracy is a pessimistic vision, a view of organization as once and for all superceding production as the master social agency. In the theory of bureaucracy, the question of which class or group of classes hold the reins of power is secondary, since the "basic" bureaucratic factor continues to grow whatever economic organization might obtain. Bureaucracy comes to be viewed as omnipotent, subject to temporary setbacks but never to any real or sizeable defeat. If such is the case, then consensus theory is indeed no less omnipotent than the organizational procedures from which it derives its originating impulse.

Consensus theory has led to such a stress on continuities and similarities in the life of an industrial complex that all real differences between democracy and autocracy, ruling and being ruled, exploiting and being exploited, are eliminated—in theory at least. The "natural history of society" technique, which sees everything in terms of functional identities, has made a universe in which only grey cats and clever hounds exist. Political systems are reduced to "quantifiable" terms of how decisions are arrived at in system *A* or system *B*. The fusion of Michels and Weber being urged upon us, a fusion between "iron laws" of oligarchy and bureaucracy respectively, is not a resolution of the crisis in consensus theory, but a symptom of that crisis.[21] Since everything is reduced to administrative techniques, goals of any specific organization vanish into functional identifications, and the individual is left with an impotence that derives from being a part of an association that has a consensual life over and above the person. Consensus becomes the ideological celebration of the corporate personality, possessing a reality which transcends human society as such.

The mystique of consensus theory is evident in the work of many students of complex organization. Here we are met with the impermeable and impenetrable sovereignty of total specialization: the narcotizing effect of role-sets, the functional value of constraint and persuasion, decision-making machinery, etc. The paradox is that consensus theory, far from acting as a

---

[21] Seymour M. Lipset, "Political Sociology," *op. cit.*, pp. 89–91.

bulwark of democratic social theory (as it starts out to be), is the very reverse. It is a theory not for reaching agreements, but one which states that harmony is intrinsic to the organization of the bureaucratic life: a harmony which exists over and above the actual accords reached by men. And such must consensus theory remain since any serious theory of agreements and decisions must at the same time be a theory of disagreements and the conditions under which decisions cannot be reached. Yet consensus theorists, starting from the metaphysical "need" for consensus as universal, can only talk about absolute and relative consensus, complete or partial integration but never about conflict as a means of expressing genuine social needs and aspirations.[22]

On this point, Gouldner has put matters rightly by pointing out that

Instead of telling men how bureaucracy might be mitigated, they insist that it is inevitable. Instead of explaining how democratic patterns may, to some extent, be fortified and extended, they warn us that democracy cannot be perfect. Instead of controlling the disease, they suggest that we are deluded, or more politely, incurably romantic for hoping to control it. Instead of assuming responsibilities as realistic clinicians, striving to further democratic potentialities wherever they can, many social scientists have become morticians, all too eager to bury men's hopes.[23]

In this connection it is interesting to note Parsons' restructuring of Merton's paper on "Social Structure and Anomie." Parsons writes that "what Merton calls 'conformity' is clearly what we here mean by the equilibriated condition of the interactive system without conflict on either side or alienative motivations."[24] But if we employ a pattern-variable scheme which admits of an equation between "rebellion" and "alienation," and "conformity" and "equilibrium," we are a priori ruling out the possibility that a condition of rebellion is consonant with equilibrium at any level, and correspondingly, that extreme states of consensus might create social or personal disequilibrium. If this formula is seriously entertained, I find it hard to fathom Parsons' sensitivity to the charge that his is a conservative doctrine that sees social change as deviant to social order, and as a phenomenon which is possible only when the "control mechanisms of the social

---

[22] See in particular, Chester I. Barnard, *The Functions of the Executive* (Cambridge: Harvard University Press, 1938); James D. Mooney and Alan C. Reiley, *The Principles of Organization* (New York: Harper & Co., 1939); Talcott Parsons, "Suggestions for a Sociological Approach to the Theory of Organizations," *Administrative Science Quarterly*, I (1956), 63–85; Philip Selznick, "Foundations of the Theory of Organization," *American Sociological Review*, XIII (1948), 25–35.

[23] Alvin W. Gouldner "Metaphysical Pathos and the Theory of Bureaucracy," *American Political Science Review*, 49 (1955), pp. 506–507.

[24] Talcott Parsons, *op. cit.*, pp. 257–259.

system" break down. Paradoxically, these remarks by Parsons are made in connection with the necessity for theory of change.[25]

The entire concept of deviant behavior itself rests on a faith that consensus is in every situation observable and functionally relevant; a statement which cannot pass inspection. From the point of view of established consensus as to the sanctity of private property, an act of juvenile vandalism might be measured in the same way as an act of political rebellion, e.g., the physical damage involved in the "Freedom Riders" actions. But from the point of view of the goals sought, what is meant by consensus needs to be spatially and temporally stipulated; and no less, the difference between means and ends must itself be considered as a factor existing over and beyond the supposed functional damage the social order sustains. Too often, deviance is ambiguously formulated so as to cover extremely different situations; i.e., a departure from the rules on the part of an isolated member of a group, and no less, defiance of group rules from those external to the specific referential set.

It cannot be stated as a theoretical first principle that consensus carries an implication of social equilibrium, or for that matter, that conflict entails disequilibrium. There is a distinction to be made between types and levels of conflict, especially between conflicts *over* the basis of consensus, and those conflicts arising *within* the consensual apparatus. There are, to draw an analogy from game theory, conflicts programmed for continuation of the game (such as parliamentary debates), and there are those programmed to end the game through a change of the rules as such (such as *coup d'états*). In neither case is a theory of conflict tied to social disorganization or to deviance from norms. This is not to say that conflict situations do not contain possibilities of social disorganization. Of course they do. For example, the absence of a formal constitution over an extended period of time can create political chaos and turmoil. But likewise, a perfect constitution, preparing the ground for every sort of contingency, can have a boomerang effect and heighten the stress situation by a failure to arrive at common standards of belief and action. In short, both consensus and conflict are phenomena which may promote or retard social cooperation or political cohesion.

Simmel caught the authentic spirit of the relation of conflict to social cooperation when he noted that

If a fight simply aims at annihilation, it does approach the marginal case of assassination in which the admixture of unifying elements is almost zero. If, however, there is any consideration, any limit to violence, there already exists a

---

[25] Talcott Parsons, *op. cit.*, pp. 320–321.

socializing factor, even though only as the qualification of violence. One unites in order to fight, and one fights under the mutually recognized control of norms and rules.[26]

It must therefore be noted that conflict, no less than consensus operates within the social structure, within the system of mutually established laws, norms, and values. . . .

If consensus and conflict occupy the same social universe and logically imply one another, what is the basis for suggesting the empirical superiority of conflict theory as an analytical tool? Fundamentally, it is the impossibility of describing any but the most permissive and tolerant communities in terms of consensus matrices. While conflict theory, with its openness to problems of coercion, pressure groups, social classes, political myths, cultural clashes, racial strife, etc., more nearly approximates the going issues in *Gesellschaft* relationships. In short, from a descriptive point of view, conflict theory covers a wider and more profound range of questions. From a prescriptivist position it is, to be sure, better for men to settle their differences on the basis of free agreement rather than external pressures. But this is an entirely different level of sociological analysis, the level of what kind of decisions make for human cooperation. In any event, consensus theorists cut themselves off from this avenue of thought because of their uniform faith in a descriptivist sociology. They are thus reduced to platitudinous statements that not enough attention has been given to the consensus apparatus in group relations. However, even admitting the validity of this claim, this does not carry with it a mandate to consider consensus as either a more virtuous— or what is more significant, a more practiced—form of arranging social affairs than custom, myth or even coercion. . . .

Why then has the great shift from conflict theory to consensus theory taken place at this juncture in American sociology? Several hypotheses suggest themselves. First, that as American society becomes more democratic, more easy-going, the search for the consensual basis becomes more pronounced. This seems to be the viewpoint adopted by Lipset. However, his view of the end of ideology seems not so much a consequence of an expanding democratic temper, as it is simply a reflection of domestic affluence, and the large share of the United States inhabitants benefitting from the affluent society.[27]

A much more powerful line of reasoning has been suggested by Morris Janowitz, when he indicates that technical bureaucracies and team-member proficiency has tended to usurp the older power of formal authority as

---

[26] Georg Simmel, *Conflict*, pp. 25–26. Quoted in Lewis A. Coser, *op. cit.*, p. 121.
[27] Seymour M. Lipset, *Political Man*, pp. 403–417; see also in this connection, Daniel Bell, *The End of Ideology* (Glencoe: The Free Press, 1960).

distinct from science. Which is to say that the older situation of science as isolated from policy making has disintegrated. With this, authority shifts from outright reliance on domination to a wider utilization of manipulation, on demonstrated managerial skills, operational proficiencies, and the capacity to develop positive organizational loyalties. Therefore, in such a context, consensus comes to be the decisive pivot upon which the success or failure of the manipulative society hangs.[28]

But perhaps the most powerful reason for the shift to consensus theory is the "enlightened" recognition that mass terror is not as powerful an instrument for extracting economic and political loyalties as mass persuasion. The entire theoretical edifice of small group theory comes to rest on the idea that the formal sanctioning of force is less potent a factor in individual or group motivation than the informal sanctions of the immediately involved reference-set. The belief in consensus as a stratagem is well articulated by Frank when he writes:

The idea has spread that employers were wasting human energy by the traditional authoritarian ways of imposing their decisions on their employees. Psychologists—collaborating with engineers and economists and, more recently, anthropologists—have made many studies concerned with the impact of physical aspects of the workplace, such as lighting, color of walls and machines, temperature and humidity ; with working conditions, such as hours, shifts, rest periods, piece rates, and especially relations of foreman and supervisors to their groups. Such studies helped to articulate a new view of corporate life.[29]

But what, it must be asked, is the content of this new view of corporate life? Is it a theory of the corporation or simply a technique of mass persuasion and manipulation? Is it a sociological statement of the nature of the corporate structure, or the uses by the corporate structure of sociological statements? The promotion of consensus as a theory has had as its asking price the conversion of sociology from a science to a tool policy. A policy which, moreover, fails to reach the goal of harmony.[30] As White recently indicated, "There is nothing new in manipulated opinion and engineered consent . . . Even the sheer bulk of distortion is not altogether new, merely

[28] Morris Janowitz, *Sociology and the Military Establishment* (New York: Russell Sage Foundation, 1959), pp. 27–38. Janowitz' remarks are confined to the military. Responsibility for enlarging the scope and context of his argument is mine.
[29] Lawrence K. Frank, "Psychology and the Social Order," in *The Human Meaning of the Social Sciences*, edited by Daniel Lerner (New York: Meridian Books, Inc., 1959), p. 230.
[30] David Riesman, Nathan Glazer, Revel Denney, *The Lonely Crowd: A Study of the Changing American Character* (Garden City: Doubleday Anchor Books, 1954), pp. 306–307.

more refined. What is new is the acceptability, the mere taken-for-grantedness of these things." [31]

I want to terminate my remarks with a plea for sharper logical and linguistic distinctions, specifically to point out that the issue of human cooperation, while related to consensus and conflict, has a quite unique dimension and operational range. It must be pointed out that a decision in favor of consensus theory is not automatically a decision on behalf of cooperation. It is simply a decision to examine social structure to the partial or total exclusion of social dynamics; a decision to act as if breaks with tradition, shifts in the culture complex, disruption of moral patterns, can be described as marginal in character. There is indeed a kind of safety in the continuing, the prolonged, the enduring. But this safety gratuitously cloaking itself in the mantle of the secularization of science is nothing but the abdication of the field of social change, and hence an abandonment of the on-going problems confronting those most directly concerned with achieving human cooperation at group, regional, national, or international levels.

The functional successes of any given social structure should not define the limits of sociological discourse. For we may find ourselves celebrating one social order one day, and another the next—and in precisely the same "functional-structural" terms. The central task of sociology is explanation and prediction, each in terms of the other, and no theory which identifies consensus with the social order as such can fail to come upon hard times.

What then is the difference between consensus and cooperation? There seem to be three distinguishable factors to be identified. First: consensus stands for agreement internally, i.e., in terms of shared perspectives, agreements on the rules of association and action, a common set of norms and values. Cooperation for its part makes no demands on role uniformity but only upon procedural rules. Cooperation concerns the settlement of problems in terms which make possible the continuation of differences and even fundamental disagreements. Thus one can legitimately speak of cooperation between labor and management, while one speaks on the degree of consensus each side brings to bear at the bargaining table. Second: consensus is agreement on the content of behavior, while cooperation necessitates agreement only on the form of behavior. We speak of consensus if all members of the Women's Christian Temperance Union agree to abstain from drinking alcoholic beverages. But we speak of cooperation when agreement is reached on the forms allowed for drinking and the forms allowed for curbing the intake of liquor. As the "Prohibition Era" dramatically showed, the substitution of consensus for cooperation did not lead to a new morality

---

[31] Howard B. White, "The Processed Voter and the New Political Science," *Social Research*, XXVIII (1961), 150.

but simply to chaos. Third: cooperation concerns toleration of differences, while consensus demands abolition of these same differences. If a game theory analogy be preferred, the distinction between cooperation and consensus might be stated in the following terms: consensus programs the termination of the game by insisting on the principle of unity and unilateral victory, whereas cooperation is pluralistic because it programs the continuation of the game by maintaining and insisting upon the legitimacy of differences.

What is required at this juncture is a more adequate sociological theory of cooperation; a stipulation of the conditions of that minimum set of beliefs about man and his social universe that is consonant with continued survival and growth. Such a theory of cooperation would insist on the need for maintaining life although leaving open the question of what to do with it; the need to secure the material and cultural needs of men although differing on the sort of social system best able to meet such needs. Beyond this, there is a need for a theory of conflict, a programming of conflict, that would allow people to shift and choose their conceptions of what constitutes progress, pleasure, etc., and the institutionalization of avenues of action to implement these conceptions. Consensus theory has done nothing to melt the present freezing of attitudes on either a national or international scale. Nor will it, unless sociologists show a willingness to expand their collective vision of the social universe beyond the confines of a dormitory or a hospital ward.

The unity required to evolve such a sociological theory of cooperation is methodological rather than systematic. It requires us to approach ideas and attitudes concerning cooperation as hypotheses whose truth content must be measured by the degree with which they can be correlated to objective circumstances. This is something quite different than placing men in a Procrustean bed of pattern variables which may or may not hold for previous or future generations—or, for that matter, for the present one. The methods of sociology do not exclude decisive choices in favor of specific objectives. It does caution us against ignoring alternative conceptual frameworks on the basis of their unpopularity or marginality. The concept of cooperation is essentially the programming of common standards in a world of conflicting interests and even different notions as to what constitutes interests. Precisely because a general theory of cooperation would offer no transcendental commitments to the eternal righteousness of any existing social order, it can place itself in the service of men. It would do well for sociology to perform a decisive role in the structuring of a theory of cooperation, both for the general values this would help establish and for a way to settle some long standing ambiguities in sociological research.

David Lockwood

Some Remarks on 'The Social System'

*I*N the "statement of general sociological theory" which is *The Social System,*[1] Professor Parsons has attempted to sift and summarize in systematic form the significant lessons of past thinking in sociology and set out a programme for the future. This enterprise is the product of a steady and consistent growth reaching back some twenty years to his initial study of eminent sociological theorists in *The Structure of Social Action*. The intention of the present essay, however, is not to give an exposition of the Parsonian system of sociology,[2] but to develop in some detail specific criticisms which might be levelled against his conceptualization of the dynamics of social systems, and, more particularly, of societies. To treat of

From David Lockwood, "Some Remarks on 'The Social System,'" *British Journal of Sociology*, 7 (June, 1956), pp. 134–146. Reprinted by permission of the author and the journal.

[1] Talcott Parsons, *The Social System*, London, Tavistock Publications; Glencoe, The Free Press, 1952.

[2] For an excellent account, see Ralf Dahrendorf, "Struktur und Funktion: Talcott Parsons und die Entwicklung der soziologischen Theorie," *Kölner Zeitschrift fur Soziologie und Sozialpsychologie*, 1955, pp. 491–519. I am much indebted to Dr. Dahrendorf for many discussions on this and other aspects of sociology.

such a large subject within so small a space is no doubt unwise in one sense; in another it is an incentive to delineate more sharply what is at issue. In particular, emphasis will be placed on the non-normative elements of social action which seem to constitute a set of variables which Parsons has ignored by concentrating on the normative elements of social structure and process. This omission may be interpreted as an accomplishment since it is the means of giving sociology a more definite status as a special social science; but whether it is a position that can be maintained in practice without inconsistency is open to severe doubt, or so it seems to the writer. This much of the vein of criticism may be anticipated.

I

In this section are to be considered those propositions put forward in *The Social System* and elsewhere[3] which illustrate Parsons' analysis of social dynamics. It is impossible to do justice in so short a space to the elaborate development and application of the conceptual scheme, of which the following outline is a mere skeleton. Thus most of what is subsequently said is not in criticism of what has been substantively accomplished within a given framework, but rather questions the appropriateness of the framework that is given. In so far as misunderstanding has not occurred, the criticism concerns what has not, rather than what has been done.

For Parsons, the social system is a system of action. It is made up of the interactions of individuals. Of special concern to sociology is the fact that such interactions are not random but mediated by common standards of evaluation. Most important among these are moral standards, which may be called norms.[4] Such norms "structure" action. Because individuals share the same "definition of the situation" in terms of such norms, their behaviour can be intermeshed to produce a "social structure." The regularity, or patterning, of interaction is made possible through the existence of norms which control the behaviour of actors. Indeed, a stabilized social system is one in which behaviour is regulated in this way, and, as such, is a major point of reference for the sociological analysis of the dynamics of social systems.[5] It is necessary in sociology, as in biology, to single out relatively

---

[3] *Towards a General Theory of Action*, edited by Talcott Parsons and Edward A. Shils, 1951; Talcott Parsons, *Essays in Sociological Theory*, 1949, second edition, 1954.
[4] Parsons' term is "standards of value-orientation." See Kingsley Davis, *Human Society*, 1949, pp. 52–82.
[5] "This integration of a set of common value patterns with the internalized need disposition structure of the constituent personalities is the core phenomenon of the dynamics of social systems. That the stability of any social system except the most

stable points of reference, or "structural" aspects of the system under consideration, and then to study the processes whereby such structures are maintained. This is the meaning of the "structural-functional" approach to social system analysis. Since the social system is a system of action, and its structural aspects are the relatively stable interactions of individuals around common norms, the dynamic processes with which the sociologist is concerned are those which function to maintain social structures, or, in other words, those processes whereby individuals come to be motivated to act in conformity with normative standards.

The equilibrium of social systems is maintained by a variety of processes and mechanisms, and their failure precipitates varying degrees of disequilibrium (or disintegration). The two main classes of mechanisms by which motivation is kept at the level and in the direction necessary for the continuing operation of the social system are the mechanisms of socialization and social control.[6] . . .

Pressures making for deviance on the other hand are regarded as being a matter for investigation in each empirical situation as it arises. In general, there are no social processes, corresponding to those stabilizing mechanisms outlined above, which systematically make for deviance and social change.

II

Although it would be tempting to begin the criticism of such a conceptual scheme by questioning the validity of some particular assumption, such as the existence of a common value system, or the meaning given to the concept of social structure, it is more rewarding to begin by asking a rather more general question. It is true to say that in principle the concepts with which we try to analyse the dynamics of social systems ought to be equally applicable to the problems of stability and instability, continuance and change of social structures; but this does not necessarily hold true of a particular conceptual scheme such as the one outlined above. It would not hold unless general concepts had been developed which would enable us to take any concrete social system and grasp the balance of forces at work in it. We may ask, therefore, is there anything about the framework just described which would suggest that a certain class of variables, vital to an understanding of the general problem—why do social structures persist and change—has in fact been ignored?

I believe there is. The first point of note in this connection is that

---

evanescent interaction process is dependent on a degree of such integration may be said to be the fundamental dynamic theorem of sociology. It is a major point of reference for all analysis which may claim to be dynamic"—*The Social System*, p. 42.

[6] *Towards a General Theory of Action*, p. 227.

Parsons' array of concepts is heavily weighted by assumptions and categories which relate to the role of *normative* elements in social action, and especially to the processes whereby motives are structured normatively to ensure social stability. On the other hand, what may be called the *substratum*[7] of social action, especially as it conditions interests which are productive of social conflict and instability, tends to be ignored as a general determinant of the dynamics of social systems. For the moment, the substratum of social action may be defined as the factual disposition of means in the situation of action which structures differential *Lebenschancen* and produces interests of a non-normative kind—that is, interests other than those which actors have in conforming with the normative definition of the situation.[8] Although, according to Parsons, such interests must be integrated with the normative patterns governing behaviour in a stabilized social system, it is inherent in the conception of deviance and social instability that non-normative interests have to be treated as a discrete and independent category in sociological analysis.[9] What then is the status of these non-normative elements in the analysis of social action? Is it useful to distinguish between norm and substratum as general points of reference in dynamic analysis? If so, why has Parsons given conceptual priority to the normative structuring of action?

Let us look at the genesis of Parsons' own concern with the normative regulation of conduct. It is the famous Hobbesian problem of order.[10] "If any two men desire the same thing, which nevertheless they cannot both enjoy, they become enemies; and in the way to their end, which is principally their own conservation, and sometimes their delectation only, endeavour to destroy, or subdue one another."[11] Relationships of power and social conflict

---

[7] The distinction between "norm" and "substratum" is made by Karl Renner in his *Mensch und Gesellschaft: Grundriss einer Soziologie*, 1952, pp. 230–33, and employed in *The Institutions of Private Law and Their Social Functions*, 1949. The terms are employed in a somewhat different sense in the present paper.

[8] In an established social relationship, and where socialization has been successful, the individual has a stake in the favourable attitudinal response of others and also acts so as to meet his internalized moral expectations about his own behavior, and these external and internal moral sanctions constitute a generalized interest in conformity with the normative patterns governing the relationship. Thus, "if any individual can be said to seek his own 'self-interest' it follows that he can do so only by conforming in some degree to the institutionalized definition of the situation"—*Essays in Sociological Theory*, 1949, p. 170. In general, "the structure of interests in a group is a function both of the structure of the realistic situations in which people act and of the 'definitions' of those situations which are institutionalized in the society"—Ibid., p. 313.

[9] "Its (the social system) stability depends on the integration of the interests of actors with the patterning of the interaction process. If interests in objects other than the attitudes of actors cannot be integrated with this mutual attitude system, such interests must constitute threats to the stability of the social system"—*The Social System*, p. 416.

[10] *The Structure of Social Action*, 1937, p. 89 et seq.

[11] Thomas Hobbes, *Leviathian*, edited with an introduction by M. Oakeshott, p. 81.

are inherent in the scarcity of means in society. The notions of power and conflict are mutually implicative: power is involved as men seek their interests against the opposition of others; and a division of interests is implicit in the relationships of power that obtain. If conflict is thus endemic in the scarcity of means and the struggle to acquire them, in the fact that the means which one man holds give him power over another man to whom they are also necessary, how then is social order possible? The answer which emerges from *The Structure of Social Action*, the proposition which is at the core of Parsons' subsequent sociology, is that order is possible through the existence of common norms which regulate "the war of all against all." The existence of the normative order, therefore, is in one very important sense inextricably bound up with potential conflicts of interest over scarce resources. This functional dependence of norm on conflict, however, does not correspond to an actual succession from a state of nature to a state of civil society: the relation is analytical, not historical. In the present context it is fundamental to the subsequent argument that the presence of a normative order, or common value system, does not mean that conflict has disappeared, or been resolved in some way. Instead, the very existence of a normative order mirrors the continual potentiality of conflict. To be sure, the degree of conflict in the social system is always a matter for empirical investigation; but so is the existence of a common value system.[12] Indeed, the varying degrees of acceptance of, or alienation from, the dominant values of the society may be regarded in large measure as reflecting the divisions of interest resulting from differential access to scarce resources. Most important of all, it would seem to follow quite naturally from this situation that when we talk of the stability or instability of a social system, we mean more than anything else the success or failure of the normative order in regulating conflicts of interest. Therefore, in an adequate view of social dynamics it is necessary to conceptualize not only the normative structuring of motives but also the structuring of interests in the substratum. In other words, it is necessary to know about the forces generated by norm *and* substratum if we wish to understand why patterns of behaviour persist or change.[13]

---

[12] "A social relationship will be referred to as 'conflict' in so far as action within it is oriented intentionally to carrying out the actor's own will against the resistance of the other party or parties ... the communal type of relationship is the most radical antithesis of conflict ... conflict and communal relationships are relative concepts"— Max Weber, *The Theory of Social and Economic Organization*, translated by A. R. Henderson and Talcott Parsons, 1947, pp. 121–6.

[13] This seems also to be the position implied in the "voluntaristic" theory of action which treats human social behavior as a function both of "normative" and of "conditional" factors; as opposed to the "positivistic" and "idealistic" theories which stress one set of factors to the exclusion of the other. *The Structure of Social Action*, pp. 77–82. Again, Parsons' position is in principle correct. The real question revolves

The step from Hobbes to Marx in this matter is a short one. The introduction of the division of labour transforms the war of all against all into the war of one class against another. Marx agrees with Hobbes that conflict is endemic in social interaction (except in communist society), and goes one step further and asserts that interests of a non-normative kind are not random in the social system, but systematically generated through the social relations of the productive process. This, as Parsons himself has acknowledged, is Marx's fundamental insight into the dynamics of social systems.[14] In a given society, so runs the recommendation, if we wish to understand the balance of forces working for stability or change we must look not only to the normative order, but also and principally to the factual organization of production, and the powers, interests, conflicts and groupings consequent on it. Here are two notions of "social structure," both characterized by "exteriority" and "constraint," the one *de jure,* the other *de facto.* Marx's own analysis tended to focus on the latter meaning. And what emerges from his thinking is a view of the social system and its operation startlingly different from the framework provided by the Parsonian theory. To pursue this theme a little further, it is not accidental for instance that the process of *exploitation* in the Marxian theory represents a radical conceptual antithesis to the social process which has a central place in Parsons' analysis: that of *socialization.* It is not accidental again that a societal typology is based in the first case on the forms of ownership and control of productive means, in the second on the dominant value patterns of the society.[15] Social stratification for Marx is the differentiation of competing economic interest groups in the society on the basis of productive relations; for Parsons it is the differentiation of individuals in terms of social superiority and inferiority on the basis of the dominant value system of the society.[16] It is unnecessary to multiply instances, for in the almost polar opposition of the two sociological systems we witness the logical outcome of fundamentally different

around his success in conceptualizing both sets of factors and relating them to societal dynamics. The uncritical criticism of structural functionalism which asserts that this standpoint is necessarily "static" does not apply in the present case at all; it is rather that there is a bias towards the conceptualization of one set of factors in the dynamics of social systems.

[14] "Social Classes and Class Conflict in the Light of Recent Sociological Theory," *Essays in Sociological Theory,* 1954, chapter XV.

[15] *The Social System,* pp. 180–200. "Value patterns" and "ownership patterns" thus have precisely the same analytical status in both theories in that they provide the link between the general concepts of "order" and "conflict" and the differentiation of types of social structure. The resulting types illustrate most clearly the widely differing foci of the two theories.

[16] "An Analytical Approach to the Theory of Social Stratification," *Essays in Sociological Theory,* 1949, chapter V II; "A Revised Analytical Approach to the Theory of Social Stratification," *Class, Status and Power,* edited by R. Bendix and S. M. Lipset, 1953, pp. 92–128.

abstractions from the nature of social action. One centres on the phemonenon of social conflict and the constraint of the factual social order; the other on that of social solidarity and the constraint of the normative social order.[17] Both theories, moreover, claim generality, both purport to be concerned with social dynamics. Such a conceptual dichotomy can only be reconciled with these claims if it is recognized that a general theory of social systems which conceptualizes one aspect of social structure and process is of necessity a particular theory. Parsons' claim that to study the forces making for stability is at the same time to grasp those making for instability and change, does not hold in his own analysis because of a selective emphasis on the normative elements of social action. The only other explanation is that the alternative system of generalized concepts is intellectually dispensable. The question here is not whether Marx was wrong or right in his specific empirical predictions (in most of them he appears nowadays to have been falsified), but whether the categories with which he approached social reality as a sociologist are generally relevant to our understanding of social process.[18] Is it possible to understand the nature of twentieth-century American society in terms of its "universalistic-achievement" value pattern without mentioning the changes which its capitalist institutions[19] are undergoing? And if the frustrated dependency needs of the middle-class male caught up in a competitive world produce "one of the focal points of strain in American society,"[20] are the relations between unions and business corporations which Professor Lindblom has recently analysed[21] of no account in the dynamics of that fateful social system?

Such questions, it is submitted, can only be asked because of the bifurcation of sociological analysis represented by the conceptual schemata just discussed. On the one hand, it is suggested that society is unthinkable without some degree of integration through common norms and that sociological theory should deal with the processes whereby this order is maintained. On

---

[17] It is interesting to note that in the ideal-type class society, solidarity is manifested as class solidarity and is a consequence not of the common value system of the society but of the divisions and conflicts of interest in the system. "Wer Klasse sagt, sagt Scheidung. Wer von sozialer Solidarität redet, bejaht die Voraussetzung sozialer Antagonismen. Dass dabei die Begriffe Scheidung und Antagonismus genetisch die primären, die Begriffe Klasse und Solidarität die sekundären, abgeleiteten, sind, ist nach logischen und empirischen Gesetzen gleich sonnenklar"—Robert Michels, *Umschichtungen in den herrschenden Klassen nach dem Kriege*, 1934, p. 1.

[18] See, for example, the recent critical evaluation by Theodor Geiger, *Die Klassengesellschaft im Schmelztiegel*, 1949.

[19] See, for example, Adolf A. Berle, Jr., *The Twentieth Century Capitalist Revolution*, 1955.

[20] *The Social System*, p. 269.

[21] Charles E. Lindblom, *Unions and Capitalism*, 1949.

the other, society is held to be unthinkable[22] without some degree of conflict arising out of the allocation of scarce resources in the division of labour, and sociological analysis is given the task of studying the processes whereby divisions of interest are structured and expressed. The latter view, which seems to be the general import of the Marxian sociology, does not necessarily imply that resources refer only to productive means, or that conflict is necessary and not contingent. In the expansion of these points it may also be shown that there is no real rivalry between the two sociological systems, but that they are on the contrary complementary in their emphases. . . .

That conflict is no more inevitable than order should be evident from the foregoing discussion of norm and substratum as the basic variables in the situation of action. Every social situation consists of a normative order with which Parsons is principally concerned, and also of a factual order, or substratum. Both are "given" for individuals; both are part of the exterior and constraining social world. Sociological theory is concerned, or should be, with the social and psychological processes whereby social structure in this dual sense conditions human motives and actions. The existence of a normative order in no way entails that individuals will act in accordance with it; in the same way the existence of a given factual order in no way means that certain kinds of behaviour result. The gap between the elements of "givenness" in the situation and individual or group action is one that is to be bridged only by the sociological appreciation of the way in which motives are structured, normatively and factually.[23]

It is evident, then, that the distinction between order and conflict is one that needs only to be maintained in so far as it illustrates the dimensions of the present problem. Order and conflict are states of the social system, indices of its operation, and to talk of the determinants of order should therefore be to talk of the determinants of conflict. It is only because the problem of order has become bound up with the functioning of the normative system in Parsons' work, that it is necessary to press for the analysis of conflict as a separate task, and especially for the recognition of those aspects

---

[22] Unthinkable in so far as "society" involves the notion of "scarce means" and therefore the problem of order; but also as a generalization about social history: "Few who consider dispassionately the facts of social history will be disposed to deny that the exploitation of the weak by the powerful, organized for purposes of economic gain, buttressed by imposing systems of law and screened by decorous draperies of virtuous sentiment and resounding rhetoric, has been a permanent feature in the life of most communities that the world has yet seen."—R. H. Tawney, *Religion and The Rise of Capitalism*, 1944, p. 286.

[23] Although there are many examples, Werner Sombart's remarkable little book, *Warum gibt es in den Vereinigten Staaten keinen Sozialismus?*, 1906, is instructive in this respect. It may be compared with the excellent discussion by Seymour M. Lipset and Reinhard Bendix, "Ideological Equalitarianism and Social Mobility in the United States," *Transactions of the Second World Congress of Sociology*, 1954, pp. 34–54.

of conflict which are non-normative. Just as the problem of order is not just a function of the existence of a normative order and the social mechanisms which procure motivation to conform with it but also of the existence of a social substratum which structures interests differentially in the social system, so the problem of conflict is not reducible to the analysis of the division of labour and the group interests consequent on it. It is rather that both conflict and order are a function of the interaction of norm and substratum. Certain kinds of normative order are more conducive to the development of conflict than others. For instance, the labour-capital conflict in its classical manifestation arose out of the actual situation of the classes under capitalistic production, but it was greatly intensified and sharpened by the existence of a dominant value system, the cardinal features of which, "freedom" and "opportunity," contrasted radically with the factual order of events. The generation of conflict, which may be taken as an index of social instability,[24] is never a simple matter of a conflict of material interest but also involves the normative definition of the situation. . . .

There is one explanation for the analytical precedence which Parsons gives to the normative structuring of social action which cannot be ignored. That is the argument that sociology should not concern itself with the dynamics of the social system as a whole, but only with some aspect thereof. To this view it is now profitable to turn.

III

That sociology should deal with a particular set of problems within the theory of social systems is the position taken by Parsons in his discussion of the division of labour between the social sciences. Here sociology is defined as having to do with the process of institutionalization of normative patterns: "that aspect of the theory of social systems which is concerned with the phenomena of institutionalization of patterns of value-orientation in the social system, and of changes in the patterns, with conditions of conformity with and deviance from a set of such patterns, and with motivational processes in so far as they are involved in all of these."[25] The sphere of "power,"

---

24 This may not seem to hold in situations where conflict is institutionalized, as in democratically organized politics, or in collective bargaining. Here there is agreement about how what shall be done is to be done, but not necessarily about what in fact shall be done. It is therefore hard to maintain the distinction between conflict *within* the system, and conflict *about* the system. There may, for example, be agreement about democratic institutions in the political field, but disagreement about capitalistic institutions in the economic field. Quite radical social change whch involves conflicts of interest about the latter may be gradually effected within the framework of the former.

25 *The Social System*, p. 552.

economic and political, precisely the factual social order, is delivered for safe keeping to the economist and political scientist.[26]

The definition of sociology which Parsons sets forth is apparently consistent with his preoccupation with the role of normative factors in social action. It provides a reasoned basis for the actual selectivity of his theoretical system. But is there consistency here; does not his very view of the scope of sociology lead to a recognition of the essential limitations of this preoccupation and selectivity? It has already been noted that the problem of conformity or nonconformity of actors with a common value pattern resolves itself into a consideration of the constraint exercised on the actors by the normative and factual orders and the processes associated with them. It is not only the continual pressure of normative expectations exerted through the processes of socialization and social control, but also the range of differential opportunities created by the division of labour, that form the effective social environment of action. Therefore, if "changes in the patterns" are to be accounted for sociologically, how is this possible without making the analysis power and means an integral part of the explanation? To take an obvious, but massive example: how is the growth of collectivistic values within the dominant individualistic ethos of British capitalism, traced in Dicey's great work,[27] to be explained without including the systematic operation of this set of factors? Or again, within this wider change of values, the trade union movement appears at its inception as a "group of deviantly motivated individuals" to use the terminology of *The Social System*. Yet is the structuring of this deviant motivation to be adequately comprehended by a system of sociological explanation so limited as that we find in this book?[28] In the analysis of actual processes of social change all the difficulties that beset a sociology whose theoretical core has developed from a concern with the normative basis of social stability become apparent.[29] Any

---

[26] Ibid., pp. 548–551, 121–127. It is economists least of all, however, who have investigated the phenomenon of "economic power" outside the limited sense of "purchasing power" in the market. For a sharp criticism of their unconcern, see Walter Eucken, *The Foundations of Economics*, 1950, p. 263 et seq. Nor is it clear, even in the case of political science, that the orthodox field of study is power in this wider societal sense and not the narrower field of formal governmental institutions. It is surely sociologists, or at least economists and political scientists with sociological orientations, who have contributed most to the study of economic and political power as it constitutes the substratum of social action. In so far as this is true, the dissociation of sociology from such problems also, means that they are ignored, at any rate so far as the formal division of labour in the social sciences is concerned.

[27] A. V. Dicey, *Lectures on the Relation between Law and Public Opinion in England During the Nineteenth Century*, 1952.

[28] Compare, for example, the approach to this type of problem in Robert Michels' "Psychologie der antikapitalistischen Massenbewegungen," *Grundriss der Sozialökonomik*, vol. IX, 1926, pp. 241–359; or G. A. Briefs, *The Proletariat*, 1936.

study of social change, defined even in terms of change in institutionalized value patterns, must be based on concepts which can interrelate the realistic and normative structure of the situation with the resultant actions of individuals and groups. In any given society, the potentialities of change are not random but systematically related to the balance of indulgence and deprivation among different social groups as this is determined by the types of normative patterns defining expected behaviour, and the types of division of labour distributing factual opportunities to realize ends. If these are elementary and readily acceptable propositions, they only serve to show that sociological analysis, even if it is formally defined as being concerned with a seemingly specialized aspect of the theory of social systems, cannot in fact avoid the role of a synthetizing discipline. In particular, sociology cannot avoid the systematic analysis of the phemonenon of "power" as an integral part of its conceptual scheme. . . .

I have no wish to deny that the sociological mode of inquiry should be made explicit by the formulation of particular sociological theories. Indeed, the process of theoretical development in sociology is one by which different factors and their interrelationships are identified and evaluated. To this development, Professor Parsons' contribution has been, and continues to be, one to which all must be indebted. This is especially true of his insistence on the necessary integration of psychological and sociological thinking around the problems of social dynamics. His claim to have provided a "statement of general sociological theory" is less acceptable, however, because it seems to have sought to clarify the status of sociology at the expense of confining it within a conceptual mould in which it does not happily fit.

---

[29] This is clear in Parsons' brief discussion of the way in which the rise of National Socialism could be approached from his theoretical standpoint. *The Social System*, pp. 520–5. When the preconditions of the movement are analysed, beyond such generalizations as the necessary presence "in the population of sufficiently intense, widely spread and properly distributed alienative motivational elements," the factors which emerge as important are the interests of economic, political and military groupings. It is hard to see that these variables can be usefully handled beyond a certain point in terms of the generalized concepts developed in the preceding theoretical discussion of social dynamics. On the other hand, they are factors which are interpreted in a penetrating way by Franz Neumann in his almost equally brief account in *Behemoth: The Structure and Function of National Socialism*, 1942, p. 17 et seq., an account which obviously owes much to the other generalized approach to social dynamics discussed in this essay.

Pierre L. van den Berghe

Dialectic and Functionalism

TOWARD A SYNTHESIS

*F*UNCTIONALISM and the Hegelian-Marxian dialect each stress one of two essential aspects of social reality, and are thus complementary to one another. My procedure will be to examine in turn the basic postulates of functionalism and the Hegelian-Marxian dialectic, show the limitations of each theory as a complete model of society, . . . and finally, by retaining and modifying elements of the two approaches, search for a unified theory.

Functionalism

With the rapidly growing body of literature on functionalism,[1] that theoretical position has become both more sophisticated and more elusive of definition. Davis even goes so far as to argue that, irrespective of what they

Reprinted from Pierre L. van den Berghe, "Dialectic and Functionalism: Toward a Theoretical Synthesis," *American Sociological Review*, 28 (October, 1963), pp. 695–705, by permission of the author and the American Sociological Association.

[1] For a sample of titles covering the last two decades see: Bernard Barber, "Structural-Functional Analysis: Some Problems and Misunderstandings," *American Sociological Review*, 21 (April, 1956), pp. 129–135; Harry C. Bredemeier, "The Methodology of Functionalism," *American Sociological Review*, 20 (April, 1955), pp. 173–

call themselves, all sociologists use much the same analytical framework.[2] Adherence to Davis' viewpoint can result in either optimism or dismay. I shall try to show, however, that functionalism is not a myth, but an important though fragmentary approach to social reality.

One must reject at the outset facile criticisms based on beating the dead horse of extreme Malinowskian functionalism. Such criticisms as that societies are never perfectly integrated, that not every element of a social system is functional or essential, and that functionalism cannot account for change, have been satisfactorily answered and shown to be untrue or irrelevant by leading exponents of the "school," notably by Merton.

Our concern, then, is with the more recent brand of functionalism in its most sophisticated and cautious form, and as represented by Parsons, Merton and Davis. Reduced to its common denominator, the functionalist or "structure-function" approach seems to involve the following postulates or elements:

1) Societies must be looked at holistically as systems of interrelated parts.

2) Hence, causation is multiple and reciprocal.

3) Although integration is never perfect, social systems are fundamentally in a state of dynamic equilibrium, i.e., adjustive responses to outside

---

180; Walter Buckley, "Social Stratification and the Functional Theory of Social Differentiation," *American Sociological Review*, 23 (August, 1958), pp. 369–375; Francesca Cancian, "Functional Analysis of Change," *American Sociological Review*, 24 (December, 1960), pp. 818–827; Kingsley Davis, "The Myth of Functional Analysis as a Special Method in Sociology and Anthropology," *American Sociological Review*, 24 (December, 1959), pp. 752–772; Kingsley Davis and Wilbert E. Moore, "Some Principles of Stratification," *American Sociological Review*, 10 (April, 1945), pp. 242–249; Ronald Philip Dore, "Function and Cause," *American Sociological Review*, 26 (December, 1961), pp. 843–853; Harold Fallding, "Functional Analysis in Sociology," *American Sociological Review*, 28 (February, 1963), pp. 5–13; Dorothy Gregg and Elgin Williams, "The Dismal Science of Functionalism," *American Anthropologist*, 50 (October–December, 1948), pp. 594–611; Carl G. Hempel, "The Logic of Functional Analysis," in Llewellyn Gross (ed.), *Symposium on Sociological Theory*, Evanston, Ill.: Row, Peterson and Co., 1959, pp. 271–307; Wayne Hield, "The Study of Change in Social Science," *British Journal of Sociology*, 5 (March, 1954), pp. 1–10; David Lockwood, "Some Remarks on the 'Social System'," *British Journal of Sociology*, 7 (June, 1956), pp. 134–146; Wilbert E. Moore, "But Some Are More Equal than Others," *American Sociological Review*, 28 (February, 1963), pp. 13–18; Richard L. Simpson, "A Modification of the Functional Theory of Stratification," *Social Forces*, 35 (December, 1956), pp. 132–137; Melvin Tumin, "On Inequality," *American Sociological Review*, 28 (February, 1963), pp. 19–26; Melvin Tumin, "Some Principles of Stratification: A Critical Analysis," *American Sociological Review*, 18 (August, 1953), pp. 387–394; Dennis H. Wrong, "The Functional Theory of Stratification: Some Neglected Considerations," *American Sociological Review*, 24 (December, 1959), pp. 772–782.

[2] Davis, *op. cit.*

[3] Robert K. Merton, *Social Theory and Social Structure*, Glencoe, Ill.: The Free Press, 1949, Chapter I.

changes tend to minimize the final amount of change within the system. The dominant tendency is thus towards stability and inertia, as maintained through built-in mechanisms of adjustment and social control.

4) As a corollary of 3), dysfunctions, tensions and "deviance" do exist and can persist for a long time, but they tend to resolve themselves or to be "institutionalized" in the long run. In other words, while perfect equilibrium or integration is never reached, it is the limit towards which social systems tend.

5) Change generally occurs in a gradual, adjustive fashion, and not in a sudden, revolutionary way. Changes which appear to be drastic, in fact affect mostly the social superstructure while leaving the core elements of the social and cultural structure largely unchanged.

6) Change comes from basically three sources: adjustment of the system to exogenous (or extra-systemic) change; growth through structural and functional differentiation; and inventions or innovations by members or groups within society.

7) The most important and basic factor making for social integration is value consensus, i.e., underlying the whole social and cultural structure, there are broad aims or principles which most members of a given social system consider desirable and agree on. Not only is the value system (or ethos) the deepest and most important source of integration, but it is also the stablest element of socio-cultural systems.

The first two postulates are useful and provisionally acceptable, although we shall formulate reservations about the first one later. Any wholesale rejection of the holistic approach leads to sterile classification of cultural items torn out of context (as represented for example by diffusionism in anthropology). A rejection of the model of multiple and reciprocal causation entails all the pitfalls of the many different brands of one-sided determinism.

The other five elements of functionalism outlined above are further reducible to two basic postulates, those of consensus and of dynamic equilibrium or integration. Both of these assumptions can be traced back to Comte, and have permeated much of British and American sociology and anthropology via Durkheim, acquiring the sanctity of tradition. The two postulates lead to a self-created *impasse* by making certain problems insoluble and by presenting a partially valid but slanted concept of social reality.

In a nutshell my argument is that, while societies do indeed show a tendency towards stability, equilibrium, and consensus, they simultaneously generate within themselves the opposites of these. Let us begin with the assumption that value consensus constitutes the most basic focus of social integration. Consensus is certainly an important basis for integration, but it is also true that societies (except perhaps the least differentiated ones) fall far short of complete consensus, and often exhibit considerable dissension[4] about basic values. To generalize from the Trobrianders and the Arunta to complex, stratified and culturally pluralistic societies is clearly unsound. Numerous societies (e.g. colonial countries) integrate widely different cultures possessing quite different value systems. Even in culturally homogeneous societies, various social groups such as classes can hold antithetical political and economic values (as shown by class conflicts in nineteenth century Europe). Conversely, consensus such as is found in charismatic movements of a revivalistic or messianistic type can precipitate the disintegration of a society, as we shall see later.

What remains then of the consensus assumption? Clearly, to make value consensus a prerequisite to the existence of a social system (as Parsons does, for example) is untenable.[5] Granting that consensus is often an important (but not a necessary) basis of social integration, one has to accept that consensus can also have disintegrative consequences, that most complex societies show considerable dissension, and that there are alternative bases of integration to consensus (e.g. economic interdependence and political coercion). Consensus, then, is a major dimension of social reality, but so are dissension and conflict. Furthermore, there is no necessary direct relation between consensus and equilibrium or integration.

The postulate of consensus, however, is logically gratuitous to functionalist theory, i.e. one could logically retain a functionalist model of integration while rejecting the consensus assumption. We must therefore examine separately the postulate of dynamic equilibrium, the real logical cornerstone of the "structure-function" approach. Here a common confusion must be dispelled at once. The concepts of equilibrium or integration are distinctly different from those of stability and inertia. Relatively integrated societies can change faster than societies in a state of strain and conflict. The model of dynamic equilibrium has change built into it, albeit a minimization thereof. Adjustive change of the social system, in response either to exogenous change, or to endogenous change in one of its parts, is a condition to the maintenance of equilibrium. Conversely, increasing disequilibrium or malintegration can result from stability and inertia in certain elements of

---

[4] In the absence of an exact antonym for "consensus," we shall use "dissension" rather than coin "dissensus."

[5] The central importance of "patterns of value-orientations" for social integration is a recurrent theme in Parsons' work. Not only must there be a substantial amount of cognitive acceptance of values by actors in a social system, but actors must internalize these values, and be motivated to act in accordance with them. Cf. Talcott Parsons, *The Social System*, Glencoe, Ill.: The Free Press, 1951, pp. 36–37, 326, 350–351; *Structure and Process in Modern Societies*, Glencoe, Ill.: The Free Press, 1960, pp. 172–176; and Max Black (ed.), *The Social Theories of Talcott Parsons*, Englewood Cliffs: Prentice-Hall, 1961, pp. 342–343.

a society (e.g. the political systems) which fail to adjust to changes in other parts of the society. However, a simple inverse relation between equilibrium and stability is likewise untenable, as not all change is adjustive. We shall return to this point later.

The usefulness of the integration or equilibrium model (in its sophisticated and minimal form) suggests that it must be salvaged, at least in part. A minimum of integration must certainly be maintained for any social system to subsist. Furthermore, far from making the analysis of change impossible, functionalism has proven a powerful instrument in dealing with at least two major types of change: growth in complexity through differentiation, and adjustment to extra-systematic changes (e.g. problems of acculturation). At the same time, the equilibrium model cannot account for certain phenomena, and, hence, cannot be accepted as a complete and satisfactory representation of society.

More specifically, a dynamic equilibrium model cannot account for the irreducible facts that:

1) reaction to extra-systematic change is not always adjustive,

2) social systems can, for long periods, go through a vicious circle of ever deepening malintegration,

3) change can be revolutionary, i.e. both sudden and profound,

4) the social structure itself generates change through internal conflicts and contradictions.

The fourth shortcoming of functionalism results from looking at social structure as the static "backbone" of society, and considering structural analysis in social science as analogous to anatomy or morphology in biology. More than anybody else, Radcliffe-Brown is responsible for this one-sided outlook which has blinded functionalism to the conflicts and contradictions inherent in social structure.[6] In short, through its incomplete emancipation from organicism, functionalism has systematically overlooked one of the crucial sources of endogenous change. Insofar as functionalists have had to take cognizance of problems of conflict and dissension, they have done so in terms of "deviance," or "variance," i.e. an unaccountable aberration from, or modification of, the "dominant pattern" which somehow tends to resolve itself through "institutionalization." To account for endogenous change through conflict and contradiction, the dialectic must be introduced to complement functionalism. We shall return to that point later.

Related to, but analytically distinguishable from, the problem of endogenous change are the difficulties arising from the functionalist assumption that social systems adjust gradually to changes from outside, and uni-

---

[6] Cf. A. R. Radcliffe-Brown, *Structure and Function in Primitive Society*, Glencoe, Ill.: The Free Press, 1952, p. 180.

formly tend towards equilibrium or integration. Basically, I believe that it is correct to speak of a long-range tendency towards integration. Functionalism is slanted in that it underrates conflict and disequilibrium, and assumes too much continuity, gradualness and uniformity in the process of change. Rather than scrapping the equilibrium model, however, we must try to modify it.

An expanded model of equilibrium has to allow for at least two alternative sequences of change. A social system can, and often does, gradually adjust to external changes, and hence, tend fairly uniformly towards integration. But a social system can also resist exogenous change and fail to adapt, either by remaining static or by introducing reactionary change. In this case, a cycle of cumulative dysfunction and increasing malintegration is initiated, which beyond a certain point, becomes irreversible, and makes drastic revolutionary change inevitable. This second alternative is compatible with a postulate of long-range tendency towards equilibrium. Indeed, revolution is fundamentally a process whereby accumulated imbalances between major elements of society (e.g. the political and the economic system) are eliminated, and a new state of relative integration achieved. This expanded equilibrium model meets the first three objections to the "classical" functionalist position: it allows the possibility of maladjustive change, of vicious circles of malintegration, and of abrupt "social mutations" through revolution.

At the same time, the revised model raises new problems which must be answered if it is to be heuristic. What forces "push" a society towards either the adjustive or the maladjustive alternative? In the latter case, what are the symptoms that the vicious circle is irreversible, short of revolution? What is the empirical range of variation on the dimension of integration (i.e. how closely can a system approximate perfect equilibrium), and, conversely, how much disequilibrium can it tolerate?

I can only suggest tentative answers. As regards the first question, we may hypothesize that the probability of entering a maladaptive cycle increases to the extent that the *status quo* is rewarding (or, conversely, that innovation is perceived as threatening) either to the society as a whole, or to its ruling group or groups (i.e. those who have the power to determine and enforce policy). While this statement appears tautological, I must stress that the notions of "reward" and "threat" are much broader and less mechanistic than the Marxian concept of "class interests," and include such diverse things as prestige, emotional or physical security, power, wealth and values. Likewise, I make no assumption that a single ruling class automatically acts in conformity with its "objective interests."

As symptoms of the inevitability of revolution (by which I do not necessarily imply physical violence), I would suggest lack of communication, unwillingness to compromise, disagreement about the "rules of the game," and reciprocal denial of legitimacy between the opposing groups. Finally, concerning societal tolerance for disequilibrium, the limits appear much wider than a functionalist position would lead one to expect. For many different reasons (such as efficient repression, strong ties of economic inter-dependence, or a complex crisscrossing of lines of conflict and cleavage), social systems can show great resilience to malintegration.

The Hegelian-Marxian Dialectic

Let us now turn to the dialectic and see what it can offer social theory. Facile rejection of the dialectic method based either on vulgar Marxism, or, at a more sophisticated level, on the failure of Marxian orthodoxy to explain certain facts and predict certain developments has led many sociologists to throw out the baby with the bath. A detailed critical examination of dialectical materialism and Hegelian idealism is plainly out of place here: first, because there is no point in beating the dead horse of orthodoxy; second, because the task has been successfully accomplished by countless people.[7]

What can usefully be salvaged of the dialectic? Marx himself shows us the way here by rejecting Hegelian idealism and retaining the dialectic out-look. The irony is that Marx then fell into the dialectic trap by advancing his own brand of one-sided determinism as an antithesis to Hegel's idealism. Clearly, Marx's economic determinism (and hence much of the complex theoretical edifice built upon it) is as untenable as the idealism of Hegel which Marx ridiculed with ponderous sarcasm. There is no logical reason, however, why the dialectic method or outlook should be tied to any one-sided determinism, and why discarding the latter should entail a rejection of the former.

Hegel's great insight consisted in conceiving of change as inherent in the nature of ideas. Marx, in turn, showed the applicability of the thesis-antithesis-synthesis sequence to social structure. Two important limitations to the dialectic suggest themselves at this point. First, any claim that the dialectical process is the *only* source of change is untenable. The dialectical analysis of change complements and does not supplant the functionalist view of change through differentiation and adaption to external conditions. Any approximation to a satisfactory model of social dynamics requires at least these three distinct sources of change (not to mention individual invention or innovation which is at a different level of analysis because of its psychological

[7] See, for example, Dahrendorf's critique of Marx from the point of view of soci-ological theory in his *Class and Class Conflict in Industrial Society*.

dimension, and which is difficult to integrate into either the dialectic or the functionalist model).

The second limitation of the dialectic is its dualistic view of social reality. The difficulty seems to be that Hegel and Marx confused an empirical tendency for contradictions and conflicts to polarize into pairs of opposites, with a logical necessity to do so. In the realm of ideas, a thesis can give rise to several different antitheses and syntheses. Similarly, Marx ran into insuperable, self-created *impasses* by trying to cling to his binary class model, and, in fact, he often was forced to speak of "intermediate" classes (e.g. the petty bourgeoisie), or remnants from precapitalistic classes (e.g. the feudal nobility). As to the peasantry, it still remains the *Poltergeist* of Marxian class analysis.

What is left of the dialectic, one may legitimately ask, if one accepts all the above restrictions? Admittedly not very much, but the residual core is of great importance. As a reformulation of a "minimum" dialectic, the following elements appear both useful and valid:

1) Change is not only ubiquitous, but an important share of it is generated within the system; i.e. the social structure must be looked at, not only as the static framework of society, but also as the source of a crucial type of change.

2) Change of intra-systemic or endogenous origin often arises from contradiction and conflict between two or more opposing factors. These "factors" can be values, ideologies, roles, institutions or groups.

This minimum dialectic approach (if it can still be called that) seems applicable at three different levels of analysis. The first level, that of values or ideas, corresponds to Hegel's use of the dialectic, and includes the study of contradictions and conflicts between values, political or religious ideologies, and scientific or philosophical theories. In short, it is concerned with all conflicts involving abstract but explicitly formulated cultural concepts, viewed in isolation from concrete participants.

The other two levels of dialectic analysis are intertwined in Marx's writings, but it is essential to distinguish between them. One of them deals with institutionalized principles or forces arising out of the social structure, or, in different words, with the internal contradictions (generally latent, i.e. unrecognized and unintended) growing out of institutionalized processes of interaction. For example, the principle of authority is essential to the maintenance of structural stability and functional efficiency of practically all human groups; but, at the same time, authority generates conflicts and tensions which can threaten the disruption of groups. Finally, the third level of analysis concerns group conflicts. In any society, different groups (defined by sex, age, "race," culture, education, relation to the means of production, wealth, power, prestige, descent, etc.) have, by virtue of their differing roles and statuses, interests which often are conflicting.

Obviously, a binary model of group opposition based on the relation to the means of production (as advanced by Marx) or on the exercise of power (Mosca), or on any other single factor, is untenable. While some oppositions are inherently dualistic (e.g. those based on sex), and while conflict often favors polarization into two camps, there is no magic in the number two. Conflicts arising from differences between age groups, for example, often follow a three-fold division (young, adult, old). Furthermore, societies invariably have several lines of cleavages which may, but often do not overlap. Neither is it permissable to assume that groups in different positions *necessarily* have conflicting interests, or that they are always *conscious* of "objectively" antagonistic interests, or that, if groups have *some* conflicting interests, they cannot simultaneously share interests that override differences. . . .

Towards a Synthesis

So far we have reduced two theories that are generally considered antithetical to a minimum form. The most ambitious task that remains is to reach a synthesis between the two. The desirability of achieving a unitary approach seems obvious. It is not enough to say that two theories are complementary and can be used *ad hoc* for different purposes; one must also show that they are reconcilable. While such an endeavor is beyond the scope of this paper, I hope to show that an attempt at synthesis offers some promise by stressing four important points of convergence and overlap.

First, both approaches are holistic, i.e. look at societies as systems of interrelated parts. On first sight, this point seems to offer little comfort, because the types of interrelation on which each theory is based seem antithetical. Functionalists have adhered to a model of multiple and reciprocal causation; they have conceived of interdependence of parts as resulting mostly from functional specialization and complementarity, and as making for equilibrium. Hegelian–Marxian analysts, on the other hand, have generally leaned toward single-factor and unidirectional causation, and viewed interdependence as a conflictual relation. Furthermore, both theories can be criticized on the ground that they tend to represent societies as *more* holistic than they are in fact. Sophisticated functionalism accepts, of course, that different parts of a social system can have varying degrees of autonomy from one another, and that their relationship can be segmental. Indeed, the interdependence of differentiated parts in a system necessarily call forth the antithetical notion of relative autonomy without which the system could not be internally structured. Nevertheless, functionalists have, like Marxian theorists, tended to stress interrelationship, and, conversely, to underrate the extent of "compartmentalization" possible in a social system.

Different elements of a society can simply coexist without being significantly complementary, interdependent or in opposition to one another. For example, a subsistence economy can independently coexist with a money economy, even though the same persons participate in both, and even though they may both produce some of the same commodities. In plural societies, two or more unrelated legal systems with overlapping jurisdictions may function side by side. Persons can move back and forth from one cultural system to another, alternately assuming different values and roles. Thus anthropologists have frequently been confronted with the apparent paradox of rapid acculturation and great conservatism and cultural resilience to outside influences.[8]

The coexistence of largely autonomous and disparate elements in a plural society can be treated in a conventional functionalist framework as a limiting case of a social system. This evasion by definition is not very helpful because such plural societies do "hang together" in spite of conflict and compartmentization. These remarks suggest that social systems can consist, at least in part, of sub-systems which are functionally unrelated and structurally discrete and disparate, but which are interlocked because they share certain elements in common. For example, in a "developing" country, the labor forces engaged in two largely unrelated economic sectors (money and subsistence) typically show considerable overlap. Similarly, the same person can occupy widely different statuses in two stratification systems (e.g. a traditional caste system and an imported Western-type class system) that arc juxtaposed but unrelated except through common personnel.

While both bodies of theory overstress interdependence and present an unsatisfactory model thereof, they also show enough overlap to point toward a more workable view of intra-systemic relations.[9] In three different ways the principle of interdependence contains its own dialectic. First, the functionalist notion of differentiated systems consisting of interrelated parts logically implies the opposite concept of relative autonomy. Secondly, parts can be interdependent in that they *adjust to* one another, or *react against* one another. In other words, interdependence and equilibrium are independently variable. Finally, tensions within a social system can arise from conflicting tendencies for the parts to seek more autonomy, and for the whole to main-

---

8 For a treatment of problems of cultural coexistence in plural societies, see J. C. Mitchell, *Tribalism and the Plural Society*, London: Oxford University Press, 1960.

9 For a detailed and useful discussion of functional autonomy and interdependence, and their relations to equilibrium, see Alvin W. Gouldner, "Reciprocity and Autonomy in Functional Theory," in Llewellyn Gross, *op. cit.*, pp. 241–270.

tain centralized control. This latter source of tension is characteristic, for example, of political systems stressing "mechanical" (as opposed to "organic") solidarity, such as those based on segmentary lineages.

A second major overlap concerns the dual role of both conflict and consensus. Whereas functionalism regards consensus as a major focus of stability and integration, and the dialectic views conflict as the source of disintegration and revolutionary change, each of those factors can have the opposite effect. Several authors, notably Coser, have stressed the integrative and stabilizing aspects of conflict.[10] For example, interdependent conflict groups and the crisscrossing of conflict lines can "sew the social system together" by cancelling each other out and preventing disintegration along one primary line of cleavage. Furthermore, in a number of societies, conflict is institutionalized and ritualized in ways that seem conducive to integration.[11] Gluckman goes so far as to argue that ritualized conflict evidences the absence of basic dissension. Such rituals, according to Gluckman, are most prominent in societies where there are rebels (who oppose the incumbents of social roles without rejecting social values), but not revolutionaries.[12]

Not only can conflict contribute to integration. Reciprocally, consensus can prevent adaptation to change and lead to maladjustive inertia, or precipitate the disintegration of a group. The high degree of consensus typical of "utopian" or "other-worldly" reform movements is related to their ephemeral character. Strict adherence to "impractical" norms (e.g. celibacy, or the destruction of means of subsistence in expectation of the coming of the messiah) can obviously be disastrous. This type of phenomenon is analogous at the social level to Durkheim's altruistic suicide, brought about by "excess" of social solidarity. In a different way, consensus on such norms as extreme competition and individualistic laissez-faire, or suspiciousness and treachery as reported of the Dobu,[13] or malevolence and resort to witchcraft is hardly conducive to social solidarity and integration.

At yet another level of analysis, consensus can be disintegrative. In com-

---

[10] Lewis A. Coser, *The Functions of Social Conflict*, Glencoe, Ill.: The Free Press, 1956. Others have stressed that "variant" values are found side by side with "dominant" values, that these "variant" values can be integrative, and that different subcultures within a society adhere to different values. See Florence R. Kluckhohn and Fred L. Strodtbeck, *Variations in Value Orientations*, Evanston, Ill.: Row, Peterson, 1961; Florence R. Kluckhohn, "Dominant and Substitute Profiles of Cultural Orientations," *Social Forces*, 28 (May, 1950), pp. 376–394; Herman Turk, "Social Cohesion Through Variant Values," *American Sociological Review*, 28 (February, 1963), pp. 28–37.

[11] See Max Gluckman, *Custom and Conflict in Africa*, Oxford: Blackwell, 1955, and *Rituals of Rebellion in South-East Africa*, Manchester: University of Manchester Press, 1954; and Pierre L. van den Berghe, "Institutionalized Licence and Normative Stability," *Cahiers d'Etudes Africaines*, 11 (1963), pp. 413–423.

[12] *Custom and Conflict in Africa*, p. 134.

[13] Reo F. Fortune, *The Sorcerers of Dobu*, London: G. Routledge and Sons, 1932.

plex and stratified societies, consensus within groups is, in part, a function of dissension between groups. In other words, in-group unity is reinforced by inter-group conflict, leading to an increasing polarization of opinion. Thus ideological polarization is a process in which growing dissension between sub-groups in a social system is intimately linked with growing consensus within the various groups. In different words, consensus is defined not only in terms of the norms of a particular group as the functionalist approach conceives of it, but also in terms of dissension with the norms of other groups. A total conception of consensus must include a dialectic of normative opposition among the constituent groups of a society.

If both conflict and consensus, as central concepts of the dialectic and functionalism, play a role opposite to that assigned to them by the respective theories, our main contention receives strong confirmation. Not only does each theory emphasize one of two aspects of social reality which are complementary and inextricably intertwined, but some of the analytical concepts are applicable to both approaches.

Thirdly, functionalism and the dialectic share an evolutionary notion of social change. For both Hegel and Marx, the dialectic process is an ascensional spiral towards progress. The functionalist concept of differentiation postulates an evolutionary growth in structural complexity and functional specificity analogous to biological evolution. Admittedly, these two evolutionary views are different, and each presents serious difficulties. We are all aware of the pitfalls of organicism, the teleological implications of "progress," and the untenabilty of assuming that evolution is unilinear or has an end-point (e.g. Marx's Communism or Comte's "positive stage"). Nevertheless, the convergence of the two theories on some form of evolutionism suggests that the concept of social evolution (in the minimal sense of change in discernable directions) may be inescapable, however ridden with problems existing brands thereof might be. More specifically, the dialectical and functionalist notions of evolution, while dissimilar, have at least one important point in common: both theories hold that a given state of the social system presupposes all previous states, and, hence, contains them, if only in residual or modified form.

Finally, (and herein probably lies the major areas of *rapprochement*) both theories are fundamentally based on an equilibrium model. In the case of functionalism, this is obvious. But the dialectic sequence of thesis-antithesis-synthesis also involves a notion of equilibrium. Indeed, synthesis is the resolution of the contradiction between thesis and antithesis. The dialectic conceives of society as going through alternating phases equilibrium and disequilibrium: the thesis is the initial equilibrated stage of the cycle; the emergence of the antithesis leads to the intermediate disequilibrated phase; finally, as the contradiction resolves itself in the synthesis, one enters the terminal, balanced stage of the cycle, which then starts anew.[14] While this model is different from the classical notion of dynamic equilibrium, the two views are not contradictory nor incompatible with a postulate of long-range tendency towards integration.

Interestingly, this theoretical convergence on equilibrium also leads to an empirical overlap in dealing with the different sources of change. Earlier, when we dealt with the inability of functionalism to account for lack of adaptation to external change and the consequences thereof, we suggested a re-formulation of the dynamic equilibrium model which is very close to the dialectic. Cumulative imbalances and abrupt qualitative changes (which are dialectic notions) were found to result from lack of adjustment to exogenous change. The traditional dialectic approach is not concerned with reactions of social systems to changes from outside, and conceives of societies as being closed systems. Conversely, the problems of interrelations between systems, exogenous change, boundary-maintenance, etc. have been dealt with by functionalism. Yet, only by introducing dialectical concepts into classical functionalist theory can one satisfactorily account for systemic reactions to outside changes.

We saw that functionalism and the dialectic converge on an equilibrium model which is compatible with an assumption of long-range tendency towards integration. So far, we have used the terms "equilibrium" and "integration" interchangeably. The functionalist concept of dynamic equilibrium does imply integration, i.e. interdependence and compatibility between the parts of a system. The dialectic, while stating that incompatibilities inevitably emerge, also stresses that they resolve themselves in the synthesis. But integration and its corollaries do not exhaust the functionalist definition of dynamic equilibrium. The latter is also defined by minimization of change, a notion outwardly alien to the dialectic which treats change as axiomatic and stability as problematical.

Empirically, one can argue as strongly for the ubiquity of inertia as for that of change. Also, as we already stressed, the amount or rate of change bears no simple relation to the degree of equilibrium. However, the facts are not at issue here, but rather the way facts have been treated by the two bodies of theory under consideration. Once more, there are similarities in outlook between functionalism and the dialectic in spite of differences in emphasis. There is, for example, little in acculturation theory (an outgrowth of anthropological functionalism) to suggest minimization of change. The concept of inertia on the other hand is not alien to Marxian class analysis.

---

[14] The term "cycle," insofar as it implies repetitiveness is, of course, somewhat misleading in reference to the dialectic process, since both Hegel and Marx conceived of social change as an ascensional spiral.

Marx considers the ruling class as inherently unwilling and unable to adjust to the forces it unleashes, and views the class struggle as a fight between the "progressive" and "reactionary" elements of society. Insofar as reaction implies action, however, the bourgeoisie under capitalism is not, according to Marx, a truly inert element, but Marx considers the petty bourgeoisie and the peasantry as largely passive and inert in the class struggle.

Inertia is thus no more alien to a dialectic approach than change is to functionalism. The maintenance or reestablishment of equilibrium implies adjustive change in both bodies of thought. If one abandons the unnecessary assumption of minimization of change, as indeed many functionalists have done, there remains no fundamental difference in the dialectical and functionalist concepts of equilibrium and disequilibrium.

Lewis Coser

The Functions of Conflict

C *ONFLICT* within a group . . . may help to establish unity or to re-establish unity and cohesion where it has been threatened by hostile and antagonistic feelings among the members. Yet, not *every* type of conflict is likely to benefit group structure, nor that conflict can subserve such functions for *all* groups. Whether social conflict is beneficial to internal adaptation or not depends on the type of issues over which it is fought as well as on the type of social structure within which it occurs. However, types of conflict and types of social structure are not independent variables.

Internal social conflicts which concern goals, values or interests that do not contradict the basic assumptions upon which the relationship is founded tend to be positively functional for the social structure. Such conflicts tend to make possible the readjustment of norms and power relations within groups in accordance with the felt needs of its individual members or subgroups.

Internal conflicts in which the contending parties no longer share the basic values upon which the legitimacy of the social system rests threaten to disrupt the structure.

One safeguard against conflict disrupting the consensual basis of the relationship, however, is contained in the social structure itself: it is provided by the institutionalization and tolerance of conflict. Whether internal conflict promises to be a means of equilibration of social relations or readjustment of rival claims, or whether it threatens to "tear apart," depends to a large extent on the social structure within which it occurs.

In every type of social structure there are occasions for conflict, since individuals and subgroups are likely to make from time to time rival claims to scarce resources, prestige or power positions. But social structures differ in the way in which they allow expression to antagonistic claims. Some show more tolerance of conflict than others.

Closely knit groups in which there exists a high frequency of interaction and high personality involvement of the members have a tendency to suppress conflict. While they provide frequent occasions for hostility (since both sentiments of love and hatred are intensified through frequency of interaction), the acting out of such feelings is sensed as a danger to such intimate relationships, and hence there is a tendency to suppress rather than to allow expression of hostile feelings. In close-knit groups, feelings of hostility tend, therefore, to accumulate and hence to intensify. If conflict breaks out in a group that has consistently tried to prevent expression of hostile feelings, it will be particularly intense for two reasons: First, because the conflict does not merely aim at resolving the immediate issue which led to its outbreak; all accumulated grievances which were denied expression previously are apt to emerge at this occasion. Second, because the total personality involvement of the group members makes for mobilization of all sentiments in the conduct of the struggle.

Hence, the closer the group, the more intense the conflict. Where members participate with their total personality and conflicts are suppressed, the conflict, if it breaks out nevertheless, is likely to threaten the very root of the relationship.

In groups comprising individuals who participate only segmentally, conflict is less likely to be disruptive. Such groups are likely to experience a multiciplicty of conflicts. This in itself tends to constitute a check against the breakdown of consensus: the energies of group members are mobilized in many directions and hence will not concentrate on *one* conflict cutting through the group. Moreover, where occasions for hostility are not permitted to accumulate and conflict is allowed to occur wherever a resolution of tension seems to be indicated, such a conflict is likely to remain focused primarily on the condition which led to its outbreak and not to revive blocked hostility; in this way, the conflict is limited to "the facts of the case."

One may venture to say that multiplicity of conflicts stands in inverse relation to their intensity.

So far we have been dealing with internal social conflict only. At this point we must turn to a consideration of external conflict, for the structure of the group is itself affected by conflicts with other groups in which it engages or which it prepares for. Groups which are engaged in continued struggle tend to lay claim on the total personality involvement of their members so that internal conflict would tend to mobilize all energies and affects of the members. Hence such groups are unlikely to tolerate more than limited departures from the group unity. In such groups there is a tendency to suppress conflict, where it occurs, it leads the group to break up through splits or through forced withdrawal of dissenters.

Groups which are not involved in continued struggle with the outside are less prone to make claims on total personality involvement of the membership and are more likely to exhibit flexibility of structure. The multiple internal conflicts which they tolerate may in turn have an equilibrating and stabilizing impact on the structure.

In flexible social structures, multiple conflicts crisscross each other and thereby prevent basic cleavages along one axis. The multiple group affiliations of individuals makes them participate in various group conflicts so that their total personalities are not involved in any single one of them. Thus segmental participation in a multiplicity of conflicts constitutes a balancing mechanism within the structure.

In loosely structured groups and open societies, conflict, which aims at a resolution of tension between antagonists, is likely to have stabilizing and integrative functions for the relationship. By permitting immediate and direct expression of rival claims, such social systems are able to readjust their structures by eliminating the sources of dissatisfaction. The multiple conflicts which they experience may serve to eliminate the causes for dissociation and to re-establish unity. These systems avail themselves, through the toleration and institutionalization of conflict, of an important stabilizing mechanism.

In addition, conflict within a group frequently helps to revitalize existent norms; or it contributes to the emergence of new norms. In this sense, social conflict is a mechanism for adjustment of norms adequate to new conditions. A flexible society benefits from conflict because such behavior, by helping to create and modify norms, assures its continuance under changed conditions. Such mechanism for readjustment of norms is hardly available to rigid systems: by suppressing conflict, the latter smother a useful warning signal, thereby maximizing the danger of catastrophic breakdown.

Internal conflict can also serve as a means for ascertaining the relative strength of antagonistic interests within the structure, and in this way constitute a mechanism for the maintenance or continual readjustment of the balance of power. Since the outbreak of the conflict indicates a rejection of a previous accommodation between parties, once the respective power of the contenders has been ascertained through conflict, a new equilibrium can be established and the relationship can proceed on this new basis. Consequently, a social structure in which there is room for conflict disposes of an important means for avoiding or redressing conditions of disequilibrium by modifying the terms of power relations.

Conflicts with some produce associations or coalitions with others. Conflicts through such associations or coalitions, by providing a bond between the members, help to reduce social isolation or to unite individuals and groups otherwise unrelated or antagonistic to each other. A social structure in which there can exist a multiplicity of conflicts contains a mechanism for bringing together otherwise isolated, apathetic or mutually hostile parties and for taking them into the field of public social activities. Moreover, such a structure fosters a multiplicity of associations and coalitions whose diverse purposes crisscross each other, we recall, thereby preventing alliances along one major line of cleavage.

Once groups and associations have been formed through conflict with other groups, such conflict may further serve to maintain boundary lines between them and the surrounding social environment. In this way, social conflict helps to structure the larger social environment by assigning position to the various subgroups within the system and by helping to define the power relations between them.

Not all social systems in which individuals participate segmentally allow the free expression of antagonistic claims. Social systems tolerate or institutionalize conflict to different degrees. There is no society in which any and every antagonistic claim is allowed immediate expression. Societies dispose of mechanisms to channel discontent and hostility while keeping intact the relationship within which antagonism arises. Such mechanisms frequently operate through "safety-valve" institutions which provide substitute objects upon which to displace hostile sentiments as well as means of abreaction of aggressive tendencies.

Safety-valve institutions may serve to maintain both the social structure and the individual's security system, but they are incompletely functional for both of them. They prevent modification of relationships to meet changing conditions and hence the satisfaction they afford the individual can be only partially or momentarily adjustive. The hypothesis has been suggested that the need for safety-valve institutions increases with the rigidity of the social structure, i.e., with the degree to which it disallows direct expression of antagonistic claims.

Safety-valve institutions lead to a displacement of goal in the actor: he need no longer aim at reaching a solution of the unsatisfactory situation, but merely at releasing the tension which arose from it. Where safety-valve institutions provide substitute objects for the displacement of hostility, the conflict itself is channeled away from the original unsatisfactory relationship into one in which the actor's goal is no longer the attainment of specific results, but the release of tension.

This affords us a criterion for distinguishing between realistic and non-realistic conflict.

Social conflicts that arise from frustrations of specific demands within a relationship and from estimates of gains of the participants, and that are directed at the presumed frustrating object, can be called realistic conflicts. Insofar as they are means toward specific results, they can be replaced by alternative modes of interaction with the contending party if such alternatives seem to be more adequate for realizing the end in view.

Nonrealistic conflicts, on the other hand, are not occasioned by the rival ends of the antagonists, but by the need for tension release of one or both of them. In this case the conflict is not oriented toward the attainment of specific results. Insofar as unrealistic conflict is an end in itself, insofar as it affords only tension release, the chosen antagonist can be substituted for by any other "suitable" target.

In realistic conflict, there exist functional alternatives with regard to the means of carrying out the conflict, as well as with regard to accomplishing desired results short of conflict; in nonrealistic conflict, on the other hand, there exist only functional alternatives in the choice of antagonists.

Our hypothesis, that the need for safety-valve institutions increases with the rigidity of the social system, may be extended to suggest that unrealistic conflict may be expected to occur as a consequence of rigidity present in the social structure.

Our discussion of the distinction between types of conflict, and between types of social structures, leads us to conclude that conflict tends to be dysfunctional for a social structure in which there is no or insufficient toleration and institutionalization of conflict. The intensity of a conflict which threatens to "tear apart," which attacks the consensual basis of a social system, is related to the rigidity of the structure. What threatens the equilibrium of such a structure is not conflict as such, but the rigidity itself which permits hostilities to accumulate and to be channeled along one major line of cleavage once they break out in conflict.

Chapter V

Functional
Needs and
System
Requisites

Introduction

SOCIOLOGY and medicine share at least one thing in the axiom that it is easier to account for illness than for health. Just as the physician is more comfortable with pathologies, sociologists are more at home with dysfunctions. Every sociologist is trained to seek out hernias in the most flourishing organizations; some have been accused of hitting below the belt to elicit instructive groans. But what is sociological health? What is necessary for a society to survive and to flourish? Is there any finite list of essential needs that must be served? If so, what kinds of needs are they, and at what level of abstraction are they best conceptualized? Functionalists have grappled with these questions at length. Non-functionalists have criticized the answers provided. We have seen these divergent views already, particularly in the discussion of "system." Thus, Parsons has specified four "system-problems" that must be solved, and others have brayed at both the choice of problems and the mechanisms of solving them. And yet Parsons is not alone in itemizing societal needs. We have included another well-known attempt here with the critical literature in its wake.

David F. Aberle, Albert K. Cohen, Arthur K. Davis, Marion J. Levy, Jr., and Francis X. Sutton are the joint authors of "The Functional Prerequisites of a Society." The article aims at a basis for cross-societal comparative analysis. Although societal needs are constant, they argue, the arrangements for fulfilling them certainly are not, and in some cases, fulfillment is lacking altogether. The essay begins by defining "society" as distinct from organization, community, and culture. It then stipulates four conditions, any one of which is sufficient to bring about societal demise. With these negative conditions in mind, the article precedes to a list of nine prerequisites that must be met to insure societal survival. These range from "provision for adequate relationship to the environment" and "sexual recruitment" to a "shared, articulated set of goals" and "the effective control of disruptive forms of behavior." The authors emphasize that the list is not definitive. Indeed Marion Levy subsequently adds one more ("adequate institutionalization") in a volume which considers the scheme in greater depth, *The Structure of Society* (Princeton, 1952). As the book's title suggests, Levy embarks upon the comparative analysis by aligning functional needs with structural fulfillments.

Barrington Moore, Jr. concentrates on Levy's volume in order to criticize the approach as a whole. Characterizing it as "splitting verbal hairs with an axe," Moore objects less to the basic strategy than to its execution. The concept of needs is undeniably useful at a concrete level. But he finds Levy's categories both abstract and abstruse; he finds the propositions often untestable and at times simply wrong. The present selection is drawn from a longer article. Its title, "The New Scholasticism and the Study of Politics," suggests Moore's ultimate concern that this tradition is more theological than scientific.

Gideon Sjoberg suggests difficulties that may be encountered once one analyzes the world on its own terms. His discussion of "Contradictory Functional Requirements and Social Systems" indicates that, while a society may indeed be conceived to have prerequisites, these often conflict to produce a festering dialectic. Sjoberg is not arguing, however, that change is inexorable or that conflict will be militant along conventional class and interest-group lines. Indeed, he suggests that the very contradictions between prerequisites often provide the tissue to sustain a society that is pulled in different ways and must respond to divergent pressures. Sjoberg analyzes three sources of contradictory demands. The first concerns the needs of the internal system alone. A second concerns the disjunctiveness between internal needs and external constraints. The third concerns the conflict among the external constraints themselves. He goes on to cite the theoretical and methodological advantages of such a perspective. These range from a more sophisticated appreciation of equilibrium in its true sense to a reduced risk of tautological reasoning and decreased seduction by the ideal-type and the false dichotomy.

George C. Homans criticizes the prerequisite approach on still different grounds. He too finds the functionalist formulations vague and unspecified. But instead of arguing that the theorist should relate more to the concrete affairs of social reality, he advocates an unabashed psychological reductionism. Homans asserts that even the most aggressive *sociologists* do this anyway when the theorizing ceases and the analysis begins. He urges an explicitly psychological approach to obviate vagaries and to maximize generalization, deductive elegance, and explanation. He suggests that true explanation can only be had at a psychological level. If our theories must deal with needs and prerequisites, psychological premises provide the only proper starting point for a properly formal theoretical system. In all of this, Homans is at pains to specify his terms closely and to confess his prior sins with candor. Nor is he merely an iconoclast. His point is not that all non-psychological approaches are worthless, but rather that they can all be improved upon.

Harry C. Bredemeier takes his psychology diluted. He agrees that psychological and motivational postulates are necessary to functionalism but asserts that a complete analysis must go on to account for these postulates in terms of the wider social and cultural context. It is not enough to rest content with motivations. They in turn depend upon socialization, internalization, conditioning, and perception—all of which are influenced by the society as a whole. After commenting on three classic functionalist studies of ignorance, stratification, and the political machine, Bredemeier concludes with a six-point paradigm for analysis. Thus, analysis should first assert a conventional statement of needs; then state the motivational conditions necessary for their satisfaction; describe the motivational conditions that actually exist; seek the social source of those motivations; compare the actual with the necessary motivations, noting strains produced by divergencies; and finally assess the way in which the need is actually met, as distinct from hypothetical ways in which it might be met. Much of this reduces to two dimensions. The first is a distinction between motivation and sources of motivation; the second is a distinction between what is and what ought to be on theoretical grounds. Of course, the latter distinction cuts a wide swath through the functionalist debate as a whole.

D. F. Aberle, A. K. Cohen, A. K. Davis,

M. J. Levy, Jr., and F. X. Sutton

The Functional Prerequisites of a Society

A COMPARATIVE social science requires a generalized system of concepts which will enable the scientific observer to compare and contrast large bodies of concretely different social phenomena in consistent terms. A promising step in furthering the development[1] of systematic social analysis is a tentative formulation of the functional prerequisities of a society. Functional prerequisites refer broadly to the things that must get done in any society if it is to continue as a going concern, i.e., the generalized conditions necessary for the maintenance of the system concerned. The specific structural arrangements for meeting the functional prerequisites differ, of course, from one society to another and, in the course of time, change in any given society.[2]

[1] Already well under way. Cf. Talcott Parsons, "The Position of Sociological Theory," *American Sociological Review*, XIII (1948), 156–64, and the references cited therein, esp. the "Discussion" by Robert K. Merton, *ibid.*, pp. 164–68.

[2] Thus all societies must allocate goods and services somehow. A particular society may change from one method, say business enterprise, to another, say a centrally

This paper offers (1) a definition of a society on the most general level; (2) a statement of four generalized conditions, the complete realization of any one of which would terminate the existence of a society as defined; (3) a list of the functional prerequisites of a society. It seeks to justify the inclusion of each prerequisite by the demonstration that in its hypothetical absence the society could not survive, since at least one of the four conditions terminating a society would occur. There is no reason to believe that the list of functional prerequisites offered here is definitive. It is subject to revision with the growth of general theory and with experience in its application to concrete situations.

Any formulation of functional prerequisites depends for its categories on the theory of action employed. Our theory of action uses the concept of an actor whose orientation to his situation is threefold: cognitive, affective, and goal-directed. The actor is an abstraction from the total human being. Many of the qualities of the human being constitute part of the situation, the set of means and conditions, within which the actor operates.[3]

Though the definition of the functional prerequisites of a society logically precedes the development of a scheme of structural prerequisites—which tell *how* the functional prerequisites may be met—in actuality the theoretic development of the two approaches is indivisible.

I. A Definition of a Society

The unit we have selected for analysis is a *society*, such as a nation, tribe, or band, and not any social system in general. The statement of the functional prerequisites of *any social system*—a monastery, a church, or a town, for example—would be on too general a level for the present discussion, though it may be an important task. Furthermore, once the functional prerequisites of a society are outlined, it becomes easier to state those of other types of social systems, often by dropping certain prerequisites from the list, since most of these other types of systems are parts of a society (or result

---

planned economy, without the destruction of the society as a society but merely with a change in its concrete structures.

We seek to avoid the limitation inherent in defining the function of a social element solely in terms of its contribution to the survival or maintenance of the particular system of which it is a component. Structural analysis, which has recently undergone notable development, is prone to focus attention on static equilibriums. We consider *what* must be done in *any* society and hope our effort may be of use in considering the alterations that take place in *how* things are done in a society while that society persists.

[3] Neither the nature of the dependence of our formulation on this theory of action nor the theory of action itself can be further elaborated here. The theory of action is outlined briefly in Talcott Parsons, *Essays in Sociological Theory* (Glencoe: Free Press, 1949), pp. 32–33.

from the interrelations of two or more societies) and depend for their perpetuation on the existence of a society.

A society is a group of human beings sharing a self-sufficient system of action which is capable of existing longer than the life-span of an individual, the group being recruited at least in part by the sexual reproduction of the members.

The identity and continuity of a society inhere in the persistence of the system of action in which the actors participate rather than in the particular set of actors themselves. There may be a complete turnover of individuals, but the society may survive. The individuals may survive, but the society may disintegrate. A system may persist in a situation while its component relationships change. Its persistence inheres in the fact that it maintains its separation from the situation, i.e., it inheres in the *integrity* of the organism, not in its fixity or unalterable character.

A system of action always exists in a situation. In the case of a society this situation includes the nonhuman environment and, in almost every case, it includes other societies. The viability of a social system and its recognition as a society within the terms of this definition depend upon the particular set of conditions in which it functions. Study of the system itself cannot alone determine whether the system meets the criteria of the definition. What is crucial is that a social system contain successful arrangements for meeting the chronic and recurrent features of its milieu.[4]

"Longer than the life-span of an individual" reminds us that a society must be able to replace its members with effectively socialized individuals from the maturing generation. The requirement of sexual reproduction excludes from consideration such groups (monasteries, cliques) as depend *solely* on types of recruitment other than sexual. But a society may be recruited in part by non-sexual means, e.g., by immigration and conquest.

The heart of the definition is "self-sufficient system of action."[5] Its full meaning will be developed in the exposition of the functional prerequisites and in the next paragraphs.

A number of questions are bound to arise in the reader's mind as to the

---

[4] This point receives further treatment below. A social system need not be copperplated to meet the definition of a society. Natural catastrophe may terminate a concrete society. Such an event does not represent a failure to meet the functional prerequisites but is rather to be considered the result of a change in the nonhuman environment beyond the limits assumed here as the setting of a society. Many concrete societies have been assimilated by the expansions of groups with which these societies had had little or no previous contact. This, too, represents an alteration in the situation of the society beyond the limits within which it had been meeting its functional prerequisites.

[5] "System" and "structure" will be used interchangeably throughout the remainder of this treatment.

application of the definition to particular social systems and as to the basis on which the decision is to be made as to whether such systems fall within the definition of a society. We emphasize that the definition is an ideal type. *A concrete aggregate is a society in so far as it approaches the generalized model.* The following examples, though not definitive, suggest the way in which the definition may be applied.

A society is not a culture. Culture is socially transmitted behavior conceived as an abstraction from concrete social groups. Two or more *societies* may have the same *culture* or similar cultures. Though the Greek city-states shared similar culture patterns, each possessed a self-sufficient structure of action and is hence to be considered a separate society. One society may be composed of groups with some marked differences in culture. The union of agricultural, industrial, and pastoral groups in a single structure of action is an example. We discuss below the limits as to the amount of diversity possible and the conditions under which such diversity may occur without the disintegration of the society.

To some degree two different societies may possess overlapping personnel and even structural elements without losing their identity as distinct societies. The fact that Englishmen live in the United States as diplomats and traders and function, in effect, as actors in both systems, does not destroy the identity or the self-sufficiency of the United States or of Great Britain as action-systems.

To be considered a society, a group need not be self-sufficient with respect to resources. It is the structure of action that must be self-sufficient. Thus, the United States is a society. While imports and exports are necessary to its maintenance, arrangements for foreign trade are part of its self-sufficient structure of action. It is this, and not the group of individuals, that is self-sufficient. Hence Chinese-American trade does not make China and America parts of a larger society. Trade relationships are limited and relatively unstable. Their existence does not involve the two aggregates in the same self-sufficient structure of action. For parallel reasons the British Empire and the United Nations are not societies but associations.

A series of difficult decisions about the relationships of various social systems can be resolved by the introduction of a point of crucial differentiation. When a social aggregate is not capable of providing a structure, structures, or parts of structures which can meet the functional prerequisites in question, it is not to be considered a society. Thus, occupied Japan does not constitute part of American society, since in the absence of American forces Japan would seem to be able to continue control and the legitimized use of force. A group of American Indians governed by the United States for a sufficient length of time may lack the crucial structures necessary for continued existence as an independent entity and therefore be considered part of American society, in spite of an important cultural variation. An American town does not constitute a society because of its thorough participation in American political, economic, value, and other structures. The early Mormon settlement in Utah, however, did constitute a society.[6]

Under what circumstances do considerations of social change lead us to speak of a "new" society? Whenever social change results in a change of social structure on the most general level under consideration, we shall speak of a "new society" having been brought about. Such transitions may be gradual (evolutionary) or sudden and chaotic (revolutionary). The determination of the exact point of change may be extremely complex but is in theory possible. This criterion for a "new society" will not ordinarily enter the study of comparative institutions unless the developmental picture of some particular society (or societies) is under consideration.

We assume that social change characterizes all societies. Change may be gradual and peaceful or characterized by severe conflicts. In either case there may be profound structural changes. Societies may split or merge peacefully or violently. In all these instances a society of some sort exists. Whether it is considered the same society or a new one depends on the relation between the level of the structural change and the level of analysis. The changes in question may be analyzed in terms of this frame of reference. We may examine the way in which a society meets its functional prerequisites, the points of tension (those functional prerequisities least effectively met), and the responses to those strains. We do not assume the perfect integration of any society.

We have omitted from our definition any statements regarding territoriality. Action, it has been pointed out, always takes place in a situation, one feature of which is a spatial dimension. The existence of two societies intermingled during a civil war, or any such example, does not negate considerations of spatiality, which are always an essential background feature of any society.

---

[6] There is no intention of making the political variable the sole criterion for the decision as to what constitutes a society. The nature of economic ties, the degree to which value-systems are shared, and the like are also crucial in making the differentiation between two systems of action.

Thus the decision as to the distinctness of two or more aggregates as societies rests on the analysis of all aspects of the systems of action, and not merely of a single variable, in their consequences for the self-sufficient character of the systems of action. Borderline cases undoubtedly exist, but the treatment made here is sufficiently refined for the purposes at hand.

II. Four Conditions Terminating the Existence
of a Society

The realization of any of the following conditions terminates the existence of a society—the existence of the structure of action, though not necessarily of the members.

A. *The biological extinction or dispersion of the members.*—To arrive at this condition, a society need not lose all its members but need only suffer such losses as to make inoperative its structure of action. Analyses of such conditions may be made at this level in terms of fertility, morbidity, and migration rates, without reference to the highly complex factors underlying them.[7]

B. *Apathy of the members.*—Apathy means the cessation of individual motivation. This condition affects some individuals to some extent in all societies and large numbers in a few societies. That migrant Polynesian laborers have died of nostalgia is well known. It is claimed that whole societies in Melanesia have withered away from ennui. In these cases, physical extinction is merely an extreme consequence of the cessation of motivation.

C. *The war of all against all.*—This condition appears if the members of an aggregate pursue their ends by means selected only on the basis of instrumental efficiency. Though the choice of means on this basis may result at times in co-operative combinations, these combinations are by definition subject to immediate dissolution if, for example, exploitation or annihilation becomes more advantageous for any one member. Hence a state of indeterminate flux, rather than a system of action, exists. The use of force is efficient only for limited purposes. Force is a sanction, but never the essence, of a society. A society based solely on force is a contradiction in terms that raises the classical question, *Quis custodiet ipsos custodes?*

D. *The absorption of the society into another society.*—This entails the partial loss of identity and self-sufficiency of the total action-system but not necessarily the extinction of the members.[8]

The more fully these four conditions are realized, the more indeterminate is the structure of action, a condition also induced when the rate of social

---

[7] In this regard certain catastrophic occurrences deriving from marked alterations in the situation are excluded from consideration in accordance with the line of reasoning previously outlined.

[8] It is worth re-emphasizing that a given society may at one time contain arrangements for maintaining its distinctness from other societies that form part of its situation, but that an alteration of that situation (the arrival of a numerically and technically superior group bent on conquest) may render these arrangements ineffective. We would not, therefore, say that the society thus absorbed had never *been* a society, but that in a *new* situation it showed a relative inadequacy of one of its functional prerequisites that resulted in its absorption.

change is very rapid. Hence we may hypothesize that fluctuations in the vital indices, in apathy, and in coercion are to some extent functions of the rate of social change. In fact, revolutions (extreme social change) are characterized by increases in mortality, morbidity, apathy, force, and fraud. The faster the change, the greater the stress, two manifestations of which are force and/or apathy. Viewing coercion as a response to stress should help us to put the discussion of the role of force in social systems on a nonideological basis.

III. The Functional Prerequisites of a Society

The performance of a given function is prerequisite to a society if in its absence one or more of the four conditions dissolving a society results. This can be demonstrated clearly in some cases. Less clearly, but still convincingly, the nonfulfilment of certain other functions can be shown at least to foster one or more of the conditions negating a society. No specific action-pattern is prerequisite to the existence of our ideal-typical society. We are concerned with *what* must get done in a society, not with *how* it is done.

A. *Provision for adequate relationship to the environment and for sexual recruitment.*—This includes modes of adapting to, manipulating, and altering the evironment in such a way as (*a*) to maintain a sufficient number and kind of members of the society at an adequate level of functioning; (*b*) to deal with the existence of other societies in a manner which permits the persistence of the system of action; and (*c*) to pattern heterosexual relationships to insure opportunities and motivation for a sufficient rate of reproduction. In the absence of these provisions, the group will suffer biological extinction through the death of the members or failure to reproduce or it will suffer absorption into another social system.

A society, however, need not provide equally for the physiological needs of all its members. Infanticide, geronticide, limitation of marriage, and birth control may be necessary to maintain certain societies. Which members, and in what proportions, are most important for the functioning of a society depends on its social organization. Every society needs enough adult members to insure reproduction and to man the essential status-positions.

A society must adapt to, manipulate, and alter its situation. Among the features thus dealt with may be chronically threatening aspects of the situation. In a dry region a society may employ techniques of food storage, irrigation, or nomadic migration. If neighboring societies are hostile, an army may be essential and the society thus dependent on the deliberate hazarding of some of its members' lives. The existence of Murngin society depends partly on the destruction of a portion of its adult males by chronic warfare. Resistance is only one possible response to hostile neighbors. Certain "men-obush" tribes of New Guinea make but little resistance to raids. These raids, however, do not threaten to extinguish the society. Only if they do can such a passive adaptation be said to be inadequate to meet the functional prerequisite.

The inclusion of such apparently disparate features as maintenance of the organism, defense, and provision for sexual reproduction under one heading is by no means arbitrary. From the point of view of a social system, the non-human environment, the biological nature of man, and the existence of other societies are all part of the situation of action. To none of these aspects of the situation is passive adaptation the only mode of adequate relationship. Thus the biological basis of society itself is molded. Individuals have constitutional differences, but the latter are variously evaluated and dealt with by societies. The biological birth-growth-death cycle is a dynamic process in its own right, yet societies both adapt to it and modify it in a number of ways. In noting the necessity for a society to meet certain biological prerequisites, we remark also upon the great plasticity of individuals. It is scarcely necessary to remark that, concretely, societies alter their modes of relationship to their situations; that technological changes occur, sometimes through loss, more often by invention and diffusion.

B. *Role differentiation and role assignment.*—This signifies the systematic and stable division of activities. We will treat under other headings role-learning and the sanctions perpetuating the role structure.

In any society there are activities which must be regularly performed if the society is to persist. If they are to be done dependably, these extensive and varied activities must be broken down and assigned to capable individuals trained and motivated to carry them out. Otherwise everyone would be doing everything or nothing—a state of indeterminacy which is the antithesis of a society and which precludes getting essential activities carried out. The universal problems of scarcity and order are insoluble without legitimized allocation of property rights and authority, and these, in turn, are unattainable without reasonably integrated role-differentiation. While a given individual is often the locus of several roles, he can never combine all the roles of his society in himself. Age and sex differences impose a degree of role-differentiation everywhere; in some societies class and occupation are additional bases of differentiation. Arguments for specialization based on differential ability, while of great force in complex societies, have no clear bearing on societies so simple that any technique can be learnd by any individual who is not feeble-minded. Whatever the society, activities necessary to its survival must be worked out in predictable, determinate ways, or else apathy or the war of each against all must prevail. Without reliable provision for child-rearing activities and without their assignment to specific persons or groups, the society invites extinction, since children at birth are helpless. The absence of role-differentiation and of role-assignment thus makes for three of the conditions negating a society. A system of role-differentiation alone is useless without a system of selection for assigning individuals to those roles.

Mention should be made of one particular type of role-differentiation that is a requirement for any society, namely, stratification. Stratification is that particular type of role-differentiation which discriminates between higher and lower standings in terms of one or more criteria. Given the universality of scarcity, some system of differential allocation of the scarce values of a society is essential. These values may consist of such desiderata as wealth, power, magic, women and ceremonial precedence. That conflict over scarce values may destroy a society will be shown in another connection below. Our present point is that the rank order must be legitimized and accepted by most of the members—at least by the important ones—of a society if stability is to be attained. Allocation of ranks may be on the basis of ascribed or achieved qualities or both.

Role-differentiation implies organization. Precedence in specialized activities must be correlated to some extent with rank order. Coercive sanctions and initiative must be vested in specified status-positions. Some individuals will thus receive more than others. These privileges are usually made acceptable to the rank and file by joining to the greater rights of the elite a larger share of responsibilities. The Brahmins stand closer to other-worldly non-existence than do the members of any other Hindu caste, but they also have to observe the most elaborate ritual obligations. The Trobriand chief enjoys a multiple share of wealth and wives; he must also finance community enterprises and exhibit at all times more generosity than anyone else.

Even the simplest societies have hierarchical sex and age grading. Modern societies are much more elaborately stratified. Symbolic activities or ritual must be carefully organized to effect successfully their latent functions of allaying anxiety and re-creating allegorically the basic meanings and affirmations of the society. In group enterprises some roles tend to rank others, though the individuals filling the roles may rotate freely, as in the case of the citizens of the Greek city-state. Regardless of the type of stratification and authority-system, a normative scale of priorities for allocating scarce values (precedence, property rights, power, etc.) is always a vital portion of the differentiation of roles in any society.

C. *Communication.*—Evidence from deaf-mutes, "wolf children," and bilinguals shows that speech, the basic form of communication, is learned and that only rudimentary communication is possible in the absence of shared, learned linguistic symbols. Without learned symbolic communication only a few highly general emotional states—e.g., anger, sexual passion—in one individual can evoke an appropriate response in another; only a few skills may be conveyed by imitation.

No society, however simple, can exist without shared, learned symbolic modes of communication, because without them it cannot maintain the common-value structure or the protective sanctions which hold back the war of each against all. Communication is indispensable if socialization and role-differentiation are to function effectively. That each functional prerequisite thus depends in part on other functional prerequisites does not vitiate our argument so long as the functional prerequisites are logically separable. But they need not be empirically distinct activities, since any action-system may contribute to several functional prerequisites.

In a simple society, where relationships are exclusively face-to-face, shared speech forms suffice. In complex societies, other than oral communication is necessary for the system as a whole, though not for subsystems. Thus, in China, writing facilitates the survival of the society despite local dialect differences too great to permit oral communication without bilingual intermediaries. Clearly, no modern society could survive without writing. Thus, communication requires language, a medium of communication, and channels.

D. *Shared cognitive orientations.*—In any society the members must share a body of cognitive orientations which (*a*) make possible adaptation to and manipulation of the situation; (*b*) make stable, *meaningful,* and predictable the social situations in which they are engaged; and (*c*) account for those significant aspects of the situation over which they do not have adequate prediction and control in such a way as to sustain and not to destroy motivation.

If the first criterion were not met, biological existence would be impossible. If the second were not, interpersonal and intergroup relations could not exist. Private definitions of social situations or the absence of such definitions could lead only to mutually incompatible actions and the war of each against all. In no society are all conditions predictable and controllable; so the frustration of expectations is a chronic feature of social life. Without a reasonable determinate explanation of such areas of existence, the individual would exist in an unstructured world and could not avoid psychological disorganization. In the absence of shared orientations, serious clashes would ensue.

Cognitive orientations must be shared, but only in so far as the actors are involved in the same situation of action. A housewife may not distinguish a colonel from a corporal; a soldier may not appreciate that he is using his hostess' "wedding silver." They must agree, however, that a foot is "so long" and that that gentleman is a "policeman." But though a farmer may pray for rain and an aviator rub a rabbit's foot for good weather with no resultant difficulties between them, both must define the American political system in a roughly similar fashion if they are to vote.

E. *A shared, articulated set of goals.*—To phrase this prerequisite in terms of ultimate ends of action produces a vague and not very useful formulation like Thomas' four wishes. It is equally difficult to operate in terms of motivations, since these are exceedingly diverse and are intricately articulated with the social structure. Our statement in terms of goals seeks a middle ground and is couched in the terms most suitable for considering a system of action.

Because there is role-differentiation in every society, we must consider a set of goals rather than a common goal. The facts of scarcity and of differential individual endowment, features of all societies, also make it necessary to speak of a set of goals. It is the range of goals, however narrow, that provides alternatives for individuals and thus reduces one serious source of conflict in societies. (The possibility of universally sought goals in a society is not ruled out.)

The goals must be sufficiently articulated to insure the performance of socially necessary activities. They must not include too much action which threatens the existence of a society. A cult of sexual abstinence, if universalized, would terminate the society. The goals must be shared to some degree, though this will vary with the differentiation of the society. Finally, the goals of one individual must be meaningful to another in so far as they share a common structure of action.

There will be both empirical and non-empirical goals. Some goals may be mutually incompatible without being destructive to the society. Without an articulated set of goals the society would invite extinction, apathy, or the war of all against all.

F. *The normative regulation of means.*—This functional prerequisite is the prescription of means for attaining the socially formulated goals of a society and its subsystems. It complements but does not overlap the functional prerequisite of "effective control of disruptive behavior." The "normative regulation of means" defines positively the means (mostly noncoercive) to the society's goals.

That these means must be stated clearly for the sake of order and the effective functioning of the society follows from (*a*) the nature of other functional prerequisites and (*b*) the *anomie* that must result from the lack of recognized legitimized means. First, role-differentiation specifies *who* is to act, while the common articulated set of goals defines *what* is to be done. The normative regulation of means tells *how* those goals may be won. Second, the absence of normative regulation of means invites apathy or the war of each against all. Without socially prescribed means, a goal must be either devalued or forcibly seized. As the loss of a bolt may cause a great machine to beat itself to pieces, so the absence of normatively regulated means operates cumulatively to destroy the social structure.

Especially in ritual and initiatory activities must procedures be normatively specified. The content of prescriptions may vary greatly among societies; what is indispensable is simply that socially accepted directives for ceremonial and symbolic action exist. This point emphasizes the necessity for the category of normative regulation of means, in addition to the effective control of disruptive behavior. Moreover, there are often alternative, non-coercive ways of realizing goals, and they must be differentially evaluated for the sake of order, or else some must be ruled out.

G. *The regulation of affective expression.*—In any society the affective states of the members must be mutually communicable and comprehensible. Furthermore, not every affect can be expressed in every situation. Some must be suppressed or repressed. Lastly, there are affects which must be produced in the members if the social structure is to survive. All these aspects are included in the regulation of affective expression.

In the absence of the first of these conditions, stability of expectations between individuals is destroyed, and apathetic or destructive reactions will occur. This is true alike of states of anger and of affection, of love, lust and the like.[9] Without comprehensibility and communicability, mutually inappropriate responses in affectively charged situations can only result in the destruction of the relationship. In a love affair, if one member's expression of affection has the intended meaning of a flirtation, while to the other it signifies willingness to consummate the affair, the relationship is headed for a crisis. The same state of affairs with respect to the expression of affect in an entire society is clearly incompatible with the continuation of that society. This is not a matter of a lack of a shared cognitive frame of reference; rather, the conflicts are potentially explosive because of the emotional involvement. The cues that make affective expression comprehensible range from obvious and subtle linguistic behavior to posture, facial expression, gesture, and tone of voice. Many of these cues are not consciously recognized by the actors themselves.

In the face of regulated competitive co-operative, and authority relationships, some of which are entailed in any conceivable system of role-allocation, taken together with disturbances of expectation and scarcity situations, no society can survive if it permits complete latitude of affective expression in all situations. The ungoverned expression of lust and rage leads to the disruption of relationships and ultimately to the war of all against all.

---

[9] It may be that gross affective states are mutually communicable in the absence of regulation, but such communication is not sufficient to obviate all the problems dealt with here.

Finally, a society must not only structure the way in which affects are expressed and restrict certain forms of emotional expression; it must actively foster some affects. Unless we adopt the view that all relationships in all societies can be rational and contractual in character, we must take the position that some relationships depend on regulated affects for their perpetuation.[10] In the absence of the production of appropriate affects, the family, for example, would not survive. The question of what effects must regularly be produced in any society is closely related to the way other functional prerequisites are fulfilled. In American society the urban middle-class conjugal family depends heavily on the establishment of strong affective ties between spouses. The American family system in meeting the demands of a highly mobile society is deprived of certain bases of stability which other family systems possess, and the mutual affection of spouses becomes of correspondingly greater importance.

H. *Socialization.*—A problem is posed for any society by the fact that its structure of action must be learned by new members. To each individual must be transmitted so much of the modes of dealing with the total situation —the modes of communication, the shared cognitive frame of reference, goal-system, attitudes involved in the regulation of means, modes of expression, and the like—as will render him capable of adequate performance in his several roles throughout life, both as respects skills and as respects attitudes. Socialization thus is a different concept from the maintenance of the child in a state of biological well-being.

Furthermore, socialization includes both the development of new adult members from infants and the induction of an individual of any age into any role of the society or its subsystems where new learning is required.

A society cannot persist unless it perpetuates a self-sufficient system of action—whether in changed or traditional form—through the socialization of new members, drawn, in part, from the maturing generation. Whatever the defects of any particular mode of socialization, a universal failure of socialization means the extinction of the society, through a combination of all four of the terminating conditions mentioned previously.[11]

One individual cannot become equally familiar with all aspects of his society; indeed, he may remain completely ignorant of some. But he must

---

[10] This argument is an example of the dependence of our system of functional prerequisites on a theory of action. A theory which includes an affective aspect in the actor's orientation can and must include this functional prerequisite.

[11] The complexities of personality development arising from the interaction of individuals of varying constitutional endowment with the modes of child care and socialization and various other aspects of the social situation, as well as with more random situations, cannot be dealt with in any way here. It is sufficient to say that no socialization system is ideally efficient, i.e., in no society are all individuals equally well socialized nor is any one individual perfectly socialized.

acquire a working knowledge of the behavior and attitudes relevant to his various roles and identify to some degree with such values as are shared by the whole society or segments thereof wherever his behavior articulates with that of other members of the society. A Brahmin and an Untouchable learn some skills and attitudes unknown to each other. Both, however, must learn that the Hindu world is made up of castes and that this is the way things should be.

I. *The effective control of disruptive forms of behavior.*—Prominent among disruptive modes of behavior are force and fraud. The extent to which such behavior will occur is dependent on the way that various other functional prerequisites are met: role-allocation, goal-system, regulation of means and of expression, and socialization being the more obvious cases in point. All these functional prerequisites, it is clear from the preceding argument, tend to prevent the occurrence of disruptive behavior. In addition to, and sparate from, these is the effective control of such behavior when it occurs. To understand why this functional prerequisite is necessary, we must ask: Why would not a perfectly integrated society exist in its absence?

The answer lies in three conditions inherent in any society: scarcity of means, frustrations of expectations, and imperfections of socialization. That many of the desiderata of life are ultimately scarce needs no emphasis. Since sexual objects are differentially evaluated by a society, those few at the top of the scale tend to be sought by a large number of the opposite sex. Wealth, however defined, is basically scarce for the mass of individuals everywhere. Force and fraud are often the most efficient methods of acquiring scarce values. Indeed, only scarce values can be objects of rationally directed coercive effort. To argue that society without coercion and deceit can exist, one must first demonstrate the absence of scarcity. Frustration of expectations is inevitable for many individuals in any society so long as there are such universal realities as unexpected consequences of purposive behavior, scarcity, and uncertainty.

Imperfect socialization results, among other things, in evasions of the normatively prescribed paths of action. Together with frustrations of expectations, it results in explosive outbursts of anger and violence.[12] Thus, both rationally directed exercise of force and fraud and less rational outbursts of emotion continually press to disrupt stable social relationships. If resort to these disruptive behaviors is restricted only by opportunity, the war of all against all will ultimately result. (Some disruptive action may also tend in the direction of an apathetic breakdown. This does not alter the nature of the argument.)

---

[12] Other disruptive modes of behavior, including apathy, also may occur. But a refined analysis of the problem of deviancy is beyond the scope of this paper.

The system of goals tells *what* must be done; the normative regulation of means prescribes *how*. It also includes pre- and proscriptions regarding the use of force and fraud. In addition, however, the society must have techniques for handling those who, for reasons outlined, use these disruptive means or are subject to these outbreaks. The form of control and the degree of efficiency may vary greatly. What type of action is directly destructive of a society depends on the nature of the society: patricide in a society founded on patriarchal clans, violation of property rights in a property-emphasizing society, and so on. Conversely, some societies can tolerate forms of these behaviors that others cannot. Chuckchee social structure, for example, withstands a high homicide rate.

IV. Conclusion

This treatment makes no claim to be final. Our list of functional prerequisites can be elaborated and altered by the reader by making explicit the elements we have left implicit. At present, a statement of the functional prerequisites of a society is primarily useful as a contribution to general social theory rather than as a tool for analyzing individual societies. It should be especially useful for constructing a general system of structural prerequisites that will tell us how the functional prerequisites may be met, and this in turn may lead to a more comprehensive and precise comparative sociology.

Even at the present stage, however, the authors have found this approach useful as a point of reference for analyses of societies and their subsystems, and for suggesting inadequacies in the analysis of given societies and in the empirical data available. It directs attention to features of social systems, relationships among institutional structures, and implications for social change which might otherwise be overlooked.

Barrington Moore, Jr.

The New Scholasticism and
the Study of Politics

*T*HE use of formal deductive methods in the study of social behavior has a venerable and respectable intellectual history. The recent return to a quasi-scholastic formalism is also partly a negative reaction to certain extremes in the empiricist tradition, particularly its older assumption that facts, once gathered, would somehow tell their own story. The story, so the deductive criticism runs, is always imposed upon the "facts" by the implicit or explicit analytical categories and hypotheses used by the investigator. Therefore, it is better to make these categories and hypotheses as explicit and logically water-tight as possible at the outset of the inquiry, in order to force the data to yield a clear-cut decision in respect to the tenability of the theory. This doctrine has gained considerable force in recent years, to the point where the old-fashioned naturalist, the scientist who is chiefly a "good observer" of social behavior, has a difficult time in justifying his scientific status. A theory that is derived from careful examination of a body of facts is liable to be dismissed with the epithet of mere *ad hoc* explanation.

Reprinted in abridged form from Barrington Moore, Jr. "The New Scholasticism and the Study of Politics," *World Politics*, (6 October, 1953), by permission of the author and the journal.

The pursuit of this doctrine to the exclusion of other considerations also leads to its own special form of exaggeration, exemplified in certain aspects of the work of Talcott Parsons and some of his students. It characterizes much of the volume by Marion J. Levy, Jr., *The Structure of Society.* I shall comment on this work in somewhat more detail shortly, but wish to set out first what seems to me some of the general difficulties inherent in this emphasis. As indicated by the appearance of Lasswell and Kaplan's *Power and Society* and Parsons' *The Social System* in 1950 and 1951 respectively, this neo-scholasticism is no isolated phenomenon, but represents a major intellectual trend among those professionally concerned with the study of human behavior.

In the first place, the development of abstract categories evidently has a seductive attraction in its own right, whether or not they are useful in ordering data. Though the formalists assert that the ultimate purpose of the development of categories is the manipulation of data, their assertion strikes me as being mostly a pious hope.[1] The actual procedure is primarily one of splitting verbal hairs with an axe. What emerges from the undertaking is a collection of verbal categories, empty file drawers, as it were, that are arranged in a neat and, at first glance, imposing pattern. All that remains, supposedly, is to fill some of the file drawers with facts, and the others will spring open with predictions. This would be quite true, and a tremendous achievement, if the relationship between the file drawers actually existed in the facts of social behavior. To permit valid inferences from one body of facts to another is the goal of any scientific theory. But in the case of the neo-scholastics, I submit, the relationship does not derive from the objective materials examined, but for the most part from the verbal symbols alone. And, for that matter, very few propositions, on the order of "if *A* is true, then *B* is also true," have come out of these reflections. In the Lasswell and Kaplan study there are a few, but they are usually so broad as to be quite meaningless. Opening this book at random I read, *"Prop:* Ruling practices are limited by the social order"; and *"Prop*: The rulers alter the regime whenever conformity to it is expected by them to constitute a significant deprivation."[2] The second one I don't think is true, and the first one can mean anything. In Parsons' work, despite the richly suggestive paragraphs that are scattered in many parts of the study, there are fewer propositions, or hypotheses as such, than in Lasswell and Kaplan.

Even though a very high proportion of the formalists' work remains so

---

[1] The reader may wish to judge for himself by examining some of the formalist writings that attempt empirical application, i.e., particularly the last three essays on political matters in Parsons, *Essays in Sociological Theory Pure and Applied*, Glencoe, Ill., 1949, or Levy, *The Family Revolution in Modern China*, Cambridge, Mass., 1949.

[2] *Power and Society*, New Haven, 1950, pp. 190–91.

far little more than a verbal juggling act, certain aspects of this approach have at least potential value. The emphasis on theory can serve as a healthy corrective to the mere accumulation of observations, without any reflection on their import. Furthermore, a system of categories or, more likely, fragments from such a system can frequently suggest new ways of looking at factual raw materials and become the source of hypotheses, even if they are not hypotheses themselves. While the great systems of the past now seem desolate intellectual ruins, important fragments from them are incorporated into what one may hope is a growing and at least partly cumulative intellectual tradition. Finally, it is certainly necessary to attempt the organization of conclusions derived from limited observations, scattered insights, and hunches into a more coherent whole that may often serve as a springboard for fruitful inquiry. It may even be argued that a set of verbal symbols can display some power to generate further symbols and ideas, as in mathematics, that eventually find their counterpart in the world of observable social behavior. Some such rationale seems to be behind much of the work now being done within the framework of the formalist and deductive tradition. At the same time, I believe that much more attention could and should be paid to the ways in which this counterpart is to be discovered, as well as to the question of whether the aspects of social behavior to be explained in this fashion are significant on other grounds. Almost any concept can be "illustrated" somehow or other, and facts picked up off the table and put into pigeonholes. This activity does not necessarily represent scientific progress.

The purpose of the set of categories developed by Levy in the course of 500-odd pages in *The Structure of Society* is "to construct from present knowledge of empirical materials on different societies a general conceptual scheme and theoretical system for beginning the comparative analysis of societies" (p. vii). As the author notes further along in his preface, the task of "determining by empirical research in what respects, if any, the system of analysis tentatively developed on a highly abstract level can be shown to offer useful concepts and relatively tenable theories" remains an undertaking for the future. What these rather elaborate preparations will amount to, in other words, remains to be seen.

There has already been a very substantial amount of comparative work done by anthropologists on preliterate societies, but relatively little on the more complex civilizations. The latter type of studies raises some new problems. Levy's book is presented primarily as a means for comparative analysis of seven recent or contemporary complex societies, the United States, Russia, China, Japan, France, England, and possibly Germany, though the author states that at least one non-literate society will be included. Except for a remark or two about the differential impact of industrialization, nothing is said about any concrete problems that are to be examined through this comparison. Just what purpose the comparison is supposed to achieve, other than as a test of the categories, is not clear. If it is merely intended to test the classification scheme, some degree of success is more or less automatically guaranteed, since the facts can be classified by this system, or by a hundred other ways. If it is also intended to test hypotheses, as the author asserts, in an attempt to construct a theory applicable to any and all societies, then it might be better strategy to use a much wider range of data.

Though Levy's work is considerably more concrete than that of Parsons, from which it derives, what hypotheses there are tend to become buried beneath an avalanche of definitions. In the chapter on politics, for example, I am able to find only two (pp. 492 and 502). Both refer to problems that have been the subject of much discussion and research in political science and economics. In addition, they are too broadly and loosely formulated to serve as starting points for any inquiry. The more specific of the two asserts that if the economic structure of society is of the capitalist type, "definite limits are placed on the degree and types of power that can be institution-alized for predominantly politically oriented structures in the society" (p. 492). Without specification of what the "definite limits" are, it is difficult to see how this hypothesis could be tested.

The key to the system of categories, the theoretical backbone of the book, is now fairly widely known under the name of structural-functional analysis. Levy gives one of the best of the recent expositions of this view. In some-what simplified and slightly inaccurate translation, this form of analysis requires asking two types of questions about any set of social institutions that is being examined. The first question is: what activities must take place if this social system is to continue to exist? Such a question can be asked about an army, a monastery, a club, or a whole society, such as the United States. The other question is: how must these activities be carried on? For an army engaged in combat, part of the answer to the first question is that it must carry on the activity of killing the enemy, and part of the answer to the second question is that in order to do this it must have a certain type of com-mand structure, a certain organization of supplies, etc. In this manner, one establishes the so-called functional imperatives of a certain type of social system.

As Levy stresses over and over again, the identification of these function-al imperatives does not yet tell us anything about the life expectancy of the institution under analysis. Marxists and others have declared that the struc-tural-functional approach is incapable of handling problems of change, because it merely tells us what is necessary for the maintenance of a particular type of status quo.[3] Levy regards this charge as unfounded. The establishment of the conditions necessary for the maintenance of a system implies neither an interest in its survival, nor an assertion that it will continue. The necessary conditions, i.e., the imperatives, may not be met, for a wide variety of reasons. History, as Levy remarks, is full of the wreckage of social systems that could not meet the requisites for their continuation. He maintains, however, as do others in this tradition, that to determine the necessary conditions of a particular set of social arrangements can be one of the most powerful first steps toward indicating the sources of internal strain in an institution and the lines of potential change.

With all of the above, I am in general agreement. In concrete research on Soviet society I have often found it useful, as a means for locating potential foci of change, to ask myself what conditions seem to be required to keep parts of this system going. It is, incidentally, a much easier question to ask than to answer, since rather complex reasoning and considerable empirical evidence may be needed to establish that one social phenomenon is really the necessary counterpart of another. Can one prove that war industry is, or is not, an essential element in present-day American prosperity?

After establishing the validity of the functional approach, this school proceeds by an attempt to draw up a list of the imperatives, first for any type of society, and then for specific types of society. Though the procedure rapidly gets into terminological complexities that need not to be pursued here, the endeavor is often suggestive. Where it goes astray, I think, is in seeking too high a level of generality. As Levy admits, it is impossible so necessary for *any* kind of social system. Likewise, I am very skeptical of far to point to any kind of concrete social arrangement that is demonstrably Talcott Parsons' attempt to classify all forms of human action as necessarily falling under one of five pairs of alternative forms. There are perhaps a few illuminating statements that can be made about *any* kind of human behavior, but most of them are likely to be banal. There is also some usefulness in an effort to encompass the whole spectrum of social and political behavior in one intellectual *tour de force,* as it were, with the aim of locating specific manifestations at their appropriate points on the spectrum. This is perhaps the strongest argument that can be made for the very high level of generality and abstraction that characterizes much of the structural-functional discourse. Until it can prove its utility on much more concrete materials, where only fragments of the scheme are likely to be applicable, the over-all system will continue to resemble a theology more than a system of scientific discourse.

[3] In this connection, see W. W. Rostow, "Toward a General Theory of Action," *World Politics*, v (July, 1953), pp. 538–43.

Gideon Sjoberg

Contradictory Functional Requirements
and Social Systems[1]

OUR primary objective is to suggest a modification of existing structural-functional theory that will enable it better to incorporate sociological findings with respect to both social change and the recurrent tensions within and among social systems. Specifically, we contend that explicit recognition must be accorded the presence of "contradictory functional requirements"—inferred from contradictory structural arrangements—which inhere within social systems or impinge upon them from without; the number and dimensions of these built-in antagonisms can be determined only through empirical investigation.

The modification we propose should have both theoretical and methodological utility, for the contradictions in social systems account in part for the recourse to typologies in sociological analysis and the persistence of some deep-seated controversies in sociology about the nature of social systems. . . .

Reprinted from Gideon Sjoberg, "Contradictory Functional Requirements and Social Systems," *Conflict Resolution*, Vol. 4, No. 2, pp. 198–208, by permission of the author and the journal.

[1] Revised and expanded version of paper delivered at the annual meeting of the American Sociological Association, Chicago, September, 1959.

339

Essentials of our Argument

We shall first state our theoretical position. . . . Our fundamental premise is that all social systems are, at one time or another, plagued by contradictory functional requirements (or imperatives) and that these are associated with the formation of mutually antagonistic structural arrangements that function to meet these requirements. Implied in this is the notion that some of these mutually contradictory structures may actually be essential to the "operation" or "maintenance" of the system. Admittedly, some writers recognize that a single structure—say, a religious one—may fulfil multiple functional imperatives; however, they generally ignore the fact that these coexisting requirements may be at odds with one another, generating tensions and change within the structure and in the broader system of which it is a part. Still less do modern structural-functional theorists[2] recognise that certain contradictory requirements, and the structures that answer to these requirements, may well sustain the system.

We step beyond this and observe that contradictory functional requirements and structures not only exist within systems but also impinge upon them from without. Still another dimension to these patterns is the contrariety between imperatives that are internal to a social system and those that derive from external sources. The antagonisms among these varied imperatives can induce either tensions or outright conflict that may eventually initiate social change.

Present-day structural functionalists, because of their inclination to divorce a system or subsystem from its broader context, tend to overlook the externally derived requirements upon a social system, to say nothing of the contradictions these may involve. Typically, a bureaucracy, a university, or even a nation is shorn from its social setting and examined in isolation. Yet structural functionalists, of all persons, should be attuned to the network of social relationships that link a system with its environment. Indeed, an explicit premise of this school is that "parts" must be related to "wholes." This failure to consider external requirements and the associated structural arrangements has resulted in a distorted view of social systems and a neglect of some fundamental issues in sociology.

Some other facets of our position should be explicated. We do not assume any "universal functionalism"—that all structures function to meet specific requirements; some structures could be eliminated without detriment to the over-all system. Moreover, we recognize that occasionally alternative

---

[2] See, for example, Marion Levy, *The Structure of Society*, Princeton, N.J.: Princeton University Press, 1952, and Talcott Parsons, *The Social System*, Glencoe, Ill.: Free Press, 1951.

structures fulfil a single requirement. Then, too, we could dispense with the rather controversial "requirement," or "need," approach and simply speak of structures as performing contradictory functions. But, even then, one is likely to postulate that these functions in turn answer to certain requirements, for a persistent question is: Why are certain functions performed?

The concept of contradictory functional requirements is not to be confused with Merton's very significant notion of "dysfunction" [3] (although the latter is not without pertinence for our discussion). Nonetheless, sociologists who deal with dysfunction are driven to concern with the static rather than the dynamic aspects of social systems, for what is considered "dysfunctional" is primarily that which is detrimental to the harmony and integration of the system. Some go so far as to equate system integration with system maintenance, assuming that a system beset with internal strains is not maintaining itself satisfactorily—though empirically just the reverse might be true.

A few writers, among them Bateson and Gluckman[4], have anticipated some of the points we develop here, although their analyses are framed within far more limited confines. Even Parsons[5], one of the most ardent champions of functionalism today, implicitly, though *not explicitly*, admits of inherent contradictions within systems. For example, he recognizes that no system may be entirely universalistic, achievement-oriented, and so on— that, for instance, along with universalism occurs a degree of particularism. Thus the concept of a universalistic, achievement-oriented social system is a limiting case—a social fiction—that finds no direct counterpart in reality. Unfortunately, Parsons and others have failed to enlarge upon the whys and wherefores of this situation or its many implications. As we detail at greater length in our conclusions, a social system is an exceedingly complex entity whose structural arrangements, reflecting mutually antagonistic functional demands upon it, are often at odds with one another; as a result, no particular social pattern—universalism, for example—can ever be realized in full-blown form. . . .

Theoretical Implications

Mere recognition of contradictory functional requirements by no means resolves some long-standing issues in structural-functional analysis—for example, the methodological question of just how functions are to be imputed to structures. Nor have we ventured to show how manifest and

---

[3] See Robert K. Merton, *Social Theory and Social Structure*, Glencoe, Ill.: Free Press, 1949.

[4] See Gregory Bateson, *Naven*, 2nd ed., Stanford, Calif.: Stanford University Press, 1958.

[5] Parsons, *op. cit.*

latent functions, for instance, are to be related to the notion of contradictory requirements. Yet the view we enunciate involves some worthwhile theoretical advances and offers us certain new leads.

Admission of the presence of contradictory requirements, and of the mutually antagonistic structures associated with these, permits the structural functionalist to pursue his customary interest in integration but adds a more realisic dimension to his analysis. It brings to the fore such strategic questions as "How does a social order maintain integration in the face of co-existent contradictory requirements and structures?" We submit that one such mechanism for sustaining internal cohesion is the employment of negative values. Dictators have frequently created external "devils" to divert the attention of the populace from contradictions within the social order, but intensification of tensions and conflicts among nation-states is the end result. An analogous process may operate within and among the subsystems of a society.[6]

Explicit recognition of the contradictory functional requirements that impinge upon a social system, or a subsystem thereof, assists the structural functionalist in analyzing the competitive struggles, conflicts, and change that beset social orders. Dahrendorf[7] argues that conflict theory should enable us to "predict" social tensions and conflicts from given structural arrangements. This is, indeed, one goal of our proposed modification of structural-functional theory.

More specifically, the theory of contradictory functional requirements illumines the self-contradictions within social systems—as the coexistence of conformity and deviation, or of stratification and egalitarianism. Nevertheless, a social system can rarely determine with any degree of precision just where the balance or equilibrium lies in developing structures to meet these mutually antagonistic requirements. A system thus tends to oscillate between emphasis upon one set of requirements and upon another. And, where several alternative structural arrangements may serve a single imperative, the picture is complicated appreciably.

A tentative explanation for this oscillation—or "dialectic"—seems to be that, when the swing is toward one "extreme," individuals or groups are likely to perceive that some vital requirements are not being met, and they initiate counteractions whose aim is the achievement of some sort of balance. Thus any excessive efforts to institutionalize egalitarianism in an industrial society would soon evoke counter demands for stratification.

We go further and hypothesize that one reason for the frequent alterna-

---

[6] See Gideon Sjoberg and Leonard D. Cain, Jr., "Negative Values and Social Action," *Alpha Kappa Deltan*, XXIX (1959), 63–70.

[7] See Ralf Dahrendorf, "Toward a Theory of Social Conflict," *Conflict Resolution*, II (1958), 175.

tion between peace and war on the international scene is that during periods of peace the contradictory requirements of societies and the structures that rise to meet these generate global instability; for, as we observed, a social system often seeks to resolve its internal dilemmas through negation of external systems. Thus is unloosed the specter of intersocietal conflict—even war. But it appears that societies cannot sustain indefinitely a garrison-state orientation; now arise further contradictions that drive the social order toward the pursuit of amicable relations with other systems. Justification of this hypothesis would necessitate a full-length treatise; here we merely suggest that it is plausible and worthy of investigation.

But qualify our observations we must! We should avoid any over-commitment to a dialectical theory of change. Aside from the logical problems posed by the theory of the dialectic (aired in numerous critiques by philosophers and logicians), it would indeed be rash, in the absence of supportive empirical data, to assume that all structures or aspects thereof are wracked by self-contradictions. We must not slight those situations wherein contradictions cannot be demonstrated—where structures are complementary rather than contradictory.

Moreover, a dialectical theory of change, to be meaningful, must be set within a structural-functional framework. The very nature of the dialectic, after all, is determined by the structural characteristics of the social system that creates it. One type of society (or subsystem) will call forth different structural arrangements, and in turn will engender divergent dialectical patterns, than will others. For instance, the demand for deviation is far more noticeable in the scientific system than in most social orders. Thus the strains, or conflicts, between the proponents of deviation and those pressing for conformity will have quite different implications in the scientific system than in some other social order. Or, as another illustration, the dialectic generated by the mutually antagonistic imperatives for stratification and for egalitarianism will diverge rather markedly in industrial and in preindustrial civilized orders, given the differing emphases upon these requirements in these two kinds of society.

We proceed beyond this to observe that the concept of "equilibrium," whether viewed as a static or a dynamic phenomenon, is most useful when cognizance is taken of the possible contrarieties among functional requirements and among their concomitant structures in social systems. Equilibrium, then, is the balance achieved in a system's response to pressures from coexistent contradictory imperatives—though the precise point at which the balance lies is well-nigh impossible to determine. . . .

Attacking this question from another vantage point, we might observe that the notion of coexisting contradictory requirements seems to be an essential ingredient of any theory of conflict. Moreover, the cross-cultural orientation propounded by structural functionalists would seem to be mandatory for conflict theorists as well. We must seek to delineate those structures that appear to be universal for societies in general or for specific types of societies and, from this information, infer the requirements these structures fulfil. We might then reverse the process, predicting the kinds of structures, within selected types of societies or systems, that answer to given requirements. But the conflict theorist cannot stop here; he must go on to determine whether contradictory sets of requirements and their concomitant structures give rise in similar situations to similar kinds of competitive struggle and conflict, particularly war. Available evidence suggests that this is the case.

Some writers[8] have warned of the deceptive ease with which the structural functionalist can lapse into tautological reasoning. Our effort, by stressing the need to determine the functional requirements of social systems through empirical investigation, attempts to side-step this pitfall. Our theoretical orientation, moreover, generates various hypotheses that are subject to empirical testing. Some of these have already been indicated. Others, phrased in question form, include: Why are some sets of contradictory requirements present in one type of social order and absent in another? How are systems best able to operate under the burden of opposing functional demands and the antagonistic arrangements that arise to meet these demands? By what mechanisms are the resulting strains neutralized? Just how many or what kinds of contradictory structural arrangements can a system endure? Moreover, are some types of systems better equipped than others to handle these dilemmas? Specifically with respect to industrial societies, is a democracy better able than a dictatorship to cope with the contradictory imperatives that operate within a given system? With those that are imposed from without? Why? Here we can touch upon one or two of these issues.

At first glance—and admittedly on the basis of limited data—democracy as a mode of government seems rather congruent with the industrial-urban system, characterized by a complex division of labor and numerous special-interest groups. One of the prime arguments for democracy is its embodiment of a "feedback" mechanism; that is, permitting the populace to voice its dissatisfaction tends to neutralize any extreme dialectical movement. Theoretically at least, a democracy can boast of a built-in alarm that warns when the system is moving too far in one direction or the other. Dictatorships, lacking such correctives upon any wide swings of the pendulum, seem to generate more violent counterreactions. Nevertheless, this corrective

---

[8] See, for example, Carl G. Hempel, "The Logic of Functional Analysis," in Llewellyn Gross, ed., *Symposium on Sociological Theory*, Evanston, Ill.: Row, Peterson & Co., 1959.

system in institutionalized democracy seems more effective for managing internal than external dilemmas, although it may be that a democracy, whatever its weaknesses, requires less hostility toward outsiders to resolve internal contradictions than does a dictatorship. Ultimately, of course, the reduction of international strife would necessitate some built-in institutional apparatus that would mediate or adjudicate the dissatisfactions that seem inevitably to arise. The United Nations, theoretically, might be viewed as a step in this direction, although, given the present autonomy of nations, it is unlikely to prove effective as a mechanism for resolving the strains that stem from the contradictory structures of nation-wide systems.

Methodological Implications

Still another implication of our approach lies in the methodological realm. The presence of contradictory sets of functional requirements accounts in large part for sociologists' frequent recourse to either ideal or constructed types, as well as for their affinity for terms like "dominant configurations" or "general patterns" when analyzing subsystems or such social orders as nation-states. Even statisticians who scorn such conceptualization are driven to their use, as a cursory examination of almost any sociological journal will confirm.

It is strange, in light of this, that no one seems to have interjected the query: Why do social scientists so often resort to these methodological devices? We believe that this is largely attributable to the persistence of contradictory requirements and structures. Their presence obviates the full realization of many types of patterns, whether within or among societies. Thus social scientists must speak of tendencies or dominant patterns (e.g., tendencies toward universalism, toward conformity, etc.).

Sociologists are frequently disturbed by their recourse to generalizations of this kind. But, instead of berating themselves, they perhaps should ask themselves *why* they are forced to do so. It is not enough to strive for neatness and simplicity. Although we, too, affirm the utility of Occam's razor, the ultimate goal, we contend, is to explain reality.

George C. Homans

Structural, Functional and Psychological Theories

*T*HERE are two classes of general theory: the normative and the non-normative. There is no good special term in use to distinguish the latter from the former. To speak very roughly, normative theories explain how men ought to behave if they are to accomplish certain results, and nonnormative theories explain how they actually do behave. . . [Editorial Note: Normative theories include "theories of applied sociology" and formal "game theories."]

Nonnormative Theories

I turn now to nonnormative general theories of which I think there are three main kinds: structural, functional, and psychological. I shall also have something to say about historical explanations, though I do not believe they

Reprinted from George C. Homans, "Contemporary Theory in Sociology," appearing in *Handbook of Modern Sociology*, edited by Robert E. L. Faris, Rand McNally & Company, Chicago, by permission. Copyright © 1964, Rand McNally & Company, all rights reserved.

constitute a distinct type of theory. I warn the reader that I do not necessarily use these words in some of the senses in which they have been used in sociology.

Structural theories explain the existence of some element of social behavior, however "element" may be defined, by its relations to other elements and the relations of these elements to one another in some configuration, a social structure or social system. In functional theories, the highest-order propositions say that a society or other social unit will not survive, remain in equilibrium, or reach its goal unless a certain element or combination of elements of social behavior occurs in the unit. In psychological theories the highest-order propositions say that some variable in the behavior of individual men as members of a species—not the behavior of societies or groups as such—is a more or less specific function of some other variable in the behavior of individual men or of the physical environment. I do not think that any one of these types of theories often occurs in its pure form in sociological writings; it is usually mixed with other types.

Structural Theories

There is no reason in principle why structural theories, which may also be called field theories, should not be used to explain the existence of any feature of any social configuration, but in sociology they have most often been used, although in sketchy form, to explain an institution as part of a social structure or social system. An institution is a rule or set of rules for behavior, conformity to which is rewarded to some degree and nonconformity punished. Structural explanations have been least sketchy in the field of social anthropology, where the following might be an example:

1. Societies that have matrilocal or avunculocal rules of residence are organized in matrilineages.

2. Societies that have avunculocal rules vest jural authority over ego in his mother's brothers.

3. Therefore, societies that vest jural authority over ego in his mother's brothers are organized in matrilineages.

4. The Trobrianders vest jural authority over ego in his mother's brothers.

5. Therefore, the Trobrianders are organized in matrilineages.

As usual, let us not worry about whether this explanation is true or about the meanings of the technical terms. Let us look only at the form of the explanation. I call it structural because its highest-order propositions (1 and 2) are general propositions about the relationships between elements in a universe of configurations (structures) of elements. In the present case, the elements are institutions and the configurations are kinship systems. This is the type of explanation social scientists have in mind when they assume, which they cannot often demonstrate, that every institution in a social system is related to all the others in the sense that if one changed the others would all change too. Then the nature of any one institution is explained by its relations with the others and by the relations of these with one another.

Now let us look at a somewhat more complex possibility. Suppose we could treat kinship systems as varying continuously along a definite number of institutional dimensions, such as "degree of matrilinearity," and that we could state a series of propositions (equations) about the relations between the variables. The propositions might well be more complicated than number 2 above, the relation between any two variables being conditioned by the values of a third, etc., so that many of the variables might enter into more than one of the equations. Then the highest-order propositions in the theory we were constructing would be relatively many in number and all (this is to say the same thing) at the same level of generality, the institutional level.

A number of concrete kinship systems, each characterized by a set of different values of the variables, would satisfy the system of propositions. If we had done our work well, they would all do so. Then if we had reason to know of a particular kinship system, like that of the Trobrianders, what the actual values of a limited number of the variables were, if these values were given as in proposition 4 above, then we could solve the system of propositions to get the values of the other variables. In this case, any one "other" feature of the Trobriand system would be explained in the sense that it could be derived from the system of propositions together with the given values.

Many sciences besides anthropology have dreamed of this type of explanation. It is the one Cuvier, for instance, had in mind when he asserted that if he possessed, say, the jaw-bone of an extinct animal he could reconstruct the rest of the animal. No rigorous structural explanation has ever, I think, been carried out in social science, but it is the type of explanation some social scientists sound as if they were groping toward, and, accordingly, I have described here what I think they would get if they groped successfully.

Structural explanation is a perfectly valid type of explanation: its propositions may be contingent and its conclusions may follow from the other propositions in a deductive system. But even at the present stage of development in social science it may not turn out to be the most general type of explanation. In my terms, it may be open at the top.

It may be possible to show that some, though at present certainly only a few, of the structural propositions like numbers 1 and 2 above are in turn derivable from still more general propositions of the psychological sort— more general in that they stand high in deductive systems that explain other features of human behavior than the interrelations of institutions. Thus Homans and Schneider[1] tried to show that a structural proposition about the relation between the loci of jural authority and the types of unilateral cross-cousin marriage could be psychologically explained. But it must be confessed that their explanation is not generally accepted.[2]

Structural explanations, if we had them fully worked out, would be valid explanations but probably not the most general possible. In this sense I call them compatible with either functional or psychological explanations, to whose ideal types I now turn.

Functional Theories

The word function has been used in so many different senses in theoretical work that I must explain what I do not mean by "functional theories" before I can explain what I do mean.[3] First, the fact that a theory contains propositions of the form "x is some function of y" in the mathematical sense of the word function does not make it a functional theory in my sense of the word, for the propositions of all real theories can be cast in this form. Nor is a theory functional that contains statements like "the function of institutions a, b, and c is to maintain institution x," when all the statement means is that institution x does not appear in a social system unless a, b, and c do too, that x is a function of a, b, and c, for this is what I have called a structural proposition.

Second, a functional theory is not the same as "functional analysis." Analysis is the word sociologists give to whatever it is they are doing when they do not want to be more specific but do want a fancy word. Sociologists are carrying out "functional analysis" when, in the course of their investigations, they examine the consequences of a particular item of social behavior or the results of a society's having adopted, for whatever reason, some particular institution. They then may call these consequences the "functions" of the behavior or the institution, further classifying them as "intended" or "unintended," as "manifest" or "latent," or as in some sense "good" or "bad" (functional or dysfunctional) consequences. Kingsley Davis[4] said that

---

[1] G. C. Homans and D. M. Schneider, *Marriage, authority, and final causes,* Glencoe, Ill.: Free Press, 1955.

[2] R. Needham, *Structure and Sentiment,* Chicago: University of Chicago Press, 1962.

[3] See, for example, E. Nagel, *The Structure of Science,* New York: Harcourt, 1961, pp. 398–446, 520–535.

[4] Kingsley Davis, "The myth of functional analysis as a special method in sociology and anthropology," *American Sociological Review,* 1959, 24, 757–773.

functional analysis cannot be distinguished from ordinary sociological analysis, that we are all functionalists now. He is right in the sense that a sociologist would be a fool not to examine the consequences of social behavior.

But to say that an item of behavior *has* consequences and that a sociologist ought to look for them is not the same thing as saying that the item exists *because* its consequences are of a particular sort. Only when the latter kind of statement is made does functional analysis begin to become functional theory, that is, functional explanation. Until then functional analysis is a rule of method (Look for consequences!) which may result in the discovery of true propositions, but the propositions themselves have yet to be explained.

Third, to say that an item of behavior occurs or an institution exists because its consequences are "good" (functional) for individual men is not enough to make this a functional theory in my sense of the word. In my terms, as we shall see, this is a psychological theory, and not a very adequate one at that, for men will do many things that are not "good" for them, such as smoking cigarettes, so long as they find the results sufficiently rewarding (valuable). Only when the occurrence of an item of behavior or the existence of an institution is explained by arguing that it is "good" not for individuals but for a society or some smaller social group as such are we in the presence of a functional theory. Merton[5] lumped individual and societal functionalism together under the rubric of functional theory. I think it well to keep them separate, because the highest-order propositions in psychological theories are in fact very different from what they are in functional ones.

Having eliminated what I do not mean by functional theories, let me turn to the characteristics of the latter as now defined. A good place to begin is Radcliffe-Brown's classic definition of *function*:

> The *function* of any recurrent activity, such as the punishment of a crime, or a funeral ceremony, is the part it plays in the social life as a whole and therefore the contribution it makes to the maintenance of the structural continuity. The concept of function as here defined thus involves the notion of a *structure* consisting of a *set of relations* amongst *unit entities*, the *continuity* of the structure being maintained by a *life-process* made up of the activities of the constituent units.[6]

Note that this definition combines at least two sorts of ideas: a notion of structure, "relations between entities"—between, for instance, the institutions of a social system—and a notion of function per se, "contribution to

---

[5] R. K. Merton, *Social Theory and Social Structure*, (rev. ed.), Glencoe, Ill.: Free Press, 1957, p. 52.

[6] A. R. Radcliffe-Brown, *Structure and Function in Primitive Society*, Glencoe, Ill.: Free Press, 1952, p. 180.

the maintenance of continuity"—for instance, the continuity of a society. This is characteristic of many functional theories, which are accordingly often called "structural-functional."

Radcliffe-Brown's[7] statement is in form a definition, and, as we know, definitions are not theories. Let me therefore set up a deductive system that will display the characteristic features of functional theories. Radcliffe-Brown spoke of "the punishment of a crime," and my example will show how a functionalist might elaborate on Durkheim's[8] famous statement that the punishment of a crime has more important societal effects on the innocent than on the criminal himself.

1. If a society is to maintain its structural continuity, its members must conform to its norms.

2. Its members' conformity to its norms is maintained by their collective horror of nonconformity.

3. Their horror of nonconformity is maintained by expressing this horror collectively.

4. The punishment of criminals, i.e., nonconformists, is the means of expressing this horror collectively.

5. Therefore, a society that maintains its structural continuity is one in which criminals are punished.

6. The Bongo are a society that maintains its structural continuity.

7. Therefore, criminals are punished among the Bongo.

The Bongo, incidentally, are a fictitious society.

Aside from the fact that proposition 1 is almost a truism, this explanation contains obvious weaknesses. It does not consider how many members "must" conform and how much. They cannot all conform or there would be no criminals to keep up the conformity of the rest. Also is the punishment of criminals the only means by which the horror of nonconformity is maintained? Functionalists try to deal with this problem through the doctrine of "functional alternatives"—different institutions that can perform the same function for a society. But I shall not dwell on these difficulties, which do not seem to me central to the problem of functionalism.

What, then, are the decisive characteristics of a theory of this sort? The *explicandum* (proposition 7) is an ordinary low-order empirical statement that a particular society possesses a particular kind of institution. It is the same sort of proposition as the one about the Trobrianders' being matrilineally organized, which I used in illustrating a structural theory. Sociological theories do not differ in what they explain but in how they explain it.

---

[7] *Ibid.*

[8] Emile Durkheim, *The Division of Labor in Society*, Glencoe, Ill.: Free Press, 1947, p. 108.

Proposition 6 is also presumed to be a low-order empirical proposition: some anthropologist must have observed that a group of people who call themselves the Bongo continue to exist at least for the time being.

More interesting are the higher-order propositions, which are of two kinds. The first, represented by propositions 2, 3, and 4, are statements, in Radcliffe-Brown's[9] terms, of relations between unit-entities, actually between types of social behavior: "horror of nonconformity" and "the punishment of criminals." I have stated these as if they were fully general, holding good of all social behavior. The deductive system might also be reconstructed so as to treat any one of them as holding good of only one type of society. In other types, the horror of nonconformity, for instance, might be maintained by other means than the punishment of criminals. In either case, these propositions could perfectly well take their place in structural theories; they are not distinctively functional. Finally, they could perhaps themselves be explained by psychological theory.

The second kind of proposition is represented by numbers 1 and 5. These are general propositions presumed to hold good of all social systems and stating one or more of the conditions under which a social system can "maintain its structural continuity" or "survive." It is the presence in deductive systems, implicitly or explicitly, of this kind of high-order proposition that makes the systems distinctively "functional." The existence of a particular institution in a particular society is explained by the function it performs in maintaining that society. A functional theory in this sense is also a "final-cause" or teleological theory in that it explains an institution by its consequences for a society rather than by its antecedents, the actual "efficient causes" that brought it into existence, which are left unexplained.

If, as I believe, functional theories provide unsatisfactory explanations in sociology, the reason must lie in their propositions like number 1, for these are the only propositions that are distinctively "functional." One difficulty is that of defining terms like "maintenance of the structural continuity" of a society. A society can maintain its structural continuity for many centuries in the sense that it is called by the same name, that its members reproduce themselves, and that it preserves its independence, while its institutions change by slow degrees, but in the long run markedly, from what they were in the beginning. Another way of putting the matter is: no method has been proposed for measuring the variable "degree of maintenance of structural continuity." Under these circumstances, a proposition containing this term becomes so weak that nothing definite can be derived from it.

For certain kinds of social groups it is conceivable that some precise measure could be developed of the degree to which a group as a whole was

---

[9]Radcliffe-Brown, *op. cit.*

successful in attaining its goals. Thus, the measure of success in industrial or commercial firms might be the profits of a firm as a percentage of capital. Then the highest-order proposition in a functional theory explaining particular features of the firm's organization might be a statement of the conditions that must be satisfied if the firm were to make a profit. But I do not know that such a proposition has actually been stated and used in a deductive system.

Another solution of the problem of defining "maintenance of the structural continuity" would be to state a proposition (equation) that the variables characterizing a social system would have to satisfy if the system were to be considered in equilibrium. The model would be provided by the science of mechanics, where some general equilibrium equation like D'Alembert's principle may be included if convenient as one of the system of equations to be solved for the values of the variables.[10] An equivalent proposition in sociology could be used as one of the propositions in a structural theory. It could be used—if we had it. In spite of the endless discussion of the "equilibrium concept" in sociology, a discussion to which I myself have contributed too much,[11] no such equilibrium proposition (not concept) has ever been both stated and rigorously used in a sociological deductive system. Unless one is both stated and used, I consider any further discussion of equilibrium to be wasted breath.

Some sociologists have tried in effect to strengthen the highest-order propositions in a functional theory by substituting "survival," which can presumably be a matter of observation, for the undefinable term "maintenance of the structural continuity." Then the propositions take the form "certain conditions must be satisfied if a society is to survive." Thus, some sociologists talk of the "functional prerequisites for the survival of a society.[12] When so strengthened these propositions run into a new kind of problem—the problem of their status as contingent propositions.

Let me say at this point that a functional theory is not unsatisfactory just because it is a "final cause" theory. In biology there are plenty of "final cause" theories that meet all the conditions of being valid theories.[13] Consider the following explanation why Canada geese fly south in winter.

1. If a species is to survive, its members (enough of them) must eat.

---

10 See E. Mach, *The Science of Mechanics*, LaSalle, Ill.: Open Court Publishing Co., 1942, pp. 421–434.

11 See G. C. Homans, *The Human Group*, New York: Harcourt, 1950, pp. 301–308.

12 D. F. Aberle, A. K. Cohen, A. K. Davis, M. J. Levy, Jr., and F. X. Sutton, "The Functional Prerequisites of a Society," *Ethics*, 1950, 60, 100–111.

13 See, for example, R. B. Braithwaite, *Scientific Explanation*, Cambridge: Cambridge University Press, 1953, Chapter 10.

2. Canada geese nest in the Arctic in the summer, but cannot get enough to eat there in the winter.

3. Yet Canada geese are a surviving species.

4. Therefore, the geese must go south in the winter to places where they can get food.

5. Flying is their method of moving long distances.

6. Therefore Canada geese fly south in the winter.

I submit that this explanation runs more or less parallel to functional explanation in sociology. Its highest-order proposition states a condition that must be met if a collectivity is to survive and makes no reference, for instance, to the motivations of individual geese. It is also, of course, a "final cause" theory, and for that reason many ornithologists would not be satisfied with it. The geese, for instance, do not wait to fly south until their northern feeding grounds freeze over, and the ornithologists would want to look for the efficient causes: how certain stimuli actually started the gaggles of geese moving on their way. I claim, nevertheless, that the explanation is perfectly valid—it meets my requirements for being a deductive system—and that we should be wholly justified in using it to explain why geese fly south, especially until we had something better, something that would explain more of the details of the phenomenon.

How then does it differ from functional explanation in sociology? It differs in the status of the higher-order propositions. In the ornithological explanation these are clearly contingent propositions: one could carry out experiments to see whether geese survive without eating and whether they can get enough to eat in the Arctic in winter. The same sort of proposition could also be tested for human societies, and indeed from such propositions important conclusions about human society can be drawn, though they are insufficient to explain its features in any detail.

But functional theorists in sociology do not confine themselves to stating such biological conditions for the survival of a society. They also state purely "social" conditions such as the one I used in illustration (the members' conformity to the norms), and the contingent status of these propositions is much more dubious.

The criteria that define a society and accordingly those that define its survival, turn out to be far less clear than might appear at first glance. Thus, the Roman Empire, as a governmental institution, has certainly not survived, but the society of Italy has otherwise maintained its structural continuity intact up to the present time. Yet there are a few groups we should usually call societies that have certainly not survived since all their members have died out. The Tasmanian aborigines are one example. Others, like the Ona, appear to be in train to dying out. Now if we look at our information on these societies and run down one of the lists specifying the functional prerequisites for survival[14] we find that these societies met all the social prerequisites on the list. Thus, their members conformed to some degree to the norms of the society—perhaps that was just the trouble. How *much* did they conform? That is another question and one irrelevant to the present discussion, for functional theorists never tell us to what degree a society must possess any of the functional prerequisites on their lists. The societies in question did meet the social prerequisites in some degree and yet failed to survive. Why? They were undone by gunfire, firewater, disease, or some combination of the three. They were undone, if you like, by failure to meet the biological prerequisites, not the social ones.

One may regard functional propositions like number 1 above as not supported by evidence. Some of the conclusions that may be drawn from them are true, but some are false: e.g., that the Tasmanians are a surviving society. One may also regard them as inherently not supportable. In either case, sociologists who implicitly or explicitly use them in deductive systems are treating them as noncontingent, as if experience were irrelevant to their truth or falsity. Accordingly the deductive systems in question are not by my definition theories at all. This does not mean that contingent functional propositions in sociology could not conceivably be devised. It is conceivable that they could be, but no such propositions are at present in sight, or anywhere near it, and current functional theories are nontheories because they are noncontingent.

Psychological Theories

I turn now to the third class of nonnormative general theories, the psychological. These are theories in which the highest-order propositions are statements about the behavior of men as members of a species and not statements about the interrelations of institutions or about the conditions some group or society must meet in order to survive or remain in equilibrium. By way of illustration let me set down a psychological explanation of the institution for which I gave a functional one above—the punishment of criminals.

1. The more rewarding men find the results of an action, the more likely they are to take this action.

2. Men who are threatened are likely to find rewarding any action that hurts the threatener.

3. A person who violates a norm of a society, that is, a criminal, threatens the other men who are members of the society.

4. Punishment is, by definition, whatever hurts the criminal.

---

14 Aberle, *et al., op. cit.*

5. Therefore, men who are members of a society are likely to punish criminals.

How does this explanation differ from a functional one? It does not deny that the punishment of criminals may have further consequences for the behavior of men, such as an increased horror for the crime, or that the increased horror may have further favorable consequences for the society as such. But it has nothing to say about consequences of this sort. Instead it explains punishment by its antecedent, the threat the criminal poses to the members of the society (proposition 3), and by two propositions (1 and 2) about the characteristics of the behavior of men as members of a species and not just as members of a particular society. But I must remind the reader of the peculiar status of the term *rewarding* (*valuable*) in proposition 1.

I call this a psychological explanation simply because propositions like these are most often formulated and tested by persons who call themselves psychologists. I shall not try to list all the essential psychological propositions here, especially as psychologists might not agree on what they are.[15] The list should certainly include propositions about how men's behavior is affected by the value of the rewards they obtain and by their degree of success in obtaining these rewards. It should also include propositions about how values themselves are acquired. It should include propositions about how men perceive the circumstances in which they act, and about the kinds of circumstances that are apt to release emotional behavior. Many of the propositions could no doubt be shown to follow as corollaries from a few more general ones. But note: to call an explanation psychological does not entail the adoption of any particular one of the many systems of psychological theory.

I claim that sociologists, even when they are sounding most "functional," use psychological explanation all the time, though they more often use it implicitly than explicitly, because propositions like numbers 1 and 2 are so obvious that they can afford to take them for granted. Let me use an example from our sister science, history. Some of the same issues over explanation have come up in history as have come up in sociology with this difference: the historians do not worry about what kind of explanation they shall use but whether they have any explanation at all. In the course of this controversy one philosopher[16] said just what I should have said, that an explanation would include general propositions or, as he called them, laws. Commenting on this view Scriven[17] wrote: "Suppose we wish to explain

15 For one example, see G. C. Homans, *Social Behavior: Its Elementary Forms*, New York: Harcourt, 1961, Chapter 4.

16 C. G. Hempel, "Explanations and Laws," in P. Gardiner (Ed.), *Theories of History*, Glencoe, Ill.: Free Press, 1959, pp. 344–356.

17 M. Scriven, "Truisms as the grounds for historical explanations," in P. Gardiner (Ed.), *Theories of History*, Glencoe, Ill.: Free Press, 1959, pp. 443–475.

why William the Conqueror never invaded Scotland. The answer, as usually given, is simple enough; he had no desire for the lands of the Scottish nobles, and he secured his northern borders by defeating Malcolm, King of Scotland, in battle and exacting homage. There seem to be no laws involved in this explanation." [18]

Scriven says that this *is* an explanation and that it does not contain any general laws. I claim that formally it is not an explanation just because it contains no general law. It is not an explanation because, with the propositions as explicitly given, no deductive system can be constructed. But if a major premise, which is now lacking, were supplied, a deductive system could be constructed, and the major premise would turn out to be a psychological proposition. I contend that the completed explanation would run something like this:

1. The more rewarding men find the results of an action, the more likely they are to take this action.

2. William the Conqueror was a man.

3. Therefore, the more rewarding William found the results of an action, the more likely he was to take this action.

4. In the given circumstances, he did not find the conquest of Scotland rewarding.

5. Therefore, he was unlikely to take action that would win him Scotland.

You see how obvious I can get if I try? The point is that the explanation as given by Scriven[19] can be turned into a real explanation only by supplying a missing major premise (proposition 1). The major premise, moreover, is a psychological proposition. In sociology as well as in history, it is our major premises that we are most apt to leave unstated, particularly when they are psychological. We leave them unstated not only because they are obvious, but also because they are so obvious that we cannot bring ourselves to take them seriously. In the social sciences, unlike other sciences, the general laws are the ones men have always known most about, though they have not always formulated them as a psychologist would—and so they can hardly believe that they *are* general laws. Laws are things that have to be discovered; something lying around in plain sight comes too cheap to be a law.

I believe that, in view of the deficiencies in functional theory, the only type of theory in sociology that stands any chance of becoming a general one is a psychological theory, in the sense that the deductive systems by which we explain social behavior would, if completed, contain among their highest-order propositions one or more of those I call psychological. The time may

18 *Ibid.*, p. 444.
19 *Ibid.*

come when they will lose their place at the top, when they in turn will be shown to be derivable from still more general propositions such as those of physiology. But the time has not come yet, and psychological propositions remain our most general ones.

What do I mean when I say that our deductive systems would "if completed" contain psychological propositions? Go back to my first illustration of a deductive system. [Editorial note: It is drawn from Emile Durkheim's *Suicide* and as formalized by Homans states:

1. In any social grouping, the suicide rate varies directly with the degree of individualism (egoism).

2. The degree of individualism varies with the incidence of Protestantism.

3. Therefore, the suicide rate varies with the incidence of Protestantism.

4. The incidence of Protestantism in Spain is low.

5. Therefore, the suicide rate in Spain is low.][20] That system was perfectly valid as far as it went, but it was open at the top. Its highest-order proposition related the suicide rate to the degree of individualism. But I think that it would be possible to construct a convincing explanation why this relationship itself should exist and that the explanation would contain psychological propositions. In the same way it has been shown that propositions about the characteristics of small groups can be psychologically explained.[21]

I said earlier that I did not think structural explanations containing, for instance, propositions about the relationships between institutions in social systems would turn out to be general explanations in sociology, though they, too, were valid as far as they went. The reason is again that some, though certainly not all, of the structural propositions can themselves be explained psychologically.[22]

An example is the study by Homans and Schneider[23] of the two forms of unilateral cross-cousin marriage: preferred marriage with father's sister's daughter, preferred marriage with mother's brother's daughter. We did not spell out our argument in full (in this respect we sinned as much as other sociologists), but in effect it ran somewhat like this. We started with the assumption that the use of punishment as a method of control would provoke in some degree reactions of fear and avoidance in the persons controlled. This is a psychological proposition for which there is good evidence. We further argued that persons in authority over others in primitive societies

---

[20] G. C. Homans, "Contemporary Theory in Sociology," in Robert E. L. Faris, *Handbook of Modern Sociology*, Chicago: Rand McNally & Company, 1964, p. 951.

[21] Homans, 1961, *op. cit.*

[22] G. P. Murdock, *Social Structure*, New York: Macmillan, 1949, p. xvi.

[23] Homans and Schneider, *op. cit.*

would be apt to use some degree of control by punishment. Then, by a series of steps too long to be reproduced here, marriage and authority would be kept separate in the sense that ego would have some tendency to marry a cross-cousin on the opposite side of the family from where authority over him lay. We finally predicted that one form of unilateral cross-cousin marriage would occur in societies where authority over ego was vested in the father, the other where it was vested in mother's brother. This hypothesis received strong statistical support.

In the long run Schneider and Homans[24] may turn out to be wrong. But no one so far has advanced hypotheses that will take care of more of the cross-cultural variance in the data than ours will. And the deductive system that explained our tested hypothesis contained at least one high-order psychological proposition. We were not, of course, able to explain everything. We were not able to explain why some societies should vest authority in the father and some in the mother's brother, nor why unilateral cross-cousin marriage should exist at all. But with these things given, we were able to explain psychologically why each of the two forms of marriage was apt to occur in certain societies and not in others.

In these cases and in others, the psychological explanations seem to be the most general, in the sense that the higher-order propositions appearing in them, besides explaining, for instance, the structural propositions themselves, can also be used to explain a wide variety of other empirical propositions about social behavior including those of elementary economics as well as those of experimental psychology. It would be easy to jump to the conclusion, as I do, that all the empirical propositions characteristic of sociology could in principle be reduced to psychology. But what is "principle"? The fact is that the reduction has not often been actually carried out, and in many cases it probably never will be if only because the necessary information is lacking. Whatever it can do in principle, psychology cannot now in fact explain every social phenomenon. Under these circumstances, "principle" is a matter of faith.

Many sociologists do not feel comfortable with psychological reductionism, and so I had better discuss some of the common objections. The position taken here does not assume that men are isolated individuals. It is wholly compatible with the doctrine that human behavior is and has always been social. What it does assume is that the general propositions of psychology, the "law of effect," for instance, do not change when the source of reward for an action changes from being, say, the physical environment to being another human. The composition effects, the ways in which the propositions work out to produce a concrete result, are much more complicated

24 *Ibid.*

when the actions of each of two or more men reward the actions of the others, but the propositions themselves do not change. When we say that the whole of social life is more than the sum of its parts, the actions of individuals, all we are referring to is the complexity of the composition effects.

The position taken here does not assume a "great man" theory of sociology, though some great men have made more difference than sociologists, many of whom know little history, are always ready to admit. It does not assume that to explain sociological phenomena one must account for the behavior of every single individual concerned. That would certainly be impossible, and in any event psychological theory certainly predicts that large numbers of individuals placed in similar circumstances, say members of a middle class in a period of economic expansion, are likely to behave in similar ways. The fact that many sociologists necessarily treat many of the phenomena they study as collective in this sense does not make the explanation of these phenomena any less psychological.

The position taken here does not assume that "human nature is the same the world over" if this old saw means that concrete human behavior is the same. It is obviously not the same but varies greatly over many dimensions. What the position does assume is something rather different: that a few general propositions hold good of human behavior, from which, under a great variety of different given conditions including those passed on to the men of a society from their ancestors, a great variety of different forms of concrete behavior follow. This capacity to explain the many through the few is the mark of a good theory.

Finally, though this is hardly a theoretical issue, the position taken here does not rob sociologists of their subject-matter. There is nothing in it to prevent sociologists, other than some kinds of theorists, from doing what they have always done, especially as the psychologists will not be doing it. Let them go on producing theories like the one of Durkheim's[25] that I started with. The fact that their theories may be open at the top, that their highest-order propositions may ultimately be derivable from psychological propositions, does not make the theories invalid. Indeed I see no great reason why any sociologist should worry at all about "general" theory, except under one condition. If sociologists come along, as they do, telling me that theirs is a general theory and that it is structural-functional, I am a mere dog in the manger, though I may be correct, when I simply deny there is any general theory. To be constructive, I must put forward an alternative. The only main type of alternative general theory is psychological.

Durkheim.—Though the position taken here does not rob sociology of its subject-matter, it does deny that it possesses any theory distinctively its own.

---

[25] E. Durkheim, *Les règles de la méthode sociologique*, (8th ed.), Paris: Alcan, 1927.

That sociology does possess such a theory was one of the convictions of that great sociologist, Durkheim, and it is still dear to many of us. Speaking of what he called social facts, he wrote: "Since their essential characteristic consists in the power they possess of exerting, from outside, a pressure on individual consciousnesses, they do not derive from individual consciousnesses, and in consequence sociology is not a corollary of psychology." [26] But does this consequence follow? When I stop at a red traffic light or obey any other convention a social fact may be said to exert from outside a pressure on my consciousness. I bet we could discover the individual consciousness from whom the idea of the traffic lights derived, but, leaving that argument aside, how do we explain the pressure the light exerts? We point out that, if I do not stop, there is some probability of certain unpleasant things hapening to me, and it is a general psychological proposition that men are apt to act so as to avoid punishment. That is, the very facts from which Durkheim drew the conclusion that sociology was not a corollary of psychology can themselves be explained only by psychological laws. When Durkheim flew away from psychology, he flew on psychological wings.

Durkheim was prepared to advance his own apparently nonpsychological form of explanation: "The determining cause of a social fact ought to be looked for among antecedent social facts, and not among the states of the individual consciousness." [27] The trouble with this is that Durkheim presented the two possibilities as alternatives rather than as complements. He may have had in mind his own finding[28] that *anomie* (a social fact) was a cause of high suicide rates (another social fact). I think it perfectly legitimate to call anomie a cause of suicide, but we are not interested just in causes but in explanations, and, were we to construct a deductive system explaining why anomie was a cause of suicide, I think the system would include psychological propositions.

Again, the price rise of the sixteenth century, which I take to be a social fact, was certainly a determining cause of the enclosure movement among English landlords. But were we to construct an explanation why this particular cause had this particular effect, we should have to say that the price rise presented English landlords both with great opportunities for monetary gain and great risks of monetary loss, that enclosure tended to increase the gain and avoid the loss, that the landlords found monetary gain rewarding (which is a state of individual consciousness, if you like), and, finally, that

---

[26] *Ibid.*, pp. 124–125.

[27] *Ibid.*, p. 135.

[28] E. Durkheim, *Suicide*, G. Simpson (Ed.), Glencoe, Ill.: Free Press, 1951, Chapter 5.

men are likely to take actions whose results they find rewarding—which, as I cannot repeat too often, is a general psychological proposition. The explanation of the price rise itself would in turn include psychological propositions and so on as far back in history as information was available. In short, the fact that social causes have social effects does not rule out psychological explanations.

Yet many able men still apparently cling to the Durkheimian[29] position. Thus Blau writes:

If we should find that, regardless of whether or not an individual has an authoritarian disposition, he is more apt to discriminate against minorities if he lives in a community where authoritarian values prevail than if he lives in one where they do not, we would have evidence that this social value exerts external constraints upon the tendency to discriminate—structural effects that are independent of the internalized value orientations of individuals.[30]

A trick is being worked here, not a deliberate trick, but a trick none the less. It consists in Blau's[31] assuming that his individual holds only one "internalized value," whereas he certainly holds many, and they are often in competition with one another. We need consider only two: antiauthoritarianism and social acceptance. The latter is just as much "internalized" as the former: both are acquired. If an individual cannot get acceptance from other members of the community except by discriminating against minorities, which is apt to be the case when the other members hold authoritarian values, the probability will increase of his foregoing the rewards of anti-authoritarianism in favor of those of social acceptance, and Blau's "structural effect" will be produced. But there are no effects here that are independent of the values of individuals, and the explanation is psychological. Psychological theory certainly does not deny that "society" exerts influence on "the individual"; it only denies that this influence must be explained through distinctively sociological propositions.

Historical theories.—Psychological theories of a simple sort, like the foregoing one on punishment of criminals, appear to be adequate to explain human institutions defined so broadly as to allow great concrete variation within the class. Thus the punishment of criminals has taken many forms in different human societies and from time to time in any one society, but a single deductive system probably explains the existence of the general category of penal institutions. The problem is different when what we have

---

29 Durkheim, 1927, *op. cit.*
30 P. M. Blau, "Structural Effects," *American Sociological Review*, 1960, 25, p. 180.
31 *Ibid.*

to explain is the existence in a particular society of a very specific institution, very narrowly defined. Thus, a simple psychological explanation, or even a functional one, might hope to explain why the United States had some kind of institution for settling disputes, but it would never explain why the jury, in particular, was part of our legal system. The deductive systems that would explain things like juries would have to include, as simple psychological explanations do not, propositions about the past historical development of a society and about the way decisions taken long ago bent the twig in directions the trunk has followed since. Yet I do not think that these theories are distinctive just because they are historical. Though they are far from "simple," though their chains of reasoning if spelled out in full must be long and complex, they are still psychological theories, especially as the complexity lies more in the history than in the psychology.

For several reasons, of which the complexity is one, sociologists have tended to avoid historical theories. One way they have of doing so is to take propositions that would require historical explanation simply as givens in their deductive systems, that is, to leave these propositions unexplained. Thus the deductive system that I used as my first illustration included the proposition, "The incidence of Protestantism in Spain is low." The proposition was part of the explanation but was itself simply taken as given, left unexplained. To have explained it in turn would have required bringing in much of the history of Spain.

I appeal to what scholars would actually do were they asked to explain why a particular institution, not just some one of a general class of institutions, existed in a particular society. If they had the historical record they would never dream of using a functional explanation. Suppose, for instance, they were asked to explain why the British Parliament or the American business corporation exist as legal entities. They would show, from one point of time to another, how men and groups of men pursuing, in a context of other institutions and of traditions passed on to them by their forebears, different, often conflicting, and by no means always material values, choosing with inadequate information between alternative courses of action on the basis of the value of the results and the prospects of success in attaining them—the scholars would show how, in these conditions, men forged the prototypes of these institutions and then modified them progressively until they took the form they have today.

Indeed the history would, in principle, only end with today. A scholar explaining the existence of the modern American corporation should end by showing what persons and groups, in the light of possible alternatives, might have an interest in modifying it, what persons and groups might have an interest in maintaining it unchanged, and what prospects in a context of other institutions each would have for success in the struggle.

The explanatory chains might be very long—so long that the scholar might take the situation at a particular time as given and start from there instead of going back to the beginning of the historical record. He would also take as given the other institutions in whose structural context the particular institution he was interested in developed, and not try to explain them in turn, even though he thought it could be done. The explanations would certainly be sketchy in many places for lack of information. Nevertheless they would always include, and include at many different points in the argument, propositions of the kind I used in explaining the behavior of William the Conqueror, propositions about how men behave as members of a species. They would then bring in as lower-order propositions the fact that the men in question held particular values and acted in particular circumstances.

The circumstances in which men are placed may differ greatly, including the ways in which they perceive the circumstances. The values they hold may also differ, though they tend to hold certain earthy ones in common. But the propositions about how they behave, given the differences in circumstances and values, are the same for all men, and the same may be true of propositions about the way values are acquired. These are the propositions I call psychological.

The historical form of explanation can obviously not be used to explain the institutions of societies that possess no historical records, which include most of the so-called primitive societies. But the primitive societies make up for their lack of history by being many in number and limited in institutional variability largely to the themes of kinship and subsistence economy. For such societies it is possible to establish statistically certain general propositions, of the kind I call structural, about the relationships between institutions, and it is sometimes possible to show that these structural propositions in turn are susceptible to psychological explanation. But here, as in historical explanation, many things may have to be taken as simply given. Thus, it may be possible to explain psychologically why men in societies that vest strong jural authority in the father should tend to have especially close and warm relationships with their mother's brothers. But in the absence of historical records it may not be possible to explain in turn why the locus of jural authority should lie where it does.

Sociologists trying to account for the nature of human institutions often feel as if there were, according to the circumstances, a number of different kinds of explanation open to them, or combinations of the different kinds. They may try to explain an institution functionally, by what it does for a society. They may try to explain it structurally, by how it is related to other institutions in a social system. They may try to explain it historically, by the way it developed over time. Or they may try to explain it psychologically, by how it follows from general characteristics of the behavior of men. I have tried to show the distinctive features of each of these forms of explanation, their strengths and weaknesses, and how they are related to one another. Even if we agree in the end that the functional explanation is not contingent, the structural not fully general, and the historical really psychological, this does not mean that any of them has failed to make its contribution to the advancement of our science.

Harry C. Bredemeier

The Functional Analysis of Motivation

(EDITOR'S INTRODUCTION: *The author reviews several specific functional
*analyses from a methodological perspective. In each instance, behavior
patterns are explained in terms of their consequences. He then asserts that
much confusion in functional analysis could be avoided if they were
explicitly formulated so that the explanatory variables are couched in
motivational terms.*)

*T*HE tendency to avoid doing this may be related to another, rather more
subtle, confusion in some functionalist thinking. This is the failure
systematically to realize that certain needs of individuals, which must be
satisfied if they are to play certain roles necessary to the operation of a
system, may themselves be generated by other aspects of the system. That is
to say, a functional analysis which concentrates only on locating the function (need-satisfaction) of a given culture pattern is very likely to be
seriously incomplete and therefore misleading. A complete understanding of
the pattern in question would require asking not only "what need does it
satisfy?" but also "what is the source of that need, i.e., what culture patterns
give rise to that need?"

For example, if one were to say that the function of a fever in a human
organism is to conserve body heat, one might be approximately correct. But
to stop there, without probing the source of the need for conserving energy
and heat (i.e., those characteristics of the organic system which generated

Reprinted from Harry C. Bredemeier, "The Methodology of Functionalism," *Ameri-
can Sociological Review, 20 (April, 1955), pp. 173–180, by permission of the author
and the American Sociological Association.

367

that need), would obviously be incomplete and possibly misleading. It could be misleading, for example, if one were led to infer that a fever is something to be encouraged.

To generalize the point, the functionality of a subsystem may always be regarded profitably as being at least partly a result of the special organization of the larger system. It is the organization of the larger system which generates the need for the subsystem to perform its function. If the above point is not explicitly kept in mind, the analyst will be conceptually blinded to the full empirical significance of the subsystem he is analyzing. A clear example of this is provided in a recent paper by Wilbert E. Moore and Melvin Tumin, who write, "Ignorance is commonly viewed today as the natural enemy of stability and orderly progress in social life."[1] Contrary to this common view, "It is the central purpose of this paper to examine explicitly some of the contexts in which ignorance . . . performs specifiable functions in social structure and action."[2] The "functions of ignorance" are then classified as follows (we summarize the grounds of the authors' reasoning, or an illustration of it, in parenthesis after each category):

(1) The preservation of a privileged position. (Ignorance on the part of customers and potential competitors contributes to the bargaining power of a specialist. It also serves to prevent jealousy when status equals receive unequal rewards.)

(2) The reinforcement of traditional values. (Ignorance of alternatives, and of the popularity of alternatives, prevents practice of alternatives.)

(3) The preservation of fair competition. (If everyone had complete knowledge of everyone else's plans and resources, the outcome would be so certain that no further action would be required.)

(4) The preservation of stereotypes. (If bureaucratic specialists had extended knowledge about one another, the limited nature of their relationships would be impaired. Also, class and ethnic stereotypes presuppose ignorance.)

(5) The maintenance of appropriate incentives. (Uncertainty produces anxiety, which is a spur to effort. Moreover, risk, as in games of chance, may be enjoyable.)

It is clear that Moore and Tumin here start from the observation of an empirical fact—ignorance—and ask about it only a limited version of a general functional question, "to the preservation of what behavior does it contribute?" The functional analysis then consists in thinking of relationships which would be different if accurate knowledge were available. More

---

[1] Wilbert E. Moore and Melvin M. Tumin, "Some Social Functions of Ignorance," *American Sociological Review*, 14 (December, 1949), p. 787.

[2] *Ibid.*, p. 788.

succinctly, the functional analysis here consists in pointing to the fact that, since people respond to their definitions of a situation, if you change their definitions their responses will change. The function of a definition is to preserve the behavior which follows from it.

But let us ask some obvious questions about the dysfunctional behavior which is alleged to follow from correct definitions of the situations considered by Moore and Tumin. If business men knew about one another's processes and plans, would no further action really be required? How about the requirement of producing goods and services? Perhaps more importantly, if one business man has a more efficient process than another, is not the contribution *to the social system* greater if all other businesses learn about and use that process?

Answer might be made, of course, that the *incentive to seek* greater efficiency is the possibility of surpassing one's competitors, and that this incentive would disappear if the business man knew that his competitors, by having knowledge of his processes, would always be just as efficient as he. But it is important to make explicit what is being assumed here, that, to secure efficiency, a very special kind of mechanism is being relied upon—the mechanism of competition for advantage. The operation of that mechanism depends upon giving each business man a special kind of *motivational orientation*—the belief that he should be richer than others. If he has such an orientation, of course, he will be motivated to keep his greater efficiency a secret and will be frustrated if the secret is violated. But there are further consequences of his keeping it a secret. Either he takes away his competitors' customers as a result of his superior efficiency (which spells the end of competition), or society does not reap the benefits of his efficiency.

The specific point we wish to make here is that the functionality of ignorance on the part of business men results from reliance upon a particular set of institutional mechanisms. It is true that ignorance is a functional necessity of American economic institutions, but to stop there is highly misleading. It is like saying that ethnic discrimination is a functional necessity of Anglo-Saxon hegemony. Both statements are true enough, but they represent the beginning, not the end, of productive functional analysis. What is the source of the functionality of ignorance or discrimination (that is, what normative orientations result in their being functional)? And what are the consequences of, and alternatives to, those orientations?

The same difficulty seems to characterize nearly all of the points made by Moore and Tumin that are not simply tautologies (as, for example, that ignorance of alternatives prevents their practice). Space limitation prevents our pursuing each in detail, but the general principle that seems relevant may be expressed as follows: functional analyses which take a subsystem as the sole point of reference are necessarily incomplete and likely to be misleading.

A thorough analysis involves asking *both* what are the consequences of the given pattern, *and* what are the conditions that make these consequences functional? The answer to the latter question must always be sought in terms of the normative orientations and symbolic definitions comprising individuals' motivations.

It will be useful to apply these considerations to another well-known piece of functional analysis, Kingsley Davis' and Wilbert E. Moore's analysis of stratification. The problem these writers set for themselves is to account for the phenomenon of inequality in the distribution of societal rewards, chiefly prestige and income; and they seek to account for it by pointing to its function for a social system. They begin by pointing to three undoubted facts: (1) Some positions in the social structure require scarcer talent or more training than others. (2) Some are functionally more important than others. (3) It is essential (for maximum efficiency) that "less essential positions . . . not compete successfully with more essential ones [for scarce talents]."[3]

Social systems, in other words, are more efficient to the degree that they evolve some mechanism for sorting their members into the functional roles for which they are comparatively best fitted, and (as Davis and Moore note further) motivate them to play those roles diligently. According to Davis and Moore, the most efficient mechanism for meeting this requirement is to attach unequal rewards to different positions, the amount of reward being greater, the greater the importance attached to a position by society and the scarcer the talent available to fill the position. This, of course, is the classical supply and demand reasoning of economic theory.

The basic logic of the Davis-Moore reasoning would seem to be this: if people are motivated to maximize their rewards, and if they can do so only by performing the most important functions their talents permit, then they will distribute themselves through the role structure in the manner most efficient for the social system.

So far, this reasoning seems impeccable. When, however, the writers go on to conclude that "Social inequality is thus an unconsciously evolved device by which societies insure that the most important positions are conscientiously filled by the most qualified persons,"[4] they assert an empirical generalization that is not at all dictated with logical compulsion by the premises. In fact, the *empirical* significance of the two "if" premises cannot be fully understood until they are conceptualized on a level which states clearly the structural sources of motivational orientations and the

---

[3] Kingsley Davis and Wilbert E. Moore, "Some Principles of Stratification," in Wilson and Kolb (eds.), *Sociological Analysis*, New York: Harcourt, Brace, and Co., 1949, p. 436.

[4] *Ibid.*, p. 430.

psychological process of adjustment to those sources. We suggest that tne following procedural canons of functional analysis might contribute to such an understanding.

(1) Needs of a system should always be stated in terms of what kinds of actions concrete individuals must manifest.
(2) The question should always be explicitly raised as to what kinds of motivations would lead people to act in the necessary manner.
(3) The psychological principles on which the answer to motivational questions is based should always be made explicit.
(4) The question should always be raised as to the full consequences of any observed motivational structures.

Applying these canons to the problem of stratification, we venture the following analysis as alternative to the Davis-Moore approach. (The numbers in parentheses after each point refer to the canon suggested above to which the proposition is intended to conform.)

If a complex division of labor is to operate efficiently, then people must play those roles for which they are best fitted and must play them to the best of their abilities (1). Since people behave so as to maximize their gratifications, gratifications must be made conditional upon diligent playing of the role for which they are best fitted (3). Since what is gratifying for human beings is chiefly the meeting of certain normative criteria of self-respect and ego-enhancement (3), the normative criteria in question should be those which make self-respect follow from playing the role for which one is best fitted (2).

If the normative criteria are something different—for example, if they are such as to make self-respect depend upon having a certain position or a certain income—then we must expect that many people will be deprived of self-respect (4). When people are deprived of self-respect, they react by attempting to minimize the damage. This leads to one or more of several types of compulsive adjustment: [5] compulsive achievement or dominance; incorrigibility or aggression; submission or ritualism; withdrawal (4). Any one of these interferes with efficiency, and constitutes a source of instability.

Confirmation of this line of reasoning comes from Merton's functional analysis of the political machine.[6] Examination of that analysis will also serve as an illustration of the utility of following the procedural canons suggested above, and will in addition permit their more detailed elaboration.

Merton's announced purpose is to account for the political machine. The logic of his procedure seems to be as follows. He begins by asking what are

---

[5] These familiar categories are taken from Talcott Parsons, *The Social System*, Glencoe, Illinois: The Free Press, 1952, Chapter 7.

[6] Robert K. Merton, *Social Theory and Social Structure*, Glencoe, Illinois: The Free Press, Chapter 1.

the needs of a social system and in partial answer points to the necessity of focusing enough power in the hands of some persons to permit them to take positive action when positive action is called for. One kind of *motivation* which would meet this requirement is the responsibility for carrying out formally prescribed role-obligations. This, however, is ruled out by the fact that the formal definitions of existing roles are designed precisely to spread power thin through checks and balances.

The result is that when different subgroups in the population need action, there is no formal structure to satisfy them. But what are such needs and where do they come from? One kind of need is the need for help, when forces beyond the individual's control defeat him—"the whole range of crises when a fellow needs a friend, and, above all, a friend who knows the score and can do something about it."[7]

Moreover, the help must not be rendered in such a way as to threaten the loss of self-respect which is often the price for legalized assistance.[8] Another kind of need of the deprived classes is the need for social mobility and economic success. The meeting of this need is also blocked in many cases by the formal institutional structure, so that the informal one of the political machine and its ally, the racket, finds a ready response.

But whence such needs? They result from the normative definitions of the dominant culture. "As is well known, the American culture lays enormous emphasis on money and power as a 'success' goal. . . . Given our cultural stigmatization of manual labor [and of dependence on charity] . . . it is clear that the result is a tendency to achieve those culturally approved objectives through whatever means are possible."[9]

Still another kind of need is the need of business men for political aid, aid which the formal structure, with its commitment to fair competition as the mechanism for distributing talent among important positions, is not able to give efficiently. "Business corporations . . . seek special political dispensation which will enable them to stabilize their situation and to near their objective of maximizing profits."[10] Whence this need? Merton quotes Lincoln Steffens: "Our economic system, which held up riches, power, and acclaim as prizes to men bold enough to buy corruptly . . . and get away with it . . ."[11] is the source.

Using Merton's analysis as a model, we might summarize and elaborate a recommended procedure for functional analysis as follows:

---

7 *Ibid.,* p. 74.
8 *Loc. cit.*
9 *Ibid.,* p. 76.
10 *Ibid.,* p. 75.
11 *Loc. cit.*

(1) Productive analysis begins with a statement of the kind of action necessary to maintain some system of inter-relationships, namely, the system of which the observed uniformity is a part.
(2) It states the motivational conditions which are necessary to produce that action (the normative criteria of gratification which will yield the relevant action).
(3) It describes the motivational patterns actually operating so as to produce the uniformity under analysis.
(4) It seeks to find the source of those patterns (to isolate the normative criteria responsible for the observed actions).
(5) It compares the consequences of the operating motivation with the motivations described as necessary, including the deviant modes of adjusting to frustration of efforts to meet the criteria in question.
(6) It finally assesses the role played by the uniformity in question in contributing to the system of which it is a part.

Chapter VI

Teleology

and

Explanation

Introduction

*T*HEORIES may be faulted for explaining too little or for explaining too much. Functionalism has been faulted for both. It is charged with explaining *too little* in using a form of explanation that is no explanation at all. For example, religion serves function *A*, and that explains why religion exists; note that this assumes a teleological purpose on the part of religion and that religion may have been "caused" by a host of extraneous circumstances regardless of the functions it does or does not serve. At the same time, functionalism is charged with explaining *too much* because, in trying to account for the total social system, it makes misleading assumptions that betray the analysis of any single element within the system. Thus, if society is to persist, function *A* must be served, and religion comes about to serve it in some way and in some fashion; note that this is both an article of faith and an incipient tautology since it assumes that function *A* will be served and religion may be defined as any institution that serves it.

Yet these examples exaggerate the culpability of contemporary functionalists. Few would demur with the logic of the accusations, but most would deny guilt by denying that their explanatory propositions follow either of the two patterns. Part of the problem is semantic. Our language is replete with teleological references of need and purpose. It is sometimes difficult to avoid them in scientific statements of causality. At times the avoidance becomes so contrived that the author slips into a natural motivational argot, trusting the reader to insert his own caveats of interpretation. As one colleague commented of "reification" or the tendency to treat conceptual abstractions as intentional beings: "I simplify; it is my opponents who reify."

But there are also real issues behind the verbal facade. Is the teleological lexicon of purpose, motivation, and "intended function" admissible in a dispassionate rhetoric of sociological explanation? Are there no sociological units whose purposes are real rather than imagined and whose consequences are intended rather than accidental? What of human beings themselves? Finally, what is the distinctively "functional mode of explanation?" How does it relate to other modes; indeed are there any real alternatives? All of these issues move beyond functionalism itself. They are all dealt with in the five readings to follow.

Kingsley Davis initiates the discussion by seeking to end it. His article on "The Myth of Functional Analysis as a Special Method in Sociology and Anthropology" argues that functionalism is simply scientific analysis writ small. It is no special cult and has no distinguishing earmarks. In the true sense, we are all functionalists and the term should be dropped as a source of spurious divisions among us. What else does scientific analysis do but assess the relations of parts to each other and to larger systemic wholes? What else does scientific analysis do but ask of the contributions of one phenomenon for the phenomena surrounding it? Alas, it is true that some functionalists have erred in the past and will err in the future. But an approach must be judged on its success rather than its mistakes, and, in general, functionalism has no mystique or stigma beyond that of science itself. Davis's article appears to attack the very justification of the present volume. But our belief is that the volume will inform larger issues for precisely the reason that Davis suggests. If functionalism is tantamount to science and theory in general, a book on functionalism has wider utility than merely airing a parochial debate. Yet Davis's view of functionalism has not gone undisputed.

Ronald Philip Dore takes explicit exception with the Davis thesis. He argues that functional explanation is not only unique but, if anything, unscientific. Dore distinguishes functionalism on two principle grounds. First, its concern with higher-order systems and deductive reasoning stands in contrast to an alternative approach that stresses lower-order empirical regularities as bricks for inductive theory-building. Second, functionalism is distinguished by its departure from the canons of causality. Its explanations are never complete, and they often account for something quite different than is intended. Thus, Dore argues that functionalism is better suited to analyze a phenomenon's persistence than its cause. He concludes that these are two quite different types of events, and that all analyses must be directed to specific "events" if scientific explanation is to be advanced. Indeed, Dore goes on to stake out his preference for a reductionism (similar to George C. Homans' argument in Chapter V) that will return us to the world of the concrete and manageable event without the onerous assumptions of the systems approach. In all of this, Dore is plainly one who faults the functionalists for seeking to explain too much. He faults sociologists for failing to develop the division of labor that is necessary to the enterprise. Biologists have long been profitably divided into those studying physiology and those studying evolution. Sociologists would do well to follow the example and adopt a similar division. Not only is there a difference between functionalism and its viable alternatives, but these differences should be stressed rather than ignored.

The remainder of the chapter departs from sociology but not from functionalism. The last three authors include two philosophers of science and a political scientist, all concerned with function, purpose, and teleology. First, Dorothy Emmet comes to a conclusion that is especially surprising in view of her approach towards it. Functionalism has long been tied to the biological concept of organismic systems; Emmet argues that there are wide differences between societies and organisms but uses this insight as a source of support for functionalism itself. Thus, biological organisms do not have purposes or motivations in the literal sense but individuals and social institutions may have such "conscious teleologies." Note that teleology has no necessary negative connotations for Emmet. She argues that such was not part of its original usage and, indeed, that teleology is scientifically acceptable. Not only do social actors and groups have such teleologies but they could scarcely survive without them. They are perfectly proper as elements of explanation for societal phenomena. Although one must be careful to distinguish the conscious purpose from the unconscious function and to note the importance of feedback in causal interaction, motivation need not be thrown out of court or out of the scientific arsenal.

Abraham Kaplan concurs in a similarly brief selection. While he cautions against either a "conspiratorial" or a "utilitarian" view of society, he asserts that there is nothing "intrinsically unscientific" about purposive explanation where there is evidence that the behavior is indeed intended. Moreover, functionalism need not be seen as a theory in the strict sense; it may be viewed as an approach to analysis without any stipulation of the analytical conclusions. Kaplan argues that the distinction between purposive explanations and causal explanations is unwarranted and "pre-Darwinian." Like

Emmet, he holds that purpose is part of nature and can be part of good causal explanation as well.

Finally, Ernst B. Haas provides a particularly ironic conclusion in using the concept of purposive behavior to guard against the more damaging aspects of functionalism such as a faith in progress, an automatically adjusted equilibrium, and the inexorability of system imperatives. Haas draws heavily upon Dorothy Emmet's insights and draws comfort from her willingness to view man as a learning, reacting, and motivated unit of analysis. To regard him otherwise would be to commit the basic flaw of a functionalism so abstract as to lose sight of man himself. Note, however, that there is a second important facet of Haas's analysis. Titled, "Functionalism and International Systems" and drawn from his book, *Beyond the Nation State*, the article is a rare example of analysis that transcends the conventional boundaries of the single society to grapple with the problem of multi-societal systems. Here is a political scientist who applies his own brand of functionalism at an undeniably important level. Haas is not alone in the venture, but his example of system building at a super-national level should raise questions to challenge both conventional functionalists and their critics.

Kingsley Davis

The Myth of Functional Analysis as a Special Method in Sociology and Anthropology

*F*OR more than thirty years now "functional analysis" has been debated among sociologists and anthropologists. Perhaps the time has come for the debate to be either settled or abandoned. My view is that it should be abandoned, because it rests on the false assumption that there is a special method or body of theory called functional analysis which can be distinguished from other methods or theories *within* sociology and social anthropology. It is not that the work done under the functional label is poor or unscientific (quite the contrary), but rather that the label itself signalizes and fosters the myth of a homogeneous mode of analysis distinct from other sociological modes of analysis. Not only is this assumption false, in my view, but it is increasingly a source of confusion. However strategic it may have been in the past, it has now become an impediment rather than a prop to scientific progress.

In seeing the rationale of this thesis, one should first realize that con-

Presidential address read at the annual meeting of the American Sociological Association, Chicago, September, 1959. Reprinted from Kingsley Davis, "The Myth of Functional Analysis as a Special Method in Sociology and Anthropology," *American Sociological Review,* 24 (December, 1959), pp 757–772, by permission of the author and the American Sociological Association.

sensus on the definition of structural-functional analysis does not exist, but that examination of the features most commonly mentioned and of the work actually done under the label shows it to be, in effect, synonymous with sociological analysis. Next, one should recognize that the issues involved in the debate over functionalism—issues with respect to problems, assumptions, methods, evidence—are the issues of sociological analysis itself. To debate them under the guise of evaluating functionalism, therefore, is to inject into the discussion a spurious obstacle to clarity and objectivity. Finally, one should undertake to see how this interpretation fits into an analysis of the history of anthropology and sociology, first with respect to the conditions under which functionalism emerged as a scholarly movement, then with respect to the subsequent circumstances that altered its role.

The Meanings of Functional Analysis

Diversity and ambiguity are easily found in conceptions of functional analysis. Characteristics that the functionalists themselves regard as either accidental faults or as totally alien to their point of view—teleology, conservatism, preoccupation with social statics, assumption of complete social integration—critics often regard as the essence of the approach. Even within each camp there are differences of definition, some as wide as those between the two sides. Among the critics we find that functionalists are described on the one hand as "primarily concerned with maintaining a stable, integrated and harmonious social equilibrium,"[1] and, on the other, as deriving " 'cultural necessities and imperatives' from physiological sources."[2] While one critic characterizes functionalism as using psychological explanations,[3] another praises it for at least not committing this error,[4] and a third berates it for neglecting motivation.[5]

The functionalists themselves exhibit scarcely more agreement. Although Firth points out that "all British social anthropology today is functionalist," and quotes Fortes to the effect that functionalism is "the generally accepted basis of theory and research in British social anthropology," he admits that

---

[1] Wayne Hield, "The Study of Change in Social Science," *British Journal of Sociology*, 5 (March, 1954), p. 1.

[2] Dorothy Gregg and Elgin Williams, "The Dismal Science of Functionalism," *American Anthropologist*, 50 (October–December, 1958), p. 597.

[3] Alexander Lesser, "Functionalism in Social Anthropology," *American Anthropologist*, 37 (July–September, 1935).

[4] Sidney Morgenbesser, "Role and Status of Anthropological Theories," *Science*, 128 (August 8, 1958), p. 285.

[5] Harry C. Bredemeier, "The Methodology of Functionalism," *American Sociological Review*, 20 (April, 1935), pp. 173–179.

the off-hand definitions and the actual practice in contemporary anthropology reveal anything but agreement or clarity as to the nature of functional analysis. There is "Redfield's description of 'the functional model' as one in which a culture or society is seen as an organization of means designed to achieve ends, . . .;" or the view that functionalism is properly the study of the "conjunction of cultural behaviors." [6] Radcliffe-Brown's distaste for Malinowski's functionalism is well known, and is hardly stronger than that of non-functionalist Kroeber.[7]

One's first impulse, when faced with this diversity, is to try to redefine structural-functional analysis clearly and consistently. But so many have tried this— notably Merton, Levy, Radcliffe-Brown—without visibly improving general usage, that one is forced to view the diversity itself as an essential rather than an accidental feature of the situation, and thus as requiring explanation. If we avoid the assumption that functionalism refers to a consistent and recognizable approach *within* sociology, and instead entertain the hypothesis that, as most commonly defined, it is as broad as sociological analysis itself, we can understand both the extent and the limits of disagreement. We can see that the lack of agreement on functionalism reflects the lack of agreement on the issues of sociological analysis, and that the features of functionalism most commonly cited are the essentials of sociological interpretation itself.

Turning from the sheer variety of conceptions to the traits most frequently cited as characterizing functional anlysis, we find that functionalism is most commonly said to *do* two things: to relate the parts of society to the whole, and to relate one part to another. Almost as common is the specification of *how* it does this relating—namely, by seeing one part as "performing a function for" or "meeting a need or requirement of" the whole society or some part of it. It strikes me that the first two traits simple describe what *any* science does. Every science describes and explains phenomena from the standpoint of a *system* of reasoning which presumably bears a relation to a corresponding *system* in nature. In the case of sociology, what is distinctive is the subject, not the method; for it deals with human societies whereas other disciplines deal with other kinds of systems. Given its subject, the

---

[6] Raymond Firth, "Function" in *Current Anthropology*, Chicago: University of Chicago Press, 1955, pp. 247–251. He gives further quotations and references showing diversity of definitions, including Fortes' claim "that the chief innovation for which the functionalist movement stands was a contribution of the Cambridge School of anthropology—the principle of the intensive study of limited areas."

[7] A. R. Radcliffe-Brown: "As for myself, I reject it entirely, regarding it as useless and worse." "Functionalism: A Protest," *American Anthropologist*, 51 (April–June, 1949), p. 321. A. L. Kroeber: "I have long considered Malinowski's whole scheme of need-derivation a verbal wish-fulfilment. . . ." "An Authoritarian Panacea," *ibid.*, p. 318.

least it could do is to relate the parts to the whole of society and to one another.

A better case for the distinctiveness of functionalism can be made on the basis of the "requirement-meeting" mode of reasoning. The distinctiveness seems to dissolve, however, when semantic problems are recognized. For this purpose Merton's characterization offers a point of departure. He describes "the central orientation of functionalism" as "the practice of interpreting data by establishing their consequences for larger structures in which they are implicated."[8] If "interpreting" here means "explanation," the sense of the statement can hardly be that in functionalism data are explained *solely* in terms of their consequences; for nothing is explained that way. Evidently the statement means that *among* the considerations used in interpretation are the consequences for larger structures. In this case, however, we have added nothing to the two characterizations discussed in the preceding paragraph. How else can data be interpreted except in relation to the larger structures *in which they are implicated?* How can data on the earth's orbit, for example, be understood except in relation to a system in which they are involved—in this case, the solar system or the earth's climatic system? Since in science some kind of system is usually being dealt with, an analysis of the effect of one factor must always be made with the possibility in mind of a possible return effect ("feedback") on that factor itself. If, for example, the increase of fish (y) in a pond has the effect of increasing the toxicity (x) of the water, the growth of the fish population (y again) will eventually cease unless other factors intervene. This is not explaining things solely by their consequences, but rather by the way their consequences react upon them.[9]

Misunderstanding in this matter seems to arise from two sources: first from the language used in describing the relationships, second from the special problems of applying systematic analysis to human societies. As to language, if the investigator uses phrases like "has the function of," "meets the need of," or simply "is for," the words have so many connotations and ambiguities that the effect is often to obstruct rather than to facilitate the conveyance of meaning. Part of the reason is that these are words borrowed from common discourse and hence mainly used to indicate moral impera- tives and volitional intent rather than sheer causal relationships. Actually, when such terms are used in natural science there is not much debate as to what is meant. An agronomist, for instance, theorizing that certain types of fruit trees die when particular trace elements are missing from the soil, may

---

[8] Robert K. Merton, *Social Theory and Social Structure*, Glencoe, Ill.: Free Press, 1957, p. 19.

[9] Cf. Bredemeier, *op. cit.*

say that the trace elements "contribute to" or "have the function of" keeping fruit trees alive. He may say this without being accused of teleology, conservatism, or worse;[10] but the same phrases used in sociological or anthropological discourse are often either actually intended this way or are so interpreted. The reason relates to the second source of difficulty—the fact that human society is being dealt with. Terms connoting moral obligation or censure, or indicating explanation by intent, are particularly unsuited for the description of causal relationships because the meanings they stand for are properly part of the *object* rather than the *basis* of explanation. It is of course extraordinarily difficult to escape from such words, not only because nearly all language is infused with them, but because they contain conceptions and values that the observer himself has as a member of society.

It thus appears that the most nearly agreed-upon traits of functionalism are those broadly characterizing scientific analysis in general. Any distinction is due, not to method *per se,* but to linguistic usage and the particular subject (society). Granted the linguistic matter is superficial,[11] we find nothing to upset the view that it is another name for sociological analysis—the interpretation of phenomena in terms of their interconnections with societies as going concerns.

What is Non-Functionalism?

The same conclusion emerges from examining that neglected concept, "non-functional analysis." Although seldom defined explicitly, this residual category seems, by implication, to include traits falling into one or the other of two classes: either they constitute some sort of reductionism and are therefore non-sociological in character, or they constitute some form of raw

---

10 For an excellent account of questionable language in textbooks of natural and physical science, see A. J. Bernatowicz, "Teleology in Science Teaching," *Science,* 128 (December 5, 1958), pp. 1402–1405. The author finds the infinitive verb is a common linguistic gateway to teleological and anthropomorphic phraseology. The *to* in these cases "is merely an abbreviation of *in order to.*" Thus atoms "strive to attain the stable arrangement of electrons . . . ," "the ultimate goal of stream erosion is to reduce the land surface to a nearly flat plain. . . ." Other key words of similar effect are "for," "has to," "must." Such language is justified as being useful in avoiding awkward circumlocutions and making for livelier reading, though Bernatowicz disagrees.

11 Sometimes commentators come perilously near to saying that functional analysis is analysis that employs the word *function.* " 'The function of religion is to relieve anxiety in a group.' This asserts nothing not asserted by 'Anxiety in a group is relieved if (or perhaps, only if) it practices religion,' or by 'A (sufficient, necessary, or sufficient and necessary) condition for relief of anxiety in a group is the practice of religion.' These latter statements are clearly nonfunctional." Walter Buckley (paraphrasing Nagel), "Structural-Functional Analysis in Modern Sociology," in Howard Becker and Alvin Boskoff, editors, *Modern Sociological Theory,* New York: Dryden, 1957, p. 247.

empiricism or sheer data manipulation and are therefore non-theoretical. In other words, whatever falls outside the domain of sociological theory falls outside the realm of functionalism.

Reductionist Theories as Non-Functional.—If the word "psychological" is construed as referring to analysis in terms of the individual as a system, especially with the implication that this system is determinative of *social* phenomena, there is general agreement that, although it may be functional psychology, it is not functional anthropology or sociology.[12] Durkheim phrased the point characteristically: "The determining cause of a social fact should be sought among the social facts preceding it and not among the states of the individual consciousness."[13] Functionalists have typically rejected explanations of social phenomena which depended on some alleged trait of the human mind rather than on the operation of a social system. Following Durkheim, for instance, they rejected the evolutionists' individualistic theory of religion as failing to account for the cultural standardization and normative obligatoriness of religious belief and behavior.[14]

If psychologistic solutions are barred from structural-functional analysis, then biologistic solutions are *a fortiori* barred. One form of biologism—explanation of social phenomena in terms of genetic inheritance—is generally considered to be at the opposite pole from functionalism.[15] Another

[12] The occasional charge that functionalism is psychological evidently arises from an ambiguity. Insofar as the word "psychological" refers simply to *mental* phenomena, such as thoughts, sentiments, and attitudes, sociology and social anthropology can hardly escape dealing with psychological phenomena. "Psychological" in the sense of treating the person as a system is a different thing. It is interesting that the science of treating the personality, or the psyche, as a system is often called "functional psychology." For this reason a disorder of the individual for which no organic cause can be found, and which is thus presumably explicable in terms of the personality system, is commonly designated a "functional disorder."

[13] Emile Durkheim, *Rules of Sociological Method*, Glencoe, Ill.: Free Press, 1950, pp. 110–111.

[14] See W. J. Goode, *Religion among the Primitives*, Glencoe, Ill.: Free Press, 1951, pp. 243–244; Kingsley Davis, *Human Society*, New York: Macmillan, 1949, p. 518; J. Milton Yinger, *Religion, Society and the Individual*, New York: Macmillan, 1957, Chapter 3. Psychoanalytic theories of religion and the family were criticized for similar reasons—Goode, *op. cit.*, pp. 247–249, and E. E. Evans-Pritchard, *Social Anthropology*, Glencoe, Ill.: Free Press, 1954, pp. 44–45. As early as 1927 B. Malinowski complained that Ernest Jones "regards the [Oedipus] complex as the *cause*, and the whole sociological structure as the *effect*." *Sex and Repression in Savage Society*, London: Paul, Trench, Trubner, 1927, pp. 139–140.

[15] Obviously, the biological character of the human species is relevant to the question of the *limits* of variation in human society—see Marion J. Levy, Jr., *The Structure of Society*, Princeton: Princeton University Press, 1952, pp. 16–17—but recognition of this fact by functionalists has not committed them to genetic interpretation of social variation itself. Admittedly the theoretical status of Malinowski's "needs" is open to dispute; although often accused of biologism (see cited articles by Gregg and Williams and by Radcliffe-Brown), his writings contain firm statements indicating that in his mind biological needs are necessary but not sufficient causes.

form—the analysis of society by treating it literally as if it were a biological organism—has sometimes been regarded as one of the precursors of functionalism, but if the only legacy is seeing society as "composed of differentiated, interrelated structures reacting on one another and constituting an integral whole on a *psycho-social*, rather than a biological, level,"[16] nothing biological is left. A third kind of biologism, social Darwinism, more an epithet for a bad ideology than a name for a scientific outlook, has seldom been charged to functionalists.[17] It is identified with Spencer and the evolutionism against which functionalists were in rebellion, and with a rugged individualism hardly compatible with an emphasis on "the functional integration of society." In fact, the critics of functionalism have accused it of paying *too little* attention to conflict and the struggle for power[18]—elements that the evolutionists and social Darwinists stressed.

The type of reductionism represented by technological or economic determinism is equally differentiated from functionalism. Although Marx, for instance, was occasionally called a functionalist,[19] his followers in sociology and anthropology quarrel with colleagues who wear this label. The reason usually given is their aversion to the functionalist concern with integration rather than conflict, but a more basic reason is the reductionism implicit in "materialism." Any view that sees all change in society as the consequence of technological or economic change offends functionalists because it reduces other aspects of society to epiphenomena and treats nonrational behavior as simply ignorance and error.

Similarly, the functionalist rebellion against trait-distributionism, signalized by Lowie's charge that Malinowski "flouts distribution studies,"[20] is understandable as a reaction of those interested in societies against those interested in culture traits. From the former standpoint the only significant aspect of a trait is its relation to the social system, and for many traits this

---

16 Buckley, *op. cit.*, pp. 239–240.

17 Richard Hofstadter's *Social Darwinism in American Thought*, revised edition, Boston: Beacon Press, 1955, contains no reference to "functionalism" or to Robertson Smith, Durkheim, Malinowski, Radcliffe-Brown. In fact, Hofstadter thinks that social Darwinism was dead by the end of World War I, which is just about the time functionalism began to emerge as a name for a self-conscious school of thought in anthropology.

18 See Ralf Dahrendorf, "Out of Utopia: Toward A Reorientation of Sociological Analysis," *American Journal of Sociology*, 64 (September, 1958); Hield, *op. cit.;* David Lockwood, "Some Remarks on 'The Social System,'" *British Journal of Sociology, 7* (June, 1956), pp. 134–146. Bredemeier, *op. cit.*, p. 175, is one of the few critics to note that the functionalists' concern with factors governing the survival of societal elements gives them a basis of linkage with biological theory.

19 Horace Kallen, "Functionalism," *Encyclopedia of the Social Sciences*, New York: Macmillan, 1931, Vol. 6, pp. 523–526.

20 Robert H. Lowie, *History of Ethnological Theory*, New York: Rinehart, 1937, pp. 234–235.

aspect is trivial. In cultural anthropology, on the other hand, the existence, form, and provenience of traits are important *per se,* whether significant for the operation of society or not.

Empiricism and Data as Non-Functional.—So far we have found that, among theories, those that explain social phenomena in terms derived from some other level tend to be classed as non-functional. Now let us recall that if a part of social science consists of theories, there must be another part that consists of observations. It appears that this part of sociology and anthropology, the sheer description and reporting of statistical relationships, is regarded as wholly outside of structural-functional analysis.

The clearest exclusion from functionalism, for instance, is the "historical approach." Insofar as this approach implies an antagonism to theoretical generalization and a preference for straight description of the past, it is opposed to the functionalists' predilection for explaining phenomena by appeal to abstract principles.[21] Of course, the attempt merely to state facts is not confined to historicism but appears in contemporary fieldwork of both the ethnographic and survey type. Such an attempt, either as methodological doctrine or as research performance, is regarded as outside of functionalism. The same is true of the empiricist doctrine that science is "nothing but" the establishment of statistical probabilities. Functional analysis is felt to involve interpretation, not simply data or data-manipulation.

Critical Issues in "Functional Analysis"

If the most frequent conceptions of functionalism make it, in effect, inclusive of sociological analysis but exclusive of reductionism and sheer description, then the scientific problems of functional analysis are the same as those of sociology in general. That this is true is suggested by the kind of questions most commonly identified with functionalism—for example: What features of social organization or behavior appear in all or nearly all societies? Why are these features so nearly universal while others are more variable? What particular features characterize each type of society, and how do they mesh together in the operation of that type? How in a concrete community are the parts of the social structure mutually congruent or incongruent, as exhibited in attitudes, roles, and conduct? Such "functional questions," when taken together, evoke a comparative science of society, because they are the most general that can be asked. The attempt to find systematic answers to them forms a framework of reasoning that can

---

[21] Evans-Pritchard characterizes functionalism as holding that "even with the best sources at his disposal, the historian can only tell us what has been the succession of accidental events by which society has become what it is." *Op. cit.,* p. 47.

enlighten any specific enquiry, no matter how limited. Such questions, then, are not peripheral to sociological analysis, but central.

It is therefore puzzling that a distinction should be assumed between sociological and functional analysis, and that once distinguished, the latter should be considered more controversial—as witness the numerous articles and chapters dealing with "functional analysis," the most famous of which opens with this statement: "Functional analysis is at once the most promising and possibly the least codified of contemporary orientations to problems of sociological interpretations."[22] Naturally, I am not interested solely in questioning the accuracy of this notion but also in trying to explain its prevalence. I think that an explanation, though hard, is possible if one bears in mind the difficulties inherent in studying society—difficulties arising mainly, if not exclusively, from the circumstance that the observer must analyze objectively the norms of conduct that he and others, as actors, react to emotionally. In pursuing this line of explanation, one can begin by examining some of the major criticisms of functionalism. These, as already indicated, are critical issues in sociological theory (a point well worth demonstrating further), but the fact that they are debated with reference to functional analysis, assumed to be a special method, is of prime significance for our argument. Let us start with the question of evidence.

Evidence and Functional Analysis—Critics note that functionalism "abounds in principles and categories" but offers little by way of verification. Relationships are established "intuitively by the structure of the observer's language, or are assumed to be in nature."[23] Since this is true of functionalist ethnography as well as comparative functionalist theory, there is no value in denial. There is value, however, in asking why the charge is true. In large part it is because functionalism is preëminently social theory. The broader and more general a theory, the less is the chance of proving or disproving it in its entirety.[24] *Social* theory, in particular, tends

---

[22] Merton, "Manifest and Latent Functions," *loc. cit.*, p. 19. Lowie, in his *History of Ethnological Theory, op. cit.*, has a chapter on the French "sociological school" including Radcliffe-Brown, followed by a chapter on "functionalism" including Malinowski. Actually, the terms "sociological" and "functional" are often used interchangeably. Most of Chapter 3 in Yinger, *op. cit.*, entitled "A Sociological Theory of Religion," is devoted to the "functional approach," which is taken for granted as the distinctively sociological approach. Radcliffe-Brown usually avoids the term "functional analysis" in favor of "comparative sociology" or simply "sociological" inquiry or theory. Malinowski was in the habit of calling his approach indifferently either sociological or functional.

[23] Buckley, *op. cit.*, p. 258, speaking particularly of Parsonian functionalism. Merton's essay, *loc. cit.*, voices similar criticism of functionalism generally.

[24] A body of theory includes a conceptual framework which, not being in the form of evidential propositions, is not subject to verification. Furthermore, disproof of specific propositions logically related to parts of the theory need not kill the system, because the latter can be modified without necessarily changing its essentials. The

to be broad and complex, because the observer, reared in a society himself, comes equipped with knowledge and opinion about social matters, including abstractions of great generality. He also intuitively understands behavior by imagining himself in the circumstances of the actor, and he constantly deals with ideological controversies woven into learned discourse. Thus the conceptual and linguistic apparatus constituting social theory becomes extremely subtle and highly ramified. By comparison, social research seems puny indeed. One reason is that much of the theory is too ambiguous to be researchable; also, public attitudes severely restrict the possible kinds of social research; and, above all, research on the non-instrumental aspects of society—on norms, values, religion, and so on—has little utility precisely because, unlike research in medicine or business, it concerns goals rather than means. Functional analysis is thus vulnerable to the charge of unverified theorizing because it has the character *par excellence* that social theory in general has.

But beyond this there is the fact that functionalism adopts a kind of language that is peculiarly close to the purposive and moralistic reasoning of ordinary discourse, yet tries to use it in the opposite way, that is, for the disinterested analysis of exactly this type of reasoning and its related behavior. Such words as "function," "dysfunction," "latent," "needs" are treacherous for the same reason that they are handy. Connected with ideas much older than sociology or anthropology, they are susceptible of easy expansion by knitting together ready-made intuitions, connotations, and ambiguities. But for this reason they are strikingly inappropriate for doing the opposite of moralistic reasoning—that is, for explaining in a detached manner the moral and religious ideas and behavior of mankind. It is this paradox that lies behind many charges against functionalism. Lack of evidence, being a good scientific objection, sometimes masks the other considerations.

Evidence is especially scarce insofar as functionalism attempts to state the requisites for the existence of any society or to explain the universals of social organization. In such matters there can be no proof by co-variation, because, by definition, all actual societies exhibit the traits in question. Nor can functionalists create experimental societies to test the effect of omitting this or that ingredient. The analysis must therefore be heavily deductive,[25]

---

broader and looser a theoretical system, the more prolific it is of propositions and the less embarrassed by their disproof. Fantastic schemes of reasoning have lasted for decades and finally died of disinterest rather than disproof. On verification and theoretical systems, see Ernest Nagel, *Logic Without Metaphysics*, Glencoe, Ill.: Free Press, 1956, Chapter 7.

25 "If we start with a social-system theory, defining and relating all the necessary concepts involved, . . . then the functional requisites, or conditions necessary for

the language of which is easily borrowed from ordinary discourse. Anybody can see, for example, that the virtually universal occurrence of incest taboos is due to their being "essential for" the nuclear family; people habitually justify basic norms in terms of their social value. The disinterestedness of functional analysis is hardly clearer when *disapproved* institutions like prostitution, social inequality, or political corruption are being explained, for this seems like either cynicism or satire. The best chance for real evidence is provided by "experimental" communities set up by political or religious sects or brought about by accidental conditions, by exceptional cases occurring in particular segments or classes of some societies, and by the inevitable normal variation in the concrete manifestation of any general rule. But unless the language of functionalism is remedied (which means eliminating the notion of "functionalism"), there seems no way for the analyst to escape having his deductions deliberately or unwittingly confused with moralizing.

The Three Postulates of Functionalism.—In criticizing the postulation of functional unity, universal functionalism, and functional indispensability, Merton seems to charge both that these abstractions are reified in functional analysis and that they lack heuristic value in any case. Whether they are actually reified depends on how one reads the evidence.[26] Our interest lies, however, in the other question, the heuristic value of the abstractions.

This question turns on what the postulates mean. As for the first two, Merton speaks of "*complete* functional unity" and of "*universal* functionalism." Certainly it would be silly to regard such propositions as literally true, and perhaps pointless to use them as abstractions. But if the intended meaning is simply that *some* order in societies is assumed and that every social form *should* be examined from the standpoint of its possible role in societal continuity (thus assuming *heuristically* that each item plays such a role), the analytic value seems plain. What else could a sociologist do? If one sets out to study societies, one presumably sets out to study something that exists. If societies exist, there must be some sense in which each one more or less

---

the persistence of such a system are, ideally, implied by the system as delineated." Buckley, *op. cit.,* p. 256.

[26] Since no functionalist has given his theory a rigorous axiomatic treatment, conclusive evidence as to whether the three abstractions are reified or even postulated cannot be produced. Merton naturally relies on quotations. Most of these are from Malinowski, whose statements are varied and careless enough to afford evidence of numerous errors. In the case of Radcliffe-Brown, a quoted statement assuming only a "degree of harmony or consistency" seems to be the evidence for Merton's implication in the next two pages that he assumes "complete functional unity." Similarly, Clyde Kluckhohn is cited (Merton, *op. cit.,* pp. 30–31) as "postulating functional value for all surviving forms of culture," but no reference is made to passages in the same book (*Navajo Witchcraft,* Cambridge, Mass.: The Museum, 1944, p. 68) where Kluckhohn discusses the "costs" and the "disruptive effects" of witchcraft.

hangs together, and the question of how this is accomplished and not accomplished is a central one.

The third postulate is, in Merton's view, a dual one: first, that certain *functions* are indispensable for the persistence of a society or group; second, "that *certain cultural or social forms are indispensable* in fulfilling each of these functions."[27] He seemingly has no objection to the first version—evidently on the ground that functions are fewer than social forms and that therefore the assumption that some of them are indispensable is a high-level abstraction serving to evoke a theory of the basis of human societies. The second version seems more specific, thus more open to empirical test, and hence more dangerous if assumed to be true concretely. Yet if a social form is actually found in all known societies, it would seem harmless to *entertain* the hypothesis that it is indispensable.[28] Such a hypothesis is not a postulate on which a system is built; it is rather a prediction *resulting* from theory and fact—a prediction that no society will be found which lacks the trait. The important thing is not the prediction but the sociological reasoning on which it is based. Equally of value is the opposite assumption, that there may be as yet undiscovered alternative structures that can perform the same function as the trait in question—provided, of couse, that this abstraction is not reified either.[29]

If Merton is correct in calling attention to the absurdity of reifying the three assumptions but not in impugning their heuristic value, the readiness of the critics of functionalism to accept and repeat the entire charge seems an over-reaction. A clue to the reason appears in the selectivity of the charge. If somebody states that a society must have economic support or biological reproduction, the proposition is taken as a harmless truism made for the purpose of facilitating a process of reasoning. If, on the other hand, it is said that normative control, attitudinal consensus, or social inequality is required, one is likely to be accused, among other things, of making an unwarranted assumption. Not only are things like consensus and inequality less tangible than economic support or reproduction, they are more closely related to ideological controversies.

The postulates are identified with functionalism, and yet Merton says

---

[27] *Op. cit.*, p. 33 (italics in original).

[28] If societies were found which *lacked* the trait, there would be no point in assuming the trait to be indispensable.

[29] In recommending the idea of functional equivalents, Merton does not call it a postulate, but simply a *concept. Op. cit.*, pp. 34, 36. Could the ideas of functional unity and functional indispensability also be called *concepts?* For interesting brief statements of the principles of functional equivalents, multi-functionality of structures, and limited possibilities, see B. Malinowski's article, "Culture," *Encyclopedia of the Social Science,* Vol. 4, pp. 621–646.

they are "unnecessary to the functional orientation."[30] The same has been said of sociology, for the latter has been perennially accused of hypostatizing something called society, of treating social solidarity as if it were the only reality or the only explanatory principle. In the case of functionalism, the idea seems to be that if the postulates can be eliminated, this orientation will be purged of some of its impurities. As I see it, the opposite course is advisable—to eliminate the notion of functionalism as a distinct method along with the confusing terminology that goes with the name, and to keep the basic heuristic assumptions that form part of a system of sociological reasoning.

A system of reasoning cannot be developed without assumptions. As long as these are not reified, it makes little difference where one starts. If one begins by asking why conflict and strife are so rife among human beings, one eventually gets around to asking why there is not even more strife than there is and hence to the problem of social control and integration. If one starts by asking how a modicum of harmony is achieved, one is soon forced to discuss conflict. Viewed in this light, there is no reason to eliminate the basic thinking represented by the three postulates discussed, but there is reason to phrase them differently and in terms less open to logical confusion and ideological attack. Also there is a need to add other assumptions.

Latent, Manifest, and Functional.—The distinction between latent and manifest functions might be described as the fourth postulate of functionalism. However, although identified with functionalism by virtue of Merton's brilliant exposition, the idea of the distinction, phrased in various ways, has long been central in sociology. It was stated in 1895 by Durkheim, who spoke of "function" versus "purpose."[31] It was developed with extreme thoroughness in Pareto's discussion, in 1916, of individual utility and utility to, of, and for the community.[32] Accordingly, the distinction in no way depends upon a special functional method or requires the use of the term "function"; yet the fact that it plays a crucial role in both sociological theory and what is called functionalism deserves careful attention.

It seems to me that the scientific issue involved is the explanatory role of subjective elements (goals, norms, knowledge) and of rational and non-rational behavior. Talcott Parsons' classic typology of theoretical positions

---

30 *Op. cit.*, p. 25.

31 "We use the word 'function,' in preference to 'end' or 'purpose,' . . . Whether there is a correspondence between the fact under consideration and the general needs of the social organism [is independent of] whether it has been intentional or not." *Rules of Sociological Method*, p. 95.

32 V. Pareto, *Mind and Society*, New York: Harcourt, Brace, 1935, Vol. 1, Chapter 2; Vol. 4, Chapter 12.

in social science rests on different ways of handling this issue.[33] For the economist, the problems are not great: he can get along analytically by taking goals as given and assuming rational behavior modified simply by ignorance and error. For the sociologist, however, the goals and sentiments and non-rational behavior are among the phenomena to be explained. He is therefore required to distinguish carefully between what the actor has in mind and what the social causes and consequences of his action may be, to keep separate always the point of view of the actor and the point of view of the observer. To the extent that he fails to do so, to the extent that he cherishes certain goals or puts his analysis in terms of them and thus adopts the role of an actor, he loses the sociological level of analysis.

Undeniably, the observer role with respect to social institutions is hard to maintain. The investigator, in trying to comprehend the subjective views of his subjects, tends to make the honest mistake of taking these views as an ultimate basis of explanation. Sometimes, in addition, social science is made to validate democracy, tolerance, peace, and other values. The functionalist movement, as I see it, represents an effort to explain social organization and behavior from a disinterested observer's point of view. This is why the manifest-latent distinction is important. Ironically, however, the movement has fallen victim to what it sought to overcome. The inability to see purposes and sentiments as objects of explanation, the unwillingness to remain detached—these have joined the inherent discomfort of analysis from a societal rather than a psychological standpoint and have riddled the weak terminology of functionalism with criticism and confusion.

Teleology and Ideology.—Teleology is one fallacy that functionalists try hard to avoid, but when they are charged with it, their language and their own and others' ambiguities make defense difficult. If we accept the dictionary definition of teleology as "the doctrine that the existence of everything in nature can be explained in terms of purpose," the distinction between manifest and latent functions is clearly contrary to it. The functional theory of incest taboos or of magical practices does not hold that these exist because their social consequences (functions) are *perceived*. On the contrary, the purposes the actors have in mind are treated as not necessarily including the consequences but as being part of the mechanisms by which the societal functions are accomplished. This refusal to take purposes at their face value as the basis of explanation often appears incomprehensible or reprehensible. One critic, for example, feels that the only way the consequences of an action can serve to explain its persistence is by the actor's *perceiving* the possible consequences and guiding his behavior accordingly.[34] To visualize the un-

---

[33] *Structure of Social Action,* New York: McGraw-Hill, 1937, Chapter 2–3.
[34] Bredemeier, *op. cit.,* pp. 173, 175. This is the utilitarian position.

recognized social consequences of an action as leading, by their unrecognized effect on the conditions, to the continuous reinforcement or minimization of that action in the society, is too much against the grain of ordinary discourse.

Those interested in social protest or reform necessarily depend upon purposes as the basis of explanation, for they must assign praise and blame. The feature of functionalism they find most objectionable is its refusal to rest with the imputation of motives. To explain anti-semitism for example, as due to the bad motives of either gentiles or Jews is to explain it in terms palatable to either the pro- or the anti-semite, whereas to explain it in "structural-functional" terms satisfies neither. Indeed, the actionist feels threatened by a system that subjects *his* motives to impersonal scrutiny. He defends himself by charging functionalism with various sins, one of which, ironically, is teleology. He sustains the charge by pointing out that *function* often means purpose or "final cause"; that words like *needs* and *requirements* are subjective; that *functional* or *disfunctional* can often be translated "approved" or "disapproved."

Similarly, the view of functionalism as disguised ideology is most often advanced by those who are themselves ideologically oriented—as shown by the selectivity of the evidence adduced and by the purport of the theories proposed as substitutes.[35] Strictly speaking, a theory's support of a moral or political bias is independent of its scientific validity. We thus have no concern with the issue except as illustrating further that functional analysis is attacked for being sociological analysis, under the guise that it is something else. Merton, noting that functional analysis has been accused of radicalism as well as conservatism, shrewdly takes this as *prima facie* evidence that it is intrinsically neither one.[36] What interests us, however, is that in making this point he unconsciously denies the premise that functionalism is a special kind of sociology. "Like other forms of sociological analysis," he says, functionalism "can be infused with any one of a wide range of ideological

---

[35] Gregg and Williams, *op. cit.*, condemn functionalism for not making a clear-cut distinction between good and bad. They say: "the cultural dichotomy which functionalism needs would at the outset distinguish *good* from *bad* goals, stultifying from liberating institutions, efficient from inefficient customs." (p. 608) See A. L. Kroeber's interesting comment on the article, "An Authoritarian Panacea," *op. cit.*, pp. 318–320.

[36] *Op. cit.*, pp. 38–46. A thoughtful analysis of why the functional theory of religion is radical is W. L. Kolb's "Values, Positivism, and the Functional Theory of Religion," *Social Forces*, 31 (May, 1953), pp. 305–311. "To spread the idea that a belief in ultimate validity of values is necessary but illusory," says Kolb, "would be to destroy society through destroying or confusing this belief." In another vein is the attack on the present writer's "functional" theory of religion by Gordon George, S.J., in "Some Sociologists Out of Bounds," *America*, 93 (January 15, 1955), pp. 397–398. "In the name of science," says George, "he [Davis] has unscientifically reduced religion to a mere device for bolstering social order." Similarly, Thomas F. O'Dea, "The Sociology of Religion," *American Catholic Sociological Review*, 15 (June, 1954), pp. 73–103.

values." The only other form of sociology he mentions is Marxism, but, curiously, he finds that the Marxist theory of religion is no different from the functional theory in method or structure of analysis.

> . . . . the functionalists, with their emphasis on religion as a *social mechanism* . . . , may not differ materially in their *analytical framework* from the Marxists who, if their metaphor of 'opium of the masses' is converted into a neutral statement of social fact, also assert that religion operates as a social mechanism. . . . The point of difference appears only when *evaluations* of this commonly accepted fact come into question.[37]

If Marxist sociology does not differ methodologically from functional analysis, it seems doubtful that *any* kind of sociology does.

Can Functionalism Handle Social Change?—The claim that functionalism cannot handle social change because it posits an integrated static society, is true by definition if "posits" means "to take literally." Here again, as with the other issues, the question for us is not who is right, but why the controversy? It seems strange indeed that the criticism should be voiced so often when in fact some of the best analyses of social change have come from people labeled as functionalists.[58] It seems even stranger when, in looking over these works, we find they do not differ in any basic way from many studies of social change by persons opposing functionalism or at least not wearing the functionalist label.[39] Perhaps the idea of incompetence in this regard is a deduction from the fact that functionalism began as a revolt against historicism. As we shall see, however, the revolt was not against the study of change itself but against the omission of sociological analysis from such study. If it is true that functionalists have devoted less attention to social change than to statics, the same can be said of sociology and of social anthropology in general in recent decades. It happens that theories of social change, for understandable reasons, are ideologically significant. Possibly the charge of incompetence in this field represents, in part at least, still another use of functionalism as a means of criticizing sociological analysis.

---

[37] *Op. cit.*, p. 44 (italics in original).

[38] A few examples: Marion J. Levy's analyses of institutional factors in Chinese and Japanese economic development; Merton's studies of the rise of science; Wilbert E. Moore's work on labor and industrialization; Bellah's study of religion and change in Japan; Bryce Ryan's historical chapters on caste in Ceylon; Geoffrey and Monica Wilson's theory of change in central Africa; Schapera's studies of native transition in South Africa.

[39] I see no basic difference of method or theory between the analysis of ideology and industrialization by Reinhard Bendix, who opposes functionalism, and the analysis of Puritanism and science by Merton or the study of the family and industrialization by Levy. Nor would I know whether to classify the work on social change by Ralph Linton, E. H. Spicer, Robert Redfield, Margaret Mead, Ralph Beals, Howard Becker, Fred Cottrell, Charles Loomis, and Philip Selznick as "functionalist" or not.

The Illusion of a Functional Method

The substantive issues so far discussed all point to the conclusion that, if there is a functional method, it is simply the method of sociological analysis. Now let us examine more directly the persistent idea that it constitutes a more special method.

Functionalism and Exact Laws.—Evans-Pritchard, following Radcliffe-Brown, says that functionalism rests on two propositions, one of which is "that social life can be reduced to scientific laws which allow prediction." [40] It is therefore startling to find another functionalist, Talcott Parsons, stating the opposite. We cannot yet "develop a complete dynamic theory" of action, he says, and "therefore, the systematization of theory in the present state of knowledge must be in 'structural-functional' terms." The latter is primitive, the highest state of theory being one "permitting deductive transitions to be made from one aspect or state of a system to another." Since this is possible only in the most fragmentary way in the sciences of action at present, "there is danger of losing all the advantages of systematic theory. But it is possible to retain some of them . . . [by] a second best type of theory," the structural-functional. [41]

These contrasting views can be reconciled if we forget functionalism and ask how we know when theory is exact. We know it when the theory is logically tight and empirically proven. Evans-Pritchard and Radcliffe-Brown are saying that a natural science of human society *can be* developed. Parsons is saying that a rather primitive state of theorizing is about *all we have now*, but he too believes that a more exact science is possible. There is actually no contradiction, but there *seems* to be one because the same term, *functional analysis*, is used with opposite meanings.

Functional versus Causal.—The occasional view that functional analysis is *not* causal analysis apparently arises from two sources: first, the image of functionalism as theory and hence as excluding raw data or pure data-manipulation; second, the Parsonian image of it as excluding exact laws too. The conclusion would not follow from the first source, except on the premise that causation is identical with evidence or statistical correlation. If, however, *causal analysis* is construed in the usual sense of discovering relationships between phenomena, there is excellent ground for stating this to be impossible in a systematic way without theory. It is the theory which provides the idea of what would be significant to test and the notion of the conditions under which a test would be conclusive.

---

[40] Evans-Pritchard, *op. cit.*, p. 49.
[41] *The Social System*, Glencoe, Ill.: Free Press, 1951, pp. 19–20.

While every experiment requires the use of principles of interpretation, the evidence for the truth of these principles comes ultimately through observation and experiment. But such further experiments once more require principles of interpretation, and this process is endless.[42]

Doubtless the feeling behind the separation of functional and causal analysis has some basis. Parsons' characterization of actual functional analysis as primitive theory is correct. Functional studies provide an intuitive grasp of how social structures fit together, of the principles somehow operative in going societies, much more than they provide logically precise or empirically proven propositions. The contribution of such work is that of bringing forth a framework, a point of view, in terms of which interpretation is possible. At the same time, as we have seen, verification is difficult. Some functionalists have seemed unwilling to discipline their language or test their propositions, taking instead the easy path of verbal tapestry. As a result, sociologists who have learned the techniques of empirical research come to feel that functionalism is a crank method, and they are encouraged in this by functionalists themselves who say they are engaged in non-causal analysis, whatever that is. But there will always be speculative sociological theory. From the standpoint of scientific discovery, the interesting part of theory is not the verified but the unverified propositions. A theory proved is no longer theory; it is fact. What is still unproved is speculation; it is, as commonly said, "theoretical." If the broadest theory in sociology is thrown out on the ground that it is "functionalism," and if what is recommended in its stead are neat single propositions whose validity is proved but whose significance is not, the result will be scientific ritualism.

Why the Myth?

Logicians habitually explain schools of thought as due to logical blunders. Thus, according to Ernest Nagel, "Functionalism in the social sciences has admittedly been inspired, and continues to be influenced, by the supposed character of functional analyses in physiology." [43] Nagel presents no evidence for this assertion, nor does he explain why the blunder happened to be committed and become popular at the particular time. The record shows that the functional lineage goes in direct line from William Robertson Smith, a philologist and Biblical and Semitic scholar, through Durkheim, a student of law and sociology, to Radcliffe-Brown and Malinowski, none of whom had any experience or interest in physiology. Radcliffe-

---

[42] Nagel, *op. cit.*, p. 152.
[43] *Op. cit.*, p. 247.

Brown drew an analogy between his mode of thinking and that of physiology, but this was merely *post hoc* rationalization of a method he had long been using and had admittedly borrowed from Durkheim.[44] Malinowski, who became identified with "functionalism" but was a late borrower of the word "function," was even less concerned with physiology.

Actually, the rise of "functionalism" can be explained sociologically, as due to the peculiar conditions found in the sociological and anthropological professions around the turn of the century. Briefly, the key fact was the absence of a sociological point of view, and the key problem (for students dimly perceiving the idea) was how to develop and establish this point of view. We have tried to state earlier the reasons why this point of view is difficult to adopt and maintain. Suffice it to realize that in the discipline called "sociology" there were, concretely, two chief obstacles—the fact that various brands of encyclopedism[45] and reductionism[46] were masquerading under the name, and the fact that ethics and social reform were woven into the analysis.[47] The situation was worse in anthropology, because that field supposedly embraced man as an organism as well as human history and all

---

[44] In *The Andaman Islanders,* Cambridge: Cambridge University Press, 1922, Radcliffe-Brown first attempted "to develop a new method in the interpretation of the institutions of a primitive people." Although the book was not published until 1922, he had written it in 1910, and he says that the new method "will not perhaps seem so novel now as it would have done then" (p. ix). In this book he shows no concern with methods in physiology, but in fact states his methodological assumptions in such a way as to make them incompatible with physiological procedures—e.g., in insisting on the importance of the "meaning" of a social custom (pp. 229–235). His article, "On the Concept of Function in Social Science," in which he spoke of "an analogy between social life and organic life," did not appear until 1935. *American Anthropologist,* 37 (July-September, 1935), pp. 395–402.

[45] Comte's concept of society included almost everything; Spencer's notion of sociology was that in included 'the other social sciences, and Ward's that it embraced all truth.

[46] Social phenomena were being "explained" in all conceivable terms except the sociological. There were organic, psychological, climatic, racial, ecological, demographic theories in abundance. After finishing two-thirds of his article on "Sociology" for the *Encyclopedia of the Social Sciences,* MacIver says: "The schools thus far discussed are distinguished by the fact that they applied to social phenomena the specific concepts or the specific methods of some other science or group of sciences." Vol. 14, pp. 232–247.

[47] Accounts of the "theories" of nineteenth-century sociologists are mostly accounts of what they "advocated." "Spencer was so busy throughout his life attempting to formulate a doctrine of what the state should not do that he failed to develop any coherent positive theory of the state." Harry E. Barnes, *Introduction to the History of Sociology,* Chicago: University of Chicago Press, 1948, p. 128. Comte's religion of positivism got in the way of his science of sociology. Le Play was mainly a social reformer who "set forth the principles of Christian morality, duty and obedience to authority as the bases of a sound economic and social organization." Gottfried Salomon, "Le Play," *Encyclopedia of the Social Sciences,* Vol. 9, p. 412.

of culture.[48] If sociological analysis was to receive recognition as an anthropological specialty in competition with archeology, physical anthropology, historical reconstruction, and cultural anthropology, it had to assert itself. As usual, a movement gains strength if it can rally under a special name. In this case the most appropriate name, sociology, was precluded, not only because it already designated a rival discipline, but also because, as just noted, it was tainted by contrary meanings. There was another term, however, which seemed to pick up the essence of what was meant. This was the term "function" which had been deliberately used by Durkheim, the founder of what has often been called the "sociological school" in anthropology. Although Radcliffe-Brown explicitly adopted the term as a key concept, it was the irrepressible Malinowski who championed it so insistently that the name "functionalism"—long used in philosophical circles to designate a focus on activity rather than structure—came to be applied to the movement.[49] Malinowski made it crystal clear that he was fighting against evolutionary theory and trait-diffusion analysis—two contrary points of view that he says had dominated anthropology. Under their dominance there was little room for the study of societies as going concerns. It was his mission to make room for it under the banner of functionalism. As soon as this term came to be applied to sociological analysis in anthropology, it was also used in sociology for the same purpose.

This interpretation of the rise of functionalism explains a paradox in its history—the fact that the hardest battle for functional analysis was fought in anthropology, whereas the most effective critical and methodological discussion of it emerged in sociology. The reason for the hard initial battle in anthropology lay in the entrenched character of competing interests in that field; the battle was for the *admission* of sociological analysis against the

---

[48] Franz Boas' article, "Anthropology," *Encyclopedia of the Social Sciences,* Vol. 2, pp. 73–110, in effect claimed for this field the whole of human knowledge.

[49] In 1931 Horace Kallen, a philosopher, noting in his article on "Functionalism," *loc. cit.,* that a trend toward functionalism was manifesting itself in architecture, law, psychology, etc., added that "Malinowski appears to be aiming at an equally thoroughgoing functionalism in anthropology," some of the means by which Malinowski became identified as the leader of functionalism are questionable. His writings, which owe many of their ideas to Durkheim and his followers, characteristically ignored or misrepresented these predecessors. His long article on "Culture" in the *Encyclopedia of the Social Sciences,* where he argued his complete case for functionalism, caricatured Durkheim and ignored Radcliffe-Brown altogether. He was so extreme and careless in his statements that the critics of functionalism found him a convenient standard-bearer for that point of view. Whenever they needed a quotation to illustrate one of the fallacies of functionalism, they could usually find one in Malinowski's writings. His readable and imaginative style of writing, his capacity for eliciting the enthusiasm of students, his prolific output—these were further factors in his acquiring the leadership of the functionalist movement.

indifference or opposition of older preoccupations.[50] Subsequently the debate died down because, once this kind of work had forced its way into anthropology as functionalism, there was no longer any question of its admission, for it was then recognized as one among a plurality of distinct anthropological interests.[51] Furthermore, having been accepted as a separate type of interest, functionalist anthropology was distracted from theoretical self-criticism by its overwhelming emphasis on ethnography—that is, on informal description and interpretation of single simple societies. "Field work" in this sense became a *mystique* among social anthropologists,[52] with the result that singularly little systematic comparison was attempted and hence not much empirically disciplined general theory. Functionalism was easily applied at the case-study level, to the analysis of particular primitive societies. Historicism in anthropology thus won a partial counter-victory over its upstart opponent, functionalism. The latter remained methodologically weak and self-satisfied as it gained success in anthropology.[53]

---

[50] The first edition of A. L. Kroeber's widely used text, *Anthropology*, New York: Harcourt, Brace, 1923, contained nothing on social anthropology. At the end of the chapter on religion (p. 325) he felt uneasy enough to admit "there must be laws underlying culture phenomena;" but he said their source must lie "obviously in the human mind. The laws of anthropological data, like those of history, are the laws of psychology." Boas, in his 40,000-word article on "Anthropology" for the *Encyclopedia of the Social Sciences* (1930), makes no mention of Malinowski or Radcliffe-Brown and refers to Durkheim and Levy-Bruhl only in the bibliography. His account of the field is preoccupied with evolution, invention, and diffusion in connection with an encyclopedic array of topics running from "food" to "art" and from "economics" to "psychological aspects."

[51] The case was somewhat like establishing a new department in a university. The new department is usually strenuously opposed when the question of its admission is raised, but, once created, it is grudgingly accepted.

[52] The chief innovation for which it [the functionalist movement] stands," says Meyer Fortes, "was . . . the principle of 'the intensive study of limited areas' as Haddon described it . . . the study and analysis of a living community in its native habitat with reference to its total social life." *Social Anthropology at Cambridge Since 1900: An Inaugural Lecture,* Cambridge: University Press, 1953, pp. 16–17.

[53] This interpretation of the anthropologists' lack of critical interest in functional analysis differs from that of Firth. The latter attributes the lack of methodological criticism in anthropology to the fact "that so much of 'functional thinking' has passed into general currency unnoticed or at least unnamed." *Op. cit.,* pp. 245–247. However, his evidence showing how inconsistently and loosely the concept of function is used in contemporary anthropology makes it clear that some additional factors must have been involved. Why would anthropologists allow such slipshod thinking to pass into general currency? The additional factor, in my view, is the concentration on informal case studies of simple communities or local societies. At this superficial level it is easy to "apply" functionalism, but if this is all that is done, there is little to offer a theoretical or methodological challenge.

The popularity of functionalism in anthropology has been due in large part to the ease of applying sociological analysis to simple local societies. The latter, small and often isolated, can be "seen" as totalities. Having relatively little specialization, they facilitate the task of studying the interrelation of the parts of society. Since primitive

In sociology, on the other hand, structural-functional analysis has been subjected to searching criticism and some codification. Since sociologists deal with complex societies, they cannot rely on informal observation and informants but have to employ a variety of research techniques. This gives them a methodological self-consciousness that makes it inevitable that any development such as functionalism will be subjected to technical scrutiny. Furthermore, the traditional interest of sociologists in systematic theory (in part a reflection of their closer ties with economics and philosophy) prompts them to examine the premises and the logic of functionalism.

In both anthropology and sociology, however, and particularly in the latter field, the intensity of the attack on functionalism suggests something more than a purely technical concern. It suggests a persistence, though in more sophisticated form, of the very factors that had originally obstructed strictly sociological analysis and had given rise to reductionism and empiricism. To understand the role of these factors, we must come back to our central historical theme. Having raised the question of how the idea of functionalism as a separate method got started, we must now ask why it is that this illusion has persisted.

In a way it is appropriate to speak of functional analysis as something *within* anthropology, because there are branches of that field that have totally different subject-matters. A similar statement with respect to *social* anthropology or sociology, however, is tautological, for the reason that structural-functional analysis *is* sociological analysis. Realization of this tautology is coming in social anthropology, particularly in Britain,[54] but is still impeded by the confusion between cultural and social anthropology. In sociology the failure to recognize the tautology is largely due, I think, to the fact that sociologists, working mainly on their own society, often take for granted the broad knowledge and interpretation (the "theory") of this society in order to concentrate on empirical fact-finding and reporting, on practical but limited applications, on social reform, or even on research techniques *per se*. To the technicians in the field, functional analysis is remote and speculative theory; their antagonism to theory in general makes them critical

---

societies also live in close dependence on nature, they can be readily regarded from the standpoint of societal survival. Being small, isolated, and relatively undifferentiated, they are more traditionalized than advanced societies, thus manifesting in startling fashion the depedence of individual behavior upon the group, the reality of society. Finally, since aboriginal societies are quite different from our own, the values and purposes of the members can be viewed by the observer as part of the phenomena to be explained, not the basis of explanation; thus the distinction between manifest and latent functions can be more easily applied. By the same token, it is easier for the ethnographer to "get away" with his interpretations. Other social scientists, being unacquainted with the society in question, cannot easily check up on him.

[54] As witness Firth's view that all of social anthropology in Britain is functionalist now.

of what seems to be the most speculative kind of all. To applied sociologists functional analysis is uncomfortable, to social reformers it is anathema, because it subjects to scrutiny the very goals for which application is made or reform intended. Such extra-scientific considerations, however, are more effective when not revealed. The belief that functionalism is some special kind of theory or method permits an attack on sociological analysis which seems to be only an attack on functionalism.

Reasons for Abandonment

The early rise of functionalism helped to make a place in sociology and anthropology for those wishing to explain social phenomena in terms of social systems, as against those who wished to make no explanation at all, to explain things in terms of some *other* system, or to plead a cause. Now, however, the movement that was once an asset has turned into a liability. The idea that functionalism is a special method has become a source of confusion and needless controversy. Above all, by a curious turn, it has become a convenient cloak under which the old enemies of sociological analysis can make their attack.

We have seen how difficult it is to say *what* functionalism is. Not only do definitions differ within each camp, but we find that so-called functionalists and professed enemies of functionalism are often *doing* the same kind of analysis. The name "functionalism" implies a difference of method or interpretation that does not exist. Not only is energy wasted in protracted discussion of this nebulous method, but the genuine issues are obscured. If a table is made of the theoretical issues in which there is a difference of opinion *on scientific grounds alone*, we shall find that the people called functionalists do not share positions, nor do the people who are non-functionalists. Yet issues are often debated as if they were an incidental battle in the warfare between the functionalists and some other camp, and some issues are meaningless apart from that supposition. For instance, we have seen that the question of "assuming" social integration or social conflict is a false issue conceived as a fight between functionalism and Marxism.[55] Once issues are understood to be those of sociological anlaysis itself, the false ones can be eliminated more effectively and the others debated more clearly.

Sociology and social anthropology are too mature to continue the archaic notion that their work is a battle between "isms." As Radcliffe-Brown says,

---

[55] To say that functionalism is wrong because it assumes integration, whereas Marxism is right because it assumes conflict, is to overlook that both are wrong as scientific theories insofar as they commit the fallacy of misplaced concreteness.

"names ending in *-ism* do not apply to scientific theories, but do apply to philosophical doctrines." [56] More importantly, we have seen that the special language that gave functionalism its name is itself, if not archaic, at least so close to ordinary moralistic discourse that it tends to lead people (even some functionalists) to do what functionalism has tried to avoid—the substitution of the actor's point of view for that of the observer. To speak of the *function* of an institution *for* a society or *for* another institution in that society is a way of asking what the institution does within the system to which it is relevant. But, having connotations that are impossible to control, the word is more of a hindrance than a help to communication.[57] Natural scientists occasionally use the term, and others like it, to convey a quick notion of how something fits into a system; but such language is acknowledged to be a way of conveying the general layout at the start of a discussion, not a medium for presenting systematic analysis. That the function of the heart is to pump blood through the body was doubtless a discovery when made, but if every time one establishes a relationship one has to say "the function of such and such is to do such and such" the circumlocution becomes tiresome. Why not say simply that the heart pumps blood through the system? Insofar as functionalism is defined as analysis that uses the term "function" and derivatives like "eufunction" and "dysfunction," it is a semantic artificiality—a fact which doubtless explains one's embarrassment when someone in a field of physical science asks what "functionalism" is. It is worth noting that economics, the most systematic of the social sciences, has not found it necessary to evolve a special method using the concept "function" or a school of thought called "functionalism."

Let me make it clear that I do not consider the myth of functionalism as a special method in sociology or anthropology to be a catastrophe. As stated earlier, in my opinion some of the sociological work wearing the functional label is the best ever done, and some of it is poor. The quality has nothing to do with the label or with use of the term *function*. The designation of a school called functionalism will doubtless die out in time anyway. My effort here has simply been based on the assumption that minor gains will be made if the process of dying is not unduly prolonged.

---

[56] He continues: "By calling his doctrine 'functionalism' Malinowski seems to have wished to emphasize that it was the product of one mind, like any philosophical doctrine, not, like a scientific theory, the product of the cooperative thinking of a succession of scientists. Might it not prevent confusion if it were renamed Malinowskianism?" "Functionalism: A Protest," *American Anthropologist*, 51 (April–June, 1949), pp. 320–323.

[57] To some persons the term has the added meaning of "good," "necessary," "sole."

Ronald Philip Dore

Function and Cause

K*INGSLEY DAVIS* has argued that we should abandon the notion that functionalism is a special form of sociological analysis.[1] It *is* sociological analysis, albeit occasionally clouded by misleading terminology. In at least one reader the effect of his thoughtful and wide-ranging paper was to stimulate reflection on our notions of function and cause and on the relations between them. The starting point of these reflections was the question: Does not Professor Davis' argument rest on a special and hardly universal view of what sociological analysis is or should be?

At one point he commends functionalism as having "helped to make a place in sociology and anthropology for those wishing to explain social phenomena in terms of social systems, as against those who wished to make no explanation at all, to explain things in terms of some other system or to plead a cause." Sociological analysis, in other words, is the explanation of

Reprinted from Ronald Philip Dore, "Function and Cause," *American Sociological Review*, 26 (December, 1961), pp. 843–853, by permission of the author and the American Sociological Association.

[1] Kingsley Davis, "The Myth of Functional Analysis as a Special Method in Sociology and Anthropology," *American Sociological Review*, 24 (December, 1959), pp. 752–772.

social phenomena in terms of social systems. But surely cause-pleading, explanation in terms of other systems and so on are not the only alternatives. There is another position, equally sociological, equally analytical, which holds that sociologists should search for regularities in the concomitant occurrences of social phenomena, seek to induce causal laws from such regularities and seek eventually to order such laws into comprehensive theory. According to this view, systematic theory (a logically consistent body of causal laws) is the end product of a long search for causal relations, not a heuristically useful starting point.

This, perhaps, betrays a preference for "neat single propositions whose validity is proved but whose significance is not," a preference which Professor Davis condemns as "scientific ritualism." It is comforting to reflect that in the natural sciences at least we would not have got far without our ritualists. Newton in developing his systematic theory of mechanics owed a good deal to Galileo's neat single proposition about the rate of acceleration of falling bodies.

The difference between these two views which we might characterize as the system approach and the piecemeal approach is not identical with the often imputed distinction between functional and non-functional analysis, but it does seem to be true that only the system approach encourages the use of the concept of function. The piecemeal approach is quite clearly bent on looking for causal relations. The system approach finds the concept of cause and causal law difficult to apply, and often finds functions easier to handle.

Perhaps the best way to justify this assertion would be to analyse closely the relations between the concepts of function and of cause. Let us take as starting point the question: In what ways can a statement about the function of an institution, a pattern of behavior, a role, or a norm be translated into a statement about causal relations?

Function—Effect

In the first place it is fairly obvious that "the function of X is to maintain Y" implies that X has some kind of causal influence on Y, and it is presumably this kind of "translation" Professor Davis had in mind when he denied that functional relations are non-causal. But an analysis of "causal influence" leads to difficulties. Can we say: "The assertion that, say, the system of stratification has the function of making the division of labor possible implies that among the causes of the division of labor is the system of stratification?" Obviously not if "the causes of the *origin* of the division of labor" is intended. We have to say something like "the causes of the persistence of the division of labor." This suggests that while one can legitimately ask the function of an institution, one cannot ask for the *cause* of an institution; one has to specify cause of origin or cause of persistence. It will be argued later that what this really amounts to is that one can legitimately ask only for the causes of *events*. Let us assume this argument for the moment and formulate this particular relation between function and cause as follows: "Institution *X* has the function of maintaining institution *Y*" implies that the recurring events referred to as institution *X* are among the causes of other events integral to the institution *Y* (or, can be related by causal laws to other events integral to institution *Y*).

Function—Cause

But this is not the kind of causal relationship implied when it is said that an institution is "explained" in terms of its function. Here (less often explicitly than implicitly as a result of the ambiguities of the word "explain") the transition is suggested not from function of *X* to the causes of something other than *X*, but from the function of *X* to the causes of *X* itself. When and how may this kind of transition be made?

A small boy's examination of the interior of a watch may lead him to conclude that the function of the balance spring is to control the movement of the balance wheel. He would have little difficulty in using his functional insight to arrive at a causal explanation of the spring's presence—it is there because the man who made the watch realized a need for something to control the movement of the wheel, and the process of ratiocination which ensued led him to put in the spring.

Sociologists are not always precluded from making the same kind of transition from function of *X* to cause of *X*. Human institutions are now purposefully designed on a scale rarely attempted before. An analysis of the functions of the Chinese communes leads easily to an explanation of the causes of their existence, for they were created by historically identifiable persons to perform these functions and there may well be minutes of committees which record the process of invention with constant reference to their intended consequences, both those which were to be manifest to the communed Chinese and those which were to be latent to them and manifest only to their leaders.

Perhaps more common is the case where human purpose, based on an awareness of function, is a causal factor not so much in the initiation of an institution as in its growth and development. The Roman circus started well before emperors realized the salutary political functions it shared with bread. It was not until the third century B.C. that, as Radcliffe-Brown has pointed out,[2] the Chinese sociologist, Hsun-Tse, realized the latent psychological and social functions of ancestral rites, but his discovery certainly prompted later Confucian scholars to encourage the deluded masses in a continued belief in the reality of the manifest functions of those rites. Nowadays, with sociologists busily ferreting out latent functions in every nook and cranny of society and their writings gaining general currency, latent functions are not likely to stay latent for long. Here indeed is the complement of the self-fulfilling prophecy—the self-falsifying assertion. The sociologist who contends that X has such and such a latent function in his own society in fact makes that function manifest. The intervention of human purpose to preserve institutions so that they may continue to fulfill their *once* latent functions is likely to occur more frequently as a result.[3]

However, modern sociologists still probably have less direct influence in moulding the institutions of their society than Hsun-Tse had in his, and in any case most sociologists are not imputing such a causal chain when they imply a connection between latent functiton of X and cause of X. Merton, for instance, clearly is thinking of something else when he speaks, apropos of the Hopi rain dances, of the analysis of their latent function as an *alternative* to describing their persistence "only as an instance of 'inertia,' 'survival' or 'manipulation by powerful subgroups'." [4]

How then, without reference to human awareness of functions, can a statement about the function of an institution be translated into a causal statement about either the origin or the persistence of that instiution?

Societal Integration

One way is to postulate an immanent tendency, universal in human societies, for the parts of the society all to be functionally integrated in the whole. Given such a tendency the function of an institution is its *raison d'être* and hence its cause. The logical grounds for such a postulate seem to be two. First there is the complementarity of roles and institutions; the role of wife

---

[2] A. R. Radcliffe-Brown, *Structure and Function in Primitive Society*, London: Cohen and West, 1952, pp. 157–159.

[3] This raises moral as well as analytical problems when the institutions concerned involve factual beliefs. At the turn of the century John Morley's liberal conscience was somewhat exercised by "the question of a dual doctrine . . . the question whether it is expedient that the more enlightened classes in a community should . . . not only possess their light in silence, but whether they should openly encourage a doctrine for the less enlightened classes which they do not believe to be true for themselves while they regard it as indispensably useful in the case of less fortunate people." *On Compromise*, London: Macmillan, 1908, p. 44.

[4] Robert K. Merton, *Social Theory and Social Structure*, Glencoe, Ill.: The Free Press, Revised Edition, 1957, p. 65.

implies the role of husband; the specialization of the executive to executive functions implies separate institutions for legislation and litigation, and so on. Such complementarities, however, are of limited range. Let an integrationist try his hand, for instance, at specifying the chains of complementarity which might link the institution of Presidential elections with that of the burlesque show. The second basis for belief in the integration of societies rests on the supposed integration of the human personality. Since the same individual occupies numerous roles in a variety of institutional contexts and since all individuals are subject to a craving for consistency, it follows that all the institutions of a society must be permeated by the same value preferences, the same modes of orientations to action, the same patterns of authority, the same world-view, the same sense of time, and so on. But how valid is the assumption of the consistent personality? Which of us, sophisticates that we are, could confidently claim that he has never been guilty of preferring value A to value B in one situation and reversing his preference in another? And even if this were not so, this argument would create an a priori expectation of social integration only in the case of very simple societies. In such simple societies the number of roles is limited. Every individual in the society may occupy at some stage of his life a high proportion of the total number of roles. In such a society integrated personalities might make for integrated institutions. But this is not the case in large complex societies, segmented into regional and class sub-cultures with specialized personality types and offering a vast multiplication of roles only a tiny fraction of which any one individual will ever find himself performing.

Obviously there are no grounds for expecting such societies to be perfectly integrated. To quote Professor Davis again, "It would be silly to regard such a proposition as literally true." And one might add that modification of the proposition from "always perfectly" to "usually somewhat" integrated (a) destroys the possibility of its empirical falsification and (b) destroys its value as an automatic means of transition from function to cause.[5]

---

[5] A less ambitious and more precise integrationist thesis such as, for instance, "the kinship structure and the occupational structure will always be integrated to the degree that the kinship structure does not impose obstacles to such free movement of individuals as the occupational structure requires" still does not allow for automatic transition from function to cause. (Would it be: the family is the way it is because of the occupational structure, or vice versa?) Such a thesis can, however, by specifying areas where causal relations are likely to be found, direct one's thinking towards such empirically testable hypotheses as those implicit in Parsons' discussion of the family. (See for example, *The Social System*, Glencoe, Ill.: The Free Press, 1951, p. 178.) Such for instance as "when industrialization proceeds the importance of the conjugal relation in the kinship structure increases."

Evolutionary Selection

There remains, however, at least one way in which the sociologist may move on from function to cause—by means of the notions of adaptation and selection developed in the theories of biological evolution. To take the example of stratification and the division of labor, the hypothesis would have to go something like this: for various reasons some societies which began the division of labor also had, or developed, a system of unequal privileges for different groups, others did not. Those which did functioned more efficiently as societies; perhaps they bred more rapidly than, acquired resources at the expense of, and eventually eliminated, the others. Perhaps (and this is an extension of the concept of selection not available to the biologist) their obvious superiority in wealth, power, the arts, standard of living, etc., induced the others to imitate their institutions wholesale, including the principle of stratification; or just conceivably (though here we slip "human awareness" back into the causal chain) the others bred sociologists who noted the importance of stratification to the superior societies and urged its adoption specifically. At any rate, by one, or a combination, of these processes it now happens that all societies with a division of labor have a system of stratification.

It is an unlikely story, but it seems to be the only kind of story which will make a statement about the latent function of X relevant to a causal explanation of X. And even this, of course, is not a complete causal explanation. The "various reasons" why some societies had stratification in the first place still need to be explained. For the biologist the place of these "various reasons" is taken by "random mutation" and some sociologists, too, are prepared to probe no further.[6]

But often the sociologist can think of specific "various reasons" which eliminate randomness. Dennis H. Wrong, in his assessment of Davis and Moore on stratification,[7] suggests, for instance, that when the division of labor takes place certain groups acquire greater power in the society by virtue of that division and consequently arrogate to themselves a larger share of material and other rewards. And in this case, if this hypothesis concerning one of the "various reasons" for the development of stratificatiton in *a* society is historically validated, or accepted on the basis of what we know in

---

[6] Ruth Benedict, for instance, remarks that "the course of life and the pressure of the environment, not to speak of the fertility of the human imagination, provide an incredible number of possible leads, all of which, it appears, may serve a society to live by" and, the implication is, it is more or less beyond precise determination why they should utilize one lead rather than another. (Ruth Benedict, *Patterns of Culture*, London: Routledge and Kegan Paul, 1949, p. 16.)

[7] Dennis H. Wrong, "The Functional Theory of Stratification," *American Sociological Review*, 24 (December, 1959), p. 774.

general of human nature, then it could equally explain the development of stratification in any and all societies. The adaptive superiority of stratification due to its function in making the division of labor workable *may* still be relevant, too, but it is only one of a number of possible causal chains, the relative importance of which can only be assessed in the light of the historical evidence.

In any case, if one is looking for the causes of (either the origination or the continuance of) X, it is better to look for causes as such; looking for the functions of X is never a necessary, and not always even a useful, first step.[8]

In point of fact we know from historical evidence that this evolutionary argument relating function to cause is irrelevant to certain social institutions which sociologists describe. The American boss-directed political machine, for instance, is said by Merton to have the functions of providing a centralization of power, of providing necessary services to those who need help rather than justice, of organizing essential, but morally disapproved, sectors of the economy etc., and as such contributes to the maintenance of the social system as a whole. However, we know that the boss-system developed long since the United States was in direct and aggressive competition with other social groups for resources; we know from historical evidence that there has been no process of selective weeding out of societies involved.

In such cases one can still appeal to a weakened form of the evolutionary argument to relate function to cause by defining causally important conditions not for the original development of the institution but for its later transmission. It would have to go something like this: if the boss system had not had these effects and so contributed to the smooth working of society, nor had these effects been neutral with respect to the smooth working of society, but had, on the contrary been positively detrimental to society's smooth working, people would have stopped doing it. In other words the fact that this feature was *not dysfunctional* to the workings of the society is a necessary condition of its present existence. It is also a necessary condition that all members of the society were not eliminated by an epidemic of

---

8 Cf., for instance, George C. Homans and David M. Schneider, *Marriage, Authority and Final Causes*, Glencoe, Ill.: The Free Press, 1955. In suggesting one "efficient cause" for the development of patrilateral cross-cousin marriage in societies of certain types, namely that such a form of marriage best conforms to the personal interests of the members of such societies, they conclude, apropos of Levy-Strauss' functional, or "final cause," explanation (that such an institution makes for a "better," because more organically integrated, society) "not ... that [it] is right or that it is wrong, but only that it is now unnecessary." (p. 59). Levy-Strauss' functional explanation did not lead them to their own causal explanation in any sense except that it prompted them to challenge his assumption that it was all there was to be said on the subject.

bubonic plague. One could think of many more such negatively defined necessary conditions, all of which play a part, but only a small part, in a full causal explanation.

Summary

This seems to exhaust the possible methods by which assertions about the functions of X can be involved in assertions about the causes of the (origin or continuance of) X. The sociologist may not be the least bit interested in any of them. Having discovered that, say, social stratification has the function of making the division of labor workable, he may be content with saying just that—and with perfect justification provided he concedes that he has said nothing about *why* societies are stratified. He may go on to point a corollary of his assertion—that if stratification were abolished the division of labor would become unworkable. This is, indeed, an eminently useful social activity and the kind of analysis which can properly precede attempts at social reform. It is also, incidentally, the kind of activity in which a good many social anthropologists in particular have been professionally engaged in colonial administrations. The practical need to assess the probable effects of changes in institutions wrought by colonial policy has provided an important application of functional analysis which perhaps explains (causally) why so many anthropologists have been content with functional analysis as a legitimate final goal of their activities.

We may sum up the argument so far as follows:

1. In a not very clearly defined way the suggestion that institution X has the function of maintaining Y implies some causal influence of X on Y.

2. Assertions about the functions of an institution X are relevant to assertions about the causes of the origin or the persistence of that same institution X if, and only if: (a) one assumes that the function is manifest to the present actors in, to the present upholders of, or to former upholders or inventors of the institution in question, and as such has played a part in their motives for performing, or inducing others to perform, the institutionalized behavior involved; (b) one postulates an immanent tendency for the functional integration of a society; (c) one postulates an adaptive superiority conferred by the institution which permitted it, having developed in one society, to spread to others.

These ideas are not particularly new.[9] The reason why they need reiterat-

---

[9] The clear differentiation of causes and consequences, for instance, and the assertion that one may argue from consequence to cause only via (a) motive or (b) evolutionary theory is to be found in Harry C. Bredemeier, "The Methodology of Function-

ing is, it seems, largely because of the ill-defined relation between function and cause suggested by the first of our two propositions. It is the main business of this paper to try to improve the definition of that relation and, in the course of doing so to make a few pertinent remarks about the use of analogies from natural science.

System and Event

Let us first examine the concept of system. "How else can data be interpreted," said Professor Davis in his paper, "except in relation to the larger structures in which they are implicated? How can data on the earth's orbit, for example, be understood except in relation to a system in which they are involved—in this case the solar system or the earth's climatic system?" Is this, however, a good analogy? There are indeed systems in nature, such as the solar system, the parts of which are in continuous interaction with each other in such a way that causal laws, expressed in the form of differential equations, allow one to predict one state of the system from another prior or later state. In human societies, however, though the money market might be somewhat similar, such systems are rare. Social systems (in the Parsonian manner) are not analogous in that the parts are not *simultaneously* affecting each other in the way in which the sun and the moon simultaneously affect each other by their gravitational attraction. The mutual relation of, say, the system of socialization to the system of political control is mediated by the personality structure, and as such it is a relation which requires a long time interval to work through the whole causal sequence. Parents may well train their children today in ways which are "significantly congruent" with the ways in which they behave politically today, but, in the other direction, the way in which they now behave politically is affected by the way in which they were trained, not today but a generation ago.

The analysis of systems such as the solar system can dispense with the notion of cause in favor of function—but this, be it noted, is strictly the mathematician's function, not that of the sociologist or of the physiologist.[10]

---

alism," *American Sociological Review*, 20 (April, 1955), p. 173. He somewhat obscures his first point, however, with the discussion, in the latter part of his paper, of the precise ways in which motives *also* have to be considered even for a discussion of consequences.

[10] See Bertrand Russell, *Mysticism and Logic*, London: Penguin Books, 1953, p. 184. It would be interesting to know whether Russell's well-known assertion in this paper that the concept of cause was useful "only in the infancy of a science" and that as a science developed it was replaced by function (mathematical) had any influence in causing sociologists and anthropologists to drop the unfashionable word cause and take up function instead. If so they were the rather naive victims of the ambiguity of

It is not, however, impossible to apply the concepts of causal law and causal event to such systems, and to do so might help to elucidate the nature of the distinction we have earlier made between the causes of the origin of, and the causes of the persistence of, institutions. If we are to give a causal explanation of the movement of the moon between 10:00 P.M. and 10:05 P.M. tonight, we would need to refer to the simultaneous events of the movements of the earth and the sun, etc., relating them to it by Newton's law of gravitation. We should also have to mention a previous event—the moon's motion at the point immediately prior to 10:00 P.M.—and relate it to the event in question (its movement between 10:00 and 10:05 P.M.) by means of Newton's first law of motion concerning momentum. Having started on this track we can regress almost indefinitely from event to event back through time (chopping our time continuum arbitrarily into "events"), the moon's velocity at any particular moment being affected by its velocity the preceding moment, until we get to an earlier traumatic event, namely the moon's supposed wrenching off from the earth. In the whole of this process it is only events which we relate to each other by causal laws and only of events that we ask: what are their causes?[11] Similarly—and this is the point of the example— when we talk of "the cause of the origin of an institution" and "the cause of the persistence of an institution" we are in both cases asking for the causes of events—in the first case the causes of the particular once-and-for-all events associated with the origin of the institution, and in the second of the recurring events which *are* the institution.

In the light of this view of causal relations, let us now look at the analogy between physiology and sociology often invoked by those who favor sociological explanation in terms of systems. It is often asserted that because the physiologist leaves questions concerning the origin of the heart to the student of evolution and concentrates on tracing its functions as it at present exists,

---

the word function, rather like the lady who heard that bearskins were replacing mink this year and though somewhat puzzled decided that fashion was fashion and went to the party naked. One might add that Russell's assertion that the concept of cause is useful only in the infancy of a science is not incompatible with the claim that "cause" is still useful for sociology.

[11] On close analysis it becomes extremely difficult, as Bertrand Russell shows, to define the concept of "event." (*Mysticism and Logic*, London: Penguin Books, 1953, pp. 176–178; *The Analysis of Mind*, London: Allen and Unwin, 1921, pp. 94–95.) The difficulties are, however, not such as to prevent Russell himself from ignoring them in his later work (see, for example, *Human Knowledge*, London: Allen and Unwin, 1948, p. 344), and the common sense notion of "event" or "happening," widened slightly perhaps to include not only "the eclipse of the moon" but also "the movement of the moon between 10:00 and 10:01 P.M." (i.e., not only common-sensically discrete events, but also arbitrarily chopped-up units of continuous processes—a legitimate extension since all "events," even eclipses, have arbitrarily defined boundaries) is adequate for the purposes of this discussion and, for the moment at least, for the purposes of sociological enquiry.

he is not concerned with causes. But this is surely not so. "The function of the heart in the human being is to pump blood" implies "The cause of the flow of this blood at this time is the pump of that heart then" and this is as much a causal assertion as "one of the reasons why animals have hearts is because when random mutation produced the first primitive heart its possessors gained the ability to out-breed the heartless."

Physiologists and students of evolution have achieved a division of labor which is not formalized among sociologists. Consequently, among sociologists the search for an "explanation" of an institution is often ambiguous. "Why is there a system of unequal rewards in this society?" may be answered by some "because parents tell (this parent and this parent told) their children that some positions in society are more worthy of respect than others, and because employers pay (this employer and this employer paid) more for some kinds of work than others, etc." This is the "physiological" explanation of the recurring events of rewarding particular people with particular acts of deference and so on which is what we mean by stratification. Alternatively the answer might be "because with the division of labor some groups became more powerful and arrogated privileges to themselves, or because differentiated societies which had systems of stratification proved more successful than those which didn't,"—the "evolutionary" explanation of the particular events which led to the institutionalization of certain patterns of behavior.

Institutions

It will be noted again that whichever way the question is taken it can be handled as if it were a question about particular events. It is the chief assertion of this paper that ultimately these are the only terms in which causal questions can be framed. But if this is the case, what then is the relation between the particular events observed by the sociologist and his concepts such as stratification, marriage, or socialization—concepts of "institutions," "norms," "behavior patterns?" Is it not exactly the same as the relation between a particular human heart and *the* human heart for the physiologist? The physiologist's statement that "the function of the heart is to pump blood" is a summary generalization of statements about the causal relations between the particular events of heart-pump and blood-flow in particular human bodies—events which nowadays recur more than two billion times a second. If the sociologist's statements are to have any empirical reference it is difficult to see how they can be different from this; how, that is to say, the relation between "John kisses Mary" and "courtship," or between "farmer George touched his cap to the lord of the manor" and "stratification" can be other than the relation between "the pump of this heart" and "the pump of the human heart."

Even sociologists who accept this are often tempted to forget it, partly because while any single heart-pump is very much like another, kisses can vary greatly in intensity, passion, and significance. This is also the reason why it is more important that the sociologist should *not* forget it; it matters very little to the physiologist if he forgets that his abstract human organ is a generalization from particular organs in particular people *because* they are all very much alike.

If it be accepted that the sociologist's "institutions" are summary generic terms for classes of particular recurring events, then it follows that his statements about the functional interrelations of institutions are generalizations about the causal relations between these recurring events. In other words that "the system of stratification functions to make the division of labor workable" is a generalized summation of a number of lower order generalizations to the effect that, for instance, "men submit to a lengthy medical training because they have the prospect of greater rewards" etc., which are themselves generalizations from statements of particular events ("Jack submitted . . . because he had . . .).

We might emphasize this assertion that statements about the functional relations between institutions are *only* generalizations about relations between particular events by means of a mathematical analogy (offered only, it might be added, as a didactic illustration and not as a proof). If it is granted that events like "John (unmarried) passionately kisses Mary (unmarried)" (a) are summarily referred to by such a term as "romantic courtship" (Σa); and events like "John (married) hits Mary (married)" (b) are summarily referred to by such a term as "pattern of marital maladjustment" (Σb), then the statement "patterns of courtship affect patterns of marital adjustment" is a summary of statements of the nature "the way John kissed Mary then affects the way he hits her now," and as such is a statement of the nature Σab, *not* of the nature $\Sigma a \times \Sigma b$.

Social Facts and Reductionism

Some sociologists would part company at this point. They might agree with the above view of the logical nature of constructs like "institution," "behavior pattern" etc., but still hold that there *is* a $\Sigma a \times \Sigma b$ kind of sense in which institutions can be related over and above the relations of the particular events they describe. It is difficult to see how this can be so. More consistent is the position of those who would hold that concepts like institutions are not, or are not only, generalizations about recurring events. Such arguments might well appeal to the Durkheimian characterization of norms and institutions as "social facts." But the position outlined above is in no way incompatible with one interpretation of the Durkheimian view. It is undoubtedly true that the members of a society do have reified concepts of, say, "marriage," "romantic love," "filial conduct" which are both more than and less than generalizations concerning particular relations between particular people. But these reified concepts are part of the *data* of sociology. Having a concept of marriage is (though normally less easily observed) as much an event in society as having a quarrel with one's wife and susceptible of the same kinds of questions and explanations. There is no more reason for the sociologist to adopt for his thinking *about* society the terms used for thinking *in* society (to take, in other words, his analytical tools straight out of his data) than there is for a carpenter to use nothing but wooden saws.

The point might be made clearer if it is stated in the terms of Maurice Mandelbaum's discussion of "societal facts." [12] His argument that societal facts are not reducible to statements concerning the actions of individuals rests on an identification of what one might call "societal (or cultural) concepts" with "sociologists' concepts." One can agree with his formulation— that there is a language *S*, in which concepts like marriage, the banking system, the Presidency, etc., appear; that there is another language *P* in which we refer to the thoughts and actions of individuals; and that sentences in *S* cannot be translated wholly into *P* because some of the thoughts and actions of individuals consist of *using S*. But the contention here is that the sociologist should be speaking in a different language—meta-*SP* if one likes—which certainly resembles *S* and was developed from *S* but is an artificial creation for the purpose of analyzing causal relations in society and can only be effective for this purpose if it *is* reducible to *P* (including all the necessary concepts of *S*—the words spoken and the thoughts thought by individuals—which *P* must incorporate). Another way of putting it would be to say that Mandelbaum's arguments that societal facts are not reducible to facts about individuals are really arguments to show that *language* is a necessary part of the sociologist's data for which there can be no substitute. And no one would wish to quarrel with that.[13]

The position outlined above is part of the thesis of "methodological

---

[12] Maurice Mandelbaum, "Societal Facts," *British Journal of Sociology*, 6 (December, 1955), pp. 305–316.

[13] In Parsonian terms the contention here could be put in the form that the analytical categories of the social system are not identical with those of the cultural system. This is indeed what Parsons says (see *The Social System*, Glencoe, Ill.: The Free Press, 1951, p. 15) but in actual practice—in, for instance, his analysis of medical practice in the same book—his method seems to be to take the definition of the role from the cultural system and "fill it out" with examples of concrete action.

individualism,"[14] the brief debate about which seems to have died down without much interest being shown by professional sociologists. The methodological individualist doctrine which holds that all sociological laws are bound to be such as can ultimately be reduced to laws of individual behavior is a hard one to refute,[15] but one which few sociologists find attractive. The reason is perhaps this: the examples we have given of the particular causal relations actually implied by statements of the functions of institutions were of the type: "Jack became a doctor because of the prospect of . . ." "The way John kissed Mary then affects the way he hits her now." All imputations of a causal relation imply a causal law. In these cases the relevant laws are laws of individual behavior—"an individual of such and such training in such and such circumstances will orient present actions to remotely deferred gratifications," "behavioral dispositions towards

---

[14] The thesis is outlined in two articles by J. W. N. Watkins, "Ideal Types and Historical Explanations," *British Journal for the Philosophy of Science*, 3 (May, 1952), pp. 22–43, and "The Principle of Methodological Individualism," *ibid.*, 3 (August, 1952), pp. 186–189.

[15] The two main attacks on Watkins articles have been those of Leon J. Goldstein ("The Inadequacy of the Principle of Methodological Individualism," *The Journal of Philosophy*, 53 (December, 1956), pp. 801–813) and E. A. Gellner ("Explanations in History" in *Dreams and Self-Knowledge*, Aristotelian Society Supplementary Volume XXX, 1956, pp. 157–176). Goldstein's objection is chiefly that the individualist position "would leave us with theories the entire content of which were the facts that suggested them in the first place, having no further power of prediction or generalization" and rests on such dubious arguments as that "to know that in such and such a society descent is reckoned in the female line or that residence is avunculocal provides no information about the aspirations and activities of particular persons." Gellner objects on several grounds; he uses the Durkheimian "social fact" argument, but eventually admits its irrelevance on approximately the same grounds as are indicated above; he argues also that in practice there may well be a Principle of Indeterminacy that makes it impossible to observe the precise individual causal sequences which account for events which can be generalized about in macroscopic statistical terms (trends in road accidents etc.), but his main point is that a statement in individualist terms *adds* nothing to a statement in holistic terms. There is, he suggests, only neatness and intelligibility to be lost and nothing to be gained in translating "the committee made this decision" into statements about the processes that went on in the minds of the individual committee members. But the individualist thesis is not one about descriptive statements, but about laws. It holds that if we knew enough such a "law" as "committees composed of equal proportions of members of low and high status in societies where a stress is placed on harmonious unanimity will tend to reach unanimous decisions reflecting the wishes of those of higher status" is reducible to a number of "laws" about individuals, the way in which they are disposed to react when faced with individuals of higher and of similar status, when faced with the demand for an expression of opinion, etc. The *advantage* of these atomistic laws over the holistic one is that they have greater explanatory power; each is applicable to a wider range of situations than just committees, much as the theory of ionization has greater explanatory power than a "law" dealing with the electrolysis of water, which states that electrodes placed in water give off hydrogen and oxygen and applies only to the specific case of water.

individual others built up under the stress of strong biological urges tend to be modified after the satiation of those urges" might be examples. These can be stated in purely behavioral terms. Nevertheless when they are so stated the possibility of further reduction to laws of psychological processes becomes apparent. Psychological reductionism has never appealed to sociologists; it has usually been conceived as a threat to the integrity and importance of sociology. It is difficult to see why. It would be as absurd to argue that because all the laws of social behavior might ultimately be reducible to psychological terms sociologists should give up sociology and take to psychology, as to hold that chemists should all abandon chemistry since their laws might ultimately be reduced to laws of physics. The antipathy towards the reductionist thesis exists, however, and sociologists have for a long time been intermittently fighting a losing battle to prove (to themselves, it seems, since no one else seems to have been particularly interested) that there *are* irreducible sociological laws *sui generis*. Is not the resort to "function" in part a continuation of this warfare by more diplomatic means?

Professor Davis noted that in their studies of social change functionalists behave no differently from other sociologists who claim to be opposed to functionalism. Now, studies of social change are explicitly looking for causes—for the causes of the particular events associated with the origination and changing of institutions. To keep one's nose equally on the scent for causes in the analysis of stable systems, however, involves constant reference to the recurring events which make up the institutional units under study and poses the problem of the kind of reductionism outlined above. The concept of function offers an escape; it blurs the precise causal relations imputed and yet descriptions in terms of functions seem somehow to be causal; it makes it easier for institutions to be treated as ultimate units without constant reference to the empirical content of such concepts;[16] in this way the sociological integrity of sociology is preserved and grand theory concerning social systems becomes possible.

Various Sociologies

What, then, of functional*ism*? It is, as Kingsley Davis points out, a name for a variety of methodological and philosophical (following Davis, following Radcliffe-Brown, though "moral" might be more apposite) positions. It might be useful to elucidate these positions with reference to the two main theses of this paper. These theses are: (1) There is a difference between

---

16 See, for example, Talcott Parsons, *op. cit.*, p. 456. The universalism of the doctor's role is spoken of as having the function of protecting the doctor from involvement in

questions about the functions of an institution and questions about the
cause(s) of (the particular once-and-for-all events leading to the origin of, or
the recurring events which make up) that institution, and answers to the
first kind of question are relevant to answers to the second kind of question
only (legitimately) via human motives or evolutionary selection, or (illegiti-
mately) by use of the postulate of necessary integration. (2) Questions about
the functions of an institution logically imply questions about the effects
of recurring particular events which make up that institution as causes of
other recurring particular events.

Functionalists, then, could be any of four types of sociologists. Type (a)
sociologists easily accept both of these propositions but find the concept of
function useful because they are chiefly concerned with the way in which
changes in one institution in a particular society would affect other institutions, for example, the social reformer or the colonial anthropologist. Type
(b) sociologists accept both of these propositions but hold the philosophical
view that sociologists should concern themselves only with the kind of
causal relationships which have a direct bearing on the equilibrium of the
social system (i.e., are [eu] functional or dysfunctional) and not with other
causal chains which, being in this special sense "non-functional," are "pragmatically unimportant";[17]

It is this particular philosophical view with its implication that "stability
is all," together with the fact that functionalists of type (a) have usually
tended in practice to give reasons for pessimism about the possible scope of
social reform, which provide the basis for the charge of functionalist conservatism. Type (c) sociologists are mainly concerned to construct models
of social systems and either deny the second of these propositions or
occasionally ignore its implications in order to reduce the difficulties of their
task. Type (d) sociologists would deny the first of these propositions (usually,
specifically the charge that the postulate of necessary integration is illegitimate[18]) and, in giving a description of the functions of an institution, would
imply that this is also, automatically, a causal explanation of that institution.

A number of alternative positions are possible if these two propositions
are accepted. There is the piecemeal approach, outlined at the beginning of

---

particularistic personal relations with his patients. This sounds like a causal relation
but would seem on closer inspection to be a matter of logic: "a doctor treats his
patients all alike" logically implies that he does not treat them as individuals. If the
universalism of the doctor's role were something *more* than his treating his patients all
alike there would be more than this to Parsons' analysis; but it does not seem that
this is the case.

[17] R. K. Merton, *op. cit.*, p. 51.

[18] This is the position from which Hempel has recently attempted to analyze the
logic of functional analysis. Carl G. Hempel "The Logic of Functional Analysis" in
Llewellyn Gross, editor, *Symposium on Sociological Theory*, Evanston, Ill.: Row,
Peterson, 1959, pp. 271–303.

this paper, which suggests that sociologists should concern themselves with searching for regularities in the concomitant occurrence of social events with a view to inducing causal laws which might ultimately be ordered in some systematic theory. There is the historical approach which is largely concerned with discovering the causes of the particular once-and-for-all events which explain the origins of institutions. There is the static approach which concentrates on societies which have been stable over long periods of time and seeks for the causal relations between the recurring events which make up their institutions. There is still possible scope for the model-system approach in so far as it seeks to build up a pattern of causal relations such as might pertain to an ideal and entirely stable society, without having recourse to the short cut of functionalists variety (c). There is, finally, the 'issue' approach, the virtues of which have recently been argued with much vehemence by C. Wright Mills. This involves starting from practical questions which actually worry people, such as "who is likely to plunge us into a world war," and using for the purpose of elucidation questions about the causes of recurring institutionalized events—so that by knowing why people do things we shall be in a better position to know how to stop them; questions about the once-and-for-all causes—so that by knowing how things got the way they are we shall be in a better position to judge whether that is the way they ought to be; and questions about functions of institutions—so that we would have a better idea of what we would be up against if we tried to change them. All kinds of questions are asked not as ends in themselves but as means to eliciting guides for judgment and action. This is not, perhaps, a scientific pursuit in the way that the other approaches outlined above are scientific, though it is one that has intermittently occupied a great many sociologists of repute.

The differences between these various positions are in part methodological—differences concerning the truth of the two propositions enunciated earlier. In part they are moral differences, about the proper scale of priorities which should guide the sociologist's use of his time. About the methodological issues there is legitimate ground for dispute. But about the "oughts" implied in these various positions, we can only preach at each other. It would be sad if we stopped preaching, but let us try to keep our sermons and our methodological discussions separate.

Dorothy Emmet

Function and Purpose

*I*F we ask why societies contain institutions which have beneficial results of an unintended kind, there are one or two suggestions which can be made, though I doubt whether any one of them can supply a general explanation. One is Natural Selection; customs which produced continual deadlocks and unresolved conflicts would be likely to lead to the elimination of the society which practised them. But there is a difficulty here: Natural Selection presupposes a very large number of unfavorable to a small number of favorable variations, and the elimination of the possessors of the unfavorable variations. Is it in fact known that a very large number of societies have died out, as distinct from carrying on somehow in a miserable, or perhaps degenerate form?[1] And if they do die out, it may be the result of an epidemic of measles or a war of extermination rather than from functional maladjust-

From Dorothy Emmet, *Function, Purpose, and Powers*, Chapter IV, Copyright © 1958, by Macmillan & Company. Reprinted with the permission of St. Martin's Press, Inc., The Macmillan Company of Canada, Limited, and Macmillan & Company, Limited, London.

[1] It might be said that the question of whether, if the social structure changes, the society is still the same society, turns on the point of logic as to how we choose to define a society as 'the same society,' and on this there is no general rule. We can,

ments in their internal institutions (though these, of course, may make them less able to withstand emergencies). At any rate, there is a question whether Natural Selection can be the whole of the story (and indeed, even in biology, Natural Selection can explain why some organisms which are functional wholes may survive, rather than others, more adequately than it can explain how organisms come to be functional wholes).

Perhaps a more hopeful approach to the problem of unconscious social function may lie along the lines of seeing how very often by doing things together in one capacity people may strengthen the ties which make them able to do other things together in other capacities, so that, from one point of view, one of the activities may be said to have the 'function' of consolidating the other. In particular joint participation in some exceptional form of activity, such as a ritual with a deep emotional content, is likely to strengthen people's powers of cooperation and self-denial in the more common activities of family life and work.

Yet to say that such activities may have this effect, and to give a functional explanation[2] of them in such terms, does not give 'underlying reasons' why the activities are undertaken, if by that is meant reasons which may be motives present in the minds of those who undertake them. What it gives is a description of how the results of certain activities help maintain a system. The teleological element in such an explanation is not the idea of a particular result to be secured, but the acceptance of the system to be maintained as an ongoing concern. Is this element of teleology simply due to the attitude of the observer, who is taking the unity of the system for granted, as he might take the organism, and explaining the functions of processes within this? Not, I think, entirely; for the maintenance of unitary organized wholes within nature seems to be an aspect of the world which, if neither teleological nor mechanistic in the senses in which these words were used in older controversies, at least calls for description in *Gestalt* terms and not in terms of

---

however, distinguish between this logical question of defining identity and continuity, and the empirical question of whether there are situations in which there is actual physical disappearance or dispersal of a whole population.

[2] "Analysis" rather than "explanation." An effect of x can only *explain* why x is as it is if it has a "feed-back" on x. (Cf. E. Nagel, "A Formalization of Functionalism," in *Logic without Metaphysics*, New York, 1956). In a chapter entitled "Sociological Explanation and Individual Responsibility" in a forthcoming book, *Rules, Roles and Relations*, I have argued that the so-called "Functional explanation" of an activity should in fact be called *structural-functional*. The "explanatory" element is primarily the structural component, tracing the reasons why some aspects of an activity are as they are to the group relationships of the participants in the society beyond the particular activity. The "functional" element is mainly heuristic; i.e. the fact that the activity has an effect in maintaining a wider social order calls attention to a problem in seeing why this should be so. If the "feedback" element is also present, producing a rare causal influence of the "function" on the continuance of the activity, the "function" can also be explanatory.

simple efficient causation. In the case of a society, there seems less reason for hesitation than in the case of an organism for describing this self-maintenance as having a teleological aspect, for the members of a society must to some extent accept its institutions if the activities which are said to have the function of helping maintain it are in fact to have this result. It may be asking too much to say (as does Professor Macbeath)[3] that in all such cases the members of a society are desiring to maintain a way of life which appeals to them as good. They may simply accept the institutions of their social system because no alternative is envisaged. But without at least this minimum readiness to take their society for granted as an ongoing concern, it is doubtful whether the institutions would have the functional effects they are said to have. That is, the element of teleology is due to the readiness of the members of the society to maintain their institutions; it is not that practices such as rituals are expressly undertaken with that end in view. If, however, such practices take place among people who are prepared to live together within a certain pattern of social relations they may in fact have this effect. When people are not prepared to accept the pattern, the practices will not have this effect. Thus, Professor Gluckman has argued that 'rituals of rebellion' in a coronation ceremony may strengthen the kingship in a society where kingship is fundamentally accepted. They would not have this effect in one in which it was being seriously challenged.[4]

This means that such functional accounts are closely dependent on the role and status model of a social system. Certain activities can be described as contributing to the maintenance of the pattern called the social system because people are acting according to the roles appropriate to their positions within the system. But, of course, this notion of the self-perpetuation of a system of interlocking role activities is very far from any society which anyone knows in the round. The elements of a social system may be institutionalized roles, but the members of a society are individuals with wills of their own. They may therefore be deemed to have purposes which cannot simply be reduced to their function, where 'function' is defined as the contribution each makes to maintaining the equilibrium of the social system. Their purposes may sometimes have a negative effect on this, or be simply indifferent. Yet individuals and institutions, such as educational, religious and recreational institutions, with their multifarious special purposes, do help nevertheless, incidentally and often unintentionally, to maintain the complex of activities we call society in a more or less stable form, so that, generally

---

[3] See his *Experiments in Living* (London, 1952), *passim*.
[4] *Rituals of Rebellion in South-East Africa*, esp. pp. 20 *seq*. (The Frazer Lecture for 1952, Manchester University Press).

speaking, and in spite of disturbances, life goes on.[5] And if it were not for this kind of 'unconscious teleology' social life would probably be impossible. Hence the interest of the functional approach to the study of institutions and of the mutual adjustments between them. The hotch-potch of different activities we call a society does somehow work together to produce a unity and an order which is not just that deliberately imposed by law and government. This is impressive, but we must not be so impressed by it as to press functional analogies drawn from more integrated kinds of system, such as organisms and sermo-mechanisms, further than they will go. For it is characteristic of human beings, as distinct from the parts of physiological organisms and servo-mechanisms, to have purposes (however misguided) as well as functions (however useful). Hence we can be less confident in leaving the system to look after itself by a kind of natural homeostasis; and hence the necd for political action, as a deliberate attempt to exercise some sort of purposive direction or control over some sides of social life. Yet it is no doubt true that no society could survive without elements both of the conscious teleology of purpose and of the unconscious teleology of function.

---

[5] This sometimes seems to be all that the grand term 'equilibrium' really means in these contexts.

Abraham Kaplan

Purpose, Function, and Motivation

*W**HAT* is characteristic . . . of explanations in behavioral science is
that they make use of interpretations in the narrow sense. This is also true,
though to a much lesser degree, of biological science; in physical science the
distinction between acts and actions has no ground, and the interpretations
called for thus have nothing to do with semantic explanation—they are interpretations only in the wide sense. In a word, behavioral science, and to some
extent biological science as well, make use of *purposive explanations*. In
these explanations, acts are given (or found to have) a meaning, and this
meaning then enters as an essential constituent of the explanations offered
for the resultant actions. The reconstruction of purposive explanations is not
necessarily limited to the pattern model. It is true that the assignment of act
meanings puts the acts into a pattern, but how the actions are thereafter
construed—that is, how they are interpreted in the context of a scientific
explanation, not a semantic one—is an open question. The deductive model

can make as good use of premises referring to purposes as the pattern model can of configurations of purposive behavior.

When an act is given a meaning it is interpreted as an action directed toward some end (though it may be an end realized in the action itself—as when an act is interpreted as being playful, for example). All act meaning, as I see it, is purposive, though this statement is by no means necessarily true of all action meaning. (The latter would be the view of certain theologies and metaphysics, for which the course of events is the fulfillment of God's purposes, the self-realization of an Absolute, and the like.) Acts that are not in some sense goal directed are precisely those, it seems to me, that are designated as meaningless. The goals, however, need not be previsioned by the actor; we may distinguish, in Dewey's phrase, between "ends" and "ends-in-view." A purposive explanation, if it makes reference to goals that the actor in some sense thinks of beforehand, may be called a *motivational explanation,* and otherwise a *functional explanation.* Goals unconsciously aimed at are treated sometimes as ends, sometimes as ends-in-view. It is my impression that for psychoanalysis the functional explanations are the more basic, but there is a tendency to formulate them always as though they were motivational: when a person acts to fulfill purposes of which he is unaware, a fictitious agent is introduced (like the "censor") to whom unconscious motives are then ascribed. I believe that the failure to appreciate this transposition of ends is responsible for the naive view of an "unconscious idea" as a contradiction in terms. I would say that the reality of the unconscious consists in the usefulness of motivational explanations of purposive behavior that does not have corresponding ends-in-view.

At any rate, I have no doubt that motivational explanations play an important part in a great deal of behavioral science, as in references to power struggles or the maximization of utility. From a methodological point of view, the objection to motivational explanations is not that they are intrinsically unscientific but that they are so often overextended and misapplied. The purposes at work may call for functional rather than motivational explanations. Functional explanations are appropriate to a great deal of animal behavior, if not to all; the imputation of motives here constitutes an anthropomorphism (which, however, is often only a manner of speaking, and not necessarily objectionable). In human affairs, the wholesale imputation of motives generates the so-called "conspiratorial theory" of society: whatever happens, it is because someone wanted it to happen, planned it that way. There is nothing "pseudo" about such explanations; they are just manifestly false, overlooking the enormous role of unanticipated and even unintended consequences of most actions, to say nothing of natural processes apart from our actions altogether. What sustains these explanations is not evidence but the secondary gain of personification, which makes such explanations so easy to see: they provide a locus for identifications and loyalties, or a target for hostilities. "The Hoover depression" thus constitutes, not merely a distinguishing label, like "the Victorian age," but an implied assignment of responsibility, as in "the Napoleonic wars."

Similar objections can be raised against functional explanations, not as such, but as being too widely applied. Corresponding to the "conspiratorial theory" is what might be called the "utilitarian theory" of society: everything in it serves a purpose. This position is somewhat less objectionable when interpreted historically: what does not now serve a purpose once did. But it seems to me that the universal generalization is maintained in the face of occasional conflicting evidence, and the more frequent absence of confirming evidence, by inventing social needs as required in order to provide a purpose. Institutions are as subject to historical accident and to the constraints of a nonpurposive natural order as are the patterns of personal action. At any rate, I do not see that to explain any item of culture *means*[1] to indicate its functional place within an institution. It may have no such place, and be explained by reference to whatever other circumstances brought it about.

But I wish to reemphasize that there is nothing intrinsically unscientific about functional explanations where evidence is forthcoming that the behavior in question *is* purposive (at the level of actions and not just of acts). Admittedly, when these explanations are applied to social phenomena rather than to individual behavior, they are often formulated in motivational terms, with "society," "culture," "institutions," and the like being spoken of as having motives just as individuals do. But this kind of formulation again may be only a manner of speaking, like the biologist's anthropomorphic locutions. Saying that society erects prisons in order to protect itself from criminals is no more objectionable, methodologically, than saying that a chameleon changes color in order to protect itself from predators. In both cases, the motivational idiom has a functional base, and "protective coloration" is a perfectly good explanatory concept. In the case of the penal system, the functional explanation may be objectionable, not because it is purposive, but because it has not addressed itself to other purposes which may also be at work, like protecting other members of society from the eruption of their own criminal impulses.

Explanations in behavioral science that do not make reference to purposes are sometimes called "structural explanations." But the two types are not necessarily mutually exclusive, to say nothing of not conflicting with

---

[1] As claimed by Malinowski, quoted in L. Gross, (Ed.), *Symposium on Sociological Theory*, Evanston, Ill., 1959, p. 282.

one another.[2] Functionalism need not be taken as a theory either of society (everything in it is purposive) or of behavioral science (only functional explanations are acceptable). It may be viewed as a program of inquiry, a set of methodological prescriptions: to find an explanation for a given pattern of behavior look first to the purposes it might be serving. This approach does not imply, however, that the explanation then arrived at will necessarily be a purposive one. The search for the ends of an action may lead to an identification of the configurations ("structures") with which it is bound up by causal laws. When certain acts are understood as a search for food we may be in a better position to discover what stimuli evoke those responses. Similarly, when certain behavior patterns are interpreted as defense mechanisms it may be easier to discover how they are learned; when we find the functions performed by an institution perhaps we can more easily discover the social forces which maintain it.

I believe that the most common objection to purposive explanations as such amounts to no more than this, that such explanations are not causal, and it is taken for granted that only causal explanations are scientific. It seems to me that there is something pre-Darwinian about this point of view, for what Darwin showed was how the purposiveness of adaptations could be accounted for by the mechanics of survival. It was his replacement of final causes by efficient causes that constituted the most radical departure from the world-view of the theologians. Yet purposive explanations were not really replaced by causal ones but were analyzed in causal terms; it is ironic that even the motivational idiom was retained, in such expressions as "natural selection." In the present century the cybernetic analysis of equilibria and of feedback systems has made possible even a mathematical treatment of purposiveness, so that purposive behavior is explained in terms of telic mechanisms rather than the other way around, as used to be done ("water seeks its own level" and "nature abhors a vacuum").

To my mind, the significance for methodology of these developments is not that purposive explanations are ruled out of science, as the mechanistic followers of Newton and Descartes had maintained against the teleologists, but precisely that the opposition between mechanism and teleology can now be seen to be a spurious one. When we explain some goal-directed behavior by reference to its goal we are not thereby assigning to the future a causal efficacy in the present; the causal agency is the present intention to reach a certain state in the future, and the workings of intentions can be described by reference to feedbacks, including symbolic processes. They "can" be so described, I say; but I am afraid that this is one of those possibilities which

---

[2] A. R. Radcliffe-Brown, *Structure and Function in Primitive Society*, London, 1952, p. 186.

is affirmed to hold only "in principle." My point is that the acceptability of purposive explanations does not depend upon our actually being able to reduce them to mechanical terms. Purposes belong to nature and can be used to explain other natural phenomena even when we are not in a position to provide in turn an explanation for the purposes. As Braithwaite says, purposive explanations are "no less worthy of credence than ordinary causal explanations. . . . It seems ridiculous to deny the title of explanation to a statement which performs both of the functions characteristic of scientific explanations—of enabling us to appreciate connections and to predict the future."[3]

---

[3] R. B. Braithwaite, *Scientific Explanation*, Cambridge (England), 1956, pp. 334–335.

Ernst B. Haas

Functionalism and International Systems

S*YSTEMS* theory is useful only when it facilitates projective thinking based on important abstractions that group and categorize important recurrent events. Hence systems that merely reinforce themselves are not useful for our purposes. It follows that extreme care must be taken not to use analogies that suggest self-reinforcement. Both the mechanistic and the organismic analogies, explicit or implicit in the majority of systems found in the literature, tempt us perpetually along the well-trod path that ends in a cozy bower called "stability," "equilibrium," or "self-maintenance." A dynamic international system must dispense with these notions and with the analogies from which they are derived. The international system most useful for our purposes is neither a machine nor a body.

A dynamic system capable of linking Functionalism with integration studies is a *concrete, actor-oriented* abstraction on recurrent relationships that can explain its own transformation into a new set of relationships, i.e. into a new system. Such a system has no defined attributes, no "needs," no *telos*. Moreover, the relationships among the units cannot be specified until the actors themselves are identified and the environment sketched in.

The actors in our international system are governments and voluntary associations. The environment consists of the beliefs, institutions, goals, and capacities of the actors. Since in past and present concrete systems international organizations have had little independent capacity, they do not contribute—as yet—to the environment. Governmental policies emanating from the environment are the inputs into the system; collective decisions are the outputs. The outputs then *may* transform the environment by being fed back into it. Whether they actually do is a central empirical question that determines whether the system is being transformed in the long run. The particular relationships which define a given system, then, are the patterns of inputs and outputs that prevail during a given epoch. The structures of the system are its body of law, its organizations, national, regional, and universal. Provisionally, international organizations are treated as structures; as a result of the feedback process, however, they may well acquire the position of an autonomous actor at some future stage. The essential purpose of our analysis is to facilitate predictions about when and how this might happen. The functions of the system are the tasks imposed on the structures by the actors. . . . It is our task now to set forth explicitly how functions relate to structures, and what we take the term "function" to mean in our system.

The way is prepared by a statement of Dorothy Emmet, to whose perceptive treatment my reconciliation of Functionalism and functional sociology owes a great deal:

For a social system is not, in fact, just a closed or repetitive system, which can be brought back into "equilibrium" by its internal functional mechanisms. Up to a point it can be studied in this way, but only up to a point. A society is a *process* with some systematic characteristics, rather than a closely integrated system, like an organism or a machine. Hence its "stability" is something more complicated than that of a biological or mechanical system. For its elements are mobile individuals with private purpose, conflicts and allegiances. Their behavior can be canalized to some extent into institutional patterns, and this is not only through the compulsory measures of law and government. Indeed, pervasive institutionalized patterns of conduct are necessary if the cohesion imposed by government itself is to be possible. . . . But similarly the cohesion of the institutionalized activities themselves is made possible by the powers of individuals. Thus the "system" so disclosed is something much less consistent and more flexible than the older functional model suggested. There will be conflicts within the system leading to periodic crises ; and few societies nowadays can be insulated against change. There will be critical occasions when adjustments, perhaps major adjustments, are called for, and these may depend largely on the initiative and resourcefulness of individuals. And not only on critical occasions. Along the line, in all sorts of social situations, adaptations, innovations and decisions will be made, with more and less success. The coherence of a society is thus not just an "equilibrium" secured by the automatic coming into opposition of countervailing tendencies ; it is something more precarious, always needing to be renewed by efforts of will and imagination.[1]

These words constitute much more than a panegyric of individual creativity and resourceful statesmanship; they are the summation of an effort to reconcile systematic determinism with the reality of social change, automatic functional adjustment with willed purpose. Although the context of Emmet's analysis is the national society, her thought applies to the international setting because of its unflinching determination to separate cognitively willed social action from action that is merely the unwilled consequence of previous choices—and yet to retain both types of action within a system that constantly changes. The crucial terms in the statement are "purpose" and "powers," in addition to "function." Before adapting the formulation to the analysis of international systems, let us follow through on Emmet's demonstration.[2]

Teleology, according to her, simply cannot be banished from functional analysis. The important thing is to be clear about the kinds of ends that are postulated. Function must mean more than that a given action has a given result, more than efficient causation; it has to mean that if a given role or action has a function, it has a result *within* the total system, the maintenance of which depends on the performance of the function. Hence, as in other examples, the preservation of the system seems to be always assumed.

But the ends imputed to various kinds of action simply cannot all be subsumed under one notion of *telos*. We must distinguish between the "blind" teleology that refers to the simple maintenance of the system, or to its adjustment to some new "equilibrium"—the type of teleology I have rejected—and the variety that refers to the end I have posited as mine: integration in the sense of movement toward a more universal type of system. As Emmet says, this would be a "natural end" in the Aristotelian sense, though we must bear in mind that the "naturalness" is posited by the

---

[1] Dorothy Emmet, *Function, Purpose, and Powers* (London: Macmillan, 1958), pp. 293–94 (italics in original).

[2] As a minor contribution to semantic confusion, let it be noted that Emmet uses the term "social structure" for what most others call the "social system" (*ibid.*, pp. 24–26). She also uses the concept of the "field" as an aspect of the "structure" selected by the observer to facilitate close attention on the particular relationships that concern him. In so doing, the observer may forego a description of the social totality and concentrate on what seems to him to be a "strategic" relationship. Emmet advocates "field" studies particularly for international relations. I hope to be true to her intent in using the concept of integration in this sense, and isolating the "field" of systemic relationships hinging on integration as my aspect of the total international system (*ibid.*, pp. 34–38).

observer. Teleology, then, can be thought of as goal-directed action, the goal in our case being integrations.[3]

But what kinds of action would qualify, and what is their relationship to the goal? At this level of analysis it becomes useful to distinguish between "purpose" and "function" more explicitly than we have done so far. In Emmett's analysis, the parts of the system as automatically interacting units have no intent, will, function, or purpose at all. They may engage in action either deliberately or not. Action based on will and intent is linked to the purposes of the acting units; the end of action is then part of the actor's explicit motivation and need not be imputed by the observer. However, action may also be considered functional in the sense of having the result postulated by the observer (e.g. the maintenance of the system), without the actor's being aware of this. The actor's motives—explicit to him—may have an *unintended*—for him—result of interest to the observer. Emmet reserves the term function for this type of action. The end, or goal, unlike the first case, is here stipulated not by the actor but by the observer. Yet, and this is the admirable portion of Emmet's treatment, the actor is never relegated to the position of a self-adjusting part in a servomechanism. He is able to "learn" from the functions; functional results become assimilated into his explicit motives, so that functions transform purposes, and observer-posited ends come to influence the ends explicitly formulated by the actor.

This brings us to the concept of "powers." The actor's capacity to learn, to intervene creatively—within the limits of what is possible in the total system—to change his mind, and to seek new ways of attaining his end is summed up by the term "powers." Men, therefore, are not condemned merely to act out a systemic tragedy because, through learning, they are able to change the system itself. Furthermore, the system is then not expected to return to a stable or metastable condition, but to transform itself.[4] What is not clear in Emmet's analysis is whether a transformed system is still the same pattern of relationships that existed before the actors learned, or whether it is something new. Since she is dealing with an image borrowed from the national polity or society, this ambiguity poses no particular problem, for the continuation of the state—albeit with new functions and structures—can be taken as sufficient evidence of the survival of the system. In international relations we have no such simple evidence, and the question can therefore not be dealt with in this fashion. Since the pattern of relationships does, demonstrably, change on the basis of different national policy inputs, and since we experimentally postulate an important transfor-

[3] *Ibid.*, p. 51.
[4] For her brilliant destruction of the notions of equilibrium and stability, see *ibid.*, pp. 60–74.

mation of the international structures, we also hold that "learning" results in the creation of a new system. The "powers" would be found in the ability of national governments to learn the art of revising their demands and seeking new ways of satisfying them without destroying themselves in the process.

Let us sum up. Unlike . . . many functional sociologists we shall reserve the term "purpose" for the action pattern consciously willed by actors in the international system; we shall reserve "function" for the results of these actions, which may bring with them unintended consequences. These may then transform the system by (1) resulting in the kind of learning that is creative in the sense that it enhances the original purposes of the actors, which implies integration; and (2) yielding the kind of learning that forces a re-examination of purposes among the actors such as to involve disintegration. Obviously, integration can be the result of intended or unintended action. Both processes must be kept in mind. But our interest is particularly aroused by the analytical force of *functions* because it enables us to posit a certain kind of international transformation without being discouraged by the prevalence of selfish national motives. The adaptive-transforming force we shall identify with the ability of governments and other actors to recast their purposes in functional terms.[5] . . .

But before summing up our sociological-functional system of the international world in its relationship to integration, we must face one major question: why, it might well be asked, cast integration into a systemic mold? Why not speak simply of the growing power of international organizations? Instead of worrying about purposes and functions, inputs and outputs, environment and feedback, we should be able simply to describe the conceivable relationships between the growing power of international organizations—if there be such—and the transformation of the national scene. We could simply state the impact of United Nations policies on the values and habits of the member states after having established the importance of these values on the policies of the United Nations.

To do so would be to commit the error of the Functionalists. Their formulation, despite its insights and sophistication with respect to the central role of welfare expectations and the trend toward technocracy, remains skewed in the direction of freedom of the will. The Functionalist separability doctrines create an impression of self-evident and automatic

---

[5] Because we are concerned with the transformation of systems, we part company with Emmet at this point. She sums up the virtues of functional analysis thus: "What can be stated in terms of the functional concepts, but not in terms of purposive ones, are the consequences of people's actions which work out in a way which helps maintain a form of society without their being intended to do so" (*ibid.*, p. 96). We would substitute the word "transform" for "maintain," and otherwise accept the formulation.

progress. The argument seems to say that if we maximize welfare tasks, and if we minimize purely diplomatic decision-making, then the latent forces making for world community will triumph manifestly. This much free will cannot be accommodated. . . .

The systemic conceptualization has the virtue of not implying automaticity or inevitable progress, provided the system used is of the concrete, actor-oriented variety. It gives us a picture of a temporally delimited world that allows for and projects probable evolutionary patterns based on empirically established forces. It helps us to imagine the future on the basis of a disciplined view of the past. It sensitizes the observer to search for the consequences flowing from the established relationships among nations. A discussion of the evolutionary potential of international organizations devoid of such a focus runs the risk of assuming unidimensionality; the projection of the role of the United Nations seen in the prism of the collective security function is as unreliable as a vision based purely on the welfare function. Only a systemic conceptualization can hope to combine these strands into one sturdy whole.

Concrete actor-oriented systems remain loyal to the historical tradition and owe more to it than to the methods of social psychology. They represent the clinical rather than the statistical mode of reasoning. Incidents of repeated historical experience are examined in the light of both the motives and the mores found to apply in the epoch in which they occurred. Conclusions are inferred from the cases, even though the cases themselves are analyzed in terms of structured interrelationships previously observed and established.[6] The statistical, as opposed to the historical-clinical, mode deduces trends and verifies hypotheses purely on the basis of quantitative aggregates, without concerning itself with clinical interrelations or historical confluences. The statistical practitioner tends to exhibit wide-eyed wonder concerning the unexpected nature of his conclusions, whereas the historically sensitized observer begins his work with a far more jaded vision.[7]

---

[6] The superiority of historical systems is clearly demonstrated by Hoffmann's discussion of the nature of international law in the current "revolutionary system." Because the current system is characterized by a whole series of specifiable and identifiable heterogeneities, certain rules of law are "obsolete" in the sense that they merely command verbal attachment and are a residue from the preceding system. Certain other rules of law, however, are "premature" in that they herald a new system which is not yet feasible because of the environmental heterogeneities. Yet this co-existence of laws has been "functional" in the sense of yielding a body of practical task-oriented rules on which nations can agree despite heterogeneity, e.g., in technical assistance, space, Antarctica, etc. In *World Politics*, XIV (1961), 229.

[7] For two pioneering efforts to generalize about international relations on the basis of manipulating large bodies of statistical data in preference to the clinical-historical approach, see Hayward R. Alker, Jr., "Dimensions of Voting in the United Nations" (unpublished Ph.D. dissertation, Yale University, 1963), and Rudolph J. Rummel,

We are now able to specify the systemic nature of the phenomena to be discussed in the language of functional sociology. The *items* to which functions are imputed in international relations are the policy demands advanced by governments and non-governmental organizations in the forum of international organizations. But, obviously, not all policy demands are important or relevant, a fact that forces us to select "strategic" items, i.e., crucial with respect to telling us something about the transformation of the system. The strategic nature of the items, however, is based on the perceptions of the actors themselves. They, not merely the observer, make claims and counterclaims concerning military security, economic development, human rights, decolonization, and stable trade patterns. These are our strategic policy demands because, in our period of history, governments consider them so.

The *motives* and *purposes* imputed to the actors are derived by studying words *and* actions, verbal pronouncements and demands as well as concrete steps taken, resolutions voted, and treaties ratified. Advocacy in addition to the subsequent steps taken to implement the results of advocacy provide the data for judging motives. When the purposes imputed to the actors include the desire for social transformation leading to system-dominance, i.e. integration, it is unnecessary to introduce the concept of *function;* in that case the overt purposes of the actors are linked to the integrative process. But when this is not the case, functions are those consequences of action noted by the observer that tend toward the integration of the system.

As Merton shows, motives and functions are easily confused. He therefore introduced the distinction between "manifest" and "latent" functions. The former "are those objective consequences contributing to the adjustment or adaptation of the system which are intended *and* recognized by participants in the system," the latter, "correlatively, being those which are *neither* intended *nor* recognized."[8] I find the distinction unnecessary in the international system because I can conceive of no unintended result of purposive action that is not eventually recognized by the actors. Functions, for us, are unintended consequences that may go unrecognized for a while, but not for very long.[9]

"Dimensions of Conflict Behavior Within and Between Nations" (unpublished Ph.D. dissertation, Northwestern University, 1963). Despite the large number of indicators used and the complexity of the factor analysis undertaken, neither study presents findings unfamiliar to the clinical-historical tradition.

[8] Robert K. Merton, *Social Theory and Social Structure*, Part I, p. 51, (my italics).

[9] Our disagreement with Merton's distinction between latent and manifest functions can be illustrated from the examples he adduces. Merton cites Veblen's treatment of conspicuous consumption as a latent function of the social-economic system being analyzed (*ibid.*, pp. 68–70). This must mean that whatever the overt purposes of the consumers, and whatever the manifest functions in terms of their eventual recognition

Since all functions are understood eventually by the actors, the unintended consequences of their purposes are "learned." Therefore, any function becomes a new purpose at a different systemic level of integration. We must merely distinguish between learning conducive to integration and learning that seeks to block the process. The difference is largely one of

---

of the unintended consequences, the "real" function remained unrecognized—"costliness = mark of higher social status"—by the American capitalist. It may be that the Fricks, Huntingtons, Vanderbilts, and Goulds were not aware of this Veblenian equation; but I doubt it. Even if we were to assume their lack of awareness, the concept of latent functions is not likely to help us in an analysis of the international system. In contrast with the myriad behavior patterns and social roles in a broad social context, in international relations we are dealing with the specific and finite demands of government. While the units being analyzed are more complex, their inputs into the system—paradoxically—are analytically simpler than the task Veblen set himself. Is it not likely that the actors will sooner or later grow aware of the unintended consequences of earlier purposes? Statesmen may be dolts, but they are not robots.

Merton uses an extended example of bossism in American urban politics to illustrate the same thesis. He puts the problem in this way: "Proceeding from the functional view, therefore, that we should *ordinarily* (not invariably) expect persistent social patterns and social structures to perform positive functions *which are at the time not adequately fulfilled by other existing patterns and structures,* the thought occurs that perhaps this publicly maligned organization is, *under present conditions,* satisfying basic latent functions" (*ibid.,* pp. 71–72, italics in original).

In terms of the manifest functions, the machine is dysfunctional for the polity because it encourages corruption and defeats the purpose of the official political structures. But it may satisfy the latent functions of underprivileged groups in the polity, who, because of ignorance, illiteracy, poverty, recent immigrant status, etc., have no opportunity to obtain redress of their demands from the official structures. Legitimate and illicit business obtain from the machine "protection" not otherwise available. Bossism then provides the informal structures for meeting these latent functions. "Put in more generalized terms," says Merton, *"the functional deficiencies of the official structure generate an alternative (unofficial) structure to fulfill existing needs somewhat more effectively.* Whatever its specific historical origins, the political machine persists as an apparatus for satisfying otherwise unfulfilled needs of diverse groups in the population" (*ibid.,* p. 73, italics in original).

In the first place, let us note that the meaning of "function" has now shifted away from "unintended consequences" to "need." Which is the latent function? The way in which the machine meets the needs of certain urban groups, or the needs themselves? Is bossism a structure that arose to meet the latent function, or the function itself? The treatment begs the question. In our paradigm it would appear as a structure. But the real problem still hinges on the issue of latency. Although bossism may have arisen as an unintended consequence, surely it did not remain unrecognized for long by politicians, the underprivileged, the racketeers, the reformers, the observers. I am not disputing Merton's argument that the machine fulfilled the positive function of meeting some of the needs of the groups studied; nor am I quarreling with his contention that functional analysis sensitizes the observer to recognizing this kind of indirect benefit from structure which, on the surface, appears to be reprehensible morally and dysfunctional for the total system. But I am disputing the adequacy of a formulation that holds these features to be both unintended *and* unrecognized by the participants, leaving the observer as the only one detached enough to be aware of the total context. Indeed, the likelihood of their recognition leads me to postulate the hiatus between the functional and dysfunctional consequences of actor purposes in international systems.

perceptions among the actors about which kind of response most nearly approximates the initial purpose.

In contrast with the difficulties encountered in the study of social systems at the national level, the identification of the unit subserved by the function is relatively simple internationally. The *unit* is whoever puts forth demands effectively, i.e. is in a position to be heard in the system's structures. This, for the most part, is a position held by governments, though for some items subject to functional analysis, national and international voluntary groups must be included. The *mechanisms* through which purposes and functions must be fulfilled are the central institutional structures of national and international bureacracies. Chief of these are the division of labor among discrete units and the delegation of power to expert bodies entrusted with the implementation of purposes. We should also include a sensitivity to the freedom of maneuver enjoyed by certain individuals with respect to the practice of creative innovation.

Suppose some item ceases to have functional significance for the transformation of the system. Suppose, indeed, it acquires a dysfunctional significance. Merton here suggests the concept of the "balance" of functional consequences of a given item and the notion of "functional equivalents." Only clinical study can disclose the existence of such phenomena in the international system. We may discover that certain items (e.g. demands for more highly institutionalized collective security) cease to have functional results at a certain time and in the setting of a certain balance of environmental conditions (e.g. the inability of revolutionary and conservative states to agree on common rules). But we may also find that another item (e.g. the demand for financial aid) takes the place of collective security in terms of functional consequences. However, it must be realized that the international system displays a relatively small number of items and thus restricts the number of functions. In addition the structural context is quite rigid. Hence the international context probably limits the available equivalents as compared with the pluralistic nation-state.

The restricted number of items and functions encountered at the international level actually simplifies the problem of *validation*. We do not as yet have to worry about locating adequate samples of social systems to be subjected to functional analysis at the international level; nor do we need to concern ourselves with huge numbers of items to be resolved into representative samples. There are as yet very few international organizations. Their activities hardly overwhelm the observer; entire "populations" of items can be studied relatively painlessly without having to resort to sampling. In recent historical systems the number of states involved has been quite manageable. Existing international structures, such as the United Nations, its specialized agencies, regional blocs and alliances, remain few enough in number to make comparison relatively simple.

A final appeal: the functional analysis of international integration is not necessarily ideologically loaded in favor of "one world." "Functional analysis has no intrinsic commitment to an ideological position," argues Merton. But he continues that "this does not gainsay the fact that particular functional analyses and particular hypotheses advanced by functionalists may have an identifiable ideological role."[10] The ideological bias is exposed by close attention to the end result of functional development postulated by the observer as being desirable. In Mitrany's case we had no difficulty in specifying the end. In rigorous functional studies the "end" (integration, in our case) is clearly postulated. This creates no ideological bias, since the reader can decide for himself whether he likes or dislikes integration. The process, conceived analytically, would exist whether one likes it or not, whether one wishes to aid it or hinder it.

---

[10] Merton, p. 54. The essay by Parsons, cited above, clearly does contain an un-avowed ideological bias in favor of an integrated world order. "The subordination of 'parochial' interests to those of a more extensive system" is deduced as systemically desirable, even though it is also clearly the author's wish that gives rise to the shape of the system he sketches. Parsons, p. 120.

Chapter VII

Values

and

Ideology

Introduction

*I*F August Comte was the father of sociology, the field has a choice of self-images. Comte had two marriages, one with a prostitute and the other unconsummated; sociology may be either a bastard son or the product of an immaculate conception. Nowadays much of the choice hinges upon one's attitude toward functionalism and one's view of the relation between sociology and ideology. According to some critics, functionalist theories are indeed "immaculately conceived" in that their view of society is utopian and unsullied by the vital events of society itself. As advocates of the status quo and political conservatism, the critics continue, functionalists turn their backs on the orgy of social change; as elegant abstractionists, they overlook processes by which passions are inflamed and men are moved. On the other hand, the so-called conflict theorists are held to be illegitimate and disreputable for their sociological indiscretions and their theoretical license. As those who would act rather than understand, some argue, they betray the normative order: as naked politicians, they are an embarrassment to the dispassionate enterprise of social science. Given such a taut polemical tone, it is no surprise that the debate has often generated more heat than light.

But perhaps the issue is false and the choice misleading. One may argue with Max Weber that sociology should be value-free. This is not to say that sociology has no relationship to values, but rather that the sociologist should be willing to declare his bias in order to counteract it methodologically. The position is central to classical sociology, but it has recently come under increasing attack from those who regard it as either irresponsible or naive. It is held to be irresponsible in that it ignores the sociologist's fundamental mandate to train his expertise upon the social problems of the day even though this necessitates value commitment. It is held to be naive in that it is impossible to be aware of all biases, let alone to counteract them. Instead of pursuing an illusory and utopian goal, how much better to take these biases at face value and pursue them honestly in their own right (cf. Alvin W. Gouldner, "Anti-Minotaur: The Myth of a Value-Free Sociology," *Social Problems,* Winter, 1962).

In the four articles that follow, there are two distinct value problems which come to the fore. The dispute between the liberals and the conservatives cross-cuts a separate dispute between those who argue that theory may be independent of values and those that view values as inevitably imbedded in theory. The four authors to follow confront these issues from diverse perspectives.

Fritz Machlup is an eminent economist who, in the selection reprinted here, explores the intrusion of values into economic analysis. His concern with "misplaced concreteness and disguised politics" indicates his aversion to value-advocacy masquerading as science. Note, however, that Machlup is not worried that the scientist will seduce the public. Rather he is fearful that the scientist will seduce himself and strip his concepts of their precision and their analytic effectiveness. In all of this, Machlup uses an example that is close to the hearts of functionalists in every discipline: equilibrium. He indicates ways in which the equilibrium model may be properly applied, but goes on to suggest improper applications as well. Thus, he cautions against interpreting equilibrium as an operational concept, as a synonym for stability, or, indeed, as a value judgment. When heuristic models are taken as reality, he argues, scientific analysis is both blunted and burlesqued.

Harold Fallding comes to the defense of an openly evaluative functionalism within sociology. He argues that evaluation is as honorable a goal as explanation within scientific circles, but he is careful to distinguish evaluation from both bias and unrefined intuition. Evaluation may be objective in spite of its intimate relation to values. Indeed, it is only by assessing the extent to which explicit values are realized that objective evaluation can proceed and functionalism may flourish. Fallding goes on to discuss the particular values at issue in the functionalist approach. He answers allegations of conservative elitism. He denies that functionalism is impervious to the needs of the individual and unalterably opposed to change or even to untidy revolution. Instead, the functionalist model of the "good" society is one in which all men are rewarded and all needs are satisfied. It is only thus that true stability can be obtained. Without such need-fulfillment, stability is hollow and wholly undesirable. In short, Fallding argues that functionalism needs a value-informed vision and has one that is justifiable in the classic liberal tradition.

Ralf Dahrendorf takes strong exception. Without speaking to Fallding directly, Dahrendorf argues that functionalism has shirked rather than stressed the central processes of society. Functionalism, he argues, is a current version of classical utopianism with one important difference: whereas the utopians used their schemes as vehicles for social satire and social criticism, the functionalists take theirs at face value as part of a general mood of "complacent conservatism." Dahrendorf is willing to concede that a model of societal equilibrium and consensus is appropriate for a very limited number of problems, but he urges an alternative approach for wider utility. This approach would substitute change for stability, conflict for consensus, and constraint for normative equilibrium. Dahrendorf has elaborated the approach in his larger work, *Class and Class Conflict in Industrial Society* (Stanford, 1959). Throughout he represents the virulent European neo-Marxism that has had such a profound impact upon the sociology of the fifties and the sixties. In this, his ideas are closely related to those of Mills, Lockwood, and Hield earlier in the volume. Not only do these authors politicize the issue but they give it a common focus in concentrating upon the work of Talcott Parsons, especially his book, *The Social System*.

The chapter's final author dissents from the common criticism of Parsons. Andrew Hacker is a political scientist and was a participant in a Cornell University symposium on Parsons (Max Black, ed., *The Social Theories of Talcott Parsons*, Prentice-Hall, 1961). Hacker uses a political yardstick in two ways. First, he argues that Parsons' analysis of political phenomena is uneven; his examination of McCarthyism is excellent, but his reply to C. Wright Mills on "the power elite" and the "mass society" is wanting. Second, Hacker assesses Parsons' own political ideology independent of his theory. Here Hacker finds that the conservative label has been misapplied. Parsons, after all, was an avid Stevenson supporter and New Dealer; he was recently among the first to issue a public call for a negotiated settlement in the Vietnam War. The important point is not that Parons is a conservative among liberals but rather that he is a liberal among radicals. Unlike Mills and Dahrendorf, Parsons retains hope that society will be equal to the task of change without a major structural realignment or revolution. The question is not whether strains exist or whether change is necessary, but rather how much alteration is needed and by what processes? In all of this, Hacker comments on a facet of Parsons that is not usually considered in the debate over functionalism. Perhaps it is unfair to examine a man's political commitments in evaluating his sociological achievements; perhaps it is unfair to single out one man for such extended treatment generally. And yet Parsons is a giant in a controversy that has become irretrievably ideological. Both the man and his ideology compel inordinate attention.

Fritz Machlup

Equilibrium and Disequilibrium

MISPLACED CONCRETENESS AND DISGUISED POLITICS

*E*CONOMISTS have used the notion of equilibrium in a variety of contexts and for a variety of purposes; in proceeding from one topic to another some have failed to note transformations in the use made of it and in the meanings read into the term. Not a few who have sensed incongruities, fallacies or outright misuse turned against all "equilibrium economics," heaping abuse on any type of analysis that employed the notion.

The Major Uses of Equilibrium Concepts in Economics

The most literal use of equilibrium or disequilibrium in the sense of equal or unequal weights on the two arms of a scale, without any analytical, explicatory, predictive or evaluative connotation, occurs only in connection with practically measurable quantities, such as income and expenditure in a budget, exports and imports in a trade balance, trade items and long-term

Reprinted from Fritz Machlup, "Equilibrium and Disequilibrium: Misplaced Concreteness and Disguised Politics," *The Economic Journal*, 68 (March, 1958), pp. 1–24, which also appeared in Fritz Machlup, *Essays on Economic Semantics*, Prentice-Hall, 1963, pp. 43–72. Reprinted by permission of the author and the Royal Economic Society.

capital transfers in a balance of payments. Yet even in these contexts economists have rarely been content with merely weighing the items on the two sides; they have usually wanted to connect them with other economic variables which they considered relevant for a more "inclusive" equilibrium or disequilibrium of the balance in question.

The most prevalent use of the equilibrium concept in economics is probably as a methodological device in abstract theory. Here "equilibrium" is employed in connection with "models" containing several interrelated variables; as a "useful fiction," it serves as a part of a mental experiment designed to analyze causal connections between "events" or "changes of variables."

It is a different use of the equilibrium idea when it is employed to refer to concrete economic situations: here it is supposed to characterize a historical situation as one that has lasted or will last for a relatively long time without significant change. The direct application of the concept to observed situations makes it "operational," as it were. The jump from equilibrium as a methodological device (useful fiction, purely mental construct to equilibrium as a characterization of a concrete historical situation (operational concept) is a big one; that many take it without noticing any strain and without noting the difference, is attributable, I shall argue, to their failure to recognise the function of the analytical concept, and is conducive to considerable confusion.

A jump in a different direction has been taken from an analytical equilibrium concept to an evaluative one. It is easy to see how it happens: the notion of equilibrium as a balance of forces acquires a connotation of "appropriateness" when the balance is thought of as one of "natural forces"; or even a connotation of "goodness" when that balance is thought of as "harmony." Once the use of equilibrium as a value judgment is condoned, the replacement of the mystical "natural" forces by "progressive" political forces appears indicated, and a variety of social goals is incorporated in the concept of equilibrium. Eventually, equilibrium comes to mean conformance with certain objectives which organised society is asked to pursue. I shall argue that such equilibrium with built-in politics often impairs the usefulness of equilibrium as a value-free analytical device.

Another evaluative equilibrium concept is used in welfare economics. In the theoretical models of the household and the firm "equilibrium" is assumed to be sought between the various items of the plans and dispositions of the individual decision maker so that he would find no reason to make further changes. The older welfare economists promoted this equilibrium from a methodological device (for the explanation of chance) to a standard of evaluation (marking the best positions attainable); and all these equilibria became "optima" and integral parts of the maximum welfare position for the whole community. Modern welfare economists deal with the value judgments that were implicit in such a procedure, and try to bring them out into the open. Propositions about conditions under which certain "allocative and distributive equilibria" in the economy as a whole would coincide with whatever is regarded as the "highest social welfare function" are then formulated and qualified with care.

The present paper will not be concerned with welfare economics. But it will be concerned, to some extent, with the use of a value-laden equilibrium concept in positive (explicatory) economics. The chief purpose of the paper is to show the dangers to clear analysis that may arise from the failure to notice the differences between analytical, descriptive and evaluative equilibrium concepts. As a prerequisite, we shall have to pay closer attention than has usually been given to the function of the purely analytical equilibrium concept in economic theorising. . . .

We have not thus far attempted to formulate a definition of equilibrium, though the meaning of the term has probably become quite clear. In the light of the preceding discussion we may define *equilibrium*, in economic analysis, as *a constellation of selected interrelated variables so adjusted to one another that no inherent tendency to change prevails in the model which they constitute.* The model as well as its equilibria are, of course, mental constructions (based on abstraction and invention).

It has been suggested to me that the phrase "balance of forces" should be a part of any definition of equilibrium. I cannot accept this suggestion; "balance of forces" is simply another metaphor, perhaps a synonym but not an explanation of "equilibrium," and sadly encumbered by the reference to "forces," which is a rather mystical concept in need of a separate time-consuming cleaning job. But if it is believed that additional metaphors can be helpful in defining or explaining equilibrium, then I should propose the phrase "peaceful co-existence" between selected variables of given magnitudes. Where such "peaceful co-existence" is not possible, where the selected variables are *not compatible* with one another in their given magnitudes, one or more of them will have to change, and will continue to change until they reach magnitudes that make it possible for them to live with each other as they are.

Thus, as an alternative definition of equilibrium we may propose *mutual compatibility of a selected set of interrelated variables of particular magnitudes.* Assume the set consists of variables A, B, C and D, and that certain inter-relationships between them are assumed (in the form of behavior equations, technological, psychological or institutional relations, as well as mere definitions). If these variables are compatible in their "present" magnitudes "everything could go on as it is." Then "something happens" which increases variable C. In its new magnitude C is no long compatible with A, B

and *D*, and "things must adjust themselves." Which of the variables will "give" and by how much will depend on the rules of the game, expressed in the relationships assumed between variables. At last, the new values of the four variables may be such that they are again compatible with one another, and "the situation calls for no further adjustments."

The crux of the matter is that the addition of another variable, somehow related to one or more of the others, would change the picture. The magnitudes in which *A, B, C* and *D* are mutually compatible when they are the only players in the game may constitute serious incompatibility when they are joined by another player, say *E*, of a certain size. But another addition, say *F*, may neutralize the "disturbing" effect of *E*, and *A, B, C, D* in their "present" magnitudes may again be compatible and "everything could go on as it is." One cannot overemphasize this *relativity* of compatibility and incompatibility regarding extra variables included in, or excluded from, the selected set. Only a complete enumeration of the variables selected and interrelations assumed makes it meaningful to assert their mutual compatibility or incompatibility, that is, the equilibrium or disequilibrium of the chosen set. And, while a *specification* of the selected variables and assumed interrelations is required for every model and every problem, the *definition* of equilibrium and disequilibrium must not narrow the freedom of choice.

Misplaced Concreteness and Disguised Politics

Although I recognized the existence of other equilibrium concepts in economics, I have discussed only the one designed for theoretical analysis. I strongly suspect that those who use equilibrium concepts for other purposes, such as the description of historical situations or their evaluation, believe that one and the same concept can do double or triple duty. This I challenge. My task in this section cannot be used for other purposes without losing much of its usefulness in analysis.

Not an Operational Concept

Equilibrium as a tool for theoretical analysis is not an operational concept; and attempts to develop operational counterparts to the construct have not been successful.[1] Some of the variables in a model usually have statistically operational counterparts; in rare instances all have. But even in this

---

[1] Schumpeter once proposed a statistically discernible "neighborhood of equilibrium," with reference to cyclical fluctuations of business activity. But he always insisted on the purely fictitious and instrumental character of the equilibrium concept

event the *compatibility* between the variables is always a question of the assumed interrelations and of the limitation of the model to the variables selected. The "real world" surely has infinitely more variables than any abstract economic model, and their "actual" interrelations are neither known nor, I fear, knowable (partly because they probably change unpredictably over time). It follows that the equilibrium between selected variables could not be observed even if each of the variables had an observable counterpart in the real world.

Some of the variables in a model which have observable and measurable counterparts can sometimes be arranged in sub-sets in the form of balance sheets, *T*-accounts or financial statements, permitting us to strike a balance between the two sides and to speak (confusingly) of an "equilibrium" or "disequilibrium" in that sub-set. For example, exports and imports can be arranged as a trade balance, or foreign-trade items and certain capital and other transfers can be arranged as an accounting-balance of payments.[2] A so-called equilibrium for these items means merely equality of the sums on each side of the account, and a so-called disequilibrium means inequality of the sums. But only when this sub-set is linked with other variables—income, consumption, investment, prices, employment, wage-rates, exchange rates, interest rates, foreign reserves, bank reserves, bank loans, etc.—does it become a factor in economic analysis. And only after the variables are selected and their interrelations assumed can we speak of equilibrium and disequilibrium in the sense in which these terms are used in economic analysis. Despite the operational sub-set, the model as a whole and its equilibrium are not observable, not operational; they remain mental constructions.

Perhaps similar, perhaps very different considerations once led Per Jacobsson to make this observation on the subject: "You can no more define equilibrium in international trade than you can define a pretty girl, but you can recognize one if you meet one." [3] I like this remark for its charm and wit, but I wonder whether it hits the mark. I think I am quite competent to recognize a pretty girl, though my taste may not be the same as that of other expert observers. But I cannot recognize an equilibrium in international trade no matter how hard I look. I can define it, at least to my own satisfaction; but I cannot recognize anything in reality—in the statistical figures representing the "facts" of a "real situation"—as an equilibrium in

---

itself. Joseph A. Schumpeter, *Business Cycles* (New York: McGraw-Hill, 1939), pp. 68–71.

[2] For an exposition of the differences between the "accounting balance," the "market balance" and the "program balance" of payments see Fritz Machlup, "Three Concepts of the Balance of Payments and the So-called Dollar Shortage," *Economic Journal*, Vol. LX (1950), pp. 46–68.

[3] Per Jacobsson, in a speech in 1949.

international trade in the sense discussed, that is, as a position where "every-thing could go on as it is" and "the situation calls for no further adjust-ments" to anything that has happened.

To characterize a concrete situation "observed" in reality as one of "equilibrium" is to commit the fallacy of misplaced concreteness. At best, the observer may mean to assert that in his opinion the observed and duly identi-fied situation corresponds to a model in his mind in which a set of selected variables determine a certain outcome, and that he finds no inherent cause of change—that is, that he believes only an outside disturbance, not in evidence at the moment, would produce a change in these variables. This, of course, is a personal judgment, meaningful only if the variables are fully enumerated and the assumptions about their inter-relations are clearly stated. As matters stand, any concrete economic situation may correspond at the same time to an equilibrium of one model and a disequilibrium of another.

The use of the analytical equilibrium concept as a designation of a con-crete historical situation is regard as "misplaced concreteness," first because of the general fallacy involved in jumping the distance between a useful fiction and particular data of observation and, second, because of the fallacy involved in forgetting the relativity of equilibrium with respect to variables and relations selected. An indefinite number of models may be found to "fit" a concrete situation in one way or another, and the choice is not dictated either by any so-called realities of life or by any conventions of the analysts.[4]

The phrase "relativity of equilibrium" gives expression to the facts that any number and combination of variables may be chosen for a model, depending on the analytical or didactic habits, skills and purposes of the economist; that the same values of variables may account both for equilib-rium or disequilibrium, depending on the other variables with which they are made to keep company and on the relations assumed to prevail between them; and that different problems (perhaps concerning the same concrete situation) may call for very different models for use in analysis.

---

[4] To be sure, there are "observed" situations which invite characterization as "dis-equilibria" without serious danger of confusion. For example, there will be little doubt about just what model and what variables are referred to when some gross instances of price fixing, either with unsold supplies not disposable at the official minimum price or with queues of would-be buyers lined up to get some of their demand satisfied at the ceiling price, are characterized as "market disequilibria." The implication, appar-ently, is that the situation could not endure were it not for the "interference." On the other hand, a model that includes government price fixing, penalties for violations, unsold stocks, unsatisfied demand, etc., among its variables would show the surplus stocks or the unsatisfied demand as the "final equilibrium"—though only as "tem-porary equilibrium" if some lagged black-market behavioral functions are added to the list of assumptions.

Not the Same as Stability

Stability in the sense of invariance over time has some connections with the notion of equilibrium which may easily lead to confusion. Since equilibrium is the position where everything is so well adjusted to everything else —in the model—that things can go on without change, this surely implies stability over time (at least until the next disturbance). And since a disturbing change must be isolated—in the model—from anything else that might require adjusting changes, this implies that "all other things remain unchanged"—particularly the interrelations assumed for the model; all in all, we presuppose the stability of a lot of things for the duration of the process that is pictured as "equilibration" in the model. With everything stable at the beginning and at the end of the imagined process, and many things stable while it goes on, the logical tie between stability and equilibrium is certainly a close one.

In addition, there is the very special meaning of "stability of equilibrium" according to which a "stable equilibrium" is distinguished from an "unstable" one depending on the presence or absence of a mechanism for the "self-correction" of random deviations from the equilibrium values of the variables involved.

However, none of these notions of stability has much to do with the stability of a price or quantity observed in actual fact. An actual price may be stable over a long time without forcing us to have it represented by an equilibrium price in the model that we may choose for explaining it. An actual price may be most unstable, jumping up and down like mad, and yet we may find it most expedient to explain these changes by means of models showing a quick succession of perfectly stable equilibria with different equilibrium prices due to a quick succession of exogenous disequilibrating changes.

We may conclude that "observed stability" and "observed instability" should not be confused with, or attributed to, equilibrium and disequilibrium, respectively, in analytic models.

Not a Value Judgment

Equilibrium as used in positive economic analysis—as distinguished from welfare economics—should not be taken as a value judgment, nor as a reference to a "desired state of affairs." Equilibrium is not a Good Thing, and disequilibrium is not a Bad Thing. Nor is the reverse association justified: equilibrium stands neither for the *status quo* nor for *laissez faire*, as some dissident economists have been inclined to think.

If equilibrium analysis is employed to explain a sad situation as the equilibrium outcome of certain conditions and events, it would be silly to transfer our dislike of the situation to the equilibrium concept used in the explanation. And if a sad situation is disliked and deemed intolerable, to call it disequilibrium on that account helps neither in analysing it nor in developing the best policy for improving it.

Of course, it is perfectly legitimate to allow our value judgments to suggest to us the problems for analysis. If we find it desirable to secure full employment at high wage-rates we may construct models to show us what conditions (interrelations between variables) would make full employment and high wage-rates compatible with given values of the other variables in the set; or what values these other variables would have to attain in order to be compatible with full employment and high wage-rates with given interrelations. If we or others advocate a certain full-employment policy we may construct models to show us what effects could be expected, in a variety of circumstances, if various institutional relationships were established to make interest rates, bank loans, government expenditures (or other employment-inducing variables) depend upon changes in (absolute or relative) unemployment. But none of these exercises, valuable and important though they are, would be aided by incorporating our moral values or political goals into the *definition* of equilibrium, as several economists have proposed. Some of these proposals require that full employment at given wage-rates and other desirable objectives be made part of the definition of equilibrium, so that any position in which these objectives are not attained would always have to be called "disequilibrium."

By infusing a value judgment, a political philosopher of programme, or a rejection of a programme or policy, into the concept of equilibrium designed for economic analysis, the analyst commits the fallacy of implicit evaluation or disguised politics. To choose the variables and interrelations suitable for an equilibrium analysis of problems that are dictated by value judgments and political objectives is one thing. It is quite another thing to insist on packaging these valuations with the definition of equilibrium. Indeed, the analysis of the possibilities of their realization may be impeded by such a restrictive definition.

Attack on Persuasive Definitions

Philosophers of science have recently shown that some definitions, supposedly stating what something is or means, are in fact devised to persuade people to do certain things or to do things in a certain way. "Persuasive definitions" is the name characterizing such definitions.[5]

---

[5] *Cf.* C. L. Stevenson, "Persuasive Definitions," *Mind*, Vol. 47 (1938), p. 331; Max

Paul Streeten, in an interesting article, showed that certain definitions of balance-of-payments equilibrium fall in the category of persuasive definitions. We have seen how stable exchange rates, full employment at given wage-rates, stable price levels and unrestricted trade have been included as additional criteria in some definitions of balance-of-payments equilibrium. This expansion of criteria, according to Streeten, amounts to "begging the question"; "conceals behind a persuasive definition value judgments not generally shared." [6]

Streeten proceeds to exemplify the dangers of persuasive definitions:

To include, say, the presence of import restrictions in the definition of "disequilibrium" produces the convenient result that the removal of these restrictions, and devaluation or deflation, become a *necessity,* although it is hoped, presumably, that the difference between logical necessity (what follows from the definition) and political or moral necessity (what ought to be done) will remain undetected. [p. 87].

It is implicitly assumed, I take it, that those who make use of a persuasive definition of equilibrium rely on the popular association of equilibrium with a Good Thing, and of disequilibrium with a Bad Thing. Thus, they hope to sell to the public the removal of import restrictions (or the adoption of full-employment policies, etc.) in the same package labelled "equilibrium." . . .

The Trouble with Built-in Politics

The objections against persuasive definitions of equilibrium are not based on the fear that gullible people may actually be persuaded to stand up for the measures or policies "deduced" from arguments in which such an equilibrium concept is employed; the real ground for objection is that an equilibrium concept so drastically restricted by built-in political criteria becomes less useful, if not useless in the analysis of most problems. Most problems that require analysis are such that not all the ideal conditions which are made "honorary criteria" of equilibrium can be "attained"; their analysis calls for a variety of policy variables and institutional (political) behavior functions combined with a less circumscribed concept of equilibrium that can be used for *any* set of variables and *any* relationships between them. This statement refers chiefly to the kind of analysis in which equilibrium is thought of as the initial and final positions in an imagined process of change involving a

Black, "The Definition of Scientific Method," *Science and Civilization* (Madison: University of Wisconsin Press, 1949), p. 69.
    [6] Paul Streeten, "Elasticity Optimism and Pessimism in International Trade," *Economia Internazionale,* Vol. VII (1954), p. 87.

chosen set of interrelated variables. But it holds also for an analysis in which equilibrium is thought of merely as the equality of certain (actual or potential) sums on the two sides of the account called "the balance of payments."

Take any change that would create an increase in the demand for foreign exchange, or a decrease in its supply. Whether it is a change in tastes at home or abroad, a change in the technical production possibilities anywhere, a change in fiscal or monetary policy (say, to accelerate economic development), a change in the wage structure (for example, giving higher wage-rates to industrial workers), a change in the flow of investment (perhaps a greater demand for foreign investment), a reduction in the desire to hold cash, or any one of a score of similar "disequilibrating changes"—the adjusting changes will involve first an accommodating outflow of foreign reserve and eventually some of the "prohibited" movements, that is, some deviations from the built-in political requirements of "equilibrium" in the persuasive sense. For example, real wages may be reduced through higher prices of wage goods; interest rates may rise, or bank loans be curtailed, with consequent reductions in employment; foreign-exchange rates may get adjusted, etc., and the final position—the new equilibrium in the analytical sense—will be a "disequilibrium" of the balance of payment in the persuasive (or rather dissuasive) sense. Since none of the results of any of the possible adjustments would qualify for the honorific title "equilibrium," the "disequilibrium" (in the dissuasive sense) could be remedied only by a *deus ex machina:* by another disequilibrating change that happened to neutralise the first disturbance and render the unpleasant adjustments unnecesasry. A virtual sabotage of economic analysis!

Harold Fallding

Evaluation, Social Systems, and Human Needs

L*IKE* other statements which have appeared in recent years,[1] the papers on functional analysis by Kingsley Davis[2] and Ronald Philip Dore[3] illustrate the amount of spadework that remains to be done here. While the contributions of Talcott Parsons[4] and Robert Merton[5] have been epoch-making, we

Reprinted from Harold Fallding, "Functional Analysis in Sociology," *American Sociological Review*, 28 (February, 1963), pp. 5–13, by permission of the author and the American Sociological Association.

[1] See Harry C. Bredemeier, "The Methodology of Functionalism," *American Sociological Review*, 20 (April, 1955), pp. 173–180; Bernard Barber, "Structural-Functional Analysis: Some Problems and Misunderstandings," *American Sociological Review*, 21 (April, 1956), pp. 129–135; Walter Buckley, "Structural-Functional Analysis in Modern Sociology," in Howard Becker and Alvin Boskoff (eds.), *Modern Sociological Theory in Continuity and Change*, New York: The Dryden Press, 1957, pp. 236–259; Francesca Cancian, "Functional Analysis of Change," *American Sociological Review*, 25 (December, 1960), pp. 818–827.

[2] Kingsley Davis, "The Myth of Functional Analysis as a Special Method in Sociology and Anthropology," *American Sociological Review*, 24 (December, 1959), pp. 752–772.

[3] Ronald Philip Dore, "Function and Cause," *American Sociological Review*, 26 (December, 1961), pp. 843–853.

[4] See especially, Talcott Parsons, *The Social System*, Glencoe, Ill.: The Free Press, 1951; Talcott Parsons, R. F. Bales, and E. A. Shils, *Working Papers in the Theory of*

have not yet the common code which Merton sought. Yet more than ever there is need for a code that would serve as scaffolding for diverse workers to build in unison. The scaffolding could always be dismembered mentally by anyone looking into basic questions,[6] but for anyone interpreting data it needs to stay provisionally fixed. The following is not the code called for but a rally to persevere in winning through to it.

The paper states in synoptic form only some of the set of assumptions which, if assembled, might orient sociologists more uniformly to their task. As it is the tradesman's last that is being fashioned, the writer does not follow into the assumptions behind the assumptions as the philosopher would—yet an exercise like this makes it easier to see what some of these postulates are. The writer is aware, moreover, that what he proposes as definite will still prove controversial. His main purpose is to represent functional analysis in sociology not as part of explanation but as a form of measurement which belongs to the natural history phase of the science. And an attempt is made to elicit some of the specific dimensions of measurement, of the kind Hempel[7] has asked for. As this proceeds, the way in which disorganization is implicated in dysfunction begins to appear plainer. The kinship connection of these two chief mourners has scarcely yet been traced.

1. Functional analysis involves evaluation.—Sociology treats behavior in situations which pose a problem of regulation, rather than dealing solely with

---

Action, Glencoe, Ill.: The Free Press, 1953; Talcott Parsons and Neil J. Smelser, *Economy and Society*, Glencoe, Ill.: The Free Press, 1956; Talcott Parsons, "An Outline of the Social System," in Talcott Parsons, Edward Shils, Kaspar D. Naegele· and Jesse R. Pitts (eds.), *Theories of Society: Foundations of Modern Sociological Theory*, Glencoe, Ill.: The Free Press, 1961, pp. 30–79.

5 See Robert K. Merton, *Social Theory and Social Structure*, Glencoe, Ill.: The Free Press, 1957; Robert K. Merton, "Social Problems and Sociological Theory," in Robert K. Merton and Robert A. Nisbet (eds.), *Contemporary Social Problems, An Introduction to the Sociology of Deviant Behavior and Social Disorganization*, New York: Harcourt, Brace and World, 1961.

6 An analysis at this basic level has been undertaken by a number of authors. See, e.g., S. F. Nadel, *The Foundations of Social Anthropology*, London: Cohen and West, 1953, pp. 368–408; Ernest Nagel, "A Formalization of Functionalism," *Logic Without Metaphysics*, Glencoe, Ill.: The Free Press, 1956, pp. 247–283; Dorothy Emmet, *Function, Purpose and Powers: Some Concepts in the Study of Individuals and Societies*, London: Macmillan, 1958; Carl G. Hempel, "The Logic of Functional Analysis," in Llewellyn Gross (ed.), *Symposium on Sociological Theory*, Evanston, Ill.: Row, Peterson and Co., 1959, pp. 271–307; Richard Bevan Braithwaite, *Scientific Explanation, a Study of the Function of Theory, Probability and Law in Science*, Cambridge: The University Press, 1959, pp. 319–341.

7 Hempel writes: "For the sake of objective testability of functionalist hypotheses, it is essential, therefore, that definitions of needs or functional prerequisites be supplemented by reasonably clear and objectively applicable criteria of what is to be considered a healthy state or a normal working order of the systems under consideration; and that the vague and sweeping notion of survival then be construed in the relativized sense of survival in a healthy state as specified." Carl G. Hempel, *op. cit.*, p. 294.

situations where regulation is achieved. But before we ever speak of social events, a system of regulated interpersonal contact either exists in some degree, or the participants are aware that one is called for and have adumbrated it—or, having lost what was won, have abrogated it. To designate the realized desideratum we can speak of "a group" or, alternatively, of "social arrangements," "social organization," "social structure," "social system." While if we speak of the function of a social system as a whole it is simply to specify what product is secured through the bridges and bonds thus established between man and man. It may be bread or bullion, music or medicine, sympathy or salvation. Then if we speak in addition of the function of any activity *contained within* a social system we refer to the effect it has in strengthening (or weakening) these productive bonds. For instance, conflict itself has been analyzed by Coser[8] as having positive functions in some social structures, and by this he simply aims to show that it can strengthen existing productive bonds by sealing their corrosions—e.g., when a hampering grievance is aired and removed and everyone is "able to get on with the job." Contained within a casket of existing bonds conflict may work like fire to purge them of imperfections; but, without these, it would presumably not even constitute a social phenomenon, much less a functional one.

The notion of function in connection with societies and their component groups has been variously employed, as Merton[9] showed. But the usage that has come to prevail takes as the function of an activity *within a system* the contribution it makes to the whole. We have therefore come to see the importance of specifying precisely both the part and the whole to which a functional statement refers. A practice which is functional within one social region need not be functional in one which is more (or less) inclusive. Other things also have to be specified if functional statements are to mean anything. As Nagel[10] stressed, we should say to what state of the whole the practice in question is contributory. But, more important than any of this, should we not bear in mind all the time what the product of the whole system is, since this itself may or may not be functional for those who bear the cost of the system and so expect to benefit? Very frequently in sociology it is whole, bounded action-systems that are being judged to be functional or dysfunctional *for man* and, only by transference, any parts within them which may make them so. And this is because social action is prompted by human need.

The examination of the properties of the "functional system" that has

---

8 Lewis A. Coser, *The Functions of Social Conflict*, Glencoe, Ill.: The Free Press, 1956.

9 Robert K. Merton, "Manifest and Latent Functions," *Social Theory and Social Structure*, Glencoe, Ill.: The Free Press, 1957, pp. 19–84.

10 Ernest Nagel, *op. cit.*

been undertaken by Nagel[11] seems to concentrate on the penultimate question of the sustained functioning of the system of action and does not ask whether, when functioning, it is functional for those who operate it. Nagel's formalization greatly facilitates our analysis of the internal processes of change and compensatory counter-change by which a system preserves equilibrium. But this has to be linked to the more ultimate question of whether the system itself is functional or dysfunctional in yielding products matched to human need. In the writer's view, asking this ultimate question is what makes it worth while to ask the penultimate one.[12] Malinowski's[13] insistence on this is one of his enduring contributions to the discussion.

Furthermore, there is a teleological residue in functional thinking that is scarcely disposed of by Nagel's[14] demonstration that the explanatory element in functionalism is simply causal explanation put in a roundabout way. Where a need-satisfaction stands at the end of a process of human endeavour it exercises some directive power over the efforts taken to achieve it. Here we have a case, then, of the kind of process for which Braithwaite[15] has striven to preserve recognition, wherein the anticipated future goal controls the present movement towards it, so that the end achieved is not the passive effect of a causal chain but, to some extent at least, the cause of its own causes. Braithwaite[16] points out that the field of study explored by cybernetics is largely concerned with teleological mechanisms like this. Such processes, once launched, may achieve the end in view—or may fail and so be "in vain." Does not the anticipation of an end to be achieved underlie all our judgments of function or dysfunction, when those judgments are made in such a way as to imply a comparison with the alternative possible outcome? In the writer's view, what we are interested in *when we make this comparison* is not explanation but evaluation.

2. *The evaluation involved in functional analysis is objective and needs*

---

[11] *Ibid.*

[12] Bredemeier suggests that functional analysis loses its point if it fails to hold in view at least the needs which are induced in the actors by the normative definitions of the dominant culture. Harry C. Bredemeier, *op. cit.*, p. 179. Cancian, on the other hand, passes over the idea that "functional" might mean "fulfilling a basic need" for no reason save that such a view is "inappropriate according to Nagel's concept of a functional system." Francesca Cancian, *op. cit.*, p. 820. Even so, one wonders whether it would be as inappropriate as Cancian says. For we would scarcely ask, as Cancian suggests, what keeps need constant but would make *need-satisfaction* our G, and ask whether or not this is maintained.

[13] B. Malinowski, *A Scientific Theory of Culture, and Other Essays*, New York: Oxford University Press, 1960.

[14] Ernest Nagel, "Teleological Explanation and Teleological Systems," in Herbert Feigl and May Brodbeck (eds.), *Readings in the Philosophy of Science*, New York: Appleton-Century-Crofts, Inc., 1953, pp. 537–558.

[15] Richard Bevan Braithwaite, *op. cit.*, pp. 328–336.

[16] *Ibid.*, p. 328.

no apology.—To ask the function of any social arrangement is to call for its justification—or alternatively for its condemnation. The positive and negative polarity inherent in the terms (eu)functional and dysfunctional should betray at once that evaluation is afoot. A great deal of unnecessary hedging in sociological work would be obviated if this could be frankly admitted. At the same time, sociological work could be more easily purged of covert, private evaluations, if it were allowed that evaluation of this objective kind is intrinsic in sociological analysis, and altogether honorable. Yet, in saying this, we have to distinguish the two meanings given to "subjective" when that state of mind is unfavorably contrasted with the "objective." It can mean biased *or* intuitive. When it has the former meaning subjectivity is to be deplored, because by it the person's perception is distorted. When it has the latter meaning it is simply to be regretted, since the person is not yet able to share his vision of what may well be the truth. The first kind of subjectivity has to be expunged from science altogether, but the second kind is the anlage of science and has to be protected and fostered till its testimony can be objectified. In saying that the evaluation in functional analysis is objective, freedom from subjectivity of the first kind is mainly what is being claimed of course. Yet this gives us grounds for believing that freedom from subjectivity of the second kind can also be achieved with time.

We imply objective evalution of two kinds, in fact, whenever we give a function. Basically, we are making a judgment as to whether the expenditure that goes into the creation and maintenance of the arrangement is worthwhile; but we determine this worthwhileness by both a backward and a forward look, as it were. The backward look tries to sum up the efficiency of the arrangement in producing its effects. To the extent that it is inefficient, wasteful, it is dysfunctional in a way. The forward look examines whether the effects themselves are valuable in terms of some schedule of needs which we postulate for the life of man in society. Some instances will make this plainer.

We may say, as Gluckman[17] has done, that the function of rituals of rebellion in Africa is to channel off the resentment that the natives feel for their chiefs and so preserve stability in the existing authority arrangements— thereby ensuring the continuing supply of everything those arrangements guarantee. We would then be implying (i) that these ritual expressions of aggression are efficient means of dissipating resentment and (ii) that it is desirable to maintain an uninterrupted need-satisfaction, and hence social stability. We may say, with Davis,[18] that the function of social stratification

---

[17] Max Gluckman, *Rituals of Rebellion in South-East Africa*, Manchester: University of Manchester Press, 1954.
[18] Kingsley Davis and Wilbert E. Moore, "Some Principles of Stratification,"

is to "insure that the most important positions are conscientiously filled by the most qualified persons." [19] We would then be implying (i) that a grading of rewards is an efficient means of motivating suitable persons to accept greater responsibilities, while a division of labor into tasks of unequal importance is an efficient means of securing common needs, and (ii) that it is desirable to satisfy common needs continuously. We may say, with Merton,[20] that the function of the political boss in the U.S.A. is "to organize, centralize and maintain in good working condition 'the scattered fragments of power' which are at present dispersed." [21] We would then be implying (i) that buying political support from diversified groups by dispensing help to them is an efficient means of concentrating power and (ii) that all such groups need some access to power and that the power secured by them needs to be concentrated to some degree. Or finally we may say, with Parsons,[22] that two functions of institutionalizing a "collectivity-orientation" in the professional role of the scientist are (a) to protect the public from arbitrary interference by men whose special knowledge gives them an advantage and (b) to expose the ideas of any scientist to the critical scrutiny of his fellows. We would then be implying (i) that role-institutionalization is an efficient means of restraining individuals who, in an intellectual sense, handle dynamite, and (ii) that society needs their contribution to knowledge.

But it would save misunderstanding if it could be appreciated that evaluation made in ways like the above is sociological evalution only. *So far as present society is concerned, X* is functional, *Y* dysfunctional—that is always the implicit stipulation. There may well be supernal heights or historical perspectives from which a socially functional arrangement can be judged bad and a dysfunctional one good—just as ill-health is sometimes recalled with gratitude because it brought spiritual blessing, or poverty because it put one in the way of great fortune at a later time—but that would not be incompatible with recognizing the arrangements as *socially* functional or dysfunctional.[23] Furthermore, this helps us to see that intellectual judgments

---

American Sociological Review, 10 (April, 1945), pp. 242–249; Kingsley Davis, *Human Society*, New York: Macmillan, 1959, pp. 364–389.

19 *Ibid.*, p. 367.

20 Robert K. Merton, *op. cit.*, pp. 70–82.

21 *Ibid.*, p. 72.

22 Talcott Parsons, *The Social System*, London: Tavistock, 1952, pp. 335–345.

23 Merton makes the same point as this when he stresses that judgments about social disorganization are not moralizing judgments but technical judgments about the working of social systems. Robert K. Merton, "Social Problems and Sociological Theory," in Robert K. Merton and Robert A. Nisbet (eds.), *Contemporary Social Problems, An Introduction to the Sociology of Deviant Behavior and Social Disorganization*, New York: Harcourt, Brace and World, 1961, pp. 719–723. Although he is referring to the notion of social disorganization, Merton attempts in this same essay to relate social disorganization to social dysfunction. He suggests that disorganization

about function and dysfunction contain no ethical imperative. We cannot pass from "The instruction of children is functional" to "Thou shalt instruct children." As sociologists we hold no whip. (Fortunately, though, our sociology is redeemed from the final futility by the fact that men exist who are not sociologists merely.)

3. *Evaluating social arrangements as functional or dysfunctional is equivalent to classifying them as normal or pathological. This is a necessary preliminary to the search for causal explanation.*—A physiologist cannot arrive at the function of the liver by generalizing directly from a random collection of livers which contains some diseased specimens. He distinguishes between the diseased and healthy organs at the outset and, setting the diseased ones aside, generalizes from the healthy ones. Certainly, *by contrast,* he gains some understanding of healthy functioning from an examination of the diseased cases, but can only do so if he first sets them in opposition by classifying them apart. His account of the liver would be altogether confounded if it simply averaged the properties of the whole collection. Distinguishing normal from pathological cases is one of his first assignments, and precedes causal knowledge of the conditions of normal or pathological functioning. Social systems are more complex than livers, of course, but the two things are alike in this respect. The instance will therefore serve to show what confusion can invade an intellectual discipline if, being concerned with things that have system-properties, it fails to recognize that character in them and evaluate them accordingly. It should show, further, that evaluation, forced upon us in this way, is simply *scientific measurement.* It amounts to quantification of those dynamic properties, possession of which defines the class of things in question. To evaluate systems is to have appropriated the dimensions for measuring them. In what follows, the three major dimensions for the significant measurement of social systems are proposed, as well as some of the minor dimensions implied in them.

It may require a titanic effort to overcome the clinging prejudice that *any* view about social desiderata will be ideologically colored and therefore

may be viewed as the resultant of multiple dysfunctions. *Ibid.,* pp. 731–737. Martindale states that all the critics of the notion of social disorganization base their objection at least partly on the fact that valuations are inherent in it. See Don Martindale, "Social Disorganization: The Conflict of Normative and Empirical Approaches," in Howard Becker and Alvin Boskoff (eds.), *Modern Sociological Theory in Continuity and Change,* New York: The Dryden Press, 1957, pp. 340–367; E. M. Lemert, *Social Pathology,* New York: McGraw-Hill Book Co., 1951, pp. 3–26; C. Wright Mills, "The Professional Ideology of Social Pathologists," *American Journal of Sociology,* 49 (Sept., 1943), pp. 165–180; Louis Wirth, "Ideological Aspects of Social Disorganization," *American Sociological Review,* 5 (Aug., 1940), pp. 472–482. But could the critics see that the need for evaluations originates from the data and not the evaluators the practice might seem less objectionable to them.

suspect, but the effort has to be made. Through the whole of modern sociology two principal objective social imperatives have been fulminating, forcing recognition for themselves. Adaptive change (which implies rationality) and stability have *both* had to be assumed necessary in the social arrangements men make. These are the two main components of efficiency which, it was said, we gauge by a kind of backward look. They are the states of the social system (Nagel's *G*'s) without which it cannot be properly productive of anything. They are, as such, nobody's political ideology; and there is no sense in calling a sociologist conservative or radical because his work illustrates the necessity of the one or the other—and as likely as not it will illustrate the necessity of both. Man, an anxious creature who looks before and after, works for his satisfactions over time and has therefore to bind time, and social organization and culture take their origin from this and must develop a certain conservatism to be of service to him. Yet, even in its most colloquial usage, stability has never meant fixity. We must not suppose that stable social arrangements mean arrangements that are fixed forever. They are simply arrangements that materialize as expected for as long as they are wanted. In no sense, either, is stability an *opposite* of change, so it would be wrong to think that combining them necessarily meant striking some mean of moderation or gradualism. Commitment to stability still leaves men free to adapt to a world which changes, or of which their knowledge changes, by various means. But to be of service stable social arrangements must yield— have a certain plasticity.

We have no choice except to take as normal, healthy or functional those social arrangements which exhibit both stability and adaptive change in the combination demanded by the time and place, and as abnormal, pathological or dysfunctional in some degree those which do not (and it is of course a matter of degree). It is admittedly a delicate calculation to make and often still largely beyond us, so we make it in a rough, rule-of-thumb way (perhaps in a way which is subjective in the second of the above senses). Yet we have no choice but to make it—and very early in our sorting of the data. To do this does not imply that the abnormal or pathological phenomenon is being pronounced "evil" in some ultimate sense. It simply means it is being classified sociologically, given a negative sociological valency so that it will not be confused with the positve counterpart which in other respects will deceptively resemble it. The well-organized family is thus not to be taken for the same sociological phenomenon as the disorganized one, the high morale department store for the same thing as the low morale store, the nation riddled with suicide and homicide for the same thing as the one where these are rare, the church or school which moves with the times for the same thing as the one made redundant through its archaisms. It is only after we have set such contrasting phenomena in classes apart that we can sample the cases in each class and arrive at causal laws about functional and dysfunctional systems. It would be a pity if the attention that has been given to functionalism were taken for an invitation to make functional analysis the end of sociological inquiry—for then it would be still-born. It is rather the end of sociology to explain—"explained" functions: to show what things have a constant association with various functional or dysfunctional operations.

[Editorial Note: Assumptions 4, 5 and 6 deal with the dynamic properties of social systems. The three major properties are identified as "stability," "adaptive change," and "integration." The author asserts in the section which follows that these can only be evaluated in terms of assumptions about human nature.]

7. *It is because the demand for need-satisfaction through them is unrelenting, that social arrangments must achieve stability, adaptive change and integration. For this reason, making judgments of function or dysfunction, normality or pathology, presupposes a whole catalogue of assumptions about human needs.*—It was said that part of our judgment that an operation is functional rests on our assumption that the product of the operation is needed by man. This must be one of the main reasons why functional thinking seems unsatisfactory to many people—for who shall say what the things are that man *must have under all circumstances?* And who shall so disentangle the inherited need from its cultural modification as to evaluate the latter as a means of supplying the former? Yet, unsatisfactory though this admittedly seems, such assumptions must be made if sociological work is to have depth and significance. These assumptions make a back-drop of our own providing to all the empirical observations we make. But the back-drop is not itself non-empirical for all that. It has been woven from the cumulative experience of mankind, as we have each been able to absorb this. We accept as human needs all those satisfactions which men have striven to repeat at many different times and places and by many different means. We assume that men need food, for example, because, under so many varied circumstances, we know they have acted *as though* they needed it. It is not for any different reason that we assume they need shelter, mutual protection, status, skillfulness, explanations of natural phenomena and the consolations of religion. What any sociologist assumes here should hardly be that minimum range of needs to which all his colleagues will give ready assent, but that whole spectrum to which his own vision has admitted him. It is precisely here that the social scientist is served by his explorations of the arts and humanities, as well as by the diversity of his experience and his range of sympathy and imagination. Perhaps it is by exceptional endowment here that the great sociologist is marked out. If he lends us his eyes for a time we may devise instruments which will compensate other men for their partial blindness.

Ralf Dahrendorf

Out of Utopia

TOWARD A REORIENTATION OF SOCIOLOGICAL ANALYSIS

*A*LL utopias from Plato's Republic to George Orwell's brave new world of 1984 have had one element of construction in common: they are all societies from which change is absent. Whether conceived as a final state and climax of historical development, as an intellectual's nightmare, or as a romantic dream, the social fabric of utopias does not, and perhaps cannot, recognize the unending flow of the historical process.[1] For the sociologist it would be an intellectual experiment both rewarding and entertaining to try

Reprinted from Ralf Dahrendorf, "Out of Utopia: Toward a Reorientation of Sociological Analysis," *American Journal of Sociology*, 64 (Sept., 1958), pp. 115–127, by permission of The University of Chicago Press. Copyright © 1958, *American Journal of Sociology*. All rights reserved.

[1] There are very many utopian constructions, particularly in recent decades. Since these vary considerably, it is doubtful whether any generalization can apply to all of them. I have tried to be careful in my generalizations on this account and to generalize without reservation only where I feel this can be defended. Thus I am prepared to argue the initial thesis of this paper even against such assertions as H. G. Wells's: "The Modern Utopia must not be static but kinetic, must shape not as a permanent state but as a hopeful stage, leading to a long ascent of stages" (*A Modern Utopia* [London: T. Nelson & Sons, 1909], chap. i, sec. 1). It seems to me that the crucial distinction to make here is that between intra-system processes, i.e., changes that are actually part of the design of utopia, and historical change, the direction and outcome of which is not predetermined.

and trace in, say, the totalitarian universe of 1984 potential sources of conflict and change and to predict the directions of change indicated in Big
Brother's society. Its originator, of course, did not do this: his utopia would
not make sense unless it was more than a passing phase of social development.

It is no accident that the catchwords of Huxley's Brave New World
—"Community, Identity, Stability"—could be applied with equal justice to
most other utopian constructions. Utopian societies have (to use a term
popular in contemporary sociological analysis) certain structural requisites;
they must display certain features in order to be what they purport to be.
First, utopias do not grow out of familiar reality following realistic patterns
of development. For most authors, utopias have but a nebulous past and no
future; they are suddenly there, and there to stay, suspended in mid-time or,
rather, somewhere beyond the ordinary notions of time. Our own society is,
for the citizens of 1984, hardly more than a fading memory. Moreover, there
is an unexplained gap, a kind of mutation somewhere between 1948 and
1984, interpreted in the light of arbitrary and permanently adapted "documents" prepared by the Ministry of Truth. The case of Marx is even more
pertinent. It is well known how much time and energy Lenin spent in trying
to link the realistically possible event of the proletarian revolution with the
image of a Communist society in which there are no classes, no conflicts, no
state, and, indeed, no division of labor. Lenin, as we know, failed, in theory
as in practice, to get beyond the "dictatorship of the proletariat," and somehow we are not surprised at that. It is hard to link, by rational argument or
empirical analysis, the wide river of history—flowing more rapidly at some
points, more slowly at others, but always moving—and the tranquil village
pond of utopia.

Nor are we surprised that in social reality the "dictatorship of the proletariat" soon turned out to be more and more of the former, involving less
and less of the latter.

A second structural characteristic of utopias seems to be the uniformity
of such societies or, to use more technical language, the existence of universal consensus on prevailing values and institutional arrangements. This,
too, will prove relevant for the explanation of the impressive stability of all
utopias. Consensus on values and institutions does not necessarily mean that
utopias cannot in some ways be democratic. Consensus can be enforced—as
it is for Orwell—or it can be spontaneous, a kind of *contrat social*—as it is
for some eighteenth-century utopian writers, and, if in a perverted way, i.e.,
by conditioned spontaneity, again for Huxley. One might suspect, on closer
inspection, that, from the point of view of political organization, the result
would in both cases turn out to be rather similar. But this line of analysis
involves critical interpretation and will be postponed for the moment. Suffice

it to note that the assumption of universal consensus seems to be built into most utopian constructions and is apparently one of the factors explaining their stability.

Universal consensus means, by implication, absence of structurally generated conflict. In fact, many builders of utopias go to considerable lengths to convince their audience that in their societies conflict about values or institutional arrangements is either impossible or simply unnecessary. Utopias are perfect—be it perfectly agreeable or perfectly disagreeable—and consequently there is nothing to quarrel about. Strikes and revolutions are as conspicuously absent from utopian societies as are parliaments in which organized groups advance their conflicting claims for power. Utopian societies may be and, indeed, often are caste societies; but they are not class societies in which the oppressed revolt against their oppressors. We may note, third, that social harmony seems to be one of the factors adduced to account for utopian stability.[2]

Some writers add to their constructions a particularly clever touch of realism: they invent an individual who does not conform to the accepted values and ways of life. Orwell's Winston Smith or Huxley's Savage are cases in point—but it is not difficult to imagine a surviving capitalist in Communist society or similar villains of the peace in other utopias. For exigencies of this kind, utopias usually have varied, though effective, means at their disposal to do away with the disturbers of unity. But how did they emerge in the first place? That question is rather more difficult to answer. Characteristically, utopian writers take refuge in chance to carry off this paradox. Their "outsiders" are not (and cannot be) products of the social structure of utopia but deviants, pathological cases infected with some unique disease.

In order to make their constructions at all realistic, utopians must, of course, allow for some activities and processes in their societies. The difference between utopia and a cemetery is that occasionally some things do happen in utopia. But—and this is the fourth point—all processes going on in utopian societies follow recurrent patterns and occur within, and as part of, the design of the whole. Not only do they not upset the status quo: they affirm and sustain it, and it is in order to do so that most utopians allow them to happen at all. For example, most writers have retained the idea that men are mortal, even in utopia.[3] Therefore, some provisions have to be made for

---

[2] R. Gerber states, in his study of *Utopian Fantasy* (London: Routledge & Paul, 1955): "The most admirably constructed Utopia fails to convince if we are not led to believe that the danger of revolt is excluded" (p. 68).

[3] Although many writers have been toying with the idea of immortality as conveyed by either divine grace or the progress of medical science. Why utopian writers should be concerned with this idea may be explained, in part, by the observations offered in this paper.

the reproduction, both physical and social, of society. Sexual intercourse (or at least artificial fertilization), the upbringing and education of children, and selection for social positions have to be secured and regulated—to mention only the minimum of social institutions required simply because men are mortal.[4] In addition to this, most utopian constructions have to cope in some way with the division of labor. These regulated processes are, however, no more than the metabolism of society; they are part and parcel of the general consensus on values, and they serve to uphold the existing state of affairs. Although some of its parts are moving in predetermined, calculable ways, utopia as a whole remains a *perpetuum immobile*.

Finally, to add a more obvious observation, utopias generally seem to be curiously isolated from all other communities (if such are indeed assumed to exist at all). We have already mentioned isolation in time, but usually we also find isolation in space. Citizens of utopia are seldom allowed to travel, and, if they are, their reports will serve to magnify, rather than bridge, the differences between utopia and the rest of the world. Utopias are monolithic and homogeneous communities, suspended not only in time but also in space, shut off from the outside world, which might, after all, present a threat to the cherished immobility of the social structure.

There are other features which most utopian constructions have in common, and which it might be interesting for the sociologist to investigate. Also, the question might be asked, Just how pleasant would it be to live in even the most benevolent of utopias? Karl Popper, in his *Open Society and Its Enemies*, has explored these and other aspects of closed and utopian societies at considerable detail, and there is little to add to his incisive analyses.[5] In any case, our concern is of a rather more specific nature than the investigation of some common structural elements of utopia. We now propose to ask the seemingly pointless, and even naïve, question whether we actually encounter all or any of these elements in *real* societies.

One of the advantages of the naïveté of this question is that it is easily answered. A society without history? There are, of course, "new societies" like the United States in the seventeenth and eighteenth centuries; there are "primitive societies" in a period of transition from pre-literate to literate culture. But in either case it would be not only misleading but downright false to say that there are no antecedents, no historical roots, no develop-

---

[4] In fact, the subjects of sex, education, role allocation, and division of labor loom large in utopian writing from its Platonic beginnings.

[5] Other authors could and should, of course, be mentioned who have dealt extensively with utopia and its way of life. Sociologically most relevant are L. Mumford, *The Story of Utopias* (New York: P. Smith, 1941); K. Mannheim, *Ideology and Utopia* (New York: Harcourt Brace & Co., 1936 [trans. by L. Wirth and E. Shils]); M. Buber, *Paths in Utopia* (New York: Macmillan, 1950 [trans. by R. F. C. Hull]).

mental patterns linking these societies with the past. A society with universal consensus? One without conflict? We know that without the assistance of a secret police it has never been possible to produce such a state and that even the threat of police persecution can, at best, prevent dissensus and conflict from finding expression in open struggles for limited periods of time. A society isolated in space and devoid of processes upsetting or changing its design? Anthropologists have occasionally asserted that such societies do exist, but it has never taken very long to disprove their assertions. In fact, there is no need to discuss these questions very seriously. It is obvious that such societies do not exist—just as it is obvious that every known society changes its values and institutions continuously. Changes may be rapid or gradual, violent or regulated, comprehensive or piecemeal, but it is never entirely absent where human beings create organizations to live together.

These are commonplaces about which even sociologists will hardly disagree. In any case, utopia means Nowhere, and the very construction of a utopian society implies that it has no equivalent in reality. The writer building his world in Nowhere has the advantage of being able to ignore the commonplaces of the real world. He can populate the moon, telephone to Mars, let flowers speak and horses fly, he can even make history come to a standstill—so long as he does not confound his imagination with reality, in which case he is doomed to the fate of Plato in Syracuse, Owen in Harmony, Lenin in Russia.

Obvious as these observations may be, it is at this point that the question arises which explains our interest in the social structure of utopia and which appears to merit some more detailed examination: If the immobility of utopia, its isolation in time and space, the absence of conflict and disruptive procesess, is a product of poetic imagination divorced from the commonplaces of reality—how is it that so much of recent sociological theory has been based on exactly these assumptions and has, in fact, consistently operated with a utopian model of society?[6] What are the reasons and what the consequences of the fact that every one of the elements we found characteristic of the social structure of utopia reappears in the attempt to systematize our knowledge of society and formulate sociological propositions of a generalizing nature?

It would evidently be both misleading and unfair to impute to any sociologist the explicit intention to view society as an unmoving entity of eternal

---

[6] In this essay I am concerned mainly with recent sociological theory. I have the impression, however, that much of the analysis offered here also applies to earlier works in social theory and that, in fact, the utopian model of society is one of two models which reappear throughout the history of Western philosophy. Expansion of the argument to a more general historical analysis of social thought might be a task both instructive and rewarding.

stability. In fact, the commonplace that wherever there is social life there is change can be found at the outset of most sociological treatises. I contend, however, in this paper that (1) recent theoretical approaches, by analyzing social structure in terms of the elements characteristic of immobile societies, have, in fact, assumed the utopian image of society; that (2) this assumption, particularly if associated with the claim to being the most general, or even the only possible, model, has been detrimental to the advancement of sociological research; and that (3) it has to be replaced by a more useful and realistic approach to the analysis of social structure and social process.

The social system, like utopia, has not grown out of familiar reality. Instead of abstracting a limited number of variables and postulating their relevance for the explanation of a particular problem, it represents a huge and allegedly all-embracing superstructure of concepts that do not describe, propositions that do not explain, and models from which nothing follows. At least they do not describe or explain (or underlie explanations of) the real world with which we are concerned. . . .

Consensus on values is one of the prime features of the social system. Some of its advocates make a slight concession to reality and speak of "relative consensus," thereby indicating their contempt for both the canons of scientific theory (in the models of which there is no place for "relatives" or "almosts") and the observable facts of reality (which show little evidence of any more than highly formal—and tautological—consensus). That societies are held together by some kind of value consensus seems to me either a definition of societies or a statement clearly contradicted by empirical evidence—unless one is concerned not so much with real societies and their problems as with social systems in which anything might be true, including the integration of all socially held values into a religious doctrine. I have yet to see a problem for the explanation of which the assumption of a unified value system is necessary, or a testable prediction that follows from this assumption.

It is hard to see how a social system based on ("almost") universal consensus can allow for structurally generated conflicts. Presumably, conflict always implies some kind of dissensus and disagreement about values. In Christian theology original sin was required to explain the transition from paradise to history. Private property has been no less a *deus ex machina* in Marx's attempt to account for the transition from an early society, in which "man felt as much at home as a fish in the water," to a world of alienation and class struggles.[7] Both these explanations may not be very satisfactory;

---

[7] Marx tackled this problem in the Paris manuscripts of 1845 on *Economics and Philosophy*. This entire work is an outstanding illustration of the philosophical and analytical problems faced in any attempt to relate utopia and reality.

they at least permit recognition of the hard and perhaps unpleasant facts of real life. Modern sociological theory of the structural-functional variety has failed to do even that (unless one wants to regard the curiously out-of-place chapter on change in Talcott Parsons' *Social System* as the original sin of this approach). By no feat of the imagination, not even by the residual category of "dysfunction," can the integrated and equilibrated social system be made to produce serious and patterned conflicts in its structure.

What the social system can produce, however, is the well-known villain of the peace of utopia, the "deviant." Even he requires some considerable argument and the introduction of a chance, or at least an undetermined variable—in this case, individual psychology. Although the system is perfect and in a state of equilibrium, individuals cannot always live up to this perfection. "Deviance is a motivated tendency for an actor to behave in contravention of one or more institutionalized normative patterns" (Parsons).[8] Motivated by what, though? Deviance occurs either if an individual happens to be pathological, or, if, "*from whatever source* [this, of course, being unspecified], a disturbance is introduced into the system." [9] In other words, it occurs for sociologically—and that means structurally—unknown and unknowable reasons. It is the bacillus that befalls the system from the dark depths of the individual psyche or the nebulous reaches of the outside world. Fortunately, the system has at its disposal certain mechanisms to deal with the deviant and to "re-equilibrate" itself, i.e., the mechanisms of social control.

The striking preoccupation of sociological theory with the related problems of reproduction, socialization, and role allocation or, on the institutional level, with (in this sequence) the family, the educational system, and the division of labor fits in well with our comparison of this type of theory and utopian societies. Plato carefully avoided Justinian's static definition of justice as *suum cuique;* in his definition the emphasis is on πράττειν, on the active and, to apply a much abused term, dynamic aspect. Similarly, the structural-functionalist insist on his concern not with a static but with a moving equilibrium. But what does this moving equilibrium mean? It means, in the last analysis, that the system is a structure not of the building type but of the organism type. Homoeostasis is maintained by the regular occurrence of certain patterned processes which, far from disturbing the tranquillity of the village pond, in fact *are* the village pond. Heraclitus' saying, "We enter the same river, and it is not the same," does not hold here. The system is the same, however often we look at it. Children are born and socialized and allocated until they die; new children are born, and the same happens all over again. What a peaceful, what an idyllic, world the system is! Of course,

---

8 *The Social System* (Glencoe, Ill.: Free Press, 1951), p. 250.
9 *Ibid.*, p. 252; my italics.

it is not static in the sense of being dead; things happen all the time; but —alas!—they are under control, and they all help to maintain that precious equilibrium of the whole. Things not only happen, but they function, and so long as that is the case, all is well.

One of the more unfortunate connotations of the word "system" is its closure. Although some structural-functionalists have tried, there is no getting away from the fact that a system is essentially something that is —even if only "for purposes of analysis"—self-sufficient, internally consistent, and closed to the outside. A leg cannot be called a system; a body can. Actually, advocates of the system have little reason to be unhappy with this term; abandoning it would rob their analyses of much of their neatness and, above all, would disable them with respect to the "whatever sources"— the villainous outsiders they can now introduce to "account" for unwanted realities. I do not want to go too far in my polemics, but I cannot help feeling that it is only a step from thinking about societies in terms of equilibrated systems to asserting that every disturber of the equilibrium, every deviant, is a "spy" or an "imperialistic agent." The system theory of society comes, by implication, dangerously close to the conspiracy-theory of history—which is not only the end of all sociology but also rather silly.[10] There is nothing logically wrong with the term "system." It begins to give birth to all kinds of undesirable consequences only when it is applied to total societies and is made the ultimate frame of reference of analysis. It is certainly true that sociology deals with society. But it is equally true that physics deals with nature, and yet physicists would hardly see an advance in calling nature a system and trying to analyze it as such. In fact, the attempt to do so would probably —and justly—be discarded as metaphysics.

To repeat, the social system as conceived by some recent sociological theorists appears to be characterized by the same features as those contained in utopian societies. This being so, the conclusion is forced upon us that this type of theory also deals with societies from which historical change is absent and that it is, in this sense, utopian. To be sure, it is utopian not because some of the assumptions of this theory are "unrealistic"—this would be true for the assumptions of almost any scientific theory—but because it is exclusively concerned with spelling out the conditions of the functioning of a utopian social system. Structural-functional theory does not introduce unrealistic assumptions for the purpose of explaining real problems; it introduces many kinds of assumptions, concepts, and models for the sole purpose

---

[10] It could, for instance, be argued that only totalitarian states display one unified value system and that only in the case of totalitarian systems do we have to assume some outside influence ("from whatever source") to account for change—an argument that clearly reduces the extreme structural-functional position to absurdity.

of describing a social system that has never existed and is not likely ever to come into being.

In thus comparing the social system with utopia, I feel I have done an injustice to the majority of utopian writers which needs to be corrected. With few exceptions, the purpose underlying utopian constructions has been one of criticism, even indictment, of existing societies. The story of utopias is the story of an intensely moral and polemical branch of human thinking, and, although, from a realistic and political point of view, utopian writers may have chosen doubtful means to express their values, they have certainly succeeded in conveying to their times a strong concern with the shortcomings and injustices of existing institutions and beliefs. This can hardly be said of modern sociological theory. The sense of complacency with—if not justification of—the status quo, which, by intention or default, pervades the structural-functional school of social thought is unheard of in utopian literature. Even as utopias go, the social system is rather a weak link in a tradition of penetrating and often radical criticism. I do not want to suggest that sociology should be primarily concerned with uncovering and indicting the evils of society; but I do want to assert that those sociologists who felt that they had to embark on a utopian venture were rather ill-advised in retaining the technical imperfections while at the same time abandoning the moral impulses of their numerous forerunners.

It is easy to be polemical, hard to be constructive, and—at least for me—impossible to be as impressively and happily catholic as those at whom my critical comments are directed. However, I do not propose to evade the just demand to specify whose work I mean when I refer to the utopian nature of sociological theory, to explain why I think that an approach of this kind is useless and even detrimental for our discipline, and to describe what better ways there are in my opinion to deal with our problems.

The name that comes to mind immediately when one speaks about sociological theory in these days is that of Talcott Parsons. Already, in many discussions and for many people, Parsons appears to be more of a symbol than a reality. Let me therefore state quite explicitly that my criticism applies neither to Parsons' total work nor only to his work. I am not concerned with Parsons' excellent and important philosophical analysis of *The Structure of Social Action,* nor am I concerned with his numerous perceptive contributions to the understanding of empirical phenomena. I do think, however, that much of his theoretical work in the last ten years represents an outstanding illustration of what I mean by the utopian bent in sociological theory. The double emphasis on the articulation of purely formal conceptual frameworks and on the social system as the point of departure and arrival of sociological analysis involves all the vices and, in his case, none of the virtues of a utopian approach. But, in stating this, one should not overlook that at some time or other many prominent American sociologists and some British anthropologists have engaged in the same kind of reasoning.

Two main remedies have been proposed in recent years against the malady of utopianism. In my opinion they have both been based on a wrong diagnosis—and by correcting this diagnostic error we may hope to get to the root of the trouble and at the same time to a path that promises to lead us out of utopia.

For some time now it has been quite popular in our profession to support T. H. Marshall's demand for "sociological stepping stones in the middle distance" or Robert K. Merton's plea for "theories of the middle range." I cannot say that I am very happy with these formulations. True, both Marshall and Merton explain at some length what they mean by their formulas. In particular, they advocate something they call a "convergence" of theory and research. But "convergence" is a very mechanical notion of a process that defies the laws of mechanics. Above all, this conception implies that sociological theory and sociological research are two separate activities which it is possible to divide and to join. I do not believe that this is so. In fact, I think that, so long as we hold this belief, our theory will be logical and philosophical, and our research will at best be sociographic, with sociology disappearing in the gorge between these two. The admonitions of Marshall and Merton may actually have led to a commendable rediscovery of empirical problems of investigation, but I venture to assert that, looking purely at their formulations, this has been an unintended consequence, a by-product rather than the content of their statements.[11]

There is no theory that can be divorced from empirical research; but, of course, the reverse is equally true. I have no sympathy with the confusion of the just demand that sociological analysis should be inspired by empirical problems and the unjust demand that it should be based on, or even exclusively concerned with, something called "empirical research." As a matter of fact, the advocates of "empirical research" and the defenders of abstract theory have been strikingly similar in one, to my mind crucial, respect (which explains, by the way, why they have been able to coexist with comparatively little friction and controversy): they have both largely dispensed with that prime impulse of all science and scholarship, with the puzzlement over specific, concrete, and—if this word must be used— empirical problems. Many sociologists have lost the simple impulse of curiosity, the desire to solve riddles of experience, the concern with problems. This, rather than anything else, explains both the success and the

---

[11] Most of the works of Marshall and Merton do display the kind of concern with problems which I am here advocating. My objection to their formulations is therefore not directed against these works but against their explicit assumption that all that is wrong with recent theory is its generality and that by simply reducing the level of generality we can solve all problems.

danger of the utopian fallacy in sociological thinking and of its smaller brother, the fallacy of empirical research.

It is perhaps fairly obvious that a book like *The Social System* displays but a minimal concern with riddles of experience. But I do not want to be misunderstood. My plea for a reinstatement of empirical problems in the central place that is due to them is by no means merely a plea for greater recognition of "facts," "data," or "empirical evidence." I think that, from the point of view of concern with problems, there is very little to choose between *The Social System* and the ever increasing number of undoubtedly well-documented Ph.D. theses on such subjects as "The Social Structure of a Hospital," "The Role of the Professional Football Player," and "Family Relations in a New York Suburb." "Areas of Investigation," "Fields of Inquiry," "Subjects," and "Topics," chosen because nobody has studied them before or for some other random reason, are not problems. What I mean is that at the outset of every scientific investigation there has to be a fact or set of facts that is puzzling the investigator: children of business-men prefer professional to business occupations; workers in the automobile industry of Detroit go on strike; there is a higher incidence of suicides among upwardly mobile persons than among others; Socialist parties in predominantly Catholic countries of Europe seem unable to get more than 30 per cent of the popular vote; Hungarian people revolt against the Communist regime. There is no need to enumerate more of such facts; what matters is that every one of them invites the question "Why?" and it is this question, after all, which has always inspired that noble human activity in which we are engaged—science.

There is little point in restating methodological platitudes. Let me confine myself, therefore, to saying that a scientific discipline that is problem-conscious at every stage of its development is very unlikely ever to find itself in the prison of utopian thought or to separate theory and research. Problems require explanation; explanations require assumptions or models and hypotheses derived from such models; hypotheses, which are always, by implication, predictions as well as explanatory propositions, require testing by further facts; testing often generates new problems.[12] If anybody wants to distinguish theory and research in this process, he is welcome to do so; my own feeling is that this distinction confuses, rather than clarifies, our thinking.

The loss of problem-consciousness in modern sociology explains many

---

[12] It is, however, essential to this approach—to add one not so trivial method-ological point—that we realize the proper function of empirical testing. As Popper has demonstrated in many of his works since 1935 (the year of publication of *Logik der Forschung*), there can be no verification in science; empirical tests serve to falsify accepted theories, and every refutation of a theory is a triumph of scientific research. Testing that is designed to confirm hypotheses neither advances our knowledge nor generates new problems.

of the drawbacks of the present state of our discipline and, in particular, the utopian character of sociological theory; moreover, it is in itself a problem worthy of investigation. How was it that sociologists, of all people, could lose touch with the riddles of experience, of which there are so many in the social world? At this point, I think, the ideological interpretation of sociological development which has recently been advanced by a number of authors is pertinent.[13] By turning away from the critical facts of experience, sociologists have both followed and strengthened the trend toward conservatism that is so powerful in the intellectual world today. What is more, their conservatism is not of the militant kind found in the so-called Left Wing of conservative parties in England, France, Germany, and the United States; it is, rather, a conservatism by implication, the conservatism of complacency. I am sure that Parsons and many of those who have joined him in utopia would disclaim being conservatives, and, so far as their explicit political convictions go, there is no reason to doubt their sincerity. At the same time, their way of looking at society or, rather, of not looking at society when they should has promoted a sense of disengagement, of not wanting to worry about things, and has, in fact, elevated this attitude of abstinence to a "scientific theory" according to which there is no need to worry. By thus leaving the job of worrying to the powers that be, sociologists have implicitly recognized the legitimacy of these powers; their disengagement has turned out to be a—however involuntary—engagement on the side of the status quo. What a dramatic misunderstanding of Max Weber's attempt to separate the vocation of politics from that of science!

Let me repeat that I am not advocating a sociological science that is politically radical in the content of its theories. In any case, there would be little sense in trying to do this, since, logically speaking, there can be no such science. I am advocating, however, a sociological science that is inspired by the moral fiber of its forefathers; and I am convinced that if we regain the problem-consciousness which has been lost in the last decades, we cannot fail to recover the critical engagement in the realities of our social world which we need to do our job well. For I hope I have made it quite clear that problem-consciousness is not merely a means of avoiding ideological biases but is, above all, an indispensable condition of progress in any discipline of human inquiry. The path out of utopia begins with the recognition of puzzling facts of experience and the tackling of problems posed by such facts.

There is yet another reason why I think that the utopian character of recent sociological theory has been detrimental to the advancement of our

---

[13] I am thinking in particular of the still outstanding articles by S. M. Lipset and R. Bendix on "Social Status and Social Structure," *British Journal of Sociology*, Vol. II (1951), and of the early parts of L. Coser's work, *The Functions of Social Conflict* (Glencoe, Ill.: Free Press, 1956).

discipline. It is quite conceivable that in the explanation of specific problems we shall at some stage want to employ models of a highly general kind or even formulate general laws. Stripped of its more formal and decorative elements, the social system could be, and sometimes has been, regarded as such a model. For instance, we may want to investigate the problem of why achievement in the educational system ranks so high among people's concerns in our society. The social system can be thought of as suggesting that in advanced industrial societies the educational system is the main, and tends to be the only, mechanism of role allocation. In this case, the social system proves to be a useful model. It seems to me, however, that even in this limited sense the social system is a highly problematic, or at least a very one-sided, model and that here, too, a new departure is needed.

It is perhaps inevitable that the models underlying scientific explanations acquire a life of their own, divorced from the specific purpose for which they have originally been constructed. The *Homo oeconomicus* of modern economics, invented in the first place as a useful, even if clearly unrealistic, assumption from which testable hypotheses could be derived, has today become the cardinal figure in a much discussed philosophy of human nature far beyond the aspirations of most economists. The indeterminacy principle in modern physics, which again is nothing but a useful assumption without claim to any reality other than operational, has been taken as a final refutation of all determinist philosophies of nature. Analogous statements could be made about the equilibrium model of society—although, as I have tried to show, it would unfortunately be wrong to say that the original purpose of this model was to explain specific empirical problems. We face the double task of having to specify the conditions under which this model proves analytically useful and of having to cope with the philosophical implications of the model itself.[14] It may seem a digression for a sociologist to occupy himself with the latter problem; however, in my opinion it is both dangerous and irresponsible to ignore the implications of one's assumptions, even if these are philosophical rather than scientific in a technical sense. The models with which we work, apart from being useful tools, determine to no small extent our general perspectives, our selection of problems, and the emphasis in our explanations, and I believe that in this respect, too, the utopian social system has played an unfortunate role in our discipline.

---

[14] The approach here characterized by the catchword "social system" has two aspects which are not necessarily related and which I am here treating separately. One is its concentration on formal "conceptual frameworks" of no relevance to particular empirical problems, as discussed in the previous section. The other aspect lies in the application of an equilibrium model of society to the analysis of real societies and is dealt with in the present section. The emphasis of advocates of the social system on one or the other of these aspects has been shifting, and to an extent it is possible to accept the one without the other. Both aspects, however, betray the traces of utopianism, and it is therefore indicated to deal with both of them in an essay that promises to show a path out of utopia.

There may be some problems for the explanation of which it is important to assume an equilibrated, functioning social system based on consensus, absence of conflict, and isolation in time and space. I think there are such problems, although their number is probably much smaller than many contemporary sociologists wish us to believe. The equilibrium model of society also has a long tradition in social thinking, including, of course, all utopian thinking but also such works as Rousseau's *Contrat social* and Hegel's *Philosophy of Law*. But neither in relation to the explanation of sociological problems nor in the history of social philosophy is it the only model, and I would strongly protest any implicit or explicit claim that it can be so regarded. Parsons' statement in *The Social System* that this "work constitutes a step toward the development of a generalized theoretical system"[15] is erroneous in every respect I can think of and, in particular, insofar as it implies that all sociological problems can be approached with the equilibrium model of society.

It may be my personal bias that I can think of many more problems to which the social system does not apply than those to which it does, but I would certainly insist that, even on the highly abstract and largely philosophical level on which Parsons moves, at least one other model of society is required. It has an equally long and, I think, a better tradition than the equilibrium model. In spite of this fact, no modern sociologist has as yet formulated its basic tenets in such a way as to render it useful for the explanation of critical social facts. Only in the last year or two has there been some indication that this alternative model, which I shall call the "conflict model of society," is gaining ground in sociological analysis.

The extent to which the social system model has influenced even our thinking about social change and has marred our vision in this important area of problems is truly remarkable. Two facts in particular illustrate this influence. In talking about change, most sociologists today accept the entirely spurious distinction between "change within" and "change of societies," which makes sense only if we recognize the system as our ultimate and only reference point. At the same time, many sociologists seem convinced that, in order to explain processes of change, they have to discover certain special circumstances which set these processes in motion, implying that, in society, change is an abnormal, or at least an unusual, state that has to be accounted for in terms of deviations from a "normal," equilibrated system. I think that

---

15 Characteristically, this statement is made in the chapter "The Processes of Change of Social System" (p. 486). In many ways I have here taken this chapter of *The Social System* as a clue to problems of structural-functionalism—an approach which a page-by-page interpretation of the amazingly weak argument offered by Parsons in support of his double claim that (*a*) the stabilized system is the central point of reference of sociological analysis and (*b*) any theory of change is impossible as the present state of our knowledge could easily justify.

in both these respects we shall have to revise our assumptions radically. A Galilean turn of thought is required which makes us realize that all units of social organization are continuously changing, unless some force intervenes to arrest this change. It is our task to identify the factors interfering with the normal process of change rather than to look for variables involved in bringing about change. Moreover, change is ubiquitous not only in time but also in space, that is to say, every part of societies is constantly changing, and it is impossible to distinguish between "change within" and "change of," "microscopic" and "macroscopic" change. Historians discovered a long time ago that in describing the historical process it is insufficient to confine one's attention to the affairs of state, to wars, revolutions, and government action. From them we could learn that what happens in Mrs. Smith's house, in a trade union local, or in the parish of a church is just as significant for the social process of history and, in fact, *is* just as much the social process of history as what happens in the White House or the Kremlin.

The great creative force that carries along change in the model I am trying to describe and that is equally ubiquitous is social conflict. The notion that wherever there is social life there is conflict may be unpleasant and disturbing. Nevertheless, it is indispensable to our understanding of social problems. As with change, we have grown accustomed to look for special causes or circumstances whenever we encounter conflict; but, again, a complete turn is necessary in our thinking. Not the presence but the absence of conflict is surprising and abnormal, and we have good reason to be suspicious if we find a society or social organization that displays no evidence of conflict. To be sure, we do not have to assume that conflict is always violent and uncontrolled. There is probably a continuum from civil war to parliamentary debate, from strikes and lockouts to joint consultation. Our problems and their explanations will undoubtedly teach us a great deal about the range of variation in forms of conflict. In formulating such explanations, however, we must never lose sight of the underlying assumption that conflict can be temporarily suppressed, regulated, channeled, and controlled but that neither a philosopher-king nor a modern dictator can abolish it once and for all.

There is a third notion which, together with change and conflict, constitutes the instrumentarium of the conflict model of society: the notion of constraint. From the point of view of this model, societies and social organizations are held together not by consensus but by constraint, not by universal agreement but by the coercion of some by others. It may be useful for some purposes to speak of the "value system" of a society, but in the conflict model such characteristic values are ruling rather than common, enforced rather than accepted, at any given point of time. And as conflict generates change, so constraint may be thought of as generating conflict. We assume that conflict is ubiquitous, since constraint is ubiquitous wherever human beings set up social organizations. In a highly formal sense, it is always the basis of constraint that is at issue in social conflict.

I have sketched the conflict model of society—as I see it—only very briefly. But except in a philosophical context there is no need to elaborate on it, unless, of course, such elaboration is required for the explanation of specific problems. However, my point here is a different one. I hope it is evident that there is a fundamental difference between the equilibrium and the conflict models of society. Utopia is—to use the language of the economist—a world of certainty. It is paradise found; utopians know all the answers. But we live in a world of uncertainty. We do not know what an ideal society looks like—and if we think we do, we are fortunately unable to realize our conception. Because there is no certainty (which, by definition, is shared by everybody in that condition), there has to be constraint to assure some livable minimum of coherence. Because we do not know all the answers, there has to be continuous conflict over values and policies. Because of uncertainty, there is always change and development. Quite apart from its merits as a tool of scientific analysis, the conflict model is essentially non-utopian; it is the model of an open society.

I do not intend to fall victim to the mistake of many structural-functional theorists and advance for the conflict model a claim to comprehensive and exclusive applicability. As far as I can see, we need for the explanation of sociological problems both the equilibrium and the conflict models of society; and it may well be that, in a philosophical sense, society has two faces of equal reality: one of stability, harmony, and consensus and one of change, conflict, and constraint.[16] Strictly speaking, it does not matter whether we select for investigation problems that can be understood only in terms of the equilibrium model or problems for the explanation of which the conflict model is required. There is no intrinsic criterion for preferring one to the other. My own feeling is, however, that, in the face of recent developments in our discipline and the critical considerations offered earlier in this paper, we may be well advised to concentrate in the future not only on concrete problems but on such problems as involve explanations in terms of constraint, conflict, and change. This second face of society may aesthetically be rather less pleasing than the social system—but, if all that sociology had to offer were an easy escape to utopian tranquillity, it would hardly be worth our efforts.

---

[16] I should not be prepared to claim that these two are the only possible models of sociological analysis. Without any doubt, we need a considerable number of models on many levels for the explanation of specific problems, and, more often than not, the two models outlined here are too general to be of immediate relevance. In philosophical terms, however, it is hard to see what other models of society there could be which are not of either the equilibrium or the conflict type.

Andrew Hacker

Sociology and Ideology

*I*N 1872 Karl Marx stood up before a public meeting at The Hague and uttered the following words: "We know that the institutions, manners and customs of the various countries must be considered, and we do not deny that there are countries, like England and America, . . . where the worker may attain his object by peaceful means."[1] It is remarks like this which turn scholarly heads gray. For in the space of several seconds Marx tore an all but fatal gash in the theory of history he had so painstakingly developed in his formal writings. The bourgeois state and society, Marx had insisted, had to be overturned by force and violence if the working class was to inaugurate an effective dictatorship as a prelude to the communist Utopia. Violent means were imperative if the values and institutions of capitalism were to be obliterated for all time: the bourgeoisie would not mend its ways voluntarily and, unless destroyed, would bend every effort to sabotage the socialist revolution. This, at least, is the substance of Marx's theory. The

---

From Andrew Hacker, "Sociology and Ideology," from Max Black, Editor, *The Social Theories of Talcott Parsons: A Critical Examination*, © 1961. Reprinted by permission of Prentice-Hall, Inc., Englewood Cliffs, New Jersey.

[1] Quoted in Hans Kelsen, *The Political Theory of Bolshevism* (Berkeley and Los Angeles: University of California Press, 1948), p. 41.

conscientious scholar, well versed in the theoretical literature of Marxism, might wish that Marx had never shown up at that meeting at The Hague: the remark about "peaceful means," despite the qualifications about national variations, simply does not fit into the general theory of history. Conscience, of course, precludes the concealing of uncomfortable evidence. Perhaps there were two Marxes—Marx the academic theorist and Marx the organizer of the First International. Perhaps, and perhaps not. At all events the scholar's position is a difficult one—and it is not irrelevant to a consideration of Talcott Parsons.

Parsons has no book entitled *Polity and Society,* and his brief remarks on politics in *The Social System* are clearly undeveloped. To gain an understanding of his political theory it is necessary to refer to his "Hague Speeches": occasional papers on a miscellany of political subjects. Four of these essays will be discussed here. All of them deal with questions of class, power, and politics as they relate to contemporary American society. Two profess to be special—that is, political—applications of the general system which is elaborated in his larger works, and all have the virtue of dealing with a specified society so that theoretical conclusions may be ranged against the available data. Insofar as Parsons' political analysis is "derived"—a favorite word of Parsons—from his formal system, an analysis of that analysis may throw some light on assumptions which underlie the larger system. But the opening *caveat* is still in order: these are occasional essays and they were written for specific purposes. Students should think twice before using them as pebbles to derail the Twentieth Century Limited. It may well be that there are two Parsonses—the political and the sociological, and the two have yet to meet in a consistent way. This paper will attempt to show a number of junctures at which his politics and sociology are significantly relevant to each other.

I

The "conservative" bias in Parsons' writings has been remarked upon by more than one commentator.[2] The central place he gives to a theory of "equilibrium" in his system is made to be convincing evidence that the emphasis is on underlying social consensus rather than on continual, even irreconcilable, conflict. Insofar as the equilibrium idea is considered here, it will be with reference to Parsons' view of American politics, and not his

---

[2] See Lewis A. Coser, *The Functions of Social Conflict* (Glencoe, Ill.: Free Press, 1956), pp. 21–24; Barrington Moore, *Political Power and Social Theory* (Cambridge: Harvard University Press, 1958), pp. 122–25; C. Wright Mills, *The Sociological Imagination* (New York: Oxford University Press, 1959), pp. 44–49.

social system as a whole. It should be pointed out right now that the epithet "conservative" is a deceptive one, and one undeserved by Parsons. While he shares some of the philosophical assumptions of a man like Edmund Burke —and these will be noted—he is on the whole a "liberal." This ideological commitment appears at two levels. On the more transitory plane Parsons' liberalism expresses itself in a partisan sense: in his approach to the proper functions of government he is sympathetic to a greater—but not over-extended—assumption of public responsibilities for the general welfare. To be specific, he is one of the liberal-intellectuals of the Democratic Party, one of the Eggheads. In a more profound sense his liberalism is more historically based: it is the ideology of John Locke and John Stuart Mill, the ideology of political liberty and a free society. The two liberalisms, of course, go hand in hand, but it is best to keep them analytically separate in this discussion. It does not matter which label is attached to an individual's political thinking so long as we are aware of the substance of his ideas. It will, for purposes of convenience, be proposed that Parsons is a liberal: that his view of society is the conventional liberal one that has characterized academic thinking in the social sciences.

In 1955 Parsons wrote an article for *The Yale Review* entitled "Social Strains in America," dealing with the problem of the attack on civil liberties which was then overt and widespread. Far from being a facile journalistic attack on the Wisconsin demagogue, it was a sophisticated analysis of tensions underlying recent American development. "McCarthyism can be understood as a relatively acute symptom of the strains which accompany a major change in the situation and structure of American society," he says. "The strains to which I refer derive primarily from conflicts between the demands imposed by the new situation and the inertia of those elements of our social structure which are most resistant to the necessary changes."[3] The new situation revolves largely about the fact that America has assumed global responsibilities which are both expensive and hazardous. By no means all Americans are as yet accustomed to this unsettled condition, and the fear of defeat at Soviet hands engenders anxieties at both conscious and unconscious levels. On the structural level there is the rapid growth of industrialization, but a growth without the stabilizing element of an ante-cedent feudal class structure. The result has been the emergence of an open society which, to put it simply, is too open. The class structure, such as it is, is based almost entirely on occupational roles: this means that individuals find their expectations in life but weakly established, and their aspirations frequently frustrated. In a more specific vein, Parsons points out that many

---

[3] Talcott Parsons, "Social Strains in America," reprinted in Daniel Bell, ed., *The New American Right* (New York: Criterion Books, 1955), pp. 117–18.

businessmen are angered about increasing government intervention in their hitherto private affairs. New men of economic power in the hinterland are jealous of the influence and prestige still possessed by the old families of the Eastern Seaboard. Children of immigrant parents are still sensitive concerning their full acceptance as first-class citizens, and tend to react by demonstrating a hyper-patriotic outlook. And a large group in American society has been able to rise in economic and social status as a result of industrial prosperity and the white-collar explosion, yet they often feel neglected when power and privileges are bestowed. This analysis is an imaginative one, and Parsons has a clear view of the sources and manifestations of serious strains in American life. He proceeds to show how these unrelieved tensions provided a large, if miscellaneous, constituency of support for McCarthyism. Compulsive concern about loyalty and security, treason and subversion, and about the softness of traditional leadership and the need for hardheaded measures—all of these were not passing political phases, but "symptoms of a process in American society of some deep and general significance."[4]

To write this way is to write of a fundamental social disequilibrium. McCarthy himself has passed from the scene. And McCarthyism has either subsided or been institutionalized in our social structure and internalized in our personalities. The importance of Parsons' essay lies in its discussion of important social forces of which McCarthyism was only a symptom. The alleviation of symptoms—in this case the censure of McCarthy—must never be confused with fundamental cure. It is of some interest that Parsons has not returned, since McCarthy's demise, to a consideration of the strains he so well outlined in 1955. If they are as deep-seated as he made them out to be, they cannot be ignored once their most disruptive symptoms have declined. It will therefore be worth the time to refer to some of the questions that Parsons raised. The McCarthyite constituency to which Parsons alluded consisted, on the whole, of two major groups: the successful and the unsuccessful, the upwardly and downwardly mobile. At the same time the movement's supporters may be divided into his vocal and virulent supporters, on the one hand, and those who gave him their tacit consent, on the other. The individuals who should be given careful attention are the successful Americans who offered their silent approval to the McCarthy crusade. There is no disputing that in the postwar years millions of individuals have experienced a rise in status. They have moved out of old neighborhoods; they have put on white collars; they have been able to surround themselves with material comforts; and they have created a new image of themselves and new expectations for their children. What has also occurred

---

[4] *Ibid.*, p. 117.

is that these Americans have begun to take seriously their status as first-class citizens. This development is more startling than it might at first glance seem. For 150 years the American creed talked the rhetoric of equality, but these sentiments were never expected to be taken at face value by the great part of the population. Now, however, new millions of Americans are in a position to demand that equality. They are no longer illiterate immigrants huddled in the urban slums, they are no longer marginal farmers forgotten in the rural countryside. They are now American citizens: middle class and not a little arrogant about it. Problems arise because there has been a political lag in the course of this social advance. The promises inherent in the rhetoric of political equality have not been fulfilled, or not delivered to the extent that first-class citizens have come to expect. In political terms the emerging middle class remains relatively powerless. It is unorganized, inarticulate, and incapable of promoting its political interests. Indeed, its "interests" are so generalized and inchoate that it is hard to know where to begin securing them.[5]

These people, although Parsons did not say much about them, were the real supporters of the McCarthy movement. Too concerned with being respectable, they did not go to meetings, join organizations, or write letters to the newspapers—either for or against him. It was their political silence and inactivity, however, which gave free rein to an era of demagogy. And it is now relevant to suggest that this constituency, fast approaching majority status in the country, will be the source of further strains. Only two will be mentioned here, but others may come to mind.

The first is in the area of race relations, especially in the North. Things are going to get a lot worse, and it is not at all self-evident that they are going to get better in the foreseeable future. If there is one sword which hangs over the heads of untold millions of white—and northern—Americans it is that they cannot afford to live in close proximity to Negroes. The single social fact which can destroy the whole image of middle class respectability is to be known to reside in a neighborhood which has Negroes nearby. Pollsters' notebooks are filled to overflow with the rationalizations supposedly impelling the flight: the danger of violence, overcrowded schools, not enough green grass and fresh air, and so forth.[6] But the simple answer is that these Americans are too insecure in their newly-won status, too fearful of the opinions of others, too ready to take the easiest and available way

---

[5] The term "interest" is being used here in the sense that James Madison intended in the Tenth and Fifty-First *Federalist Papers*. For a further explanation see Andrew Hacker, *Politics and the Corporation* (New York: Fund for the Republic, 1958), pp. 4–11.

[6] See the Report of the Commission on Race and Housing entitled *Where Shall We Live?* (Berkeley and Los Angeles: University of California Press, 1958).

out. Not simply our great cities, but all urban areas are developing racial ghettoes with inadequate social services and slender opportunities for escape for those who must stay behind. And our burgeoning suburbs have become monuments to white anxiety. The problem is a national one, and it is bound to become exacerbated as more white Americans are drawn into the middle class. For this class-status is too easily attained, too unstructured, to give those who enter it a sense of psychological security. The decision to move to a suburb is no solution to the basic problem. The answer must be political and is yet to emerge.

The second area of strain has to do with the quality of culture. At one time in our history the constituency for knowledge and serious learning was a small one. The proportion of the population which went to college, which read important books and periodicals and which generally partook of high culture was comparatively minute. With such a small and appreciative clientele, disciplined standards could be both set and met. All of this is being altered, and for good reason. The citizens of the new social democracy demand not only a high-school education, but also college admission for themselves and their children. And the simple fact is that most of these people—*Fortune* magazine calls them "the new masses"[7]—are not equipped for serious or disciplined learning. When culture has a small, selective, and privileged constituency, it is possible to keep standards high: as the constituency is enlarged to many times its original size, the distribution of aptitudes and motivations is bound to be far wider and the mean far lower. Nevertheless, these new citizens demand admission to the citadels of knowledge, and once they are there they pull requirements down to a level they can handle. The point, in short, is that the new middle class is too large and too poorly motivated to live by the traditional injunctions of quality. Arguments about the number of "classical" records and local symphony orchestras, about the number of "good" paperback books and local little theatres, are more wishful thinking than serious analysis.[8] American culture is increasingly yielding to majority wishes, increasingly being defined in mass terms. Even the most venerable of schools and universities cannot but be swayed by the demands of a buyers' market. This, then, is another consequence of making real the doctrine of equality of opportunity. Social democracy and cultural majority rule produce strains less virulent than McCarthyism and less noisome than the race discrimination, but serious enough to warrant attention. And these tensions, too, ultimately have a political content.

---

[7] Daniel Seligman, "The New Masses," *Fortune*, 59:106 ff. (1959).

[8] See Bernard Rosenberg and David Manning White, eds., *Mass Culture* (Glencoe, Ill.: Free Press, 1957), especially the essays by Rosenberg, Dwight MacDonald, and Melvin Tumin, at pp. 3–12, 59–73, and 548–56 respectively.

II

It is no criticism of Parsons to point out that since the time of McCarthy he has not written articles on other strains in American life. But what is of interest is that since that time he has all but forgotten the structural factors which underpinned his analysis of the McCarthyite tensions. It has been suggested that these forces still exist and that they will continue to manifest themselves for a long period to come. And the key question for theory, of course, concerns what is going to emerge in the future. The writings of the great political theorists had two characteristics. On the one hand they were startling: they told us something new and unorthodox about the society we thought we understood. And on the other hand they stuck their necks out: they ventured a prediction about the future direction of social and political development. Parsons' work, if it is to have lasting value, must be assessed on both of these grounds.

There is, first, the question of social class. In a paper entitled "Social Classes and Class Conflict," delivered before the American Economic Association, he offered a critical and yet sympathetic analysis of some features of Marxian theory. After examining the strengths and weaknesses of Marx's approach, Parsons then proceeds to his own consideration of class conflict in modern, industrialized societies. The root of the matter, as he sees it, lies in the tension between the emphasis on individual attainment and the imperatives of bureaucratic organization. "The status of the individual," he says, "must be determined on grounds essentially peculiar to himself, notably his own personal qualities, technical competence, and his own decisions about his occupational career and with respect to which he is not identified with any solidary group." (Essays II 327) At the same time there arises a complex of organizational structures which have the power to direct significant elements in the lives of individuals. "Organization on an ever increasing scale . . . naturally involves centralization and differentiation of leadership and authority," Parsons says, "so that those who take responsibility for coordinating the actions of many others must have a different status in important respects from those who are essentially in the role of carrying out specifications laid down by others." (Essays II 327) Apart from the empirical question of how many individuals are affected by these organizational imperatives and to what degree, there is little to argue about in these descriptive propositions. There then follows a listing of the "principal aspects of the tendency to develop class conflict in our type of social system." (Essays II 329–32) These may be summarized: (1) In a competitive occupational system there will be losers as well as winners. (2) Organization entails discipline and authority, and there will be resistance to the exercise of this power. (3) Individuals favored by strategic location can exploit those less fortunately placed. (4) Varied and conflicting ideologies emerge in a differentiated social structure. (5) Patterns of family life and attitude-formation in the young will vary as between social classes. (6) The promise of equal opportunity for all will be thwarted.

Parsons acknowledges his indebtedness to Marx wherever appropriate (and it would be pleasant if more social scientists were secure enough to be able to do the same), and he also quite properly indicates that Marx's theory is insufficient to explain the contemporary world. Indeed, what social science most surely needs is a new Marxism: a new systematic theory which postulates cause and effect and which commits itself on the future development of society. Such a theory, however, needs what for lack of a better term may be called a source of energy. The common criticism of Marx is that he had but a single, determinist idea at the core of his thinking. But at least it was an idea of some power, and he was able to develop the rest of his thoughts around it. The difficulty with Parsons' scheme is that he has too many ideas which interact on a parity of causal significance. It might be asked which one of the six "principal aspects" of class conflict is most important, which one of the six "principal aspects" of class conflict is most important, which one—if any—is causal with relation to the rest. One is tempted to conclude that until Parsons is prepared to be a little less conventional, a little more daring, we will not have a pioneering explanation of social strains or class conflict. We might, indeed, ask whether the social strains America has been experiencing are instances of class conflict in modern dress. The new middle class has many of the attributes of an alienated proletariat, albeit a proletariat with white collars. However, there is lacking a class-conciousness in any political sense; and the exploitation of a bourgeois class has been replaced by the discipline and authority of impersonal corporate institutions. Many important political questions are raised here, and it may be hoped that Parsons will turn to them before long.

III

One obstacle to a Parsonian theory of class and power may not be easy to overcome. Social scientists, whether they acknowledge it or not, cannot help being bearers of an ideology—although the ideology will, of course, differ from person to person. Ideology, for present purposes, may be thought of as having two components. It is, first of all, purportedly normative, composed of philosophical propositions which are actually rationalizations for preserving the status quo or attaining a new set of social arrangements. Second, ideology is purportedly scientific: an unintentionally distorted picture of social reality, the distortion arising because the observer sees what he wants to see. Any theory which combines fact and norm, whether by accident or design, runs the risk of forcing descriptive reality into the Procrustean bed of ideology. This is probably inevitable, and it is certainly not to be condemned out of hand. Indeed, the real test is not whether fact or norm is tainted with ideology, but whether the ideology itself is a viable one.[9]

The ideological overtones in Parsons' political thinking come to light most vividly in his essay on " 'Voting' and the Equilibrium of the American Party System." This is ostensibly a review-article, drawing on the Elmira study of Berelson, Lazarsfeld, and McPhee.[10] Actually, however, Parsons uses only those data which are helpful to his own analysis of the party system in the United States; and he gives no evidence of a familiarity with the voluminous literature on party politics which has accumulated in the postwar years. His particular interest is the process of representative government as it relates to social stability. "My point of reference will be the capacity of a social system to get things done in its collective interest," Parsons says. "Hence power involves a special problem of the integration of the system, including the binding of its units, individual and collective, to the necessary commitments."[11] It is Parsons' view that things do get done through the medium of the party system and that the system does remain integrated. To conclude this, however, is to make a number of important assumptions: about what ought to be done, what can be done, and the effectiveness of what is done. There is, furthermore, the assumption that what we see at work is actually the process of representative government. To begin with the last of these, Parsons believes that the institutions of political democracy play an important and effective role in the exercise of power in society. The chief of these institutions is the vote as it is exercised through the party system. "Voting is the central focus of the process of selection of leadership and hence in one sense all other influences must channel their effects through the voting process," he says. "The two-party system may be regarded as a mechanism that makes possible a certain balance between effectiveness through a relative centralization of power, and mobilization of support

---

[9] Jeremy Bentham put it this way: "No wonder then, in a treatise partly of the *expository* class, and partly of the *censorial*, that if the latter department is filled with imbecility, symptoms of kindred weakness should characterize the former." *A Fragment on Government*, edited by Wilfrid Harrison (Oxford: Blackwell, 1948), p. 14.

[10] Bernard R. Berelson, Paul F. Lazarsfeld, and William N. McPhee, *Voting: A Study of Opinion Formation in a Presidential Campaign* (Chicago: University of Chicago Press, 1954).

[11] Talcott Parsons, " 'Voting' and the Equilibrium of the American Political System," Eugene Burdick and Arthur J. Brodbeck, eds., *American Voting Behavior* (Glencoe, Ill.: Free Press, 1959), p. 81.

from different sources in such a way that . . . the supporter is offered a real alternative."[12] While this description of voting and the party system in America is admirable from the standpoint of normative democratic theory— the writings of Robert MacIver or Ernest Barker, for example—it bears small relation to how these institutions operate.

The point is not that Parsons has got his facts wrong: actually the interpretation of reality is far from settled in this area. What is important is that Parsons has come to his particular interpretation and that he has seen fit to reject other alternatives. And it follows that he has chosen to emphasize certain facts and to ignore others. The question, to repeat, is why he sees what he does and why he turns a blind eye in other directions. A few comments on matters of fact—or the interpretation of fact—may be in order. The selection of leadership by means of the vote, it may be argued, only assumes significance in limited cases: if the two individuals on the slate of candidates selected by the two party organizations offer a real choice in terms of their stands on matters of policy. Usually they do not. In most parts of the country the bearer of the party label traditional to that area wins automatically. In most contested districts the tendency is for candidates to be essentially similar because both must appeal to the same heterogeneous electorate. On the national scene it is possible to claim that American voters have not been offered a "real alternative" since Bryan ran against McKinley in 1896. (It turned out that they had a real choice in 1932, but the voters did not know it while the campaign was going on.) Furthermore, it is quite plausible to suggest that the major interests which exercise an influence in the making of public policy make their weight felt regardless of the candidates the voters happen to put in office. Such interests are studiously non-partisan and they are quite ready to approach policy-makers no matter which party label they happen to bear. These are only a few alternative interpretations of the voting and party processes, and space forbids elaborating on these or others at this time.

The reason why Parsons presents such a one-sided picture can only be a subject for speculation. His chief concern, it would appear, is to show that the American political system is a democratic one at base. He wishes to present a persuasive case to the effect that the public has power and that it uses this power to govern itself. The voter, in short, can use his ballot as an instrument for compelling his rulers to make policy responsive to his wishes. "He receives the expectation that many kinds of measure that he approves will be implemented if his candidate wins, but without exact specification of particular policies," Parsons says.[13] But even this carefully qualified state-

---

12 *Ibid.*, pp. 86, 87.
13 Parsons, " 'Voting' and the Equilibrium of the American Party System," p. 90.

ment, it may once again be suggested, describes the ideal rather than the real. Voters continue to expect that promises will be delivered—their faith, although occasionally tinged by cynicism, is self-renewing—but even those who support the victors are usually disappointed. Taxes are not cut, the cost of living continues to rise, unemployment is never fully abolished, peace with honor remains an unfulfilled hope. And when it comes to even more subtle issues, issues between the lines of the formal platforms and speeches, our political institutions have shown themselves incapable of rising to the challenge. Parsons, however, is content with what he sees. In terms of the mechanisms of representative government and in terms of the substance of public policy, he sets his standard for optimum performance at a fairly low level. "The essential point is that new things do get done and that the consequences do come to be accepted," he says. "In view of what sociologists now know of the intensity of the tensions and stresses generated by major processes of social change, the relative effectiveness of this set of mechanisms is impressive."[14] What makes them look impressive is that Parsons believes they have been subjected to a rigorous test and have passed that examination successfully.

An example of this testing is the New Deal, with business regulation and social welfare legislation. "The Federal Reserve Act, the Securities Exchange Act, the Wagner Act, and the Social Security Act, were all Democratic measures—every one of which was strongly contested by the Republican party," Parsons says. "Every one of them has come to be fundamentally accepted by that party with no attempt to undo the work."[15] As a factual proposition this is of course true. What Parsons finds impressive is the fact that the Republicans accepted these laws, that the business community in particular did not resort to extra-constitutional means when they were put on the statute books. An alternative view would suggest that the limits of the American political consensus has not been tested since the close of the Civil War. What Parsons and other liberals like to think of as business regulation is, despite the predictable complaints of businessmen, more a paper tiger than an effective system of economic controls in the public interest. A few questions may be asked about these supposed powers of the national government. Can any public agency determine the level of wages, of

---

14 *Ibid.*, p. 112.

15 *Ibid.*, p. 111. The "Democratic party" which Parsons refers to in generalized terms is actually the liberal—and minority—wing of the party. Like most liberal Democrats, Parsons would like to believe that his image of the party is the real one. The record of the Democrats in the Congress over the past twenty years, however, shows that the reality lies elsewhere.

prices, of profits? Can it, perhaps more important, specify the level and direction of capital investment? Can any government bureau allocate raw materials or control plant location? Can it in any way guarantee full employment or the rate of economic growth? Has any suit of the Anti-Trust Division actually broken up one of our large corporations in an appreciable way? The simple answer is that measures such as these are neither possible under the laws nor do we know what the reaction to them would be. And what Parsons chooses to call welfare legislation is, despite the partisan panegyrics of New Deal Democrats, more a humane hope than a realized system of economic security. Several questions may once again be posed. What proportion of low-income Americans live in rural or urban slums and what proportion are in government housing projects? What source of income is there for a man who is out of work after his 13 or 26 weeks of unemployment compensation expires? What standard of life can be maintained on the social security pension an individual may receive at 65 and how many Americans do not have additional sources of income? If a family is visited with a really serious and extended illness, where can a citizen get medical care other than in a charity ward? Just what can a widow or a deserted mother with three small children expect as a right from her government? Any serious study of these matters will show that the so-called welfare state offers a slender mite indeed.

In making judgments in an area like this, one can be a Burke or a Bentham, but in neither case is one a social scientist. To a Burkean what has been done looks impressive; to a Benthamite what remains to be done looks formidable. Parsons is pleased with what has been accomplished: to his mind it is quite a feat that so much has been done without rending the Republic. His evidence that the limit has been reached is that businessmen complained so bitterly about even minimal regulation and welfare measures. This, it may be suggested, is no test at all. Businessmen complain without surcease, and have been doing so since the time of Adam Smith.[16] We do

---

16 More than a century ago Charles Dickens could report: "Surely there never was such a fragile china-ware as that of which the millers of Coketown were made. Handle them never so lightly, and they fell to pieces with such ease that you might suspect them of having been flawed before. They were ruined, when they were required to send labouring children to school; they were ruined when inspectors were appointed to look into their works; they were ruined, when such inspectors considered it doubtful whether they were quite justified in chopping people up with their machinery; they were utterly undone, when it was hinted that perhaps they need not always make quite so much smoke.... Whenever a Coketowner felt he was ill-used—that is to say, whenever he was not left entirely alone, and it was proposed to hold him accountable for the consequences of any of his acts—he was sure to come out with the awful menace, that he would 'sooner pitch his property into the Atlantic.' This had terrified the Home Secretary within an inch of his life, on several occasions." From *Hard Times* (1854).

not know how much they will take without resorting to counterrevolution. Parsons' political "equilibrium" is, on the one hand, an acceptance of the economic status quo in its major outlines, and, on the other, a cautious espousal of traditional liberalism. The latter will be examined more carefully later on. It might also be asked whether the government is in a position to do anything about the "tensions and stresses generated by major processes of social change" which Parsons himself has discussed. Here the focus is not on regulatory or welfare problems, but on the larger social strains. If it is not government's, then whose responsibility is it to remedy the status anxieties, the fragmentation of personality, and the sense of individual powerlessness brought on by contemporary institutions and events?

Parsons has said that the instrumentality of the vote is important, but surely there are limits to solving such problems via the ballot box. The forces which led to McCarthyism were not exorcised by the censure and death of McCarthy. Racial tensions will not be solved by pleas for tolerance, and the cultural level will not be raised by pleas for internal discipline. Our political institutions, as now constituted, are too free and too democratic to handle these problems of staus and personality. Serious questions must be raised about democracy and freedom. What is revealing is that Parsons evades these questions altogether. The solutions provided by communism and fascism are abhorrent; those proposed by classical conservatism and socialism are pre-industrial and hence Utopian. There is nothing wrong with talk of "equilibrium" if its base point is reasonably up to date. Parsons may, like many of us, be fearful of what the future will bring. But that is no excuse for designing a political theory which stands still.

IV

Parsons' nostalgia for the past and his acceptance of present arrangements are brought out most clearly in his article-review of C. Wright Mills' *The Power Elite*.[17] Mills' book, one of the most challenging to appear since the end of World War II, speaks a language which is harsh and alien to Parsons' ears. It is interesting to see what Parsons makes of these arguments, for in a real sense we have here a confrontation of liberal and radical thinking. It is not surprising that Parsons fails to understand much of what Mills has to say. The discussion of who the members of the power elite are is neglected in order to make the rather obvious point that America is no longer ruled by a property-owning class. And as for Mills' important chapter on mass society, Parsons thinks it has to do mainly with mass media and he

---

[17] C. Wright Mills, *The Power Elite* (New York: Oxford University Press, 1956).

does not know what to make of it. There are comments on the role of women and physicians (they are socially important); on government economic controls (they are genuine because businessmen object to them); on Adlai Stevenson (a favorite of Parsons'); and on the fact that Americans have friends and relations and go to church (so they cannot be as anomic as is made out). Finally Parsons says that he is not really interested in how power is distributed—who exercises it over whom and who has it at whose expense—but rather in how it is produced. "Power is a generalized facility or resource in the society," he says. "It has to be divided or allocated, but it also has to be produced and it has collective as well as distributive functions."[18] It is clear that Parsons, for the symmetry of his larger social system, wants to set up a wealth-power analogy in order to underpin an economics-politics model. The scheme dictates that if wealth must be created before it is distributed, so must power. Until Parsons can show that it is important to make this analytic separation, it will probably be better to follow men like Machiavelli and Hobbes who find the production and distribution of power an identical process. For Parsons, however, the dichotomy serves the useful purpose of allowing him to evade the controversial questions raised by asking who in America has power and who has not.

Mills' book is more complex than it seems on the surface and is not easy for someone reared on liberalism to understand. Parsons understands that something akin to a power elite exists. "The rise to prominence within the firm of specialized executive functions," he says, "is a normal outcome of a process of growth in size and in structural differentiation."[19] This is true enough. But Mills' concern is with the great influence that the decisions of these top executives have on the lives of Americans, a power in no way made institutionally responsible. Parsons skirts this problem, and in doing so implies that he does not think it important. And the idea of the mass society, the other side of Mills' theory, receives even less attention from Parsons. There are millions of Americans—the Americans described in *White Collar, The Organization Man, The Lonely Crowd,* and *The Status Seekers*—who have no significant access to power.[20] To Parsons' mind they have the vote, and this makes them masters of their destiny. Mills juxtaposes the anonymous and non-responsible men who lead the great corporate institutions and the cheerful and anxious Americans who are recipients of commands. All

---

18 Talcott Parsons, "The Distribution of Power in American Society," *World Politics,* 10:141 (October, 1957).

19 *Ibid.,* p. 129.

20 "No social scientist has yet come up with a theory of mass society that is entirely satisfying," Irving Howe says; but he himself gives a cogent description of its bare outlines. See his "Mass Society and Post-War Modern Fiction," *Partisan Review,* 26:426–28 (Summer, 1959).

this and more is in Mills' book, but Parsons is unable or unwilling to see it. Mills is not so much describing the present as he is picking out future tendencies. Because Parsons has no view of the future himself, he can only quarrel over details. And he can also criticize Mills' tone. "There is," Parsons says, "the tendency to think of power as presumptively illegitimate; if people exercise considerable power, it must be because they have somehow unsurped it where they had no right and they intend to use it to the detriment of others." [21] When Mills finds both irresponsibility and immorality in the conduct of the power elite, Parsons becomes a realist and decries Jeffersonian Utopianism. What is required, he says, is "objective analysis."

V

We have now come full circle. C. Wright Mills is called a Utopian because he would prefer it if a power elite did not exist. The question which now has to be put is why Parsons prefers that McCarthyism and the power behind it not exist. "McCarthyism," he says, "is perhaps the major type of 'pathology' of our system and, if not controlled, may have highly disruptive consequences."[22] If McCarthyism is "pathological," why not also the Higher Immorality of a power elite? The use of a clinical term can be deceptive. (Are race prejudice and mass culture also "pathologies"? What about labor disputes, juvenile delinquency, isolationism in foreign affairs, and the dearth of good conversation?) It is clear that Parsons is assuming that certain social arrangements are healthy and others are not. A good idea of his conception of normality may be gained if we look at his prescription for the McCarthyite disease. Power must be met with power: in this case the power of the populace with the power of—yes—the power elite. "Under American conditions, a politically leading stratum must be made up of a combination of business and non-business elements," Parsons says. "The role of the economy in American society and of the business element in it is such that political leadership without prominent business participation is doomed to ineffectiveness and to the perpetuation of dangerous internal conflict. It is not possible to lead the American people against the leaders of the business world." [23] Parsons suggests that business leaders be brought into politics and that they use their social power to quash the popular attack on civil liberties. This prescription probably reveals better than anything which has been said up to now Parsons' view of political and social normality. It is his hope that the men in the higher ranks of America's corporate world are potential defenders of the traditional liberal values.

---

[21] Parsons, "The Distribution of Power in American Society," p. 140.
[22] Parsons, " 'Voting' and the Equilibrium of the American Political System," p. 103.
[23] Parsons, "Social Strains in America," p. 139.

Historically speaking, such a view of the business class is justified. The growth of political liberty in the Western world was accompanied by, even caused by, the ascent to power of men of property. This class was informed that wisdom, virtue, and social responsibility were its proper attributes; and in many ways it lived up to these expectations. Its members put their power and prestige behind the Constitution, the Bill of Rights, and the Common Law. They were able to do this because they were accorded unquestioning deference by a public which acknowledged that their betters ought to attend to matters as important as these. The source of this class' power lay in its property ownership and its members' personal control over elements of the economy. They also supplied the nation's diplomats and cabinet members, lawmakers and judges, financiers and industrialists, churchmen and scholars. While this class was the custodian of the country's liberty, it was careful not to overextend its resources in their defense of the rights of individuals. The railroaded Wobbly in Montana and the emasculated Negro in Alabama were not encompassed by their power: and they could not find it in their jurisdiction to defend two Italian anarchists named Sacco and Vanzetti. By and large the freedoms which this class created were for their own use; but they were phrased in universalistic and equalitarian terms, and there was a residue for the rest of society. This class, also, was the major support of higher learning and serious culture: here too it was for their own benefit, but the standards stood for the community as a whole. The need for such a ruling class is implicit in Parsons' notion of political equilibrium, although it is doubtful if he would acknowledge it—or if he even realizes it. What is "pathological" about McCarthyism—and racial discrimnation and mass culture— is that the man in the street is no longer deferring to his betters. In his essay on voting Parsons says, "In constructing this model I have of course leaned heavily on the literature of political theory."[24] That literature, from Plato and Aristotle through Locke and Mill, relies on the power of a secure ruling class to protect the traditional liberties of a society. Scholars who have benefited from this shield, who reside in institutions which continue to feed on prescriptive deference, may be excused if they generalize from their particular good fortune.[25]

This America, the creation of the liberal ideology and class structure, is passing rapidly from the scene. Already the old class has had to share its power with the new elite. This is an elite of talent, but specialized talent. They are the men Mills excoriates and the men Parsons calls on to take up

[24] Parsons, " 'Voting' and the Equilibrium of the American Political System," p. 113.

[25] For a further development of the ideas in this paragraph and the one following see Andrew Hacker, "Liberal Democracy and Social Control," *The American Political Science Review,* 51:1009–26 (December, 1957).

the defense of political freedom. However, if any examination is given to the kind of men they are, their interests in life and their social backgrounds, the basis on which they were selected and their own definition of their roles, and above all to their unwillingness to entangle with controversy—if such study is made, it soon becomes apparent that these men have neither the concern nor the motivation to use the power of their institutions to defend the freedoms so cherished by traditional liberalism. They define their responsibilities to society in only the most cautious and conventional of terms. For all the rhetoric about "the conscience of the corporation" and "the social responsibilities of business," when the chips are down the elite has shown itself unwilling to oppose the pathological strains which Parsons deplores. While this might be expected of the old ruling class, it is quite another thing to ask such deeds from the new elite. They simply would not understand what Parsons is talking about.

Concurrently with the rise of the elite, the children and grandchildren of a once deferential public are beginning for the first time to feel their democratic oats. The democracy is more social than political, but its consequences cannot be ignored. Experiencing tensions as they move into a place in the sun, these people are compelled for the benefit of their own well-being to act in ways that are inimical to traditional freedoms. Overt political populism is only sporadic: the defense of a white neighborhood in one instance, the defeat of a school bond issue in another, obscurantist legislation from time to time as a third. But society is too bureaucratized for populist politics to damage the structure itself: what is far more fragile is the delicate fabric of traditional liberty, and here the cost can be high. The new masses, furthermore, have no vested interest in such protections as the First Amendment freedoms. For them freedom is not the right to make a heretical speech, but the right to move to the suburbs and buy a motorboat. The new and burgeoning middle class, unlike the old and selective middle class, is without commitment to political liberty or a culture of quality. And the new elite, while it exercises control over much of the economy and society, makes no effort to contain the "pathological" behavior of the new democracy. The chief explanation for this is that elite and mass are really not much different so far as tastes or interests are concerned: the former simply have more important jobs than the latter. Politically and culturally they are quite similar. Both subscribe to *Life* magazine.

The ideology underlying Parsons' political theory is a worthy one in many respects. But liberalism of the eighteenth and nineteenth centuries no longer has the structural basis which gave it its strength. The political era into which we are moving will create its own equilibrium: and both a power elite and a mass society will play crucial roles in its definition. Neither Mills' socialism nor Marx' communism, and least of all Parsons' liberalism, will be of much theoretical help. The ideological components of Parsons' thought do him a disservice not because they are ideological, but because they refer to a world we have put behind us and to which we cannot return. The politics he depicts are the politics he would like to exist, not those we are going to have to live with. Whether this nostalgia for an age of civility infuses the larger outlines of his social system is a question that all students of Parsons ought to ponder.

Epilogue

A<small>NY</small> volume that airs a controversy might also be expected to end it. Where is the *truth* in the flurry of allegations? What is the *correct* theoretical posture and what are the *proper* theoretical assumptions? Alas, we have no answers, or at least none with illusions of definitiveness. The debate will persist long after this volume and, perhaps, long after the demise of functionalism itself. Its issues form the very heart of contemporary sociological theory. Indeed a cynic might argue that the theory will only remain vital as long as the issues remain unresolved.

This final article offers a perspective rather than a panacea. It was written before the volume was planned, but it is fitting as the volume's conclusion. Having witnessed charges and countercharges, it is appropriate to evaluate both while identifying with neither. As we have seen, both critics and defenders tend to regard structural-functionalism as a single school with a distinct identity and a common strategy. This paper argues that the illusion of unity has obfuscated the discussion. It suggests that structural-functionalism harbors at least two quite different approaches. While both are "legitimate," they lead to different conclusions with different vulnerabilities. Thus, it matters whether one is primarily concerned with the *structural part* or the *systemic whole*. In each case there are advantages and disadvantages, but errors of Panglossian unity, functional indispensability, static analysis, and ideological conservatism do not apply equally to both. Each is exposed to biases, but the biases are neither identical nor inevitable.

N. J. Demerath III

Synecdoche and Structural-Functionalism

*T*HE debate over structural-functionalism now involves at least three positions. First, there are those who defend the school as a distinct approach to sociological phenomena. Second, there are those who are hostile to structural-functionalism and would temper assumptions of harmony with assumptions of conflict[1] Third, there are others who feel that all science is structural-functional; we should do away with the debate to get on with the

Reprinted from N. J. Demerath III, "Synecdoche and Structural-Functionalism," *Social Forces*, 44 (March, 1966), pp. 390–401, by permission of the author and the journal.

[1] Two leading spokesmen for this view are David Lockwood, "Some Remarks on the 'Social System,'" *British Journal of Sociology*, 7 (June 1956), pp. 134–146, and Ralf Dahrendorf, "Out of Utopia: Toward a Reorientation of Sociological Analysis," *American Journal of Sociology*, 64 (September 1958), pp. 115–127. Dahrendorf's *Class and Class Conflict in Industrial Society* (Stanford: Stanford University Press, 1959) is similar in tack but milder in tone. It actually applauds Parsons on some points and feels that "system analysis," even "static analysis," is appropriate for some situations. As this suggests, not all "conflict theories" are inimical to structural-functionalism. Lewis Coser's reworking of Simmel's insights, *The Functions of Social Conflict* (Glencoe, Illinois: The Free Press, 1956), is avowedly within the structural-functional school. Here conflict is often seen as leading to ultimate harmony and stability.

analysis.[2] There are clear differences between these positions, but there is also common ground as well. Each tends to view structural-functionalism as an almost seamless whole. Each sees it as a single theoretical stance that can be evaluated in its entirety. It is here that the present paper suggests a departure. If structural-functionalism is open to charges of analytic myopia and omnipresent utopia, some of its forms are more vulnerable than others. If there are no distinctions between structural-functionalism and sociology in general, there are certainly distinctions within structural-functionalism itself.

The term "synecdoche," in suggesting a confusion of the whole with its parts,[3] is doubly apt in this context. First, structural-functionalism includes distinct subspecies with distinct consequences, and we should not judge the "whole" on the basis of only one of its "parts." Second, a crucial difference between subspecies is whether the analyst is primarily interested in a particular "part" (a discrete institution) or in the configuration of the "whole" the total society). In elaborating these points, the paper seeks a measure of clarity but has no pretense of ending the debate. Because the present approach is non-partisan and methodological, it can have little hope of ceasing a dialogue that has taken on ideological overtones. Its only pretension is to make the dialogue more understandable to the audience at large.

Previous Discussions of Heterogeneity Within Structural Functionalism

Having noted the tendency to view structural-functionalism monotonically, it is important to introduce the exceptions. Several other commentators have also pointed to diversity within the school. These authors are a sparse minority and their insights are sometimes asides rather than major arguments. Nevertheless, they reinforce the argument that divergences exist, and some even agree about one particular dimension along which the differences occur.

---

[2] The leading figure here, of course, is Kingsley Davis, "The Myth of Functional Analysis as a Special Method in Sociology and Anthropology," *American Sociological Review,* 24 (December 1959), pp. 752–772. But while Davis makes the point as part of an attack, it had earlier statements as part of the functionalist's defense. Talcott Parsons has long argued that "function" is the dynamic element in sociology's scientific equation; it is an effort to maintain the general scientific tradition rather than a departure from it. Marion Levy echoes Parsons and anticipates Davis in *The Structure of Society* (Princeton, New Jersey: Princeton University Press, 1952), p. 28.

[3] For a discussion of the term in another sociological context, see Robert Wenkert, "Reply to the Critical Exchange on 'Working-Class Authoritarianism,'" *Berkeley Journal of Sociology,* 6 (Spring 1961), p. 110. Wenkert accounts for a "tempest in a teapot" in terms of the "synecdochic fallacy." A similar relation might be drawn in the literature on structural-functionalism.

orate distinctions occur in Melford Spiro's "typology of func-
Spiro derived no less than 12 varieties from the non-exhaustive
ve dimensions. One of these dimensions relates to the part-
on of Homans, Kluckhohn, and Levy. Thus, one can separate
ctionalism from "configurational" functionalism. Where the
erned with the growth and maintenance of a single structure,
erested in the total constellation of structures.
demeier's essay on "The Methodology of Functionalism" [11]
gument. Although the article is primarily concerned with the
function" and "cause," it is noteworthy for two other reasons.
suggests that functionalism can be considered on other than
evaluative grounds. The self-conscious use of the term "meth-
ts to an assessment of practical consequences instead of puta-
hauungs." [12] Secondly, Bredemeier is another who detects dif-
1 the camp:

l approach to sociology consists basically of an attempt to under-
enomena in terms of their relationship to some system. At least
ds of procedures, however, seem to be covered by that statement.
attempt to assess that part played by an observed pattern of
e maintenance of some larger system in which it included. . . .
of functional analysis should be clearly distinguished from the
, is an attempt to *explain the persistence* of an observed pattern of
is, to approach an observed phenomenon with the question of its
. [author's italics][13]

ergence revolves about the part-whole distinction. Is the object
ne particular observed pattern of behavior? Or is the goal to
ther patterns to examine the larger system in which they are

ldner has taken the further step of aligning the two options with

Spiro, "A Typology of Functional Analysis," *Explorations*, 1 (1953).
Bredemeier, "The Methodology of Functionalism," *American Socio-*
20 (April 1955), pp. 173–180.
his paper is primarily concerned with differences within structural-
self, a sequel might consider differences in its interpreters. Here it
whether one considers the approach a "theory" or a "method." In
ho opt for the former are critical; those who opt for the latter are
tic. Thus, Lockwood, Dahrendorf, and Mills have all identified
onalism with a theoretical "weltanschauung" that rankles. Merton,
Davis consider it a method and explore it on analytical rather than
nds. There are, however, exceptions. Harold Fallding, "Functional
ology," *American Sociological Review*, 28 (February 1963), pp. 5–13,
ctionalism is openly evaluative and worthy of applause on that score.
, *op. cit.*, p. 173.

As early as 1931, Horace K
structural-functionalism in his e
Sciences.[4] As if to account for t
their legacies in *The Structure o*
"voluntarism," an important fac
spring of a marriage between i
functionalism includes strands o
Weber, its diversity is understand

Four years later, George Ho
contemporary structural-function
difference.[6] While both Radcliff
early "functionalists" each was a
Homans traced this to an essen
Whereas Radcliffe-Brown was n
society as a whole, Malinowski wa
of the society and the particular i

By 1944, this concern with lev
embrace both Malinowski and R
the structural-functionalist must
cate.[8] First, there is the language
of particular structures into the t
guage of "adaptation" that conc
societal gestalt.

Marion Levy implied a si
general rubric of "structural-func
species. It is possible to interpret
concerning the requirements for
The analysis of "structural requ
tions for maintaining any single

More ela
tionalism." [10]
interplay of
whole distinc
"genetic" fu
former is con
the latter is ir

Harry Br
adds to the a
confusion of
First, the title
theoretical or
odology" poi
tive "weltans
ferences with

The function
stand social p
two distinct k

One is an
behavior in t
A second typ
foregoing. Th
behavior, that
causes in min

Again the div
to explain so
use this and
implicated?

Alvin Go

---

[4] Horace Kallen, "Functionalism,"
York: The Macmillan Co., 1931), V
[5] Talcott Parsons, *The Structure o*
Free Press, 1949).
[6] George Caspar Homans, "Anxiet
Radcliffe-Brown," *American Anthro*
printed in *Sentiments and Activities* (
201.
[7] For Radcliffe-Brown's views, see
Elgin Williams, "The Dismal Science
(October-December 1948), pp. 594–6
and Radcliffe-Brown summon righted
terizes Malinowski's brand of functi
[8] Clyde Kluckhohn, "Navaho Wi
Archaeology and Ethnology, Harvar
[9] Levy, *op. cit.*, pp. 62–76.

[10] Melford E
[11] Harry C.
logical Review
[12] Although
functionalism
plainly matters
general, those
more sympath
structural-func
Gouldner, and
ideological gro
Analysis in So
argues that fu
[13] Bredemeie

As early as 1931, Horace Kallen cited a variety of interpretations of structural-functionalism in his essay for the *Encyclopedia of the Social Sciences*.[4] As if to account for these differences, Talcott Parsons analyzed their legacies in *The Structure of Social Action*,[5] published in 1937. Thus, "voluntarism," an important facet of structural-functionalism, was the off-spring of a marriage between idealism and positivism. Since structural-functionalism includes strands of Pareto, Marshall, Marx, Durkheim, and Weber, its diversity is understandable.

Four years later, George Homans examined two other predecessors of contemporary structural-functionalism and uncovered another systematic difference.[6] While both Radcliffe-Brown and Malinowski are considered early "functionalists" each was anxious to expel the other from the school.[7] Homans traced this to an essential difference in their levels of analysis. Whereas Radcliffe-Brown was more Durkheimian in his concern for the society as a whole, Malinowski was more interested in the individual member of the society and the particular institutions that cater to his needs.

By 1944, this concern with levels had become more pronounced. As if to embrace both Malinowski and Radcliffe-Brown, Kluckhohn suggested that the structural-functionalist must learn two different languages to communicate.[8] First, there is the language of "adjustment" that deals with the fitting of particular structures into the total environment. Second, there is the language of "adaptation" that concerns the articulation of all structures in a societal gestalt.

Marion Levy implied a similar specification in 1952.[9] Under the general rubric of "structural-functional requisite analysis" he noted two sub-species. It is possible to interpret the analysis of "functional requisites" as concerning the requirements for maintaining the system in a given state. The analysis of "structural requisites" can be seen as involving the conditions for maintaining any single unit within that system.

---

[4] Horace Kallen, "Functionalism," *The Encyclopedia of the Social Sciences* (New York: The Macmillan Co., 1931), Vol. 6.

[5] Talcott Parsons, *The Structure of Social Action* (2d ed.; Glencoe: Illinois: The Free Press, 1949).

[6] George Caspar Homans, "Anxiety and Ritual: The Theories of Malinowski and Radcliffe-Brown," *American Anthropologist* 43 (April-June 1941), pp. 164–172, re-printed in *Sentiments and Activities* (Glencoe, Illinois: The Free Press, 1962), pp. 192–201.

[7] For Radcliffe-Brown's views, see the exchange prompted by Dorothy Gregg and Elgin Williams, "The Dismal Science of Functionalism," *American Anthropologist,* 50 (October-December 1948), pp. 594–611. In the following issue, both A. L. Kroeber and Radcliffe-Brown summon righteous indignation. It is here that the latter characterizes Malinowski's brand of functionalism as mere "Malinowskianism."

[8] Clyde Kluckhohn, "Navaho Witchcraft," Papers of the Peabody Museum of Archaeology and Ethnology, Harvard University, Vol. 22, no. 2 (1944).

[9] Levy, *op. cit.*, pp. 62–76.

More elaborate distinctions occur in Melford Spiro's "typology of functionalism." [10] Spiro derived no less than 12 varieties from the non-exhaustive interplay of five dimensions. One of these dimensions relates to the part-whole distinction of Homans, Kluckhohn, and Levy. Thus, one can separate "genetic" functionalism from "configurational" functionalism. Where the former is concerned with the growth and maintenance of a single structure, the latter is interested in the total constellation of structures.

Harry Bredemeier's essay on "The Methodology of Functionalism" [11] adds to the argument. Although the article is primarily concerned with the confusion of "function" and "cause," it is noteworthy for two other reasons. First, the title suggests that functionalism can be considered on other than theoretical or evaluative grounds. The self-conscious use of the term "methodology" points to an assessment of practical consequences instead of putative "weltanschauungs." [12] Secondly, Bredemeier is another who detects differences within the camp:

> The functional approach to sociology consists basically of an attempt to understand social phenomena in terms of their relationship to some system. At least two distinct kinds of procedures, however, seem to be covered by that statement.
> One is an attempt to assess that part played by an observed pattern of behavior in the maintenance of some larger system in which it included. . . . A second type of functional analysis should be clearly distinguished from the foregoing. This is an attempt to *explain the persistence* of an observed pattern of behavior, that is, to approach an observed phenomenon with the question of its causes in mind. [author's italics][13]

Again the divergence revolves about the part-whole distinction. Is the object to explain some particular observed pattern of behavior? Or is the goal to use this and other patterns to examine the larger system in which they are implicated?

Alvin Gouldner has taken the further step of aligning the two options with

---

10 Melford E. Spiro, "A Typology of Functional Analysis," *Explorations,* 1 (1953).

11 Harry C. Bredemeier, "The Methodology of Functionalism," *American Sociological Review,* 20 (April 1955), pp. 173–180.

12 Although this paper is primarily concerned with differences within structural-functionalism itself, a sequel might consider differences in its interpreters. Here it plainly matters whether one considers the approach a "theory" or a "method." In general, those who opt for the former are critical; those who opt for the latter are more sympathetic. Thus, Lockwood, Dahrendorf, and Mills have all identified structural-functionalism with a theoretical "weltanschauung" that rankles. Merton, Gouldner, and Davis consider it a method and explore it on analytical rather than ideological grounds. There are, however, exceptions. Harold Fallding, "Functional Analysis in Sociology," *American Sociological Review,* 28 (February 1963), pp. 5–13, argues that functionalism is openly evaluative and worthy of applause on that score.

13 Bredemeier, *op. cit.,* p. 173.

particular theorists. His excellent "Reciprocity and Autonomy in Functional Theory" distinguishes between the approaches of Merton and Parsons as follows:

. . . system concepts play a pivotal role in both their formulations of functional theory. It will be noted, however, that the nature of their commitment to a system model differs, Parsons' being what may be called a total commitment, while Merton's can be regarded as a strategy of minimal commitment. . . . In brief, for Merton functional analysis is focused on some delimited unit of human behavior or belief, with a view to accounting either for its persistence or change by establishing its consequences for environing social or cultural structures. . . .
In contrast to Merton, Parsons does not focus on the explanation of empirically delimited units of social behavior or belief, but instead centers attention directly on analysis of the contextual structure as a system. . . . Parsons' assumption is that it is impossible to understand adequately any single pattern except by referring it to some larger systemic whole. He, therefore, assumes that the *whole* system must be conceptually constituted prior to the investigation and analysis of specific patterns. In consequence, Parsons is led forthwith to the analysis of the *total* anatomy of social systems in an effort to identify their constituent elements and relationships.[14]

In focusing on the part-whole alternative, Gouldner had company. And there are several more recent companions to be considered.

In exploring "The Idea of a Social System," Philip and Gertrude Selznick distinguish two ways of working with the concept.[15] "Interpretation" seeks to understand a particular element against the backdrop of the totality. "Generalization" involves a comparative inspection of systems as wholes. And if the debate over functionalism is confusing, Thomas Ford Hoult has sought to dispel misunderstanding by a pedagogic metaphor.[16] He introduces two community consultants, Professors "Due" and "It." The former is a "structuralist" who simply wants to describe individual institutions in detail. The latter is a "functionalist" who wants to examine institutions only as they contribute to the whole. In a happy denouement, the two pool their efforts, thus producing "structural-functionalism" as the best of both worlds.

---

[14] Alvin W. Gouldner, "Reciprocity and Autonomy in Functional Theory" in Gross (ed.), *Symposium on Sociological Theory* (Evanston, Illinois: Row, Peterson & Co., 1959), pp. 242–245.

[15] Philip and Gertrude Selznick, "The Idea of a Social System," paper read to the American Sociological Association, September, 1959. See also the latter's "Functionalism, the Freudian Theory, and Philosophy of Value," unpublished Ph.D. dissertation, U.C.L.A., 1960, in which a distinction is drawn between Titchener and Freud in terms of structuralism *vs.* functionalism as I will use them later.

[16] Thomas Ford Hoult, "Functionalism: A Brief Clarification," *Sociological Inquiry*, 33 (Winter 1963), pp. 31–33. But see also Ben Singer, "A Clarification of a Clarification: Functionalism." *Sociological Inquiry*, 33 (Spring 1963), pp. 141–143.

A final, most recent, and most peculiar perception of diversity is Pierre van den Berghe's synthesis of "Dialectic and Functionalism." [17] Although the cynic may cite this as forcing a marriage to gloat over the divorce, van den Berghe argues that both Marx and the functionalists utilize part-whole relations and the concept of system equilibrium. It is just that they accord their emphases differently. Reading between the author's lines, the Marxist tack can be seen as more "part-oriented" in two senses. First, its dialectical postulate assumes the importance of specific parts at war with each other. Second, in locating the dialectic within the economic sector, the Marxists stress one particular segment of society rather than the system as a whole. By contrast, the functionalists are more catholic. Precisely because their primary focus is on the integrity of the system, they turn to the wider society as a source of explanation and a locus of consequence. As an example, consider Smelser's rebuttal to the Marxists on the role of the working class in industrial change in England. [18]

In summary, while it is common to regard structural-functionalism as a single theoretical stance with easily identified characteristics,[19] it is also possible to find heterogeneity within it. Several previous authors have agreed not only that diversity exists but that a large part of it revolves about the part-whole distinction. On the one hand, it is possible to concentrate on the "part," using the "whole" as a kind of backboard off of which to bounce effects and consequences. On the other hand, one can concentrate on the whole itself. Here the various parts are constituent elements and only really interesting as they contribute to the entirety. Put into more rococo terms, one can focus on a particular structure, using its contributions to the system as a source of information about the structure itself. Or one can stress the system and the relationships which compose it and make or break its equilibrium. Here individual structures are means to the end but not analytic ends in themselves. Here the level of analysis is shifted to a higher, but not necessarily more valid or significant plane. Using Hoult's language, the first option can be termed "structuralism," and the second may be called "functionalism," thus giving new life to a once moribund hyphen.

---

[17] Pierre L. van den Berghe, "Dialectic and Functionalism," *American Sociological Review,* 28 (October 1963), pp. 695–705.

[18] Neil J. Smelser, *Social Change in the Industrial Revolution* (Chicago: University of Chicago Press, 1959), chap. 14.

[19] It is logically impudent to discuss subspecies without defining the specie itself. It is partly symptomatic of the foregoing that no succinct description of structural-functionalism can escape cavilling or serious criticism. Nevertheless, some definition is called for, and my own would be the following: structural-functionalism is a general methodology that focuses on the functional articulation between structural parts and a systemic whole. This is not to say that the articulation is always perfect, that an equilibrium always occurs, or that conflict is not present. It is a statement of what to look at instead of what to find.

Structuralism vs. Functionalism in their Analytic Consequences

Anyone presuming to elaborate a distinction must heed Homans' warning of the perils of "being split by a false dichotomy." It is clearly one thing to cite a distinction and quite another to demonstrate its importance. In fact, while the aforementioned authors are already a minority in noting the diversity within structural-functionalism, still fewer argue that the diversity is ultimately significant. Some, like Hoult, see the distinction as more artificial than real and contrive a Panglossian finale in which the two sides cannot help but merge to complement each other. Others, like Homans himself, feel that there has been a troublesome gulf in the past but that it can be bridged by the discourse of gentlemen who are willing to talk to instead of past each other. Finally, still others like Spiro, are confident that the audience can resolve the dilemma. From this perspective, one need only tip off the reader to the particular approach in use and communication will proceed in a euphonious flow.

And yet there are two important exceptions who indicate not only that the distinction is firmly rooted but that its fruits may be bitter. Thus, Gouldner suggests that Merton—and perhaps "structuralism" generally—is better able to cope with the problematics of "reciprocity and autonomy" than are Parsons and the "functionalists." He does not go on to deny the legitimacy of the latter; he simply suggests that here is one area in which the divergence has real consequences. As if to supply other areas, van den Berghe traces the ramifications of the distinction between Marxists and non-Marxists to such isues as uni- vs. multiple-causality, perceptions of conflict, and the nature of change. Here again the attempt is not to denigrate one approach to the advantage of the other. Nor is it to indicate a past danger that will be overcome in the more reasoned future. Instead, both Gouldner and van den Berghe are arguing that the distinction is far from false or insignificant. It is something that must be confronted in its consequences.

This, of course, is the present thesis as well. Without opting for one approach rather than the other, the paper will argue that many of the charges flung at structural-functionalism apply to only one of its forms instead of both. Fallacies such as "functional unity," "indispensability," static analysis, and ideological conservatism have all been key issues in the debate. But it is possible that the critics are at fault in chopping at the tree rather than the branches. It is also possible that the defenders have erred in defending too much.

The remainder of the argument falls under four headings. In each case, the heading represents a procrustean polarity. Thus, one may be alert to the possibilities of conflict *or* one may be attuned to functional unity; one may risk the fallacy of indispensability *or* one may explore for functional alternatives; one may stress changes in the system as a whole *or* one may focus on internal processes designed to maintain it; one may court one form of conservatism *or* court another. The argument, in brief, is that structuralism has an affinity for the first element in each pair, while functionalism leans more to the second.

Before examining the propositions in detail, three caveats are important. *First,* the conclusions are not grounded in an empirical survey or an ineluctable logic. They are more properly hunches in a perverse sociology of knowledge where methodology is given the force customarily ascribed to class position. *Second,* it follows that the issue is not one of certainty, but rather of probability. To say that an approach "risks" a bias is not to say that all of its representatives will succumb. And, *third,* there is the question of illustration, evidence, and scope. It is possible to see the distinction cutting a wide swath through the history of sociological theory. It may inform not only the difference between Merton and Parsons, but also the discrepancies between such contemporaries as Marx and Comte, Weber and Durkheim, Malinokswi and Radcliffe-Brown, and even the logicians Hempel and Nagel, since the first member of each pair can be seen as a structuralist and the second as a functionalist. But whole careers are erratic. Although the alignment is elegant, it is a pyrrhic victory of oversimplification. Instead, for the present, I will simply express a series of hypotheses with some clarifying examples. An argument of this sort is perhaps better judged by its resonance in others than by the evidence it contrives. Forewarnings aside, consider the following issues and their articulation with the current distinction.

Conflict Versus Functional Unity

Perhaps no dimension of the debate over structural-functionalism is as hotly contested as this one. Certainly none is as ideologically impassioned. The phrase "fallacy of functional unity" is, of course, Merton's.[20] Its disqualifying assumption is that the system not only esteems harmony but actually achieves it. On the other hand, undue emphasis on conflict can be a fallacy as well. It may occur not only among those who see anarchy or overt struggle, but also those who simply see no grounds for mutuality and posit centrifugal rather than centripetal tendencies. Yet this is not to say that unity is nonexistent or that perceptions of conflict are inevitably in error. It is simply that, holding the reality "constant," perceptions of it will be influenced by one's approach. In this case, the structuralist may have one preconception and the functionalist may have quite another.

---

[20] Robert K. Merton, *Social Theory and Social Structure* (Glencoe, Illinois: The Free Press, 1957), pp. 25–30.

Pairing the approaches with the risks, functionalism should be sensitive to unity, while structuralism should conduce to conflict. The functionalist has already invested in an abstraction when he makes his primary commitment to the whole instead of the part. The use of "system" almost necessarily involves reification, if only for grammatical reasons. The reification should lead to concretization and justification by documenting unity as a prime ingredient of the system concept. It is always tempting to treat expectations as actualities and metaphors as reality; the functionalist must be sorely tempted indeed.

By contrast, the structuralist is not primarily concerned with the system. While it is a useful device, he can carry on even where the "whole" is wracked by conflict and disunity. Indeed his analysis often becomes more revealing when the "part" is exposed to discrepant demands in a fragmented context. Here problems of decision-making, commitment, leadership, and efficiency come to a boil. Not only is the structure exposed in its detail, but it also has an opportunity to make a cavalry-like entrance to justify the researcher's own faith in its importance.

Support for these contentions begins with Merton himself. As a structuralist, it is not surprising that his category of errors should begin with the "fallacy of functional unity." As contrasted with Parsons, operating at a higher than "middle-range" level. Merton's work on early science, the political machine and the conditions of anomie shows a greater proportion of concern with conflict. While Parsons has also examined system strain and conflict, these issues are much less prominent in an output designed to produce a paradigmatic answer to the Hobbesian question of order. Gouldner's analysis explicates the differences here in much greater detail. While wider difference could be demonstrated between Marx and Parsons or even Dahrendorf and Parsons on the issue, the important thing is that the distinction applies as well between Merton and Parsons as the two foremost exponents of structural-functionalism in the popular view.

A second and more substantive example concerns religion and the approaches of Weber and Durkheim. I suggested earlier that an over-simplification would have Weber as the structuralist and Durkheim as the functionalist. While it would be dangerous to extend the labels categorically, they do make sense in the realm of religion. Weber, whose structuralism grew out of his twin background as lawyer and historiographer, was wary of overarching formulations and preferred to treat particular structures and institutions as discrete. Durkheim, coming out of positivism, had a commitment to the society *sui generis* and his functionalism was an attempt to bolster the assertion of society as a social fact. Thus, Weber treated Protestantism as an unique occurrence and saw it as an abrasive agent for change in a traditional society.[21] Durkheim pictured the "church" in quite different terms. Indeed, his identification of religion with society was a circular formulation that overstepped conflict by demonstrating unity at the expense of a tautology.[22] Without suggesting that Weber was a "conflict theorist" in the contemporary sense or that Durkheim was constitutionally unable to perceive strain, this may help to illumine part of their differences in approaching religion. Structuralists and functionalists are not *necessarily* at odds on the issue of conflict *vs.* functional unity, but they are exposed to different temptations with frequently different consequences.

STRUCTURAL INDISPENSABILITY VERSUS FUNCTIONAL ALTERNATIVES

The error of overestimating a part's significance to the whole occurs in two of Merton's three fallacies: the postulates of "universal functionalism" and "indispensability." The first assumes that every structure makes a positive contribution; the second asserts that the structure is not only positive but non-expendable. There are, of course, differences here, but I have elected to treat them under a single heading because they share both the common sin of overestimation and a common antidote in the functional alternative. Thus, political institutions may replace or complement the church in providing social integration and value reinforcement. Schools may aid the family in a "structurally differentiated" socialization process. But note that an assumption of alternatives may also be an error. It is possible to ascribe an undue flexibility to the constellation of parts, while overlooking arrangements that are subjectively necessary if not logically dictated. In any event, here as before, the structuralist and the functionalist should have different penchants.

Every researcher seeks to justify his concerns to himself and to the field. In the case of the structuralist, this means justifying the importance of the part or institution which launched his analysis in the first place. If one is studying the family, it is satisfying to judge that the family is indispensable for society. If one is concerned with religion, there is nothing more shaking than evidence of irrelevance. In an age where the scholar is expected to provide practical results, there is stigma in being identified with the trivial. As overcompensation, the structuralist may be tempted to bloat the significance of the structure in question.

On the other hand, the functionalist has no commitment to a particular pattern or institution. Because his concern is with the system as a whole, he

---

[21] Max Weber, *The Protestant Ethic and the Spirit of Capitalism* (New York: Charles Scribner's Sons, 1958).

[22] Emile Durkheim, *The Elementary Forms of the Religious Life* (Glencoe, Illinois: The Free Press, 1956).

has an opposite stake. In order to show that the systemic analog is not erroneous, he must demonstrate that the totality can sustain itself even when the parts are shifted or disrupted. The concept of functional alternatives provides an analytic safety-valve. In addition to bolstering the system, it precludes undue dependency upon any of its constituent elements.

Consider once again Merton the structuralist and Parsons the functionalist. Here the risks of pat categorization become evident. According to the hypothesis, Merton should manifest the error of indispensability, but, of course, he is one of the foremost exponents of the functional alternative. Still, it is important to note that Parsons' "system analysis" employs the alternative with the widest latitude. Parsons has continually cautioned against aligning specific structures with the functions of a, g, i, and l. The model gains much of its comparative advantage in providing a framework for noting, say, the school's predominantly integrative functions in one context and its predominantly adaptive functions in another. Parsons' much-maligned neology can be seen as an attempt to transcend the common structural vocabulary to talk in more purely functional terms.[23]

Here as before, however, a better illustration comes from a specific substantive area. Since the paper is concerned with the distinction's practical consequences, concrete illustrations are preferable. Turning again to religion, studies can be divided into two camps, though both are concerned with the structural-functional problem of "religion in society." On the one hand, there are the structuralists who identify religion with the church as a specific structure. On the other hand, there are the functionalists who speak of religion in terms of system needs and their fulfillment, needs such as societal integration, normative sanctions, value inculcation and reinforcement. Troeltsch, Niebuhr, and Will Herberg are more structural; Durkheim, LaPiere, and Glock are more functional.

For a time, the sociology of American religion was dominated by the structuralists, and Durkheim was either restricted to the primitives or ignored. During this phase, there was a great deal of analysis on the conditions for church growth and survival.[24] There was also an undertone which

---

[23] Note, however, that the victory of scope is won at the expense of operationalization. Precisely because there are no strict conjunctions between function and structure in Parsons' model, it is difficult to enter an empirical wedge. On which structures does one test his propositions? If they do not work for one, at what point may we cease to examine alternatives? The problem in Parsons is less the absence of propositions and more their rhetorical form. Instead of being couched in the language of testing, they are often presented in the abstract and circuitously self-fulfilling logic used to such advantage by the Marxists and the Freudians.

[24] Perhaps the best example of this tradition is H. Paul Douglass and Edmund deS. Brunner, *The Protestant Church as a Social Institution* (New York: Harper & Bros., 1935).

suggested that the church was indeed indispensable for society. Just as Troeltsch ended his two volume history of the Western European churches with a hope for resurgence,[25] so did Niebuhr conclude that denomination-alism threatened society itself by splintering the church as a structure,[26] and Herberg similarly deplored the rooting of creedal ecumenicism in "the American way of life." [27]

The functionalists have countered with a different approach. Although Durkheim identified religion with society, he also predicted a more secular and philosophical religion in the West that would adequately replace the conventional church.[28] Much the same argument was made before him by Jean Marie Guyau in a recently re-issued volume, *The Non-Religion of the Future*.[29] LaPiere and Glock add contemporary reinforcement. Thus, LaPiere makes the following remarks in his study of *Collective Behavior:*

> If the important aspect of any social structure is its functions, it follows that no structure can be judged in terms of structure alone. . . . The functional approach will, undoubtedly, affront all those who believe that specific socio-psychological structures have inherent values. Thus, to those who believe that a church service is good because it is a church service, the statement that some church services are formal motions which are devoid of religious significance, that others are functionally comparable to theatrical performances, and that still others are a form of revelry and are therefore comparable to a drunken spree will be an affront to common sense, an attack upon the integrity of decent people, or, at the least, the ravings of a poor fool.[30]

A similar but less strident comment comes from Charles Y. Glock's evaluation of the study of religion in *Sociology Today:*

> The unintended consequence of focusing on religion was a tendency to ignore the functional alternatives to religion in meeting societal needs. There was at least an implicit propensity to view religious beliefs and the rites and practices which accompany them as the exclusive means by which these needs are met. For certain primitive societies, this view may have been justified. It soon becomes apparent, however, that it is highly tenuous when applied to more complex societies. It is difficult, for example, to defend the proposition that religion alone

25 Ernst Troeltsch, *The Social Teachings of the Christian Churches* (New York: Harper & Bros., Torchbooks, 1960), Vol. 2, pp. 1010–1013.

26 H. Richard Niebuhr, *The Social Sources of Denominationalism* (New York: Henry Holt & Co., 1929).

27 Will Herberg, *Protestant, Catholic, Jew* (rev. ed.; Garden City: Doubleday Anchor Books, 1960).

28 Durkheim, *op. cit.,* pp. 445–447.

29 Jean Marie Guyau, *The Non-Religion of the Future* (New York: Schocken Books, 1962).

30 Richard LaPiere, *Collective Behavior* (New York: McGraw-Hill Book Co., 1938), pp. 55–56, cited by Merton, *op. cit.,* p. 39.

supports social integration or social control in American, British, or even Indian society.[31]

Both LaPiere and Glock are concerned with a different kind of analysis when compared to the structuralists. An emphasis upon functions such as "social integration or social control" is at odds with a stress on the church as an ultimate structure. While both approaches examine structures and functions, the functionalist asks "What structures are available to fulfill one or more functions important to the system?" The structuralist asks "What functions does this particular structure serve and what are the consequences for the structure itself?"

A final example concerns a more celebrated debate. Although Melvin Tumin is ambivalent in his structural-functional allegiance, his dispute with Davis and Moore[32] can be seen in terms of the present distinction. While both parties are concerned with a part-whole relationship in considering the role of stratification in the society-at-large, they ask quite different questions. Davis and Moore are more structural in seeking an explanation of the stratification structure by asking of its contributions to the whole. Tumin, the more functional, is concerned not with explaining stratification but rather with examining the needs of the system itself. He thereby approaches the issue from the opposite side and, predictably emerges with a different answer. There are functional alternatives to stratification as a structure; it is therefore neither explained nor justified. Now it is true that Moore and Tumin have recently neared a rapprochement by reducing the issue from stratification to inequality.[33] Nevertheless, that the debate lasted for as long as it did is partial testimony to the consequences of disparate goals and assumptions. Surely there are ideological factors at play here, but the present distinction adds additional light to the controversy.

SOCIAL CHANGE VERSUS SOCIAL PROCESS

Merton's fallacies do not relate to change explicitly. Presumably, without the errors of unity and indispensability, the analysis of change would be unobstructed. Still, since the functionalists are more vulnerable to the fallacy of unity and the structuralists more threatened by indispensability, both errors

---

[31] Charles Y. Glock, "The Sociology of Religion," in Merton, Broom and Cottrell (eds.), *Sociology Today* (New York: Basic Books, 1959), p. 155.

[32] For the opening salvos see Kingsley Davis and Wilbert E. Moore, "Some Principles of Stratification," *American Sociological Review*, 10 (April 1945), pp. 242–249, and Melvin M. Tumin, "Some Principles of Stratification: A Critical Analysis," *American Sociological Review*, 18 (August 1953), pp. 387–394.

[33] See Moore, "But Some Are More Equal Than Others," Tumin, "On Equality," and Moore, "Rejoinder," all in *American Sociological Review*, 28 (February 1963), pp. 13–28.

are rarely absent at once. Since each position appears to solve only half of the problem, what are the consequences for their particular approaches to social change?

It is tempting to simply label one approach "static" and the other "dynamic." Yet the issue is more complex. A number of recent commentators have suggested that structural-functionalism is not inherently static and that it has, in fact, demonstrated a capacity to deal with dynamics of several sorts.[34] This raises the fundamental question of "what sorts?" Change is certainly not a single phenomenon. Structuralism may be more compatible with one variety, while functionalism conduces to another. For example, Talcott Parsons is largely responsible for a distinction between the dynamics necessary to maintain a system in a given state or equilibrium (process) and dynamics that involve wholesale shifts in the system itself (change).[35] Pursuing this further, one can postulate a linkage between process and functionalism, on the one hand, and between change and structuralism, on the other.

I suggested earlier that whether one focuses primarily on the part or the whole, there is an urge to both concretize and justify the commitment. In the case of the structuralist, this may lead to two outcomes. He can treat the "part" as intrinsically stable but caught up in "external" changes in the larger system. Or he can treat the part as the active agent in the change itself. In both cases, the structuralist is apt to see change, like conflict, as an analytic wedge into the most interesting aspects of his study. In both cases, he is concerned with wholesale change as opposed to process.

The functionalist, however, has a different commitment. Again to concretize and justify his interest in the system as a whole, he is apt to "hold external changes constant" and turn his attention to internal processes which maintain the homeostatic balance. Moreover, with his broader perspective, he is in a better position to inspect the institutional interaction that is so crucial to societal processes, whether socialization, social control, political administration, or economic production and distribution.

The most common juxtaposition of change and process involves Marx

---

[34] See, for example, Wilbert Moore, "A Reconsideration of Theories of Social Change," *American Sociological Review,* 25 (December 1960), pp. 810–818; Ernest Nagel, "A Formalization of Functionalism," in *Logic Without Metaphysics* (Glencoe, Illinois: The Free Press, 1960); Francesca Cancian, "Functional Analysis of Change," *American Sociological Review,* 25 (December 1960), pp. 818–827; and van den Berghe, *op. cit.* Even Ralf Dahrendorf, the conflict theorist extraordinaire, has defended structural-functionalism against charges of a static bias. He notes that it has made a particular contribution to the study of process, if not in the study of wholesale change and cites Parsons as a case in point. See Dahrendorf, *Class and Class Conflict in Industrial Society, op. cit.,* p. 161 n.

[35] Talcott Parsons, *The Social System* (Glencoe, Illinois: The Free Press, 1951), chap. 10.

and Parsons. It is important to note, however, that the gap is not as wide as is customarily assumed. As van den Berghe points out, the dialectics and the functionalists have always shared an evolutionary approach. Furthermore, the later works of both Marx and Parsons point to even greater convergence. Marx's "Hague Speeches"[36] in 1872 marked a retreat from the revolutionary theory of change espoused in the "Manifesto" of 1848. Parsons' recent statement in *Theories of Society*[37] and his work with Smelser in *Economy and Society*[38] indicate continued refinement of the earlier concept of structural differentiation. But this is not to say that Marx and Parsons are now indistinguishable. While they have approached agreement on the *means* of change, they remain apart on the *ends*. Marx retained the Hegelian view of change in discrete stages between which society changes its external form as well as its internal alignment. Parsons, however, retains an equilibrium model. As a functionalist, he sees structural differentiation as "institutional change" but not a change in the system as a whole. Although the economy was altered with the separation of ownership and management, Parsons has elsewhere commented on the continuity of values that overarched the process.

Turning from economics back to religion, Weber and Durkheim offer a similar comparison. Weber, the more structural, emphasized religion as one among many agents in the change from pre-capitalism, through traditional capitalism, to rational-capitalism. Nor was this change an easy transition. It was precisely because it necessitated a wholesale shift in values that it concerned Weber. He prophesied that ultimately rationalism would return to haunt one of its "necessary but not sufficient" conditions. The Puritan Ethic would lose its force as economic values and the secular bureaucracy gained sway.[39]

Durkheim's functional approach had a different consequence. Although Robert Bellah has criticized the view that Durkheim lacked a sense of history,[40] it remains true that Durkheim had a poorly developed theory of social change, one that was overly dependent on population density as an

---

[36] Hans Kelson, *The Political Theory of Bolshevism* (Berkeley: University of California Press, 1948), p. 41 ff. Cited in Andrew Hacker, "Sociology and Ideology," in Max Black (ed.), *The Social Theories of Talcott Parsons* (Englewood Cliffs, New Jersey: Prentice-Hall, 1961), pp. 289–290.

[37] Talcott Parsons, "An Outline of the Social System," in Parsons, Shils, Naegele, and Pitts (eds.), *Theories of Society* (Glencoe, Illinois: The Free Press, 1961), Vol. 1, esp. pp. 70–79.

[38] Talcott Parsons and Neil J. Smelser, *Economy and Society* (Glencoe, Illinois: The Free Press, 1956), pp. 246–294.

[39] Weber, *op. cit.*, pp. 181–183. See also Max Weber, *General Economic History* (New York: Collier Books, 1961), p. 270.

[40] Robert N. Bellah, "Durkheim and History," *American Sociological Review*, 24 (August 1959), pp. 447–461. See also the exchange that followed in the same issue.

energizer.[41] Durkheim was primarily concerned with the world of the "social fact" and portrayed it as concrete in order to justify the stability that the term "fact" suggests. Certainly his analysis of religion concerns process rather than change.[42] Although he later saw functional alternatives to Christianity in the West, he did not envision a disjunctive change in the contours of the overall society. Unlike Marx, he had abandoned his own predecessors' conceptions of change through distinct epochs. While it is worth repeating that examples offer no proof, the foregoing offers two cele-brated differences to illustrate the structuralist's penchant for change and the functionalist's affinity for process. Neither approach is necessarily static, but they differ in the kind and degree of dynamics that concern them.

CONSERVATISM VERSUS LIBERALISM

This issue is plainly related to the foregoing, though it has been singled out for particular fervor in the debate. For the most part, structural-functionalism is charged with an encrusted conservatism that not only toler-ates the existing order but legitimates it. And yet there are dissenting voices. Andrew Hacker has argued not that Parsons is a new conservative but rather that he is an old liberal who espouses change through all too temperate means.[43]

As this suggests, ideological labels find squirming subjects among con-temporary theorists. Moreover, the labels themselves are far from clear-cut. The distinction between conservatism and liberalism traverses a number of dimensions. It matters which dimension you choose as to how you will label the object. Indeed, it is possible to show that *both* structuralism and func-tionalism are *both* conservative and liberal.

If, for example, one defines the liberal as an advocate of change and the conservative as an advocate of the status quo, then the structuralist is more likely to be read into the former camp and the functionalist into the latter. But suppose a conservative is one who is concerned with the rugged indi-vidual and the particular institution whereas a liberal is more oriented to the welfare of the whole. Here the functionalist may be considered the liberal and the structuralist the conservative. Or consider the concept of teleology. Presumably, a conservative is one who will justify an institution's future by pointing to its past, whereas a liberal is open to alternatives. Once again, the structuralist should be the more conservative and the functionalist should

---

[41] Emile Durkheim, *The Division of Labor in Society* (Glencoe, Illinois: The Free Press, 1960), pp. 256–283.

[42] Durkheim, *The Elementary Forms of the Religious Life, op. cit.,* pp. 427–431. See also Durkheim's later work on moral education as an alternative to the traditional church.

[43] Hacker, *op. cit.,* pp. 290–310.

be more liberal, according to the earlier logic dealing with indispensability and functional alternatives.

Finally, one can define a conservative as the armchair observer who is seldom moved to action, while defining the liberal as one whose analyses move himself and others on behalf of a specific objective. On this score, the tables turn again and revert back to the initial alignment. Here the structuralist should be more liberal since his analytic commitment to a particular structure may shade into an ideological commitment as well. The functionalist should be more conservative since his broader perspective lessens the temptations of particularism.

In short, a single label applied to either structuralism or functionalism will be inaccurate. Since both conservatism vs. liberalism and structuralism vs. functionalism are multi-faceted distinctions, it is impossible to capture their mutual essence in a solitary equation. This does not mean that either structuralism or functionalism are non-ideological; any sociological theory should impinge upon some ideology or run the risk of irrelevance. The important point is that ideological characterizations are often misleading in their spellbinding simplicity.

Summary and Conclusions

In arguing that structural-functionalism is not all of a piece, this paper has distinguished "structuralism" from "functionalism" according to their allocation of emphasis in the part-whole relationship. The structuralist is primarily concerned with the analysis of a particular part in the system; the functionalist is guided by an interest in the system as a whole. To anticipate charges of a "false dichotomy" or abstract hair-splitting, the paper went on to trace some practical consequences of the distinction. Thus, the *structuralist* is more likely to envisage social conflict or disunity, more likely to err towards the fallacy of indispensability, more likely to detect wholesale social change, more likely to be conservative in his emphasis on the individual and his vulnerability to teleology, and, finally, more likely to be liberal in his affinity for change and ideological activism. On the other hand, the *functionalist* has the reverse proclivities. He runs the risk of overestimating system unity, is more drawn to the functional alternative, is more concerned with internal process than external change, is conservative in his de-emphasis of change and his lack of particularism, but is liberal in his stress on the collectivity and his aversion to teleology.

But, in any paper of this sort, the most fitting conclusion is a whimper and not a bang. Surely the present distinction is not the only one that is meaningful within structural-functionalism, though it does have the advantage of consensual validation in the comments of previous authors. Nor are the correlates of the distinction to be taken on faith. They are neither logically foolproof nor empirically buttressed, and their illustrations provide credibility rather than certainty. Then too, there may be other consequences that have been neglected here. For example, the structuralist may be more ideographic while the functionalist is more nomothetic, or the structuralist may be more descriptive while the functionalist is more explanatory.

Whatever the qualifications, it is hoped that the primary aims have been realized. These are not to take sides for or against structural-functionalism or either of its subspecies. Instead, one intent is to indicate the consequences of multidimensionality and another is to suggest that debate on the issue need not be a tempest in a teapot. Abstract theoretical sympathies do have consequences at a practical level. We can better appreciate these consequences by treating structural-functionalism less as a theoretical "weltanschauung" and more as a methodological approach.

Indexes

Name

Index

Subject Index